Collins

Primary illustrated Dictionary

Published by Collins
An imprint of HarperCollins Publishers
Westerhill Road
Bishopbriggs
Glasgow G64 2QT

Second Edition 2015

10 9 8 7 6 5 4 3 2

PB ISBN 978-0-00-757875-7
HB ISBN 978-0-00-812690-2

www.collinsdictionary.com
www.collins.co.uk/childrensreference

Typeset by Davidson Publishing Solutions

Printed and Bound by Printing Express Ltd, Hong Kong

A catalogue record for this book is available from the British Library.

If you would like to comment on any aspect of this book, please contact us at the given address or online.
E-mail: dictionaries@harpercollins.co.uk
@Collins4Parents

Acknowledgements
We would like to thank those authors and publishers who kindly gave permission for copyright material to be used in the Collins Corpus. We would also like to thank Times Newspapers Ltd for providing valuable data.

Contents

Using this dictionary

A dictionary helps you to find out what a word means and how to spell it correctly. The words in a dictionary are arranged in alphabetical order.

How to find a word

An **alphabet line** has been printed at the side of each page, and the letter in the blue box tells you which letter the words on that page begin with. So if you want to find the word **maximum**, use the alphabet line to look for words beginning with **m**.

At the top of each page there is a **guide word**. On a left-hand page the guide word tells you the first word on the page. On a right-hand page the guide word tells you the last word on the page. This means that when you open your dictionary, you can see straight away if you are at the right place. For example, if you are looking up **maximum**, you know that it must come on the pages with the guide words **marvel** and **maze**, because the words in the dictionary always come in alphabetical order.

When you think you have the right page, look at the headwords until you find the word you want.

Finding your way around the dictionary

① The **alphabet line** shows the first letter of the word.

② The **guide word** shows the first word on the page if it is a left-hand page and the last word on the page if it is a right-hand page.

③ The **headword** is the word you are looking up.

④ After the headword there can be **other forms** of the word, such as plural nouns, verb tenses, and comparative and superlative adjectives.

⑤ The **part of speech** tells you what type of word the headword is, such as a noun, verb, adjective, adverb, or pronoun.

⑥ The **definition** tells you what the word means.

⑦ Sometimes there is an **example** to show how the word is used.

⑧ If the headword has more than one meaning, each meaning has a different **number**.

⑨ A **pronunciation** shows you how to say a difficult word.

⑩ Some entries have a **related word**, such as a noun, adjective, or adverb made from the headword.

⑪ A **word history** tells you where a word originally came from.

⑫ **Synonyms**, or words that you can use instead, are given for some words.

⑬ **Antonyms**, or words that have the opposite meaning, are given for some words.

Using this dictionary

maze (2)

(3) **material** **materials**
NOUN **1** cloth
2 anything from which something else can be made • *artists' **materials***

maternal
ADJECTIVE **1** used to describe things relating to a mother • *My **maternal** grandfather was Welsh.*
(8) **2** A woman who is **maternal** has strong motherly feelings.

maternity
(5) ADJECTIVE relating to or involving pregnant women and childbirth • *The baby was born in the **maternity** wing of the hospital.*

mathematics
NOUN the study of numbers, quantities and shapes
(10) **mathematical** ADJECTIVE
mathematically ADVERB
mathematician NOUN

maths
NOUN an abbreviation of *mathematics*

matinee **matinees**
(9) *Said* "**mat**-i-nay" NOUN an afternoon performance at a theatre or cinema

matrix **matrices**
Said "**may**-trix, **may**-tri-sees" NOUN In mathematics, a **matrix** is a set of numbers or letters set out in rows and columns.

matt
ADJECTIVE dull rather than shiny • *Mum painted the front door **matt** green.*

matter **matters, mattering, mattered**
NOUN **1** a task or situation that you have to attend to • *We will have to discuss the **matter** with the head teacher.*
(12) SYNONYMS: affair, business, subject
2 any substance • *The scientists explored how **matter** behaves at high temperatures.*
VERB **3** If something **matters**, it is important.
PHRASE **4** If you ask **What's the matter?**, you want to know what is wrong.

mattress **mattresses**
NOUN a large, flat, spongy pad that is put on a bed to make it comfortable to sleep on

mature **matures, maturing, matured**
VERB **1** When a child or other young animal **matures**, it becomes an adult.
ADJECTIVE **2** fully grown or developed
maturely ADVERB **maturity** NOUN

maul **mauls, mauling, mauled**
VERB If an animal **mauls** someone, they savagely attack and badly injure them. (6)

mauve
Rhymes with "stove" NOUN OR ADJECTIVE a light purple colour

maximum
ADJECTIVE **1** The **maximum** amount is the most that is possible or allowed. • *The **maximum** score for this question is five marks.*
ANTONYM: minimum (13)
NOUN **2** the most that is possible or allowed • *Pupils are allowed a **maximum** of two pounds to spend on the school trip.*
ANTONYM: minimum

may
VERB **1** If something **may** happen, it is possible that it will happen.
2 If you **may** do something, you are allowed to do it.

May
NOUN the fifth month of the year. **May** has 31 days.
[probably from the Roman goddess *Maia*] (11)

maybe
ADVERB If you think there is a possibility that something will happen, but you are not sure, you use **maybe**. • ***Maybe** we will be allowed to go to the cinema tonight.* (7)

mayonnaise
NOUN a thick salad dressing made with egg yolks and oil

mayor **mayors**
NOUN someone who has been elected to represent the people of a town at official functions

maze **mazes** (4)
NOUN a system of complicated passages which it is difficult to find your way through

a b c d e f g h i j k l m (1) n o p q r s t u v w x y z

243

Using this dictionary

Other features of this dictionary

- Some headwords can be spelt in more than one way.

medieval; also spelt **mediaeval**

age **ages, ageing** or **aging, aged**

- Sometimes definitions include a label, such as FORMAL, INFORMAL, or TRADEMARK. This tells you a little more about the word or how it is used.

mum **mums**
NOUN INFORMAL mother

- Sometimes a photo or an illustration is included.

mollusc **molluscs**
NOUN an animal with a soft body and no backbone. Snails, slugs, clams and mussels are all **molluscs**.

- Grammar and spelling tips provide extra information on the spelling or use of words.

different
ADJECTIVE If one thing is **different** from another, it is not like it.

There are two *es* in *different*.

- Some definitions tell you where to find more information at another headword.

convex
ADJECTIVE A **convex** surface bulges outwards, rather than being level or curving inwards.
See **concave**

Extra help for you

Word Wizard is a special section at the back of this book to help you with your writing. It contains information on things like parts of speech, prefixes, suffixes, and punctuation. It also tells you how you can improve your spelling. There are interesting facts about where some words come from. It even has information on shapes, numbers, fractions, and angles, along with pictures.

The Earth and Space is a fact-filled section with colourful pictures. This is where to look if you want to know more about the Solar System, the Earth, the Moon, the continents, and the world's mountains, rivers, and oceans. There are also pages showing you the flags of some of the nations of the world.

Aa

a **an**
ADJECTIVE **A** and **an** are used when you talk about one of something. **A** is used when the next sound is a consonant: ***a*** *car,* ***a*** *dog.* **An** is used when the next sound is a vowel (a, e, i, o or u): ***an*** *apple,* ***an*** *elephant.*

abacus **abacuses**
NOUN a frame with beads that slide along rods, used for counting
[from Greek *abax* meaning board covered with sand for doing sums on]

abandon **abandons, abandoning, abandoned**
VERB If you **abandon** someone or something, you leave them or give them up for good. • *He* ***abandoned*** *all hope of catching the train on time.*

abbey **abbeys**
NOUN a church with buildings attached to it in which monks or nuns live

abbreviation **abbreviations**
NOUN a short form of a word or phrase • *N is an* ***abbreviation*** *for North.*

abdomen **abdomens**
NOUN the front part of your body below your chest, containing your stomach and intestines
abdominal ADJECTIVE

ability **abilities**
NOUN If you have **ability**, you have the intelligence and skill to do things.

able
ADJECTIVE If you are **able** to do something, you can do it.
ANTONYM: unable

abnormal
ADJECTIVE not normal or usual
abnormally ADVERB

aboard
PREPOSITION OR ADVERB If you are **aboard** a plane or a ship you are on it.

Aborigine **Aborigines**
NOUN someone descended from the people who were living in Australia before the European settlers arrived

about
PREPOSITION OR ADVERB **1** If you talk or write **about** a particular thing, you say things that are to do with that subject. • *a book* ***about*** *London*
2 You say **about** in front of a number to show it is not exact. • ***about*** *two o'clock*
PHRASE **3** If you are **about to** do something, you are just going to do it. • *He was* ***about to*** *leave.*

above
PREPOSITION OR ADVERB If one thing is above another, it is higher up. • *The plane was flying* ***above*** *the clouds.*
ANTONYM: below

abroad
ADVERB If you go **abroad**, you go to another country.

abscess **abscesses**
NOUN a painful swelling on the body, which contains pus

abseil **abseils, abseiling, abseiled**
VERB If you **abseil** down a rock face, you use ropes to go down it.

absent
ADJECTIVE If you are **absent** from a place, you are not there.
ANTONYM: present

absolute
ADJECTIVE **1** total and complete • ***absolute*** *darkness*
2 having total power • *an* ***absolute*** *ruler*

absolutely
ADVERB If you are **absolutely** sure about something, you are completely sure of it.

absorb **absorbs, absorbing, absorbed**
VERB If something **absorbs** liquid or gas, it soaks it up. • *Plants* ***absorb*** *moisture from the soil.*

a b c d e f g h i j k l m n o p q r s t u v w x y z

A B C D E F G H I J K L M N O P Q R S T U V W X Y Z

absorbent
ADJECTIVE If something is **absorbent**, it soaks up liquids easily.

abstract
ADJECTIVE **1** An **abstract** idea is based on thoughts and ideas rather than on real objects or happenings, for example *bravery* and *happiness*.
2 Abstract art uses shapes rather than images of people or objects.

an abstract painting

3 In grammar, **abstract** nouns refer to qualities or ideas, rather than physical objects, for example *happiness*.
See **noun**

absurd
ADJECTIVE Something that is **absurd** is stupid or ridiculous.

abuse **abuses, abusing, abused**
Said "ab-**yooss**" NOUN **1** cruel treatment of someone
2 rude and unkind remarks
Said "ab-**yooz**" VERB **3** To **abuse** someone is to treat them cruelly.
4 If you **abuse** someone, you speak to them in a rude and insulting way.

abysmal
ADJECTIVE very bad
abysmally ADVERB

academic **academics**
ADJECTIVE **1 Academic** work is done in school, college and university.
NOUN **2** someone who teaches or does research in a college or university

academy **academies**
NOUN **1** a school or college, usually one that specializes in a particular subject
• *the Royal **Academy** of Arts*
2 an organization of scientists, writers, artists or musicians

accelerate **accelerates, accelerating, accelerated**
VERB To **accelerate** is to speed up.
ANTONYM: decelerate

acceleration
NOUN the rate at which the speed of something increases

accent **accents**
NOUN a way of pronouncing a language
• *She had an Australian **accent**.*

accept **accepts, accepting, accepted**
VERB **1** If you **accept** something, you say yes to it or you take it from someone.
• *She **accepted** our invitation to the party.*
2 If you **accept** a situation, you realize that it cannot be changed. • *I **accepted** that I would have to work hard before my exams.*

acceptable
ADJECTIVE satisfactory

access
NOUN If you have **access** to a place, you may enter it. If you have **access** to a thing, you may use it.

accessible
ADJECTIVE **1** easy to reach or to see
• *The beach was **accessible** by a narrow path.*
2 Books that are **accessible** are easy to understand.

accident **accidents**
NOUN **1** something that happens suddenly or unexpectedly, causing people to be hurt or killed
PHRASE **2** Something that happens **by accident** has not been planned.
• *We met **by accident** in the supermarket.*

accidental
ADJECTIVE Something that is **accidental** has not been planned.
accidentally ADVERB

accommodation
NOUN a place where you can live, work or sleep

accompany **accompanies, accompanying, accompanied**
VERB **1** If you **accompany** someone, you go with them.
2 If you **accompany** a singer, you play an instrument while they sing.

accomplice **accomplices**
NOUN a person who helps someone else to commit a crime

accomplish **accomplishes, accomplishing, accomplished**
VERB If you **accomplish** something, you succeed in doing it.

according to
PREPOSITION If something is true **according to** a particular person, that person says that it is true. • ***According to*** *my grandad, that castle is haunted.*

account **accounts, accounting, accounted**
NOUN **1** a written or spoken report of something
2 money that you keep at a bank
PHRASE **3** **On account of** means because of. • *He couldn't play football,* ***on account of*** *a sore throat.*
VERB **4** To **account for** something is to explain it. • *The bad weather* ***accounts for*** *the cancellation of the barbecue.*

accountant **accountants**
NOUN someone whose job is to look after the financial affairs of people and companies

accumulate **accumulates, accumulating, accumulated**
VERB If things **accumulate**, or if you **accumulate** things, they collect over a period of time. • *While they were away, a large pile of letters* ***accumulated*** *on the doormat.*
accumulation NOUN

accurate
ADJECTIVE absolutely correct
accuracy NOUN

accuse **accuses, accusing, accused**
VERB If you **accuse** someone of doing something wrong, you say they have done it.
accusation NOUN

ace **aces**
NOUN **1** In a pack of cards, the **ace** is a card with a single symbol on it.
2 In tennis, an **ace** is a serve that the other player is unable to return.
ADJECTIVE **3** INFORMAL good or skilful
• *an* ***ace*** *squash player*

ache **aches, aching, ached**
NOUN **1** a continuous, dull pain
VERB **2** If a part of your body **aches**, you feel a continuous, dull pain there.

achieve **achieves, achieving, achieved**
VERB If you **achieve** something, you are successful at doing it or at making it happen.

> The *i* comes before the *e* in *achieve.*

acid **acids**
NOUN **1** a chemical substance. Strong **acids** can damage skin, cloth and metal, for example sulphuric **acid**. Other **acids**, such as those found in citrus fruit and vinegar, are harmless.
ANTONYM: alkali
ADJECTIVE **2** If something has an **acid** taste, it tastes sharp or bitter.
ANTONYM: alkaline
[from Latin *acidus* meaning sour]

acid rain
NOUN rain that has been polluted by the burning of fossil fuels, such as coal and oil

acknowledge **acknowledges, acknowledging, acknowledged**
VERB **1** If you **acknowledge** a fact or a situation, you admit that it is true.
2 If you **acknowledge** someone, you show that you have seen and recognized them, by waving or saying *hello*.
3 If you **acknowledge** a message or a letter, you tell the person who sent it that you have received it.

A B C D E F G H I J K L M N O P Q R S T U V W X Y Z

acne
NOUN a skin disease that causes spots on the face and neck. **Acne** is common among teenagers.

acorn **acorns**
NOUN a nut that grows on oak trees

acquaintance **acquaintances**
NOUN someone you know slightly but not well

acre **acres**
NOUN a unit for measuring land. One acre is equal to 4840 square yards or about 4047 square metres.

acrobat **acrobats**
NOUN an entertainer who performs difficult gymnastic acts
[from Greek *akrobates* meaning someone who walks on tiptoe]
acrobatic ADJECTIVE
acrobatics PLURAL NOUN

acronym **acronyms**
NOUN a word made up of the initial letters of a phrase • *NATO is an **acronym**, and stands for North Atlantic Treaty Organization.*

across
PREPOSITION OR ADVERB **1** If you go **across** a place, you go from one side of it to the other. • *We walked **across** Hyde Park.*
2 Something that is situated **across** a road or river is on the other side of it.

act **acts, acting, acted**
VERB **1** If you **act**, you do something.
• *We have to **act** quickly in an emergency.*
2 If you **act** in a particular way, you behave in that way. • *You're **acting** like a baby.*
3 If you **act** in a play or film, you play a role in it.
NOUN **4** a single thing someone does
• *The rescue was a brave **act**.*
5 An **Act** of Parliament is a law passed by the government.
6 Stage plays are divided into parts called **acts**.

action **actions**
NOUN **1** something you do for a particular purpose
2 a physical movement, such as jumping

active
ADJECTIVE **1** Someone who is **active** moves around a lot or does a lot of things.
2 In grammar the **active**, or the **active** voice, is the form of the verb in which the subject of the sentence is the person or thing doing the action, rather than having it done to them. For example, the sentence *The dog bit Ben* is in the **active** voice. In the passive voice the subject is acted upon: *Ben was bitten by the dog.*
ANTONYM: passive

activity **activities**
NOUN **1** a situation in which a lot of things are happening at the same time • *There was a great deal of **activity** in the hall as we got ready for the school play.*
2 something you do for pleasure, such as gymnastics or music

actor **actors**
NOUN a man or woman whose job is performing in plays or films

actress **actresses**
NOUN a woman whose profession is acting

actual
ADJECTIVE real, rather than imaginary or guessed at • *You guessed I was eleven – my **actual** age is twelve.*
actually ADVERB

acute
ADJECTIVE **1** severe or intense • *She had an **acute** pain in her arm.*
2 In mathematics, an **acute** angle measures less than 90 degrees.
3 Someone who is **acute** is intelligent.

AD
ADJECTIVE You use **AD** in dates to show the number of years after the birth of Jesus Christ.
[an abbreviation of the Latin *Anno Domini* meaning the year of Our Lord]

adapt **adapts, adapting, adapted**
VERB **1** If you **adapt** to something, you get used to it.
2 If you **adapt** something, you change it so that it can be used in a new way.

adaptable
ADJECTIVE If you are **adaptable**, you change

easily in a new situation or to suit new circumstances.

add **adds, adding, added**
VERB **1** If you **add** something to a number of things, you put it with those things. • *Each girl **added** more wood to the pile.*
2 If you **add** numbers together, or **add** them up, you work out the total. • *Two and three **added** together are five* (2 + 3 = 5).

adder
adders
NOUN a small, poisonous snake

addiction
addictions
NOUN If you have an **addiction** to something, you cannot stop doing it or wanting it.

addition **additions**
NOUN **1** the process of adding two or more numbers together
2 something that is added to something else • *The **addition** of sugar would improve the taste of these plums.*

additional
ADJECTIVE extra or more

additive **additives**
NOUN something that is added to something else, such as food

address **addresses, addressing, addressed**
NOUN **1** Your **address** is the number of the house where you live, together with the name of the street and the town or village.
VERB **2** If someone **addresses** a letter to you, they write your name and address on it.
3 If you **address** a group of people, you speak to them formally.

There are two *d*s and two *s*s in *address.*

adenoids
PLURAL NOUN small lumps of flesh at the back of the throat

adequate
ADJECTIVE just enough for what is needed
SYNONYMS: enough, satisfactory, sufficient

adhesive **adhesives**
NOUN **1** a substance used to stick things together, such as glue
ADJECTIVE **2** If something is **adhesive**, it sticks to other things.

adjective **adjectives**
NOUN a word that adds to the description of a noun. For example, *large* and *old* are both **adjectives**.

adjust **adjusts, adjusting, adjusted**
VERB **1** If you **adjust** something, you change its position or alter it in some other way. • *She **adjusted** her pillow to make herself more comfortable.*
2 If you **adjust** to a new situation, you get used to it.
adjustment NOUN

administration **administrations**
NOUN the work of managing and supervising an organization

admiral **admirals**
NOUN a senior officer in the navy

admire **admires, admiring, admired**
VERB If you **admire** someone or something, you respect and approve of them.
admirer NOUN

admission **admissions**
NOUN **1** If you are allowed **admission** to a place, you may go into it.
2 If you make an **admission**, you confess to something or agree that it is true.

admit **admits, admitting, admitted**
VERB **1** If you **admit** something, you agree that it is true.
2 If you **admit** to something, you agree that you did something you shouldn't have done.
3 To **admit** someone or something to a place is to allow them to enter it.

admittance
NOUN the right to enter somewhere • *There will be no **admittance** to the party after eight o'clock.*

A B C D E F G H I J K L M N O P Q R S T U V W X Y Z

adolescent **adolescents**
NOUN a young person who is no longer a child, but is not yet an adult
[from Latin *adolescere* meaning to grow up]
adolescence NOUN

adopt **adopts, adopting, adopted**
VERB If someone **adopts** a child, they take them into their family as their son or daughter by a legal process.
[from Latin *adoptare* meaning to choose for oneself]

adorable
ADJECTIVE loveable and attractive

adore **adores, adoring, adored**
VERB If you **adore** someone, you feel deep love and admiration for them.
adoration NOUN

adult **adults**
NOUN a mature and fully developed person or animal

advance **advances, advancing, advanced**
VERB **1** To **advance** is to move forward.
NOUN **2** An **advance** is progress in something. • *There have been many scientific **advances** in the past century.*
PHRASE **3** If you do something **in advance** of something, you do it beforehand. • *We booked our holiday well **in advance**.*

advanced
ADJECTIVE If something is **advanced**, it is at a high level, or ahead in development or progress. • *The children in the top group do **advanced** maths exercises.*

advantage **advantages**
NOUN **1** a benefit, or something that puts you in a better position • *The **advantage** of e-mail is that it is quicker than the post.*
PHRASE **2** If you **take advantage** of someone, you treat them unfairly for your own benefit.
3 If you **take advantage** of something, you make use of it.

adventure **adventures**
NOUN something that is exciting, and perhaps even dangerous

adverb **adverbs**
NOUN a word that tells you how, when, where or why something happens or something is done. For example, she walked *slowly*, he came *yesterday*, they live *here*.
[from Latin *adverbium* meaning added word]

advert
NOUN an abbreviation for *advertisement*

advertise **advertises, advertising, advertised**
VERB If you **advertise** something, you tell people about it in a newspaper, on a poster or on TV.

advertisement **advertisements**
NOUN a notice in a newspaper, on a poster or on TV about a job or things for sale

advice
NOUN a suggestion from someone about what you should do

The noun *advice* ends in *ce*.

advisable
ADJECTIVE If it is **advisable** to do something, it is a sensible thing to do and will probably give the results that you want. • *It is **advisable** to wear a helmet when cycling.*

advise **advises, advising, advised**
VERB If you **advise** someone to do something, you tell them you think they should do it.

The verb *advise* ends in *se*.

aerial **aerials**
NOUN **1** a piece of wire for receiving television or radio signals
ADJECTIVE **2** happening in the air
• *We watched the **aerial** displays at the RAF airshow.*

aero-
PREFIX to do with the air, for example **aero**plane
[from Greek *aer* meaning air]

aerobics
NOUN a type of fast physical exercise that increases the oxygen in your blood and

strengthens your heart and lungs
aerobic ADJECTIVE

aeroplane **aeroplanes**
NOUN a vehicle with wings and engines that enable it to fly

aerosol **aerosols**
NOUN a small, metal container in which liquid is kept under pressure so that it can be forced out as a spray

affair **affairs**
NOUN **1** an event or series of events • *The wedding was a happy* ***affair****.*
2 If something is your own **affair**, then it is your concern only.

affect **affects, affecting, affected**
VERB When something **affects** someone or something, it causes them to change. • *Computers* ***affect*** *our lives in many ways.*

affection
NOUN a feeling of love and fondness for someone
affectionate ADJECTIVE

affluent
ADJECTIVE People who are **affluent** have a lot of money and possessions.

afford **affords, affording, afforded**
VERB **1** If you can **afford** something, you have enough money to pay for it.
2 If you can **afford** to relax, you feel you have done enough work for the moment, and have time to take things easy.

afloat
ADVERB If something or someone is **afloat**, they are floating.

afraid
ADJECTIVE **1** If you are **afraid**, you are frightened.
SYNONYM: scared
2 If you are **afraid** something might happen, you worry that it might happen.

after
PREPOSITION OR ADVERB **1** later than a particular time, date or event • *She left just* ***after*** *breakfast.* • *Soon* ***after****, he went to work.*
PREPOSITION **2** If you come **after** someone or something, you are behind them and following them. • *They ran* ***after*** *her.*

afternoon **afternoons**
NOUN the part of the day between twelve noon and about six o'clock

afterwards
ADVERB after an event or time • *We went swimming, and* ***afterwards*** *we had an ice cream.*

again
ADVERB happening one more time • *The film was so good that we went to see it* ***again****.*
SYNONYM: once more

against
PREPOSITION **1** touching and resting on • *He leaned the ladder* ***against*** *the wall.*
2 in opposition to • *France played* ***against*** *England.*

age **ages, ageing** or **aging, aged**
NOUN **1** The **age** of something or someone is the number of years they have lived or existed.
2 a particular period in history • *the Iron* ***Age***
PLURAL NOUN **3** INFORMAL **Ages** means a very long time. • *He's been talking for* ***ages****.*
VERB **4** To **age** is to grow old or to appear older.

Ageing and *aging* are both correct spellings.

agency **agencies**
NOUN an organization or business that provides special services • *detective* ***agency*** • *advertising* ***agency***

agenda **agendas**
NOUN a list of items to be discussed at a meeting

agent **agents**
NOUN **1** someone who does business or arranges things for other people • *a travel* ***agent***
2 someone who works for their country's secret service

aggravate **aggravates, aggravating, aggravated**
VERB **1** If you **aggravate** something, you make it worse.

2 INFORMAL If you **aggravate** someone, you annoy them.
aggravating ADJECTIVE **aggravation** NOUN

aggressive
ADJECTIVE full of hostility and violence
• *Some breeds of dog are more **aggressive** than others.*
SYNONYMS: belligerent, hostile

agile
ADJECTIVE able to move quickly and easily
• *He is as **agile** as a cat.*
agilely ADVERB **agility** NOUN

agitated
ADJECTIVE worried and anxious
agitation NOUN

ago
ADVERB in the past • *She bought her flat three years **ago**.*

agony
NOUN very great physical or mental pain
SYNONYMS: suffering, torment

agree **agrees, agreeing, agreed**
VERB **1** If you **agree** with someone, you have the same opinion as they do.
2 If you **agree** to do something, you say you will do it.

agreeable
ADJECTIVE **1** pleasant or enjoyable
2 If you are **agreeable** to something, you are willing to allow it or to do it.
agreeably ADVERB

agreement **agreements**
NOUN If you reach an **agreement** with one or more people, you make a decision with them or come to an arrangement with them.

agriculture
NOUN farming

ahead
ADVERB **1** in front • *He looked **ahead** as he cycled down the road.*
2 more advanced than someone or something else • *Some countries are **ahead** of others in space travel.*
3 in the future • *I can't think that far **ahead**.*

aid **aids**
NOUN **1** money, equipment or services provided for people in need
2 something that makes a job easier
• *The whiteboard is a useful teaching **aid**.*

ailment **ailments**
NOUN a minor illness

aim **aims, aiming, aimed**
VERB **1** If you **aim** at something, you point a weapon at it.
2 If you **aim** to do something, you are planning to do it.
SYNONYMS: intend, mean
NOUN **3** Your **aim** is what you intend to achieve. • *The **aim** of the jumble sale is to raise money for charity.*
SYNONYMS: goal, objective

aimless
ADJECTIVE If you are **aimless**, you have no clear purpose or sense of direction.
aimlessly ADVERB

air
NOUN **1** the mixture of oxygen and other gases that we breathe and that forms the earth's atmosphere
2 the space around things or above the ground • *The balloons floated up into the **air**.*
3 used to refer to travel in aircraft
• *My uncle often travels by **air**.*

air conditioning
NOUN a way of keeping cool, fresh air in a building

aircraft
NOUN any vehicle that can fly

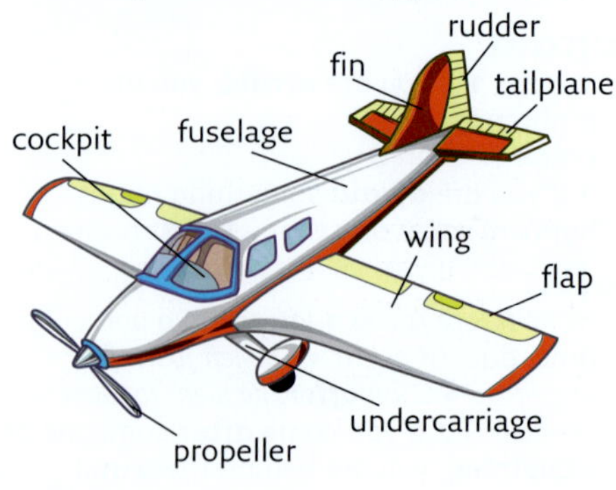

air force **air forces**
NOUN the part of a country's armed services that fights using aircraft

airline **airlines**
NOUN a company that provides air travel

airmail
NOUN the system of sending letters and parcels by air • *He sent letters from Hong Kong to Britain by **airmail**.*

airport **airports**
NOUN a place where people go to catch aeroplanes

airtight
ADJECTIVE If something is **airtight**, no air can get in or out.

aisle **aisles**
NOUN a long, narrow gap that people can walk along between rows of seats or shelves • *The ticket collector was coming down the **aisle**.*

ajar
ADJECTIVE A door or window that is **ajar** is slightly open.

alarm **alarms, alarming, alarmed**
NOUN **1** a feeling of fear and worry • *The cat sprang back in **alarm**.*
2 an automatic device used to warn people of something • *The burglar **alarm** went off accidentally.*
VERB **3** If something **alarms** you, it makes you worried and anxious.

album **albums**
NOUN **1** a CD, cassette or record with a number of songs on it
2 a book in which you keep a collection of things, such as photographs or stamps

alcohol
NOUN the name for drinks such as beer, wine and spirits

alert **alerts, alerting, alerted**
ADJECTIVE **1** If you are **alert**, you are paying full attention to what is happening.
SYNONYMS: vigilant, watchful
VERB **2** If you **alert** someone to a problem or danger, you warn them of it.

algebra
NOUN a branch of mathematics in which symbols and letters are used to represent unknown numbers

alias **aliases**
NOUN a false name

alibi **alibis**
NOUN If you have an **alibi**, you have evidence proving you were somewhere else when a crime was committed.

alien **aliens**
NOUN **1** In science fiction, an **alien** is a creature from outer space.
ADJECTIVE **2** Something that is **alien** to you seems strange because it is not part of your normal experience. • *The desert is an **alien** environment to many people.*
[from Latin *alienus* meaning foreign]

alight **alights, alighting, alighted**
ADJECTIVE **1** Something that is **alight** is burning.
VERB **2** If something **alights** somewhere, it lands there.
3 If someone **alights** from a vehicle, they get out of it.

alike
ADJECTIVE **1** Things that are **alike** are very similar in some way.
ADVERB **2** If people or things are treated **alike**, they are treated the same.

alive
ADJECTIVE If someone or something is **alive**, they are living.

alkali **alkalis**
NOUN a chemical substance sometimes used in cleaning materials. **Alkalis** can neutralize acids.
ANTONYM: acid
alkaline ADJECTIVE

all
ADJECTIVE, NOUN OR ADVERB **1** the whole of something • *She told us **all** about it.*
• *He ate **all** the chocolate.*
ADVERB **2** also used to show that both sides in a game or contest have the same score
• *The final score was three points **all**.*

Allah
PROPER NOUN the Muslim name for God

a b c d e f g h i j k l m n o p q r s t u v w x y z

allege **alleges, alleging, alleged**
VERB If you **allege** that something is true, you say it's true, but you cannot prove it.

allergy **allergies**
NOUN If you have an **allergy** to something, it makes you ill to eat or touch it.
allergic ADJECTIVE

alley **alleys**
NOUN a narrow street or passageway between buildings

alliance **alliances**
NOUN a group of countries, organizations or people who have similar aims and who work together to achieve them

alligator **alligators**
NOUN a large, scaly reptile, similar to a crocodile
[from Spanish *el lagarto* meaning lizard]

alliteration
NOUN the use of several words together that begin with the same letter or sound. For example, *the slithery snake slid silently across the sand.*

allotment **allotments**
NOUN a piece of land that people rent to grow fruit and vegetables on

allow **allows, allowing, allowed**
VERB If someone **allows** you to do something, they let you do it.

all right
ADJECTIVE **1** If something is **all right**, it is satisfactory, but not especially good.
• *Do you like mushrooms? They're **all right**.*
2 If someone is **all right**, they are safe and not harmed.
3 You say **all right** if you agree to something. • *Will you help? **All right**.*

ally **allies**
NOUN a person or a country that helps and supports another
SYNONYMS: friend, partner

almond **almonds**
NOUN an oval edible nut, cream in colour

almost
ADVERB very nearly • *I have **almost** as many points as you.*
SYNONYMS: just about, practically

alone
ADJECTIVE not with other people or things

along
PREPOSITION **1** moving forward • *We strolled **along** the road.*
2 from one end of something to the other • *The cupboards stretched **along** the wall.*

alongside
PREPOSITION OR ADVERB next to something
• *We tied our boat **alongside** the jetty.*

aloud
ADVERB When you read **aloud**, you read so that people can hear you.

alphabet **alphabets**
NOUN all the letters used to write words in a language. The letters of an **alphabet** are written in a special order.

alphabetical
ADJECTIVE If something is in **alphabetical** order, it is arranged according to the letters of the alphabet.
alphabetically ADVERB

already
ADVERB If you have done something **already**, you did it earlier. • *Josh has **already** gone to bed.*

also
ADVERB in addition to something that has just been mentioned • *I bought an ice cream, and I **also** bought a drink.*

altar **altars**
NOUN a holy table in a church or temple

alter **alters, altering, altered**
VERB If something **alters**, or if you **alter** it, it changes.

alternate **alternates, alternating, alternated**
Said "ol-**ter**-nut" ADJECTIVE **1** If something happens on **alternate** days, it happens on one in every two days.
Said "**ol**-ter-nayt" VERB **2** If two things **alternate**, they regularly happen one after the other.

alternative **alternatives**
NOUN something you can do or have instead of something else • *Is there an **alternative** to meat on the menu?*

although
CONJUNCTION in spite of the fact that • *He wasn't well-known in America, **although** he had made a film there.*

altitude **altitudes**
NOUN height above sea level • *The mountain range reaches an **altitude** of 1330 metres.*

altogether
ADVERB **1** completely or entirely • *The car got slower, then stopped **altogether**.*
2 in total – used of amounts • *I have two cats and two dogs. That's four pets **altogether**.*

aluminium
NOUN a silvery-white, lightweight metal

always
ADVERB **1** all the time • *He's **always** late.*
2 forever • *I'll **always** remember this day.*

a.m.
a.m. is used to show times in the morning
[an abbreviation of the Latin *ante meridiem* meaning before noon]

am
VERB a present tense of **be**

amateur **amateurs**
NOUN someone who does something without being paid for it • *He began playing football as an **amateur**, but now he is a professional.*

amaze **amazes, amazing, amazed**
VERB If something **amazes** you, it surprises you very much.
SYNONYMS: astonish, astound
amazement NOUN

amazing
ADJECTIVE If something is **amazing**, it is very surprising.
amazingly ADVERB

ambassador **ambassadors**
NOUN a person sent to a foreign country as the representative of their own government

amber
NOUN **1** a hard, yellowish-brown substance from trees, used in making jewellery
NOUN OR ADJECTIVE **2** an orange-brown colour

ambiguous
ADJECTIVE If something is **ambiguous**, it can have more than one meaning.
ambiguously ADVERB **ambiguity** NOUN

ambition **ambitions**
NOUN If you have an **ambition** to do something, you want very much to do it.

amble **ambles, ambling, ambled**
VERB If you **amble**, you walk along in a slow, relaxed way.

ambulance **ambulances**
NOUN a vehicle for taking sick and injured people to hospital

ambush **ambushes, ambushing, ambushed**
NOUN **1** a surprise attack
VERB **2** If one group of people **ambushes** another, they hide and lie in wait, and then make a surprise attack.

ammonia
NOUN a strong-smelling, colourless liquid or gas, often used in cleaning substances

ammunition
NOUN anything that can be fired from a gun or other weapon, for example bullets and shells

amoeba **amoebas** or **amoebae**
NOUN a tiny living organism that has only one cell. An **amoeba** reproduces by dividing into two.

among or **amongst**
PREPOSITION **1** surrounded by
2 in the company of • *He was **among** friends.*
3 between more than two • *The money will be divided **among** seven charities.*

amount **amounts**
NOUN how much there is of something • *You need a large **amount** of flour for this recipe.*

a b c d e f g h i j k l m n o p q r s t u v w x y z

A B C D E F G H I J K L M N O P Q R S T U V W X Y Z

amphibian **amphibians**
NOUN a creature that lives partly on land and partly in water, for example a frog or a newt
amphibious ADJECTIVE

frog

newt

amplify **amplifies, amplifying, amplified**
VERB If you **amplify** a sound, you make it louder.
amplifier NOUN

amputate **amputates, amputating, amputated**
VERB If a surgeon **amputates** part of the body, such as an arm or a leg, they cut it off.
amputation NOUN

amuse **amuses, amusing, amused**
VERB **1** If something **amuses** you, you think it is funny.
2 If you **amuse** yourself, you find things to do that stop you from being bored.
amused ADJECTIVE **amusing** ADJECTIVE

amusement **amusements**
NOUN **1** the feeling you have when you think that something is funny or you have pleasure
2 a mechanical device used for entertainment, at a fair for example
3 **Amusements** are ways of passing the time pleasantly.

an
ADJECTIVE **An** is used instead of *a* in front of words that begin with the vowels a, e, i, o, or u. • ***an** apple* • ***an** egg*

anaemia
NOUN a medical condition in which there are too few red cells in the blood. It makes you feel tired and look pale.
anaemic ADJECTIVE

anaesthetic **anaesthetics**; also spelt **anesthetic**
NOUN a substance that stops you feeling pain. A general **anaesthetic** stops you from feeling pain in the whole of your body by putting you to sleep. A local **anaesthetic** makes just one part of your body go numb.

anagram **anagrams**
NOUN a word or phrase formed by changing the order of the letters of another word or phrase. For example, *draw* is an **anagram** of *ward* and *dear* is an **anagram** of *read*.

analogue
ADJECTIVE An **analogue** watch or clock shows the time with pointers that move round a dial.
ANTONYM: digital

analogy **analogies**
NOUN a comparison between two things that are similar in some ways

analyse **analyses, analysing, analysed**
VERB If you **analyse** something, you investigate it carefully to understand it or to find out what it consists of.

anatomy **anatomies**
NOUN the study of the structure of bodies, both animal and human, to find out how they work
anatomical ADJECTIVE

ancestor **ancestors**
NOUN a member of your family who lived many years ago • *He could trace his **ancestors** back 700 years.*
[from Latin *antecessor* meaning one who goes before]

anchor **anchors, anchoring, anchored**
NOUN **1** a heavy, hooked object at the end of a chain. It is dropped from a boat into the water to keep the boat from floating away.
VERB **2** If you **anchor** something, you hold it down firmly.

ancient
ADJECTIVE Things that are **ancient** existed or happened a very long time ago.
ANTONYM: modern

and
CONJUNCTION You use **and** to link two or more parts of a sentence together. • *Let's go to the cinema **and** then have pizza.*

anecdote **anecdotes**
NOUN a short, sometimes entertaining story about a person or an event

angel **angels**
NOUN a being who, some people believe, lives in heaven and acts as a messenger for God
[from Greek *angelos* meaning messenger]

anger
NOUN the strong feeling you get about something unfair or cruel
SYNONYMS: fury, rage, wrath

angle **angles**
NOUN **1** the distance between two lines at the point where they join together. **Angles** are measured in degrees.
• *an **angle** of 90 degrees*
2 the direction from which you look at something • *He painted pictures of the garden from all **angles**.*

angry **angrier, angriest**
ADJECTIVE very annoyed
SYNONYMS: furious, cross

anguish
NOUN great suffering

animal **animals**
NOUN any living being that is not a plant

animation **animations**
NOUN a way of making films using drawings that appear to move when you watch them
animated ADJECTIVE

ankle **ankles**
NOUN the joint that connects your foot to your leg

annihilate **annihilates, annihilating, annihilated**
VERB If someone or something **annihilates** someone or something else, they destroy them completely.
annihilation NOUN

anniversary **anniversaries**
NOUN a date that is remembered because something special happened on that date in a previous year • *We celebrated Mum and Dad's twelfth wedding **anniversary**.*

announce **announces, announcing, announced**
VERB If you **announce** something, you tell people about it publicly or officially.
• *They **announced** the team on Friday morning.*
SYNONYM: make known
announcement NOUN

annoy **annoys, annoying, annoyed**
VERB If someone or something **annoys** you, they make you angry or impatient.
SYNONYMS: bother, irritate
annoyance NOUN

annual **annuals**
ADJECTIVE **1** happening once a year • *our **annual** sports day*
NOUN **2** a book that is published once a year for children

anonymous
ADJECTIVE If something is **anonymous**, nobody knows who is responsible for it.
• *The charity received an **anonymous** donation.*

anorak **anoraks**
NOUN a warm, waterproof jacket, usually with a hood
[an Eskimo word]

anorexia
NOUN a psychological illness in which the person refuses to eat
[from Greek *an* + *orexis* meaning no appetite]

another
ADJECTIVE OR PRONOUN one more person or thing

answer **answers, answering, answered**
VERB **1** If you **answer** someone, you reply to them in speech or writing.
NOUN **2** the reply you give when you

answer someone • *I received an **answer** to my letter.*
3 a solution to a problem

ant **ants**
NOUN **Ants** are small insects that live in large groups.

antagonize **antagonizes, antagonizing, antagonized**
VERB If you **antagonize** someone, you upset them and make them feel angry.

Antarctic
NOUN the area around the South Pole

antelope **antelopes**
NOUN a hoofed animal, similar to a deer

antenna **antennae** or **antennas**
NOUN **1** one of the two long, thin parts attached to the head of an insect or other animal, which it uses to feel with. The plural is **antennae**.
2 In Australian, New Zealand and American English, an **antenna** is a radio or television aerial. The plural is **antennas**.

anthem **anthems**
NOUN usually a song of celebration, and sometimes a religious song

anther **anthers**
NOUN the part of the stamen in a flower where the pollen matures

anthology **anthologies**
NOUN a collection of writings by various authors, published in one book
[from Greek *anthologia* meaning flower gathering]

anti-
PREFIX against or opposite • *an **anti**malaria tablet*
ANTONYM: pro-

antibiotic **antibiotics**
NOUN a drug or chemical used in medicine to kill bacteria and cure infections

anticipate **anticipates, anticipating, anticipated**
VERB If you **anticipate** an event, you are expecting it and are getting prepared for it.
anticipation NOUN

anticlimax **anticlimaxes**
NOUN If something is an **anticlimax**, it disappoints you because it is not as exciting as you expected, or because it occurs after something that was more exciting.

anticlockwise
ADJECTIVE OR ADVERB moving in the opposite direction to the hands of a clock
ANTONYM: clockwise

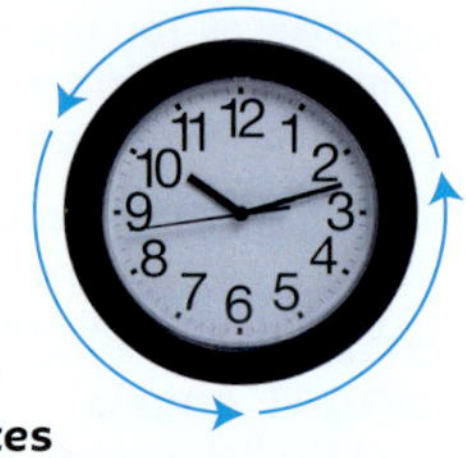

antidote **antidotes**
NOUN a chemical substance that works against the effects of a poison

antique **antiques**
NOUN an object from the past that is collected because of its value or beauty

antiseptic
ADJECTIVE Something that is **antiseptic** can kill some germs.

antler **antlers**
NOUN **Antlers** are the branched horns on the top of a male deer's head.

antonym **antonyms**
NOUN a word that means the opposite of another word • *Happy is the **antonym** of sad.*

anxiety **anxieties**
NOUN nervousness or worry

anxious
ADJECTIVE **1** If you are **anxious**, you are nervous or worried.
2 If you are **anxious** to do something, you very much want to do it. • *She was **anxious** to pass her ballet exam.*

any
ADJECTIVE OR PRONOUN **1** one, some or several • *Have you **any** sausages?*
2 even the smallest amount or even one • *She can't eat nuts of **any** kind.*
3 no matter which or what • *I'm so thirsty, **any** drink will do.*

anybody
PRONOUN any person

anyhow
ADVERB **1** in any case • *It's still early, but I'm going to bed **anyhow**.*
2 in a careless way • *They were all shoved in **anyhow**.*

anyone
PRONOUN any person • *I won't tell **anyone**.*

anything
PRONOUN any object, event, situation or action • *Can you see **anything**?*

anyway
ADVERB in any case • *It's raining, but I'm going out **anyway**.*

anywhere
ADVERB in, at or to any place • *Can you see him **anywhere**?* • *We haven't got **anywhere** to play.*

apart
ADVERB OR ADJECTIVE **1** When something is **apart** from something else, there is a space or a distance between them. • *The gliders landed about seventy metres **apart**.*
ADVERB **2** If you take something **apart**, you separate it into pieces.

apartment **apartments**
NOUN a set of rooms for living in, usually on one floor of a building

ape **apes, aping, aped**
NOUN **1** a large animal similar to a monkey, but without a tail. **Apes** include chimpanzees and gorillas.
VERB **2** If you **ape** someone's speech or behaviour, you imitate it.

apex **apexes** or **apices**
NOUN The **apex** of something is its pointed top. • *the **apex** of a cone*
SYNONYM: vertex

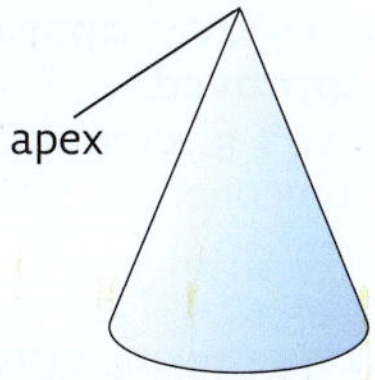

apologize **apologizes, apologizing, apologized**; also spelt **apologise**
VERB When you **apologize** to someone, you say you are sorry for something you have said or done.
apology NOUN

apostrophe **apostrophes**
NOUN **1** a punctuation mark (') used to show that one or more letters have been missed out of a word, for example *he's* for *he is*
2 **Apostrophes** are also used with *-s* at the end of a noun to show that what follows belongs to or relates to the noun. If the noun already has an *-s* at the end, for example because it is plural, the **apostrophe** comes after the *s*. For example, *my brother's books* (one brother), *my brothers' books* (more than one brother).

apparatus
NOUN the equipment used for a particular task • *The firefighters wore breathing **apparatus**.*

apparent
ADJECTIVE **1** An **apparent** situation seems to exist, although you cannot be certain of it.
2 clear and obvious • *It was **apparent** they would get on well together.*
apparently ADVERB

appeal **appeals, appealing, appealed**
VERB **1** If you **appeal** for something, you make an urgent request for it. • *The police **appealed** for witnesses to come forward.*
2 If something or someone **appeals** to you, you find them attractive or interesting.
NOUN **3** a formal or serious request • *an **appeal** for funds to help people in need*

appear **appears, appearing, appeared**
VERB **1** When something **appears**, it moves from somewhere you could not see to somewhere you can see it. • *The sun **appeared** from behind the clouds.*
2 If something **appears** to be a certain way, it seems or looks that way.

appearance **appearances**
NOUN **1** Someone's or something's **appearance** is the way they look to other people.
2 If a person makes an **appearance** in a film or a show, they take part in it.

a b c d e f g h i j k l m n o p q r s t u v w x y z

A B C D E F G H I J K L M N O P Q R S T U V W X Y Z

3 The **appearance** of something is the time it begins to exist.

appendicitis
NOUN a painful illness in which a person's appendix becomes infected

appendix **appendices** or **appendixes**
NOUN **1** Your **appendix** is a small, closed tube forming part of your digestive system.
2 extra information that comes at the end of a book

> When *appendix* means the body part, the plural is *appendixes*. When it means the part of a book, the plural is *appendices*.

appetite **appetites**
NOUN a desire to eat
[from Latin *appetere* meaning to desire]

appetizing
ADJECTIVE When food is **appetizing**, it looks or smells good and you want to eat it.

applause
NOUN the sound of people clapping to show their enjoyment or approval of something

apple **apples**
NOUN a round fruit with smooth skin and firm white flesh

appliance **appliances**
NOUN any machine in your home that you use to do a job like cleaning or cooking. For example, a toaster is a kitchen **appliance**.

application **applications**
NOUN If you make an **application** for something, you make a formal request, usually in writing.

apply **applies, applying, applied**
VERB **1** If you **apply** for something, you ask for it formally, usually by writing a letter. • *My brother is **applying** for jobs.*
2 If you **apply** something to a surface, you put it on or rub it into the surface.
• *She **applied** sun cream to her face.*
3 If you **apply** yourself to a task, you give it all of your attention.

appoint **appoints, appointing, appointed**
VERB If a person **appoints** someone to a job or position, they formally choose them for it. • *The teacher **appointed** Sunita as team captain.*

appointment **appointments**
NOUN an arrangement you have with someone to meet them

appreciate **appreciates, appreciating, appreciated**
VERB If you **appreciate** something that someone has done for you, you are grateful to them for it.

apprehensive
ADJECTIVE If you are **apprehensive** about something, you feel worried and unsure about it.

apprentice **apprentices**
NOUN someone who works with another person for a length of time to learn that person's job or skill

approach **approaches, approaching, approached**
VERB If you **approach** something, you come near or nearer to it.

appropriate
ADJECTIVE suitable or acceptable for a particular situation

approval
NOUN If you ask for **approval** for something that you want to do, you ask for agreement with your plans.

approve **approves, approving, approved**
VERB **1** If you **approve** of something or someone, you think they are acceptable or good.
SYNONYMS: favour, like
2 If someone **approves** a plan or idea, they agree to it. • *The council **approved** plans for the new swimming pool.*
SYNONYMS: agree to, permit

approximate
ADJECTIVE near but not exactly right • *What was the **approximate** time you arrived?*

apricot **apricots**
NOUN a small, soft, yellowish-orange fruit

April
NOUN the fourth month of the year. **April** has 30 days.

apron **aprons**
NOUN a piece of clothing worn over the front of normal clothing to protect it

aquarium **aquaria** or **aquariums**
NOUN a glass tank filled with water in which fish and other aquatic animals or plants are kept

aquatic
ADJECTIVE An **aquatic** animal or plant lives in water.

aqueduct **aqueducts**
NOUN a bridge with many arches, which carries a water supply over a valley

arable
ADJECTIVE **Arable** land is used for growing crops.

arc **arcs**
NOUN **1** a smoothly curving line
2 In geometry, an **arc** is a section of the circumference of a circle.

arcade **arcades**
NOUN a covered passageway where there are shops or market stalls

arch **arches, arching, arched**
NOUN **1** a structure that has a curved top, supported on either side by a pillar or wall
VERB **2** If something **arches**, or if you **arch** it, it forms a curved line or shape. • *The cat **arched** its back.*

archaeology; also spelt **archeology**
NOUN the study of the past by digging up and examining the remains of things such as buildings, tools, and pots
[from Greek *arkhaios* meaning ancient]

archbishop **archbishops**
NOUN a bishop of the highest rank in a Christian Church • *the **Archbishop** of Canterbury*

archery
NOUN a sport in which people shoot at a target with a bow and arrow

architect **architects**
NOUN a person who designs buildings

architecture
NOUN the art or practice of designing buildings

arctic
NOUN **1** The **Arctic** is the region north of the Arctic Circle.
ADJECTIVE **2** very cold indeed • *You need specially warm clothes for **arctic** conditions.*

are
VERB a present tense of **be**

area **areas**
NOUN **1** a particular part of a place, country, or the world • *a built-up **area** of the city*
SYNONYMS: district, region, zone
2 the measurement of a flat surface
• *The **area** of the playground is 1500 square metres (1500 m^2).*

arena **arenas**
NOUN a place where sports and other public events take place
[from Latin *harena* meaning sand, because of the sandy centre of an amphitheatre where gladiators fought]

aren't
VERB a contraction of *are not*

argue **argues, arguing, argued**
VERB **1** If you **argue** with someone about something, you disagree with them about it, sometimes in an angry way.
2 If you **argue** that something is true, you give reasons why you think that it is.

a b c d e f g h i j k l m n o p q r s t u v w x y z

A B C D E F G H I J K L M N O P Q R S T U V W X Y Z

argument **arguments**
NOUN a talk between people who do not agree

arid
ADJECTIVE **Arid** land is very dry because there has been very little rain.
ANTONYM: fertile

arise **arises, arising, arose, arisen**
VERB When something such as an opportunity or a problem **arises**, it begins to exist.

aristocrat **aristocrats**
NOUN someone whose family has a high social rank, and who has a title such as Lord or Lady
aristocratic ADJECTIVE **aristocracy** NOUN

arithmetic
NOUN the part of mathematics that is to do with the addition, subtraction, multiplication and division of numbers [from Greek *arithmos* meaning number]
arithmetical ADJECTIVE
arithmetically ADVERB

arm **arms, arming, armed**
NOUN **1** the part of your body between your shoulder and your wrist
PLURAL NOUN **2** **Arms** are weapons used in a war.
VERB **3** If a country **arms** itself, it prepares for war.

armada **armadas**
NOUN a large fleet of warships • *The Spanish **Armada** was the fleet sent to destroy the English in 1588.*

armchair **armchairs**
NOUN a large chair with a support on each side for your arms

armistice **armistices**
NOUN In war, an **armistice** is an agreement to stop fighting.

armour
NOUN **1** In the past, **armour** was metal clothing worn for protection in battle.
2 In modern warfare, tanks are often referred to as **armour**.

army **armies**
NOUN a large group of soldiers who are trained to fight on land

aroma **aromas**
NOUN a strong, pleasant smell
[a Greek word meaning spice]
aromatic ADJECTIVE

around
PREPOSITION **1** situated at various points in a place or area • *There are several post boxes **around** the town.*
2 from place to place inside an area • *We walked **around** the stalls at the summer fair.*
3 surrounding or encircling a place or object • *We were sitting **around** the table.*
4 at approximately the time or place mentioned • *The jumble sale began **around** noon.*

arrange **arranges, arranging, arranged**
VERB **1** If you **arrange** to do something, or **arrange** something for someone, you make plans for it or make it possible.
• *I **arranged** to meet him later.* • *Dad **arranged** a trip to the circus for us.*
2 If you **arrange** objects, you set them out in a particular way. • *We **arranged** the books in alphabetical order.*

array **arrays**
NOUN **1** a large number of different things displayed together
2 a mathematical way of grouping. For example, 3 × 2 is shown as ⁝⁝⁝ and 2 × 3 is shown as ⁝⁝.

arrest **arrests, arresting, arrested**
VERB **1** If the police **arrest** someone, they take them to a police station because they believe they may have committed a crime.
NOUN **2** An **arrest** is the act of arresting someone.

arrive **arrives, arriving, arrived**
VERB **1** When you **arrive** at a place, you reach it at the end of your journey.
2 When you **arrive** at a decision you make up your mind.
arrival NOUN

arrogant
ADJECTIVE **Arrogant** people behave as if they are better than other people.

arrow **arrows**
NOUN a long, thin weapon with a sharp point at one end, shot from a bow

arsenal **arsenals**
NOUN a place where weapons and ammunition are stored or produced

arsenic
NOUN a strong, dangerous poison that can kill

arson
NOUN the crime of deliberately setting fire to something, especially a building

art **arts**
NOUN **1** the creation of objects, such as paintings and sculptures, that are thought to be beautiful or that express a particular idea • *He wanted to take **art** classes to learn how to draw and paint well.*
2 **Art** is also used to refer to the objects themselves. • *We saw lots of interesting paintings and sculptures at the **art** exhibition.*
3 something that needs special skills or ability • *I would like to master the **art** of sewing.*

artery **arteries**
NOUN the tubes that carry blood from your heart to the rest of your body
See **vein**
arterial ADJECTIVE

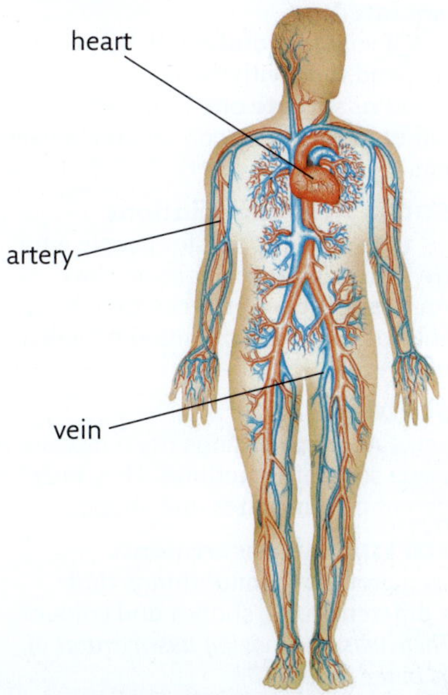

arthritis
NOUN a condition in which the joints in someone's body become painful, and sometimes swollen
arthritic ADJECTIVE

article **articles**
NOUN **1** a piece of writing in a newspaper or magazine
2 a particular item • *an **article** of clothing*

artificial
ADJECTIVE Something **artificial** is created by people rather than occurring naturally.
ANTONYM: natural

artillery
NOUN **1** **Artillery** consists of large, powerful guns and rockets.
2 The **artillery** is the branch of an army that uses these weapons.

artist **artists**
NOUN a person who draws or paints or produces other works of art

as
CONJUNCTION **1** at the same time that • *We watched television **as** we ate our sandwiches.*
2 because • ***As** I like school I get there early.*
PHRASE **3** You use **as if** *or* **as though** when you are giving an explanation for something. • *Shane walked past **as if** he didn't know me.*

ascend **ascends, ascending, ascended**
VERB FORMAL If someone or something **ascends**, they move or lead upwards. • *We **ascended** the stairs to the second floor.*
ANTONYM: descend

ash **ashes**
NOUN the grey or black powdery remains of anything that has been burnt • *We put the **ashes** from the bonfire on the compost heap.*

ashamed
ADJECTIVE **1** If you are **ashamed**, you feel embarrassed or guilty.
2 If you are **ashamed** of someone, you feel embarrassed to be connected with them.

a b c d e f g h i j k l m n o p q r s t u v w x y z

A B C D E F G H I J K L M N O P Q R S T U V W X Y Z

ashore
ADVERB If someone or something comes **ashore**, they come on to the land from the sea or a river.

aside
ADVERB If you move something **aside**, you move it to one side. • *She closed the book and laid it **aside**.*

ask **asks, asking, asked**
VERB **1** If you **ask** someone something, you put a question to them.
2 If you **ask** someone to do something, you tell them you want them to do it. • *We **asked** him to do his card trick.*
3 If you **ask** for something, you say you would like to have it. • *She **asked** for a drink of water.*
4 If you **ask** someone to come or go somewhere, you invite them there.

asleep
ADJECTIVE If you are **asleep**, your eyes are closed and your whole body is resting.

aspect **aspects**
NOUN one of many ways of seeing or thinking about something

aspirin **aspirins**
NOUN **1** a white drug used to relieve pain, fever and colds
2 a small white tablet of this drug

ass **asses**
NOUN another word for **donkey**

assassinate **assassinates, assassinating, assassinated**
VERB If someone **assassinates** an important person, they murder them.
assassination NOUN

assault **assaults**
NOUN a violent attack on someone
[from Latin *assalire* meaning to leap upon]

assemble **assembles, assembling, assembled**
VERB **1** If people **assemble**, they gather together. • *We **assembled** in the playground to watch the display.*
2 If you **assemble** something, you fit the parts of it together. • *It took us ages to **assemble** the model car.*

assembly **assemblies**
NOUN a group of people who have gathered together for a meeting

assess **assesses, assessing, assessed**
VERB If you **assess** something, you consider it carefully and make a judgement about it. • *She tried to **assess** how much further they had to walk.*
SYNONYMS: judge, size up

asset **assets**
NOUN **1** If someone or something is an **asset**, they are useful or helpful. • *He's an **asset** to the school.*
2 The **assets** of a person or a company are all the things they own that could be sold to raise money.

assignment **assignments**
NOUN a job you are given to do

assist **assists, assisting, assisted**
VERB If you **assist** someone, you help them to do something.

assistant **assistants**
NOUN someone who helps another person to do their job

associate **associates, associating, associated**
VERB **1** If you **associate** with someone, you spend time with them.
2 If you **associate** one thing with another, you make a connection between them.

association **associations**
NOUN **1** an organization for people who have similar interests, jobs or aims
2 An **association** between two things is a link you make in your mind between them.

assorted
ADJECTIVE **Assorted** things are a mixture of various sorts of something. They may be different colours, sizes and shapes.

assortment **assortments**
NOUN a group of similar things that are different sizes, shapes and colours • *There was an amazing **assortment** of toys in the shop.*

assume **assumes, assuming, assumed**
VERB **1** If you **assume** that something is true, you believe it, even if you have not thought carefully about it.
2 If you **assume** responsibility for something, you decide to do it. • *I **assumed** responsibility for feeding the hamster.*

assure **assures, assuring, assured**
VERB If you **assure** someone of something, you say something to make them less worried about it. • *I **assured** him that I wouldn't be late.*

asterisk **asterisks**
NOUN a symbol (*) used in writing and printing to draw attention to something that is explained somewhere else, usually at the bottom of the page

asteroid **asteroids**
NOUN one of the large number of very small planets that move around the sun between the orbits of Jupiter and Mars

asthma
NOUN a disease of the chest that causes wheezing and difficulty in breathing [from Greek *azein* meaning to breathe hard]
asthmatic ADJECTIVE

astonish **astonishes, astonishing, astonished**
VERB If something **astonishes** you, it surprises you very much.
astonished ADJECTIVE **astonishing** ADJECTIVE **astonishingly** ADVERB **astonishment** NOUN

astrology
NOUN the study of the sun, moon and stars in the belief that their movements can influence people's lives

astronaut **astronauts**
NOUN a person who operates a spacecraft [from Greek *astron* meaning star and *nautes* meaning sailor]

astronomy
NOUN the scientific study of stars and planets
astronomer NOUN

at
PREPOSITION **1** where someone or something is • *John waited for me **at** the bus stop.*
2 the direction something is going in • *I threw the snowball **at** my brother.*
3 when something happens • *The party starts **at** six o'clock.*

ate
VERB the past tense of **eat**

atheist **atheists**
NOUN someone who does not believe in any form of God

athlete **athletes**
NOUN a person who is very good at sport and who takes part in sporting competitions

athletics
NOUN sporting events such as running, long jump and discus

Atlantic
NOUN the ocean that separates North and South America from Europe and Africa

atlas **atlases**
NOUN a book of maps
[from the giant *Atlas* in Greek mythology, who supported the sky on his shoulders]

atmosphere **atmospheres**
NOUN **1** gases that surround a planet
2 the general mood of a place • *There was a friendly **atmosphere** at the party.*

atom **atoms**
NOUN the smallest part of an element that can take part in a chemical reaction

atrocity **atrocities**
NOUN an extremely shocking and cruel act

attach **attaches, attaching, attached**
VERB If you **attach** something to something else, you join or fasten the two things together.

attachment **attachments**
NOUN **1** a feeling of love and affection for someone
2 a file attached to an e-mail

a b c d e f g h i j k l m n o p q r s t u v w x y z

A B C D E F G H I J K L M N O P Q R S T U V W X Y Z

attack **attacks, attacking, attacked**
VERB **1** If someone **attacks** another person or animal, they use violence in order to hurt or kill them. • *The lion **attacked** the zebra in order to kill it for food.*
2 In a game such as football or hockey, players **attack** to get the ball into a position from which a goal can be scored.
NOUN **3** violent, physical action against someone

attempt **attempts, attempting, attempted**
VERB **1** If you **attempt** to do something, you try to do it.
NOUN **2** the act of trying to do something • *He made a brave **attempt** to help.*

attend **attends, attending, attended**
VERB **1** If you **attend** school, church or hospital, you go there regularly.
2 If you **attend** an event, you are present at it.

attend to
VERB If you **attend to** something, you deal with it. • *We should **attend to** our homework before going to the park.*

attendant **attendants**
NOUN someone whose job is to help people in a place such as a museum or shop

attention
NOUN the thought or care that you give to someone or something • *I paid a lot of **attention** to my homework.*

attentive
ADJECTIVE When you are **attentive**, you pay close attention.
attentively ADVERB

attic **attics**
NOUN a room at the top of a house immediately below the roof

attitude **attitudes**
NOUN the way you think about someone or something and behave towards them • *I'm not going in that shop again. I don't like their **attitude**.*

attract **attracts, attracting, attracted**
VERB **1** If something **attracts** people, it interests them and makes them want to go to it.
2 If someone **attracts** you, you like them and are interested in them.
3 When magnetic materials are **attracted** to a magnet, they are pulled towards it.

attraction **attractions**
NOUN **1** If you feel an **attraction** for someone, you like them very much.
2 somewhere people like to visit for interest or pleasure, such as a fun fair or a stately home
3 A force of **attraction** pulls magnetic materials towards a magnet.

attractive
ADJECTIVE **1** Someone who is **attractive** is good-looking or has an exciting personality.
2 If something is **attractive**, it is interesting.

aubergine **aubergines**
NOUN a dark purple, pear-shaped vegetable. It is also called an eggplant.

auburn
ADJECTIVE a red-brown hair colour

auction **auctions, auctioning, auctioned**
NOUN **1** a public sale in which goods are sold to the person who offers the highest price
VERB **2** to sell something in an auction

audible
ADJECTIVE If something is **audible**, you can hear it.

audience **audiences**
NOUN **1** the group of people who are watching or listening to a performance

2 a private or formal meeting with an important person • *The winners of the bravery awards had an **audience** with the Queen.*

audition **auditions**
NOUN a short performance by an actor or musician, so that a director can decide whether they are suitable for a part in a play or a film, or for a place in an orchestra

auditorium **auditoriums** or **auditoria**
NOUN the part of a theatre or concert hall where the audience sits

August
NOUN the eighth month of the year. **August** has 31 days.

aunt **aunts**
NOUN Your **aunt** is the sister of your mother or father, or the wife of your uncle.

author **authors**
NOUN The **author** of a book is the person who wrote it.

authority **authorities**
NOUN **1** the power to tell other people what to do • *The teacher had the **authority** to give me detention.*
2 an organization that controls public interests • *the local health **authority***
3 Someone who is an **authority** on something, knows a lot about it.

authorize **authorizes, authorizing, authorized**
VERB If someone **authorizes** something, they give official permission for it.
authorization NOUN

auto-
PREFIX **1** self or same • ***auto**biography*
2 self-propelling • ***auto**matic car*

autobiography **autobiographies**
NOUN an account of someone's life that they have written themselves
autobiographical ADJECTIVE

autograph **autographs**
NOUN the signature of a famous person
[from Greek *auto* meaning self and *graphos* meaning written]

automatic **automatics**
ADJECTIVE **1** An **automatic** machine is programmed to perform tasks without needing a person to operate it.
NOUN **2** a car in which the gears change automatically as the car's speed changes

autumn **autumns**
NOUN the season between summer and winter, when the leaves fall off the trees • *I love the golden colours of the trees in **autumn**.*

available
ADJECTIVE **1** If something is **available**, it is easy to get or to buy.
2 A person who is **available** is ready for work or free to talk to.

avalanche **avalanches**
NOUN a huge mass of snow and ice that falls down a mountainside

avenue **avenues**
NOUN a street, especially one with trees along it

average **averages**
NOUN **1** a result obtained by adding several amounts together and then dividing the total by the number of different amounts • *If I shared 36 sweets between four children, the **average** would be nine sweets per child.*
ADJECTIVE **2** standard or usual • *The **average** teenager is interested in pop music.*
SYNONYMS: normal, ordinary, typical
PHRASE **3** You say **on average** when mentioning what usually happens in a situation. • *Men are, **on average**, taller than women.*

aviary **aviaries**
NOUN a large cage or group of cages in which birds are kept

aviation
NOUN the science of flying aircraft

avocado **avocados**
NOUN a pear-shaped fruit with dark green skin, soft greenish-yellow flesh, and a large stone

avoid **avoids, avoiding, avoided**
VERB **1** If you **avoid** someone or something, you keep away from them. • *To **avoid** him, she went home the other way.*
2 If you **avoid** doing something, you make an effort not to do it.
SYNONYMS: dodge, shirk

awake
ADJECTIVE Someone who is **awake** is not sleeping.

award **awards, awarding, awarded**
NOUN **1** a prize or certificate for doing something well
VERB **2** If someone **awards** you something, they give it to you formally or officially. • *He was **awarded** the prize for fastest runner.*

aware
ADJECTIVE **1** If you are **aware** of something, you know about it.
2 If you are **aware** of something, you can see, hear, smell or feel it.

away
ADVERB **1** moving from a place • *I saw them walk **away** from the house.*
2 at a distance from a place • *The nearest supermarket is 12 kilometres **away**.*
3 in its proper place • *He put his CDs **away**.*
4 not at home, school or work • *My friend's been **away** from school for a week.*

awe
NOUN FORMAL a feeling of great respect mixed with amazement, and sometimes slight fear • *Looking up at the mountains, we felt a sense of **awe**.*

awful
ADJECTIVE very unpleasant or very bad • *Isn't the weather **awful**?*
SYNONYMS: dreadful, terrible

awkward
ADJECTIVE **1** difficult to deal with • *an **awkward** situation*
2 clumsy and uncomfortable • *The large bag was **awkward** to carry.*
[from Old Norse *ofugr* meaning turned the wrong way]

axe **axes**
NOUN a tool with a handle and a sharp blade, used for chopping wood

axis **axes**
NOUN **1** an imaginary line through the middle of something, around which it moves • *The earth turns on its **axis**.*
2 one of the two sides of a graph

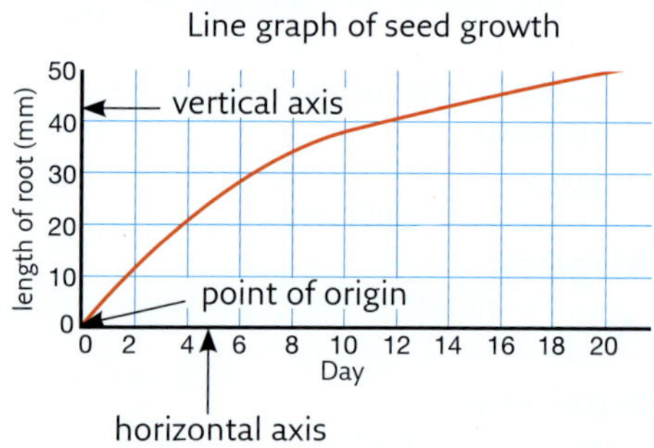

axle **axles**
NOUN the long bar that connects a pair of wheels on a vehicle

Bb

babble **babbles, babbling, babbled**
VERB If someone **babbles**, they talk in a quick and confused way that is difficult to understand.

baboon **baboons**
NOUN an African monkey with a pointed face, large teeth and a long tail

baby **babies**
NOUN a child in the first year or two of its life

baby-sit **baby-sits, baby-sitting, baby-sat**
VERB If you **baby-sit** for someone, you look after their children while they are out.

bachelor **bachelors**
NOUN a man who has never been married

back **backs, backing, backed**
ADVERB **1** When people or things move **back**, they move in the opposite direction to the one they are facing.
2 When you go **back** to a place or situation, you return to it. • *She went **back** to sleep.*
NOUN **3** the rear part of your body
ADJECTIVE **4** The **back** parts of something are the ones at the rear. • *the dog's **back** legs*
VERB **5** If a building **backs** on to something, the back of it faces in that direction.

backbone **backbones**
NOUN the column of linked bones along the middle of the back of a human and other vertebrates

background **backgrounds**
NOUN **1** the things in a picture or scene that are less noticeable than the main things
2 the kind of home you come from, and your education and experience

backstroke
NOUN a style of swimming movement on your back

backward
ADJECTIVE If you take a **backward** look, you look behind you.

backwards
ADVERB **1** If you move **backwards**, you move to a place behind you.
2 If you do something **backwards**, you do it opposite to the usual way. • *He told them to count **backwards** from 20 to 5.*

bacon
NOUN meat from the back or sides of a pig, which has been salted or smoked

bacteria
PLURAL NOUN very tiny organisms that can cause disease
[from Greek *bakterion* meaning little rod; some bacteria are rod-shaped]
bacterial ADJECTIVE

bad **worse, worst**
ADJECTIVE **1** **Bad** things are harmful or upsetting. • *I have some **bad** news.*
SYNONYMS: distressing, grave, terrible
2 not enough or of poor quality • *We thought the film was very **bad**.*
3 **Bad** food is not fresh.
SYNONYMS: rotten, decayed

badge **badges**
NOUN a piece of plastic or metal with a design or message on it that you can pin to your clothes

badger **badgers, badgering, badgered**
NOUN **1** a nocturnal mammal that has a white head with two black stripes on it
VERB **2** If you **badger** someone, you keep asking them questions or pestering them to do something.

badly **worse, worst**
ADVERB **1** not well, poorly • *The script was **badly** written.*
2 seriously • *She was **badly** hurt in the accident.*

badminton
NOUN a game in which two or four players use rackets to hit a feathered object, called a shuttlecock, over a high net

bag **bags**
NOUN a container for carrying things in
[From Old Norse *baggi* meaning bundle]

baggage
NOUN Your **baggage** is all the suitcases, holdalls and bags that you take with you when you travel.

bagpipes
PLURAL NOUN a musical instrument played by squeezing air out of a leather bag and through pipes

baguette **baguettes**
NOUN a long, thin French loaf of bread

bail **bails**
NOUN **1** In cricket, the **bails** are the two small pieces of wood placed on top of the stumps to form the wicket.
2 a sum of money paid to a court to allow an accused person to go free until the time of the trial • *The accused man was released on* ***bail****.*

bait **baits, baiting, baited**
NOUN **1** a small amount of food placed on a hook, or in a trap, to attract and catch a fish or wild animal
VERB **2** If you **bait** a hook or a trap, you put some food on it to catch a fish or wild animal.

bake **bakes, baking, baked**
VERB **1** When you **bake** food, you cook it in an oven without using extra liquid or fat.
2 If you **bake** earth or clay, you heat it until it becomes hard.

baker **bakers**
NOUN a person who makes and sells bread and cakes

balance **balances, balancing, balanced**
VERB **1** When someone or something **balances**, they remain steady and do not fall over.
2 used in mathematics when weighing and comparing two weights. If two weights are equal, they **balance**.
NOUN **3** the state of being upright and steady • *She lost her* ***balance*** *and fell.*
4 the amount of money in someone's bank account

balcony **balconies**
NOUN **1** a platform on the outside of a building, with a wall or railing round it
2 an area of upstairs seats in a theatre or cinema

bald **balder, baldest**
ADJECTIVE A **bald** person has little or no hair on their head.
[from Middle English *ballede* meaning having a white patch]

bale **bales, baling, baled**
NOUN **1** a large bundle of something, such as paper or hay, tied tightly
VERB **2** If you **bale** water from a boat, you remove it using a container; also spelt **bail**.

ball **balls**
NOUN **1** a round object used in games such as tennis, soccer, and hockey
2 The **ball** of your foot or thumb is the rounded part where your toes join your foot or your thumb joins your hand.

ballad **ballads**
NOUN **1** a long song or poem that tells a story
2 a slow, romantic pop song

ballerina **ballerinas**
NOUN a female ballet dancer

ballet
NOUN a type of artistic dancing based on precise steps
[from Italian *balletto* meaning little dance]

balloon **balloons**
NOUN **1** a small bag made of thin rubber that you blow into until it becomes larger. **Balloons** are often used as party decorations.
2 a large, strong bag filled with gas or hot air, that travels through the air carrying passengers in a basket underneath it • *They went on a hot air* ***balloon*** *flight over the city.*

ballpoint **ballpoints**
NOUN a pen with a small, metal ball at the writing point

bamboo
NOUN a tall tropical grass with hard, hollow stems used for making furniture

ban **bans, banning, banned**
VERB **1** If you **ban** something, you forbid it to be done.
SYNONYMS: forbid, prohibit
NOUN **2** If there is a **ban** on something, it is not allowed.

banana **bananas**
NOUN a long, curved fruit with a yellow skin

band **bands**
NOUN **1** a group of musicians who play jazz or pop music together
2 a group of people who share a common purpose
3 a narrow strip of something used to hold things together • *She tied her hair back with an elastic **band**.*

bandage **bandages**
NOUN a strip of cloth wrapped round a wound to protect it

bang **bangs, banging, banged**
NOUN **1** a sudden, short, loud noise
2 a hard, painful bump against something
VERB **3** If you **bang** something, you hit it or put it down violently so that it makes a loud noise.
4 If you **bang** a part of your body against something, you accidentally bump it.

banish **banishes, banishing, banished**
VERB **1** If someone is **banished**, they are sent away and never allowed to return.
2 If you **banish** something from your thoughts, you try not to think about it.
banishment NOUN

banister **banisters**
NOUN a rail supported by posts up the side of a staircase

banjo **banjos** or **banjoes**
NOUN a musical instrument, like a small guitar with a round body

bank **banks, banking, banked**
NOUN **1** a business that looks after people's money
2 the raised ground along the edge of a river or lake
VERB **3** If you **bank on** something happening, you rely on it. • *I know we said we'd go swimming, but don't **bank on** it.*

banner **banners**
NOUN **1** a long strip of cloth with a message or slogan on it • *We saw **banners** advertising the fair.*
ADJECTIVE **2** A **banner** headline is a headline printed right across the page of a newspaper.

banquet **banquets**
NOUN a grand, formal dinner, often followed by speeches
[from Old French *banquet*, originally meaning little bench]

baptism **baptisms**
NOUN the ceremony in which someone has water sprinkled on them, or they are immersed in water, as a sign that they have become a Christian

baptize **baptizes, baptizing, baptized**; also spelt **baptise**
VERB When a church official **baptizes** someone, they sprinkle water on them, or immerse them in water, as a sign that they have become a Christian.

bar **bars, barring, barred**
NOUN **1** a long, straight piece of metal
VERB **2** If you **bar** someone's way, you stop them going somewhere by standing in front of them.
NOUN **3** a counter or room where alcoholic drinks are served
4 a piece of something made in a rectangular shape • *a **bar** of soap*

barbecue **barbecues**
NOUN **1** a grill with a charcoal fire on which you cook food, usually outdoors
2 an outdoor party where you eat food cooked on a **barbecue**
[from a Caribbean word meaning framework]

barber **barbers**
NOUN a man who cuts men's hair

bar chart **bar charts**
NOUN a kind of graph where the information is shown in rows or bars

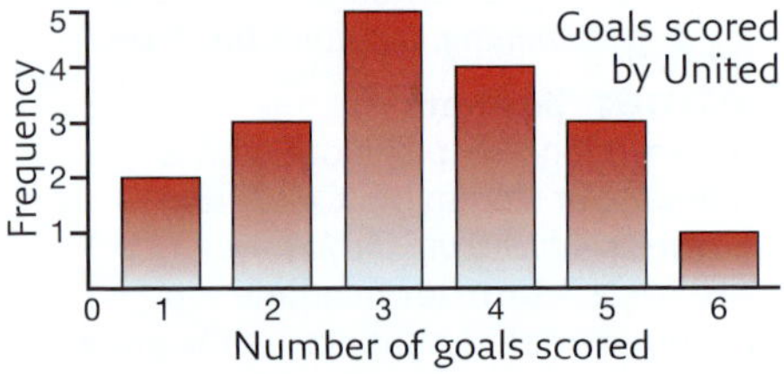

bar code **bar codes**
NOUN a pattern of lines and numbers on something that is for sale, so that the price can be read by a machine

bare **barer, barest**
ADJECTIVE **1** If a part of your body is **bare**, it is not covered by any clothing. • ***bare*** *feet*
SYNONYMS: naked, uncovered
2 If something is **bare**, it is not covered or decorated with anything. • ***bare*** *wooden floors*
3 The **bare** minimum, or the **bare** essentials, means the very least that is needed.

barely
ADVERB If you **barely** manage to do something, you only just succeed in doing it.

bargain **bargains, bargaining, bargained**
NOUN **1** an agreement in which two people or groups discuss and agree what each will do, pay or receive
2 something that is sold at a low price and that is good value • *The apples are a* ***bargain*** *at this price.*
VERB **3** When people **bargain** with each other, they discuss and agree terms about what each will do, pay or receive.

barge **barges, barging, barged**
NOUN **1** a boat with a flat bottom used for carrying heavy loads, especially on canals
VERB **2** INFORMAL If you **barge** into a place, you push into it in a rough or rude way.

bark **barks, barking, barked**
VERB **1** When a dog **barks**, it makes a short, loud noise, once or several times.
NOUN **2** the tough material that covers the outside of a tree

barley
NOUN a cereal that is grown for food and is also used for making beer and whisky

bar mitzvah
NOUN A Jewish boy's **bar mitzvah** is a ceremony that takes place on his 13th birthday, after which he is regarded as an adult.

barn **barns**
NOUN a large farm building used for storing crops or animal food
[from Old English *beren* meaning barley room]

barnacle **barnacles**
NOUN a small shellfish that fixes itself to rocks and to the bottom of boats

barometer **barometers**
NOUN an instrument that measures air pressure and shows when the weather is changing

barrel **barrels**
NOUN **1** a wooden container with rounded sides and flat ends
2 The **barrel** of a gun is the long tube through which the bullet is fired.

barricade **barricades, barricading, barricaded**
NOUN **1** a temporary barrier put up to stop people getting past
VERB **2** If you **barricade** yourself inside a room or building, you put something heavy against the door to stop people getting in.
[from Old French *barriquer* meaning to block with barrels]

barrier **barriers**
NOUN a fence or wall that prevents people or animals getting from one area to another

barrister **barristers**
NOUN a lawyer who is qualified to represent people in the higher courts

barrow **barrows**
NOUN **1** another word for **wheelbarrow**
2 a large cart from which fruit or other goods are sold in the street

base **bases, basing, based**
NOUN **1** the lowest part of something
• *The waves crashed at the **base** of the cliffs.*
2 The **base** of a triangle or a square-shaped pyramid is the bottom.
3 a place where part of an army, navy or air force works from
VERB **4** If you **base** one thing on another, you develop from it. • *She **based** the film on a true story.*
5 If you are **based** somewhere, you live there or work from there. • *My dad is **based** in Cardiff, but spends a lot of time abroad.*

baseball
NOUN a team game played with a bat and a ball. It is popular in the USA.

basement **basements**
NOUN a room or set of rooms below the level of the street • *My aunt lives in the **basement** of our house.*

basic
ADJECTIVE **1** The **basic** aspects of something are the most necessary ones. • *The **basic** ingredients of bread are flour, yeast and water.*
2 having only the essentials, and no extras or luxuries
basically ADVERB

basin **basins**
NOUN **1** a round, wide container which is open at the top
2 A river **basin** is a bowl of land from which water runs into the river.

basis **bases**
NOUN If something is the **basis** of something else, it is the main principle on which it is based, and from which other points and ideas can be developed.

bask **basks, basking, basked**
VERB If you **bask** in hot weather, you lie in the sun and enjoy the warmth.

basket **baskets**
NOUN a container made of thin strips of wood or metal woven together
• *a shopping **basket***

basketball
NOUN a game in which two teams try to score goals by throwing a large ball through one of two circular nets that are suspended high up at each end of the **basketball** court

bass **basses**
NOUN **1** a man with a very deep singing voice
ADJECTIVE **2** In music, a **bass** instrument produces a very deep sound. • *a **bass** guitar*

bassoon **bassoons**
NOUN a large woodwind instrument

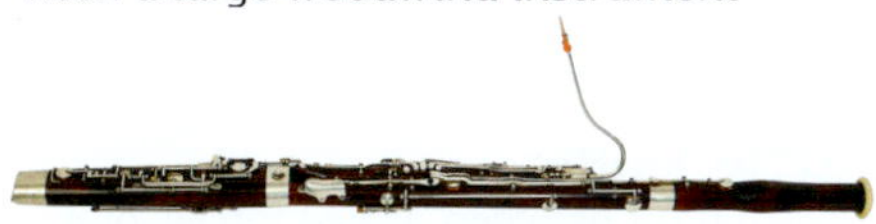

bat **bats, batting, batted**
NOUN **1** a specially shaped piece of wood with a handle, used for hitting a ball in games such as table tennis or cricket
2 a small animal like a mouse with leathery wings. **Bats** fly at night and sleep hanging upside down.
VERB **3** If you are **batting** in cricket, baseball or rounders, it is your turn to hit the ball.

batch **batches**
NOUN A **batch** of things is a group of things that are all the same or are being dealt with at the same time. • *They delivered the first **batch** of books at the start of term.*

bath **baths**
NOUN a long container that you fill with water and sit in to wash yourself

bathe **bathes, bathing, bathed**
VERB When you **bathe** in a sea, river or lake, you swim or play there.

bathroom **bathrooms**
NOUN a room with a bath or shower, a washbasin and often a toilet in it

A B C D E F G H I J K L M N O P Q R S T U V W X Y Z

baton **batons**
NOUN **1** a light, thin stick that a conductor uses to direct an orchestra or choir
2 a short stick passed from one runner to another at the changeover in a relay race

battalion **battalions**
NOUN an army unit consisting of three or more companies

batter **batters, battering, battered**
NOUN **1** a mixture of flour, eggs and milk, used to make pancakes, or to coat food before frying it
VERB **2** When someone or something **batters** someone or something, they hit them many times. • *The waves **battered** the sides of the ship.*

battery **batteries**
NOUN a device for storing energy and producing electricity, for example in a torch or a car

battle **battles**
NOUN a fight between armed forces, or a struggle between two people or groups with different aims

battlefield **battlefields**
NOUN a place where a battle has been fought or is being fought

battlements
PLURAL NOUN the top part of a castle where there are openings through which arrows or guns could be fired

battleship **battleships**
NOUN a large fighting ship carrying powerful guns

bawl **bawls, bawling, bawled**
VERB If someone **bawls**, they shout or cry loudly.

bay **bays, baying, bayed**
NOUN **1** part of the coastline where the land curves
2 a space or an area used for a particular purpose • *a loading **bay***
3 a tree with dark green leaves. The leaves are used for flavouring food.
VERB **4** When a dog or a wolf **bays**, it makes a deep, howling sound.
PHRASE **5** If you keep something **at bay**, you stop it hurting you. • *Try eating an orange to keep a cold **at bay**.*

bayonet **bayonets**
NOUN a sharp blade that can be fixed to the end of a rifle

bazaar **bazaars**
NOUN **1** an area with many small shops and stalls, especially in Eastern countries
2 a sale to raise money for charity
• *a Christmas **bazaar***
[from Persian *bazar* meaning market]

BC
ADJECTIVE You use **BC** to show the dates before the birth of Jesus Christ. It is an abbreviation for *before Christ.*

be **am, is, are; being; was, were; been**
VERB **1** You can use **be** with the present participle of other verbs. • *Look! I **am** riding on my own!*
2 You can also use **be** to say that something will happen. • *I will **be** nine in November.*
3 You use **be** to say more about something or somebody. • *His name **is** Tom.*

beach **beaches**
NOUN an area of sand or pebbles beside the sea

beacon **beacons**
NOUN In the past, a **beacon** was a light or fire on a hill, which acted as a signal or warning.

bead **beads**
NOUN **1** a small, shaped piece of glass, stone or wood with a hole through the middle. **Beads** are strung together with others to make necklaces or bracelets.
2 a drop of liquid • ***beads** of perspiration*

beak **beaks**
NOUN the hard part of a bird's mouth that sticks out. It is used for pecking up food and for carrying things such as twigs.

beam **beams, beaming, beamed**
NOUN **1** a long, thick bar of wood or metal, especially one that supports a roof
2 a band of light that shines from something such as a torch or the sun
VERB **3** If you **beam**, you smile broadly.

bean **beans**
NOUN the seed or pod of a plant, eaten as a vegetable or used for other purposes
• *runner **beans*** • *coffee **beans*** • *soya **beans***

bear **bears, bearing, bore, borne**
NOUN **1** a large, strong, wild mammal with thick fur and sharp claws • *polar **bear***
• *grizzly **bear***
VERB **2** If someone or something **bears** something, they carry it or support its weight. • *The ice wasn't thick enough to **bear** their weight.*
3 If something **bears** a mark or typical feature, it has it. • *The room **bore** all the signs of a violent struggle.*
4 If you **bear** something difficult, you accept it and are able to deal with it.
• *The loneliness was hard to **bear**.*

beard **beards**
NOUN the hair that grows on the lower part of a man's face

beast **beasts**
NOUN **1** an old-fashioned word for a large, wild animal
2 INFORMAL If you call someone a **beast**, you mean that they are cruel or spiteful.

beat **beats, beating, beat, beaten**
VERB **1** If someone or something **beats** someone or something else, they hit them hard and repeatedly. • *The rain was **beating** against the window.*
2 If you **beat** someone in a race or game, you defeat them or do better than them.
3 When your heart **beats**, it pumps blood with a regular rhythm.
NOUN **4** the main rhythm of a piece of music or poetry

beautiful
ADJECTIVE very attractive or pleasing
SYNONYM: lovely

beauty **beauties**
NOUN **1** the quality of being beautiful
• *the **beauty** of the stars on a clear night*
2 The **beauty** of an idea or a plan is what makes it attractive or worth doing.
• *The **beauty** of going in September is that the sea will be warmer for swimming.*

beaver **beavers**
NOUN a mammal with a big, flat tail and webbed hind feet. **Beavers** build dams.

because
CONJUNCTION **1** **Because** is used with other words to give the reason for something.
• *I went home **because** I was tired.*
PHRASE **2** **Because of** is used with a noun that gives the reason for something.
• *I had to stay late **because of** detention.*

beckon **beckons, beckoning, beckoned**
VERB If you **beckon** to someone, you make a sign to them with your hand, asking them to come to you.

become **becomes, becoming, became, become**
VERB If someone or something **becomes** something else, they start feeling or being that thing. • *I **became** more and more angry.*
[from Old English *becuman* meaning to happen]

bed **beds**
NOUN **1** a piece of furniture that you lie on when you sleep
2 an area of ground in a garden which has been dug and prepared for planting
3 The **bed** of the sea or a river is the bottom of it.

bedraggled
ADJECTIVE If a person or animal is **bedraggled**, they are wet, dirty and messy.

bedroom **bedrooms**
NOUN a room for sleeping in

bedtime **bedtimes**
NOUN the time when you go to bed

bee **bees**
NOUN a winged insect that makes honey. Many types of **bee** live in large groups.

beech **beeches**
NOUN a tree with a smooth, grey trunk and shiny leaves

beef
NOUN the meat of a cow, bull or ox

beehive **beehives**
NOUN a specially designed structure in which bees are kept so that their honey can be collected

been
VERB the past participle of **be**

beer **beers**
NOUN an alcoholic drink made from malt and flavoured with hops

beetle **beetles**
NOUN a flying insect with hard wings that cover its body when it is not flying [from Old English *bitan* meaning to bite]

beetroot **beetroots**
NOUN a round, dark red root vegetable

before
ADVERB, PREPOSITION OR CONJUNCTION If something happens **before**, it happens earlier than something else. • *Can I see you* ***before*** *you go?*
ANTONYM: after

beg **begs, begging, begged**
VERB **1** When people **beg**, they ask for food or money, because they are very poor.
2 If you **beg** someone to do something, you ask them very anxiously to do it.
• *David* ***begged*** *his dad to take him to the cinema.*

began
VERB the past tense of **begin**

begin **begins, beginning, began, begun**
VERB If you **begin** something, you start it.

beginner **beginners**
NOUN someone who has just started to learn something
SYNONYM: learner

beginning **beginnings**
NOUN The **beginning** of something is when or where it starts.

begun
VERB the past participle of **begin**

behalf
PHRASE If you do something **on behalf of** someone or something, you do it for them or in their name. • *We did the sponsored swim* ***on behalf of*** *various charities.*

behave **behaves, behaving, behaved**
VERB **1** If you **behave** in a particular way, you act in that way. • *He knew that he'd* ***behaved*** *badly.*
2 If you **behave** yourself, you act correctly or properly.

behind
PREPOSITION **1** at the back of • *The moon disappeared* ***behind*** *a cloud.*
2 supporting someone • *The whole school was* ***behind*** *him in the competition.*
ADVERB **3** If you stay **behind**, you remain after other people have gone.
4 If you leave something **behind**, you do not take it with you.

beige
ADJECTIVE a cream-brown colour

being
VERB the present participle of **be**

belch **belches, belching, belched**
VERB **1** If you **belch**, you make a sudden noise in your throat because air has risen up from your stomach.
2 If something **belches** smoke or fire, it sends it out in large amounts. • *Smoke* ***belched*** *from the factory chimneys.*
NOUN **3** the noise you make when you belch

belief **beliefs**
NOUN If you have a **belief** in something, you are certain that it is right or true.

believe **believes, believing, believed**
VERB **1** If you **believe** that something is true, you think that it is true.
2 If you **believe** someone, you accept that they are telling the truth.

bell **bells**
NOUN **1** a cup-shaped metal object with a piece inside it called a clapper that hits the side and makes a ringing sound
2 an electrical device that you can ring or buzz to get attention

bellow **bellows, bellowing, bellowed**
VERB If a human or other animal **bellows**, they shout very loudly or make a very loud, deep noise like a roar.

belly **bellies**
NOUN the part of your body, especially your stomach, that holds and digests food

belong **belongs, belonging, belonged**
VERB **1** If something **belongs** to you, it is yours and you own it.
2 If you **belong** to a group, you are a member of it.
3 If something **belongs** in a particular place, that is where it should be. • *That book* ***belongs*** *on the top shelf.*

belongings
PLURAL NOUN Your **belongings** are all the things that you own.

below
PREPOSITION OR ADVERB **1** If something is **below** something else, it is in a lower position. • *We could hear music coming up from the flat two floors* ***below****.*
ANTONYM: above
2 If something is **below** a particular amount or level, it is less than it.
• ***below*** *average rainfall*
ANTONYM: above

belt **belts**
NOUN a strip of leather or cloth that you fasten round your waist to hold your trousers or skirt up

bench **benches**
NOUN a long seat that two or more people can sit on

bend **bends, bending, bent**
VERB **1** When you **bend** something, you use force to make it curved or angular.
2 When you **bend**, you move your head and shoulders forwards and downwards.
• *I* ***bent*** *over to pick up my glasses.*
NOUN **3** a curved part of something
• *a* ***bend*** *in the road*

beneath
PREPOSITION OR ADVERB FORMAL underneath

benefit **benefits, benefiting, benefited**
NOUN **1** the advantage that something brings to people • *the* ***benefit*** *of a good education*
VERB **2** If you **benefit** from something, it helps you. • *He'll* ***benefit*** *from some extra tuition.*
[from Latin *benefactum* meaning good deed]

bent
ADJECTIVE curved or twisted out of shape

bereaved
ADJECTIVE FORMAL You say that someone is **bereaved** when a close relative of theirs has recently died.
bereavement NOUN

berry **berries**
NOUN a small, round fruit that grows on bushes or trees

berserk
ADVERB If somebody goes **berserk**, they lose control of themselves and become extremely violent.
[from Icelandic *berserkr* meaning a Viking who wore a shirt made from the skin of a bear and who worked himself into a mad frenzy before going into battle]

berth **berths**
NOUN **1** a space in a harbour where a ship stays when it is being loaded or unloaded
2 In a boat or caravan, a **berth** is a bed.
PHRASE **3** If you give someone or something **a wide berth**, you avoid them because they are unpleasant or dangerous.

beside
PREPOSITION If one thing is **beside** another thing, it is next to it.

A B C D E F G H I J K L M N O P Q R S T U V W X Y Z

besides
ADVERB also or in addition to

best
ADJECTIVE **1** the superlative of *good* and *well* • *That was one of the **best** films I've ever seen.*
ANTONYM: worst
ADVERB **2** The thing that you like **best** is the thing that you prefer to everything else.

bet **bets, betting, bet**
VERB If you **bet** on the result of an event, you will win money if what you bet on happens and lose money if it does not.

betray **betrays, betraying, betrayed**
VERB If you **betray** someone who trusts you, you tell people something secret about them.

better
ADJECTIVE **1** the comparative of *good* and *well* • *I am feeling **better** today.*
2 If you are **better** after an illness, you are no longer ill.
SYNONYM: cured

between
PREPOSITION OR ADVERB **1** If something is **between** two other things, it is situated or happens in the space or time that separates them. • *He was head teacher **between** 1989 and 2000.*
2 A relationship or a difference **between** two people or two things is one that involves them both. • *the difference **between** frogs and toads*

beware
VERB If you tell someone to **beware** of something, you are warning them that it might be dangerous or harmful.

bewilder **bewilders, bewildering, bewildered**
VERB If something **bewilders** you, it confuses and muddles you so that you can't understand.
bewilderment NOUN

beyond
PREPOSITION **1** If something is **beyond** a certain place, it is on the other side of it. • ***Beyond** the mountains was the secret valley.*
2 If something is **beyond** you, you cannot do it or understand it.

bi-
PREFIX added to a word to mean two or twice. For example, someone who is **bi**lingual can speak two languages.

bib **bibs**
NOUN a piece of cloth or plastic put under a baby's chin to protect its clothes from stains

Bible **Bibles**
NOUN the sacred book of the Christian religion • *I read about Noah and the Ark in the **Bible**.*

bibliography **bibliographies**
NOUN a list of books or articles

bicycle **bicycles**
NOUN a two-wheeled vehicle that you ride by pushing two pedals with your feet

bid **bids, bidding, bid**
VERB If you **bid** for something, you offer to buy it for a certain sum of money.
• *He **bid** for an old bike at the auction.*

big **bigger, biggest**
ADJECTIVE large or important
ANTONYMS: small, tiny, little

bike **bikes**
NOUN an abbreviation for *bicycle*

bikini **bikinis**
NOUN a small, two-piece swimming costume worn by women

bilingual
ADJECTIVE involving or using two languages
• ***bilingual** street signs*
[from Latin *bis* meaning two and *lingua* meaning tongue]

bill **bills**
NOUN **1** a written statement of how much is owed for goods or services • *a phone **bill***
2 a formal statement of a proposed new law that is discussed and then voted on in Parliament
3 A **bill** can be a piece of paper money.
• *a dollar **bill***
4 A bird's **bill** is its beak.

billiards

NOUN a game in which a long stick called a cue is used to move balls on a table

billion **billions**

NOUN a thousand million • *You can write one **billion** like this: 1,000,000,000.*

billow **billows, billowing, billowed**

VERB **1** When things made of cloth **billow**, they swell out and flap slowly in the wind.
2 When smoke or cloud **billows**, it spreads upwards and outwards.
NOUN **3** a large wave

billy goat **billy goats**

NOUN a male goat

bin **bins**

NOUN a container, especially one that you put rubbish in

binary

ADJECTIVE The **binary** system is a number system used when working with computers. It uses only two digits, 0 and 1.

bind **binds, binding, bound**

VERB **1** If you **bind** something, you tie rope or string round it so that it is held firmly.
2 If you **bind** a wound, you wrap bandages round it.
3 When a book is **bound**, the pages are joined together and a cover is put on.

bingo

NOUN a game in which players aim to match the numbers that someone calls out with the numbers on the card they have been given

binoculars

PLURAL NOUN an instrument with lenses for both eyes, which you look through in order to see objects far away • *They used **binoculars** for bird watching.*

biodegradable

ADJECTIVE **Biodegradable** materials can be broken down naturally, and so they are not dangerous to the environment.

biography **biographies**

NOUN the history of someone's life, written by someone else

biology

NOUN the study of living things
[from Greek *bios* + *logos* meaning life study]

birch **birches**

NOUN a tall, deciduous tree with thin branches and thin bark

bird **birds**

NOUN an egg-laying animal with feathers, two wings, two legs and a beak

birth **births**

NOUN Your **birth** was when you were born.

birthday **birthdays**

NOUN Your **birthday** is the anniversary of the date on which you were born.

birthmark **birthmarks**

NOUN a mark on your skin that has been there since you were born

biscuit **biscuits**

NOUN a small, flat cake that is crisp and usually sweet

bisect **bisects, bisecting, bisected**

VERB to divide a line or an area in half

bishop **bishops**

NOUN a high-ranking clergyman in some Christian Churches

bison

NOUN a large, hairy animal, related to cattle, with a large head and shoulders. **Bison** used to be very common on the prairies in North America, but they are now almost extinct.

bit **bits**

VERB **1** the past tense of **bite** • *She **bit** into the toast.*
NOUN **2** A **bit** of something is a small amount of it.
PHRASE **3** INFORMAL **A bit** means slightly or to a small extent. • *That's **a bit** difficult.*

bitch **bitches**
NOUN a female dog

bite **bites, biting, bit, bitten**
VERB If you **bite** something, you cut into it with your teeth.

bitter **bitterest**
ADJECTIVE **1** A **bitter** taste is sharp and unpleasant.
2 A **bitter** wind is extremely cold.
3 If you are **bitter** about something, you feel angry and resentful.

bizarre
ADJECTIVE very strange and weird
SYNONYMS: odd, peculiar

black **blacker, blackest**
NOUN OR ADJECTIVE the darkest possible colour, like the sky at night when there is no light

blackberry **blackberries**
NOUN a small, soft black fruit that grows on brambles

blackbird **blackbirds**
NOUN a common European bird, the male of which has black feathers and a yellow beak

blackboard **blackboards**
NOUN a dark-coloured board in a classroom, which teachers write on using chalk

blackcurrant **blackcurrants**
NOUN **Blackcurrants** are very small, dark, purple fruits that grow in bunches on bushes.

black hole **black holes**
NOUN the empty space made by the collapse of a star

bladder **bladders**
NOUN the part of your body where urine is held until it leaves your body

blade **blades**
NOUN **1** the sharp part of a knife, axe or saw
2 a single piece of grass

blame **blames, blaming, blamed**
VERB If someone **blames** a person for something bad that has happened, they believe that person caused it.
SYNONYM: accuse

blank **blanker, blankest**
ADJECTIVE **1** Something that is **blank** has nothing on it. • *a **blank** sheet of paper*
2 If you look **blank**, your face shows no feeling or interest.

blanket **blankets**
NOUN a large rectangle of thick cloth that is put on a bed to keep people warm [from Old French *blancquete* meaning little white thing]

blare **blares, blaring, blared**
VERB to make a loud, unpleasant noise • *The radio **blared** from the flat below.*

blast **blasts, blasting, blasted**
VERB **1** When people **blast** a hole in something, they make a hole with an explosion. • *They're using dynamite to **blast** away rocks.*
NOUN **2** a big explosion, especially one caused by a bomb

blaze **blazes, blazing, blazed**
NOUN **1** a large, hot fire
VERB **2** If something **blazes**, it burns or shines brightly. • *The fire **blazed** in the fireplace.*

blazer **blazers**
NOUN a kind of jacket, often in the colours of a school or sports team

bleach **bleaches, bleaching, bleached**
NOUN **1** a chemical that is used to make material white or to clean thoroughly and kill germs
VERB **2** If you **bleach** material or hair, you make it white, usually by using a chemical.

bleak **bleaker, bleakest**
ADJECTIVE **1** If a place is **bleak**, it is cold, bare and exposed to the wind. • *a **bleak** mountain top*
2 If a situation is **bleak**, it is bad and seems unlikely to improve.

bleat **bleats, bleating, bleated**
VERB When sheep or goats **bleat**, they make a high-pitched cry.

bleed **bleeds, bleeding, bled**
VERB When you **bleed**, you lose blood as

a result of an injury. • *My hand **bled** a lot after I cut it.*

blend **blends, blending, blended**
VERB **1** When you **blend** substances, you mix them together to form a single substance. • ***Blend** the butter with the sugar.*
2 When colours or sounds **blend**, they combine in a pleasing way.

bless **blesses, blessing, blessed** or **blest**
VERB When a priest **blesses** people or things, he or she asks God to give his protection to them.
[from Old English *bloedsian* meaning to sprinkle with sacrificial blood]

blew
VERB the past tense of **blow**

blind **blinds, blinding, blinded**
ADJECTIVE **1** Someone who is **blind** cannot see.
VERB **2** If something **blinds** you, it stops you seeing, either for a short time or permanently.
NOUN **3** a roll of cloth or paper that you pull down over a window to keep out the light

blindfold **blindfolds**
NOUN a strip of cloth tied over someone's eyes to stop them seeing

blink **blinks, blinking, blinked**
VERB When you **blink**, you close your eyes quickly for a moment.

bliss
NOUN a state of complete happiness
blissful ADJECTIVE **blissfully** ADVERB

blister **blisters**
NOUN a small bubble on your skin containing watery liquid, caused by a burn or rubbing

blizzard **blizzards**
NOUN a heavy snowstorm with strong winds

bloated
ADJECTIVE Something that is **bloated** is much larger than normal, often because there is a lot of liquid or gas inside it.

block **blocks, blocking, blocked**
NOUN **1** a large building containing flats or offices
2 In a town, a **block** is an area of land with streets on all its sides.
3 a large, rectangular, three-dimensional piece of something
VERB **4** If someone or something **blocks** a road or channel, they put something across it so that nothing can get through.
SYNONYM: obstruct

block capitals
PLURAL NOUN large upper-case letters.
THESE ARE BLOCK CAPITALS.

block graph **block graphs**
NOUN another name for **bar chart**

blog **blogs, blogging, blogged**
NOUN **1** a person's online diary that they put on the internet so that other people can read it
VERB **2** If you **blog** about something, you write about it in a blog. • *He **blogs** about cooking and restaurants.*

blonde **blondes**
ADJECTIVE **1** **Blonde** hair is pale yellow in colour. The spelling **blond** is used when referring to men.
NOUN **2** A **blonde** *or* **blond** is a person with pale yellow hair.

blood
NOUN the red liquid that is pumped by the heart round the bodies of human beings and other vertebrates

bloodstream
NOUN the flow of blood through your body

bloodthirsty
ADJECTIVE Someone who is **bloodthirsty** enjoys using or watching violence.

bloom **blooms, blooming, bloomed**
NOUN **1** a flower on a plant
VERB **2** When a plant **blooms**, it produces flowers.

blossom **blossoms, blossoming, blossomed**
NOUN **1** all the flowers that appear on a tree before the fruit

a b c d e f g h i j k l m n o p q r s t u v w x y z

A B C D E F G H I J K L M N O P Q R S T U V W X Y Z

VERB **2** When a tree **blossoms**, it produces flowers.

blot **blots**
NOUN a mark made by a drop of liquid, especially ink

blouse **blouses**
NOUN a light shirt, worn by a girl or a woman

blow **blows, blowing, blew, blown**
VERB **1** When the wind **blows**, the air moves.
2 If you **blow**, you send a stream of air from your mouth.
3 If you **blow** your nose, you force air out of it through your nostrils in order to clear it.
NOUN **4** If you receive a **blow**, someone or something hits you.

blow up
VERB **1** If something **blows up**, it is destroyed by an explosion.
2 If you **blow up** a balloon or a tyre, you fill it with air.

blubber
NOUN the layer of fat beneath the skin of animals such as whales and seals that protects them from the cold

blue **bluer, bluest**
ADJECTIVE OR NOUN the colour of the sky on a clear, sunny day

bluebell **bluebells**
NOUN a woodland plant with blue, bell-shaped flowers

bluff **bluffs, bluffing, bluffed**
NOUN **1** an attempt to make someone believe that you will do something when you do not really intend to do it
VERB **2** If you are **bluffing**, you are trying to make someone believe that you are in a strong position when you are not.
[from Dutch *bluffen* meaning to boast]

blunder **blunders, blundering, blundered**
NOUN **1** a silly mistake
VERB **2** If you **blunder**, you make a silly mistake.

blunt **blunter, bluntest**
ADJECTIVE **1** A **blunt** object has a rounded point or edge, rather than a sharp one. • *My pencil was **blunt** so I could not write with it.*
2 If you are **blunt**, you say exactly what you think, without trying to be polite.
SYNONYMS: outspoken, straightforward

blur
NOUN If something is a **blur**, you can't see it clearly. • *The mountain was a **blur** through the mist.*

blurb **blurbs**
NOUN the description of a book printed on the back cover

blurt out **blurts out, blurting out, blurted out**
VERB If you **blurt out** something, you say it suddenly, after trying to keep it a secret.

blush **blushes, blushing, blushed**
VERB If you **blush**, your face becomes red, because you are embarrassed or ashamed.
[from Old English *blyscan* meaning to glow]

boa **boas**
NOUN a large snake that kills its prey by coiling round it and crushing it

boar **boars**
NOUN **1** a male wild pig
2 a male domestic pig used for breeding

board **boards, boarding, boarded**
NOUN **1** a long, flat piece of wood
2 a flat piece of wood, plastic or cardboard, which is used for a particular purpose • *a chess**board*** • *a surf**board***
3 the group of people who control a company or organization • *My mum is on the **board** of governors.*
4 the meals provided when you stay in a hotel or guesthouse • *The price includes full **board**.*
VERB **5** If you **board** a ship or aircraft, you get on it or in it.
PHRASE **6** If you are **on board** a ship or aircraft, you are on it or in it.

Do not confuse *board* with *bored*.

boarder **boarders**
NOUN **1** a pupil who lives at school during term
2 a lodger

boast **boasts, boasting, boasted**
VERB If you **boast**, you talk proudly about what you have or what you can do.
SYNONYM: brag

boat **boats**
NOUN a small vehicle for travelling across water

body **bodies**
NOUN **1** Your **body** is all of you, from your head to your feet.
2 You can say **body** when you mean just the main part of a human or other animal, not counting head, arms and legs.

bodyguard **bodyguards**
NOUN a person employed to protect someone

bog **bogs**
NOUN an area of wet, spongy ground

boil **boils, boiling, boiled**
VERB **1** When a hot liquid **boils**, or when you **boil** it, it starts to bubble and to give off steam.
2 When you **boil** food, you cook it in boiling water.

boiler **boilers**
NOUN a piece of equipment that burns fuel to provide hot water

boisterous
ADJECTIVE Someone who is **boisterous** is noisy and lively.
SYNONYMS: loud, rowdy
boisterously ADVERB

bold **bolder, boldest**
ADJECTIVE **1** brave or confident • *He was **bold** enough to ask for her autograph.*
2 clear and noticeable • *The sign was painted in **bold** colours.*
[from Old Norse *ballr* meaning dangerous or terrible]

bollard **bollards**
NOUN a short, thick post used to stop vehicles from entering a road

bolt **bolts, bolting, bolted**
NOUN **1** a metal object that screws into a nut and is used to fasten things together

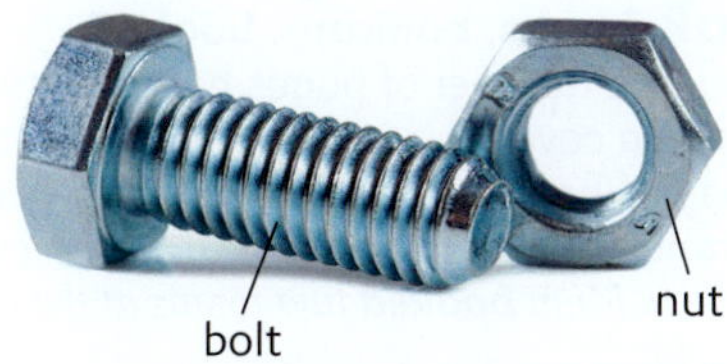

VERB **2** If you **bolt** one thing to another, you fasten them together using a bolt.
• *They **bolted** the chair to the floor.*
3 If you **bolt** a door or window, you slide a metal bar across in order to fasten it.

bomb **bombs, bombing, bombed**
NOUN **1** a container filled with material that explodes when it hits something or when it is set off by a timer
VERB **2** If you **bomb** something, you attack it with a bomb.
[from Greek *bombos* meaning a booming sound]

bond **bonds**
NOUN a close relationship between people
• *the **bond** between mothers and babies*

bone **bones**
NOUN the hard parts that form the framework of a person's or animal's body

bonfire **bonfires**
NOUN a large fire made outdoors, to burn rubbish or to celebrate something
[from *bone* + *fire* – bones were used as fuel in the Middle Ages]

bonnet **bonnets**
NOUN **1** the metal cover over a car's engine
2 a baby's or woman's hat tied under the chin

bonus **bonuses**
NOUN **1** an amount of money added to a person's usual pay
2 a good thing that you get in addition to something else

A B C D E F G H I J K L M N O P Q R S T U V W X Y Z

bony **bonier, boniest**
ADJECTIVE **Bony** people or animals are very thin, with not much flesh covering their bones.

book **books, booking, booked**
NOUN **1** a number of pages held together inside a cover
VERB **2** When you **book** something, you arrange to have it or use it at a particular time. • *Mum **booked** two rooms at the hotel.*

bookcase **bookcases**
NOUN a piece of furniture where you keep books

booklet **booklets**
NOUN a small book with a paper cover

boom **booms, booming, boomed**
NOUN **1** a deep, echoing sound
2 a fast increase in something • *There has been a **boom** in the sale of sun cream this summer.*
VERB **3** If something **booms**, it makes a loud booming sound. • *We heard the foghorn **boom** in the distance.*

boomerang **boomerangs**
NOUN a curved, wooden missile that can be thrown so that it returns to the thrower. **Boomerangs** were traditionally used as weapons by Australian Aborigines.

boost **boosts, boosting, boosted**
VERB If someone **boosts** something, they improve or increase it. • *The teacher **boosted** Juliet's confidence when she praised her story.*

boot **boots**
NOUN **1** strong shoes that come up over your ankle, and sometimes your calf
2 the covered space in a car, usually at the back, for carrying things in

booth **booths**
NOUN **1** a small, partly-enclosed area • *a telephone **booth***
2 a stall where you can buy things, for example at a market or a fair

border **borders**
NOUN **1** the dividing line between two countries
2 a strip or band round the edge of something
3 flower beds round the edges of a garden

borderline **borderlines**
NOUN If someone or something is on the **borderline**, they are on the division between two different categories.

bore **bores, boring, bored**
VERB **1** If something **bores** you, you find it dull and uninteresting.
2 If you **bore** a hole in something, you make it using a tool such as a drill.
3 the past tense of **bear**
NOUN **4** someone or something that bores you

bored
ADJECTIVE If you are **bored**, you are miserable because you have nothing interesting to do.

Do not confuse *bored* with *board.*

boring
ADJECTIVE dull and uninteresting
ANTONYM: interesting

born
VERB When an animal such as a human baby is **born**, it comes out of its mother's body and starts to live.

borrow **borrows, borrowing, borrowed**
VERB If you **borrow** something that belongs to someone else, they let you have it for a period of time. • *I **borrowed** a book from my friend.*

boss **bosses, bossing, bossed**
NOUN **1** Someone's **boss** is the person in charge of the place where they work.
VERB **2** If someone **bosses** you, they keep telling you what to do.

bossy **bossier, bossiest**
ADJECTIVE If you are **bossy**, you like to order other people around.

botany
NOUN the study and classification of plants

both
ADJECTIVE OR PRONOUN **Both** is used when saying something about two things or two people. • *You can* ***both*** *come to my party.*

bother **bothers, bothering, bothered**
VERB **1** If you don't **bother** to do something, you don't do it because it takes too much effort or it's not important.
2 If something **bothers** you, you are worried about it.
3 If you are not **bothered** about something, you don't care about it.
4 If you **bother** someone, you interrupt them when they are busy.
NOUN **5** trouble, fuss or difficulty • *Mum's having a bit of* ***bother*** *with the car.*

bottle **bottles, bottling, bottled**
NOUN **1** a glass or plastic container for keeping liquids in
VERB **2** If you **bottle** something, you put it in a bottle to store it.

bottom **bottoms**
NOUN **1** the lowest part of something • *It sank to the* ***bottom*** *of the pond.*
2 Your **bottom** is the part of your body that you sit on.

bottomless
ADJECTIVE If something is **bottomless**, it has no bottom or it is very deep.

bough **boughs**
Rhymes with "cow" NOUN a large branch of a tree

bought
VERB the past tense and past participle of **buy**

Do not confuse *bought* with *brought*.

boulder **boulders**
NOUN a large, rounded rock

bounce **bounces, bouncing, bounced**
VERB When an object **bounces**, it springs back from something after hitting it. • *The ball* ***bounced*** *high off the ground.*

bound **bounds, bounding, bounded**
ADJECTIVE **1** If you say that something is **bound** to happen, you mean that it is certain to happen. • *He's* ***bound*** *to find out.*
NOUN **2** a large leap
VERB **3** When humans or other animals **bound**, they move quickly with large leaps.

boundary **boundaries**
NOUN the limit of an area

bouquet **bouquets**
NOUN an attractively arranged bunch of flowers

bout **bouts**
NOUN **1** something that lasts for a short period of time • *I had a* ***bout*** *of flu.*
2 a boxing or wrestling match

boutique **boutiques**
NOUN a small shop that sells fashionable clothes

bow **bows, bowing, bowed**
Rhymes with "now" VERB **1** When you **bow**, you bend your body or lower your head as a sign of respect or greeting.
NOUN **2** the movement you make when you **bow**
3 the front part of a ship
Rhymes with "low" NOUN **4** a knot with two loops and two loose ends • *The ribbon was tied in a* ***bow****.*
5 a long, thin piece of wood with horsehair strings stretched along it, used to play some stringed instruments, such as the violin and the cello
6 a long, flexible piece of wood used for shooting arrows

bowel **bowels**
NOUN the tubes leading from your stomach, through which waste passes before it leaves your body
[from Latin *botellus* meaning little sausage]

bowl **bowls, bowling, bowled**
NOUN **1** a round container with a wide, uncovered top, used for holding liquid or for serving food • *a* ***bowl*** *of soup*

A B C D E F G H I J K L M N O P Q R S T U V W X Y Z

2 the hollow, rounded part of something • *a toilet* ***bowl***
VERB 3 When you **bowl** in cricket and rounders, you throw the ball towards the batsman.

bowling
NOUN a game in which you roll a heavy ball down a narrow track towards a set of wooden objects called pins, and try to knock them down

bowls
NOUN a game in which the players try to roll large wooden balls as near as possible to a small ball

box **boxes, boxing, boxed**
NOUN 1 a container with a firm base and sides, and usually a lid
VERB 2 If someone **boxes**, they fight according to special rules.

boxer **boxers**
NOUN 1 a person who boxes
2 a medium-sized, smooth-haired dog with a flat face

Boxing Day
NOUN the day after Christmas Day

boy **boys**
NOUN a male child

boyfriend **boyfriends**
NOUN Someone's **boyfriend** is the man or boy with whom they are having a romantic relationship.

bra **bras**
NOUN a piece of underwear worn by a woman to support her breasts

brace **braces, bracing, braced**
NOUN 1 an object fixed to something to straighten or support it • *I wore a* ***brace*** *on my teeth for two years.*
PLURAL NOUN 2 **Braces** are elastic straps worn over the shoulders to hold trousers up.
VERB 3 If you **brace** yourself, you stiffen your body to steady yourself. • *We* ***braced*** *ourselves as the bus went round the corner.*
4 If you **brace** yourself for something unpleasant, you prepare yourself to deal with it.

bracelet **bracelets**
NOUN a chain or band worn around someone's wrist as an ornament
[from Old French *bracel* meaning little arm]

bracken
NOUN a plant like a large fern that grows on hills and in woods

bracket **brackets**
NOUN a pair of written marks, ( ), { } or [ ], placed round a word or sentence that is not part of the main text, or to show that the items inside the **brackets** belong together

brag **brags, bragging, bragged**
VERB If you **brag**, you boast about something.

Braille
NOUN a system of printing for blind people in which letters are represented by raised dots that can be felt with the fingers

brain **brains**
NOUN the organ inside your head that controls your body and enables you to think and feel

brainstorm **brainstorms**
NOUN 1 a clever idea that you think of suddenly
2 If you have a **brainstorm**, you become confused and cannot think clearly.

brainy **brainier, brainiest**
ADJECTIVE clever and good at learning things

brake **brakes, braking, braked**
NOUN 1 a device for making a vehicle stop or slow down
VERB 2 When drivers **brake**, they make a

vehicle stop or slow down by using its brakes.

bramble **brambles**
NOUN a wild, trailing bush with thorns, which produces blackberries

branch **branches, branching, branched**
NOUN **1** part of a tree that grows out from the trunk
2 A **branch** of a business or organization is one of its offices or shops.
VERB **3** A road that **branches** off from another road splits off from it to lead in a different direction.

brand **brands**
NOUN a particular kind or make of something

brandy
NOUN a strong, alcoholic drink, often drunk after a meal
[from Dutch *brandewijn* meaning burnt wine]

brass
NOUN OR ADJECTIVE **1** a yellow-coloured metal made from copper and zinc
2 In an orchestra, the **brass** section consists of instruments such as trumpets and trombones.

brave **braver, bravest; braves, braving, braved**
ADJECTIVE **1** A **brave** person is willing to do dangerous things and does not show any fear.
SYNONYMS: courageous, daring
VERB **2** If you **brave** an unpleasant or dangerous situation, you face up to it in order to do something. • *We **braved** the snow to go to the party.*
[from Italian *bravo* meaning courageous or wild]

brawl **brawls, brawling, brawled**
NOUN **1** a rough fight
VERB **2** When people **brawl**, they take part in a rough fight.

bread
NOUN a very common food made from flour, and baked in an oven

breadth **breadths**
NOUN the distance between two sides of something • *I can swim the **breadth** of the pool.*
See **width**

break **breaks, breaking, broke, broken**
VERB **1** When an object **breaks**, or when you **break** it, it becomes damaged or separates into pieces.
2 If you **break** a rule or promise, you fail to keep it.
3 To **break** a record means to do better than the previous recorded best. • *She **broke** the record for the long jump.*
NOUN **4** a short period during which you rest or do something different

break down
VERB When a machine or a vehicle **breaks down**, it stops working.

break up
VERB When schools **break up**, the term ends. • *We **break up** on Thursday.*

breakable
ADJECTIVE easy to break

breakdown **breakdowns**
NOUN If there is a **breakdown** in a system, it stops working.

breakfast **breakfasts**
NOUN the first meal of the day

breast **breasts**
NOUN A woman's breasts are the two soft, fleshy parts on her chest, which produce milk after she has had a baby.

breast-feed **breast-feeds, breast-feeding, breast-fed**
VERB If a woman **breast-feeds** her baby, she feeds it with milk from her breasts.

breath **breaths**
NOUN **1** the air you take into your lungs and let out again when you breathe
• *He took a deep **breath** before jumping into the pool.*
PHRASE **2** If you are **out of breath**, you are breathing with difficulty after doing something energetic.

A B C D E F G H I J K L M N O P Q R S T U V W X Y Z

breathe **breathes, breathing, breathed**
VERB When you **breathe**, you take air into your lungs and let it out again.

breathless
ADJECTIVE If you are **breathless**, you are breathing very fast or with difficulty. • *I was **breathless** after running to catch the bus.*
breathlessly ADVERB
breathlessness NOUN

breed **breeds, breeding, bred**
NOUN **1** a particular type of animal. For example, an Alsatian is a **breed** of dog.
VERB **2** Someone who **breeds** animals or plants keeps them in order to produce more animals or plants with particular qualities. • *He used to **breed** dogs for the police.*
3 When animals **breed**, they produce young.
SYNONYM: reproduce

breeze **breezes**
NOUN a gentle wind
breezy ADJECTIVE

brewery **breweries**
NOUN a place where beer is made, or a company that makes beer

bribe **bribes, bribing, bribed**
NOUN **1** a gift or money given to an official to persuade them to allow you to do something
VERB **2** If someone **bribes** someone else, they give them a bribe.

brick **bricks**
NOUN a rectangular block of baked clay used in building

bride **brides**
NOUN a woman who is getting married or who has just got married

bridegroom **bridegrooms**
NOUN a man on or near his wedding day

bridesmaid **bridesmaids**
NOUN a woman or girl who helps a bride on her wedding day

bridge **bridges**
NOUN **1** a structure built over a river, road or railway so that vehicles and people can cross
2 a card game for four players

bridle **bridles**
NOUN a set of straps round a horse's head and mouth, which the rider uses to control the horse

brief **briefer, briefest; briefs, briefing, briefed**
ADJECTIVE **1** Something that is **brief** lasts only a short time. • *We only had time for a **brief** visit.*
VERB **2** When you **brief** someone on a task, you give them all the necessary instructions or information about it.

briefcase **briefcases**
NOUN a small, flat case for carrying papers

bright **brighter, brightest**
ADJECTIVE **1** strong and startling • *a **bright** light*
SYNONYMS: brilliant, dazzling
2 clever • *That's a **bright** idea.*
SYNONYMS: intelligent, quick

brighten **brightens, brightening, brightened**
VERB If something **brightens**, it becomes brighter.

brighten up
VERB If you **brighten up** something, you make it look brighter and more attractive.

brilliant
ADJECTIVE **1** A **brilliant** person is extremely clever.
2 INFORMAL Something that is **brilliant** is extremely good or enjoyable.
3 A **brilliant** colour or light is extremely bright.

brim **brims**
NOUN **1** the wide part of a hat that sticks outwards from the head
2 If a container is filled to the **brim**, it is filled right to the top.

bring **brings, bringing, brought**
VERB If you **bring** something or someone

with you when you go to a place, you take them with you.

bring up
VERB When someone **brings up** children, they look after them while they grow up.

brink
NOUN **1** the edge of a deep hole, cliff or ravine
PHRASE **2** If you are **on the brink** of something, you are about to do it. • *They were **on the brink** of discovering a cure for the common cold.*

brisk **brisker, briskest**
ADJECTIVE **1** quick and energetic • *a **brisk** walk*
2 If someone's manner is **brisk**, it shows that they want to get things done quickly and efficiently.
briskly ADVERB **briskness** NOUN

bristle **bristles, bristling, bristled**
NOUN **1 Bristles** are strong animal hairs used to make brushes.
VERB **2** If the hairs on an animal's body **bristle**, they rise up because it is frightened.
bristly ADJECTIVE

brittle
ADJECTIVE An object that is **brittle** is hard but breaks easily.

broad **broader, broadest**
ADJECTIVE **1** A **broad** river is wide.
2 The **broad** outline of a story gives the main points, but no details.

broadband
NOUN a digital system for sending data to and from televisions, computers and telephones • *What is the **broadband** speed like here?*

broadcast **broadcasts, broadcasting, broadcast**
NOUN **1** a programme or announcement on radio or television
VERB **2** When someone **broadcasts** something, they send it out by radio waves, so that it can be seen on television or heard on radio.

broccoli

NOUN a vegetable with green stalks and green or purple flower buds

brochure **brochures**
NOUN a booklet that gives information about a product or a service • *holiday **brochure***

broke
VERB **1** the past tense of **break**
ADJECTIVE **2** If you are **broke**, you have no money.

broken
ADJECTIVE A **broken** object is damaged in some way.

bronchitis
NOUN an illness in which the tubes connecting your windpipe to your lungs become infected, making you cough

brontosaurus **brontosauruses**
NOUN a very large, plant-eating dinosaur

bronze
NOUN a yellowish-brown metal that is a mixture of copper and tin

brooch **brooches**
Rhymes with "coach" NOUN a piece of jewellery with a pin at the back for attaching to clothes

brood **broods, brooding, brooded**
NOUN **1** a family of baby birds
VERB **2** If you **brood** about something, you are worried about it and can't stop thinking about it.

brook **brooks**
NOUN a stream

broom **brooms**
NOUN a long-handled brush

brother **brothers**
NOUN Your **brother** is a boy or man who has the same parents as you.

brother-in-law **brothers-in-law**
NOUN Someone's **brother-in-law** is the brother of their husband or wife, or their sister's husband.

brought
VERB the past tense and past participle of **bring**

Do not confuse *brought* with *bought*.

brown **browner, brownest**
ADJECTIVE OR NOUN the colour of earth or wood

Brownie **Brownies**
NOUN a junior member of the Girl Guides

bruise **bruises, bruising, bruised**
NOUN **1** a purple mark that appears on your skin after something has hit it
VERB **2** If something **bruises** you, it hits you so that a bruise appears on your skin.

brunette **brunettes**
NOUN a girl or a woman with dark brown hair

brush **brushes, brushing, brushed**
NOUN **1** an object with bristles. There are **brushes** for cleaning things, painting or tidying your hair.

VERB **2** If you **brush** something, you clean it or tidy it with a brush.

Brussels sprout **Brussels sprouts**
NOUN a vegetable that looks like a tiny cabbage

brutal
ADJECTIVE **Brutal** behaviour is violent and cruel.
brutally ADVERB **brutality** NOUN

bubble **bubbles, bubbling, bubbled**
NOUN **1** a ball of air in a liquid
VERB **2** When a liquid **bubbles**, bubbles form in it.

buck **bucks, bucking, bucked**
NOUN **1** the male of various animals, including deer and rabbits
VERB **2** If a horse **bucks**, it jumps into the air with all four feet off the ground.

bucket **buckets**
NOUN a deep, round container with an open top and a handle

buckle **buckles, buckling, buckled**
NOUN **1** a fastening on the end of a belt or strap
VERB **2** If you **buckle** a belt or strap, you fasten it.
3 If metal **buckles**, it crumples up.

bud **buds**
NOUN a small, tight swelling on a tree or plant, which develops into a flower or leaf

Buddhist
NOUN someone who follows the religious teachings of Buddha, who taught in India in the fifth century. **Buddhists** believe that the way to end suffering is by overcoming our desires.
Buddhism NOUN

budgerigar **budgerigars**
NOUN a small, brightly-coloured pet bird. **Budgerigars** originated in Australia.
[an Australian Aboriginal name, from *budgeri* + *gar* meaning good cockatoo]

budget **budgets, budgeting, budgeted**
NOUN **1** a plan showing how much money will be available and how it will be spent
VERB **2** If you **budget** for something, you plan how you use your money carefully, so as to be able to afford what you want.

buffalo **buffaloes**
NOUN **1** a wild animal like a large cow with long curved horns
2 another word for **bison**

buffet **buffets**
NOUN **1** a café at a station or on a train
2 a meal at which people serve themselves

bug **bugs, bugging, bugged**
NOUN **1** a small insect, especially one that causes damage
2 an infection or virus that makes you ill
3 a small error in a computer programme that stops it working properly
VERB **4** If a place is **bugged**, tiny microphones are hidden there to pick up what people are saying.

build **builds, building, built**
VERB If you **build** something, you make it from all its parts.

builder **builders**
NOUN a person whose job is to build buildings

building **buildings**
NOUN a structure with walls and a roof

bulb **bulbs**
NOUN **1** the glass part of an electric lamp
2 an onion-shaped root from which a flower or plant grows. Tulips and daffodils are grown from **bulbs**.
[from Greek *bolbos* meaning onion]

bulge **bulges, bulging, bulged**
VERB **1** If something **bulges**, it swells out.
NOUN **2** a lump on a normally flat surface

bulk **bulks**
NOUN **1** a large mass of something
PHRASE **2** If you buy something **in bulk**, you buy it in large quantities.

bulky **bulkier, bulkiest**
ADJECTIVE Something that is **bulky** is large and heavy and sometimes difficult to move.

bull **bulls**
NOUN the male of some animal species including cattle, elephants and whales

bulldozer **bulldozers**
NOUN a powerful tractor with a broad blade in front, which is used for moving earth or knocking things down

bullet **bullets**
NOUN a small piece of metal fired from a gun

bulletin **bulletins**
NOUN a short news report on radio or television

bullion
NOUN gold or silver bars

bullock **bullocks**
NOUN a young male bull that is reared for meat

bully **bullies, bullying, bullied**
NOUN **1** someone who uses their strength or power to hurt or frighten other people
VERB **2** If someone **bullies** you into doing something, they make you do it by using force or threats.
[a sixteenth-century word meaning fine fellow or hired ruffian]

bump **bumps, bumping, bumped**
VERB **1** If you **bump** into something, you knock into it accidentally.
NOUN **2** a soft noise made by something knocking into something else
3 a raised, uneven part of a surface
SYNONYMS: bulge, lump

bumper **bumpers**
NOUN a bar on the front or back of a vehicle that protects it if it bumps into something

bumpy **bumpier, bumpiest**
ADJECTIVE Something that is **bumpy** has a rough, uneven surface. • *a **bumpy** road*

bun **buns**
NOUN a small, round bread roll or cake

bunch **bunches**
NOUN a group of things together • *a **bunch** of flowers*

bundle **bundles, bundling, bundled**
NOUN **1** a number of things tied together or wrapped up in a cloth
VERB **2** If you **bundle** someone or something somewhere, you push them there quickly and roughly.

bungalow **bungalows**
NOUN a one-storey house
[from Hindi *bangla* meaning house]

bunk **bunks**
NOUN a bed fixed to a wall in a ship or caravan

bunk beds
PLURAL NOUN two beds fixed together, one above the other

buoy **buoys**
NOUN a floating object anchored to the bottom of the sea, marking a channel or warning of danger

buoyancy
NOUN Something that has **buoyancy** is able to float in liquid or in the air.

buoyant
ADJECTIVE **1** Something that is **buoyant** is able to float.
2 Someone who is **buoyant** is lively and cheerful.

burden **burdens**
NOUN a heavy load

burger **burgers**
NOUN a flat fried cake of meat, vegetables or cheese, served in a bread roll

burglar **burglars**
NOUN someone who breaks into buildings and steals things
burgle VERB

burn **burns, burning, burned** or **burnt**
VERB **1** If something is **burning**, it is on fire.
2 To **burn** something means to damage or destroy it with fire.
3 People often **burn** fuel, such as coal, to keep warm.
NOUN **4** A **burn** is an injury caused by fire or by something hot.

> You can write either *burned* or *burnt* as the past form of *burn*.

burqa **burqas**; also spelt **burka**
Said "**bur**-ka" NOUN a long garment worn by some Muslim women in public, covering everything except the eyes

burrow **burrows, burrowing, burrowed**
NOUN **1** a tunnel or hole in the ground dug by a small animal
VERB **2** When an animal **burrows**, it digs a burrow.

burst **bursts, bursting, burst**
VERB **1** When something **bursts**, or when you **burst** it, it splits open suddenly.
2 When you **burst** into a room, you enter suddenly and with force.
NOUN **3** A **burst** of something is a sudden short period of it. • *a **burst** of applause*

bury **buries, burying, buried**
VERB **1** If you **bury** something, you put it in a hole in the ground and cover it with earth.
2 If something is **buried** under something, it is covered by it. • *My trainers were **buried** under a pile of clothes.*

bus **buses**
NOUN a large motor vehicle that carries passengers
[from Latin *omnibus* meaning for all]

bush **bushes**
NOUN **1** a large plant, smaller than a tree and with a lot of woody branches
2 In Australia and South Africa, an uncultivated area outside a town or city is called the **bush**.
3 In New Zealand, the **bush** is land covered by rainforest.

bushy **bushier, bushiest**
ADJECTIVE **Bushy** hair or fur grows very thickly. • *My dad has **bushy** eyebrows.*

business **businesses**
NOUN **1** work relating to the buying and selling of goods and services
2 an organization that produces or sells goods, or provides a service
SYNONYMS: company, firm, organization

busker **buskers**
NOUN someone who sings or plays music in public places for money

bus stop **bus stops**
NOUN a place where the bus stops regularly for passengers to get on or off, usually marked with a sign

busy **busier, busiest**
ADJECTIVE **1** If you are **busy**, you are doing something and are not free to do

anything else. • *She was too **busy** to come to the cinema with us.*
2 A **busy** place is full of people doing things or moving about.

but
CONJUNCTION **1** used to introduce an idea that is opposite to what has gone before • *I love cooking, **but** I hate washing up afterwards.*
2 used when you apologize for something • *Sorry, **but** I can't come to play tomorrow.*
PREPOSITION **3** except • *There was nothing to eat **but** potatoes.*

butcher **butchers**
NOUN a shopkeeper who prepares and sells meat

butter
NOUN a soft, fatty food made from cream, which is spread on bread and used in cooking

buttercup **buttercups**
NOUN a wild plant with bright yellow flowers

butterfly **butterflies**
NOUN a type of insect with large, colourful wings. **Butterflies** develop from caterpillars.

buttocks
PLURAL NOUN Your **buttocks** are the part of your body that you sit on.
[from Old English *buttuc* meaning rounded slope]

button **buttons, buttoning, buttoned**
NOUN **1** a small, hard round object sewn on to clothing such as shirts • *My new jeans fasten with **buttons** instead of a zip.*
2 a small object on a piece of equipment that you press to make it work • *You must push the **button** down to switch the video on.*
VERB **3** If you **button** a garment, you fasten it using its buttons.

buy **buys, buying, bought**
VERB If you **buy** something, you get it by paying money for it.

buzz **buzzes, buzzing, buzzed**
VERB If something **buzzes**, it makes a humming sound, like a bee.

buzzer **buzzers**
NOUN a device that makes a buzzing sound. **Buzzers** are used to attract attention. • *I pressed the door **buzzer** but nobody was home.*

by
PREPOSITION **1** used to show who or what has done something • *The announcement was made **by** the head teacher.*
2 used to show how something is done • *He cheered us up **by** taking us to the cinema.*
3 next to or near to • *They live **by** the park.*
4 before a particular time • *We should finish **by** tea time.*
PREPOSITION OR ADVERB **5** going past • *We drove **by** her house.*

bypass **bypasses**
NOUN a road that takes traffic around the edge of a town instead of through the middle • *The centre of town is much quieter since they built the **bypass**.*

byte **bytes**
NOUN a unit of storage in a computer

A B C D E F G H I J K L M N O P Q R S T U V W X Y Z

Cc

cab **cabs**
NOUN **1** a taxi
2 The **cab** is where the driver sits in a lorry, bus or train.

cabbage **cabbages**
NOUN a large, green, leafy vegetable

cabin **cabins**
NOUN **1** a room in a ship where a passenger sleeps
2 a small wooden house, usually in the country

cabinet **cabinets**
NOUN **1** a small cupboard • *a medicine **cabinet***
2 The **cabinet** in a government is a group of ministers who advise the leader and decide policies.

cable **cables**
NOUN **1** a strong, thick rope or chain
2 a bundle of wires with a rubber covering, which carries electricity

cable television
NOUN a television service that comes through underground wires

cactus **cacti** or **cactuses**
NOUN a thick, fleshy plant that grows in deserts. **Cactuses** are usually covered in spikes.

cadet **cadets**
NOUN a young person being trained in the armed forces or police

café **cafés**
NOUN a place where you can buy light meals and drinks
[from the French *café* meaning coffee or coffee house]

caffeine; also spelt **caffein**
NOUN a chemical in coffee and tea that makes you more active

cage **cages**
NOUN a box or room made with bars, in which birds or animals are kept
caged ADJECTIVE

cake **cakes, caking, caked**
NOUN **1** a sweet food made from eggs, flour, butter and sugar
2 a block of a hard substance such as soap
VERB **3** If something is **caked**, it becomes covered with a solid layer of something else. • *My shoes were **caked** in mud.*

calamity **calamities**
NOUN something terrible that happens, causing destruction and misery • *The earthquake was a terrible **calamity**.*
SYNONYMS: disaster, catastrophe

calcium
Said "**kal**-see-um" NOUN a soft white mineral found in bones and teeth and in some foods. Milk and cheese are good sources of **calcium**.

calculate **calculates, calculating, calculated**
VERB If you **calculate** something, you work it out, usually by doing some arithmetic. • *We **calculated** how much money we had raised from the sponsored walk.*
[from Latin *calculus* meaning stone or pebble, which the Romans used for counting]

calculation **calculations**
NOUN something that you think about carefully and work out mathematically, or that you do on a machine such as a calculator

calculator **calculators**
NOUN a small electronic machine used for doing mathematical calculations

calendar **calendars**
NOUN a chart, usually organized month by month, showing the date of each day in a particular year • *We marked the end of term on the **calendar** in red.*

calf **calves**
NOUN **1** a young cow
2 Your **calves** are the backs of your legs between your knees and ankles.

call **calls, calling, called**
VERB **1** If you **call** someone or something a particular name, that is their name.
• *I will **call** my dog Spot.* • *That type of machine is **called** a combine harvester.*
2 If you **call** someone, you telephone them.
3 If you **call** someone, you shout their name loudly.
NOUN **4** A **call** is a shout or a cry. • *We heard a **call** for help.*

call off
VERB If something is **called off** it is cancelled. • *The party was **called off**.*

call on
VERB If you **call on** someone, you pay them a short visit.

calm **calmer, calmest**
ADJECTIVE **1** Someone who is **calm** is quiet and does not show any worry or excitement.
2 If the sea is **calm**, the water is not moving very much.

calorie **calories**
NOUN The amount of energy that food gives you is measured in **calories**.

came
VERB the past tense of **come**

camel **camels**
NOUN a large mammal with either one or two humps on its back. **Camels** live in hot desert areas and are used for carrying people and things.

camera **cameras**
NOUN a piece of equipment used for taking photographs or for filming

camouflage **camouflages, camouflaging, camouflaged**
NOUN **1** a way of avoiding being seen by having the same colour or appearance as the surroundings
VERB **2** To **camouflage** something is to hide it by giving it the same colour or appearance as its surroundings.

camp **camps, camping, camped**
NOUN **1** a place where people live in tents or stay in tents for a holiday
VERB **2** If you **camp**, you stay in a tent.
NOUN **3** a collection of buildings for soldiers or prisoners
camper NOUN

campaign **campaigns, campaigning, campaigned**
VERB When people **campaign**, they take action in order to achieve something.
• *She **campaigned** against the export of live animals.*
campaign NOUN

can **could; cans**
VERB **1** If someone says you **can** do something, you are allowed to do it.
2 If you **can** do something, you are able to do it. • *I **can** say "hello" in French.*
NOUN **3** a metal container, often sealed, with food or drink inside

canal **canals**
NOUN a long, narrow, man-made stretch of water

canary **canaries**
NOUN a yellow songbird

cancel **cancels, cancelling, cancelled**
VERB If you **cancel** something that has been arranged, you stop it from happening. • *They **cancelled** the school trip.*

cancer **cancers**
NOUN a serious disease in which abnormal cells in a part of the body increase rapidly, causing growths

a b c d e f g h i j k l m n o p q r s t u v w x y z

A B C D E F G H I J K L M N O P Q R S T U V W X Y Z

candidate **candidates**
NOUN a person who is being considered for a job

candle **candles**
NOUN a stick of hard wax with a piece of string called a wick through the middle. You light the wick to produce a flame.

cane **canes**
NOUN **1** the long, hollow stem of a plant such as bamboo
2 strips of **cane** used for weaving baskets and other containers
3 a long, narrow stick used to support plants

canine **canines**
ADJECTIVE **1** relating to dogs
NOUN **2** a **canine** is one of the pointed teeth near the front of the mouth in humans and some animals

cannibal **cannibals**
NOUN a person who eats human flesh

cannon **cannons** or **cannon**
NOUN a large gun, usually on wheels, which fires heavy iron balls

cannot
VERB the same as *can not*

canoe **canoes**
NOUN a small, narrow boat that you row using a paddle
canoeing NOUN **canoeist** NOUN

can't
VERB a contraction of *cannot*

canteen **canteens**
NOUN a place to eat in a school or workplace

canvas **canvases**
NOUN **1** strong, heavy cloth used for making things such as sails and tents
2 a piece of **canvas** on which an artist does a painting

canyon **canyons**
NOUN a narrow river valley with steep sides

cap **caps**
NOUN **1** a soft, flat hat, often with a peak at the front
2 a bottle top
3 a small explosive used in toy guns

capable
ADJECTIVE **1** If you are **capable** of doing something, you are able to do it.
2 Someone who is **capable** is able to do something well.

capacity **capacities**
NOUN the maximum amount that something can hold or produce • *The arena has a seating **capacity** of two thousand.*

capital **capitals**
NOUN **1** The **capital** of a country is the city where the government meets. • *Paris is the **capital** of France.*
2 A **capital**, or a **capital** letter, is a larger, upper-case letter used at the beginning of a sentence or a name: **C**arol, **T**im.

capsize **capsizes, capsizing, capsized**
VERB If a boat **capsizes**, it turns upside down.

capsule **capsules**
NOUN **1** a small container with medicine inside, which you swallow
2 the part of a spacecraft in which astronauts travel
[from Latin *capsula* meaning little box]

captain **captains**
NOUN **1** the officer in charge of a ship or aeroplane
2 the leader of a sports team

caption **captions**
NOUN a title printed underneath a picture or a photograph

captive **captives**
NOUN someone who is locked up and kept prisoner

capture **captures, capturing, captured**
VERB If someone **captures** someone or something, they take them prisoner.

car **cars**
NOUN **1** a four-wheeled road vehicle with an engine and room to carry a few passengers

2 a railway carriage used for a particular purpose • *the buffet **car***

caravan **caravans**
NOUN **1** a vehicle pulled by a car in which people live or spend their holidays
2 a group of people and animals travelling together, usually across a desert

carbohydrate **carbohydrates**
NOUN a substance that gives you energy. It is found in foods like sugar and bread.

carbon
NOUN a chemical found in coal, diamonds and graphite. All living things contain **carbon**.

carbon dioxide
NOUN the gas that human beings and other animals breathe out

carbon footprint **carbon footprints**
NOUN the amount of carbon monoxide produced by a person, company or country

card **cards**
NOUN **1** a piece of stiff paper or plastic with a message or information on it
• *birthday **card*** • *credit **card***
2 When you play **cards**, you play a game using special playing **cards**.
3 strong, stiff paper

cardboard
NOUN thick, stiff paper, which is stronger than card

cardigan **cardigans**
NOUN a knitted jacket that fastens up the front

care **cares, caring, cared**
VERB **1** If you **care** about something or someone, you are concerned about them and interested in them.
2 If you **care** for a person or an animal, you look after them.
NOUN **3** worry or trouble • *She didn't have a **care** in the world.*
4 If you do something with **care**, you concentrate very hard on it so that you don't make mistakes. • *He wrote the telephone number down with great **care**.*
PHRASE **5** If you **take care of** a person or an animal, you look after them. • *Shakira said she would **take care of** the hamsters while we were on holiday.*

career **careers**
NOUN Your **career** is the series of jobs you have in life, often in the same occupation.
• *a teaching **career***

careful
ADJECTIVE acting sensibly and with care
ANTONYM: careless
carefully ADVERB

careless
ADJECTIVE not paying attention to what you are doing
SYNONYMS: slapdash, sloppy
carelessly ADVERB **carelessness** NOUN

caretaker **caretakers**
NOUN a person who looks after a large building such as a school

cargo **cargoes**
NOUN goods carried on a ship or plane

Caribbean
Said "carib-**ee**-un" NOUN **1** short for the **Caribbean** Sea, which lies between the West Indies and South America
ADJECTIVE **2** to do with the **Caribbean** Sea or the islands in it • *I love **Caribbean** food.*

carnation **carnations**
NOUN a plant with thin leaves and scented white, pink or red flowers

carnival **carnivals**
NOUN a public festival with music, processions and dancing

carnivore **carnivores**
NOUN an animal that eats meat
carnivorous ADJECTIVE

carol **carols**
NOUN a religious song sung at Christmas time

carpenter **carpenters**
NOUN a person who makes and repairs wooden things
carpentry NOUN

carpet **carpets**
NOUN a thick floor covering usually made of material like wool

carriage **carriages**
NOUN **1** one of the separate sections of a passenger train
2 an old-fashioned vehicle for carrying passengers, usually pulled by horses

Carroll diagram **Carroll diagrams**
NOUN a way of sorting and displaying information in the form of a grid

	Walk	Do not walk
Travel less than 1km	(3) Fiona, Sophie, Poppy	(3) John, Gavin, Anita
Travel 1km or more	(4) Kay, Rabi, Aaran, Rajeev	(4) Nina, Mark, George, Krishna

How Class 4 travel to school

carrot **carrots**
NOUN a long, thin, orange-coloured root vegetable

carry **carries, carrying, carried**
VERB **1** If you **carry** something, you hold it and take it somewhere.
2 When a vehicle **carries** people, they travel in it.
3 If people or animals **carry** a germ or a disease, they can pass it on to others.
4 If a sound **carries** it can be heard a long way off. • *Their voices **carried** across the valley.*

cart **carts**
NOUN a vehicle with wheels, used for carrying things and usually pulled by horses or cattle

carton **cartons**
NOUN a cardboard or plastic container

cartoon **cartoons**
NOUN **1** a humorous drawing in a newspaper, comic or magazine
2 a film in which all the characters and scenes are drawn

cartridge **cartridges**
NOUN **1** a tube containing a bullet and an explosive substance, used in guns
2 a small plastic container filled with ink that you put in a pen or a printer

cartwheel **cartwheels**
NOUN an acrobatic movement in which you lift both arms in the air then throw yourself sideways on to one hand, swinging your body around in a circle with your legs straight until you land on your feet again

carve **carves, carving, carved**
VERB If you **carve** something, you shape it or slice it with a knife.

cascade **cascades, cascading, cascaded**
NOUN **1** a small waterfall or group of waterfalls flowing down a rocky hillside
VERB **2** When water **cascades**, it flows very fast down a hillside or over rocks.

case **cases**
NOUN **1** a box for keeping or carrying things in
2 a particular situation or event • *a bad **case** of measles*
3 A crime that the police are investigating is called a **case**.

cash
NOUN money in notes and coins

cashier **cashiers**
NOUN the person who deals with money in a place such as a shop or a bank

casserole **casseroles**
NOUN **1** a stew made with meat, vegetables or fish that is baked in the oven
2 a dish with a lid, which is used for cooking

cast **casts, casting, cast**
NOUN **1** all the people who act in a play or film
2 an object made by pouring a liquid such as plaster into a container and leaving it to harden
VERB **3** If an object **casts** a shadow on to a place, it makes a shadow fall there.

castaway **castaways**
NOUN someone who has been shipwrecked but manages to survive on a lonely shore or an island

castle **castles**
NOUN a large building with walls or ditches round it to protect it from attack
[from Latin *castellum* meaning small fort]

casual
ADJECTIVE **1** happening by chance and without planning • *I made a **casual** remark.*
2 **Casual** clothes are suitable for informal occasions.

casualty **casualties**
NOUN a person killed or injured in an accident or a war • *There were many **casualties** after the motorway crash.*

cat **cats**
NOUN a small, furry mammal with whiskers, a tail and sharp claws, often kept as a pet

catalogue **catalogues**
NOUN a list of things, such as the goods you can buy from a company, the objects in a museum, or the books in a library • *I ordered my trainers from a mail order **catalogue**.*

catastrophe **catastrophes**
NOUN a terrible disaster
catastrophic ADJECTIVE

catch **catches, catching, caught**
VERB **1** If you **catch** an object that is moving through the air, you grasp it with your hands.
2 If you **catch** a person or animal, you capture them. • *The police **caught** the thief.*
3 If you **catch** a bus, train or plane, you get on it and travel somewhere.
4 If you **catch** a cold or a disease, you become ill with it.
NOUN **5** a hook that fastens or locks a door or window

catching
ADJECTIVE If a disease or illness is **catching** it spreads very quickly. • *Measles is **catching**.*

catchy **catchier, catchiest**
ADJECTIVE Something that is **catchy**, such as a tune, is pleasant and easy to remember.

category **categories**
NOUN a group of things that have something in common

caterpillar **caterpillars**
NOUN the larva of a butterfly or moth. **Caterpillars** look like small, coloured worms and feed on plants.

cathedral **cathedrals**
NOUN an important church with a bishop in charge of it • *Canterbury **Cathedral***

Catholic **Catholics**
ADJECTIVE OR NOUN a Roman **Catholic**, or belonging to that religion

cattle
PLURAL NOUN cows and bulls kept by farmers

caught
VERB the past tense of **catch**

cauldron **cauldrons**
NOUN a large, round metal cooking pot, especially one that sits over a fire
[from Latin *caldarium* meaning hot bath]

cauliflower **cauliflowers**
NOUN a large, round, white vegetable surrounded by green leaves

cause **causes, causing, caused**
VERB **1** To **cause** something means to make it happen.
NOUN **2** The **cause** of something is the thing that makes it happen. • *The **cause** of the explosion was a gas leak.*

cautious
ADJECTIVE Someone who is **cautious** acts carefully in order to avoid danger or disappointment.

cavalry
NOUN The **cavalry** is the part of an army that fights on horseback or in armoured vehicles such as tanks.

cave **caves, caving, caved**
NOUN a large hole in the side of a cliff or under the ground

cave in
VERB If a roof **caves in**, it collapses inwards.

caveman or **cavewoman** **cavemen** or **cavewomen**
NOUN **Cavemen** and **cavewomen** were people who lived in caves in prehistoric times.

cavity **cavities**
NOUN a small hole in something solid • *There were* ***cavities*** *in his back teeth.*

CD
NOUN an abbreviation for *compact disc*

CD-ROM
NOUN a way of storing video, sound or text on a compact disc that can be played on a computer. **CD-ROM** is an abbreviation for *compact disc read-only memory.*

cease **ceases, ceasing, ceased**
VERB **1** If something **ceases**, it stops.
2 If you **cease** doing something, you stop doing it.

ceiling **ceilings**
NOUN the roof inside a room

celebrate **celebrates, celebrating, celebrated**
VERB If you **celebrate** something, you do something special and enjoyable because of it. • *We felt like* ***celebrating*** *the end of exams.*
celebration NOUN

celebrity **celebrities**
NOUN a famous person

celery
NOUN a vegetable with long, pale green stalks

cell **cells**
NOUN **1** In biology, a **cell** is the smallest part of an animal or plant that can exist by itself. Humans, animals and plants are made up of millions of **cells**.
2 a small room in a prison or police station where a prisoner is locked up

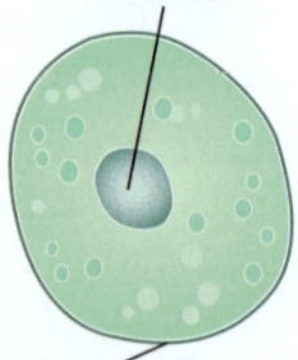

cellar **cellars**
NOUN a room underneath a building

cello **cellos**
Said "**chel**-oh" NOUN a large, stringed musical instrument that you play sitting down
cellist NOUN

Celsius
NOUN a scale for measuring temperature in which water freezes at 0 degrees (0 °C) and boils at 100 degrees (100 °C)
[named after Anders *Celsius* (1701–1744) who invented it]

cement
NOUN a grey powder that is mixed with sand and water to make concrete

cemetery **cemeteries**
NOUN an area of land where dead people are buried

census **censuses**
NOUN an official survey of the population of a country

cent **cents**
NOUN In some countries a **cent** is a unit of currency.

centenary **centenaries**
NOUN the hundredth anniversary of something

centigrade
NOUN another word for **Celsius**

centimetre **centimetres**
NOUN a unit of length (cm). One **centimetre** is equal to ten millimetres (mm).

centipede **centipedes**
NOUN a long, thin creature with many pairs of legs
[from Latin *centum* + *pedes* meaning a hundred feet]

central
ADJECTIVE **1** Something **central** is in the middle.
2 An idea that is **central** is the main idea.

central heating
NOUN a heating system in which water or air is heated and passed round a building through pipes and radiators

centre **centres**
NOUN **1** the middle of an object or area
2 a building where people go for activities, meetings, or help • *We played badminton at the sports* ***centre****.*

century **centuries**
NOUN a period of one hundred years

ceramic **ceramics**
Said "ser-**ram**-ic" NOUN **1** a hard material made by baking clay at very high temperatures
PLURAL NOUN **2** **Ceramics** is the art of making objects out of clay.

cereal **cereals**
NOUN **1** a food made from grain, often eaten with milk for breakfast
2 a plant that produces edible grain, such as wheat, oats, barley and rye

ceremony **ceremonies**
NOUN a formal event such as a wedding or prizegiving

certain
ADJECTIVE **1** If you are **certain** about something, you are sure it is true. • *She is* ***certain*** *she wants to be a vet.*
2 You use **certain** to refer to a particular person, place or thing. • *I like* ***certain*** *animals, for example cats and dogs.*

certainly
ADVERB without any doubt • *"Will you be at the party?" "I* ***certainly*** *will."*

certificate **certificates**
NOUN an official piece of paper that proves that something took place • *a birth* ***certificate***

chaffinch **chaffinches**
NOUN a small European bird with black and white wings

chain **chains**
NOUN **1** a number of metal rings linked together in a line
2 a number of things in a series or connected to each other • *a* ***chain*** *of shops* • *a* ***chain*** *of events*

chair **chairs**
NOUN a seat for one person to sit on, with a back and four legs

chalet **chalets**
NOUN a small wooden house with a sloping roof, especially found in mountain areas or holiday camps

chalk
NOUN a soft, white rock. Small sticks of **chalk** are used for writing or drawing on a blackboard.
chalky ADJECTIVE

challenge **challenges, challenging, challenged**
NOUN **1** something new and exciting that needs a lot of effort • *Learning how to cook is a new* ***challenge*** *for me.*
VERB **2** If someone **challenges** you, they suggest that you compete with them.
• *She* ***challenged*** *me to a game of table tennis.*

challenging
ADJECTIVE If you find something **challenging**, you find it quite difficult.

chameleon **chameleons**
NOUN a lizard that is able to change the colour of its skin to match the colour of its surroundings
[from Greek *khamai* + *leon* meaning ground lion]

champagne **champagnes**
NOUN a sparkling white wine made in France

champion **champions**
NOUN a person who wins a competition

championship **championships**
NOUN a competition to find the best player or players of a particular sport

chance **chances**
NOUN **1** how possible or likely something is • *I think we've got a good* ***chance*** *of winning.*
2 an opportunity to do something • *This is your* ***chance*** *to be a TV star!*
3 a possibility that something dangerous or unpleasant may happen
PHRASE **4** Something that happens **by chance** happens unexpectedly, without being planned.

a b c d e f g h i j k l m n o p q r s t u v w x y z

chancellor **chancellors**
NOUN the head of government in some European countries

Chancellor of the Exchequer
NOUN the government minister in charge of finance and taxes in Britain

change **changes, changing, changed**
NOUN **1** money you get back when you pay for something with more money than it costs
VERB **2** When something **changes**, or you **change** it, it becomes different. • *The wind **changed** direction.*

channel **channels**
NOUN **1** a wavelength on which television programmes are broadcast. It can also be the television station itself.
2 a passage for water or other liquid
3 The **Channel**, or the English **Channel**, is the stretch of sea between England and France.

chaos
NOUN a state of complete disorder
• *The demonstration ended in **chaos**.*
chaotic ADJECTIVE

chapel **chapels**
NOUN **1** a section of a church or cathedral with its own altar
2 a type of small church

chapter **chapters**
NOUN one of the parts into which a book is divided

character **characters**
NOUN **1** all the qualities that make a person or a place special • *She has a gentle **character**.*
2 The **characters** in a film, play or book are the people in it.

characteristic **characteristics**
NOUN **1** a special quality about a person, place or thing
ADJECTIVE **2** typical of a place or person
• *Noise and traffic fumes are **characteristic** of cities.*

charades
NOUN a party game where one team guesses what the other team is acting out

charcoal
NOUN burnt wood used as a fuel. **Charcoal** is also used for drawing.

charge **charges, charging, charged**
VERB **1** If someone **charges** you money, they ask you to pay for something you have bought or received.
2 rush forward • *She **charged** into the room.*
PHRASE **3** If you are **in charge of** someone or something, you are responsible for them. • *I left him **in charge of** the shop while I went out.*

chariot **chariots**
NOUN a two-wheeled open vehicle pulled by horses in ancient times

charity **charities**
NOUN **1** an organization that raises money to help people in need
2 money or other help given to people in need

charm **charms, charming, charmed**
NOUN **1** something you wear for good luck
2 the quality of being attractive and pleasant
VERB **3** If you **charm** someone, you use your charm to please them.

chart **charts**
NOUN a diagram or table showing information

chase **chases, chasing, chased**
VERB If you **chase** someone, you run after them or follow them in order to catch them or make them leave a place.

chat **chats, chatting, chatted**
NOUN **1** a friendly talk with someone
VERB **2** When people **chat**, they talk to each other in a friendly way about things that are not very important.
chatty ADJECTIVE

chatroom **chatrooms**
NOUN an internet site where users have discussions using e-mail

chatter **chatters, chattering, chattered**
VERB **1** When people **chatter**, they talk about unimportant things.

2 If your teeth **chatter**, they knock together and make a clicking noise because you are cold.

chauffeur **chauffeurs**
NOUN a person whose job is to drive another person's car • *He had a **chauffeur** to drive him everywhere.*

cheap **cheaper, cheapest**
ADJECTIVE **1** Something that is **cheap** costs very little money.
2 **Cheap** sometimes means of poor quality.
cheaply ADVERB

cheat **cheats, cheating, cheated**
VERB If someone **cheats** in a game or exam, they break the rules in order to do better.

check **checks, checking, checked**
VERB **1** If you **check** something, you examine it to make sure that everything is all right. • ***Check** your work carefully when you finish.*
NOUN **2** an inspection to make sure that everything is all right
3 **Checks** are different coloured squares that form a pattern.

checkout **checkouts**
NOUN the place in a supermarket where you pay for your goods

cheek **cheeks**
NOUN **1** Your **cheeks** are the sides of your face below your eyes.
2 speech or behaviour that is rude and disrespectful • *Their grandparents won't stand any **cheek** from them.*
cheeky ADJECTIVE **cheekily** ADVERB

cheer **cheers, cheering, cheered**
VERB When people **cheer**, they shout loudly and happily. • *We **cheered** our team when they won.*

cheerful
ADJECTIVE A **cheerful** person is happy.
cheerfully ADVERB

cheese **cheeses**
NOUN a solid savoury food made from milk

cheetah **cheetahs**
NOUN a wild mammal like a large cat with black spots, mainly found in Africa
[from Sanskrit *citra* + *kaya* meaning speckled body]

chef **chefs**
NOUN a head cook in a restaurant or hotel
[from French *chef* meaning head]

chemical **chemicals**
NOUN **1** a substance made by the use of chemistry • *Dangerous **chemicals** should be handled carefully.*
ADJECTIVE **2** involved in chemistry or using chemicals • *a **chemical** reaction*

chemist **chemists**
NOUN a shop that sells medicines and cosmetics

chemistry
NOUN the scientific study of substances and the ways in which they change when they are combined

cheque **cheques**
NOUN a printed piece of paper that people can use to pay for things

cherry **cherries**
NOUN a small, juicy fruit with a red, yellow or black skin and a hard stone in the centre

chess
NOUN a game played on a board with 64 squares. Each player has 16 pieces.

chest **chests**
NOUN **1** the front part of your body between your shoulders and your waist
2 a large wooden box used for storing things

chestnut **chestnuts**
NOUN **1** a reddish-brown nut that grows inside a prickly, green outer covering
2 the tree that produces these nuts
ADJECTIVE **3** Something that is **chestnut** is reddish-brown in colour.

A B C D E F G H I J K L M N O P Q R S T U V W X Y Z

chew **chews, chewing, chewed**
VERB When you **chew** something, you use your teeth to break it up in your mouth before swallowing it.

chewing gum
NOUN a kind of sweet that you chew for a long time, but which you do not swallow

chick **chicks**
NOUN a young bird

chicken **chickens**
NOUN a bird kept on a farm for its eggs and meat; also the meat of this bird

chickenpox
NOUN an illness that causes a fever and blister-like spots to appear on the skin

chief **chiefs**
NOUN **1** the leader of a group or organization
ADJECTIVE **2** main or most important

chilblain **chilblains**
NOUN a sore, itchy swelling on a finger or toe, which causes discomfort in cold weather

child **children**
NOUN **1** a young person who is not yet an adult
SYNONYMS: kid, youngster
2 Someone's **child** is their son or daughter.

childhood **childhoods**
NOUN Your **childhood** is the time when you are a child.

childish
ADJECTIVE If someone is **childish**, they are not acting in an adult way.
ANTONYM: adult
childishly ADVERB

childminder **childminders**
NOUN a person who is paid to look after children while their parents are at work

children
PLURAL NOUN the plural of **child**

chill **chills, chilling, chilled**
VERB **1** When you **chill** something, you make it cold. • ***Chill** the orange juice before you drink it.*
NOUN **2** a feverish cold
3 a feeling of cold • *the **chill** of early morning*

chilli **chillies**
NOUN the red or green seed pod of a type of pepper that has a very hot, spicy taste

chilly **chillier, chilliest**
ADJECTIVE **1** **Chilly** weather is rather cold.
2 If people behave in a **chilly** way, they are not very friendly.

chime **chimes, chiming, chimed**
VERB **1** When a bell **chimes**, it makes a clear ringing sound.
NOUN **2** **Chimes** are a set of bells or other objects that make ringing sounds.

chimney **chimneys**
NOUN a pipe above a fireplace or furnace through which smoke from the fire can escape

chimpanzee **chimpanzees**
NOUN a small ape with dark fur that lives in forests in Africa

chin **chins**
NOUN the part of your face below your mouth

china
NOUN plates, cups, saucers and other dishes that are made from fine clay

chink **chinks**
NOUN **1** a small, narrow opening • *a **chink** in the fence*
2 a small ringing sound, like glasses touching each other

chip **chips, chipping, chipped**
NOUN **1** **Chips** are thin strips of fried potato.
2 a tiny piece of silicon inside a computer, which is used to form electronic circuits • *computer **chips***
VERB **3** If you **chip** an object, you break a small piece off it.

chirp **chirps, chirping, chirped**
VERB When a bird **chirps**, it makes a short, high-pitched sound.

chisel **chisels, chiselling, chiselled**
NOUN **1** a tool with a long metal blade and a sharp edge at the end. **Chisels** are used for cutting and shaping wood, stone or metal.

VERB **2** If you **chisel** wood, stone or metal, you cut or shape it using a chisel.

chlorine
NOUN a poisonous greenish-yellow gas with a strong, unpleasant smell. It is used to disinfect water and to make bleach.

chocolate **chocolates**
NOUN a sweet food made from cocoa beans [from Aztec *xococ* + *atl* meaning bitter water]

choice **choices**
NOUN **1** a range of different things that are available to choose from
SYNONYMS: range, variety
2 something that you choose • *You made a good **choice** when you bought this book.*

choir **choirs**
NOUN a group of singers, for example in a church

choke **chokes, choking, choked**
VERB If you **choke** on something, it prevents you from breathing properly. • *He **choked** on a fish bone.*

cholesterol
NOUN a substance found in all animal fats, tissues and blood

choose **chooses, choosing, chose, chosen**
VERB If you **choose** something, you decide to have it or do it.
SYNONYMS: pick, select

chop **chops, chopping, chopped**
VERB **1** If you **chop** something, you cut it with quick, heavy strokes using an axe or a knife. • *Mum **chopped** the logs for firewood.*
NOUN **2** a small piece of pork or lamb that contains a bone • *We had **chops** and broccoli for dinner.*

choppy
ADJECTIVE When the sea or a stretch of water is **choppy**, there are a lot of waves on it because it is windy.

chopstick **chopsticks**
NOUN **Chopsticks** are a pair of thin sticks used for eating Chinese and Japanese food.

choral
Said "**kor**-al" ADJECTIVE for a choir

chord **chords**
NOUN a group of three or more musical notes played together

chore **chores**
NOUN an uninteresting job that has to be done

chorus **choruses**
NOUN **1** a part of a song that is repeated after each verse
2 a large group of singers

chose
VERB the past tense of **choose**

chosen
VERB **1** the past participle of **choose**
2 When you are **chosen**, you are picked to do something. • *I was **chosen** for the volleyball team.*

christen **christens, christening, christened**
VERB When a priest **christens** someone, they name them in a ceremony where water is poured over their head as a sign that they are a member of the Christian church.
christening NOUN

Christian **Christians**
NOUN a person who believes in Jesus Christ and his teachings
Christianity NOUN

Christmas **Christmases**
NOUN a Christian festival held on December 25th to celebrate the birth of Jesus Christ

chrome
Said "**krome**" NOUN metal plated with chromium, a hard, silver-grey metal

chromosome **chromosomes**
Said "**krome**-uh-soam" NOUN the part of a cell in living things that contains the genes that determine what characteristics the animal or plant will have

chronic
ADJECTIVE lasting a very long time or never stopping • *He suffers from **chronic** hay fever.*

chronological
ADJECTIVE arranged in the order in which things happened • *Tell me the whole story in **chronological** order.*
chronologically ADVERB

chrysalis **chrysalises**
NOUN a butterfly or moth when it is developing from being a caterpillar to being a fully grown adult

chrysanthemum
chrysanthemums
NOUN a plant with large, brightly-coloured flowers

chuckle **chuckles, chuckling, chuckled**
VERB When you **chuckle**, you laugh quietly.

chunk **chunks**
NOUN a thick piece of something
SYNONYMS: hunk, lump, piece

church **churches**
NOUN a building where Christians go for religious services and worship

churchyard **churchyards**
NOUN an area of land around a church, often used as a graveyard

churn **churns, churning, churned**
NOUN **1** a container used for making milk or cream into butter
VERB **2** When you **churn** something, you stir it vigorously, for example when making milk into butter.

churn out
VERB If you **churn out** something, you produce it quickly in large numbers.
• *They **churned out** hundreds of leaflets advertising the dance.*

chutney
NOUN a strong-tasting, thick sauce made from fruit, vinegar and spices

cider
NOUN an alcoholic drink made from apples

cigar **cigars**
NOUN a roll of dried tobacco leaves, which people smoke

cigarette **cigarettes**
NOUN a thin tube of paper containing tobacco, which people smoke

cinder **cinders**
NOUN **Cinders** are small pieces of burnt material left after something such as wood or coal has burned.

cinema **cinemas**
NOUN a place where people go to watch films

circle **circles, circling, circled**
NOUN **1** a regular, two-dimensional round shape. Every point on the edge is the same distance from the centre.
VERB **2** to move around in a circle
• *Seagulls **circled** overhead.*
circular ADJECTIVE

circuit **circuits**
NOUN **1** the path of an electric current
2 a racecourse
3 A training **circuit** is a course of physical activities.

circulation **circulations**
NOUN **1** the movement of blood around a body
2 the number of copies of a newspaper or magazine that are sold each time it is issued

circumference
circumferences
NOUN **1** the outer line or edge of a circle
2 The length of this line is also called the **circumference**.

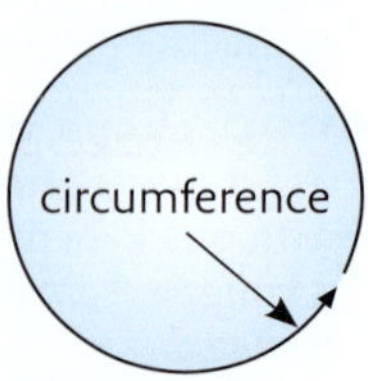

circumstance **circumstances**
NOUN The **circumstances** of a situation or event are the conditions that affect

what happens. • *He did well under difficult **circumstances**.*

circus **circuses**
NOUN a travelling show performed in a large tent, with performers such as clowns and acrobats

cistern **cisterns**
NOUN a tank in which water is stored, such as in the roof of a house, or above a toilet

citizen **citizens**
NOUN The **citizens** of a country or city are the people who live in it or belong to it.

citrus fruit **citrus fruits**
NOUN **Citrus fruits** are juicy, sharp-tasting fruits such as oranges, lemons and grapefruit.

city **cities**
NOUN a large town where many people live and work

civil
ADJECTIVE **1** relating to the citizens of a place
2 Someone who is **civil** is polite.

civilian **civilians**
NOUN a person who is not in the armed forces

civilization **civilizations**; also spelt **civilisation**
NOUN **1** a large group of people with a high level of organization and culture
• *We're learning about the ancient **civilizations** of Greece, Rome and Egypt.*
2 a highly developed and organized way of life

civilized; also spelt **civilised**
ADJECTIVE **1** A **civilized** society is one with a highly developed social organization and a comfortable way of life.
2 A **civilized** person is polite and reasonable.

civil war **civil wars**
NOUN a war between groups of people who live in the same country

claim **claims, claiming, claimed**
VERB **1** If you **claim** that something is the case, you say that it is so.
2 If you **claim** something, you ask for it because you believe you have a right to it.

clamber **clambers, clambering, clambered**
VERB If you **clamber** somewhere, you climb there with difficulty. • *We **clambered** over the rocks to get to the beach.*

clammy **clammier, clammiest**
ADJECTIVE unpleasantly damp and sticky
• *The weather was very **clammy**.*

clamp **clamps, clamping, clamped**
NOUN **1** a device that holds something firmly in place
VERB **2** When you **clamp** one thing to another, you fasten them together with a clamp.

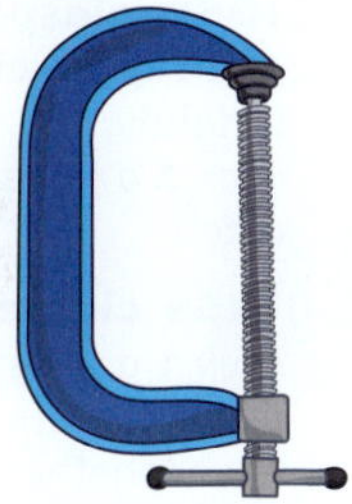

clan **clans**
NOUN a group of families related to each other by being descended from the same ancestor

clang **clangs, clanging, clanged**
VERB When something made of metal **clangs**, or when you **clang** it, it makes a loud, ringing sound.

clank **clanks, clanking, clanked**
VERB When something **clanks**, it makes a loud, metallic sound.

clap **claps, clapping, clapped**
VERB **1** When you **clap**, you hit your hands together loudly to show that you have enjoyed something or that you approve of something.
NOUN **2** a sudden loud noise of thunder

clarify **clarifies, clarifying, clarified**
VERB If you **clarify** something, you make it clear and easier to understand.
clarification NOUN

clarinet **clarinets**
NOUN a woodwind instrument with a straight tube and a single reed in its mouthpiece

clarity
NOUN The **clarity** of something is its clearness. • *The **clarity** of the water made me think it was very clean.*

a b c d e f g h i j k l m n o p q r s t u v w x y z

clash **clashes, clashing, clashed**
VERB **1** Colours or ideas that **clash** are so different that they do not go together.
• *Debbie's red shirt **clashed** with her green shorts.*
2 If one event **clashes** with another, they happen at the same time, so you cannot go to both.
3 If people **clash** with each other, they fight or argue.

clasp **clasps, clasping, clasped**
VERB **1** If you **clasp** something, you hold it tightly.
NOUN **2** a fastening such as a hook or a catch

class **classes**
NOUN **1** a group of pupils or students taught together, or a lesson that they have together
2 A **class** of people or things is a group of them of a particular type. • *Beetles and ants belong to different **classes** of insect.*
SYNONYMS: group, kind, type

classic
ADJECTIVE Something described as **classic** is considered a high quality example of something. • *He has a **classic** car.*

classical
ADJECTIVE **1** traditional in style and content
• ***classical** ballet*
2 Classical music is serious music thought to be of lasting value.

classify **classifies, classifying, classified**
VERB to arrange things into groups with something in common • *We **classified** the foods into three groups: fruits, vegetables and meats.*
classification NOUN

classroom **classrooms**
NOUN a room in a school where lessons take place

clatter **clatters, clattering, clattered**
VERB **1** When things **clatter**, they hit each other with a loud, rattling noise.
NOUN **2** a loud noise made by hard things hitting against each other • *There was a great **clatter** when the waitress dropped the tray.*

clause **clauses**
NOUN In grammar, a **clause** is a group of words with a subject and a verb, which may be a complete sentence or part of a sentence.

claw **claws, clawing, clawed**
NOUN **1** An animal's **claws** are the hard, curved nails at the end of its feet.
2 The **claws** of a crab or a lobster are the two jointed parts at the end of the leg, used for holding things.
VERB **3** 3 If an animal claws something, it digs its claws into it

clay
NOUN a type of earth that is soft and sticky when wet and hard when baked dry. It is used to make pottery and bricks.

clean **cleaner, cleanest; cleans, cleaning, cleaned**
ADJECTIVE **1** free from dirt or unwanted marks
VERB **2** to remove dirt from something

clear **clearer, clearest; clears, clearing, cleared**
ADJECTIVE **1** easy to understand, see or hear
• *The instructions on the packet were very **clear**.*
2 easy to see through • *a **clear** liquid*
VERB **3** To **clear** unwanted things from a place is to remove them. • *We **cleared** the dirty dishes from the table.*
4 If you **clear** a fence or other obstacle, you jump over it without touching it.
clearly ADVERB

clear up
VERB When you **clear up** a place, you tidy it and put things away.

clench **clenches, clenching, clenched**
VERB **1** When you **clench** your fist, you curl your fingers up tightly.
2 When you **clench** your teeth, you squeeze them together tightly, either in pain or in anger.

clerk **clerks**
NOUN a person who keeps records or accounts in an office, bank or law court

clever **cleverer, cleverest**
ADJECTIVE **1** intelligent and quick to understand things
SYNONYMS: bright, intelligent, smart
2 very effective or skilful • *We came up with a **clever** plan.*

cliché **clichés**
NOUN an idea or phrase that is no longer effective because it has been used so much. For example, *in this day and age* and *over the moon.*

click **clicks, clicking, clicked**
VERB **1** When something **clicks** or when you **click** it, it makes a short snapping sound.
NOUN **2** a sound of something clicking

client **clients**
NOUN someone who pays a professional person or company for a service

cliff **cliffs**
NOUN a high area of land with a very steep side, usually next to the sea

cliffhanger **cliffhangers**
NOUN a very exciting or frightening situation, usually in a television or radio serial, where you are left not knowing what is going to happen next

climate **climates**
NOUN the general weather conditions that are typical of a place

climax **climaxes**
NOUN the most exciting moment of something, usually near the end

climb **climbs, climbing, climbed**
VERB **1** If you **climb** something, such as a tree, mountain or ladder, you move towards the top of it.
2 If you **climb** somewhere, you move there with difficulty. • *We **climbed** over the high wall.*
NOUN **3** a movement upwards • *I was tired after the long **climb** to the top of the hill.*
climber NOUN

cling **clings, clinging, clung**
VERB If you **cling** to something, you hold on to it tightly.

clinic **clinics**
NOUN a place where people go for medical advice or treatment

clip **clips, clipping, clipped**
NOUN **1** a small metal or plastic object used for holding things together
2 a short piece of a film shown by itself
VERB **3** If you **clip** something, you cut bits from it to shape it.

clipboard **clipboards**
NOUN a stiff piece of board or plastic, with a clip at the top to keep papers in place

clippers
PLURAL NOUN a tool used for cutting • *hedge **clippers***

cloak **cloaks, cloaking, cloaked**
NOUN **1** a wide, loose coat without sleeves
VERB **2** If something **cloaks** something else, it covers or hides it. • *The mist **cloaked** the land.*

cloakroom **cloakrooms**
NOUN **1** a room where you can leave coats and luggage for a while
2 a room with toilets and washbasins in a public building

clock **clocks**
NOUN an instrument that measures and shows the time

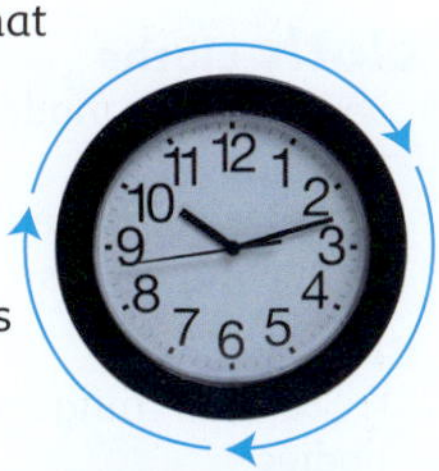

clockwise
ADVERB in the same direction as the hands on a clock

clockwork
NOUN **1** Toys that move by **clockwork** are wound up with a key.
PHRASE **2** If something goes **like clockwork**, it happens with no problems or delays.

clog **clogs, clogging, clogged**
VERB **1** When something is **clogged**, or when you **clog** something up, it becomes blocked and doesn't work properly or

a b c d e f g h i j k l m n o p q r s t u v w x y z

A B C D E F G H I J K L M N O P Q R S T U V W X Y Z

doesn't allow things to move freely. • *The traffic was **clogging** the roads.*
NOUN **2** a shoe made entirely of wood, originally from the Netherlands

clone **clones**
NOUN an animal or plant that is an identical copy of another animal or plant

close **closes, closing, closed; closer, closest**
Said "**klohz**" VERB **1** If you **close** something, you move it so that it is no longer open. • *He **closed** the door behind him.*
2 If a shop or other building **closes** at a certain time, it does not do business after that time.
Said "**klohss**" ADJECTIVE **3** Something that is **close** to something else is near to it.
SYNONYMS: near, nearby
4 People who are **close** are very friendly with each other and know each other well.
5 If the weather is **close**, it is uncomfortably warm and stuffy.
NOUN **6** a street that is closed at one end • *We live in Park **Close**.*
closely ADVERB

close-up **close-ups**
Said "**klohss**-up" NOUN A **close-up** in a film or a photograph is taken at very close range and shows things in great detail.

cloth **cloths**
NOUN **1** fabric made by a process such as weaving
2 a piece of material used for wiping or protecting things

clothes
PLURAL NOUN things people wear on their bodies

cloud **clouds**
NOUN **1** a mass of water vapour that is seen as a white or grey patch in the sky
2 A **cloud** of smoke or dust is a mass of it floating in the air.

cloudy **cloudier, cloudiest**
ADJECTIVE **1** full of clouds • *The sky was **cloudy**.*
SYNONYMS: dull, overcast
2 difficult to see through • *a **cloudy** liquid*
SYNONYM: murky

clover
NOUN a small plant with leaves made up of three similar parts

clown **clowns**
NOUN a circus performer who wears funny clothes and make-up and does silly things to make people laugh

club **clubs**
NOUN **1** a group of people with similar interests, who meet regularly. The place where they meet is also called a **club**.
• *a youth **club***
2 a team that competes in sports competitions

clue **clues**
NOUN something that helps solve a problem or mystery • *Police have found **clues** to the robbery.*

clueless
ADJECTIVE INFORMAL If you say that someone is **clueless**, you think they are stupid and not able to do things properly.

clump **clumps**
NOUN a small group of things growing or standing close together • *a **clump** of trees*

clumsy **clumsier, clumsiest**
ADJECTIVE moving awkwardly and carelessly
SYNONYMS: awkward, ungainly
clumsily ADVERB

clung
VERB the past tense and past participle of **cling**

cluster **clusters, clustering, clustered**
NOUN **1** a group of things together
• *There is a **cluster** of houses by the lake.*
VERB **2** If people **cluster** together, they stay together in a close group.
[from Old English *clyster* meaning bunch of grapes]

clutch **clutches, clutching, clutched**
VERB If you **clutch** something, you hold it tightly or seize it.

clutter **clutters, cluttering, cluttered**
NOUN **1** an untidy mess
VERB **2** Things that **clutter** a place fill it and make it untidy.

coach **coaches, coaching, coached**
NOUN **1** a large bus that takes passengers on long journeys
2 a section of a train that carries passengers
VERB **3** If someone **coaches** you, they help you to get better at a sport or a subject.
SYNONYMS: instruct, train
NOUN **4** someone who coaches a person or sports team

coal
NOUN a hard, black rock taken from under the ground and burned as a fuel

coarse **coarser, coarsest**
ADJECTIVE **1** Something that is **coarse** is rough in texture.
2 Someone who is **coarse** talks or behaves in a rude, offensive way.
coarsely ADVERB **coarseness** NOUN

coast **coasts, coasting, coasted**
NOUN **1** the edge of the land where it meets the sea
VERB **2** If a vehicle **coasts** somewhere, it moves there with the engine switched off. • *The car **coasted** quietly down the hill.*
coastal ADJECTIVE

coastguard **coastguards**
NOUN an official who watches the sea near a coast to get help for sailors when they need it

coat **coats, coating, coated**
NOUN **1** a piece of outdoor clothing with sleeves, which you wear over other clothes
2 An animal's **coat** is the fur or hair on its body.
3 A **coat** of paint or varnish is a layer of it.
VERB **4** If you **coat** something, you cover it with a thin layer of something. • *We **coated** the biscuits with chocolate.*

coating **coatings**
NOUN a thin layer of something spread over a surface

coax **coaxes, coaxing, coaxed**
VERB If you **coax** someone to do something, you persuade them gently to do it.

cobble **cobbles**
NOUN **Cobbles** or cobblestones are stones with a rounded surface that were used in the past for making roads.

cobra **cobras**
NOUN a type of large poisonous snake from Africa and Asia

cobweb **cobwebs**
NOUN the very thin net that a spider spins to catch insects

cock **cocks**
NOUN an adult male chicken, or any other male bird

cockerel **cockerels**
NOUN a young cock

cockle **cockles**
NOUN a type of small, edible shellfish

Cockney **Cockneys**
NOUN someone who was born in the East End of London

cockpit **cockpits**
NOUN **1** the area in a plane where the pilot sits in control
2 the driver's compartment in a racing car

cockroach **cockroaches**
NOUN a large, dark-coloured insect often found in dirty rooms
[from Spanish *cucaracha*]

cocky **cockier, cockiest**
ADJECTIVE INFORMAL If you are **cocky**, you are sure of yourself and sometimes rather cheeky.

cocoa
NOUN **1** a brown powder made from the seeds of a tropical tree and used for making chocolate
2 a hot drink made from this powder

A B C D E F G H I J K L M N O P Q R S T U V W X Y Z

coconut **coconuts**
NOUN a very large nut with white flesh, milky juice, and a hard hairy shell

cocoon **cocoons**
NOUN a silky covering over the larvae of moths and some other insects

cod
NOUN a large, edible fish

The plural of *cod* is *cod*.

code **codes**
NOUN **1** a system of replacing the letters or words in a message with other letters or words, so that nobody can understand the message unless they know the system • *They wrote messages in **code**.*
2 a group of numbers and letters used to identify something • *the telephone **code** for Falmouth*

coeducation
NOUN **Coeducation** is a system where girls and boys are taught together at the same school.
coeducational ADJECTIVE

coffee
NOUN **1** a powder made by roasting and grinding the beans of the **coffee** plant
2 a hot drink made from **coffee**

coffin **coffins**
NOUN a box in which a dead body is buried or cremated

cog **cogs**
NOUN a wheel with teeth, which turns another wheel or part of a machine

coil **coils, coiling, coiled**
NOUN **1** a length of rope or wire wound into a series of loops
2 A single loop is also called a **coil**.
VERB **3** If something **coils**, or if you **coil** it, it winds into a series of loops.
• *The snake **coiled** around the branch.*

coin **coins, coining, coined**
NOUN **1** a small metal disc used as money
VERB **2** If you **coin** a word or a phrase, you invent it.

coinage
NOUN the coins that are used in a particular country

coincide **coincides, coinciding, coincided**
VERB When two things **coincide**, they happen at the same time. • *Auntie's visit **coincided** with my birthday.*

coincidence **coincidences**
NOUN what happens when two or more things occur at the same time by chance

coke
NOUN a grey fuel produced from coal

cola **colas**
NOUN a sweet, brown fizzy drink, like Coca-Cola

colander **colanders**
NOUN a bowl-shaped container with holes in it, used for washing or draining food

cold **colder, coldest; colds**
ADJECTIVE **1** If something is **cold**, it has a very low temperature.
2 If the weather is **cold**, the air temperature is very low.
NOUN **3** a minor illness that makes you sneeze and cough, and sometimes gives you a sore throat

cold-blooded
ADJECTIVE **1** A **cold-blooded** animal has a body temperature that changes according to the surrounding temperature.
2 Someone who is **cold-blooded** does not show any pity.
cold-bloodedly ADVERB

coleslaw
NOUN a salad of chopped cabbage and other vegetables in mayonnaise

collaborate **collaborates, collaborating, collaborated**
VERB When people **collaborate**, they work together to produce something. • *The two schools **collaborated** to produce a play.*
collaboration NOUN **collaborator** NOUN

collage **collages**
NOUN a picture made by sticking pieces of paper or cloth on to a surface

collapse **collapses, collapsing, collapsed**
VERB **1** If something such as a building **collapses**, it falls down suddenly.
2 If a person **collapses**, they fall down suddenly because they are ill.

collapsible
ADJECTIVE A **collapsible** object can be folded flat when it is not in use.
• ***collapsible** chairs*

collar **collars**
NOUN **1** the part around the neck of something, such as a coat or shirt
2 a leather band round the neck of a dog or cat

colleague **colleagues**
NOUN A person's **colleagues** are the people they work with.

collect **collects, collecting, collected**
VERB **1** If you **collect** things, you gather them together for a special purpose or as a hobby.
2 If you **collect** someone or something from a place, you call there and take them away. • *We **collected** Ali from school.*
3 When things **collect** in a place, they gather there over a period of time. • *Dust **collects** in corners.*

collection **collections**
NOUN **1** a group of things you have gathered over a period of time • *a stamp **collection***
2 the organized collecting of money, for example for charity, or the money collected

collective noun **collective nouns**
NOUN a noun that refers to a group of people or things. For example, a flock, a herd, and a shoal are all **collective nouns**.

college **colleges**
NOUN a place where students study after they have left school

collide **collides, colliding, collided**
VERB If a moving object **collides** with something, it hits it. • *They **collided** with each other as they rushed through the door.*

collision **collisions**
NOUN A **collision** is when a moving object hits something.
SYNONYM: crash

colon **colons**
NOUN **1** the punctuation mark (:). It is used to introduce a list, a quotation or an explanation of a statement. • *We need to buy several things: bread, milk, fruit and toothpaste.*
2 part of your intestine

colonel **colonels**
NOUN an army officer with a fairly high rank

colony **colonies**
NOUN **1** a country that is controlled by another country
2 a group of people or animals living together

colossal
ADJECTIVE very large indeed
[from Greek *kolossos* meaning huge statue]

colour **colours**
NOUN the appearance something has as a result of reflecting light • *Red, blue and yellow are the primary **colours**.*

colour blind
ADJECTIVE Someone who is **colour blind** is not able to see the difference between certain colours.

colourful
ADJECTIVE **1** Something that is **colourful** has a lot of different colours or bright colours.
ANTONYMS: dull, colourless
2 A **colourful** story is very exciting and interesting.
ANTONYMS: dull, boring

colourless
ADJECTIVE **1** without colour
2 dull and uninteresting

colt **colts**
NOUN a young male horse

column **columns**
NOUN **1** a tall, solid, upright cylinder, especially one supporting part of a building

A B C D E F G H I J K L M N O P Q R S T U V W X Y Z

2 In a newspaper or magazine, a **column** is a vertical section of writing.
3 a group of people or vehicles moving in a long line

coma **comas**
NOUN a state of deep unconsciousness

comb **combs, combing, combed**
NOUN **1** a flat object with long, thin, pointed parts, which you use for tidying your hair
VERB **2** When you **comb** your hair, you tidy it with a comb.

combat **combats, combating, combated**
NOUN **1** fighting • *In the Falklands War many soldiers had to take part in armed* ***combat****.*
VERB **2** If someone **combats** something, they try to stop it happening. • *We need new ways to* ***combat*** *crime.*

combination **combinations**
NOUN **1** a mixture of things • *Fatima won the competition through a* ***combination*** *of skill and determination.*
2 a series of numbers or letters used to open a special lock

combine **combines, combining, combined**
VERB If you **combine** things, you mix them together. • ***Combine*** *the butter and sugar, then add the eggs.* • *The book* ***combines*** *adventure and mystery.*

combine harvester **combine harvesters**
NOUN a large machine used on farms to cut, sort and clean grain

combustion
NOUN the process of burning

come **comes, coming, came**
VERB **1** If you **come** to a place, you move or arrive there.
2 If something **comes** to a particular point, it reaches that point. • *The water* ***came*** *up to her waist.*
3 When a particular time **comes**, it happens. • *Spring* ***came*** *early this year.*

comedian **comedians**
NOUN an entertainer whose job is to make people laugh

comedy **comedies**
NOUN a play, film, or television programme that is intended to make people laugh

comet **comets**
NOUN an object that travels around the sun leaving a bright trail behind it
[from Greek *kometes* meaning long-haired]

comfort **comforts, comforting, comforted**
NOUN **1** the state of being pleasantly relaxed
2 a feeling of relief from worry or unhappiness • *It's a* ***comfort*** *to me to know that they are safe.*
VERB **3** If you **comfort** someone, you make them less worried or unhappy.

comfortable
ADJECTIVE **1** If you are **comfortable**, you are at ease and relaxed.
2 Something that is **comfortable** makes you feel relaxed. • *a* ***comfortable*** *chair*
comfortably ADVERB

comic **comics**
NOUN **1** a magazine that contains stories told in pictures
ADJECTIVE **2** funny • *a* ***comic*** *song*

comma **commas**
NOUN the punctuation mark (,). It can show a short pause, or it can separate items in a list or words in speech marks from the rest of the sentence.

command **commands, commanding, commanded**
NOUN **1** an order to do something
VERB **2** If you **command** someone to do something, you order them to do it.

commemorate **commemorates, commemorating, commemorated**
VERB If you **commemorate** something, you do something special to show that you remember it. • *On Remembrance Day we* ***commemorate*** *all the people who died in the two World Wars.*

comment **comments, commenting, commented**
NOUN **1** a remark about something
VERB **2** If you **comment** on something, you make a remark about it.

commentary **commentaries**
NOUN a description of an event that is broadcast on radio or television while the event is happening • *The **commentary** on the match was on the radio.*

commentator **commentators**
NOUN someone who gives a radio or television commentary

commerce
NOUN the buying and selling of goods

commercial **commercials**
NOUN **1** an advertisement on television or radio
ADJECTIVE **2** **Commercial** activities involve producing large amounts of goods to sell and make money.

commit **commits, committing, committed**
VERB When someone **commits** a crime or sin, they do it. • *The police know who **committed** the burglary.*

committee **committees**
NOUN a group of people who make decisions on behalf of a larger group

common **commoner, commonest; commons**
ADJECTIVE **1** Something that is **common** exists in large numbers or happens often.
NOUN **2** an area of grassy land where everyone can go
ADJECTIVE **3** If something is **common** to two or more people, they all have it or use it. • *We had a **common** interest in butterflies.*
PHRASE **4** If two things or people have something **in common**, they both have it. • *Sarah and I have a lot **in common**.*

common noun **common nouns**
NOUN **Common nouns** name things in general. They begin with lower-case letters: *girl, boy, animal, picture.*
See **noun**

common sense
NOUN knowing how to behave sensibly in any situation

Commonwealth
NOUN The **Commonwealth** is a group of countries that used to be ruled by Britain.

commotion
NOUN a lot of noise and excitement

communal
ADJECTIVE shared by a group of people • *The shop had **communal** changing rooms.*

communicate **communicates, communicating, communicated**
VERB When people **communicate**, they exchange information, usually by talking or writing to each other.

communication **communications**
NOUN **1** the act of exchanging information, usually by talking, writing or, in the case of animals, making sounds • *the **communication** of ideas*
PLURAL NOUN **2** **Communications** are electrical or radio systems that allow people to broadcast or communicate information.

communion
NOUN **1** a Christian religious service in which people share holy bread and wine
2 the sharing of thoughts and feelings

community **communities**
NOUN all the people living in a particular area

commuter **commuters**
NOUN a person who has to travel a long way to work every day

compact
ADJECTIVE Something that is **compact** takes up very little space, or no more space than is necessary.

compact disc **compact discs**
NOUN a music or video recording in the form of a small plastic disc

companion **companions**
NOUN someone you travel or spend time with

company **companies**
NOUN **1** a business that sells goods or provides a service

2 If you have **company**, you have a friend or visitor with you.
PHRASE **3** If you **keep someone company**, you spend time with them.

comparative **comparatives**
ADJECTIVE **1** You use **comparative** to show that something is true only when compared with something else.
NOUN **2** In grammar, the **comparative** is the form of an adjective or adverb that shows an increase in size, quality or amount. It is usually formed by adding *-er* to a word, for example, *bigger*, *faster*, or by putting *more* before the word, for example, *more difficult*.

compare **compares, comparing, compared**
VERB When you **compare** things, you see in what ways they are different or similar. • *We **compared** our hair to see whose was longest.*

comparison **comparisons**
NOUN When you make a **comparison**, you consider two things together and decide in what ways they are different or similar.

compartment **compartments**
NOUN **1** a section of a railway carriage
2 one of the separate sections of something such as a bag or a box

compass **compasses**
NOUN **1** an instrument with a magnetic needle that always points north. You use a **compass** to find your way.
PLURAL NOUN **2 Compasses** are a hinged instrument for drawing circles.

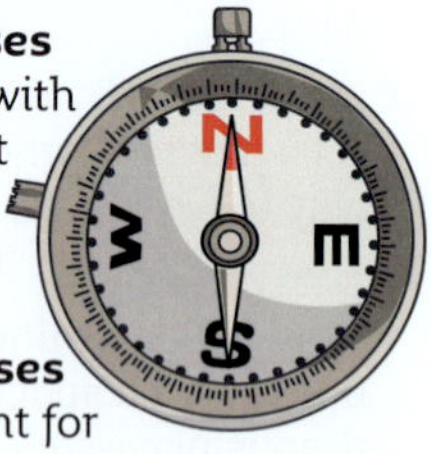

compassion
NOUN pity and sympathy for someone who is suffering
compassionate ADJECTIVE

compass point **compass points**
NOUN one of the 32 marks on the dial of a compass that show direction • *North, south, east and west are **compass points**.*

compel **compels, compelling, compelled**
VERB **1** If you **compel** someone to do something, you force them to do it.
ADJECTIVE **2** A **compelling** story or event is extremely interesting.
3 A **compelling** argument or reason makes you believe that something is true.

compensate **compensates, compensating, compensated**
VERB **1** To **compensate** someone means to give them money to replace something that has been lost or damaged.
2 If one thing **compensates** for another, it cancels out the bad effects of it. • *The trip to Disneyland **compensated** for her long illness.*

compete **competes, competing, competed**
VERB **1** If you **compete** in a contest or game, you take part in it.
2 If you **compete**, you try to do better than others.

competent
ADJECTIVE Someone who is **competent** at something can do it satisfactorily. • *He is a **competent** nurse.*

competition **competitions**
NOUN an event in which people take part to find out who is the best at something

compile **compiles, compiling, compiled**
VERB When you **compile** information, you collect it and put it together.

complain **complains, complaining, complained**
VERB **1** If you **complain**, you say that you are not happy about something. • *The neighbours **complained** about the noise.*
2 If you **complain** of pain or illness, you say that you have it.
complaint NOUN

complement **complements, complementing, complemented**
VERB **1** If one thing **complements** another, the two things go well together. • *Her piano music **complements** the poem.*

NOUN **2** In grammar, a **complement** is a word or phrase that gives information about the subject or object of a sentence. For example, in the sentence *Rover is a dog*, *is a dog* is the **complement**.

Do not confuse *complement* with *compliment*.

complete **completes, completing, completed**
VERB **1** If you **complete** something, you finish it. • *She has just* ***completed*** *her third short story.*
ADJECTIVE **2** If something is **complete**, none of it is missing.

completely
ADVERB totally
SYNONYM: utterly

complex **complexes**
ADJECTIVE **1** **Complex** things have many different parts and are hard to understand.
NOUN **2** a group of buildings used for a particular purpose, such a sports **complex**

complexion **complexions**
NOUN the quality of the skin on your face

complicated
ADJECTIVE Something that is **complicated** is hard to understand.

complication **complications**
NOUN something that makes a situation more difficult to deal with

compliment **compliments**
NOUN If you pay someone a **compliment**, you tell them you admire or like something about them.

Do not confuse *compliment* with *complement*.

component **components**
NOUN The **components** of something are the parts it is made of.

compose **composes, composing, composed**
VERB **1** If you **compose** a piece of music, a letter, or a speech, you write it.
2 If something is **composed** of particular things or people, it is made up of them.

composer **composers**
NOUN someone who writes music

composition **compositions**
NOUN **1** a piece of music or writing
2 the things that something is made up of

compost
NOUN a mixture of rotted plants and manure that gardeners add to the soil to help plants grow

compound word **compound words**
NOUN a word with a single meaning, but made up of two or more words. For example, *gingerbread*, *housework* and *teapot* are all **compound words**.

comprehend **comprehends, comprehending, comprehended**
VERB If you **comprehend** something, you understand it.

comprehensive **comprehensives**
ADJECTIVE **1** Something that is **comprehensive** includes everything that you need to know.
NOUN **2** a school where children of all abilities are taught together
comprehensively ADVERB

compress **compresses, compressing, compressed**
VERB If you **compress** something, you squeeze it or shorten it. • *She* ***compressed*** *her story into one page.*

compromise **compromises, compromising, compromised**
NOUN **1** an agreement in which people accept less than they really wanted
VERB **2** When people **compromise**, they settle for less than they really wanted.

compulsory
ADJECTIVE If something is **compulsory**, you have to do it.

computer **computers**
NOUN an electronic machine that stores information and makes calculations

computerize **computerizes, computerizing, computerized**; also spelt **computerise**
VERB When a system or process is

computerized, such as train timetables or bank accounts, the work is done by computers.

comrade **comrades**
NOUN a companion, especially in battle

con **cons, conning, conned**
VERB **1** If someone **cons** you, or you are **conned**, you are tricked into doing something. • *He **conned** me into buying the tickets.*
NOUN **2** a trick that makes you believe or do something that you would not normally believe or do

concave
ADJECTIVE A **concave** surface curves inwards, rather than being level or bulging outwards.
ANTONYM: convex

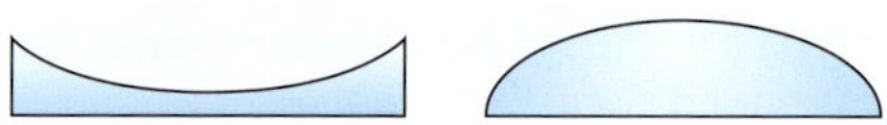

concave convex

conceal **conceals, concealing, concealed**
VERB If you **conceal** something, you hide it.

conceited
ADJECTIVE Someone who is **conceited** is too proud of their appearance or abilities.
SYNONYMS: bigheaded, self-important

conceive **conceives, conceiving, conceived**
VERB **1** If you can't **conceive** of something, you can't imagine it or believe it. • *He couldn't **conceive** of anything more fun than surfing.*
2 If you **conceive** something such as a plan, you think of it and work out how it could be done. • *Alex **conceived** the idea while eating his lunch.*
3 When a woman **conceives**, she becomes pregnant.

concentrate **concentrates, concentrating, concentrated**
VERB **1** If you **concentrate** on something, you give it all your attention. • *I need to **concentrate** on my homework.*
2 When something is **concentrated** in one place, it is all there rather than in several places. • *The shops were **concentrated** in the town centre.*

concentrated
ADJECTIVE A **concentrated** liquid has been made stronger by having water removed from it. • ***concentrated** orange juice*

concentration **concentrations**
NOUN **1** the ability to give your full attention to something you do or hear
2 A **concentration** of something is a large amount of it in one place.

concept **concepts**
NOUN an abstract or general idea

conception **conceptions**
NOUN the idea you have of something

concern **concerns, concerning, concerned**
NOUN **1** worry about something or someone
2 If something is your **concern**, it is your duty or responsibility.
VERB **3** If something **concerns** you or if you are **concerned** about it, it worries you.
concerned ADJECTIVE

concerning
PREPOSITION You use **concerning** to show what something is about. • *an article **concerning** fox hunting*

concert **concerts**
NOUN a public performance by musicians

concession **concessions**
NOUN If you make a **concession**, you agree to let someone have or do something.

concise
ADJECTIVE giving all the necessary information using as few words as possible • *a **concise** explanation*
SYNONYMS: brief, short
concisely ADVERB

conclude **concludes, concluding, concluded**
VERB **1** If you **conclude** something, you

examine the facts and decide what your opinion is. • *We **concluded** that the letter was a fake.*
2 When you **conclude** something, you finish it.

conclusion **conclusions**
NOUN **1** the end of something
2 a final decision about something
• *We wanted to go for a swim in the sea, but we came to the **conclusion** that it was too cold.*

concrete
NOUN **1** a building material made by mixing cement, sand and water
ADJECTIVE **2** real and physical, rather than abstract • *He had no **concrete** evidence.*

concussion
NOUN damage to the brain caused by a blow or a fall, which causes confusion, sickness or unconsciousness
concussed ADJECTIVE

condemn **condemns, condemning, condemned**
VERB **1** If you **condemn** something, you say it is bad and unacceptable.
2 If someone is **condemned** to a punishment, they are given it. • *The burglar was **condemned** to five years in prison.*

condensation
NOUN a coating of tiny drops of liquid formed on a cold surface by steam or vapour

condense **condenses, condensing, condensed**
VERB **1** If you **condense** a piece of writing or a speech, you shorten it.
2 When a gas or vapour **condenses**, it changes into a liquid.

condition **conditions**
NOUN **1** the state someone or something is in • *The antique clock was still in good **condition**.*
2 something that must happen in order for something else to be possible • *I can go swimming on Saturday on the **condition** that I do my homework first.*

conduct **conducts, conducting, conducted**
Said "**kon**-duct" NOUN **1** behaviour
Said "kon-**duct**" VERB **2** When you **conduct** an activity, you carry it out.
3 When someone **conducts** an orchestra, a band or a choir, they direct it in a piece of music.
4 If something **conducts** heat or electricity, heat or electricity can pass along it. • *Copper **conducts** electricity well.*

conductor **conductors**
NOUN **1** someone who conducts an orchestra or choir
2 someone who moves round a bus or train selling and checking tickets
3 a substance that conducts heat or electricity

cone **cones**
NOUN **1** a regular three-dimensional shape with a circular base and a point at the top
2 the fruit of a fir or pine tree

conference **conferences**
NOUN a meeting at which formal discussions take place

confess **confesses, confessing, confessed**
VERB If you **confess** to something, you admit that you did it.

confession **confessions**
NOUN **1** If you make a **confession**, you admit that you have done something wrong.
SYNONYM: admission
2 the act of confessing something, especially as a religious act, where people confess their sins to a priest

confetti
NOUN small pieces of coloured paper thrown over the bride and groom at a wedding [from Italian *confetto* meaning a sweet]

confide **confides, confiding, confided**
VERB If you **confide** in or to someone, you tell them a secret.

confidence
NOUN **1** If you have **confidence** in someone, you feel you can trust them.
2 Someone who has **confidence** is sure of their own abilities or qualities.

confident
ADJECTIVE **1** If you are **confident** about something, you are sure it will happen the way you want it to.
2 Someone who is **confident** is very sure of themselves and their own abilities.
confidently ADVERB

confidential
ADJECTIVE **Confidential** information is meant to be kept secret.

confine **confines, confining, confined**
VERB **1** If someone **confines** you to a place, you can't leave it. • *The doctor **confined** Debbie to bed for two weeks as she had pneumonia.*
2 If you **confine** yourself to doing something, you do only that thing. • *On their trip abroad, they **confined** themselves to drinking bottled water.*

confirm **confirms, confirming, confirmed**
VERB **1** If you **confirm** something, you say or show that it is true. • *The teacher **confirmed** that we had all passed our spelling test.*
2 If you **confirm** an arrangement or appointment, you say it is definite.
• *Dad **confirmed** our holiday booking.*

confiscate **confiscates, confiscating, confiscated**
VERB If someone **confiscates** something, they take it away from someone as a punishment.
[from Latin *confiscare* meaning to seize for the public treasury]
confiscation NOUN

conflict **conflicts, conflicting, conflicted**
NOUN **1** disagreement and argument
2 a war or battle
VERB **3** When two ideas or interests **conflict**, they are different and it seems impossible for them both to be true.

conform **conforms, conforming, conformed**
VERB **1** If you **conform**, you behave the way people expect you to.
2 If something **conforms** to a law or to someone's wishes, it does what is required or wanted.
conformist NOUN OR ADJECTIVE

confront **confronts, confronting, confronted**
VERB **1** If you are **confronted** with a problem or task, you have to deal with it.
2 If you **confront** someone, you meet them face to face, especially when you are going to fight or argue with them.

confrontation **confrontations**
NOUN a serious dispute between two people or groups of people who come face to face

confuse **confuses, confusing, confused**
VERB **1** If you **confuse** two people or things, you mix them up and are not sure which is which.
2 If you **confuse** someone, you make them uncertain about what is happening or what to do.
confusion NOUN

congested
ADJECTIVE **1** When a road is **congested**, it is so full of traffic that normal movement is impossible.
2 If your nose is **congested**, it is blocked and you cannot breathe properly.
congestion NOUN

congratulate **congratulates, congratulating, congratulated**
VERB If you **congratulate** someone, you say that you're pleased about something good that has happened to them, or praise them for something they have done. • *He **congratulated** us on winning the competition.*
congratulations NOUN

congregation **congregations**
NOUN the people attending a service in a church

congruent
ADJECTIVE In mathematics, things that are **congruent** are exactly the same size and shape, and would fit exactly on top of each other. • ***congruent** triangles*

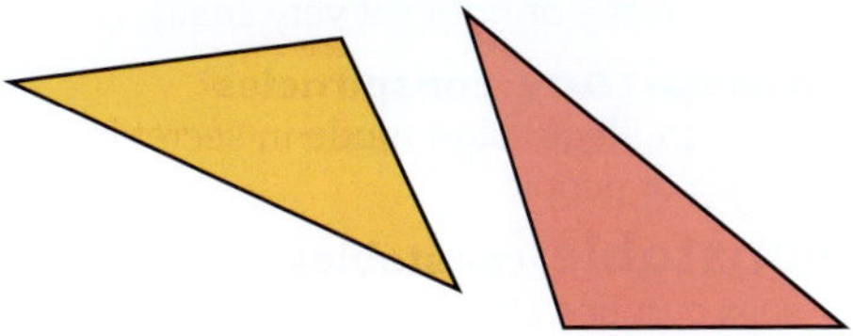

conifer **conifers**
NOUN any type of evergreen tree that produces cones
coniferous ADJECTIVE

conjunction **conjunctions**
NOUN In grammar, a **conjunction** is a word that links two other words or two clauses, such as *and*, *but*, *or*, *while* and *that*. For example: "I love bacon *and* eggs." "I'm happy, *but* my brother is not".

conjurer **conjurers**
NOUN someone who entertains people by doing magic tricks

conker **conkers**
NOUN a brown nut from a horse chestnut tree

connect **connects, connecting, connected**
VERB **1** If you **connect** two things, you join them together.
2 If one thing or person is **connected** with another, there is a link between them.

connection **connections**
NOUN **1** the point where two things are joined together
2 If you make a **connection** at a station or airport, you continue your journey by catching another train, bus or plane.
• *Our train was late, so we missed our **connection**.*

connective **connectives**
NOUN a word that connects phrases, clauses or words together
See **conjunction**

conquer **conquers, conquering, conquered**
VERB **1** If you **conquer** something difficult or dangerous, you succeed in controlling it. • *She **conquered** her fear of spiders.*
2 to take control of a country by force
conqueror NOUN

conscience
NOUN the part of your mind that tells you what is right or wrong

conscientious
ADJECTIVE Someone who is **conscientious** takes great care over their work.
conscientiously ADVERB

conscious
ADJECTIVE **1** Someone who is **conscious** is awake, rather than asleep or unconscious.
2 If you are **conscious** of something, you are aware of it.
3 A **conscious** action or effort is done deliberately.

consecutive
ADJECTIVE **1** **Consecutive** events or periods of time happen one after the other. • *We had eight **consecutive** days of rain.*
2 **Consecutive** numbers follow each other in order. For example, 1, 2, 3, 4 are **consecutive** numbers.
consecutively ADVERB

consent **consents, consenting, consented**
NOUN **1** permission to do something
2 agreement between two or more people
• *By common **consent** we went to France for the holiday.*
VERB **3** If you **consent** to something, you agree to do it or allow it to happen.

consequence **consequences**
NOUN result or effect

conservation
NOUN the preservation of the environment
conservationist NOUN OR ADJECTIVE

conservative **conservatives**
NOUN **1** a member or supporter of the **Conservative** Party in Britain
ADJECTIVE **2** Someone who is **conservative** does not like change or new ideas.

A B C D E F G H I J K L M N O P Q R S T U V W X Y Z

3 A **conservative** estimate or guess is a cautious or moderate one.

conservatory **conservatories**
NOUN a room with glass walls and a glass roof in which plants are kept

conserve **conserves, conserving, conserved**
VERB **1** If you **conserve** a supply of something, you make it last as long as possible. • *I switched off my torch to* ***conserve*** *the battery.*
2 If you **conserve** something, you keep it as it is and do not change it. • *We should* ***conserve*** *this old building.*

consider **considers, considering, considered**
VERB If you **consider** something, you think about it carefully.

considerable
ADJECTIVE A **considerable** amount of something is a lot of it.

considerate
ADJECTIVE Someone who is **considerate** thinks of other people's needs and feelings.

consideration **considerations**
NOUN **1** careful thought about something
2 something that should be thought about when you are planning or deciding something
3 Someone who shows **consideration** pays attention to the needs and feelings of other people.

consist **consists, consisting, consisted**
VERB Something that **consists** of certain things is made up of them. • *This bread* ***consists*** *of flour, yeast and water.*

consistent
ADJECTIVE Something that is **consistent** does not change.

console **consoles, consoling, consoled**
Said "kon-**sole**" VERB **1** If you **console** someone who is unhappy, you comfort them and cheer them up.
Said "**kon**-sole" NOUN **2** a panel with switches or knobs for operating a machine

consonant **consonants**
NOUN all the letters of the alphabet that are not vowels

conspicuous
ADJECTIVE If something is **conspicuous**, you can see or notice it very easily.

conspiracy **conspiracies**
NOUN an illegal plan made in secret by a group of people

constable **constables**
NOUN a police officer of the lowest rank

constant
ADJECTIVE **1** Something that is **constant** happens all the time or is always there.
• *We could hear the* ***constant*** *sound of the waves pounding the shore.*
2 If an amount or level is **constant**, it stays the same.

constellation **constellations**
NOUN a group of stars

constipated
ADJECTIVE Someone who is **constipated** finds it difficult to empty their bowels. [from Latin *constipare* meaning to press together]
constipation NOUN

constitution **constitutions**
NOUN **1** The **constitution** of a country is the system of laws and principles by which it is governed.
2 Your **constitution** is your health.

construct **constructs, constructing, constructed**
VERB If you **construct** something, you build or make it.

construction **constructions**
NOUN **1** the process of building or making something
2 something built or made

constructive
ADJECTIVE helpful • *The tennis coach made some* ***constructive*** *comments about my backhand.*

consult **consults, consulting, consulted**
VERB **1** If you **consult** someone, you ask for their opinion or advice.

2 If you **consult** a book or map, you look at it for information.
consultation NOUN

consultant **consultants**
NOUN an experienced doctor who specializes in one type of medicine
• *a **consultant** heart surgeon*

consume **consumes, consuming, consumed**
VERB **1** If you **consume** something, you eat or drink it.
2 To **consume** fuel or energy is to use it up.

consumer **consumers**
NOUN someone who buys things or uses services • *magazines aimed at teenage **consumers***

consumption
NOUN The **consumption** of fuel or food is the using of it, or the amount used. • *The **consumption** of ice cream rises in hot weather.*

contact **contacts, contacting, contacted**
NOUN **1** If you are in **contact** with someone, you talk or write to them regularly. • *I am in **contact** with a pen pal in France.*
2 When things are in **contact**, they are touching each other.
VERB **3** If you **contact** someone, you telephone them or write to them.

contact lens **contact lenses**
NOUN small plastic lenses that you put in your eyes instead of wearing glasses, to help you see better

contagious
ADJECTIVE A **contagious** disease can be caught by touching people or things infected with it. • *Measles is **contagious**.*

contain **contains, containing, contained**
VERB **1** If a substance **contains** something, that thing is a part of it.
2 The things a box or room **contains** are the things inside it.

container **containers**
NOUN something that you keep things in, such as a box or a jar

contaminate **contaminates, contaminating, contaminated**
VERB If dirt, chemicals or radiation **contaminate** something, they make it impure and harmful.
contamination NOUN

contemplate **contemplates, contemplating, contemplated**
VERB **1** If you **contemplate**, you think very carefully about something. • *She **contemplated** what she would do at the weekend.*
2 If you **contemplate** something, you look at it for a long time.

contemporary
ADJECTIVE **1** produced or happening now
2 A **contemporary** work is one that was written at the time of the events it describes.

contempt
NOUN If you treat someone with **contempt**, you show no respect for them at all.

content
Said "kon-**tent**" ADJECTIVE **1** If you are **content**, you are happy and satisfied with your life.
2 If you are **content** to do something, you are willing to do it.

contents
Said "**kon**-tents" PLURAL NOUN **1** The **contents** of something like a box or a cake are the things in it.
2 The **contents** page of a book tells you what is in it.

contest **contests**
NOUN a competition or game

contestant **contestants**
NOUN someone who takes part in a competition
SYNONYMS: competitor, player

context **contexts**
NOUN The **context** of a word or sentence is the words or sentences that come before and after it, which help to make the meaning clear.

continent **continents**
NOUN **1** a very large area of land, such as Africa or Asia
2 In Britain, the mainland of Europe is sometimes called the **Continent**.
[from Latin *terra continens* meaning continuous land]

continental
ADJECTIVE In Britain, **continental** means on, belonging to or typical of the mainland of Europe. • ***continental*** *breakfast*

continual
ADJECTIVE happening again and again
• *Mum had a **continual** stream of phone calls.*

continue **continues, continuing, continued**
VERB **1** If you **continue** to do something, you keep doing it.
2 If something **continues**, it does not stop.
3 You say something **continues** when it starts again after stopping. • *She paused for a moment, then **continued**.*

continuous
ADJECTIVE happening all the time without stopping • *The television made a **continuous** buzzing noise.*

contour **contours**
NOUN **1** The **contour** of something is its general shape or outline.
2 On a map, a **contour** is a line joining points of equal height.

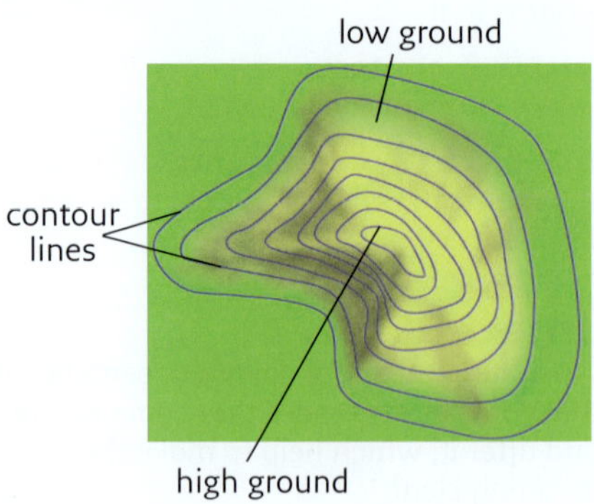

contract **contracts, contracting, contracted**
Said "**con**-trakt" NOUN **1** a legal agreement about the sale of something or work done for money • *He was given a two-year **contract**.*
Said "con-**trakt**" VERB **2** When something **contracts**, it gets smaller or shorter.
• *Metals **contract** with cold and expand with heat.*
ANTONYM: expand

contraction **contractions**
NOUN a shortened form of a word or words, often marked by an apostrophe • *"I've" is a **contraction** of "I have".*

contradict **contradicts, contradicting, contradicted**
VERB If you **contradict** someone, you say that what they have just said is wrong.
contradiction NOUN

contrary
ADJECTIVE **1** **Contrary** ideas, opinions or attitudes are completely different from each other.
PHRASE **2** **On the contrary** is used to contradict something that has just been said.

contrast **contrasts, contrasting, contrasted**
Said "**con**-trast" NOUN **1** a great difference between things • *the **contrast** between town and country*
Said "con-**trast**" VERB **2** If you **contrast** things, you describe or emphasize the differences between them.

contribute **contributes, contributing, contributed**
VERB **1** If you **contribute** to something, you do something to make it successful.
• *Everyone **contributed** to the class project.*
2 If you **contribute** money to something, you help to pay for it. • *We **contributed** some money to the appeal for the homeless.*
SYNONYMS: donate, give
contribution NOUN

control **controls, controlling, controlled**
NOUN **1** If you have **control** over something,

you are able to make it work the way you want it to.
2 The **controls** on a machine are the knobs or other devices used to work it.
VERB **3** If someone **controls** a country or an organization, they make the decisions about how it is run.
4 If someone **controls** something such as a machine, they make it work the way they want it to.
PHRASE **5** If something is **out of control**, nobody has any power over it. • *The fire was* ***out of control****.*

controversial

ADJECTIVE Something that is **controversial** causes a lot of discussion and argument, because many people disapprove of it.
• *The film was* ***controversial****.*

convalescent **convalescents**

NOUN someone who is resting while recovering from an illness

convenient

ADJECTIVE If something is **convenient**, it is easy to use or it makes something easy to do. • *It's* ***convenient*** *living close to the bus stop.*
convenience NOUN

convent **convents**

NOUN **1** a building where nuns live
2 a school run by nuns

conventional

ADJECTIVE Someone who is **conventional** thinks or behaves in an ordinary and accepted way.

converge **converges, converging, converged**

VERB When things meet or join at a particular place, they **converge**. • *The roads* ***converge*** *after three kilometres.*
convergence NOUN

conversation **conversations**

NOUN When people have a **conversation**, they talk to each other.

convert **converts, converting, converted**

VERB **1** If you **convert** something, it changes from one thing to another.
• *Dad* ***converted*** *the loft into a workshop.*
2 If someone **converts** you, they persuade you to change your religious or political beliefs.
3 In mathematics, **convert** means to change a number from one form to another. These are equal to each other. For example, you can **convert** a fraction to a decimal ($^1/_2 = 0.5$).

convex

ADJECTIVE A **convex** surface bulges outwards, rather than being level or curving inwards.
See **concave**
ANTONYM: concave

convey **conveys, conveying, conveyed**

VERB **1** If someone **conveys** people or things to a place, they take them there.
2 If you **convey** information, ideas or feelings, you tell people about them.

conveyor belt **conveyor belts**

NOUN a moving strip used in factories for moving objects along

convict **convicts, convicting, convicted**

Said "kon-**vikt**" VERB **1** If a law court **convicts** someone of a crime, it says they are guilty of it.
Said "**kon**-vikt" NOUN **2** someone serving a prison sentence

convince **convinces, convincing, convinced**

VERB If you **convince** someone of something, you persuade them to do it or that it is true. • *I* ***convinced*** *mum and dad to let me go on the school trip.*

convoy **convoys**

NOUN a group of ships or vehicles travelling together

cook **cooks, cooking, cooked**

VERB **1** When you **cook**, you prepare food for eating by boiling, baking or frying it.
NOUN **2** a person whose job is to prepare food

cooker **cookers**

NOUN an apparatus for cooking food

A B C D E F G H I J K L M N O P Q R S T U V W X Y Z

cookery
NOUN the art of preparing and cooking food

cookie **cookies**
NOUN **1** a sweet biscuit • *a chocolate* ***cookie***
2 a small file placed on a user's computer by a website • *This website uses* ***cookies****.*

cool **cooler, coolest; cools, cooling, cooled**
ADJECTIVE **1** Something **cool** has a low temperature but is not cold.
2 If you are **cool** in a difficult situation, you stay calm.
VERB **3** When something **cools**, it becomes less warm.

cooperate **cooperates, cooperating, cooperated**
VERB **1** When people **cooperate**, they work or act together.
2 If you **cooperate**, you do what someone asks you to do.

cooperative **cooperatives**
ADJECTIVE **1** A **cooperative** person does what they are asked to do willingly and cheerfully.
NOUN **2** a business or organization run by the people who work for it, and who share its profits

coordinates
PLURAL NOUN a pair of numbers or letters that tell you exactly where a point is on a grid, map or graph

cop **cops**
NOUN INFORMAL a policeman

cope **copes, coping, coped**
VERB If you **cope**, you are able to do something even if the circumstances are difficult. • *I managed to* ***cope*** *with my homework and with looking after my little brother at the same time.*

copper
NOUN a soft, reddish-brown metal

copy **copies, copying, copied**
NOUN **1** something made to look like something else • *a* ***copy*** *of a famous painting*
2 A **copy** of a book, newspaper or record is one of many identical ones produced at the same time. • *a* ***copy*** *of today's newspaper*
VERB **3** If you **copy** what someone does, you do the same thing.
4 If you **copy** something, you make a copy of it.

copyright **copyrights**
NOUN If someone has the **copyright** on a piece of writing or music, it cannot be copied or performed without their permission.

coral **corals**
NOUN a hard substance that forms in the sea from the skeletons of tiny animals called **corals**

cord **cords**
NOUN **1** strong, thick string
2 electrical wire covered in rubber or plastic

corduroy
NOUN heavy, ribbed cloth made of cotton

core **cores**
NOUN the most central part of an object or place • *an apple* ***core*** • *the earth's* ***core***

cork **corks**
NOUN **1** a soft, light substance that forms the bark of a Mediterranean tree
2 a piece of **cork** pushed into the end of a bottle to close it

corkscrew **corkscrews**
NOUN a device for pulling corks out of bottles

corn
NOUN **1** crops such as wheat and barley
2 the seeds of these crops

corner **corners, cornering, cornered**
NOUN **1** the point where two sides or edges of something meet • *The TV was in the **corner** of the room.*
See **vertex**
VERB **2** If someone **corners** a person or animal, they get them into a place they can't escape from. • *The police **cornered** the thief.*

cornet **cornets**
NOUN a small, brass instrument used in brass and military bands

coronation **coronations**
NOUN the ceremony at which a king or queen is crowned

coroner **coroners**
NOUN an official who investigates the deaths of people who have died in a violent or unusual way

corporal **corporals**
NOUN an officer of low rank in the army or air force

corporal punishment
NOUN punishing of people by beating them

corps
Said "**kor**" NOUN part of an army with special duties • *the Medical **Corps***

corpse **corpses**
NOUN a dead body

correct **corrects, correcting, corrected**
ADJECTIVE **1** If something is **correct**, there are no mistakes in it.
VERB **2** If you **correct** something that is wrong, you make it right. • *She **corrected** my maths homework.*
correction NOUN

correspond **corresponds, corresponding, corresponded**
VERB **1** If one thing **corresponds** with another, it is similar to it or it matches it in some way.
2 If numbers or amounts **correspond**, they are the same.
3 When people **correspond**, they write to each other.

correspondence
NOUN **1** letters or the writing of letters
2 If there is a **correspondence** between two things, there is a similarity between them.

correspondent **correspondents**
NOUN a newspaper, radio or television reporter

corridor **corridors**
NOUN a passage in a building or train [from Old Italian *corridore* meaning place for running]

corrode **corrodes, corroding, corroded**
VERB When something **corrodes**, it is eaten away. When iron and steel are **corroded**, rust is formed.
corrosion NOUN **corrosive** ADJECTIVE

corrugated
ADJECTIVE **Corrugated** metal or cardboard has parallel folds to make it stronger.

corrupt **corrupts, corrupting, corrupted**
ADJECTIVE **1** People who are **corrupt** act dishonestly or illegally in return for money or power.
SYNONYM: dishonest
VERB **2** If you **corrupt** someone, you make them dishonest.
3 If a bug in a computer spoils files, it **corrupts** them.
corruption NOUN

cosmetics
PLURAL NOUN lipstick, face powder and other make-up

cosmic
ADJECTIVE belonging to or relating to the whole universe

cosmos
NOUN the universe

A B C D E F G H I J K L M N O P Q R S T U V W X Y Z

cost **costs, costing, cost**
NOUN **1** the amount of money needed to buy, do or make something
VERB **2** You use **cost** to talk about the amount of money you have to pay for things. • *You can't have that – it **costs** too much.*

costume **costumes**
NOUN **1** a set of clothes worn by an actor
2 the clothing worn in a particular place or during a particular period

cosy **cosier, cosiest**
ADJECTIVE warm and comfortable

cot **cots**
NOUN a small bed for a baby, with bars or panels round it to stop the baby falling out

cottage **cottages**
NOUN a small house, especially in the country

cotton
NOUN **1** cloth made from the soft fibres of the **cotton** plant • *a **cotton** shirt*
2 thread used for sewing • *a needle and **cotton***

couch **couches**
NOUN a long, soft piece of furniture for sitting or lying on

cough **coughs, coughing, coughed**
VERB When you **cough**, you force air out of your throat with a sudden harsh noise.

could
VERB **1** the past tense of **can**
2 You use **could** to say that something might happen or might be true. • *It **could** rain later.*
3 You use **could** when you are asking for something politely. • ***Could** you tell me the way to the station, please?*

couldn't
VERB a contraction of *could not*

council **councils**
NOUN a group of people elected to look after something, especially the affairs of a town, district or county

counsel **counsels, counselling, counselled**
NOUN **1** advice
VERB **2** If someone **counsels** people, they give them advice about their problems.

count **counts, counting, counted**
VERB **1** When you **count**, you say all the numbers in order up to a particular number.
2 If you **count**, or **count** up, all the things in a group, you add them up to see how many there are.
3 If you can **count** on someone or something, you can rely on them. • *You can **count** on me to help.*
PHRASE **4** If you **keep count** of something, you keep a record of how often it happens. • *Who's **keeping count** of the score?*
5 If you **lose count** of something, you cannot remember how often it has happened.

counter **counters**
NOUN **1** a long, flat surface in a shop, over which goods are sold
2 a small, flat, round object used in board games

counterfeit **counterfeits, counterfeiting, counterfeited**
Said "**kown**-ter-fit" ADJECTIVE
1 **Counterfeit** things are not genuine, but have been made to look genuine in order to deceive people. • ***counterfeit** money*
VERB **2** If someone **counterfeits** something, they make an exact copy of it in order to trick people.

countless
ADJECTIVE too many to count

country **countries**
NOUN **1** one of the political areas the world is divided into
2 land away from towns and cities • *It is peaceful living in the **country**.*

countryside
NOUN land away from towns and cities

county **counties**
NOUN a region with its own local government • *The **county** of Lincolnshire is in the east of England.*

couple **couples**
NOUN **1** two people who are married or having a romantic relationship
2 A **couple** of things or people means two of them, or not very many.

couplet **couplets**
NOUN two lines of poetry together that usually rhyme

coupon **coupons**
NOUN **1** a piece of printed paper that entitles you to pay less than usual for something
2 a form you fill in to ask for information or to enter a competition

courage
NOUN the quality shown by people who do things that they know are dangerous or difficult • *She showed great **courage** in her efforts to save them from the burning house.*
courageous ADJECTIVE
courageously ADVERB

courgette **courgettes**
NOUN a vegetable that looks like a small green marrow

courier **couriers**
NOUN **1** someone employed by a travel company to look after people on holiday
2 someone employed to deliver letters and parcels quickly

course **courses**
NOUN **1** a series of lessons or lectures
2 a piece of land where races take place or golf is played
3 the route something such as a ship or a river takes • *The captain changed **course** to avoid the storm.*
4 one of the parts of a meal • *The first **course** was soup.*
PHRASE **5** If you say **of course**, you are showing that you are absolutely sure about something. • ***Of course** she wouldn't do a thing like that.*

court **courts**
NOUN **1** a place where legal matters are decided by a judge and jury or a magistrate. The judge and jury or magistrate can also be referred to as the **court**. • *He is due to appear in **court** next week.* • *The **court** awarded him ten thousand pounds in compensation.*
2 a place where a game such as tennis or badminton is played
3 the place where a king or queen lives and works

courteous
ADJECTIVE **Courteous** behaviour is polite and considerate.
courteously ADVERB

courtyard **courtyards**
NOUN a flat area of ground surrounded by buildings or walls

cousin **cousins**
NOUN Your **cousin** is the child of your uncle or aunt.

cove **coves**
NOUN a small bay on the coast

cover **covers, covering, covered**
VERB **1** If you **cover** something, you put something else over it to protect it or hide it.
2 If something **covers** something else, it forms a layer over it.
3 If you **cover** a particular distance, you travel that distance.
4 If you **cover** a subject, you discuss it in a lesson, course or book. • *We **covered** the Vikings in today's lesson.*
NOUN **5** something put over an object to protect it or keep it warm
6 The **cover** of a book or magazine is its outside.
7 **Cover** is trees, rocks or other places where you can shelter or hide. • *When it started raining they ran for **cover**.*

coverage
NOUN The **coverage** of something in the news is the reporting of it. • *There was complete **coverage** of the Wimbledon finals on television.*

A B C D E F G H I J K L M N O P Q R S T U V W X Y Z

cow **cows**
NOUN a large female mammal kept on farms for its milk and meat

coward **cowards**
NOUN a person who is easily frightened and avoids dangerous situations
cowardly ADJECTIVE **cowardice** NOUN

cowboy **cowboys**
NOUN a man employed to look after cattle in America

coy **coyer, coyest**
ADJECTIVE If someone behaves in a **coy** way, they pretend to be shy and modest.

crab **crabs**
NOUN a crustacean with four pairs of legs, two claws, and a flat, round body covered by a shell

crack **cracks, cracking, cracked**
VERB **1** If something **cracks**, or if something **cracks** it, it becomes damaged, with lines appearing on its surface.
2 If you **crack** a joke, you tell it.
3 If you **crack** a problem or code, you solve it.
NOUN **4** one of the lines appearing on something when it cracks
5 a narrow gap • *My ring fell into a **crack** in the pavement.*

cracker **crackers**
NOUN **1** a thin, crisp biscuit that is often eaten with cheese
2 a paper-covered tube that pulls apart with a bang, and usually has a toy and paper hat inside

crackle **crackles, crackling, crackled**
VERB **1** something **crackles**, it makes a series of short sharp sounds • *The bonfire started to **crackle** as the flames grew higher.*
NOUN **2** a short sharp sound

cradle **cradles, cradling, cradled**
NOUN **1** a box-shaped bed for a baby
VERB **2** If you **cradle** something in your arms or hands, you hold it there carefully.

craft **crafts**
NOUN **1** an activity that needs skill with the hands, such as weaving, carving or pottery
2 a boat, plane or spacecraft

craftsman or **craftswoman**
craftsmen or **craftswomen**
NOUN a person who makes things skilfully with their hands
craftsmanship NOUN

crafty **craftier, craftiest**
ADJECTIVE **Crafty** people get what they want by tricking other people in a clever way.
SYNONYMS: cunning, wily

crag **crags**
NOUN a steep, rugged rock or peak

cram **crams, cramming, crammed**
VERB If you **cram** people or things into a place, you put more in than there is room for. • *I **crammed** my dirty washing into the washing machine.*

cramp **cramps**
NOUN pain caused when muscles contract

cramped
ADJECTIVE If a room or a building is **cramped**, it is not big enough for the people or things in it.

crane **cranes, craning, craned**
NOUN **1** a machine that moves heavy things by lifting them in the air
2 a large bird with a long neck and long legs
VERB **3** If you **crane** your neck, you extend your head in a particular direction to see or hear something better.

crash **crashes, crashing, crashed**
NOUN **1** an accident in which a moving vehicle hits something and is damaged
2 a sudden, loud noise
VERB **3** If a vehicle **crashes**, it hits something and is badly damaged.

crate **crates**
NOUN a large box used for transporting or storing things

crater **craters**
NOUN a wide hole in the ground caused by something hitting it or by an explosion
• *The surface of the moon has many **craters**.*
[from Greek *krater* meaning mixing-bowl]

crave **craves, craving, craved**
VERB If you **crave** something, you want it very much. • *I **craved** a bar of chocolate.*
craving NOUN

crawl **crawls, crawling, crawled**
VERB **1** When you **crawl**, you move forward on your hands and knees.
2 When an insect or vehicle **crawls** somewhere, it moves there very slowly.

crayon **crayons**
NOUN a coloured pencil or a stick of coloured wax

craze **crazes**
NOUN something that is very popular for a short time

crazy **crazier, craziest**
ADJECTIVE INFORMAL **1** very strange or foolish
2 If you are **crazy** about something or someone, you like them very much.

creak **creaks, creaking, creaked**
VERB **1** If something **creaks**, it makes a harsh sound when it moves or when you stand on it.
NOUN **2** a harsh, squeaking noise
creaky ADJECTIVE

cream **creams**
NOUN **1** a thick, yellowish-white liquid taken from the top of milk
2 a substance that you can rub into your skin to make it soft or protect it
ADJECTIVE **3** a yellowish-white colour

crease **creases, creasing, creased**
NOUN **1** an irregular line that appears on cloth or paper when it is crumpled
2 a straight line on something that has been pressed or folded neatly
• *Dad ironed a sharp **crease** in his best trousers.*
VERB **3** If you **crease** something, you make lines appear on it.

create **creates, creating, created**
VERB If someone **creates** something, they cause it to happen or exist.
creation NOUN

creative
ADJECTIVE **Creative** people are good at inventing and developing new ideas.

creature **creatures**
NOUN any living thing that is not a plant

crèche **crèches**
NOUN a place where small children are looked after while their parents are working
[from old French *crèche* meaning crib or manger]

credit **credits**
NOUN **1** a system where you pay for something in small amounts, regularly over a period of time
2 praise given to you for good work
PLURAL NOUN **3** **Credits** are the list of people who helped make a film, record or television programme.
PHRASE **4** If your bank account is **in credit**, you have money in it.

credit card **credit cards**
NOUN a plastic card that allows someone to buy goods on credit rather than paying with cash

creek **creeks**
NOUN a narrow inlet where the sea comes a long way into the land

creep **creeps, creeping, crept**
VERB If you **creep** somewhere, you move there quietly and slowly.

creepy **creepier, creepiest**
ADJECTIVE strange and frightening • *The film was **creepy**.*
SYNONYMS: eerie, spooky

A B C D E F G H I J K L M N O P Q R S T U V W X Y Z

cremate **cremates, cremating, cremated**
VERB If someone is **cremated** when they die, their body is burned instead of buried.

crematorium **crematoriums** or **crematoria**
NOUN a building in which people are cremated

crescent **crescents**
NOUN a curved shape that is wider in the middle than at the ends, like a new moon

cress
NOUN a plant with small, strong-tasting leaves, used in salads

crest **crests**
NOUN **1** the highest part of a hill or wave
2 a tuft of feathers on top of a bird's head
3 a special sign of something, such as a school or other organization

crevice **crevices**
NOUN a narrow crack or gap in rock

crew **crews**
NOUN The **crew** of a ship, aeroplane or spacecraft are the people who operate it.

cricket **crickets**
NOUN **1** an outdoor game played by two teams, who take turns at scoring runs by hitting a ball with a bat
2 a small, jumping insect that produces sounds by rubbing its wings together

cried
VERB the past tense and past participle of **cry**

crime **crimes**
NOUN an action for which you can be punished by law

criminal **criminals**
NOUN **1** someone who has committed a crime
ADJECTIVE **2** involving or related to crime

crimson
NOUN OR ADJECTIVE dark, purplish-red

crinkle **crinkles, crinkling, crinkled**
VERB **1** If something **crinkles**, it becomes slightly creased or folded.
NOUN **2** a small crease or fold

cripple **cripples, crippling, crippled**
VERB If someone is **crippled** by something, they are injured so severely that they can never move properly again.
crippling ADJECTIVE

crisis **crises**
NOUN a serious or dangerous situation
• *The food **crisis** was caused by drought.*

crisp **crisper, crispest; crisps**
ADJECTIVE **1** pleasantly fresh and firm
• ***crisp** lettuce leaves*
NOUN **2** a thin slice of potato that has been fried until it is hard and crunchy

critic **critics**
NOUN **1** someone who writes reviews of books, films, plays or musical performances for newspapers or magazines
2 a person who criticizes someone or something publicly

critical
ADJECTIVE **1** A **critical** time or situation is a very important and serious one when things must be done correctly.
2 If the state of a sick or injured person is **critical**, they are in danger of dying.
3 Someone who is **critical** judges people and things very severely.

criticism **criticisms**
NOUN **1** spoken or written disapproval of someone or something
2 A **criticism** of a book, film or play is an examination of its good and bad points.

criticize **criticizes, criticizing, criticized**; also spelt **criticise**
VERB If you **criticize** someone or something, you say what you think is wrong with them.

croak **croaks, croaking, croaked**
VERB **1** When animals and birds **croak**, they make harsh, low sounds.
NOUN **2** a harsh, low sound
croaky ADJECTIVE

crochet **crochets, crocheting, crocheted**
Said "**kroh**-shay" NOUN **1** a kind of knitting done with a hooked needle and cotton or wool

VERB **2** If you **crochet**, you use a hooked needle and wool or cotton to make lacy material for things such as clothes and shawls.

crockery
NOUN things you use for eating and drinking, such as plates, cups, bowls and saucers

crocodile **crocodiles**
NOUN a large, scaly, meat-eating reptile that lives in tropical rivers
[from Greek *krokodeilos* meaning lizard]

crocus **crocuses**
NOUN **Crocuses** are yellow, purple or white flowers that grow in early spring.

crook **crooks**
NOUN **1** a criminal
2 The **crook** of your arm or leg is the soft, inside part of your elbow or your knee.
3 a long stick with a hooked end used by shepherds

crooked
ADJECTIVE **1** bent or twisted
2 dishonest

crop **crops, cropping, cropped**
NOUN **1** plants such as wheat and potatoes that are grown for food
2 the plants collected at harvest time
• *They gather two* ***crops*** *of rice a year.*
VERB **3** If you **crop** something such as your hair, you cut it very short.

cross **crosses, crossing, crossed; crosser, crossest**
VERB **1** If you **cross** something, such as a room or a road, you go to the other side of it.
2 Lines or roads that **cross** meet and go across each other.
3 If you **cross** your arms, legs or fingers, you put one on top of the other.
NOUN **4** a mark or a shape like + or ×
ADJECTIVE **5** Someone who is **cross** is rather angry.

cross out
VERB If you **cross out** words on a page, you draw a line through them.

cross-country
NOUN the sport of running across open countryside, rather than on roads or a track

crossing **crossings**
NOUN **1** a place where you can cross the road, a railway or a river
2 a journey by ship to a place across the sea

crossroads
NOUN a place where two roads meet and cross each other

cross-section **cross-sections**
NOUN **1** the flat part of something that you see when you cut straight through it to see inside • *We looked at* ***cross-sections*** *of kiwi fruit and oranges.*

2 a typical sample of people or things
• *We interviewed a* ***cross-section*** *of teenagers.*

crossword **crosswords**
NOUN a word puzzle in which you work out answers to clues and write them in a grid

crouch **crouches, crouching, crouched**
VERB If you **crouch**, you lower your body with your knees bent.

crow **crows, crowing, crowed**
NOUN **1** a large black bird that makes a loud, harsh sound
VERB **2** When a cock **crows**, it makes a series of loud sounds, usually early in the morning.

crowbar **crowbars**
NOUN a heavy, iron bar used as a lever or for forcing things open

crowd **crowds, crowding, crowded**
NOUN **1** a large group of people gathered together

a b c d e f g h i j k l m n o p q r s t u v w x y z

A B C D E F G H I J K L M N O P Q R S T U V W X Y Z

VERB **2** When people **crowd** around someone or something, they gather closely together around them.

crown **crowns, crowning, crowned**
NOUN **1** a circular ornament made of gold or jewels, which a king or queen wears on their head
VERB **2** When a king or queen is **crowned**, a crown is put on their head and they are officially made king or queen.

crucial
ADJECTIVE Something that is **crucial** is very important.

crucify **crucifies, crucifying, crucified**
VERB When a person is **crucified** they are tied or nailed to a cross and left there to die.
crucifixion NOUN

crude **cruder, crudest**
ADJECTIVE **1** rough and simple • *a **crude** shelter made of old boxes*
2 rude and vulgar

cruel **crueller, cruellest**
ADJECTIVE **Cruel** people deliberately cause pain or distress to other people or to animals.
SYNONYMS: brutal, unkind
cruelly ADVERB **cruelty** NOUN

cruise **cruises, cruising, cruised**
NOUN **1** a holiday in which you travel on a ship and visit places
VERB **2** When a vehicle **cruises**, it moves at a constant, moderate speed.

crumb **crumbs**
NOUN a very small piece of bread or cake

crumble **crumbles, crumbling, crumbled**
VERB When something **crumbles**, or when you **crumble** it, it breaks into small pieces.

crumple **crumples, crumpling, crumpled**
VERB If you **crumple** paper or cloth, you squash it so that it is full of creases and folds.

crunch **crunches, crunching, crunched**
VERB If you **crunch** something, you crush it noisily, for example between your teeth or under your feet.

crusade **crusades**
NOUN **1** In the Middle Ages, the **Crusades** were a number of expeditions to Palestine by Christians who were attempting to recapture the Holy Land from the Muslims.
2 a long and determined attempt to achieve something
[from Spanish *cruzar* meaning to take up the cross]
crusader NOUN

crush **crushes, crushing, crushed**
VERB **1** If you **crush** something, you squeeze it hard until its shape is destroyed. • *He **crushed** the empty can.*
2 If you **crush** against someone or something, you press hard against them.
• *We **crushed** against each other in the crowded bus.*

crust **crusts**
NOUN **1** the hard outside part of a loaf
2 a hard layer on top of something
• *the earth's **crust***

crustacean **crustaceans**
Said "krus-**tay**-shun" NOUN an animal with a hard outer shell and several pairs of legs, which usually lives in water
• *Crabs, lobsters and shrimps are **crustaceans**.*

crutch **crutches**
NOUN a support like a long stick that you lean on if you have injured your leg or foot • *I was on **crutches** while my ankle healed.*

cry **cries, crying, cried**
VERB **1** When you **cry**, tears come from your eyes because you are unhappy or hurt.
2 If you **cry** something, you shout it or say it loudly.
NOUN **3** a shout or other loud sound made with your voice

crypt **crypts**
NOUN an underground room beneath a church, usually used as a burial place

crystal **crystals**
NOUN **1** a piece of a mineral that has formed naturally into a regular shape
2 a type of transparent rock, used in jewellery
3 a type of very high quality glass
crystalline ADJECTIVE

cub **cubs**
NOUN **1** the young of some wild animals
• *a fox* ***cub*** • *a lion* ***cub***
2 The **Cubs** is an organization for young boys before they join the Scouts.

cube **cubes**
NOUN a solid shape with six square faces that are all the same size

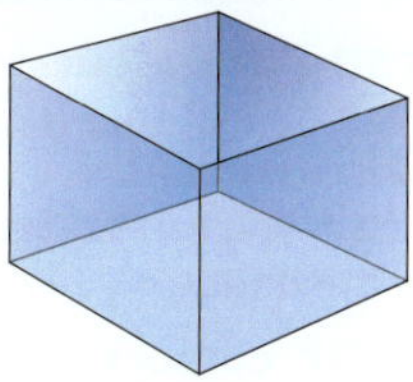

cubic
ADJECTIVE **1** shaped like a cube
2 used to describe volume when you measure height, width and depth
• *a* ***cubic*** *metre*

cubicle **cubicles**
NOUN a small enclosed area in a place such as a sports centre or a shop, where you can dress and undress

cuboid **cuboids**
NOUN a rectangular, three-dimensional box shape. A **cuboid** has six faces, all of which are rectangles.

cuckoo **cuckoos**
NOUN a grey bird with a two-note call. **Cuckoos** lay their eggs in other birds' nests.

cucumber **cucumbers**
NOUN a long, thin, green vegetable that is eaten raw

cud
NOUN food that has been chewed and digested more than once by cows, sheep or other animals that have more than one stomach

cuddle **cuddles, cuddling, cuddled**
VERB **1** If you **cuddle** someone, you hold them closely in your arms as a way of showing your affection.
NOUN **2** If you give someone a **cuddle**, you cuddle them.
cuddly ADJECTIVE

cuff **cuffs**
NOUN the end part of a sleeve, especially a shirt sleeve

cul-de-sac **cul-de-sacs**
NOUN a road that does not lead to any other roads because one end is blocked off [from French *cul* + *de* + *sac* meaning bottom of the bag]

culprit **culprits**
NOUN someone who has done something harmful or wrong

cult **cults**
NOUN **1** a small religious group, especially one that is considered strange
ADJECTIVE **2** very popular or fashionable among a particular group of people
• *It became a* ***cult*** *film.*

cultivate **cultivates, cultivating, cultivated**
VERB When someone **cultivates** land, they grow crops on it.
cultivation NOUN

culture **cultures**
NOUN the ideas, customs and art of a particular society

cunning
ADJECTIVE A **cunning** person or plan achieves things in a clever way, often by deceiving people.
SYNONYMS: crafty, sly, wily

cup **cups, cupping, cupped**
NOUN **1** a small, round container with a handle, which you drink from
2 a large metal container with two handles, which is given as a prize
VERB **3** If you **cup** your hands, you put them together to make a shape like a cup.

cupboard **cupboards**
NOUN **1** a piece of furniture with doors and shelves

a b c d e f g h i j k l m n o p q r s t u v w x y z

A B C D E F G H I J K L M N O P Q R S T U V W X Y Z

2 a very small room for storing things in • *The broom is in the **cupboard** under the stairs.*

curator **curators**
NOUN the person in a museum or art gallery in charge of its contents

curb **curbs, curbing, curbed**
VERB If you **curb** something, you keep it within limits. • *You must **curb** your spending on comics.*

curdle **curdles, curdling, curdled**
VERB When milk **curdles**, it turns sour.

cure **cures, curing, cured**
VERB **1** If a doctor **cures** someone of an illness, they help them get better.
NOUN **2** something that heals or helps someone to get better
VERB **3** If someone **cures** meat or fish, they smoke it to give it flavour and preserve it.

curfew **curfews**
NOUN a rule or a law stating that people must stay indoors between particular times at night

curiosity **curiosities**
NOUN **1** the desire to know something or about many things
2 something unusual and interesting

curious
ADJECTIVE **1** Someone who is **curious** wants to know more about something.
SYNONYMS: inquisitive, nosy
2 Something that is **curious** is unusual or difficult to understand.
SYNONYMS: strange, peculiar

curl **curls, curling, curled**
NOUN **1** **Curls** are lengths of hair shaped in tight curves and circles.
2 a curved or spiral shape • *A **curl** of smoke rose from the chimney.*
VERB **3** If something **curls**, it moves in a curve or spiral. • *Smoke **curled** up the chimney.*
curly ADJECTIVE

currant **currants**
NOUN a small, dried grape. **Currants** are often used in cakes and puddings.

currency **currencies**
NOUN A country's **currency** is its coins and banknotes.

current **currents**
NOUN **1** a steady continuous flowing movement of water or air
NOUN **2** An electric **current** is a flow of electricity through a wire or circuit.
ADJECTIVE **3** Something that is **current** is happening now. • ***current** fashion trends*

curriculum **curriculums** or **curricula**
NOUN the different courses taught at a school or university

curry **curries**
NOUN an Indian dish made with hot spices

curse **curses, cursing, cursed**
NOUN **1** an evil spell • *She said the old house had a **curse** on it.*
VERB **2** If you **curse**, you swear because you are angry.

cursor **cursors**
NOUN a sign on a computer monitor that shows where the next letter or symbol is

curtain **curtains**
NOUN a hanging piece of material that can be pulled across a window

curtsy **curtsies, curtsying, curtsied**
NOUN **1** a little bobbing bow to show respect • *I made a little **curtsy** to the Queen.*
VERB **2** the action of making a curtsy

curve **curves, curving, curved**
NOUN **1** a smooth, gradually bending line

VERB **2** When something **curves**, it moves in a curve or has the shape of a curve. • *The lane **curved** to the right.*
curved ADJECTIVE

cushion **cushions, cushioning, cushioned**
NOUN **1** a soft object that you put on a seat to make it more comfortable
VERB **2** When something **cushions** something else, it reduces its effect. • *The pile of leaves **cushioned** his fall.*

custard
NOUN a sweet, yellow sauce made from milk and eggs

custody
NOUN **1** If someone has **custody** of a child, they have the legal right to keep it and look after it.
PHRASE **2** Someone who is **in custody** is being kept in prison until they can be tried in a court.
[from Latin *custos* meaning a guard]
custodial ADJECTIVE

custom **customs**
NOUN something that people usually do • *the **custom** of decorating the house for Christmas*

customary
ADJECTIVE usual

customer **customers**
NOUN a person who buys things from a shop or firm

customs
NOUN the place at a border, airport or harbour where you declare any goods that you are bringing into the country

cut **cuts, cutting, cut**
VERB **1** If you **cut** something, you use a pair of scissors, a knife or another sharp tool to mark it or remove parts of it.
2 If you **cut** yourself, you injure yourself with a sharp object.
NOUN **3** a mark made with a knife or a sharp tool
4 a reduction in something • *There were lots of price **cuts** during the sales.*

cutlery
NOUN knives, forks and spoons

cycle **cycles, cycling, cycled**
NOUN **1** a bicycle
2 a series of events that is repeated again and again • *the **cycle** of the seasons*
VERB **3** When you **cycle**, you ride a bicycle.
cyclist NOUN

cyclone **cyclones**
NOUN a violent wind that blows in a spiral like a corkscrew

cygnet **cygnets**
NOUN a young swan

cylinder **cylinders**
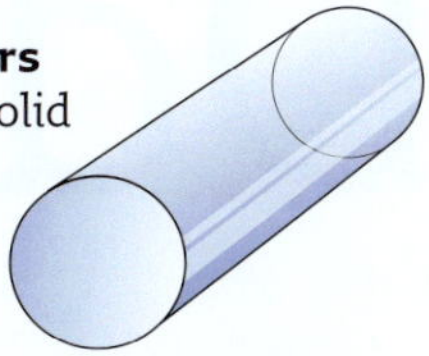
NOUN **1** a hollow or solid shape with straight sides and equal circular faces
See **prism**
2 the part of an engine that the piston moves in
cylindrical ADJECTIVE

cymbal **cymbals**
NOUN a circular brass plate used as a percussion instrument. **Cymbals** are clashed together or hit with a stick.
See **percussion**

A B C D E F G H I J K L M N O P Q R S T U V W X Y Z

Dd

dabble **dabbles, dabbling, dabbled**
VERB If you **dabble** in something, you work or play at it without being seriously involved in it.

dad or **daddy** **dads** or **daddies**
NOUN INFORMAL Your **dad** or your **daddy** is your father.

daffodil **daffodils**
NOUN a plant with yellow, trumpet-shaped flowers that blooms in spring

daft **dafter, daftest**
ADJECTIVE silly and not very sensible

dagger **daggers**
NOUN a weapon like a short knife

daily
ADJECTIVE occurring every day

dainty **daintier, daintiest**
ADJECTIVE very delicate and pretty

dairy **dairies**
NOUN **1** a shop or company that supplies milk and milk products
2 In New Zealand, a **dairy** is a small shop selling groceries.
ADJECTIVE **3** **Dairy** products are foods made from milk, such as butter, cheese, cream and yogurt.

daisy **daisies**
NOUN a small, wild flower with a yellow centre and small, white petals
[from Old English *deagesege* meaning day's eye, because the daisy opens in the daytime and closes at night]

Dalmatian **Dalmatians**
NOUN a large, smooth-haired white dog with black or brown spots

dam **dams**
NOUN a barrier built across a river to hold back water

damage **damages, damaging, damaged**
VERB If you **damage** something, you harm or spoil it.

damp **damper, dampest**
ADJECTIVE slightly wet
dampness NOUN

damson **damsons**
NOUN **1** a small, blue-black plum
2 the tree that damsons grow on

dance **dances, dancing, danced**
VERB **1** When you **dance**, you move around in time to music.
NOUN **2** a series of rhythmic movements that you do in time to music
3 a social event where people dance with each other

dandelion **dandelions**
NOUN a wild plant with yellow flowers that form a ball of fluffy seeds
[from Old French *dent de lion* meaning lion's tooth, referring to the shape of the leaves]

dandruff
NOUN small, loose scales of dead skin in someone's hair

danger **dangers**
NOUN the possibility that someone may be harmed or killed
SYNONYMS: peril, risk

dangerous
ADJECTIVE If something is **dangerous**, it is likely to cause hurt or harm. • *It is **dangerous** to walk close to the edge of the cliff.*
SYNONYMS: unsafe, hazardous
dangerously ADVERB

dangle **dangles, dangling, dangled**
VERB When something **dangles**, or when you **dangle** it, it swings or hangs loosely. • *We sat by the pool and **dangled** our legs in the water.*

dappled
ADJECTIVE marked with patches of a different or darker shade • *The lawn was **dappled** with the shadows of the leafy trees.*

dare **dares, daring, dared**
VERB **1** If you **dare** to do something, you have the courage to do it.
2 If you **dare** someone to do something, you challenge them to do it. • *I **dare** you to ask him his name.*
[from Old English *durran* meaning to venture or to be bold]

daredevil **daredevils**
NOUN a person who enjoys doing dangerous things

daring
ADJECTIVE **1** bold and willing to take risks
NOUN **2** the courage required to do things that are dangerous
daringly ADVERB

dark **darker, darkest**
ADJECTIVE **1** If it is **dark**, there is not enough light to see properly.
2 **Dark** colours have a lot of black, grey or brown tones in them.
dark NOUN

darken **darkens, darkening, darkened**
VERB If something **darkens**, it becomes darker than it was before. • *The sky **darkened** as the storm approached.*

darkness
NOUN being dark

darling **darlings**
NOUN You call someone **darling** if you love them or like them very much.

darn **darns, darning, darned**
VERB **1** When you **darn** a hole in a garment, you mend it with crossing stitches.
NOUN **2** A **darn** is the part of a garment that has been darned.

dart **darts, darting, darted**
NOUN **1** a small, pointed arrow
2 **Darts** is a game in which the players throw **darts** at a round board divided into numbered sections.
VERB **3** If you **dart** somewhere, you move there quickly and suddenly.

dash **dashes, dashing, dashed**
VERB **1** If you **dash** somewhere, you rush there.
NOUN **2** the punctuation mark (–) which may be used instead of brackets

dashboard **dashboards**
NOUN the instrument panel in a car

data
NOUN information, usually in the form of facts or statistics

> *Data* is really a plural word, but is usually used as a singular word: *Customer data is stored here.*

database **databases**
NOUN a collection of information stored in a computer

date **dates**
NOUN **1** a particular day or year that can be named • *What is your **date** of birth?*
2 If you have a **date**, you have an appointment to meet someone.
3 a small, brown, sticky fruit with a stone inside. **Dates** grow on palm trees.

daughter **daughters**
NOUN Someone's **daughter** is their female child.

dawdle **dawdles, dawdling, dawdled**
VERB If you **dawdle**, you are slow about doing something or going somewhere. • *Don't **dawdle**, we have to be there in ten minutes.*

dawn **dawns**
NOUN the time in the morning when light first appears in the sky

day **days**
NOUN **1** the time taken between one midnight and the next. There are 24 hours in one **day**.

a b c d e f g h i j k l m n o p q r s t u v w x y z

A B C D E F G H I J K L M N O P Q R S T U V W X Y Z

2 the period of light between sunrise and sunset

daydream **daydreams, daydreaming, daydreamed**
NOUN **1** pleasant thoughts about things that you would like to happen
VERB **2** When you **daydream**, you drift off into a daydream.

daylight
NOUN the part of the day when it is light

daytime
NOUN the part of the day when it is light

daze
PHRASE If you are **in a daze**, you are confused and bewildered.

dazzle **dazzles, dazzling, dazzled**
VERB If a bright light **dazzles** you, it blinds you for a moment.
dazzling ADJECTIVE

de-
PREFIX added to some words to mean removal or reversal of something • *She* ***de****bugged the computer program.* • *We had to* ***de****frost the windscreen before leaving.*

dead
ADJECTIVE **1** no longer living
2 no longer functioning • *The phone went* ***dead****.*
ADVERB **3** precisely or exactly • *We arrived* ***dead*** *on eight o'clock.*

deadly **deadlier, deadliest**
ADJECTIVE **1** likely or able to cause death • *a* ***deadly*** *disease*
ADVERB OR ADJECTIVE **2** used to emphasize how serious or unpleasant something is • ***deadly*** *dangerous* • ***deadly*** *serious*

deaf **deafer, deafest**
ADJECTIVE **Deaf** people are unable to hear anything or unable to hear well.

deafening
ADJECTIVE A **deafening** sound is so loud that you cannot hear anything else.

deal **deals, dealing, dealt**
NOUN **1** an agreement or arrangement, especially in business
VERB **2** If you **deal** with something, you do what is necessary to sort it out.
3 When you **deal** cards, you give them out to the players.
PHRASE **4** **A good deal** *or* **a great deal** of something is a lot of it.

dear **dearer, dearest**
NOUN **1** You call someone **dear** as a sign of affection.
ADJECTIVE **2** Something that is **dear** is very expensive.
3 You use **dear** at the beginning of a letter, with the name of the person you are writing to. • ***Dear*** *Sunita.*

death **deaths**
NOUN the end of the life of a human being or other animal or plant

debate **debates, debating, debated**
NOUN **1** argument or discussion
2 a formal discussion in which opposing views are expressed
VERB **3** When people **debate** something, they discuss it in a formal way.

debit card **debit cards**
NOUN a plastic card that allows someone to buy goods using the money in their bank account

debris
NOUN fragments or rubble left after something has been destroyed • *After the eruption, volcanic* ***debris*** *was found scattered for miles.*

debt **debts**
NOUN a sum of money that someone owes

debut **debuts**
NOUN a performer's first public appearance

decade **decades**
NOUN a period of ten years

decaffeinated
ADJECTIVE **Decaffeinated** coffee or tea has had most of the caffeine removed.

decathlon **decathlons**
NOUN an athletic competition in which competitors take part in ten different events

decay **decays, decaying, decayed**
VERB When things **decay**, they rot or go bad.

deceased
ADJECTIVE FORMAL A **deceased** person is someone who has recently died.

deceit
NOUN behaviour that makes people believe something to be true that is not true

deceive **deceives, deceiving, deceived**
VERB If you **deceive** someone, you make them believe something that is not true.

December
NOUN the twelfth month of the year. **December** has 31 days.

decent
ADJECTIVE honest and respectable

deception **deceptions**
NOUN **1** something that is intended to trick or deceive someone
2 the act of deceiving someone

deceptive
ADJECTIVE likely to make people believe that something is true when it is not

decide **decides, deciding, decided**
VERB If you **decide** to do something, you choose to do it, usually after thinking about it carefully.
SYNONYM: make up one's mind
decision NOUN

deciduous
ADJECTIVE **Deciduous** trees lose their leaves in the autumn every year.

decimal **decimals**
ADJECTIVE **1** A **decimal** system involves counting in units of ten.
NOUN **2** A **decimal**, or **decimal** fraction, is a fraction in which a dot, called a decimal point, separates the whole numbers on the left from tenths, hundredths and thousandths on the right. For example, 0.5 represents $^{5}/_{10}$ (or $^{1}/_{2}$); 0.05 represents $^{5}/_{100}$ (or $^{1}/_{20}$).

decision **decisions**
NOUN a choice or judgement that is made about something

decisive
ADJECTIVE **1** A **decisive** person is able to make decisions quickly.
2 having an important influence on the result of something • *The first goal was a **decisive** moment in the match.*

deck **decks**
NOUN a downstairs or upstairs area on a bus or ship

declare **declares, declaring, declared**
VERB **1** If you **declare** something, you say it firmly and forcefully.
SYNONYMS: announce, proclaim, state
2 FORMAL If something is **declared**, it is announced publicly. • *War was **declared** in 1939.*

decline **declines, declining, declined**
VERB **1** If something **declines**, it becomes smaller or weaker. • *The number of students has **declined** this year.*
2 If you **decline** something, you politely refuse to accept it or do it.

decode **decodes, decoding, decoded**
VERB If you **decode** a coded message, you convert it into ordinary language.

decompose **decomposes, decomposing, decomposed**
VERB If something **decomposes**, it rots after it dies.

decorate **decorates, decorating, decorated**
VERB **1** If you **decorate** something, you make it more attractive by adding things to it.
2 If you **decorate** a room or building, you paint or wallpaper it.

decoy **decoys**
NOUN something used to lead a person or animal into a trap

decrease **decreases, decreasing, decreased**
VERB If something **decreases**, or if you **decrease** it, it becomes less. • *The number of children in the class **decreased** rapidly.*

a b c d e f g h i j k l m n o p q r s t u v w x y z

decree **decrees, decreeing, decreed**
NOUN **1** an official order by the government, church or the rulers of a country
VERB **2** If someone **decrees** something, they announce formally that it will happen.

dedicate **dedicates, dedicating, dedicated**
VERB **1** If you **dedicate** yourself to something, you give your time and energy to it.
2 If you **dedicate** a book or piece of music to someone, you say that it is written for them.

deduct **deducts, deducting, deducted**
VERB If you **deduct** an amount from a total, you take it away.

deed **deeds**
NOUN **1** something that is done • *a good **deed***
2 an important piece of paper or document that an agreement is written on

deep **deeper, deepest**
ADJECTIVE **1** going a long way down from the surface • *a **deep** hole*
2 great or intense • ***deep** affection*
3 a low sound • *a **deep** voice*

deer
NOUN a large, fast-running, graceful mammal with hooves, that lives wild in parts of Britain and other countries. Male **deer** have antlers.

deface **defaces, defacing, defaced**
VERB If you **deface** something, you damage its appearance in some way. • *The gang **defaced** the walls with spray paint.*

defeat **defeats, defeating, defeated**
VERB **1** If you **defeat** someone or something, you win a victory over them, or cause them to fail.
NOUN **2** the state of being beaten or of failing • *The team was downhearted after its **defeat**.*

defect **defects, defecting, defected**
NOUN **1** a fault or flaw in something
VERB **2** If someone **defects**, they leave their own country or organization and join an opposing one.
defection NOUN **defector** NOUN

defective
ADJECTIVE Something that is **defective** is not perfect or has something wrong with it.

defence **defences**
NOUN **1** something that protects you against attack • *She carried an alarm as a **defence** against muggers.*
2 A country's **defences** are its armed forces and its weapons.

defend **defends, defending, defended**
VERB **1** If you **defend** someone or something, you protect them from harm or danger.
2 If you **defend** a person or their ideas, you argue in support of them.

defendant **defendants**
NOUN a person in a court of law who is accused of a crime

defer **defers, deferring, deferred**
VERB If you **defer** something, you put off doing it until later.

defiant
ADJECTIVE If you are **defiant**, you behave in a way that shows you are not willing to obey someone.
defiance NOUN **defiantly** ADVERB

deficient
ADJECTIVE lacking in something
deficiency NOUN

define **defines, defining, defined**
VERB If you **define** something, you say what it is or what it means.

definite
ADJECTIVE **1** clear and unlikely to be changed • *We must arrange a **definite** date for the party.*
2 true rather than being someone's guess or opinion

There is no *a* in *definite*.

definitely
ADVERB OR EXCLAMATION certainly; without doubt • *I am **definitely** going on holiday next week.*

definition **definitions**
NOUN a statement explaining the meaning of a word or an idea

deflate **deflates, deflating, deflated**
VERB If you **deflate** something, such as a tyre or balloon, you let all the air or gas out of it.
ANTONYMS: inflate, blow up

deforestation
NOUN the cutting down or the destruction of all the trees in an area

deformed
ADJECTIVE disfigured or abnormally shaped

defrost **defrosts, defrosting, defrosted**
VERB **1** If you **defrost** frozen food, you let it thaw out.
2 If you **defrost** a freezer or refrigerator, you remove the ice from it.

defuse **defuses, defusing, defused**
VERB **1** If someone **defuses** a bomb, they remove its fuse or detonator so that it cannot explode.
2 If you **defuse** a dangerous or tense situation, you make it less dangerous or tense.

defy **defies, defying, defied**
VERB If you **defy** a person or a law, you openly refuse to obey.

degree **degrees**
NOUN **1** a unit of measurement for temperatures, angles, and longitude and latitude, written as ° after a number • *The temperature was 20 °C.* • *A right angle is a ninety-**degree** angle.*
2 an amount of a feeling or quality • *As captain you have a high **degree** of responsibility.*
3 a university qualification gained after completing a course of study there

dehydrated
ADJECTIVE If someone is **dehydrated**, they are weak or ill because they have lost too much water from their body.

deity **deities**
NOUN a god or goddess

dejected
ADJECTIVE If you are **dejected**, you are sad and gloomy.
dejection NOUN

delay **delays, delaying, delayed**
VERB **1** If you **delay** doing something, you put it off until later.
SYNONYM: postpone
2 If something **delays** you, it makes you late or slows you down.
NOUN **3** If there is a **delay**, something does not happen until later than planned or expected.

delete **deletes, deleting, deleted**
VERB If you **delete** something written, you cross it out or remove it.

deliberate
ADJECTIVE **1** done on purpose or planned in advance
2 slow and careful in speech and action • ***deliberate** movements*
deliberately ADVERB

delicate
ADJECTIVE **1** light and attractive • *a **delicate** perfume*
2 fragile and needing to be handled carefully • *a **delicate** china cup*
3 precise or sensitive • ***delicate** instruments*
delicately ADVERB

delicatessen **delicatessens**
NOUN a shop selling unusual or imported foods

delicious
ADJECTIVE **Delicious** food or drink has an extremely pleasant taste.
SYNONYMS: delectable, scrumptious

delight **delights, delighting, delighted**
NOUN **1** great pleasure or joy
VERB **2** If something **delights** you, or if you are **delighted** by it, it gives you a lot of pleasure.
delighted ADJECTIVE

A B C D E F G H I J K L M N O P Q R S T U V W X Y Z

delinquent **delinquents**
NOUN a young person who commits minor crimes
delinquency NOUN

delirious
ADJECTIVE **1** unable to speak or act in a rational way because of illness or fever
2 wildly excited and happy
deliriously ADVERB

deliver **delivers, delivering, delivered**
VERB **1** If you **deliver** something to someone, you take it and give it to them.
2 If someone **delivers** a baby, they help the woman who is giving birth.

delta **deltas**
NOUN a triangular piece of land at the mouth of a river where it divides into separate streams

deluge **deluges**
NOUN a sudden, heavy downpour of rain

demand **demands, demanding, demanded**
VERB **1** If you **demand** something, you ask for it forcefully.
NOUN **2** If there is **demand** for something, a lot of people want to buy it or have it.

democracy **democracies**
NOUN a system of government in which the people choose their leaders by voting for them in elections
democratic ADJECTIVE

demolish **demolishes, demolishing, demolished**
VERB If someone **demolishes** a building, they knock it down.
demolition NOUN

demon **demons**
NOUN a devil or an evil spirit

demonstrate **demonstrates, demonstrating, demonstrated**
VERB **1** If you **demonstrate** something to somebody, you show them how to do it or how it works.
2 If people **demonstrate**, they march or gather together to show that they oppose or support something.

demonstration **demonstrations**
NOUN **1** If someone gives a **demonstration**, they show how to do something or how something works.
2 a march or a gathering of people to show publicly what they think about something

den **dens**
NOUN **1** a home or hiding place of a wild animal
2 a special place where you can do what you want without being disturbed

denial **denials**
NOUN **1** A **denial** of something is a statement that it is untrue.
2 The **denial** of a request is the refusal to grant it.

denim **denims**
NOUN strong, cotton cloth used for making clothes, especially jeans
[from French *serge de Nîmes*, meaning serge (a type of cloth) from Nîmes]

denominator **denominators**
NOUN In mathematics, the **denominator** is the bottom number of a fraction.

dense **denser, densest**
ADJECTIVE **1** Something that is **dense** contains a lot of things or people in a small area. • *We cut our way through the **dense** forest.*
2 difficult to see through • *The **dense** fog prevented us from enjoying the view over the hills.*
densely ADVERB

density **densities**
NOUN **1** thickness
2 the proportion of mass to volume

dent **dents, denting, dented**
VERB **1** If you **dent** something, you damage its surface by hitting it.
NOUN **2** a hollow in the surface of something

dental
ADJECTIVE to do with teeth

dentist **dentists**
NOUN a person who is qualified to treat people's teeth

dentures
PLURAL NOUN false teeth

deny **denies, denying, denied**
VERB **1** If you **deny** something, you say that it is not true.
2 If you are **denied** something, you are refused it.

deodorant **deodorants**
NOUN a substance used to hide or prevent the smell of sweat on your body

depart **departs, departing, departed**
VERB When you **depart**, you leave.
departure NOUN

department **departments**
NOUN one of the sections into which a large shop or an organization is divided

department store **department stores**
NOUN a very large shop divided into departments, each selling different types of goods

depend **depends, depending, depended**
VERB **1** If one thing **depends** on another, it is influenced by it. • *The cooking time **depends** on the size of the potato.*
2 If you **depend** on someone or something, you trust them and rely on them.

dependable
ADJECTIVE If someone is **dependable**, you can trust them to be helpful, sensible and reliable.

depict **depicts, depicting, depicted**
VERB If you **depict** someone or something, you paint, draw or describe them.

deport **deports, deporting, deported**
VERB If someone is **deported** from a country they are sent out of it, either because they have no right to be there, because they have done something wrong or because they did not ask permission to be there.

deposit **deposits, depositing, deposited**
VERB **1** If you **deposit** something, you put it down or leave it somewhere.
NOUN **2** a sum of money given in part payment for goods or services

depot **depots**
NOUN **1** a place where supplies of food or equipment are stored until they are needed
2 A bus **depot** is a bus station.

depressed
ADJECTIVE sad and gloomy

depression **depressions**
NOUN **1** a state of mind in which someone feels unhappy and has no energy or enthusiasm for anything
2 a hollow in the ground or on any other surface
3 a time when there is a lot of unemployment and poverty

deprive **deprives, depriving, deprived**
VERB If you **deprive** someone of something, you take it away from them or prevent them from having it.

depth **depths**
NOUN **1** the measurement or distance between the top and bottom of something, or the back and front of something • *The **depth** of the swimming pool at the deep end is 1.5 m.*
PHRASE **2** **In depth** means thoroughly.
• *We studied the poem **in depth**.*

deputy **deputies**
NOUN a person who helps someone in their job and acts on their behalf when they are away

derail **derails, derailed, derailing**
VERB If a train is **derailed**, it comes off the railway tracks.

A B C D E F G H I J K L M N O P Q R S T U V W X Y Z

derivation **derivations**
NOUN The **derivation** of something is where it has come from.

derive **derives, deriving, derived**
VERB **1** FORMAL If you **derive** something from someone or something, you get it from them. • *He* ***derives*** *great pleasure from music.*
2 If something is **derived** from something else, it comes from that thing. • *His name is* ***derived*** *from a Greek word.*

descant **descants**
NOUN **1** The **descant** to a tune is another tune played at the same time but at a higher pitch.
ADJECTIVE **2** A **descant** musical instrument plays the highest notes in a range of instruments. • *a* ***descant*** *recorder*

descend **descends, descending, descended**
VERB If someone or something **descends**, they move downwards. • *We* ***descended*** *to the basement in the lift.*
ANTONYM: ascend

descendant **descendants**
NOUN A person's **descendants** are all the people in later generations who are related to them.

describe **describes, describing, described**
VERB If you **describe** someone or something, you say what they are like.

desert **deserts, deserting, deserted**
Said "**dez**-ert" NOUN **1** an area of land, usually in a hot region, that has almost no water, rain, trees or plants • *the Sahara* ***Desert***

Said "de-**zert**" VERB **2** If someone **deserts** you, they leave you and no longer help or support you.

deserted
ADJECTIVE A **deserted** building or place is one that people have left and never come back to.

deserve **deserves, deserving, deserved**
VERB If you **deserve** something, you earn it or have a right to it.

design **designs, designing, designed**
VERB **1** If you **design** something new, you plan what it should be like.
NOUN **2** a drawing from which something can be built or made
3 a decorative pattern of lines or shapes

desire **desires, desiring, desired**
VERB **1** If you **desire** something, you want it.
NOUN **2** a strong feeling of wanting something
SYNONYMS: longing, want, wish

desk **desks**
NOUN a piece of furniture with a flat or sloping top, which you sit at to write, read or work

desktop
ADJECTIVE small enough to be used at a desk • *a* ***desktop*** *computer*

desolate
ADJECTIVE **1** deserted and bleak • *a* ***desolate*** *mountain top*
2 lonely, very sad, and without hope
desolation NOUN

despair **despairs, despairing, despaired**
NOUN **1** a total loss of hope
VERB **2** If you **despair**, you lose hope.

desperate
ADJECTIVE **1** If you are **desperate**, you are in such a bad situation that you will try anything to change it.
2 A **desperate** situation is extremely dangerous or serious.

despicable
ADJECTIVE Something that is **despicable** is nasty, cruel or evil.

despise **despises, despising, despised**
VERB If you **despise** someone or something, you have a very low opinion of them.

despite
PREPOSITION If you do something **despite** some difficulty, you manage to do it anyway.

dessert **desserts**
NOUN a sweet food that you eat at the end of a meal

destination **destinations**
NOUN the place you are going to

destined
ADJECTIVE meant to happen • *They were **destined** to meet.*

destiny **destinies**
NOUN Your **destiny** is your fate: the things that will happen to you in the future.

destitute
ADJECTIVE without money or possessions, and therefore in great need
destitution NOUN

destroy **destroys, destroying, destroyed**
VERB If you **destroy** something, you damage it so much that it is completely ruined.
SYNONYMS: demolish, ruin, wreck
destruction NOUN

destructive
ADJECTIVE Something that is **destructive** can cause great damage, harm or injury.
SYNONYM: damaging

detach **detaches, detaching, detached**
VERB If you **detach** something, you remove or unfasten it.
detachable ADJECTIVE

detached
ADJECTIVE separate or standing apart • *It was a **detached** house, standing alone at the top of the hill.*

detail **details**
NOUN **1** an individual fact or feature of something • *I remember every **detail** of that film.*
PLURAL NOUN **2** **Details** about something are information about it. For example, your **details** might be your name and address.

detain **detains, detaining, detained**
VERB If you **detain** someone, you keep them from going somewhere or doing something.

detect **detects, detecting, detected**
VERB If you **detect** something, you notice or find it. • *X-rays can **detect** broken bones.*

detective **detectives**
NOUN a person, usually a police officer, whose job is to investigate crimes

detector **detectors**
NOUN an instrument used to detect the presence of something • *a metal **detector***

detention
NOUN **1** a form of punishment in which a pupil is made to stay in school for extra time when other children do not have to **2** arrest or imprisonment

deter **deters, deterring, deterred**
VERB If you **deter** someone from doing something, you persuade them not to do it or try to stop them in some way.

detergent **detergents**
NOUN a chemical substance used for washing or cleaning things

deteriorate **deteriorates, deteriorating, deteriorated**
VERB If something **deteriorates**, it gets worse.
deterioration NOUN

determination
NOUN a great strength and will to do something

determined
ADJECTIVE having your mind firmly made up • *She was **determined** to pass her exams.*

a b c d e f g h i j k l m n o p q r s t u v w x y z

A B C D E F G H I J K L M N O P Q R S T U V W X Y Z

deterrent **deterrents**
NOUN something that prevents people from doing something, usually by making them afraid to do it • *We have a car alarm as a* ***deterrent*** *to car thieves.*

detest **detests, detesting, detested**
VERB If you **detest** someone or something, you dislike them intensely.
[from Latin *detestari* meaning to curse]
detestable ADJECTIVE

detonate **detonates, detonating, detonated**
VERB If someone **detonates** a bomb or mine, they cause it to explode.
detonation NOUN **detonator** NOUN

detour **detours**
NOUN If you make a **detour** on a journey, you go by a longer or less direct route.

devastate **devastates, devastating, devastated**
VERB A place that has been **devastated** has been severely damaged or destroyed.
devastation NOUN

develop **develops, developing, developed**
VERB **1** When something **develops**, it grows or becomes more advanced.
2 If you **develop** photographs or film, you produce a visible image from them.

development **developments**
NOUN gradual growth or progress • *There have been great* ***developments*** *in technology over the past fifty years.*

device **devices**
NOUN a machine or tool that is used for a particular purpose

devil **devils**
NOUN an evil spirit

devious
ADJECTIVE **Devious** people behave in an underhand, nasty and secretive way.

devise **devises, devising, devised**
VERB If you **devise** something, you invent it or design it.

devoted
ADJECTIVE very loving and loyal

devour **devours, devouring, devoured**
VERB **1** If you **devour** food, you eat it quickly and greedily.
2 If one creature **devours** another, it eats it.
3 If you **devour** a book, you read it very quickly.

devout
ADJECTIVE very deeply religious

dew
NOUN drops of moisture that form on the ground and other cool surfaces at night

diabetes
NOUN a condition in which a person has too much sugar in their blood
diabetic NOUN OR ADJECTIVE

diagnose **diagnoses, diagnosing, diagnosed**
VERB If someone **diagnoses** an illness or problem, they identify what is wrong.

diagonal **diagonals**
NOUN **1** a straight line that slopes from one corner of a shape to another
ADJECTIVE **2** in a slanting direction
• *a* ***diagonal*** *line*
[from Greek *diagonios* meaning from angle to angle]

diagram **diagrams**
NOUN a drawing that shows or explains something • *Carroll or Venn* ***diagram***

dial **dials, dialling, dialled**
NOUN **1** the part of a clock or meter where the time or a measurement is shown
VERB **2** If you **dial** a telephone number, you press the buttons to select the number you want.

dialect **dialects**
NOUN the form of a language spoken in a particular area

dialogue **dialogues**
NOUN In a novel, play or film, **dialogue** is conversation.

diameter
diameters
NOUN the length of a straight line drawn across a circle through its centre

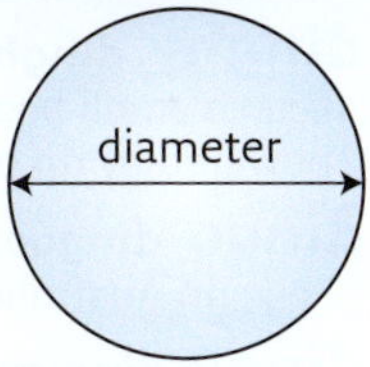

diamond **diamonds**
NOUN **1** a precious stone made of pure carbon
2 a shape with four straight sides of equal length that are not at right angles to each other
See **rhombus**

diarrhoea
NOUN an illness that attacks your bowels so that you can't stop going to the lavatory

diary **diaries**
NOUN a notebook with a separate space or page for each day of the year

dice **dices, dicing, diced**
NOUN **1** a small cube with dots on each of its six faces
VERB **2** If you **dice** food, you cut it into small cubes.

dictate **dictates, dictating, dictated**
VERB **1** If you **dictate** something, you say it or read it aloud for someone else to write down.
2 If you **dictate** to someone, you give them orders in a bossy way.
dictation NOUN

dictionary **dictionaries**
NOUN a book in which words are listed alphabetically and their meanings explained

did
VERB the past tense of **do**

didgeridoo **didgeridoos**
NOUN an Australian wind instrument made from a long, hollowed-out piece of wood

didn't
VERB a contraction of *did not*

die **dies, dying, died**
VERB **1** When humans, other animals or plants **die**, they stop living.
2 When something **dies**, **dies away** *or* **dies down**, it becomes less intense and disappears. • *The wind **died down**.*

diesel **diesels**
NOUN **1** a heavy fuel used in trains, buses and lorries
2 a vehicle with a diesel engine

diet **diets**
NOUN **1** the food you usually eat
2 If you are on a **diet**, you eat only certain foods for health reasons or to lose weight.

difference **differences**
NOUN **1** the way in which things are unlike each other
2 the amount by which one number is less than another
3 a change in someone or something

different
ADJECTIVE If one thing is **different** from another, it is not like it.

> There are two *e*s in *different*.

difficult
ADJECTIVE **1** **Difficult** things are not easy to do, understand or solve.
2 Someone who is **difficult** behaves in an unreasonable way.

difficulty **difficulties**
NOUN a problem

dig **digs, digging, dug**
VERB **1** If you **dig**, you make a hole in earth or sand, especially with a spade.
2 If you **dig** something, you poke it.

digest **digests, digesting, digested**
VERB To **digest** food means to break it down in the gut so that it can be easily absorbed and used by the body.
digestible ADJECTIVE

digit **digits**
Said "**dij**-it" NOUN **1** a written symbol for any of the numbers from zero (0) to nine (9) • *A two-**digit** number: 46.*
2 a finger or toe

A B C D E F G H I J K L M N O P Q R S T U V W X Y Z

digital
ADJECTIVE **Digital** instruments, such as watches, have changing numbers instead of a dial with hands.
ANTONYM: analogue

dignified
ADJECTIVE **Dignified** people are calm, and behave in a way that other people admire and respect.

dilemma **dilemmas**
NOUN a situation where you have to choose between two alternatives that are equally difficult or unpleasant

diligent
ADJECTIVE hard-working and showing care
diligently ADVERB **diligence** NOUN

dilute **dilutes, diluting, diluted**
VERB If you **dilute** a liquid, you add water or another liquid to it to make it weaker.

dim **dimmer, dimmest; dims, dimming, dimmed**
ADJECTIVE **1** lacking in brightness and badly lit
VERB **2** If lights **dim**, or are **dimmed**, they become less bright.

dimension **dimensions**
NOUN The **dimensions** of something are its measurements or its size.

diminish **diminishes, diminishing, diminished**
VERB If something **diminishes**, or you **diminish** it, it reduces in size or importance.

diminutive **diminutives**
ADJECTIVE **1** very small
NOUN **2** You can make **diminutives** by adding the suffixes *-kin*, *-let* or *-ette* to other words. For example *lambkin*, *piglet*, *diskette*.

dimple **dimples**
NOUN a small hollow in someone's cheek or chin

din
NOUN a very loud and unpleasant noise

dine **dines, dining, dined**
VERB FORMAL When you **dine**, you eat dinner in the evening.

dinghy **dinghies**
NOUN a small boat that is rowed, sailed or powered by an outboard motor

dingo **dingoes**
NOUN an Australian wild dog

dingy **dingier, dingiest**
ADJECTIVE shabby and dirty to look at

dinner **dinners**
NOUN the main meal of the day, eaten either in the evening or in the middle of the day

dinosaur **dinosaurs**
NOUN a large reptile that lived in prehistoric times
[from Greek *deinos* + *sauros* meaning fearful lizard]

dip **dips, dipping, dipped**
VERB **1** If you **dip** something into a liquid, you lower it in and take it out again quickly.
2 If something **dips**, it slopes downwards or goes below a certain level. • *The road **dipped** suddenly.*
NOUN **3** a downward slope or hollow
• *There was a **dip** in the road.*
4 a quick swim
5 a savoury mixture for eating, in which you dip crisps, crackers or vegetables

diploma **diplomas**
NOUN a certificate that is awarded to a student who has successfully completed a course of study

diplomat **diplomats**
NOUN an official who negotiates with another country on behalf of his or her own country

diplomatic
ADJECTIVE If you are **diplomatic**, you are tactful and say and do things without offending people.

direct **directs, directing, directed**
ADVERB **1** If you go **direct** to a place, you go straight there. • *This train goes **direct** to Paris.*
ADJECTIVE **2** If someone's speech or behaviour is **direct**, they are honest and say what they mean.
SYNONYMS: frank, open, straightforward
VERB **3** If you **direct** someone to a place, you show them how to get there.
4 Someone who **directs** a film or play decides the way it is made and performed.

direction **directions**
NOUN **1** the way that someone or something is moving or pointing
PLURAL NOUN **2** instructions that tell you how to do something or how to get somewhere

director **directors**
NOUN **1** a senior manager of a company
2 the person who decides how a film or play is made and performed

directory **directories**
NOUN a book that gives lists of information, such as people's names, addresses and telephone numbers

dirt
NOUN **1** any unclean substance such as mud, dust or stains
2 earth or soil

dirty **dirtier, dirtiest**
ADJECTIVE **1** marked or covered with dirt
SYNONYMS: filthy, grubby, mucky
2 unfair or dishonest

dis-
PREFIX added to some words to make them mean the opposite. For example, **dis**contented means not content.

disability **disabilities**
NOUN a condition or illness that limits the way in which someone can use their body

disabled
ADJECTIVE **Disabled** people have an illness or injury that can restrict their way of life.
disable VERB

disadvantage **disadvantages**
NOUN something that makes things difficult

disagree **disagrees, disagreeing, disagreed**
VERB **1** If you **disagree** with someone, you have a different opinion or view from them.
2 If you **disagree** with an action or proposal, you believe it is wrong.

disagreeable
ADJECTIVE unpleasant or unhelpful and unfriendly • *The woman was very **disagreeable** and did not even offer to help.*

disappear **disappears, disappearing, disappeared**
VERB **1** If someone or something **disappears**, they go where they cannot be seen or found.
2 If something **disappears**, it stops existing or happening.

disappoint **disappoints, disappointing, disappointed**
VERB If someone or something **disappoints** you, they fail to live up to what you expected.

disapprove **disapproves, disapproving, disapproved**
VERB If you **disapprove** of something or someone, you believe they are wrong or bad.
disapproval NOUN **disapproving** ADJECTIVE

disaster **disasters**
NOUN **1** a very bad accident, such as an earthquake or a plane crash
SYNONYMS: calamity, catastrophe
2 a complete failure • *The party was a **disaster**.*

disc **discs**; also spelt **disk**
NOUN **1** anything with a flat, circular shape, such as a compact **disc**

a b c d e f g h i j k l m n o p q r s t u v w x y z

A B C D E F G H I J K L M N O P Q R S T U V W X Y Z

2 a storage device used in computers
• *Please insert a **disc** into the drive.*

discard **discards, discarding, discarded**
VERB If you **discard** something, you throw it away because it is of no use to you anymore.

discharge **discharges, discharging, discharged**
VERB **1** If a doctor **discharges** someone from hospital, they allow them to leave.
2 If something **discharges** or is **discharged**, it is given or sent out.
• *Cars **discharge** exhaust fumes into the atmosphere.*

disciple **disciples**
NOUN a follower of someone or something
[from Latin *discipulus* meaning pupil]

discipline **disciplines, disciplining, disciplined**
NOUN **1** making people obey rules, by training them and by punishing them when they break the rules
2 the ability to behave and work in a controlled way
VERB **3** If a parent **disciplines** a child, they punish them.

disc jockey **disc jockeys**
NOUN someone who introduces and plays pop records on the radio or at a night club

disco **discos**
NOUN a party or a club where people go to dance to pop music

discomfort
NOUN slight pain or worry

disconnect **disconnects, disconnecting, disconnected**
VERB If you **disconnect** something, you detach it from something else or break its connection.

discontinue **discontinues, discontinuing, discontinued**
VERB If you **discontinue** something, you stop doing it.

discount **discounts**
NOUN a reduction in the price of something

discourage **discourages, discouraging, discouraged**
VERB **1** If you **discourage** someone, you take away their enthusiasm for doing something.
2 If you **discourage** someone from doing something, you try to persuade them not to do it.
discouraging ADJECTIVE
discouragement NOUN

discover **discovers, discovering, discovered**
VERB If you **discover** something, you find it or learn about it for the first time.
• *She **discovered** that they'd escaped.*

discreet
ADJECTIVE If you are **discreet**, you keep private things to yourself and can be trusted with a secret.
discretion NOUN

discriminate **discriminates, discriminating, discriminated**
VERB **1** If you **discriminate** between people, you treat them differently – often unfairly – because of their race, religion or gender.
2 If you are **discriminating**, you can recognise differences between things and use your judgement to make choices.
discrimination NOUN

discus **discuses**
NOUN a flat, circular weight that athletes throw in a competition

discuss **discusses, discussing, discussed**
VERB When people **discuss** something, they talk about it in detail.
discussion NOUN

disease **diseases**
NOUN an illness that affects human beings, other animals or plants

disgrace **disgraces, disgracing, disgraced**
NOUN **1** something unacceptable
• *Tidy your room – it's a **disgrace**.*

VERB **2** If you **disgrace** yourself, you do something that others disapprove of.

disgruntled
ADJECTIVE If you are **disgruntled**, you are cross and discontented about something.

disguise **disguises, disguising, disguised**
VERB **1** If you **disguise** yourself, you change your appearance so that people will not recognize you.
NOUN **2** something you wear or a change you make to your appearance so that people will not recognize you

disgust **disgusts, disgusting, disgusted**
NOUN **1** a very strong feeling of dislike and loathing
VERB **2** If you **disgust** someone, you make them feel a strong sense of dislike and disapproval.
disgusting ADJECTIVE

dish **dishes**
NOUN **1** a shallow container for cooking or serving food
2 a particular kind of food, or food cooked in a particular way • *a vegetarian **dish***

disheartened
ADJECTIVE If you are **disheartened**, you feel disappointed.

dishonest
ADJECTIVE not truthful or fit to be trusted
dishonestly ADVERB

dishwasher **dishwashers**
NOUN a machine that washes crockery, cutlery, pots and pans

disinfectant **disinfectants**
NOUN a chemical substance that kills germs

disintegrate **disintegrates, disintegrating, disintegrated**
VERB If an object **disintegrates**, it breaks into many pieces and so is destroyed.
disintegration NOUN

disk
NOUN another spelling of **disc**

dislike **dislikes, disliking, disliked**
VERB If you **dislike** something or someone, you think they are unpleasant.

dislocate **dislocates, dislocating, dislocated**
VERB If you **dislocate** a bone in your body, you put it out of its usual position by accident.

disloyal
ADJECTIVE not loyal

dismal
ADJECTIVE depressing and bleak • *It was a **dismal** day, with rain pouring down and cold winds blowing.*

dismantle **dismantles, dismantling, dismantled**
VERB If you **dismantle** something, you take it apart.

dismay **dismays, dismaying, dismayed**
VERB **1** If something **dismays** you, it worries and alarms you.
NOUN **2** a feeling of fear and worry

dismiss **dismisses, dismissing, dismissed**
VERB **1** If you **dismiss** something, you decide that it is not important enough for you to think about.
2 If someone is **dismissed**, they are told to leave a place or leave their job. • *She **dismissed** the class.*

dismount **dismounts, dismounting, dismounted**
VERB to get off a horse or a bicycle

disobey **disobeys, disobeying, disobeyed**
VERB If you **disobey** the rules, you break them. If you **disobey** a person, you refuse to do as they say.
disobedience NOUN **disobedient** ADJECTIVE

disorder **disorders**
NOUN **1** a state of untidiness
2 lack of organization
3 an illness • *a stomach **disorder***
disorderly ADJECTIVE

A B C D E F G H I J K L M N O P Q R S T U V W X Y Z

disorganized; also spelt **disorganised**
ADJECTIVE Someone or something that is **disorganized** is muddled, confused or badly prepared.

dispatch **dispatches, dispatching, dispatched**
VERB **1** If you **dispatch** someone or something to a particular place, you send them there for a particular reason.
NOUN **2** an official message

dispensary **dispensaries**
NOUN a place where medicines are prepared and given out

dispersal
NOUN The **dispersal** of something is its spreading or scattering out in many directions.

disperse **disperses, dispersing, dispersed**
VERB If someone **disperses** people, they send them away.

display **displays, displaying, displayed**
NOUN **1** an arrangement of things designed to attract people's attention • *a firework **display***
VERB **2** If you **display** something, you put it on show.
3 If you **display** an emotion, you behave in a way that shows how you feel.

disposable
ADJECTIVE **Disposable** things are designed to be thrown away after they have been used.

dispose **disposes, disposing, disposed**
VERB If you **dispose** of something, you get rid of it. • *We **disposed** of our litter carefully.*

disprove **disproves, disproving, disproved**
VERB If you **disprove** something, you show that it is not true.

dispute **disputes, disputing, disputed**
NOUN **1** an argument
VERB **2** If you **dispute** a fact or theory, you say that it is incorrect or untrue.

disqualify **disqualifies, disqualifying, disqualified**
VERB If someone **disqualifies** someone from a competition or activity, they officially stop them from taking part in it. • *The team was **disqualified** from the competition for cheating.*

disregard **disregards, disregarding, disregarded**
VERB **1** If you **disregard** someone or something, you take no notice of them.
NOUN **2** If you show **disregard** for something, you show that you do not care for it.

disrespect
NOUN contempt or lack of respect
disrespectful ADJECTIVE

disrupt **disrupts, disrupting, disrupted**
VERB If you **disrupt** something, you break it up or throw it into confusion. • *Rain **disrupted** the school's sports day.* [from Latin *dirumpere* meaning to smash to pieces]
disruption NOUN **disruptive** ADJECTIVE

dissatisfied
ADJECTIVE not pleased or contented
dissatisfaction NOUN

dissect **dissects, dissecting, dissected**
VERB When you **dissect** a plant or part of the body of an animal, you cut it up carefully so that you can examine it closely.

dissolve **dissolves, dissolving, dissolved**
VERB If you **dissolve** something, or if something **dissolves** in a liquid, it mixes with the liquid and becomes part of it.

distance **distances**
NOUN **1** The **distance** between two points is the amount of space between them.
2 the fact of being far away • *My friend's house is a great **distance** from mine.*

distant
ADJECTIVE far away in space or time
• *a **distant** planet*

distil **distils, distilling, distilled**
VERB When you **distil** a liquid, you purify it by boiling it and condensing the vapour.

distinct
ADJECTIVE **1** If one thing is **distinct** from another, there is an important difference between them. • *The word "chest" has two **distinct** meanings.*
2 If something is **distinct**, you can hear, smell, see or sense it clearly.

distinction **distinctions**
NOUN **1** a difference between two things
2 a quality of excellence and superiority
• *a woman of **distinction***
3 the highest level of achievement in an examination

distinctive
ADJECTIVE If something is **distinctive**, it has a special quality that makes it recognisable. • *Peppermint has a **distinctive** smell.*

distinguish **distinguishes, distinguishing, distinguished**
VERB **1** If you can **distinguish** one thing from another, you can see or understand the difference between them.
2 If you can **distinguish** something, you can see, hear or taste it. • *I heard shouting but couldn't **distinguish** the words.*

distort **distorts, distorting, distorted**
VERB **1** If you **distort** something, you twist it out of shape.
2 If you **distort** an argument or the truth, you alter the facts to suit yourself.

distract **distracts, distracting, distracted**
VERB If you **distract** someone, you take their attention away from what they are doing.
distraction NOUN

distress **distresses, distressing, distressed**
NOUN **1** **Distress** is suffering caused by pain or sorrow.
VERB **2** If something **distresses** you, it causes you to be upset or worried.
PHRASE **3** If someone or something is **in distress**, they are in danger and need help.

distribute **distributes, distributing, distributed**
VERB **1** If you **distribute** things, you hand them out or deliver them.
2 If you **distribute** something, you share it among a number of people.

district **districts**
NOUN an area of a town or country

distrust **distrusts, distrusting, distrusted**
VERB **1** If you **distrust** someone, you are suspicious of them because you are not sure whether they are honest.
NOUN **2** suspicion
distrustful ADJECTIVE **distrustfully** ADVERB

disturb **disturbs, disturbing, disturbed**
VERB If you **disturb** someone, you interrupt their peace or privacy.
disturbance NOUN

disused
ADJECTIVE If something is **disused**, it is neglected or no longer used.
disuse NOUN

ditch **ditches**
NOUN a channel cut into the ground at the side of a road or field

dive **dives, diving, dived**
VERB **1** If you **dive**, you plunge head first into deep water.
2 If something or someone **dives**, they move suddenly and quickly. • *The birds **dived** to catch the insects.*

diver **divers**
NOUN **1** a person who uses breathing apparatus to swim or work under water
2 a person who takes part in diving competitions
3 a bird that catches its food by diving into water

diverse
ADJECTIVE If things are **diverse**, they show a wide range of differences. • *There was a **diverse** collection of paintings in the gallery.*

a b c d e f g h i j k l m n o p q r s t u v w x y z

A B C D E F G H I J K L M N O P Q R S T U V W X Y Z

diversion **diversions**
NOUN **1** an alternative road you can use if the main one is blocked
2 something that takes your attention away from what you are doing
divert VERB

divide **divides, dividing, divided**
VERB **1** When you **divide** something, or when it divides, it separates into two or more parts. • *We **divided** the cake into six equal slices.*
ANTONYM: multiply
2 If something **divides** two areas, it forms a barrier between them. • *A tall hedge **divided** the two gardens.*
3 If you **divide** a larger number by a smaller number, or into a smaller number, you calculate how many times the larger number contains the smaller number.
• *Thirty-five **divided** by five is seven (35 ÷ 5 = 7). Six **divided** into three is two.*
ANTONYM: multiply

divine
ADJECTIVE having the qualities of a god or goddess

divisible
ADJECTIVE A number that is **divisible** can be divided by another number. • *8, 20, 46 and 166 are all **divisible** exactly by two.*

division
NOUN the process of dividing numbers or things

divorce **divorces, divorcing, divorced**
VERB When married couples **divorce**, they end their marriage legally.

Diwali
NOUN a Hindu festival of light, celebrated in the autumn

DIY
NOUN the activity of making or repairing things yourself. **DIY** is an abbreviation for *do-it-yourself.*

dizzy **dizzier, dizziest**
ADJECTIVE If you feel **dizzy**, you feel that you are losing your balance and are about to fall.

do **does, doing, did, done**
VERB **1** If you **do** something, you get on and finish it. • *I've **done** my homework.*
2 You can use **do** with other verbs.
• ***Do** you like ice cream?*
3 If you ask people what they **do**, you want to know what their job is.

docile
ADJECTIVE A **docile** person or other animal is calm and unlikely to cause any trouble.

dock **docks**
NOUN an enclosed space in a harbour where ships go to be loaded, unloaded or repaired

doctor **doctors**
NOUN a person who is qualified in medicine and treats people who are ill

document **documents, documenting, documented**
NOUN **1** a piece of paper that provides an official record of something
VERB **2** If you **document** something, you make a detailed record of it.

documentary **documentaries**
NOUN a radio or television programme, or a film, that gives information about real events

dodge **dodges, dodging, dodged**
VERB If you **dodge** something, you move suddenly to avoid being seen, hit or caught.

dodgy
ADJECTIVE INFORMAL dangerous, risky or unreliable

doe **does**
NOUN a female deer, rabbit or hare

does
Said "**duz**" VERB a present tense of **do**

doesn't
VERB a contraction of *does not*

dog **dogs**
NOUN a mammal that is often kept as a pet or used to guard or hunt things

dole **doles, doling, doled**
VERB If you **dole** something out, you give a certain amount of it to each individual in a group.

doll **dolls**
NOUN a toy that looks like a baby or a person

dollar **dollars**
NOUN a unit of money in the USA, Australia, Canada, New Zealand and some other countries. A **dollar** is worth 100 cents.

dolphin **dolphins**
NOUN a mammal that lives in the sea

dome **domes**
NOUN a rounded roof

domestic
ADJECTIVE involving or concerned with the home and family
• *Dogs and cats are often kept as **domestic** pets.*

dominant
ADJECTIVE most powerful or important

dominate **dominates, dominating, dominated**
VERB **1** If someone or something **dominates** a situation or an event, they are the most powerful or important thing in it.
2 If one person **dominates** another, they have power and control over them. [from Latin *dominari* meaning to be lord over]

domino **dominoes**
NOUN a small, rectangular block marked with two groups of spots on one side, used for playing the game called **dominoes**

donate **donates, donating, donated**
VERB If you **donate** something, you give it, especially to a charity.

done
VERB the past participle of **do**

donkey **donkeys**
NOUN an animal like a horse, but smaller and with longer ears

donor **donors**
NOUN someone who donates something, such as a blood **donor** or someone who gives to charity

don't
VERB a contraction of *do not*

doodle **doodles, doodling, doodled**
NOUN **1** a drawing done when you are thinking about something else or when you are bored
VERB **2** When you **doodle**, you draw doodles.

doomed
ADJECTIVE If someone or something is **doomed** to an unhappy or unpleasant experience, they are certain to suffer it.

door **doors**
NOUN a swinging or sliding panel for opening or closing the entrance to something

dormitory **dormitories**
NOUN a large bedroom where several people sleep

dormouse **dormice**
NOUN a mammal, like a large mouse, with a furry tail

dose **doses**
NOUN a measured amount of a medicine or drug

dot **dots, dotting, dotted**
NOUN **1** a very small, round mark, such as a full stop or a decimal point
VERB **2** When things **dot** a place or an area they are scattered all over it. • *The hillside was **dotted** with trees.*
PHRASE **3** If you arrive somewhere **on the dot**, you arrive at exactly the right time.

double **doubles, doubling, doubled**
ADJECTIVE **1** twice the usual size
2 consisting of two parts
VERB **3** If something **doubles**, or if you **double** it, it becomes twice as large.
• *The number of pupils has **doubled** over the last year.*
NOUN **4** Your **double** is someone who looks exactly like you.

A
B
C
D
E
F
G
H
I
J
K
L
M
N
O
P
Q
R
S
T
U
V
W
X
Y
Z

double bass
double basses
NOUN a very large stringed instrument • *My brother plays the* ***double bass*** *in a jazz band.*

doubt **doubts, doubting, doubted**
VERB If you **doubt** something, you think that it is probably not true or possible.
• *I* ***doubt*** *if I'll be allowed to go to the party.*

doubtful
ADJECTIVE uncertain or unlikely

doubtless
ADVERB certainly; without any doubt

dough
NOUN a mixture of flour and water used to make bread, pastry or biscuits

doughnut **doughnuts**
NOUN a ring of sweet dough cooked in hot fat

dove **doves**
NOUN a bird of the pigeon family that makes a soft, cooing sound

down
PREPOSITION OR ADVERB **1** towards the ground, towards a lower level, or in a lower place
ADVERB **2** If you put something **down**, you place it on a surface.
3 If an amount of something goes **down**, it decreases. • *The water level in the river has gone* ***down****.*
NOUN **4** the tiny, soft feathers on baby birds

downcast
ADJECTIVE If you are **downcast**, you feel sad and without hope.

downhill
ADVERB down a slope

download **downloads, downloading, downloaded**
VERB When you **download** a program from a disk or from the internet, you move it into a file on your own computer.

downpour **downpours**
NOUN a very heavy shower of rain

downstairs
ADVERB **1** If you go **downstairs**, you go towards the ground floor.
ADJECTIVE **2** on a lower floor

doze **dozes, dozing, dozed**
VERB When you **doze**, you sleep lightly for a short period.

dozen **dozens**
NOUN OR ADJECTIVE A **dozen** or a **dozen** things are twelve of them.

Dr
NOUN an abbreviation for *Doctor*

drab
ADJECTIVE plain, dull and unattractive

draft **drafts**
NOUN an early plan for a story, a book, a letter or a speech that you are going to write

drag **drags, dragging, dragged**
VERB If you **drag** a heavy object somewhere, you pull it there slowly and with difficulty.

dragon **dragons**
NOUN In stories and legends, **dragons** are large, fire-breathing, lizard-like creatures with claws and leathery wings.

dragonfly
dragonflies
NOUN a colourful insect that is often found near water

drain **drains, draining, drained**
NOUN **1** a pipe that carries water or sewage away from a place, or an opening in a surface that leads to the pipe
VERB **2** If you **drain** something, or if it **drains**, liquid flows out of it or off it.

drake **drakes**
NOUN a male duck

drama **dramas**
NOUN **1** a serious play for the theatre, television or radio

2 You can refer to the exciting aspects of a situation as **drama**.

dramatic
ADJECTIVE Something **dramatic** is very exciting, interesting and impressive.

drank
VERB the past tense of **drink**

drape **drapes, draping, draped**
VERB If you **drape** a piece of material over something, you hang it loosely.

drastic
ADJECTIVE A **drastic** course of action is very severe and is usually taken urgently.

draught **draughts**
Said "**draft**" NOUN **1** a current of cold air
PLURAL NOUN **2** **Draughts** is a game for two people, played on a chessboard with round pieces.
draughty ADJECTIVE

draw **draws, drawing, drew, drawn**
VERB **1** When you **draw** something, you use a pen or pencil to make a picture of it.
2 If you **draw** the curtains, you pull them so that they cover or uncover the window.
NOUN **3** the result of a game or competition in which both sides have the same score, so nobody wins

draw lots
PHRASE If you **draw lots**, you decide who will do something by a method that depends on chance, such as taking names out of a hat.

drawback **drawbacks**
NOUN a problem that upsets a plan • *One **drawback** of eating too much chocolate is that you feel sick.*

drawer **drawers**
NOUN part of a desk or other piece of furniture that is shaped like a box and slides in and out

drawing **drawings**
NOUN a picture made with a pencil, pen or crayon

drawing pin **drawing pins**
NOUN a short nail with a broad flat top. You pin papers to a board by pressing a **drawing pin** through them with your thumb.

dread **dreads, dreading, dreaded**
VERB If you **dread** something, you feel very worried and frightened about it.

dreadful
ADJECTIVE very bad or unpleasant • *The weather has been **dreadful** this week.*
SYNONYMS: atrocious, awful, terrible

dreadlocks
PLURAL NOUN a hairstyle where the hair is grown long and twisted into tightly curled strands

dream **dreams, dreaming, dreamed** or **dreamt**
NOUN **1** a series of events that you experience in your mind while asleep
2 a hope or ambition that you often think about because you would very much like it to happen
VERB **3** When you **dream**, you see events in your mind while you are asleep.

You can write either *dreamed* or *dreamt* as the past form of *dream*.

dreary **drearier, dreariest**
ADJECTIVE extremely dull and boring

drenched
ADJECTIVE soaking wet

dress **dresses, dressing, dressed**
NOUN **1** a piece of clothing worn by women and girls, made up of a top and skirt joined together
2 **Dress** is used to describe clothing or costumes in general, such as national **dress** or fancy **dress**.
VERB **3** When you **dress**, you put on your clothes.
4 When you **dress** a wound, you clean it and treat it.

dress up
VERB When you **dress up**, you put on clothes that make you look like something else. • *Let's **dress up** as witches for the party.*

dressing **dressings**
NOUN **1** a bandage or plaster to put on a wound

A B C D E F G H I J K L M N O P Q R S T U V W X Y Z

2 a mixture of oils and spices that can be added to salads and other dishes to heighten the flavour

dressing gown **dressing gowns**
NOUN a long, warm garment, usually worn over night clothes

drew
VERB the past tense of **draw**

dribble **dribbles, dribbling, dribbled**
VERB **1** If a person or animal **dribbles**, saliva trickles from their mouth.
2 In sport, when you **dribble** a ball, you move it along by repeatedly tapping it with your foot or a stick.

drift **drifts, drifting, drifted**
VERB **1** When something **drifts**, it is carried along by the wind or by water.
2 When people **drift**, they move aimlessly from one place or one activity to another.
NOUN **3** snow or sand piled up by the wind
4 INFORMAL the general meaning of something

drill **drills, drilling, drilled**
NOUN **1** a tool for making holes
2 a routine exercise or routine training
VERB **3** If you **drill** a hole, you make a hole using a drill.

drink **drinks, drinking, drank, drunk**
VERB **1** When you **drink** a liquid, you take it into your mouth and swallow it.
NOUN **2** A **drink** is an amount of liquid for drinking.

drip **drips, dripping, dripped**
VERB **1** When liquid **drips**, it falls in small drops.
2 When an object **drips**, drops of liquid fall from it. • *Stop that tap **dripping**.*
NOUN **3** a drop of liquid that is falling

drive **drives, driving, drove, driven**
VERB **1** When someone **drives** a vehicle, they operate it and control its movements.
2 If something **drives** a machine, it supplies the power that makes it work.
NOUN **3** a journey in a vehicle
4 a private road that leads from a public road to a person's house
driver NOUN

drizzle
NOUN light rain

drone **drones, droning, droned**
VERB **1** If something **drones**, it makes a low, continuous humming noise.
NOUN **2** a continuous, low, dull sound
3 a male bee

drool **drools, drooling, drooled**
VERB If someone **drools**, saliva drips from their mouth continuously.

droop **droops, drooping, drooped**
VERB If something **droops**, it hangs or sags downwards with no strength or firmness.

drop **drops, dropping, dropped**
VERB **1** If you **drop** something, you let it fall.
2 If something **drops**, it falls straight down.
3 If the level or the amount of something **drops**, it becomes less.
NOUN **4** a very small, round quantity of liquid
5 the distance between the top and the bottom of something • *There was a fifty-metre **drop** to the river below.*

drought **droughts**
NOUN a long period during which there is no rain

drove
VERB the past tense of **drive**

drown **drowns, drowning, drowned**
VERB When someone **drowns**, or when they are **drowned**, they die because they have gone under water and cannot breathe.

drowsy **drowsier, drowsiest**
ADJECTIVE feeling sleepy

drug **drugs**
NOUN **1** a chemical used by the medical profession to treat people with illnesses or diseases
2 a substance that some people smell, smoke, inject or swallow because of its

stimulating or calming effects. **Drugs** can be harmful to health and may be illegal.

drum **drums**
NOUN **1** a musical instrument consisting of a skin stretched tightly over a round frame
2 an object or container shaped like a **drum** • *an oil* ***drum***

drunk **drunker, drunkest**
VERB **1** the past participle of **drink**
ADJECTIVE **2** If someone is **drunk**, they have consumed too much alcohol.

dry **drier** or **dryer, driest; dries, drying, dried**
ADJECTIVE **1** Something that is **dry** is not wet, and contains no water or liquid.
VERB **2** When you **dry** something, or when it **dries**, liquid is removed from it.

dual
ADJECTIVE having two parts, functions or aspects • *This is a* ***dual****-purpose room – it is both the office and the spare bedroom.*

dual carriageway **dual carriageways**
NOUN a road with several lanes in each direction

dubious
ADJECTIVE **1** not entirely honest, safe or reliable
2 doubtful • *I felt* ***dubious*** *about the idea.*
dubiously ADVERB

duchess **duchesses**
NOUN a woman who has the same rank as a duke, or who is a duke's wife or widow

duck **ducks, ducking, ducked**
NOUN **1** a bird that lives in water and has webbed feet and a large flat bill

VERB **2** If you **duck**, you move your head quickly downwards in order to avoid being hit by something.
3 If you **duck** someone, you push them under water for a very short time.

duckling **ducklings**
NOUN a young duck

due
ADJECTIVE expected to happen or arrive • *The train is* ***due*** *at eight o'clock.*

duel **duels**
NOUN a fight arranged between two people

duet **duets**
NOUN a piece of music sung or played by two people

dug
VERB the past tense of **dig**

duke **dukes**
NOUN a nobleman with a rank just below that of a prince

dull **duller, dullest**
ADJECTIVE **1** not interesting • *I thought the story was rather* ***dull****.*
2 not bright, sharp or clear • *a* ***dull*** *day*

dumb **dumber, dumbest**
ADJECTIVE **1** unable to speak • *She was so shocked that she was momentarily struck* ***dumb****.*
2 INFORMAL stupid

dumbfounded
ADJECTIVE If you are **dumbfounded**, you are so shocked or surprised about something that you cannot speak.

dummy **dummies**
NOUN **1** a rubber or plastic teat given to a baby to suck to keep it happy
2 an imitation or model of something that is used for display • *I first saw the jacket on a* ***dummy*** *in a shop window.*

dump **dumps, dumping, dumped**
VERB **1** If you **dump** something somewhere, you put it there in a careless way.
NOUN **2** a place where rubbish is left
3 INFORMAL You refer to a place as a **dump** when it is unattractive and unpleasant to live in.

dune **dunes**
NOUN a hill of sand near the sea or in the desert

A B C D E F G H I J K L M N O P Q R S T U V W X Y Z

dung
NOUN body waste excreted by large animals

dungarees
PLURAL NOUN trousers that have a bib covering the chest and straps over the shoulders
[named after *Dungri* in India, where dungaree material was first made]

dungeon **dungeons**
NOUN an underground prison

dunk **dunks, dunking, dunked**
VERB If you **dunk** something, you dip it into water or some other liquid for a short time.

duo **duos**
NOUN any two people who do something together, especially a pair of musical performers

duplicate **duplicates, duplicating, duplicated**
Said "**dyoo**-pli-kayt" VERB **1** If someone **duplicates** something, they make an exact copy of it.
Said "**dyoo**-pli-kut" NOUN **2** something that is identical to something else, or an exact copy
duplication NOUN

durable
ADJECTIVE Things that are **durable** are very strong and last a long time.

duration
NOUN the length of time during which something happens or exists

during
PREPOSITION happening throughout a particular time or while something else is going on • *We had an ice cream **during** the interval.*

dusk
NOUN the time just before nightfall when it is not completely dark

dust **dusts, dusting, dusted**
NOUN **1** dry, fine, powdery material such as particles of earth, dirt or pollen
VERB **2** When you **dust** furniture or other objects, you remove dust from them using a duster.
3 If you **dust** a surface with something powdery, you cover it lightly with that substance. • ***Dust** the top of the cake with icing sugar.*

dustbin **dustbins**
NOUN a large container for rubbish

duster **dusters**
NOUN a cloth for dusting things

dusty **dustier, dustiest**
ADJECTIVE covered with dust

duty **duties**
NOUN **1** Your **duty** is what you should do because it is part of your job or because it is expected of you.
PHRASE **2** When workers are **on duty**, they are at work.

duvet **duvets**
NOUN a large bed cover filled with feathers or similar material, which you use instead of sheets and blankets

DVD **DVDs**
NOUN a type of compact disc that can store large amounts of video and sound information. **DVD** is an abbreviation for *digital video* or *versatile disc*.

dwarf **dwarfs, dwarfing, dwarfed**
NOUN **1** a person or thing that is smaller than average
VERB **2** If one thing **dwarfs** another, it is so much bigger that it makes it look very small. • *The mountains **dwarfed** the village.*

dwindle **dwindles, dwindling, dwindled**
VERB If something **dwindles**, it becomes smaller or weaker. • *Their supplies of firewood **dwindled**.* • *As it got later the light **dwindled**.*

dye **dyes, dyeing, dyed**
VERB **1** If you **dye** something, you change its colour by soaking it in a special liquid.
NOUN **2** a substance used to change the colour of something such as cloth or hair

dying
VERB the present participle of **die**

dyke **dykes**; also spelt **dike**
NOUN a thick wall or barrier that prevents a river or the sea from flooding the land

dynamic
ADJECTIVE A **dynamic** person is full of energy, ambition and new ideas.

dynamite
NOUN a powerful explosive

dynamo **dynamos**
NOUN a device that uses movement to produce electricity. A **dynamo** can be used for lighting bicycle lamps.

dynasty **dynasties**
NOUN a series of rulers of a country, all belonging to the same family

dyslexia
NOUN a certain type of difficulty with reading and writing
dyslexic ADJECTIVE OR NOUN

Ee

each
ADJECTIVE OR PRONOUN every one of a group

eager
ADJECTIVE If you are **eager**, you are keen to do something.
SYNONYM: enthusiastic
eagerly ADVERB

eagle **eagles**
NOUN a large bird of prey

ear **ears**
NOUN Your **ears** are the parts of your body on either side of your head, with which you hear sounds.

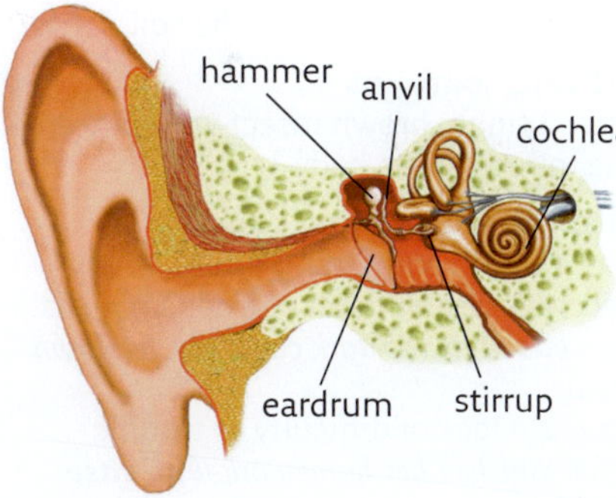

earache
NOUN a pain in your ear

early **earlier, earliest**
ADJECTIVE OR ADVERB **1** before the arranged or expected time
ADJECTIVE **2** near the beginning of something • *I like to go for a walk in the **early** morning.*

earn **earns, earning, earned**
VERB **1** If you **earn** money, you receive it in return for work that you do.
2 If you **earn** something such as praise, you receive it because you deserve it.

a b c d e f g h i j k l m n o p q r s t u v w x y z

A B C D E F G H I J K L M N O P Q R S T U V W X Y Z

earnest
ADJECTIVE If you are **earnest** about something, you are very serious about it.
earnestly ADVERB

earnings
PLURAL NOUN the money or payment that you receive for working

earphone **earphones**
NOUN a very small speaker worn in your ear so you can listen to a radio or MP3 player

earring **earrings**
NOUN a piece of jewellery that you wear on your ear

earth
NOUN **1** The **earth** is the planet we live on. **2** another word for **soil**

earthquake **earthquakes**
NOUN a violent shaking of the ground caused by movement of the earth's crust

earthworm **earthworms**
NOUN a worm that lives in the soil

earwig **earwigs**
NOUN a small, brown insect with pincers at the tail end of its body

ease **eases, easing, eased**
VERB **1** When something **eases**, it becomes less difficult or intense. • *The rain **eased** as the dark clouds were blown away.*
NOUN **2** a lack of difficulty or trouble • *She finished her homework with **ease**.*
VERB **3** If you **ease** something, you move it gently and slowly. • *He **eased** himself into the chair.*

easel **easels**
NOUN an upright frame that supports a picture that someone is painting

easily
ADVERB If you do something **easily**, you do it without difficulty.

east
NOUN one of the four main points of the compass. The sun rises in the **east**. The abbreviation for **east** is E.

Easter
NOUN a Christian religious festival celebrating Christ's return to life after his death
[from Old English *Eostre*, a goddess whose festival was at the spring equinox]

eastern
ADJECTIVE in or from the east

easy **easier, easiest**
ADJECTIVE If something is **easy**, you can do it without difficulty.

eat **eats, eating, ate, eaten**
VERB When you **eat** food, you chew it and swallow it.

ebb **ebbs, ebbing, ebbed**
VERB When the sea or the tide **ebbs**, it goes out.

ebony
NOUN a hard, dark-coloured wood

e-book **e-books**
NOUN a book for reading on an electronic device

eccentric
ADJECTIVE Someone **eccentric** has habits or opinions that other people think are odd or peculiar.
eccentricity NOUN **eccentrically** ADVERB

echo **echoes, echoing, echoed**
NOUN **1** the repeat of a sound caused by the sound being reflected off a surface
VERB **2** When a sound **echoes**, it is reflected off a surface so that it can be heard again. • *Their cries **echoed** back from the mountain.*

eclipse **eclipses**
NOUN An **eclipse** of the sun happens when the moon passes between the sun and the earth and part or all of the sun is hidden from view.

ecology
NOUN the relationship between living

things and their environment, or the study of this relationship
ecological ADJECTIVE **ecologically** ADVERB
ecologist NOUN

economical
ADJECTIVE If you are **economical**, you are not wasteful with money or things.
economically ADVERB

economics
NOUN the system of organizing the money, production and trade of a country, region or group

economy **economies**
NOUN The **economy** of a country or region is the way in which the industries, banks and businesses are organized to make money.
economist NOUN

ecosystem **ecosystems**
NOUN the relationship between plants and animals and their environment

ecstasy
NOUN a feeling of extreme happiness
ecstatic ADJECTIVE

eczema
NOUN a skin disease that makes the skin rough and itchy

edge **edges**
NOUN the part along the side or end of something

edible
ADJECTIVE Things that are **edible** are safe to eat.

edit **edits, editing, edited**
VERB **1** If you **edit** a piece of writing, you correct it.
2 If you **edit** a film or a television programme, you select different parts of it and arrange them in a particular order.

edition **editions**
NOUN An **edition** of a book or newspaper is one or all of the copies printed at one time.

editor **editors**
NOUN **1** someone who is responsible for the contents of a newspaper or magazine
2 someone who edits a piece of writing, a film or a television programme

editorial **editorials**
NOUN an article in a newspaper or magazine which expresses the opinion of the editor

educate **educates, educating, educated**
VERB If you **educate** someone about something, you teach them so that they learn about it.

education
NOUN When you receive an **education**, you gain knowledge and understanding through learning.
educational ADJECTIVE
educationally ADVERB

eel **eels**
NOUN a long, thin fish shaped like a snake

eerie **eerier, eeriest**
ADJECTIVE strange and frightening • *There was an **eerie** silence after the thunderstorm.*

effect **effects**
NOUN **1** something that happens as a result of something else • *The **effects** of global warming are now becoming clear.*
2 the impression something makes • *The **effect** of the moonlight in the mist was eerie.*

effective
ADJECTIVE If something is **effective**, it works well and gives the results that were intended.
effectively ADVERB

efficient
ADJECTIVE capable of doing something well, without wasting time or energy
efficiently ADVERB **efficiency** NOUN

effort **efforts**
NOUN the physical or mental energy needed to do something

effortless
ADJECTIVE done easily and without much effort
effortlessly ADVERB

eg or **e.g.**
Eg means *for example*.

A B C D E F G H I J K L M N O P Q R S T U V W X Y Z

egg **eggs**
NOUN **1** a rounded object produced by female birds, reptiles, fish and insects. The young animal develops in the **egg** until it is ready to hatch.
2 a hen's **egg** used as food

Eid
Said "**eed**" NOUN a festival at the end of the Muslim fast of Ramadan

eight
NOUN **Eight** is the number 8.
eighth NOUN OR ADJECTIVE

eighteen
NOUN **Eighteen** is the number 18.
eighteenth NOUN OR ADJECTIVE

eighty
NOUN **Eighty** is the number 80.
eightieth NOUN OR ADJECTIVE

either
ADJECTIVE, PRONOUN OR CONJUNCTION **1** You use **either** to refer to each of two possible alternatives. • *You can **either** come with me or stay here.*
ADJECTIVE **2** You use **either** to refer to both of two things. • *There were fields on **either** side of the road.*

eject **ejects, ejecting, ejected**
VERB If you **eject** someone or something, you push or send them out of something with force. • *They **ejected** the children from the cinema because they were making too much noise.*
ejection NOUN

elaborate
ADJECTIVE having many different parts, often very detailed or complicated
elaborately ADVERB **elaboration** NOUN

elastic
NOUN rubber material that stretches when you pull it, and returns to its original shape when you let it go

elated
ADJECTIVE very happy or excited

elbow **elbows**
NOUN the joint where your arm bends in the middle

elder
ADJECTIVE Your **elder** brother or sister is older than you.

elderly
ADJECTIVE Someone who is **elderly** is old.

eldest
ADJECTIVE If you are the **eldest** in a family, you are the oldest.

elect **elects, electing, elected**
VERB If you **elect** someone, you choose them as your representative by voting for them.

election **elections**
NOUN When there is an **election**, people choose someone to represent them by voting for them.
[from Latin *eligere* meaning to select]

electric
ADJECTIVE powered or produced by electricity
electrical ADJECTIVE

electrician **electricians**
NOUN a person whose job it is to install and repair electrical equipment

electricity
NOUN a form of energy that provides power for heating, lighting and machines
[from Greek *elektron* meaning amber. In early experiments, scientists rubbed amber in order to get an electrical charge]

electrocute **electrocutes, electrocuting, electrocuted**
VERB If someone **electrocutes** themselves, they accidentally kill themselves or injure themselves badly by touching a strong electric current.
electrocution NOUN

electronic
ADJECTIVE An **electronic** device contains transistors or silicon chips that control an electric current. • *Computers and televisions are examples of **electronic** devices.*
electronically ADVERB

electronic mail
NOUN the sending of messages and documents from one computer to another

elegant
ADJECTIVE attractive and graceful
elegantly ADVERB **elegance** NOUN

element **elements**
NOUN **1** a part of something that combines with others to make a whole
2 In chemistry, an **element** is a substance that is made up of only one atom.
3 The **elements** are the weather, especially when it is bad.

elephant **elephants**
NOUN a very large mammal with a long trunk, large ears, thick skin and ivory tusks

eleven
NOUN **Eleven** is the number 11.
eleventh NOUN OR ADJECTIVE

elf **elves**
NOUN a small, mischievous creature in fairy stories

eligible
ADJECTIVE If you are **eligible** for something, you are suitable or have the right qualifications. • *You are **eligible** to enter the under-twelves competition.*
eligibility NOUN

eliminate **eliminates, eliminating, eliminated**
VERB If you **eliminate** something or someone, you get rid of them.

ellipse **ellipses**
NOUN a regular oval shape

elm **elms**
NOUN a tall tree with broad leaves

else
ADJECTIVE **1** besides or as well as • *What **else** do you see?*
PHRASE **2** **Or else** means otherwise. • *You'd better hurry, **or else** you'll miss the bus.*

elsewhere
ADVERB If you do something **elsewhere**, you do it in another place.

e-mail **e-mails**; also spelt **email**
NOUN **1** the short form for **electronic mail**
2 When you send an **e-mail**, you send a message from one computer to another.

embark **embarks, embarking, embarked**
VERB **1** When you **embark**, you go on to a ship at the start of your journey.
2 When you **embark** on a project, you start it.

embarrass **embarrasses, embarrassing, embarrassed**
VERB If you **embarrass** someone, you make them feel ashamed or awkward.

> There are two *r*s and two *s*s in *embarrass*.

embarrassed ADJECTIVE
embarrassing ADJECTIVE
embarrassment NOUN

embassy **embassies**
NOUN the building in which an ambassador and his or her staff work

emblem **emblems**
NOUN an object or a design representing an organization or a country

embrace **embraces, embracing, embraced**
VERB If you **embrace** someone, you put your arms round them to show your affection for them.

embroider **embroiders, embroidering, embroidered**
VERB If you **embroider** fabric, you sew a decorative design on to it.
embroidery NOUN

embryo **embryos**
NOUN an unborn animal, such as a human being, in the very early stages of development

emerald **emeralds**
NOUN **1** a bright-green precious stone
NOUN OR ADJECTIVE **2** bright green

emerge **emerges, emerging, emerged**
VERB If you **emerge** from somewhere, you come out from it.
emergence NOUN

A B C D E F G H I J K L M N O P Q R S T U V W X Y Z

emergency **emergencies**
NOUN an unexpected and serious situation that must be dealt with quickly

emigrate **emigrates, emigrating, emigrated**
VERB If you **emigrate**, you leave your native country and go to live permanently in another one.
ANTONYM: immigrate
emigration NOUN

eminent
ADJECTIVE If someone is **eminent**, they are well known and respected for what they do.
eminently ADVERB

emit **emits, emitting, emitted**
VERB If something **emits** light, sound, heat or smell, it produces it or lets it out.
emission NOUN

emotion **emotions**
NOUN a strong feeling, such as love or fear
emotional ADJECTIVE

emperor **emperors**
NOUN a male ruler of an empire

emphasis **emphases**
NOUN the special importance or stress put on something • *When you read out the poem, you must put* ***emphasis*** *on the important words.*

emphasize **emphasizes, emphasizing, emphasized**; also spelt **emphasise**
VERB If you **emphasize** something, you make it look or sound more important than the things around it. • *He* ***emphasized*** *the word by underlining it.*

empire **empires**
NOUN a group of countries controlled by one ruler • *The Roman* ***Empire*** *covered many lands.*
[from Latin *imperium* meaning rule]

employ **employs, employing, employed**
VERB If you **employ** someone, you pay them to work for you.

employee **employees**
NOUN someone who works for someone else

employer **employers**
NOUN the person or company that someone works for

employment
NOUN the state of having a paid job

empress **empresses**
NOUN **1** a female ruler of an empire
2 the wife or widow of an emperor

empty **emptier, emptiest; empties, emptying, emptied**
ADJECTIVE **1** having nothing or nobody inside
VERB **2** If you **empty** something, you remove the contents.
emptiness NOUN

emu **emus**
NOUN a large, Australian bird that can run fast but cannot fly

enable **enables, enabling, enabled**
VERB If you **enable** something to happen, you make it possible. • *The ramp* ***enables*** *people in wheelchairs to use the library.*

enchanted
ADJECTIVE If you are **enchanted** by something or someone, you are fascinated or charmed by them. • *The audience were* ***enchanted*** *by her dancing.*

encircle **encircles, encircling, encircled**
VERB If you **encircle** someone or something, you surround them completely.

enclose **encloses, enclosing, enclosed**
VERB **1** If you **enclose** something with a letter, you put it in the same envelope.
2 If you **enclose** an object or area, you surround it with something solid. • *They* ***enclosed*** *the garden with a strong fence.*
enclosed ADJECTIVE

encore **encores**
NOUN an extra item at the end of a performance, when the audience asks for more
[from French *encore* meaning again]

encounter **encounters, encountering, encountered**
VERB **1** If you **encounter** someone or something, you meet them or are faced with them. • *Did you **encounter** any problems?*
NOUN **2** a meeting, especially when it is difficult or unexpected

encourage **encourages, encouraging, encouraged**
VERB If you **encourage** someone, you give them the confidence to do something.
encouraging ADJECTIVE
encouragement NOUN

encyclopedia **encyclopedias**; also spelt **encyclopaedia**
NOUN a book or set of books that gives information about a number of different subjects

end **ends, ending, ended**
NOUN **1** The **end** of something is the furthest point of it.
2 The **end** of an event is the last part of it.
VERB **3** When something **ends**, it finishes.

endanger **endangers, endangering, endangered**
VERB If someone **endangers** something, they cause it to be in a dangerous or harmful situation.
endangered ADJECTIVE

endeavour **endeavours, endeavouring, endeavoured**
VERB If you **endeavour** to do something, you try very hard to do it.

ending **endings**
NOUN The **ending** of something is when it finishes.

endless
ADJECTIVE Something that is **endless** has, or seems to have, no end. • *His **endless** chatter was very boring.*
endlessly ADVERB

endure **endures, enduring, endured**
VERB **1** If you **endure** someone or something unpleasant, you put up with them.
2 If something **endures**, it continues or lasts.
enduring ADJECTIVE

enemy **enemies**
NOUN Your **enemy** is someone who is very much against you and may wish to harm you.

energetic
ADJECTIVE full of energy
SYNONYMS: active, lively

energy **energies**
NOUN **1** the physical strength needed to do active things • *He is saving his **energy** for next week's race.*
2 the power that makes things move, light up, make a sound or get hotter • *electrical **energy*** • *nuclear **energy***

engage **engages, engaging, engaged**
VERB **1** If you **engage** in an activity, you take part in it.
2 If you **engage** someone to do something, you pay them to do it.

engaged
ADJECTIVE **1** If two people are **engaged**, they have agreed to marry each other.
2 If someone or something is **engaged**, they are busy. • *Every time I tried to telephone you, your number was **engaged**.*

engine **engines**
NOUN **1** the part of a vehicle that produces the power to make it move
2 the large vehicle that pulls a railway train

engineer **engineers**
NOUN a person trained in designing and building machinery and electrical devices, or roads and bridges

engineering
NOUN the job of designing and building machinery and electrical devices

engrave **engraves, engraving, engraved**
VERB If you **engrave**, you cut letters or designs into a hard surface with a tool. • *He **engraved** the stone with an unusual design.*
engraving NOUN

a b c d e f g h i j k l m n o p q r s t u v w x y z

A B C D E F G H I J K L M N O P Q R S T U V W X Y Z

enjoy **enjoys, enjoying, enjoyed**
VERB **1** If you **enjoy** something, it gives you pleasure.
2 If you **enjoy yourself**, you are happy and have fun.
enjoyable ADJECTIVE **enjoyment** NOUN

enlarge **enlarges, enlarging, enlarged**
VERB When you **enlarge** something, you make it bigger.
enlargement NOUN

enormous
ADJECTIVE very large in size or amount
SYNONYMS: vast, huge, massive

enough
ADJECTIVE OR ADVERB as much or as many as is necessary • *Do you have **enough** money to buy that?*

enquire **enquires, enquiring, enquired**
VERB If you **enquire** about something or someone, you ask for information about them.

enrol **enrols, enrolling, enrolled**
VERB If you **enrol** for something, such as a course or a society, you register to join or become a member of it.

ensure **ensures, ensuring, ensured**
VERB If you **ensure** that something happens, you make certain that it happens. • *I will **ensure** that I arrive on time.*

enter **enters, entering, entered**
VERB **1** To **enter** a place means to go into it.
2 If you **enter** a competition, you take part in it.
3 If you **enter** something in a diary or a list, you write it down.

enterprise **enterprises**
NOUN **1** something new and exciting that you try to do
2 a large business or company
enterprising ADJECTIVE

entertain **entertains, entertaining, entertained**
VERB If you **entertain** someone, you do something to amuse them.

enthusiasm
NOUN If you show **enthusiasm** for something, you show much interest and excitement.

enthusiastic
ADJECTIVE If you are **enthusiastic** about something, you are very keen on it and talk or behave in an excited and eager way that shows how much you like it.
enthusiastically ADVERB

entire
ADJECTIVE whole, complete • *The **entire** class went on the trip.*

entirely
ADVERB wholly and completely • *My sister and I are **entirely** different.*

entrance **entrances**
NOUN the doorway or gate to a building or area

entry **entries**
NOUN **1** the act of entering a place • *No **entry** after 11 p.m.*
2 something you write in order to take part in a competition • *Send your **entry** to the address below.*
3 something written in a diary or list • *the **entry** for March 23 in her diary*

envelope **envelopes**
NOUN the paper cover in which you put a letter

envious
ADJECTIVE If you are **envious**, you wish you could have what someone else has.
enviously ADVERB

environment **environments**
NOUN **1** Your **environment** is your surroundings, especially the conditions in which you live or work.
2 the natural world around us • *Many people are keen to preserve the **environment**.*

> There is an *n* before the *m* in *environment.*

envy **envies, envying, envied**
VERB If you **envy** someone, you wish that you had what they have.

epidemic **epidemics**
NOUN an outbreak of a disease that takes place in one area, spreading quickly and affecting many people

epilepsy
NOUN a condition of the brain that causes fits and periods of unconsciousness
epileptic NOUN OR ADJECTIVE

episode **episodes**
NOUN **1** one of the programmes in a serial on television or radio
2 an event or period of time, especially one that is important or unusual

epitaph **epitaphs**
NOUN words about a person who has died, usually found on their gravestone

equal **equals, equalling, equalled**
ADJECTIVE **1** being the same in size, number or amount
VERB **2** In mathematics, the symbol (=) stands for **equals**. The numbers before it equal the numbers after it. For example, 3 + 3 = 6.

equally
ADVERB to the same extent or in the same amounts • *We shared the sweets **equally** between the three of us.*

equation **equations**
NOUN a mathematical number sentence stating that two amounts or values are the same • 3 + 6 = 9 *is an **equation** because what is on the left equals what is on the right.*

equator
NOUN an imaginary line drawn round the middle of the earth, lying halfway between the north and south poles
See **tropic**
equatorial ADJECTIVE

equilateral
ADJECTIVE An **equilateral** triangle has sides that are all the same length, and angles that are all the same size.

equinox **equinoxes**
NOUN one of the two days in the year when the day and night are of equal length. The spring **equinox** occurs in March and the autumn **equinox** in September.
[from Latin *aequinoctium* meaning equal night]

equip **equips, equipping, equipped**
VERB If you **equip** yourself, you collect together everything that you need to do a particular thing.

equipment
NOUN all the things that are needed or used for a particular job or activity
• *camping **equipment***

equivalent **equivalents**
ADJECTIVE **1** equal in use, size, value or effect
2 In mathematics, **equivalent** means of equal value. Fractions can be **equivalent** if they are of equal value, for example $2/4=1/2$. Different forms can be **equivalent**, for example 0.5 = $1/2$ =50%.
NOUN **3** Something that has the same use, size, value or effect as something else.
• *One metre is the **equivalent** of 1.094 yards.* • *An example of **equivalent** fractions is $2/4 = 1/2$.*

erase **erases, erasing, erased**
VERB If you **erase** writing, you rub it out.

erect **erects, erecting, erected**
VERB If you **erect** something, you put it up or construct it. • *They **erected** the tent in the garden.*

errand **errands**
NOUN If you run an **errand** for someone, you go a short distance to do a job for them, such as taking a message or fetching something.

erratic
ADJECTIVE not following a regular pattern
• *His attendance at school was **erratic**.*
erratically ADVERB

a b c d e f g h i j k l m n o p q r s t u v w x y z

A B C D E F G H I J K L M N O P Q R S T U V W X Y Z

error **errors**
NOUN a mistake, or something that is wrong

erupt **erupts, erupting, erupted**
VERB **1** When a volcano **erupts**, it throws out a lot of hot lava and ash.
2 When a situation **erupts**, it begins suddenly and violently. • *A family row **erupted**.*

escalator **escalators**
NOUN a mechanical, moving staircase

escape **escapes, escaping, escaped**
VERB **1** If you **escape** from someone or something, you succeed in getting away from them.
2 If you **escape** something unpleasant or difficult, you succeed in avoiding it. • *She was lucky to **escape** serious injury.*
NOUN **3** If you make an **escape** from somewhere, you manage to get away.

escort **escorts, escorting, escorted**
NOUN **1** a person or vehicle that travels with another in order to protect or guide them
VERB **2** If you **escort** someone, you go with them somewhere, especially in order to protect or guide them. • *I will **escort** you round the new buildings.*

Eskimo **Eskimos**
NOUN a member of a group of people who live in North America, Greenland and eastern Siberia. Eskimos who come from North America and parts of Greenland are called Inuits.

especially
ADVERB You say **especially** to show that something applies more to one thing, person or situation than to others. • *It is always cold at the top of the mountain, **especially** when the wind is blowing.*

espionage
NOUN the act of spying to get secret information, especially to find out military or political secrets
[from French *espionner* meaning to spy]

essay **essays**
NOUN a short piece of writing on a particular subject, especially one written as an exercise by a student

essential **essentials**
ADJECTIVE **1** Something that is **essential** is absolutely necessary.
NOUN **2** something that is very important or necessary

establish **establishes, establishing, established**
VERB **1** If you **establish** something, you set it up and keep it going.
2 If you **establish** a fact, you confirm that it is definitely correct.
established ADJECTIVE **establishment** NOUN

estate **estates**
NOUN **1** a large area of land in the country, owned by one person or organization
2 an area of land that has been developed for housing or industry
• *a housing **estate***

estate agent **estate agents**
NOUN a person who works for a company that sells houses and land

estimate **estimates, estimating, estimated**
Said "**ess**-ti-mayt" VERB **1** If you **estimate** an amount or quantity, you calculate it approximately. • *They **estimated** that the trip would take around three hours.*
Said "**ess**-ti-mit" NOUN **2** an approximate calculation of an amount or quantity
• *The final cost was twice the original **estimate**.*

estuary **estuaries**
NOUN the wide part of a river near where it joins the sea, and where fresh water mixes with salt water

etc.
a written abbreviation for *et cetera*

et cetera
Et cetera means *and so on* or *and similar things*.
[from Latin, meaning and others]

eternal
ADJECTIVE lasting forever, or seeming to last forever
SYNONYMS: endless, everlasting, perpetual
eternally ADVERB

a b c d e f g h i j k l m n o p q r s t u v w x y z

ethnic
ADJECTIVE connected with a particular racial group of people • *There were many different **ethnic** groups in the school.*
[from Greek *ethnos* meaning race]
ethnically ADVERB

EU
NOUN an abbreviation for *European Union*

euro **euros**
NOUN the unit of currency used in many countries in Europe, including Germany, France, Italy, Ireland, Spain and the Netherlands

euthanasia
NOUN causing someone to die painlessly and gently, so that they do not suffer during an incurable illness
[from Greek *eu* meaning well and *thanatos* meaning death]

evacuate **evacuates, evacuating, evacuated**
VERB If people **evacuate**, or are **evacuated**, they move from somewhere dangerous to a place of safety. • *The police **evacuated** shoppers from a store after a bomb scare.*
evacuee NOUN

evaluate **evaluates, evaluating, evaluated**
VERB If you **evaluate** something, you assess its quality or value.
evaluation NOUN

evaporate **evaporates, evaporating, evaporated**
VERB When a liquid **evaporates**, it gradually changes from a liquid into a gas or vapour.
[from Latin *vapor* meaning steam]
evaporation NOUN

even
ADJECTIVE **1** An **even** number is one that can be divided into two equal halves, such as two, four and six.
ANTONYM: odd
2 An **even** surface is level, smooth and flat.
3 An **even** measurement or rate stays at about the same level. • *Keep the cooker at an **even** temperature.*
ADVERB **4 Even** is used to say that something is greater in degree than something else. • *He was speaking **even** more slowly than usual.*
PHRASE **5 Even if** *or* **even though** are used to introduce something that is surprising in relation to the rest of the sentence. • *She did not say anything, **even though** she had been left out again.*

evening **evenings**
NOUN the part of the day between the end of the afternoon and the time you go to bed

event **events**
NOUN **1** something that happens, especially when it is unusual or important
SYNONYMS: happening, incident, occurrence
2 an organized activity, such as a sports match or a concert

eventually
ADVERB in the end • *It was a long way, but we got there **eventually**.*

ever
ADVERB at any time in the past or future • *That's the biggest dog I've **ever** seen.*

evergreen **evergreens**
NOUN An **evergreen** is a plant that does not lose its leaves in the winter.

every
ADJECTIVE **1 Every** is used to refer to all the members of a group or all the parts of something. • ***Every** shop in the town was closed.*
2 Every is also used to indicate that something happens at regular intervals. • *The clock strikes **every** hour.*
PHRASE **3** If something happens **every other** day or week, it happens on alternate days or weeks. • *Practice sessions are held **every other** week.*

everybody
PRONOUN every person

everyone
PRONOUN all the people in a group

everything
PRONOUN all or the whole of something

everywhere
ADVERB in many or most places

evict **evicts, evicting, evicted**
VERB To **evict** someone means to officially force them to leave a place they are occupying.
eviction NOUN

evidence
NOUN **1** anything that causes you to believe that something is true or exists
2 the information used in a court of law to try to prove something

evident
ADJECTIVE If something is **evident**, it is clear and obvious.
evidently ADVERB

evil **evils**
NOUN **1** **Evil** is used to refer to all the wicked or bad things that happen in the world.
ADJECTIVE **2** Someone or something **evil** is very bad and causes harm to people.

evolution
NOUN a process that takes place over many generations. During this time, living things slowly change as they adapt to different environments.
evolutionary ADJECTIVE

evolve **evolves, evolving, evolved**
VERB When living things **evolve**, they gradually change and develop into different forms. • *Many people believe that man **evolved** from apes.*

ewe **ewes**
NOUN a female sheep

ex-
PREFIX former • *the **ex**-prime minister*

exact
ADJECTIVE If something is **exact**, it is accurately measured or made.
exactly ADJECTIVE

exaggerate **exaggerates, exaggerating, exaggerated**
VERB If you **exaggerate**, you make something seem better, worse, bigger or more important than it really is.

> There are two *g*s but only one *r* in *exaggerate*.

exaggeration NOUN

exam **exams**
NOUN an official test that aims to find out your knowledge in a subject • *a science **exam***

examination **examinations**
NOUN **1** the full word for **exam**
2 If someone makes an **examination** of something, they look at it very carefully.

examine **examines, examining, examined**
VERB **1** If you **examine** something, you inspect it carefully.
2 If a doctor **examines** you, he or she checks your body to find out how healthy you are.
examiner NOUN

example **examples**
NOUN **1** something that is typical of a particular group of things
SYNONYMS: sample, specimen
2 Someone who is an **example** to others is worth imitating.
PHRASE **3** You use **for example** to give an example of something you are talking about. • *large mammals, **for example** whales*
[from Latin *exemplum* meaning pattern]

exasperate **exasperates, exasperating, exasperated**
VERB If someone or something **exasperates** you, they annoy and frustrate you.
exasperating ADJECTIVE **exasperation** NOUN

excavate **excavates, excavating, excavated**
VERB When someone **excavates**, they remove earth from the ground by digging. When archaeologists **excavate** objects, they carefully uncover remains in the ground to discover information about the past. • *They found some interesting Roman artefacts while they were* ***excavating****.*
excavation NOUN **excavator** NOUN

exceed **exceeds, exceeding, exceeded**
VERB If something **exceeds** a particular amount, it is greater than that amount.

excel **excels, excelling, excelled**
VERB If someone **excels** in something, they are very good at doing it.

excellent
ADJECTIVE very good indeed
SYNONYMS: first-rate, outstanding, superb
excellence NOUN

except
PREPOSITION apart from or not including someone or something • *Everyone laughed* ***except*** *Ben.*

exception **exceptions**
NOUN somebody or something that is not included in a general rule • *All my family are musicians, with the* ***exception*** *of my father.*

exceptional
ADJECTIVE If someone or something is **exceptional**, they are unusual or remarkable in some way. For example, they may be very clever or have special talents.
exceptionally ADVERB

excerpt **excerpts**
NOUN a short piece of writing, music or film that is taken from a longer piece

excess **excesses**
NOUN too much of something

excessive
ADJECTIVE more than is needed or allowed
excessively ADVERB

exchange **exchanges, exchanging, exchanged**
VERB If you **exchange** something for something else, you replace it with something. • *I took the shoes back to the shop and* ***exchanged*** *them for another pair.*

excite **excites, exciting, excited**
VERB If something **excites** you, it makes you feel very happy and enthusiastic.
excited ADJECTIVE **excitedly** ADVERB
exciting ADJECTIVE **excitement** NOUN

exclaim **exclaims, exclaiming, exclaimed**
VERB When you **exclaim**, you cry out suddenly or loudly because you are excited or shocked.
exclamation NOUN

exclamation mark **exclamation marks**
NOUN a punctuation mark (!) used in writing to show a strong feeling

exclude **excludes, excluding, excluded**
VERB If you **exclude** someone from a place or activity, you prevent them from entering or taking part.
ANTONYM: include
exclusion NOUN

exclusive
ADJECTIVE **1** available to a small group of rich or privileged people
2 belonging to a particular person or group only • *Our group will have* ***exclusive*** *use of the pool.*
exclusively ADVERB

excruciating
ADJECTIVE extremely painful
excruciatingly ADVERB

excursion **excursions**
NOUN a short journey or outing

excuse **excuses, excusing, excused**
Said "ex-**kyooss**" NOUN **1** a reason you give to explain why something has been done, has not been done, or will not be done
Said "ex-**kyooz**" VERB **2** If you **excuse** someone's behaviour, you give reasons for why they behaved in that way.
PHRASE **3** You say **excuse me** to try to catch somebody's attention or to apologize for an interruption.

A B C D E F G H I J K L M N O P Q R S T U V W X Y Z

execute **executes, executing, executed**
VERB To **execute** somebody means to kill them as a punishment for a crime.
execution NOUN

executive **executives**
NOUN a person who works at a senior level in a company

exercise **exercises, exercising, exercised**
NOUN **1** any activity that you do in order to get fit or stay healthy
2 a piece of work that you do for practice
VERB **3** When you **exercise**, you do activities that help you to get fit and stay healthy.

exert **exerts, exerting, exerted**
VERB If you **exert** yourself, you make a great deal of effort to do something.

exhale **exhales, exhaling, exhaled**
VERB When you **exhale**, you breathe out.
ANTONYM: inhale

exhaust **exhausts, exhausting, exhausted**
VERB **1** If something **exhausts** you, it makes you very tired.
NOUN **2** the pipe that carries the gas or steam out of the engine of a vehicle
exhaustion NOUN

exhausted
ADJECTIVE If you are **exhausted**, you are very tired.

exhibit **exhibits, exhibiting, exhibited**
VERB **1** If someone **exhibits** something, they put it on show for others to see, especially in a gallery or museum.
NOUN **2** something that is put on show for others to see, especially in a gallery or museum

exhibition **exhibitions**
NOUN a public display of works of art, products or skills

exile **exiles, exiling, exiled**
NOUN **1** a person who is not allowed to live in their own country
VERB **2** If someone is **exiled**, they are sent away from their own country, usually as a punishment.

exist **exists, existing, existed**
VERB If something **exists**, it is in the world as a real thing.
existence NOUN

exit **exits, exiting, exited**
NOUN **1** a doorway through which you can leave a public place
ANTONYM: entrance
2 If you make an **exit**, you leave a place.
ANTONYM: entrance
VERB **3** If you **exit** a place, you leave it.

exotic
ADJECTIVE If something is **exotic**, it is unusual and interesting, usually because it comes from another country.

expand **expands, expanding, expanded**
VERB If something **expands**, or if you **expand** it, it becomes larger.
expansion NOUN

expanse **expanses**
NOUN a large area of something such as the sky or land

expect **expects, expecting, expected**
VERB **1** If you **expect** something to happen, you believe that it will happen.
2 If you are **expecting** someone, you are waiting for them to arrive.
3 If you **expect** something, you believe that you ought to get it or have it. • *I'm **expecting** you to help me.*
expectation NOUN

expedition **expeditions**
NOUN **1** an organized journey made for a special purpose, often to explore
2 the party of people who go on an expedition • *The **expedition** set out through the rainforest.*

expel **expels, expelling, expelled**
VERB **1** If someone **expels** a person from a school or club, they tell them officially to leave because they have behaved badly.
2 If a gas or liquid is **expelled** from a place, it is forced out of it.

expulsion NOUN

expense **expenses**
NOUN the amount of money it costs to do something or buy something • *They could not afford the **expense** of the school trip.*

expensive
ADJECTIVE If something is **expensive** it costs a lot of money.
expensively ADVERB

experience **experiences, experiencing, experienced**
NOUN **1** all the things that you have done or that have happened to you
2 something that you do or something that happens to you, especially something new or unusual
VERB **3** If you **experience** something, it happens to you or you are affected by it. • *We had never **experienced** this kind of holiday before.*

experiment **experiments, experimenting, experimented**
NOUN **1** a scientific test that aims to prove or discover something
VERB **2** If you **experiment** with something or on something, you do a scientific test to prove or discover something about it.
experimentation NOUN
experimental ADJECTIVE
experimentally ADVERB

expert **experts**
NOUN a person who is very skilled at something or who knows a lot about a particular subject
SYNONYMS: authority, specialist
expertly ADVERB

expire **expires, expiring, expired**
VERB If something **expires**, it comes to an end and you can no longer use it.

explain **explains, explaining, explained**
VERB If you **explain** something, you give information about it or reasons for it so that it can be understood.
SYNONYMS: clarify, make clear
explanatory ADJECTIVE

explanation **explanations**
NOUN An **explanation** explains something.

explode **explodes, exploding, exploded**
VERB If something such as a bomb **explodes**, it bursts with great force.
explosion NOUN **explosive** ADJECTIVE

exploit **exploits, exploiting, exploited**
Said "ex-**ploit**" VERB **1** If somebody **exploits** a person or a situation, they take advantage of them for their own ends.
Said "**ex**-ploit" NOUN **2** something daring or interesting that somebody has done

explore **explores, exploring, explored**
VERB If you **explore** a place, you travel around it to discover what it is like.
exploration NOUN **exploratory** ADJECTIVE
explorer NOUN

explosive **explosives**
ADJECTIVE **1** If something is **explosive**, it is likely to explode.
NOUN **2** something that can cause an explosion

export **exports, exporting, exported**
Said "ex-**port**" VERB **1** If someone **exports** goods, they sell them to another country.
Said "**ex**-port" NOUN **2** **Exports** are goods that are sold to another country.

expose **exposes, exposing, exposed**
VERB **1** If you **expose** something, you uncover it so that it can be seen.
2 If a person is **exposed** to something dangerous, they are put in a situation that might harm them. • *The patients were isolated so that no one else would be **exposed** to the disease.*

exposure **exposures**
NOUN **1** the harmful effect of the weather on the body if a person is outside too long without any protection
2 a single photograph on a film

express **expresses, expressing, expressed**
VERB **1** When you **express** an idea or feeling, you show what you think or feel by saying or doing something.
• *She **expressed** her gratitude by giving me a hug.*
ADJECTIVE **2** very fast • *an **express** train*

expression **expressions**
NOUN **1** Your **expression** is the look on your face that shows what you are thinking or feeling.
2 The **expression** of ideas or feelings is the act of showing them through words, actions or art.
3 An **expression** is a phrase with a special meaning, such as *nosy parker*.
expressive ADJECTIVE

exquisite
ADJECTIVE Something that is **exquisite** is extremely beautiful and pleasing.

extend **extends, extending, extended**
VERB If you **extend** something, you make it longer or bigger.

extension **extensions**
NOUN **1** a room or building that is added on to an existing building
2 an additional telephone connected to the same line as another telephone

extensive
ADJECTIVE **1** covering a large area • *The gardens are **extensive**.*
2 very great in effect • *After the storm the house required **extensive** repairs.*
extensively ADVERB

extent **extents**
NOUN The **extent** of something is its length or the area it covers.

exterior **exteriors**
NOUN the outside of something

exterminate **exterminates, exterminating, exterminated**
VERB To **exterminate** people or animals means to kill them deliberately.
extermination NOUN

external
ADJECTIVE existing or happening on the outside of something • *The **external** walls of the house need painting.*

extinct
ADJECTIVE **1** An **extinct** species of animal or plant is no longer in existence.
2 An **extinct** volcano is no longer likely to erupt.
extinction NOUN

extinguish **extinguishes, extinguishing, extinguished**
VERB If you **extinguish** a light or fire, you put it out.

extra
ADJECTIVE OR ADVERB more than is usual, necessary or expected
SYNONYMS: added, additional, further

extract **extracts, extracting, extracted**
Said "ex-**trakt**" VERB **1** If you **extract** something from a place you get it out, often by force. • *The dentist had to **extract** my loose tooth.*
Said "**ex**-trakt" NOUN **2** a small section taken from a book or a piece of music

extraordinary
ADJECTIVE very unusual or surprising
SYNONYMS: exceptional, remarkable
extraordinarily ADVERB

extraterrestrial
ADJECTIVE If something is **extraterrestrial**, it happens or exists beyond the earth's atmosphere.

extravagant
ADJECTIVE spending or costing more money than is reasonable or affordable
extravagantly ADVERB **extravagance** NOUN

extreme **extremes**
ADJECTIVE **1** very great in degree or intensity
• ***extreme** cold*
NOUN **2** the furthest point or edge of something
3 the highest or furthest degree of something • *You experience **extremes** of temperature in the desert, where it is very cold at night and very hot during the day.*
extremely ADVERB

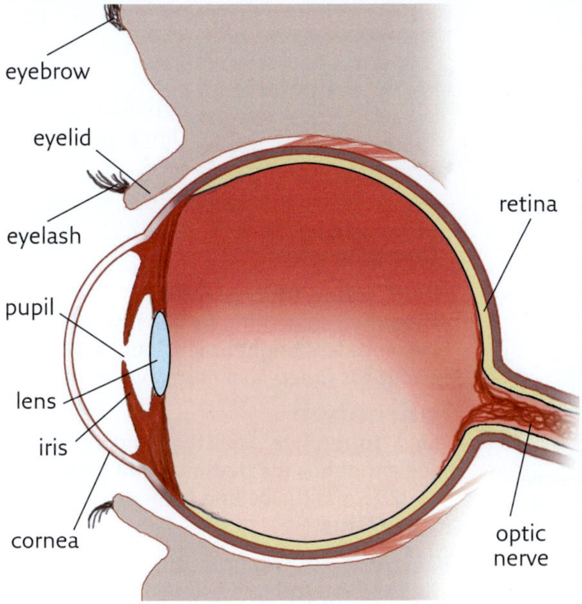

The **pupil** is a hole that changes size to control the amount of light that enters the eye. When it is light the pupil is small and when it is dark the pupil is large.

The **iris** is the coloured part of the eye.

The **cornea** is a clear, tough covering over the iris and pupil that helps protect the eye and begins focusing the light.

The **lens** bends the rays of light coming into the eye so that they fall on the back of the eye.

The back of the eye is called the **retina**, and this is where the light rays are focused.

The **optic nerve** connects the retina to the brain.

eye **eyes, eyeing** or **eying, eyed**
NOUN **1** the parts of your body with which you see
VERB **2** To **eye** something means to look at it. • *They **eyed** each other's new shoes with interest.*

eyebrow **eyebrows**
NOUN Your **eyebrows** are the lines of hair that grow on the ridges of bone above your eyes. • *She raised her **eyebrows** in surprise when she saw her dad's new hat.*

eyelash **eyelashes**
NOUN Your **eyelashes** are the hairs that grow on the edges of your eyelids.

eyelid **eyelids**
NOUN Your **eyelids** are the folds of skin that cover your eyes when they are closed. • *I was so tired that my **eyelids** started to droop.*

eyesight
NOUN the ability to see • *His **eyesight** is not very good, so he wears glasses.*

eyewitness **eyewitnesses**
NOUN someone who has seen something happen and can describe it, especially an accident or a crime • *The police appealed for any **eyewitnesses** to the crash to come forward.*

Ff

fable **fables**
NOUN a story intended to teach a moral lesson • *the **fable** of the tortoise and the hare*

fabric **fabrics**
NOUN cloth • *Silk is a delicate **fabric**.*

fabulous
ADJECTIVE **1** wonderful or very impressive
2 Fabulous creatures are only found in legends or fairy tales.

face **faces, facing, faced**
NOUN **1** the front part of your head, from your chin to your forehead
2 a surface or side of something • *We could see the north **face** of the mountain.*
VERB **3** If you **face** something or someone, you are opposite them and look in their direction.
4 If you **face** in a certain direction, you look there.

facility **facilities**
NOUN a piece of equipment or a service that is provided for a particular purpose • *The school has excellent sports **facilities**.*

fact **facts**
NOUN **1** a piece of information that is true, or something that has actually happened
PHRASE **2 In fact** and **as a matter of fact** mean *actually* or *really* and are used for emphasis. • ***As a matter of fact**, I do like the idea.*

factor **factors**
NOUN **1** something that affects an event or situation • *One of the main **factors** in our success was our strong team.*
SYNONYMS: element, part
2 The **factors** of a number are the whole numbers that will divide exactly into it. • *Two and five are **factors** of 10*: 2 × 5 = 10, 10 ÷ 5 = 2, 10 ÷ 2 = 5.

factory **factories**
NOUN a building or group of buildings where goods are made in large quantities

factual
ADJECTIVE If something is **factual**, it has actually happened.
factually ADVERB

fade **fades, fading, faded**
VERB When something **fades**, it slowly becomes less bright or less loud. • *The colour has **faded** from my favourite T-shirt.*

Fahrenheit
Said "**fa**-ren-hite" NOUN the temperature scale that has the freezing point for water at 32 °F and the boiling point at 212 °F
See **Celsius**

fail **fails, failing, failed**
VERB **1** If you **fail** to do something, you do not succeed in doing it.
ANTONYM: succeed
2 If you **fail** an exam, your marks are too low and you do not pass.
3 If someone or something **fails** to do something that they should have done, they do not do it. • *The bomb **failed** to explode.*
PHRASE **4 Without fail** means definitely or regularly. • *He plays football every Sunday **without fail**.*

failure **failures**
NOUN **1** a lack of success in doing something • *Her attempt to win the race ended in **failure**.*
2 an unsuccessful person, thing or action

faint **fainter, faintest; faints, fainting, fainted**
ADJECTIVE **1** A sound, colour or feeling that is **faint** is not strong or intense. • *Their voices grew **fainter** as they moved away.*
2 If you feel **faint**, you feel dizzy and unsteady. • *I was feeling **faint**, so I sat down.*
VERB **3** If you **faint**, you lose consciousness for a short time.
faintly ADVERB

fair **fairer, fairest; fairs**
ADJECTIVE **1** Something that is **fair** seems reasonable to most people.
2 If the weather is **fair** it is fine.
3 quite good or moderate • *I think I have a **fair** chance of passing my exams.*
4 People who are **fair** have light-coloured hair.
NOUN **5** a form of entertainment that takes place outside, with stalls, games and rides
fairly ADVERB **fairness** NOUN

fairground **fairgrounds**
NOUN an open piece of ground where fairs are held

fairly
ADVERB quite or rather • *My room's **fairly** small.*

fairy **fairies**
NOUN In stories, **fairies** are small, supernatural creatures with magical powers.

fairy tale **fairy tales**
NOUN a story of magical events

faith **faiths**
NOUN **1** If you have **faith** in someone, you trust them.
2 a religious belief

faithful
ADJECTIVE If you are **faithful** to someone or something, you are loyal and continue to support them. • *He is one of my most **faithful** friends.*
faithfully ADVERB

fake **fakes, faking, faked**
NOUN **1** an imitation of something, made to trick people into thinking that it is genuine
ADJECTIVE **2** imitation and not genuine • *The coat was made of **fake** fur.*
VERB **3** If you **fake** a feeling, you pretend that you are experiencing it. • *I **faked** illness to avoid the games lesson.*

fall **falls, falling, fell, fallen**
VERB **1** If someone or something **falls**, or **falls** over, or **falls** down, they drop towards the ground. • *The snow **fell** all day, covering the fields and trees.*
2 to become lower or less • *The temperature usually **falls** at night.*
3 If you **fall ill**, you become ill.
4 If you **fall asleep**, you begin to sleep.
5 If you **fall in love**, you begin to love someone.
6 If you **fall out** with someone, you disagree and quarrel with them.
NOUN **7** If you have a **fall**, you fall over.

false
ADJECTIVE **1** untrue or incorrect
2 not real or genuine, but intended to seem real • *Grandad has **false** teeth.*
falsely ADVERB

fame
NOUN the state of being very well known

familiar
ADJECTIVE **1** well-known or easy to recognize • *The room was full of **familiar** faces.*
ANTONYM: unfamiliar
2 If you are **familiar with** something, you know it or understand it well. • *He was very **familiar with** the local area.*
ANTONYM: unfamiliar

family **families**
NOUN a group of people who are related to each other, especially parents and their children

family tree **family trees**
NOUN a diagram that shows how different members of a family are related to each other

famine **famines**
NOUN a serious shortage of food that may cause many deaths
[from Latin *fames* meaning hunger]

famished
ADJECTIVE very hungry

famous
ADJECTIVE very well-known
famously ADVERB

fan **fans, fanning, fanned**
NOUN **1** If you are a **fan** of something or someone famous, you like them very much.
2 a hand-held or mechanical device that moves air to make it cooler

A B C D E F G H I J K L M N O P Q R S T U V W X Y Z

VERB **3** If you **fan** yourself, you cool the air around you with a fan.

fancy **fancies, fancying, fancied; fancier, fanciest**
VERB **1** If you **fancy** something, you want to have it.
ADJECTIVE **2** highly decorated and special

fancy dress
NOUN clothing worn for a party at which people dress up to look like a particular character or animal

fang **fangs**
NOUN a long, sharp tooth

fantastic
ADJECTIVE **1** wonderful and very pleasing
SYNONYM: marvellous
2 strange or unusual, like a fantasy
[from Greek *phantasia* meaning imagination]
fantastically ADVERB

fantasy **fantasies**
NOUN an imaginative story that is unlikely to happen in real life

far **farther** or **further, farthest** or **furthest**
ADVERB **1** a long distance away
ANTONYMS: near, close
ADJECTIVE **2** You can use **far** to ask questions about distance. • *How **far** is the nearest supermarket?*
ANTONYMS: near, close

fare **fares**
NOUN the amount that you pay to travel on a bus, train or plane

farewell
EXCLAMATION goodbye

far-fetched
ADJECTIVE unlikely to be true

farm **farms, farming, farmed**
NOUN **1** an area of land and buildings, used for growing crops or raising animals
VERB **2** If someone **farms** land, they plant crops or keep animals there.
farming NOUN

farmer **farmers**
NOUN someone who looks after a farm

fascinate **fascinates, fascinating, fascinated**
VERB If something **fascinates** you, it interests and attracts you.
fascinating ADJECTIVE

fashion **fashions**
NOUN a style of dress or way of behaving that is popular at a particular time
fashionable ADJECTIVE **fashionably** ADVERB

fast **faster, fastest; fasts, fasting, fasted**
ADJECTIVE OR ADVERB **1** If something is **fast**, or is happening **fast**, it is happening quickly or with great speed. • *Our car is very **fast**.*
2 If a clock is **fast**, it shows a time that is ahead of the real time.
PHRASE **3** If you are **fast asleep**, you are in a deep sleep.
VERB **4** If you **fast**, you eat no food for a period of time, usually for religious reasons.

fasten **fastens, fastening, fastened**
VERB If you **fasten** something, you close it or attach it firmly to something else.
fastener NOUN **fastening** NOUN

fat **fatter, fattest**
ADJECTIVE **1** having a lot of flesh on the body
NOUN **2** the greasy, white substance that animals and humans have under their skin. It is used to store energy and helps to keep them warm.
3 the greasy or oily substance from animals and plants that is used in cooking

fatal
ADJECTIVE A **fatal** accident or illness causes someone's death.
fatally ADVERB

fate **fates**
NOUN **1** a power that some people believe controls events
2 Someone's **fate** is what becomes of them.

father **fathers**
NOUN a male parent

father-in-law **fathers-in-law**
NOUN the father of someone's husband or wife

fatigue
NOUN extreme tiredness

fault **faults, faulting, faulted**
NOUN **1** a mistake or something wrong with the way something is made
2 If something bad is your **fault**, you are to blame for it.
VERB **3** If you **fault** someone or something, you find something wrong with them.
• *You can't **fault** his piano playing.*
faultless ADJECTIVE

faulty
ADJECTIVE If something is **faulty**, there is something wrong with it.

favour **favours, favouring, favoured**
NOUN **1** If you do someone a **favour**, you do something to help them.
VERB **2** If you **favour** someone or something, you prefer them to others.

favourite **favourites**
ADJECTIVE **1** Your **favourite** person or thing is the one you like best. • *Peaches are my **favourite** fruit.*
NOUN **2** Someone's **favourite** is the person or thing they like best. • *I like all sports, but soccer is my **favourite**.*

fawn **fawns**
NOUN **1** a young deer
NOUN OR ADJECTIVE **2** a light-brown colour

fax **faxes, faxing, faxed**
NOUN **1** a machine that sends and receives documents electronically along a telephone line
2 a document sent in this way
VERB **3** If you **fax** a document, you send it electronically along a telephone line.

fear **fears, fearing, feared**
NOUN **1** the feeling of worry you have when you think that you are in danger or that something bad might happen
VERB **2** If you **fear** someone or something, you are afraid of them.

fearful
ADJECTIVE If you are **fearful** of someone or something, you are afraid of them.
fearfully ADVERB

fearless
ADJECTIVE If you are **fearless**, you are brave and have no fear.
fearlessly ADVERB

fearsome
ADJECTIVE frightening or terrible

feast **feasts**
NOUN a large and special meal for many people

feat **feats**
NOUN a difficult and impressive achievement

feather **feathers**
NOUN A bird's **feathers** are the light, soft growths covering its body.

feature **features**
NOUN **1** a particular part or characteristic of something that is interesting or important
PLURAL NOUN **2** Your **features** are your eyes, nose, mouth and other parts of your face.
• *Your **features** are similar to your mother's.*

February
NOUN the second month of the year.
February usually has 28 days, but has 29 days in a leap year.

> There is an *r* after the *b* in *February*.

fed
VERB the past participle of **feed**

fed up
ADJECTIVE INFORMAL unhappy or bored • *I'm **fed up** with this rainy weather.*

fee **fees**
NOUN a charge or payment for a job, service or activity

feeble **feebler, feeblest**
ADJECTIVE weak, with no strength or power

feed **feeds, feeding, fed**
VERB **1** If you **feed** a person or animal,

A B C D E F G H I J K L M N O P Q R S T U V W X Y Z

you give them food. • *She **feeds** the pigeons every day.*
2 When an animal or baby **feeds**, it eats. • *These insects **feed** on wood.*
3 If you **feed** something into a machine, you put it in there. • *They **fed** the information into a computer.*

feel **feels, feeling, felt**
VERB **1** If you **feel** an emotion or sensation, you experience it. • *I **felt** very happy on my birthday.*
2 If you **feel** something, you touch it. • *The doctor **felt** my forehead.*
PHRASE **3** If you **feel like** doing something, you want to do it.

feeler **feelers**
NOUN **Feelers** are long, thin antennae on the heads of some insects, used to sense things around them.

feeling **feelings**
NOUN **1** an emotion • *Finishing my homework gave me a **feeling** of satisfaction.*
2 a physical sensation • *I had a **feeling** of pins and needles in my foot.*
3 Your **feelings** about something are your general attitudes or thoughts about it.

feet
PLURAL NOUN the plural of **foot**

feline
ADJECTIVE relating to the cat family, or catlike • *The dancer moved with **feline** grace.*

felt
VERB **1** the past tense and past participle of **feel**
NOUN **2** a thick cloth made by pressing short threads together

female **females**
NOUN **1** a person or animal that belongs to the gender that can have babies or young
ADJECTIVE **2** concerning or relating to females
[from Latin *femina* meaning woman]

feminine
ADJECTIVE relating to women or considered to be typical of women

fence **fences**
NOUN a wooden or wire barrier between two areas of land

ferment **ferments, fermenting, fermented**
VERB When beer, wine or fruit **ferments**, a chemical change takes place and alcohol is often produced.

fern **ferns**
NOUN a plant with long, feathery leaves and no flowers

ferocious
ADJECTIVE violent and fierce
ferociously ADVERB **ferocity** NOUN

ferret **ferrets**
NOUN a small mammal that can be trained to hunt rabbits or rats

ferry **ferries, ferrying, ferried**
NOUN **1** a boat that carries people and vehicles across short stretches of water
• *We took the **ferry** across to France.*
VERB **2** If someone **ferries** people or goods somewhere, they transport them there, usually on a short, regular journey. • *A fleet of buses **ferried** people to the concert.*

fertile
ADJECTIVE **1** If soil is **fertile** it can produce strong, healthy plants.
2 If a human or other animal is **fertile**, they are able to have babies or young.
fertility NOUN

fertilize **fertilizes, fertilizing, fertilized**; also spelt **fertilise**
VERB **1** When an egg is **fertilized**, the process of reproduction has begun.
• *Pollen **fertilizes** the female part of a plant.*
2 When you **fertilize** land, you put manure or chemicals on to it to help the growth of plants.
fertilizer; also spelt **fertiliser** NOUN

festival **festivals**
NOUN **1** an organized series of events and performances • *The film **festival** at Cannes in France is very famous.*

2 a time when something special is celebrated • *Harvest **festival** is in the autumn.*

fetch **fetches, fetching, fetched**
VERB If you **fetch** something, you go to where it is and bring it back. • *She **fetched** a towel from the bathroom.*

fête **fêtes**; also spelt **fete**
Said "**fayt**" NOUN an outdoor event with games, displays and goods for sale • *The school **fête** was a big success.*
[from the French *feste* meaning feast]

feud **feuds, feuding, feuded**
Said "**fyood**" NOUN **1** a long-running and bitter quarrel, especially between families
VERB **2** When people **feud**, they quarrel over a long period of time.

fever **fevers**
NOUN If you have a **fever**, your temperature is higher than usual because you are ill.

feverish
ADJECTIVE If you are **feverish**, you have a higher body temperature than usual.
feverishly ADVERB

few **fewer, fewest**
ADJECTIVE OR NOUN not many or a small number of things or people • *I saw him a **few** moments ago.*

> Use *fewer* to talk about things that can be counted and *less* for things that can't be counted: *fewer apples; less time.*

fiancé **fiancés**
Said "fee-**on**-say" NOUN A woman's **fiancé** is the man to whom she is engaged to be married.
[from Old French *fiancer* meaning to promise or betroth]

fiancée **fiancées**
Said "fee-**on**-say" NOUN A man's **fiancée** is the woman to whom he is engaged to be married.
[from Old French *fiancer* meaning to promise or betroth]

fiasco **fiascos**
Said "fee-**ass**-koh" NOUN When something is a **fiasco**, it fails completely, especially in a ridiculous or disorganized way.

fib **fibs, fibbing, fibbed**
VERB If you **fib** about something, you tell a small lie about it.

fibre **fibres**
NOUN **1** a thin thread of a substance used to make cloth • *Many fabrics today are made from artificial **fibres**.*
2 a part of plants that can be eaten but not digested by your body • ***Fibre** is good for your digestive system.*

fickle
ADJECTIVE If you are **fickle**, you keep changing your mind about what you want.

fiction
NOUN stories about imaginary people and events
ANTONYM: non-fiction
fictional ADJECTIVE

fiddle **fiddles, fiddling, fiddled**
VERB **1** If you **fiddle** with something, you keep touching it and playing with it in a restless way.
NOUN **2** another word for **violin**

fidget **fidgets, fidgeting, fidgeted**
VERB If you **fidget**, you keep changing your position or making small restless movements because you are nervous or bored.
fidgety ADJECTIVE

field **fields**
NOUN **1** an area of land where crops are grown or animals are kept
2 an area of land where sports are played • *a football **field***
3 a particular subject or area of interest

fiend **fiends**
Said "**feend**" NOUN **1** a devil or evil spirit
2 a very wicked or cruel person

fierce **fiercer, fiercest**
ADJECTIVE very aggressive or intense • *a **fierce** dog* • ***fierce** competition*
fiercely ADVERB

A B C D E F G H I J K L M N O P Q R S T U V W X Y Z

fiery **fierier, fieriest**
ADJECTIVE If you are **fiery**, you show great anger, energy or passion in what you do.

fifteen
NOUN **Fifteen** is the number 15.
fifteenth NOUN OR ADJECTIVE

fifth
NOUN OR ADJECTIVE The **fifth** or the **fifth** thing in a series is the one counted as number five.

fifty
NOUN **Fifty** is the number 50.
fiftieth NOUN OR ADJECTIVE

fig **figs**
NOUN a very sweet fruit that is full of seeds and can be eaten dried

fight **fights, fighting, fought**
VERB **1** When people **fight**, they take part in a battle, a boxing match, or in some other attempt to hurt or kill someone.
2 If you **fight** something, or if you fight against it, you try in a determined way to stop it happening. • *I've **fought** all my life against cruelty to animals.*
NOUN **3** a situation in which people hit or try to hurt each other
SYNONYMS: battle, conflict

figurative
ADJECTIVE If you use a word or expression in a **figurative** sense, you use it for effect, with a more abstract or imaginative meaning than its usual one. For example, you could write about a person as if he or she was a bird. • *He flew down the stairs.* • *She perched on a chair.*

figure **figures**
NOUN **1** a written number • *He wrote the **figures** down and then added them up.*
2 Your **figure** is the shape of your body.
3 a diagram or table in a book or a magazine

figure of speech **figures of speech**
NOUN an expression, such as a metaphor or a simile, where the words should not be taken literally. *She was as cold as ice* (simile). *The road was a ribbon of moonlight* (metaphor).

file **files, filing, filed**
NOUN **1** a box or folder in which papers are kept
2 In computing, a **file** is a set of related data with its own name. • *He copied the **file** on to a floppy disk.*
3 a tool with rough surfaces, used for smoothing and shaping hard materials
VERB **4** When someone **files** something, they put it in its correct place with others that are similar. • *They **filed** the students' papers alphabetically.*
5 When a group of people **file** somewhere, they walk one behind the other in a line. • *The children **filed** out of the school.*
PHRASE **6** If people walk **in single file**, they walk one behind the other.

fill **fills, filling, filled**
VERB **1** If you **fill** something, or if it **fills** up, it becomes full. • *The arena soon began to **fill** up.*
2 If something **fills** a space, there is very little room left. • *The water **filled** the jug.*

fill in
VERB If you **fill in** a form, you write information in the spaces on it.

filling **fillings**
NOUN **1** the mixture inside a sandwich, cake or pie
2 a small amount of metal or plastic that a dentist puts into a hole in a tooth

film **films, filming, filmed**
NOUN **1** a series of moving pictures that can be shown in a cinema or on television
2 a strip of thin plastic that you use in a camera to take photographs
3 a very thin layer of powder or liquid • *A **film** of dust covered every surface.*

VERB **4** If you **film** someone or something, you use a camera to take moving pictures of them.

filter filters, filtering, filtered

NOUN **1** a device that allows some substances, lights or sounds to pass through it, but not others • *The suntan cream acted as a **filter** against the harmful rays of the sun.*

VERB **2** If you **filter** something, you pass it through a filter to remove tiny particles from it.

filtration NOUN

filthy filthier, filthiest

ADJECTIVE very dirty

fin fins

NOUN a flat object on the body of a fish that helps it to swim and keep its balance *See* **fish**

final finals

ADJECTIVE **1** The **final** thing in a series is the last one, or the one that happens at the end. • *the **final** chapter of a book*

2 A decision that is **final** cannot be changed or questioned. • *The judges' decision is **final**.*

NOUN **3** The **final** is the last game or contest in a series, that decides the overall winner.

finalist finalists

NOUN someone who takes part in the final of a competition

finally

ADVERB **1** If something **finally** happens, it happens after a long delay. • ***Finally**, he answered the phone.*

SYNONYMS: at last, eventually

2 You use **finally** to introduce the last point or topic. • ***Finally**, I would like to thank everyone for coming.*

SYNONYMS: in conclusion, lastly

finance finances, financing, financed

NOUN **1** **Finance** describes affairs to do with money.

VERB **2** If someone **finances** something, they provide the money for it.

find finds, finding, found

VERB **1** If you **find** someone or something, you see them or discover where they are. • *He eventually **found** the book under his bed.*

2 If you **find** something, you know it from experience. • *I **find** that air travel tires me.*

find out

VERB If you **find out** something, you learn or discover something. • *He wants to **find out** what really happened.*

fine finer, finest; fines

ADJECTIVE **1** Something that is **fine** is very good or very beautiful.

2 If something is **fine** it is satisfactory or suitable. • *That outfit is **fine** for the party.*

3 If you are **fine**, you are well and happy.

4 **Fine** sand or powder is made up of very small particles.

5 When the weather is **fine**, it is bright and sunny.

NOUN **6** a sum of money that must be paid as a punishment

finger fingers

NOUN one of the four long structures at the end of your hands that you use to feel and hold things

fingernail fingernails

NOUN the hard coverings at the ends of your fingers

fingerprint fingerprints

NOUN the unique marks made by the tip of your fingers when you touch something

finish finishes, finishing, finished

VERB **1** When you **finish** something, you do the last part of it and complete it.

2 When something **finishes**, it ends. • *The film **finished** at eight o'clock.*

NOUN **3** The **finish** of something is the last part of it. • *There was a very exciting **finish** to the match.*

SYNONYMS: close, conclusion, end

fir firs

NOUN an evergreen tree with thin, needle-like leaves and cones

fire **fires, firing, fired**
NOUN **1** the flames produced when something burns
2 a mass of burning material • *We lit a **fire** on the beach.*
3 a device that uses electricity, coal, gas or wood to heat a room
VERB **4** If someone **fires** a gun, they shoot a bullet. • *He **fired** the gun into the air.*
5 INFORMAL If an employer **fires** someone, that person loses their job.
PHRASE **6** If something is **on fire**, it is burning.

fire brigade **fire brigades**
NOUN the organization that has the job of putting out fires

fire engine **fire engines**
NOUN a vehicle used by firefighters to help them put out fires

fire escape **fire escapes**
NOUN an emergency exit or staircase for use if there is a fire

fire extinguisher **fire extinguishers**
NOUN a device that contains water or foam that is sprayed on to fires to put them out

firefighter **firefighters**
NOUN a person whose job is to put out fires

fireplace **fireplaces**
NOUN the opening beneath a chimney where a fire can be lit

fireproof
ADJECTIVE If something is **fireproof**, it is resistant to fire.

firework **fireworks**
NOUN a small object that produces coloured sparks or smoke when lit

firm **firmer, firmest; firms**
ADJECTIVE **1** Something that is **firm** is fairly hard and does not change shape very much when it is pressed. • *I like sleeping on a **firm** mattress.*
2 A **firm** grasp or push is strong or controlled. • *His handshake was **firm** and confident.*
3 Someone who is **firm** behaves in a fairly strict way and will not change their mind.
NOUN **4** a business that sells or produces something • *an engineering **firm***

first **firsts**
ADJECTIVE OR ADVERB **1** happening, coming or done before all the others • *Andrea came **first** in the 100 metres race.*
NOUN **2** the person or thing that happens or comes before all the others • *I was the **first** to arrive.*
ADJECTIVE **3** the most important • *Her painting won **first** prize.*
ADVERB **4** for the first time • *They **first** met in 1995.*
PHRASE **5** You use **at first** to refer to what happens to start with, or what happens at the beginning of something.

first aid
NOUN simple treatment given as soon as possible to a person who is injured or who suddenly becomes ill

first class
ADJECTIVE Something that is **first class** is of the highest quality or standard.

first person
NOUN In grammar, the **first person** refers to yourself when you are speaking or writing. It is expressed as I or me.
• *William wrote his story in the **first person**.*

fish **fishes, fishing, fished**
NOUN **1** an animal with a tail and fins that lives in water

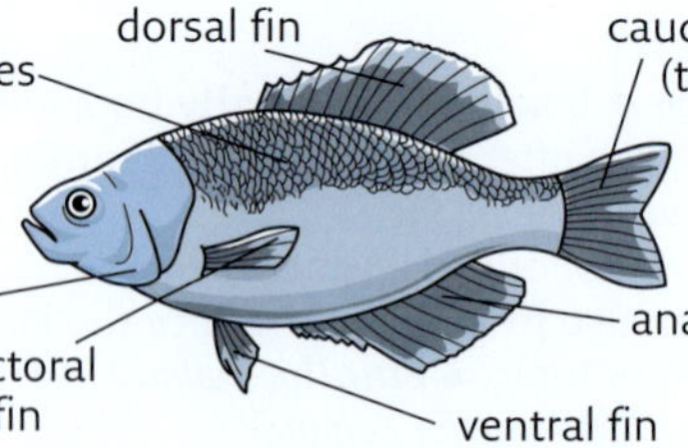

VERB **2** If you **fish**, you try to catch fish.

> The plural of the noun *fish* can be either *fish* or *fishes*, but *fish* is more common.

fishing NOUN

fisherman **fishermen**
NOUN someone who catches fish for a living or as a sport

fist **fists**
NOUN a hand with the fingers curled tightly towards the palm

fit **fits, fitting, fitted; fitter, fittest**
VERB **1** If something **fits**, it is the right shape or size for a particular person or position. • *There is now a computer that **fits** into your pocket.*
2 If you **fit** something, you put it securely in place. • *We need to **fit** a new pane of glass in the broken window.*
3 If something **fits** a particular situation, person or thing, it is suitable or appropriate.
NOUN **4** A **fit** of laughter, coughing, rage, or panic is a sudden, uncontrolled outburst of it. • *They collapsed in a **fit** of laughter.*
5 If someone has a **fit**, they lose consciousness and their body makes uncontrollable movements. • *epileptic **fit***
ADJECTIVE **6** Someone who is **fit** is healthy and physically strong.
fitness NOUN

five
NOUN **Five** is the number 5.

fix **fixes, fixing, fixed**
VERB **1** If you **fix** something somewhere, you attach it there securely. • *He **fixed** the clock to the wall.*
2 If you **fix** something that is broken, you repair it.
SYNONYM: mend

fixture **fixtures**
NOUN **1** a sports event that takes place on a particular date
2 an object such as a cupboard or a bath that is fixed in position in a building

fizz **fizzes, fizzing, fizzed**
VERB When something **fizzes** it makes a hissing or bubbling sound.

fizzy **fizzier, fizziest**
ADJECTIVE A **fizzy** drink has a gas called carbon dioxide in it to make it bubbly.

flag **flags**
NOUN a piece of cloth that has a particular colour or design, and is used as the symbol of a country or as a signal

flake **flakes, flaking, flaked**
NOUN **1** a small, thin piece of something • ***Flakes** of rust came off the old bicycle.*
VERB **2** When something such as paint **flakes**, small, thin pieces of it come off.
flaky ADJECTIVE **flaked** ADJECTIVE

flame **flames**
NOUN a hot, bright stream of burning gas • *The **flames** of the fire flickered.*

flamingo **flamingos** or **flamingoes**
NOUN a long-legged wading bird with pink feathers and a long neck

flammable
ADJECTIVE likely to catch fire and burn easily

flan **flans**
NOUN a flat, open tart that can be sweet or savoury

flannel **flannels**
NOUN **1** a small square of towelling, used for washing yourself. In Australian English it is called a *washer.*
2 a lightweight woollen fabric

flap **flaps, flapping, flapped**
VERB **1** If something **flaps**, or if you **flap** it, it moves quickly up and down or from side to side. • *The flag was **flapping** in the wind.*
NOUN **2** a loose piece of something, such as cloth or plastic, that is attached at one edge • *a cat **flap***

flare **flares, flaring, flared**
NOUN **1** a device that produces a brightly coloured flame, used especially as an emergency signal
VERB **2** If a fire **flares**, it suddenly burns much more vigorously.

flash **flashes, flashing, flashed**
NOUN **1** a sudden, short burst of light • *There was a **flash** of lightning in the middle of the storm.*
VERB **2** If a light **flashes**, or if you **flash** it, it shines suddenly and briefly. • *The light*

A B C D E F G H I J K L M N O P Q R S T U V W X Y Z

*from the lighthouse **flashed** in the night.*
3 If something **flashes**, it moves or happens very quickly. • *A car **flashed** past the window.*

flask **flasks**
NOUN a special bottle used for keeping drinks hot or cold, and for carrying around with you. It is an abbreviation for *vacuum flask* or *Thermos flask*.

flat **flats; flatter, flattest**
NOUN **1** a set of rooms for living in. A **flat** is part of a larger building. • *We live in a block of **flats**.*
ADJECTIVE **2** Something that is **flat** is level and smooth.
3 A **flat** tyre or ball has not got enough air in it.
4 A **flat** battery has lost its electrical charge.

flatten **flattens, flattening, flattened**
VERB If you **flatten** something, you make it flat or flatter.

flatter **flatters, flattering, flattered**
VERB If you **flatter** someone, you praise them in an exaggerated way, either to please them or to persuade them to do something. • *When she **flatters** me I know she wants me to do something for her.*
flattering ADJECTIVE **flattery** NOUN

flaunt **flaunts, flaunting, flaunted**
VERB If you **flaunt** something, you show it off to others.

flavour **flavours, flavouring, flavoured**
NOUN **1** the taste of food and drink • *This cheese has a very strong **flavour**.*
VERB **2** If you **flavour** food, you add something to it to give it a particular taste. • *You can **flavour** the pasta sauce with herbs.*

flaw **flaws**
NOUN a fault or weakness in something
flawed ADJECTIVE **flawless** ADJECTIVE

flax
NOUN a plant that is used for making rope and cloth

flea **fleas**
NOUN a small, wingless, jumping insect that feeds on blood

fleece **fleeces**
NOUN A sheep's **fleece** is its coat of wool.

fleet **fleets**
NOUN a group of ships or vehicles owned by the same organization, or travelling together

flesh
NOUN the soft part of your body between the bones and the skin
fleshy ADJECTIVE

flew
VERB the past tense of **fly**

flex **flexes, flexing, flexed**
NOUN **1** a length of wire covered in plastic, that carries electricity to an appliance
VERB **2** If you **flex** your muscles, you bend and stretch them.

flexible
ADJECTIVE Something that is **flexible** can be bent easily without breaking.
flexibility NOUN

flick **flicks, flicking, flicked**
VERB **1** If you **flick** something, you move it sharply with your finger. • *He **flicked** through the pages of the book to find where he was up to.*
NOUN **2** a sudden, quick movement or sharp touch with the finger • *The cat gave a sudden **flick** of its tail.*

flicker **flickers, flickering, flickered**
VERB If a light or a flame **flickers**, its brightness comes and goes.

flies
PLURAL NOUN the plural of **fly**

flight **flights**
NOUN **1** a journey made by aeroplane
2 the action of flying or the ability to fly
3 A **flight** of stairs or steps is a row of them.
4 the action of running away • *The girl took **flight** when she saw the big dog.*

flight attendant **flight attendants**
NOUN a person who looks after the passengers on an aeroplane

flimsy **flimsier, flimsiest**
ADJECTIVE made of something very thin and easily damaged • *The shelter they made in the garden was very **flimsy**.*

flinch **flinches, flinching, flinched**
VERB If you **flinch**, you make a sudden, small movement in fear or pain. • *She **flinched** when the dentist's drill started.*
SYNONYMS: cringe, wince

fling **flings, flinging, flung**
VERB If you **fling** something somewhere, you throw it there using a lot of force. • *He **flung** his shoes into the corner.*

flint **flints**
NOUN a very hard, grey-black stone used for building

flip **flips, flipping, flipped**
VERB If you **flip** something, you turn it over quickly. • *He **flipped** open the book to start his homework.*

flipper **flippers**
NOUN one of the flat limbs of an animal like a penguin or seal that they use for swimming

float **floats, floating, floated**
VERB **1** Something that **floats** is supported by liquid. • *A branch **floated** down the river.*
2 If something **floats** in the air, it hangs in the air or moves slowly through it. • *A leaf **floated** on the breeze.*
NOUN **3** an object attached to a fishing line to keep the hook floating in the water
4 an amount of money that a shop or stall keeps for change

flock **flocks, flocking, flocked**
NOUN **1** a group of birds, sheep or goats
VERB **2** If people **flock** somewhere, they go there in large numbers.

flood **floods, flooding, flooded**
NOUN **1** If there is a **flood**, a large amount of water covers an area that is usually dry.
2 A **flood** of something is a large amount of it occurring suddenly. • *There was a **flood** of letters after the programme.*
VERB **3** If water **floods** an area that is usually dry, or if the area **floods**, it becomes covered with water. • *He left the tap running and **flooded** the kitchen.*

floodlight **floodlights**
NOUN a very powerful outdoor light that is used to illuminate sports fields and public buildings

floor **floors**
NOUN **1** the part of a room that you walk on
2 one of the levels in a building • *Our flat is on the fifth **floor** of the building.*

flop **flops, flopping, flopped**
VERB **1** If someone or something **flops**, they fall loosely and heavily. • *He **flopped** down on to the sofa when he got home.*
2 INFORMAL If something **flops**, it fails. • *The play **flopped** after it had some bad reviews.*

florist **florists**
NOUN a person or shop selling flowers

flour
NOUN a white or brown powder made by grinding grain. It is used for making bread, cakes and pastry.

flourish **flourishes, flourishing, flourished**
VERB Something that **flourishes** develops or grows successfully or healthily.
[from Latin *florere* meaning to flower]

flow **flows, flowing, flowed**
VERB **1** If something **flows** somewhere, it moves there in a steady and continuous manner. • *The river **flows** south from the town.*
NOUN **2** A **flow** of something is a steady, continuous movement of it. • *There is a constant **flow** of traffic down the main road.*

flow chart **flow charts**
NOUN a diagram that shows the sequence of steps and choices that lead to various results and courses of action

flower **flowers, flowering, flowered**
NOUN **1** the part of a plant that grows at the end of a stem. It carries the reproductive parts of the plant from which the fruit and seeds develop.

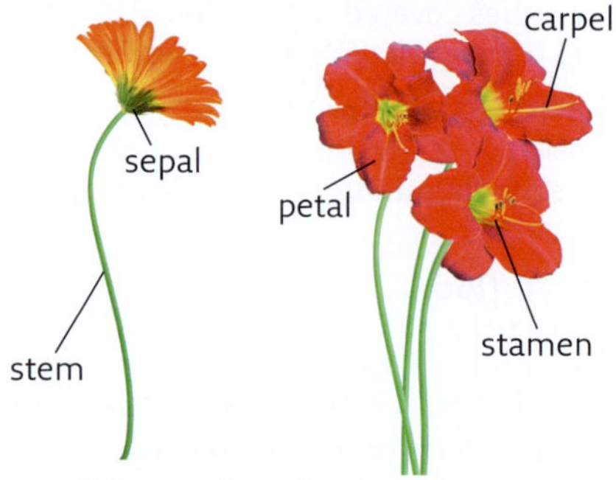

VERB **2** When a plant **flowers**, its flowers open.

flown
VERB the past participle of **fly**

flu
NOUN an abbreviation of *influenza*. **Flu** is an illness similar to a bad cold, but more serious.

fluent
ADJECTIVE Someone who is **fluent** in a foreign language can speak it correctly and without hesitation.
fluently ADVERB

fluff
NOUN soft, light, woolly threads or fibres bunched together

fluffy **fluffier, fluffiest**
ADJECTIVE soft and woolly

fluid **fluids**
NOUN a liquid • *Drink plenty of **fluids** in hot weather.*

fluke **flukes**
NOUN an accidental success • *It must be a **fluke** that I did so well in my exams.*

fluorescent
ADJECTIVE **1** When something is **fluorescent**, it gives out its own light when another light is shone on it.
2 A **fluorescent** light is in the form of a tube that shines with a harsh, bright light.

fluoride
NOUN a chemical mixture that is often added to drinking water and to toothpaste because it is thought to prevent tooth decay

flush **flushes, flushing, flushed**
VERB **1** If you **flush**, your face goes red.
2 If you **flush** a toilet or something such as a pipe, you force water through it to clean it.

flute **flutes**
NOUN a musical wind instrument in the shape of a long tube with holes along it. You play it by blowing over a hole near one end while holding it sideways to your mouth.

flutter **flutters, fluttering, fluttered**
VERB If something **flutters**, it flaps or waves with small, quick movements. • *I felt the bird **flutter** in my hands.*

fly **flies, flying, flew, flown**
NOUN **1** an insect with two pairs of wings
VERB **2** When a bird, insect or aircraft **flies**, it moves through the air. • *The bird **flew** away.*
3 If you **fly** somewhere, you travel there in an aircraft.
flying ADJECTIVE OR NOUN **flyer** NOUN

flyover **flyovers**
NOUN a bridge that takes one road over the top of another one

foal **foals**
NOUN a young horse

foam **foams, foaming, foamed**
NOUN **1** a mass of tiny bubbles • *The bubble bath produced a lot of **foam**.*
VERB **2** When something **foams**, it forms a mass of small bubbles. • *The powder **foamed** in the washing machine.*

focus **focuses, focusing, focused** or **focusses, focussing, focussed**
VERB **1** If you **focus** your eyes or a camera on something, you adjust your eyes or the camera so that the image is clear. • *She **focused** her eyes on the ball.*
2 If you **focus** on a particular topic, you concentrate on it.

PHRASE **3** If an image is **in focus**, the edges of the image are clear and sharp. If it is **out of focus**, the edges are blurred. [from Latin *focus* meaning hearth, which was seen as the centre of a Roman home]

> You can spell the inflections of *focus* with one *s* or two *ss* in the middle but the spellings with one *s* are much more common: *focuses, focusing, focused.*

fodder
NOUN food given to horses and cattle

foe **foes**
NOUN If someone is your **foe**, they are your enemy.

foetus **foetuses**; also spelt **fetus**
NOUN A **foetus** is an unborn child or other animal in the womb.

fog
NOUN a thick mist caused by tiny drops of water in the air

foil **foils, foiling, foiled**
VERB **1** If you **foil** someone's attempt at something, you prevent it from succeeding. • *The policeman **foiled** the robbery.*
NOUN **2** thin, paper-like sheets of metal used to wrap food

fold **folds, folding, folded**
VERB **1** If you **fold** something, you bend it so that one part lies over another. • *He **folded** the letter and put it back in the envelope.*
NOUN **2** a crease or bend in paper or cloth

folder **folders**
NOUN a thin piece of folded cardboard used for keeping papers together

foliage
NOUN the leaves of plants

folk
PLURAL NOUN **1** people • *These are the **folk** I was telling you about.*
ADJECTIVE **2** **Folk** music and art are traditional or typical of the people of a particular area. • *My dad likes Irish **folk** music.*

folklore
NOUN the traditional stories and beliefs of a community

follow **follows, following, followed**
VERB **1** If you **follow** someone or something, you move along behind them. • *We **followed** him up the steps.*
2 If you **follow** a path or a sign, you go somewhere using the path or sign to direct you. • *I **followed** the signs to the dining room.*
3 If you **follow** instructions or advice, you do what you are told.
4 If you **follow** an explanation or the plot of a story, you understand each stage of it.
follower NOUN

fond **fonder, fondest**
ADJECTIVE If you are **fond** of someone or something, you like them.

font **fonts**
NOUN **1** a large, stone bowl in a church that holds the water for baptisms
2 a style of printed writing. There are many **fonts** to choose from, such as: Helvetica, Times, Courier or Frutiger.

food **foods**
NOUN what people and other animals eat

food chain **food chains**
NOUN a series of living things that are linked together because each one feeds on another in the chain

fool **fools, fooling, fooled**
NOUN **1** someone who is silly and is not sensible
VERB **2** If you **fool** someone, you deceive or trick them. • *Don't be **fooled** by his appearance.*

foolish
ADJECTIVE stupid or silly

foolproof
ADJECTIVE If something is **foolproof**, it cannot fail.

foot **feet**
NOUN **1** the part of your body at the end of your leg

A B C D E F G H I J K L M N O P Q R S T U V W X Y Z

2 the part of something that is farthest from the top • *The hotel was at the **foot** of the mountain.*
3 a unit of length equal to 12 inches or about 30.5 centimetres

football **footballs**
NOUN **1** a game such as soccer and American **football**, in which the ball can be kicked and two teams try to score goals
2 a ball used in these games
footballer NOUN

foothold **footholds**
NOUN a place where you can put your foot when climbing

footpath **footpaths**
NOUN a path for people to walk on, especially in the countryside

footprint **footprints**
NOUN the mark made by a foot on the ground

footstep **footsteps**
NOUN the sound made by someone's feet when they are walking • *They heard **footsteps** in the corridor.*

for
PREPOSITION **1** to be used by or given to a particular person • *I bought a present **for** my brother.*
2 **For** is used when explaining the reason, cause or purpose of something. • *I'm going shopping **for** a pair of shoes.*
3 You use **for** to show a distance, time or quantity. • *I have been waiting here **for** ages.*
4 If you are **for** something, you support it. • *My parents are all **for** the new school.*
ANTONYM: against

forbid **forbids, forbidding, forbade, forbidden**
VERB If someone **forbids** you to do something, they order you not to do it.
forbidden ADJECTIVE

force **forces, forcing, forced**
VERB **1** If you **force** someone to do something, you make them do it.
NOUN **2** violence or great strength • *He used a lot of **force** to pull the wall down.*
3 an organized group of people, especially soldiers or police • *The police **force** helped to maintain order at the football match.*
4 a push or pull. **Forces** are measured in newtons.
forceful ADJECTIVE **forcefully** ADVERB

forecast **forecasts, forecasting, forecast** or **forecasted**
NOUN **1** A **forecast** says what is likely to happen. • *the weather **forecast***
VERB **2** If you **forecast** an event, you say what is likely to happen. • *We **forecast** that we would win the game.*

foreground **foregrounds**
NOUN In a picture, the **foreground** is the part that seems nearest to you.

forehead **foreheads**
NOUN the area at the front of your head, above your eyebrows and below your hair

foreign
ADJECTIVE belonging to or involving a country that is not your own • *It is useful to learn a **foreign** language.*
foreigner NOUN

forest **forests**
NOUN a large area of trees growing close together

forever
ADVERB permanently or continually

forfeit **forfeits, forfeiting, forfeited**
VERB If you **forfeit** something, you have to give it up as a penalty.

forgave
VERB the past tense of **forgive**

forge **forges, forging, forged**
NOUN **1** a place where a blacksmith works making metal goods by hand
VERB **2** If someone **forges** metal, they hammer and bend it into shape while it is hot.
3 Someone who **forges** money, documents or paintings makes illegal copies of them.

forgery **forgeries**
NOUN **1** the crime of making false copies of something
2 an illegal false copy of something

forget **forgets, forgetting, forgot, forgotten**
VERB If you **forget** something, you do not remember it.
forgetful ADJECTIVE

forgive **forgives, forgiving, forgave, forgiven**
VERB If you **forgive** someone who has done something wrong, you stop being angry with them.

fork **forks**
NOUN **1** an instrument with prongs on the end of a handle, used for eating food or for digging earth
2 If there is a **fork** in a road or river, it divides into two or more parts.

forlorn
ADJECTIVE If you are **forlorn**, you are unhappy and lonely.

form **forms, forming, formed**
NOUN **1** a particular type or kind of something • *Running is a **form** of exercise.*
2 the shape or pattern of something • *Cut out your paper in the **form** of a star.*
3 a class in school
4 a piece of paper with questions and spaces where you fill in your answers
VERB **5** If you **form** something, you make it or give it a particular shape. • *Please all stand up and **form** a circle.*
6 If something **forms**, it develops or comes into existence. • *The puddles **formed** on the pavement after the rain.*

formal
ADJECTIVE **1** **Formal** speech, writing or behaviour is correct and serious, rather than relaxed and friendly. • *At the prizegiving everyone wore **formal** clothes.*
ANTONYM: informal
2 A **formal** action or event is an official one that follows accepted rules.
ANTONYM: informal
formally ADVERB

format **formats**
NOUN the way something is arranged and presented • *The **format** of the book is easy to follow.*

formation **formations**
NOUN **1** the start or creation of something
2 the pattern or shape of something

former
ADJECTIVE **1** happening or existing before now, or in the past • *The **former** tennis champion presented the trophy to the new champion.*
2 **Former** refers to the first of two things mentioned. • *Exams and coursework are both important, but the **former** must take priority this term.*
formerly ADVERB

formula **formulae** or **formulas**
NOUN a group of letters, numbers or symbols that stand for a mathematical or scientific rule

fort **forts**
NOUN a strong, fortified building built for defence

fortify **fortifies, fortifying, fortified**
VERB If someone **fortifies** a building, they make it stronger against attack.

fortnight **fortnights**
NOUN a period of two weeks

fortress **fortresses**
NOUN a very strong and well-protected castle or town

fortunate
ADJECTIVE lucky
fortunately ADVERB

fortune **fortunes**
NOUN **1** luck
2 a lot of money

forty
NOUN **Forty** is the number 40.
fortieth NOUN OR ADJECTIVE

forward **forwards**
ADVERB **1** If you move something **forward**, you move it towards the front.
NOUN **2** In a game like hockey or football, a **forward** is someone in an attacking position.

fossil **fossils**
NOUN the remains or impression of an animal or plant from a previous age, which has been preserved in rock
fossilize VERB

foster **fosters, fostering, fostered**
VERB If someone **fosters** a child, they look after the child for a period in their home, but do not become his or her legal parent.
foster child NOUN **foster home** NOUN
foster parent NOUN

fought
VERB the past tense of **fight**

foul **fouler, foulest; fouls**
ADJECTIVE **1** very unpleasant, especially because it is dirty or obscene • *There was a **foul** smell coming from the drains.*
NOUN **2** In sport, a **foul** is an action that breaks the rules.

found **founds, founding, founded**
VERB **1** the past tense and past participle of **find**
2 If someone **founds** an organization or company, they create it. • *He **founded** the charity ten years ago.*

foundation **foundations**
NOUN **1** the basic ideas on which something is based • *A good education is the **foundation** for a successful life.*
PLURAL NOUN **2** The **foundations** of a building are the layer of concrete or bricks below the ground on which it is built.
NOUN **3** the founding of something

fountain **fountains**
NOUN an ornamental structure in which a jet of water is forced into the air by a pump

fountain pen **fountain pens**
NOUN a pen that has a nib which is supplied with ink from a container inside the pen

four
NOUN **Four** is the number 4.
fourth NOUN OR ADJECTIVE

fourteen
NOUN **Fourteen** is the number 14.
fourteenth NOUN OR ADJECTIVE

fowl **fowls**
NOUN a bird, such as chicken or duck, that is kept or hunted for its meat or eggs

fox **foxes**
NOUN a wild mammal that looks like a dog and has reddish-brown fur and a thick tail

foyer **foyers**
Said "**foy**-ay" NOUN a large entrance hall just inside the main doors of a cinema, hotel or public building

fraction **fractions**
NOUN **1** In mathematics, a **fraction** is a part of a whole number.
2 a tiny proportion or amount of something

fracture **fractures, fracturing, fractured**
NOUN **1** a crack or break in something, especially a bone
VERB **2** If something **fractures**, or if you **fracture** it, it breaks. • *She **fractured** her arm while playing netball.*

fragile
ADJECTIVE easily broken or damaged
fragility NOUN

fragment **fragments**
NOUN a small piece or part of something • *There were **fragments** of glass on the floor after I dropped the vase.*
fragmentation NOUN
fragmented ADJECTIVE

fragrant
ADJECTIVE Something that is **fragrant** smells sweet or pleasant.

frail **frailer, frailest**
ADJECTIVE weak or fragile
frailty NOUN

frame **frames, framing, framed**
NOUN **1** the structure surrounding a door, window or picture
VERB **2** If you **frame** a picture, you make a frame for it.

framework **frameworks**
NOUN a structure that forms a support or frame for something • *wooden shelves on a steel **framework***

frantic
ADJECTIVE If you are **frantic**, you behave in a wild, desperate way because you are anxious or frightened.
frantically ADVERB

fraud **frauds**
NOUN the crime of getting money by deceit

fraught
ADJECTIVE **1** If a situation is **fraught**, it is full of potential problems or difficulties.
2 If someone is **fraught**, they are tense and upset.

frayed
ADJECTIVE If material is **frayed**, the edges are worn and ragged.

freak **freaks**
NOUN **1** A **freak** is someone whose appearance or behaviour is very unusual.
ADJECTIVE **2** A **freak** event is very unusual. • *We had a **freak** storm in the middle of the summer.*

freckle **freckles**
NOUN a small, light-brown spot on someone's skin, especially their face
freckled ADJECTIVE

free **freer, freest; frees, freeing, freed**
ADJECTIVE **1** If something is **free**, you can have it without paying for it.
2 Someone who is **free** is no longer a prisoner.
3 If someone is **free**, they are not busy. • *Are you **free** on Saturday afternoon?*
VERB **4** If you **free** someone or something that is trapped, you release them.

freedom
NOUN If you have the **freedom** to do something, you are free to do it.

free verse
NOUN poetry that does not use patterns of rhyme or rhythm

freeway **freeways**
NOUN In Australia, South Africa and the USA, a **freeway** is a road for fast-moving traffic.

freeze **freezes, freezing, froze, frozen**
VERB **1** When a liquid **freezes**, or when something **freezes** it, it becomes solid because it is very cold.
2 If you **freeze** food, you make it very cold to preserve it.
3 If you **freeze**, you suddenly stop moving because there is danger.
ADJECTIVE **4** You say you are **freezing** when you are very cold.

freezer **freezers**
NOUN a refrigerator in which you can store food for a long time at very low temperatures

freight
NOUN goods moved by lorries, ships or other transport

frenzy **frenzies**
NOUN If someone is in a **frenzy**, their behaviour is wild and uncontrolled.
frenzied ADJECTIVE

frequency **frequencies**
NOUN **1** The **frequency** of an event is how often it happens.
2 The **frequency** of a sound or radio wave is the rate at which it vibrates.

frequency table **frequency tables**
NOUN a chart where you write down how often something happens

frequent
ADJECTIVE If something happens at **frequent** intervals, it happens often.
frequently ADVERB

fresh **fresher, freshest**
ADJECTIVE **1** Something that is not old or

used. • *We put **fresh** towels out for the guests.*
2 Fresh food has been made or picked recently, and is not tinned or frozen.
3 Fresh water is water that is not salty. • *The water in a river or lake is **fresh** water.*

freshwater
ADJECTIVE A **freshwater** animal lives in a river, lake or pool and not in the sea.

fret **frets, fretting, fretted**
VERB **1** If you **fret** about something, you worry about it.
NOUN **2** The **frets** on a stringed instrument, such as a guitar, are the metal ridges across its neck.

friction
NOUN **1** the force that slows things down and can stop them from moving
2 Friction between people is disagreement and quarrels. • *There was a lot of **friction** between the two families.*

Friday **Fridays**
NOUN the sixth day of the week, coming between Thursday and Saturday
[from Old English *Frigedæg* meaning Freya's day, the Norse goddess of love]

fridge **fridges**
NOUN a short form of *refrigerator*

friend **friends**
NOUN someone you know well and like, but who is not related to you

friendly **friendlier, friendliest**
ADJECTIVE A **friendly** person is kind and pleasant to others.

friendship **friendships**
NOUN the state of being friends with someone • *Her **friendship** means a lot to me.*

fright
NOUN a sudden feeling of fear

frighten **frightens, frightening, frightened**
VERB If something or someone **frightens** you, they make you afraid.
frightened ADJECTIVE **frightening** ADJECTIVE

frill **frills**
NOUN a strip of material with a lot of folds in it, that is attached to something as decoration

fringe **fringes**
NOUN **1** the hair that hangs over a person's forehead • *She had a long **fringe** that almost covered her eyes.*
2 a decoration on clothes and other objects, consisting of a row of hanging threads • *There is a **fringe** along the bottom of the curtains.*
fringed ADJECTIVE

frivolous
ADJECTIVE Someone who is **frivolous** behaves in a silly or light-hearted way, especially when they should be serious or sensible.
frivolously ADVERB **frivolity** NOUN

frizzy **frizzier, frizziest**
ADJECTIVE **Frizzy** hair has tight, wiry curls.

frog **frogs**
NOUN a small, amphibious animal with long back legs

frolic **frolics, frolicking, frolicked**
VERB When children and other young animals **frolic**, they run around and play in a lively way. • *In the spring, the lambs **frolic** in the fields.*

from
PREPOSITION **1 From** tells you where someone or something started. • *The river flows **from** the north.*
2 If you take something **from** an amount, you reduce the amount by that much. • *If you take five **from** 20 you are left with 15.*
3 You use **from** to state the range of something. • *Lunchtime is **from** 12 o'clock to 1 o'clock.*

front **fronts**
NOUN **1** the part of something that faces forward • *a jacket with buttons down the **front***
ADJECTIVE **2** The **front** part of something is the part that is furthest forward. • *I like to sit in the **front** seats of the cinema.*
NOUN **3** In a war, the **front** is the place where two armies are fighting.
4 At the seaside, the **front** is the road or promenade that runs alongside the beach.

frontier **frontiers**
NOUN a border between two countries
• *Their passports were checked at the* ***frontier****.*

frost **frosts**
NOUN powdery, white ice that forms on the ground when the temperature outside falls below freezing

frosty **frostier, frostiest**
ADJECTIVE When it is **frosty**, the temperature outside falls below freezing and powdery, white ice forms on the ground.

froth **froths, frothing, frothed**
NOUN **1** a mass of small bubbles on the surface of a liquid
VERB **2** If a liquid **froths**, small bubbles appear on its surface.
frothy ADJECTIVE

frown **frowns, frowning, frowned**
VERB **1** If you **frown**, you move your eyebrows closer together and wrinkle your forehead, usually because you are annoyed, worried or puzzled.
NOUN **2** an expression on the face of someone who is frowning

froze
VERB the past tense of **freeze**

frozen
VERB **1** the past participle of **freeze**
ADJECTIVE **2** If you say you are **frozen**, you mean you have become very cold.

fruit **fruits**
NOUN the part of a plant that develops after the flower has been fertilized, that contains the seeds. Apples, oranges and bananas are all **fruit**.
[from Latin *fructus* meaning produce or benefit]

frustrate **frustrates, frustrating, frustrated**
VERB **1** If something **frustrates** you, it prevents you doing what you want and makes you upset.
2 If you **frustrate** something, such as a plan, you prevent it. • *They deliberately* ***frustrated*** *my attempts to do my homework.*
frustrated ADJECTIVE **frustrating** ADJECTIVE
frustration NOUN

fry **fries, frying, fried**
VERB When you **fry** food, you cook it in a pan containing hot fat.

fudge
NOUN a soft, brown sweet made from butter, milk and sugar

fuel **fuels**
NOUN a substance such as coal, gas, oil or wood that is burned to provide heat or power

fugitive **fugitives**
NOUN someone who is running away or hiding, especially from the police

fulfil **fulfils, fulfilling, fulfilled**
VERB **1** If you **fulfil** a promise, you keep it.
2 If something **fulfils** you, it gives you satisfaction.
fulfilling ADJECTIVE **fulfilment** NOUN

full **fuller, fullest**
ADJECTIVE **1** Something that is **full** contains as much as it is possible to hold. • *The bus was* ***full*** *so we had to wait for the next one.*
ANTONYM: empty
2 to the greatest possible extent • *The radio was playing at* ***full*** *volume.*
3 complete or whole • *I will tell you the* ***full*** *story later.*
ADVERB **4** completely or wholly • *Turn the taps* ***full*** *on.*
fullness NOUN **fully** ADVERB

full stop **full stops**
NOUN the punctuation mark (.) used at the end of a sentence and after an abbreviation or initial

A B C D E F G H I J K L M N O P Q R S T U V W X Y Z

full-time
ADJECTIVE If you have a **full-time** job, you work for the whole of each normal working week.

fumble **fumbles, fumbling, fumbled**
VERB If you **fumble**, you feel or handle something clumsily. • *I **fumbled** with the door handle because it was so dark.*

fume **fumes, fuming, fumed**
PLURAL NOUN **1** **Fumes** are unpleasant-smelling gases and smoke that are sometimes poisonous, and are produced by burning and by some chemicals.
VERB **2** If something **fumes**, it produces smoke or gas.
3 If you **fume**, you are very angry.

fun
NOUN **1** pleasant, enjoyable and light-hearted activity • *Let's have some **fun**!*
ADJECTIVE **2** If someone or something is **fun**, you enjoy being with them or you enjoy doing it. • *She is always **fun** to be with.*
PHRASE **3** If you **make fun** of someone or something, you tease them or make jokes about them.

function **functions, functioning, functioned**
VERB **1** If a thing **functions**, it works as it should.
NOUN **2** The **function** of someone or something is their purpose or the work they are supposed to do.
functional ADJECTIVE

fund **funds**
NOUN an amount of money that is collected for a particular purpose

fundamental
ADJECTIVE If something is **fundamental**, it is basic and necessary. • *You must understand the **fundamental** rules of the game before you can progress.*

funeral **funerals**
NOUN a ceremony for the burial or cremation of someone who has died

fungus **fungi** or **funguses**
NOUN an organism, such as a mushroom or mould, that does not have flowers or leaves
fungal ADJECTIVE

funnel **funnels**
NOUN **1** an open cone that narrows to a tube, and is used to pour substances into containers
2 a metal chimney on a ship or steam engine

funny **funnier, funniest**
ADJECTIVE **1** causing amusement or laughter • *He told us a **funny** story.*
SYNONYMS: amusing, comical, humorous
2 strange or puzzling • *We could hear a **funny** noise.*
SYNONYMS: odd, peculiar

fur
NOUN the thick hair that grows on the bodies of many animals • *Polar bears have white **fur**.*
furry ADJECTIVE

furious
ADJECTIVE extremely angry
furiously ADVERB

furnace **furnaces**
NOUN a very large, hot oven used for heating glass and melting metal

furnish **furnishes, furnishing, furnished**
VERB If you **furnish** a house or a room, you put furniture into it.

furniture
NOUN movable objects such as tables, chairs and wardrobes that you need inside a building • *bedroom **furniture***

furrow **furrows**
NOUN a shallow, straight channel dug into the earth by a plough

further **furthest**
ADJECTIVE OR ADVERB another word for *farther*
See **far**

furtive
ADJECTIVE secretive, sly and cautious
furtively ADVERB

fury
NOUN violent or extreme anger
[from Latin *furia* meaning madness]

fuse **fuses, fusing, fused**
NOUN **1** a safety device in an electrical plug or appliance, consisting of a piece of wire that melts to stop the electric current if a fault occurs
VERB **2** When an electrical appliance **fuses**, it stops working because the fuse has melted to protect it.

fuss **fusses, fussing, fussed**
NOUN **1** unnecessarily anxious or excited behaviour
VERB **2** If someone **fusses**, they behave with unnecessary anxiety and concern for unimportant things.

fussy **fussier, fussiest**
ADJECTIVE If you are **fussy**, you worry too much about unnecessary details.

future **futures**
NOUN **1** the period of time after the present
• *He is already making plans for his* ***future****.*
ADJECTIVE **2** relating to or occurring at a time after the present
PHRASE **3** **In future** means from now on.
• *Be more careful* ***in future****.*

fuzzy **fuzzier, fuzziest**
ADJECTIVE **1** soft and fluffy
2 If a picture is **fuzzy**, it is not clear.

Gg

gadget **gadgets**
NOUN a small mechanical device or tool

gain **gains, gaining, gained**
VERB **1** If you **gain** something, you get more of it or get something you didn't have before. • *She was pleased when she began to* ***gain*** *better marks.*
2 If a clock or watch **gains** time, it starts telling a later time than it is.
• *I think my watch has* ***gained*** *five minutes. It says five past one and the clock says one o'clock.*

gala **galas**
NOUN a special, public celebration or performance • *a swimming* ***gala***

galaxy **galaxies**
NOUN a huge group of stars that extends over millions of kilometres

Our galaxy, the Milky Way

gale **gales**
NOUN an extremely strong wind

gallant
ADJECTIVE brave and honourable
gallantly ADVERB **gallantry** NOUN

galleon **galleons**
NOUN a large Spanish sailing ship in the sixteenth and seventeenth centuries

a b c d e f g h i j k l m n o p q r s t u v w x y z

A B C D E F G H I J K L M N O P Q R S T U V W X Y Z

gallery **galleries**
NOUN a building where paintings and other works of art are shown

gallon **gallons**
NOUN a measure of liquid that is equal to eight pints or 4.55 litres

gallop **gallops, galloping, galloped**
VERB When a horse **gallops**, it runs very fast, so that during each stride all four feet are off the ground at the same time.

gallows
NOUN a framework on which criminals used to be hanged

gamble **gambles, gambling, gambled**
VERB When someone **gambles**, they bet money on the result of a contest or race.

game **games**
NOUN **1** an activity with a set of rules that is played by individuals or teams against each other
2 a term for wild birds and animals that are hunted for food or sport, such as pheasant or boar

gammon
NOUN cured meat from a pig, similar to bacon but usually in thicker and larger slices

gander **ganders**
NOUN a male goose

gang **gangs, ganging, ganged**
NOUN **1** a group of people who join together for some purpose, for example to commit a crime
VERB **2** INFORMAL If people **gang up** on you, they join together to oppose you. • *The children finally **ganged up** on the bully.*

gangster **gangsters**
NOUN a violent criminal who is a member of a gang

gangway **gangways**
NOUN **1** a space left between rows of seats, for example in a train or cinema, for people to walk through
2 a movable passenger bridge between a ship and the shore

gaol
NOUN OR VERB another spelling of **jail**

gap **gaps**
NOUN a space between two things or a hole in something solid • *He was just able to squeeze through the **gap** in the hedge.*

gape **gapes, gaping, gaped**
VERB **1** If you **gape**, you stare with your mouth wide open.
2 If something **gapes**, it is wide open.

garage **garages**
NOUN **1** a building in which you can keep a car
2 a place where cars are repaired or where petrol is sold

garbage
NOUN In American English, **garbage** is rubbish, especially waste from a kitchen.

garden **gardens**
NOUN an area of land next to a house, with plants, trees and grass

gardener **gardeners**
NOUN a person who looks after a garden as a job or as a hobby

gargle **gargles, gargling, gargled**
VERB When you **gargle**, you rinse the back of your throat by putting some liquid in your mouth and making a bubbling sound without swallowing the liquid.

gargoyle **gargoyles**
NOUN a stone carving below the roof of an old building, in the shape of an ugly person or animal

garlic
NOUN the small, white bulb of an onion-like plant that has a strong taste and smell and is used in cooking

garment **garments**
NOUN an item of clothing

gas **gases**
NOUN a substance that is not a liquid or a solid. Air is a mixture of **gases**. The bubbles in fizzy lemonade contain a **gas** called carbon dioxide.

gasp **gasps, gasping, gasped**
VERB If you **gasp**, you quickly draw in your breath through your mouth because you are surprised or in pain.

gate **gates**
NOUN a barrier that can be opened or shut and is used to close off the entrance to a field, garden or path

gateau **gateaux**
NOUN a rich, layered cake with cream in it [from French *gâteau* meaning cake]

gather **gathers, gathering, gathered**
VERB **1** If you **gather** things, you collect or pick them. • *I **gathered** some flowers from the garden.*
2 When people **gather**, they come together in a group. • *We **gathered** at my house before we went to the party.*
3 If you **gather** information, you learn it, often from hearing or reading about it. • *I **gather** you passed your exams.*

gathering **gatherings**
NOUN a meeting of people who gather together for a particular purpose

gauge **gauges, gauging, gauged**
VERB **1** If you **gauge** something, you estimate or work out how much of it there is or how much is required.
NOUN **2** an instrument used for measuring • *The fuel **gauge** shows that we need more petrol.*

gauze
NOUN a thin, cotton cloth, often used for bandages

gave
VERB the past tense of **give**

gaze **gazes, gazing, gazed**
VERB If you **gaze** at something, you look steadily at it for a long time. • *We **gazed** up at the stars.*

gazelle **gazelles**
NOUN a small antelope found in Africa and Asia

gear **gears**
NOUN **1** The **gears** in a car or on a bicycle are a set of cogs that work together to send power to the wheels.
2 the clothes or equipment that you need for an activity • *climbing **gear***

geese
PLURAL NOUN the plural of **goose**

gel **gels**
NOUN a smooth, soft, jelly-like substance • *hair **gel***

gem **gems**
NOUN a jewel or precious stone

gender **genders**
NOUN The **gender** of a person or animal is whether they are male or female.

gene **genes**
Said "**jeen**" NOUN one of the parts of the chromosomes found inside the cells of an organism. Offspring inherit **genes** from their parents.
genetic ADJECTIVE **genetically** ADVERB

general **generals**
ADJECTIVE **1** relating to the whole of something or to most things in a group • *There has been a **general** improvement in your work.*
2 including or involving a range of different things • *There was a **general** knowledge quiz at the end of term.*
NOUN **3** an army officer of very high rank
PHRASE **4 In general** is used to indicate that a statement is true in most cases, or that it applies to most people or things. • ***In general**, people take their holidays over the summer.*
generally ADVERB

general election **general elections**
NOUN an election in which people vote for who they want to represent them in the national parliament

generate **generates, generating, generated**
VERB If someone or something **generates** something else, they produce or create it.

• *They built a new power station to **generate** more electricity.*

generation **generations**
NOUN **1** all the people of a similar age • *the younger **generation***
2 the length of time that it takes for children to grow up and have children of their own • *The next **generation** will see a lot more changes.*

generator **generators**
NOUN a machine that produces electricity from another form of energy, such as wind or water power

generous
ADJECTIVE A **generous** person gives or shares what they have, especially time or money.
generously ADVERB

genie **genies**
NOUN a magical being that obeys the wishes of the person who controls it • *Aladdin rubbed his magic lamp and the **genie** appeared.*
[from Arabic *jinni* meaning demon]

genitals
PLURAL NOUN The **genitals** are the reproductive organs. The technical name is **genitalia**.

genius **geniuses**
NOUN a highly intelligent, creative or talented person • *a mathematical **genius***

gentle **gentler, gentlest**
ADJECTIVE Someone or something that is **gentle** is mild and calm. • *A **gentle** breeze blew across the field.*
ANTONYMS: violent, rough

gentleman **gentlemen**
NOUN **1** a man who is polite and well-educated
2 a polite way of referring to any man

genuine
ADJECTIVE real and exactly what it appears to be • *It's a **genuine** diamond.*

geography
NOUN the study of the physical features of the earth, its countries, climate and people
geographical ADJECTIVE

geology
NOUN the study of the earth's structure, especially the layers of rock and soil that make up the surface of the earth
geological ADJECTIVE **geologist** NOUN

geometry
NOUN that part of mathematics that deals with lines, angles, curves and shapes

geranium **geraniums**
NOUN a plant with bright red, pink or white flowers

gerbil **gerbils**
NOUN a small rodent with long back legs that is often kept as a pet

germ **germs**
NOUN a very small organism that can cause disease

germinate **germinates, germinating, germinated**
VERB When a seed **germinates**, it starts to grow.
germination NOUN

gesture **gestures, gesturing, gestured**
NOUN **1** a movement of your hands or head that suggests a message or feeling • *She made an angry **gesture** with her fist.*
VERB **2** If you **gesture**, you move your hands or head in order to communicate a message or feeling. • *She **gestured** to me to come over.*

get **gets, getting, got**
VERB **1** If you **get** something, you fetch it or receive it. • *He **got** his report on the last day of term.*
2 If you **get** a bus, you travel on it.
3 If you **get** a meal ready, you prepare it.
4 If you **get** someone to do something for you, you persuade them to do it.
5 If you **get** a joke, you understand it.
6 If you **get** ill, you become ill.
7 If you **get** to a place, you arrive there.

geyser **geysers**
NOUN a natural spring out of which hot water and steam gush in spurts. There are many geysers in Iceland and New Zealand.
[from Old Norse *geysa* meaning to gush]

ghastly **ghastlier, ghastliest**
ADJECTIVE extremely horrible and unpleasant

ghost **ghosts**
NOUN the spirit of a dead person that appears to someone who is still alive • *She believes she saw a **ghost** in the old house.*

giant **giants**
NOUN **1** a huge person in a myth or legend
ADJECTIVE **2** much larger than other similar things • *There was a **giant** Christmas tree in the town centre.*

giddy **giddier, giddiest**
ADJECTIVE If you feel **giddy**, you feel unsteady on your feet, usually because you are ill.
giddily ADVERB **giddiness** NOUN

gift **gifts**
NOUN **1** something that you give someone as a present
2 a natural skill or ability • *He has a **gift** for acting.*

gifted
ADJECTIVE If you are **gifted**, you have special talents. • *She is a **gifted** musician.*

gigantic
ADJECTIVE extremely large • *She was keen to ride on the **gigantic** big wheel.*
SYNONYMS: huge, massive, enormous

giggle **giggles, giggling, giggled**
VERB If you **giggle**, you laugh in a nervous, quiet way.

gill **gills**
NOUN the organs on the sides of a fish that it uses for breathing

gimmick **gimmicks**
NOUN something that is not really necessary, but is unusual and used to attract interest • *The new shop needed a **gimmick** to attract customers.*
gimmicky ADJECTIVE

gin
NOUN a strong, colourless alcoholic drink made from grain and juniper berries

ginger
NOUN **1** a plant root with a hot, spicy flavour, used in cooking
ADJECTIVE **2** bright orangey-brown

Gipsy
NOUN another spelling of **Gypsy**

giraffe **giraffes**
NOUN a large African mammal with a very long neck, long legs and yellowish skin with dark patches

girder **girders**
NOUN a strong metal or concrete beam used in building

girl **girls**
NOUN a female child

girlfriend **girlfriends**
NOUN Someone's **girlfriend** is the woman or girl with whom they are having a romantic relationship.

give **gives, giving, gave, given**
VERB **1** If you **give** something to someone, you hand it to them or provide it for them.

a b c d e f g h i j k l m n o p q r s t u v w x y z

A B C D E F G H I J K L M N O P Q R S T U V W X Y Z

• *Please would you **give** me back the book I lent to you?*
2 If you **give** a party, you host it.
3 Give can be used to express an action.
• ***give** a speech* • ***give** the door a push*
PHRASE **4** If something **gives way**, it collapses.

glacier **glaciers**
NOUN a huge, frozen river of slow-moving ice

glad **gladder, gladdest**
ADJECTIVE happy or pleased

gladiator **gladiators**
NOUN In ancient Rome, **gladiators** were slaves trained to fight in arenas to provide entertainment.

glance **glances, glancing, glanced**
VERB **1** If you **glance** at something, you look at it quickly. • *He **glanced** at his watch.*
NOUN **2** a quick look

gland **glands**
NOUN an organ in your body which produces and releases special chemicals. Some **glands** help to get rid of waste products from your body. Sweat **glands** are small **glands** in your skin that produce sweat.
glandular ADJECTIVE

glare **glares, glaring, glared**
VERB **1** If you **glare** at someone, you look at them angrily.
NOUN **2** a hard, angry look

glass **glasses**
NOUN **1** the hard, transparent substance that windows and bottles are made of
2 a container made of glass, from which you can drink • *a **glass** of water*

glasses
PLURAL NOUN two lenses in a frame, that some people wear over their eyes to improve their eyesight

glaze **glazes, glazing, glazed**
NOUN **1** a smooth, shiny surface on pottery or food
VERB **2** If you **glaze** pottery or food, you cover it with a glaze.
3 If someone **glazes** a window, they fit a sheet of glass into the window frame.

gleam **gleams, gleaming, gleamed**
VERB **1** If something **gleams**, it shines and reflects light. • *He polished the silver teapot until it **gleamed**.*
NOUN **2** a pale, shining light • *There was a **gleam** of light at the end of the dark tunnel.*

glide **glides, gliding, glided**
VERB **1** If you **glide**, you move smoothly.
• *The skater **glided** across the ice.*
2 When birds or aeroplanes **glide**, they float on air currents.

glider **gliders**
NOUN an aeroplane without an engine, that flies by floating on air currents

glimmer **glimmers, glimmering, glimmered**
NOUN **1** a faint, unsteady light • *There was a **glimmer** of light ahead.*
VERB **2** If something **glimmers**, it produces a faint, unsteady light.

glimpse **glimpses, glimpsing, glimpsed**
NOUN **1** a brief sight of something
VERB **2** If you **glimpse** something, you see it briefly. • *They **glimpsed** a rare bird through the trees.*

glisten **glistens, glistening, glistened**
VERB If something **glistens**, it shines or sparkles. • *The frost **glistened** in the moonlight.*

glitter **glitters, glittering, glittered**
VERB **1** If something **glitters**, it shines in a sparkling way. • *The diamond **glittered** in the sunlight.*
NOUN **2** sparkling light

gloat **gloats, gloating, gloated**
VERB If you **gloat**, you cruelly show how pleased you are about your own success or someone else's failure.

global
ADJECTIVE to do with the whole world
• *Pollution of the atmosphere is a **global** concern.*

global warming
NOUN an increase in the world's overall temperature, believed to be caused by a thinning of the ozone layer

globe **globes**
NOUN **1** the earth, the planet you live on
2 a sphere fixed to a stand, with a map of the world on it
global ADJECTIVE

gloom
NOUN **1** darkness or dimness • *I could not see in the **gloom** of the forest.*
2 a feeling of unhappiness or despair

gloomy **gloomier, gloomiest**
ADJECTIVE **1** Something that is **gloomy** is dull and dark, and sometimes depressing. • *It was a **gloomy** winter day.*
2 If you are **gloomy**, you are unhappy.
gloomily ADVERB

glorious
ADJECTIVE beautiful and splendid • *We were lucky to have **glorious** weather while we were on holiday.*

glory **glories**
NOUN something considered splendid or admirable • *They enjoyed the **glory** of their son's success.*

gloss
NOUN a bright shine on a smooth surface

glossary **glossaries**
NOUN a list of explanations of specialist words, usually found at the back of a book

glossy **glossier, glossiest**
ADJECTIVE smooth and shiny • *This new shampoo makes my hair **glossy**.*

glove **gloves**
NOUN **Gloves** cover your hands and keep them warm or give them protection.

glow **glows, glowing, glowed**
VERB **1** If something **glows**, it shines with a dull, steady light.
NOUN **2** a dull, steady light
3 a strong feeling of pleasure or happiness

glucose
NOUN a natural sugar found in plants and produced in the bodies of animals, including humans, to give them energy

glue **glues, gluing** or **glueing, glued**
NOUN **1** a substance used for sticking things together
VERB **2** If you **glue** one object to another, you stick them together using glue. • *She **glued** the picture into her book.*

glutton **gluttons**
NOUN a person who eats too much
gluttony NOUN

gnarled
ADJECTIVE If something is **gnarled** it is old, twisted and rough. • *There is a big, **gnarled** tree in the churchyard.*

gnash **gnashes, gnashing, gnashed**
VERB If you **gnash** your teeth, you make a noise with them by grinding them together because you are angry or upset.

gnat **gnats**
NOUN a tiny flying insect that bites

gnaw **gnaws, gnawing, gnawed**
VERB If someone or something **gnaws** at something, they chew and bite at it repeatedly. • *The hamster **gnawed** at the bars of its cage.*

gnome **gnomes**
NOUN a tiny old man in fairy stories, who usually lives underground

go **goes, going, went, gone**
VERB **1** If you **go** somewhere, you walk, move or travel there.
2 If something **goes** well, it is a success.
3 If you **go**, you start to move. • *When you hear the whistle, **go** as fast as you can.*
4 If something **goes** somewhere, it leads there. • *This road **goes** to the centre of town.*
5 If something **goes**, it works properly. • *My watch doesn't **go** any more.*
6 become • *This fruit has **gone** bad.*

a b c d e f g h i j k l m n o p q r s t u v w x y z

NOUN **7** an attempt or a turn at doing something
VERB **8** disappear • *The mist has **gone**.*
9 If you are **going** to do something, you will do it.

go down
VERB **1** If you **go down** with an illness, you catch it.
2 If something **goes down** well, people like it. If it **goes down** badly, they do not like it.

go off
VERB **1** If you **go off** someone or something, you stop liking them.
2 If a bomb **goes off**, it explodes.
3 If food **goes off**, it becomes unsafe and has begun to decompose.

go on
VERB **1** If you **go on** doing something, you continue to do it.
2 If you **go on** about something, you keep talking about it in a rather boring way.
3 If something is **going on**, it is happening.

go through
VERB If you **go through** an unpleasant event, you experience it.

goal **goals**
NOUN **1** In games like football and hockey, the **goal** is the space into which the players try to get the ball to score a point.

2 In games like football and hockey, if a player scores a **goal**, they get the ball into the **goal**.
3 something that you hope to achieve • *Our **goal** is to raise as much money as possible for charity.*

goat **goats**
NOUN an animal similar to a sheep, with shaggy hair, a beard and horns

gobble **gobbles, gobbling, gobbled**
VERB **1** If you **gobble** food, you eat it very quickly.
2 When a turkey **gobbles**, it makes a loud gurgling sound.

goblet **goblets**
NOUN a kind of drinking cup or glass

goblin **goblins**
NOUN a small, ugly and mischievous creature found in fairy stories

god **gods**
PROPER NOUN **1** God is the being worshipped by Christians, Jews and Muslims as the creator and ruler of the world.
NOUN **2** any of the beings that are believed in many religions to have power over an aspect of the world • *Mars was the Roman **god** of war.*

goddess **goddesses**
NOUN a female god

godparent **godparents**
NOUN someone who agrees, at a child's christening, to be responsible for their religious upbringing

goggles
PLURAL NOUN special glasses that fit closely round your eyes to protect them • *I usually wear **goggles** when I go swimming.*

go-kart **go-karts**
NOUN a small motorized vehicle that can be raced

gold
NOUN **1** a valuable, yellow-coloured metal, used for making jewellery and as an international currency
ADJECTIVE **2** made of gold • *a **gold** necklace*

golden
ADJECTIVE gold in colour or made of gold

goldfish
NOUN a small, orange fish, often kept as a pet in a bowl or pond

golf
NOUN a game in which players use special clubs to hit a ball into holes that are spread out over a large area of grassy land

gondola **gondolas**
NOUN a long, narrow boat used on the canals in Venice. **Gondolas** are propelled by using a long pole.

gone
VERB the past participle of **go**

gong **gongs**
NOUN a flat, circular piece of metal that is hit with a hammer to make a loud sound, often as a signal for something • *They sounded the **gong** for dinner.*

good **better, best**
ADJECTIVE **1** pleasant or enjoyable • *The weather turned out to be **good**.*
2 of a high quality • *The food was very **good**.*
3 sensible or valid • *The rain gives me a **good** reason for staying at home.*
4 well-behaved • *Have the children been **good**?*
PHRASE **5** **For good** means forever.

goodbye
GREETING You say **goodbye** when you are leaving someone or ending a telephone conversation.

goodness
NOUN the quality of being good and kind

good night
GREETING You say **good night** to someone when you are leaving them at night.

goods
PLURAL NOUN things that are bought and sold in a shop or warehouse

google **googles, googling, googled**
VERB If you **google** a person or thing, you search the internet for information about them.

goose **geese**
NOUN a fairly large bird, with webbed feet and a long neck

gooseberry **gooseberries**
NOUN a round, green berry that grows on a bush and has a sharp taste

gore **gores, goring, gored**
NOUN **1** the blood from a wound
VERB **2** If an animal **gores** someone, it wounds them by sticking a horn or tusk into them.

gorge **gorges, gorging, gorged**
NOUN **1** a deep, narrow valley
VERB **2** If you **gorge** yourself, you eat a lot of food greedily.

gorgeous
ADJECTIVE extremely pleasant or attractive
• *a **gorgeous** dress*

gorilla **gorillas**
NOUN a very strong, large ape, that lives in family groups

gory **gorier, goriest**
ADJECTIVE involving a lot of blood and violence • *a **gory** film*

gosling **goslings**
NOUN a young goose

gospel **gospels**
NOUN one of the four books in the New Testament that describe the life and teachings of Jesus Christ

gossip **gossips, gossiping, gossiped**
NOUN **1** informal conversation, often about people's private affairs
VERB **2** If you **gossip**, you talk informally with someone, especially about other people.

got
VERB the past tense of **get**

gouge **gouges, gouging, gouged**
VERB If you **gouge** something out, you scoop it out forcefully with a pointed object. • *She **gouged** a hole in the apple with a knife.*

govern **governs, governing, governed**
VERB When someone **governs** something, they rule or control it, especially a country or state.

A B C D E F G H I J K L M N O P Q R S T U V W X Y Z

government **governments**
NOUN The **government** is the group of people who officially control a country.

There is an *n* before the *m* in *government.*

governor **governors**
NOUN **1** someone who controls or helps to run a state or organization
2 In Australia, New Zealand and other commonwealth countries the **Governor** represents the British King or Queen.

GP **GPs**
NOUN an abbreviation of *general practitioner*. A **GP** is a doctor who treats all kinds of illnesses, and sends people to a specialist if necessary.

grab **grabs, grabbing, grabbed**
VERB If you **grab** something, you take it or pick it up quickly and roughly. • *He **grabbed** a sandwich before running for the bus.*

grace **graces**
NOUN **1** an elegant and attractive way of moving
2 a short prayer before or after a meal
3 a pleasant and kind way of behaving

graceful
ADJECTIVE If you are **graceful**, you move in a smooth and elegant way.
gracefully ADVERB

gracious
ADJECTIVE kind, polite and pleasant • *He always acts in a **gracious** and thoughtful manner.*
graciously ADVERB

grade **grades, grading, graded**
VERB **1** If someone **grades** things, they judge them according to their quality.
NOUN **2** the mark that you get in an exam

gradient **gradients**
NOUN a slope or the steepness of a slope • *The **gradient** of this hill means it will be difficult to climb.*

gradual
ADJECTIVE happening or changing slowly over a long period of time • *Her spelling showed **gradual** improvement.*
gradually ADVERB

graduate **graduates**
NOUN someone who has a degree from a university or college

graffiti
NOUN slogans or drawings scribbled on walls

grain **grains**
NOUN **1** a cereal plant, such as wheat, that is grown and harvested for food
2 a seed from a cereal plant such as wheat or rice
3 a tiny, hard particle of something • *I have got **grains** of sand in my shoes from walking on the beach.*
4 the natural pattern of lines in a piece of wood, made by the fibres in it

gram **grams**
NOUN a unit of mass and weight (g). There are one thousand **grams** in a kilogram (kg).

grammar
NOUN the rules of a language that state how words can be combined to form sentences

grand **grander, grandest**
ADJECTIVE splendid or impressive

grandad **grandads**
NOUN INFORMAL grandfather

grandchild **grandchildren**
NOUN Someone's **grandchildren** are the children of their son or daughter.

granddaughter **granddaughters**
NOUN Someone's **granddaughter** is the daughter of their son or daughter.

grandfather **grandfathers**
NOUN Your **grandfather** is your father's father or your mother's father.

grandmother **grandmothers**
NOUN Your **grandmother** is your father's mother or your mother's mother.

grandparent **grandparents**
NOUN Your **grandparents** are the parents of your father or mother.

grandson **grandsons**
NOUN Someone's **grandson** is the son of their son or daughter.

granite
NOUN a very strong, hard rock often used in building

granny **grannies**
NOUN INFORMAL grandmother

grant **grants, granting, granted**
NOUN **1** an amount of money that an official body gives to someone for a particular purpose • *He was given a* ***grant*** *to go to university.*
VERB **2** If you **grant** something to someone, you allow them to have it. • *I will* ***grant*** *you a wish.*

grape **grapes**
NOUN a small, green or purple fruit that grows in bunches on vines. **Grapes** are eaten raw or used to make wine.

grapefruit **grapefruits**
NOUN a large, round, yellow citrus fruit

graph **graphs**
NOUN a diagram that gives information about how two sets of numbers and measurements are related

Block graph of class 5 test marks

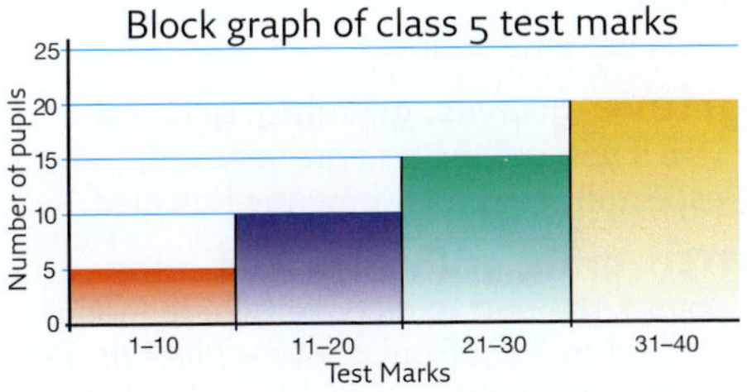

Line graph of seed growth

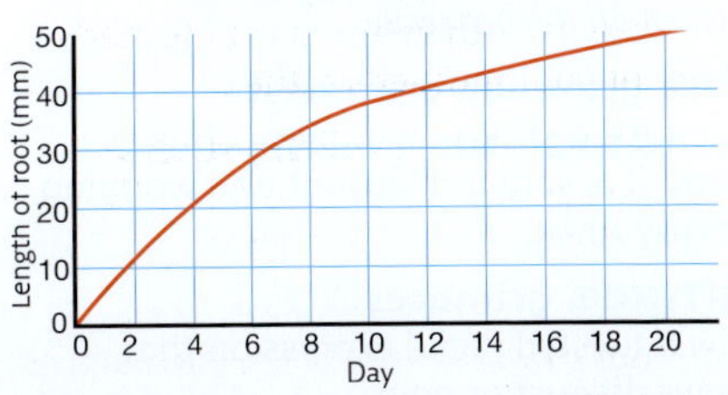

graphic **graphics**
ADJECTIVE **1** A **graphic** description is very detailed and clear.
PLURAL NOUN **2** **Graphics** are drawings, designs and diagrams. • *computer* ***graphics***

grasp **grasps, grasping, grasped**
VERB **1** If you **grasp** something, you hold it firmly. • *He* ***grasped*** *both my hands.*
2 If you **grasp** an idea, you understand it. • *She finally* ***grasped*** *the answer.*

grass **grasses**
NOUN the common green plant that grows on lawns and in parks

grasshopper **grasshoppers**
NOUN an insect with long back legs that it uses for jumping and making a high-pitched sound

grate **grates, grating, grated**
VERB **1** If you **grate** food, you shred it into small pieces by rubbing it against a tool called a grater.
NOUN **2** a framework of metal bars in a fireplace for holding coal or wood • *A wood fire burned in the* ***grate***.

grateful
ADJECTIVE If you are **grateful** for something, you feel thankful for it. • *I'm* ***grateful*** *to you for your help.*
SYNONYM: appreciative
gratefully ADVERB

gratitude
NOUN If you show **gratitude** to someone for something, you are thankful.
SYNONYMS: thankfulness, appreciation

grave **graves; graver, gravest**
NOUN **1** a place where a dead person is buried
ADJECTIVE **2** FORMAL very serious • *We are in* ***grave*** *danger.*

gravel
NOUN small stones used for making roads and paths

graveyard **graveyards**
NOUN a place where people are buried, usually in a churchyard

A B C D E F G H I J K L M N O P Q R S T U V W X Y Z

gravity
NOUN the force that pulls things down towards the earth

gravy
NOUN a brown sauce made from meat juices

graze **grazes, grazing, grazed**
VERB **1** When animals **graze**, they eat grass that is growing. • *The cows **grazed** in the field.*
2 If something **grazes** a part of your body, it scrapes against it, injuring you slightly.
NOUN **3** a slight injury caused by something scraping against your skin

grease **greases, greasing, greased**
NOUN **1** a substance used for oiling machines
2 animal fat used in cooking
VERB **3** If you **grease** something, you put grease on it. • *Lightly **grease** a baking tray.*

great **greater, greatest**
ADJECTIVE **1** very large in size, amount or degree • *She had **great** difficulty in staying awake.*
2 very important • *a **great** artist*
3 very good • *That's a **great** idea.*

greedy **greedier, greediest**
ADJECTIVE Someone who is **greedy** wants more of something than is necessary or fair.
greedily ADVERB

green **greener, greenest; greens**
ADJECTIVE OR NOUN **1** a colour between yellow and blue on the spectrum. Grass and leaves are usually **green**.
NOUN **2** a smooth, flat area of grass • *We played cricket on the village **green**.*

greengrocer **greengrocers**
NOUN a shopkeeper who sells fruit and vegetables

greenhouse **greenhouses**
NOUN a glass building in which people grow plants that need to be kept warm

greenhouse effect
NOUN the gradual increase in the temperature of the earth's atmosphere because the heat absorbed from the sun is not able to escape

greet **greets, greeting, greeted**
VERB If you **greet** someone, you say something friendly and welcoming to them when you meet them.

greeting **greetings**
NOUN the words or actions that you use when you meet someone

grenade **grenades**
NOUN a small bomb that can be thrown by hand
[from Spanish *granada* meaning pomegranate, which is a similar shape to a grenade]

grew
VERB the past tense of **grow**

grey **greyer, greyest**
ADJECTIVE OR NOUN the colour of ashes or of clouds on a rainy day

grid **grids**
NOUN a pattern of lines crossing each other to form squares

grief
NOUN extreme sadness

grieve **grieves, grieving, grieved**
VERB If you **grieve** you are very sad, especially because someone has died.

grill **grills, grilling, grilled**
NOUN **1** the part of a cooker where food is cooked by heat from above • *Place the fish under a hot **grill**.*
VERB **2** If you **grill** food, you cook it under or over direct heat. • *We **grilled** the chicken on the barbecue.*

grim **grimmer, grimmest**
ADJECTIVE If a situation or piece of news is **grim**, it is very unpleasant and worrying.
grimly ADVERB

grimace **grimaces**
NOUN a twisted facial expression that shows disgust or pain

grime
NOUN thick dirt that gathers on the surface of something
grimy ADJECTIVE

grin **grins, grinning, grinned**
VERB **1** If you **grin**, you have a broad smile.
NOUN **2** a broad smile

grind **grinds, grinding, ground**
VERB **1** If you **grind** something, you crush it into a fine powder. • *He **ground** the mud into the carpet.*
2 If you **grind** your teeth, you rub your upper and lower teeth together.
PHRASE **3** If something **grinds to a halt**, it slows down and stops.

grip **grips, gripping, gripped; grips**
VERB **1** If you **grip** something, you hold it firmly. • *He **gripped** his mother's hand tightly.*
NOUN **2** a handle on a bat or racket • *The **grip** on his tennis racket needed repairing.*

gristle
NOUN the tough, rubbery part of meat that is difficult to eat

groan **groans, groaning, groaned**
VERB **1** If you **groan**, you make a long, low sound of pain, unhappiness or disapproval.
NOUN **2** the sound you make when you groan

grocer **grocers**
NOUN a person who runs a shop that sells all kinds of food and household supplies

groceries
PLURAL NOUN the goods that you buy in a grocer's shop

groove **grooves**
NOUN a deep line cut into a surface
grooved ADJECTIVE

grope **gropes, groping, groped**
VERB If you **grope** for something, you feel for it with your hands because you cannot see it.

gross **grosser, grossest**
ADJECTIVE **1** extremely bad • *I made a **gross** error on my exam paper.*
2 Gross language or behaviour is very rude.
3 The **gross** amount of something is its total, without anything taken away. For example, the **gross** weight of something is the total weight, including the weight of its container.
4 unpleasantly fat or ugly

grotesque
ADJECTIVE **1** exaggerated and absurd
2 very strange and ugly
grotesquely ADVERB

grotto **grottoes** or **grottos**
NOUN a small cave that people visit because it is attractive

ground **grounds**
NOUN **1** the surface of the land • *They sat on the **ground**.*
2 an area of land, especially land that is used for a particular purpose • *a football **ground***
PLURAL NOUN **3** The **grounds** of a large building are the garden or area of land that surrounds it. • *We camped in the **grounds** of the stately home.*
4 FORMAL The **grounds** for something are the reason for it. • *I had **grounds** to believe that he was telling the truth.*
VERB **5** the past tense and past participle of *grind*

group **groups, grouping, grouped**
NOUN **1** a number of things or people that are linked in some way • *a small **group** of friends*
VERB **2** When things or people **group** together, they are linked in some way. • *We **grouped** together for the school photograph.*

grovel **grovels, grovelling, grovelled**
VERB If you **grovel**, you behave in an unpleasantly humble way towards someone you think is important.
[from Middle English *on grufe* meaning lying on your belly]

grow **grows, growing, grew, grown**
VERB **1** When someone or something **grows**, it gets bigger or increases. • *Children **grow** at different rates.*
2 When people **grow** plants, they plant them and look after them.

3 You use **grow** to say that someone or something gradually changes into a different state. • *He's **growing** old.*

grow up
VERB When a child **grows up**, they become an adult.

growl **growls, growling, growled**
VERB **1** When an animal **growls**, it makes a low rumbling sound, usually because it is angry.
NOUN **2** the sound an animal makes when it growls

grown-up **grown-ups**
NOUN an adult

growth
NOUN The process by which something develops to its full size.

grub **grubs**
NOUN **1** a worm-like creature that is the young of some insects, after it has hatched but before it becomes an adult
2 INFORMAL food

grubby **grubbier, grubbiest**
ADJECTIVE rather dirty • *That shirt looks a bit **grubby**.*

grudge **grudges**
NOUN If you have a **grudge** against someone, you resent them because they have harmed or upset you in the past.

gruelling
ADJECTIVE difficult and exhausting • *It was a long and **gruelling** race.*

gruesome
ADJECTIVE shocking and horrible • *The film was unsuitable for the children because it was so **gruesome**.*

gruff **gruffer, gruffest**
ADJECTIVE If someone's voice is **gruff**, it sounds rough and unfriendly.
gruffly ADVERB

grumble **grumbles, grumbling, grumbled**
VERB **1** If you **grumble**, you complain in a bad-tempered way.
NOUN **2** a bad-tempered complaint

grumpy **grumpier, grumpiest**
ADJECTIVE bad-tempered and fed-up • *She is often **grumpy** in the morning.*
grumpily ADVERB

grunt **grunts, grunting, grunted**
VERB **1** If a person or a pig **grunts**, they make a short, low, gruff sound.
NOUN **2** the sound a person or a pig makes when they grunt

guarantee **guarantees, guaranteeing, guaranteed**
NOUN **1** a promise by a company to do something, especially to replace or repair a product free of charge within a given time period if it develops a fault • *This television has a five-year **guarantee**.*
VERB **2** If something or someone **guarantees** something, they promise that it will happen. • *I **guarantee** that after all your hard work the day will be a success.*

guard **guards, guarding, guarded**
VERB **1** If you **guard** a person or object, you watch them carefully, either to protect them or to stop them from escaping.
NOUN **2** a person whose job is to guard a person, object or place

guardian **guardians**
NOUN someone who has been legally appointed to look after a child, but is not the child's parent

guerrilla **guerrillas**; also spelt **guerilla**
NOUN a member of a small, unofficial army fighting an official army

guess **guesses, guessing, guessed**
VERB **1** If you **guess** something, you form an opinion about it without knowing all the relevant facts. • *She **guessed** that he was probably older than her.*
NOUN **2** an attempt to give an answer or opinion about something without knowing all the relevant facts • *If you don't know the answer, have a **guess**.*

guest **guests**
NOUN someone who has been invited to stay at your home or attend an event

guide **guides, guiding, guided**
NOUN **1** someone who shows you round places, or leads the way through difficult country
VERB **2** If you **guide** someone somewhere, you lead them there.

guidebook **guidebooks**
NOUN a book that gives information about a place

guillotine **guillotines**
NOUN **1** In the past, the **guillotine** was a machine used for beheading people, especially in France.
2 a piece of equipment with a long, sharp blade, used for cutting paper [named after Joseph-Ignace *Guillotin*, who first recommended the guillotine as a way of executing people]

guilt
NOUN **1** the unhappy feeling of having done something wrong
2 Someone's **guilt** is the fact that they have done something wrong. • *After hearing the evidence, the jury felt that his **guilt** was clear.*

guilty **guiltier, guiltiest**
ADJECTIVE If you are **guilty** of doing something wrong, you did it.
guiltily ADVERB

guinea pig **guinea pigs**
NOUN **1** a small, furry mammal without a tail, often kept as a pet
2 a person used to try something out • *You will be a **guinea pig** in this experiment.*

guitar **guitars**
NOUN a musical instrument with six strings and a long neck

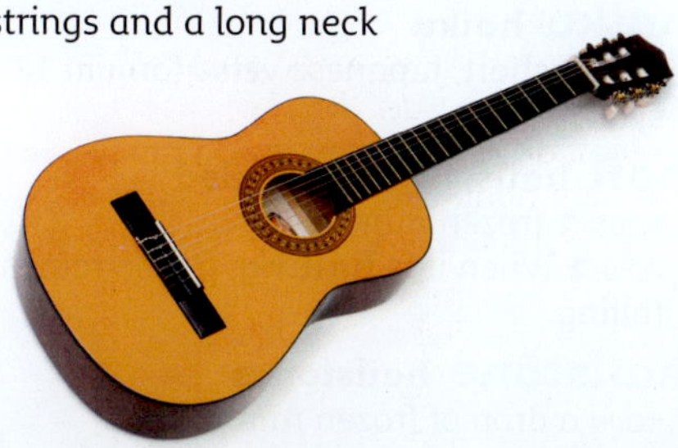

gulf **gulfs**
NOUN a very large bay

gull **gulls**
NOUN a sea bird with long wings, white and grey or black feathers, and webbed feet

gullible
ADJECTIVE If someone is **gullible**, they are easily tricked.

gulp **gulps, gulping, gulped**
VERB **1** If you **gulp** food or drink, you swallow large quantities of it quickly and noisily.
NOUN **2** a large quantity of food or drink swallowed quickly and noisily

gum **gums**
NOUN **1** Your **gums** are the firm flesh in which your teeth are set.
2 a soft, flavoured substance that people chew but do not swallow
3 glue

gumboot **gumboots**
NOUN a wellington boot

gumtree **gumtrees**
NOUN a eucalyptus or other tree that produces gum

gun **guns**
NOUN a weapon that fires bullets or shells

gunpowder
NOUN a powder that explodes when it is lit. It is used for making things such as fireworks.

gurdwara **gurdwaras**
NOUN a Sikh place of worship

gust **gusts**
NOUN a sudden rush of wind • *A **gust** of wind blew his hat off.*

gutter **gutters**
NOUN the edge of a road next to the pavement, where rain collects and flows away

gym **gyms**
NOUN a hall or room for sports and exercise. It is short for *gymnasium*.

A
B
C
D
E
F
G
H
I
J
K
L
M
N
O
P
Q
R
S
T
U
V
W
X
Y
Z

gymkhana gymkhanas
Said "jim-**kah**-na" NOUN a competition in which people take part in horse-riding contests

gymnasium gymnasiums
NOUN a room with special equipment for physical exercises

gymnastics
NOUN physical exercises, especially ones using equipment such as bars and ropes

Gypsy Gypsies; also spelt **Gipsy**
NOUN a member of an ethnic group scattered across most countries of Europe, the Middle East and the Americas. They migrated from north-west India in the 9th century and still have a nomadic lifestyle, although some are settled on sites and in houses. The **Gypsy** language is Romani.
[from *Egyptian* because in the 16th century they were thought to have come from Egypt]

Hh

habit habits
NOUN something that you do often or regularly

habitat habitats
NOUN the natural home of a plant or animal

hack hacks, hacking, hacked
VERB If you **hack** at something, you cut it using rough strokes.

had
VERB the past participle of **have**

haddock
NOUN an edible sea fish

hadn't
VERB a contraction of *had not*

haggard
ADJECTIVE A person who is **haggard** looks very tired and ill.

haggis haggises
NOUN a Scottish dish made of the minced internal organs of a sheep, boiled together with oatmeal and spices in a skin

haggle haggles, haggling, haggled
VERB If you **haggle** with someone, you argue with them about the price of something.

haiku haiku
NOUN a short, Japanese verse form in 17 syllables

hail hails, hailing, hailed
NOUN **1** frozen rain
VERB **2** When it is **hailing**, frozen rain is falling.

hailstone hailstones
NOUN a drop of frozen rain

hair **hairs**
NOUN one of the large number of fine threads that grow on your head and body. **Hair** grows on the bodies of some other animals.

haircut **haircuts**
NOUN the cutting of someone's hair and the style into which it is cut

hairdresser **hairdressers**
NOUN a person who is trained to cut and style hair

hairstyle **hairstyles**
NOUN the way in which your hair is arranged or cut

hairy **hairier, hairiest**
ADJECTIVE covered in a lot of hair

hajj
NOUN the pilgrimage to Mecca that every Muslim must make at least once in their life, if they are healthy and wealthy enough to do so
[from Arabic *hajj* meaning pilgrimage]

halal; also spelt **hallal**
NOUN meat from animals that have been killed according to Muslim law

half **halves**
NOUN OR ADJECTIVE **1** one of two equal parts that make up a whole. It can be written as $^1/_2$. • *the second **half** of the match* • *My cup is only **half** full.*
ADVERB **2** You can use **half** to say that something is only partly true. • *I **half** expected to see the teacher walk in.*
PHRASE **3** **Half past** refers to a time that is thirty minutes after a particular hour. • ***half past** twelve*

halfway
ADVERB If something is **halfway** between two points or two times, it is at the middle point between them.

hall **halls**
NOUN **1** the room just inside the front entrance of a house that leads into the other rooms
2 a large room or building for public events • *a school **hall***

hallo
EXCLAMATION OR GREETING another spelling of **hello**

Halloween
NOUN **Halloween** is October 31st. In the past people thought that ghosts and witches would be about on this night, and it is now celebrated by children dressing up, often as ghosts and witches.

hallucinate **hallucinates, hallucinating, hallucinated**
VERB If someone **hallucinates**, they imagine that they see strange things, for example because they are ill.

halo **haloes** or **halos**
NOUN a circle of light around something, especially the head of a holy person in a picture

halt **halts, halting, halted**
VERB **1** When someone or something **halts**, they stop. • *They **halted** a short distance from the house.*
PHRASE **2** When something **comes to a halt**, it stops.

halter **halters**
NOUN a strap fastened round a horse's head so that it can be led easily

halve **halves, halving, halved**
VERB If you **halve** something, you divide it into two equal parts.

ham
NOUN meat from the hind leg of a pig

hamburger **hamburgers**
NOUN a flat disc of minced meat, fried and eaten in a bread roll
[named after *Hamburg* in Germany, the city where they were first made]

hammer **hammers, hammering, hammered**
NOUN **1** a tool consisting of a heavy piece of metal at the end of a handle, used for hitting nails into things
VERB **2** If you **hammer** something, you hit it repeatedly with a hammer.

hammock **hammocks**
NOUN a piece of net or canvas hung between two supports and used as a bed

hamper **hampers, hampering, hampered**
NOUN **1** a large basket with a lid, used for carrying food
VERB **2** If something **hampers** you, it makes it difficult for you to do what you are trying to do. • *The bad weather **hampered** their expedition.*

hamster **hamsters**
NOUN a small, furry rodent, often kept as a pet

hand **hands, handing, handed**
NOUN **1** the part of your body at the end of your arm, below the wrist

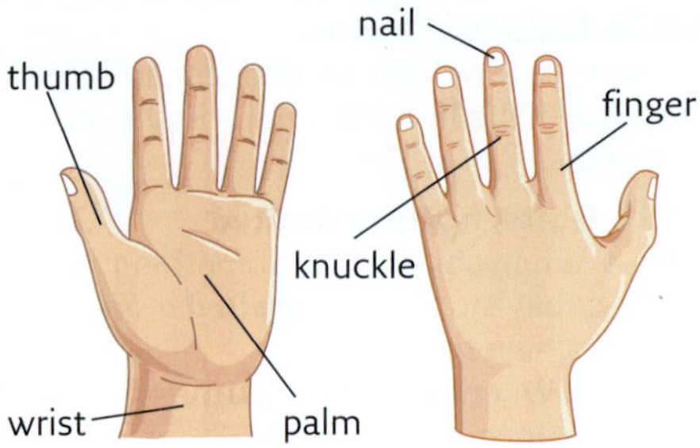

2 The **hands** of a clock or watch are the pointers that indicate what time it is.
3 In a game of cards, a **hand** is the set of cards dealt to each player.
VERB **4** If you **hand** something to someone, you pass it to them.
PHRASE **5** If you **give a hand**, you help someone to do something.
6 If you do something **by hand**, you do it using your hands rather than a machine.
7 If something gets **out of hand**, it becomes beyond your control.

handbag **handbags**
NOUN a small bag, usually carried by a woman

handcuffs
PLURAL NOUN two strong metal rings joined by chains that are locked round a prisoner's wrists

handful **handfuls**
NOUN **1** A **handful** of something is the amount of it you can hold in your hand.
2 a small number or quantity of something • *Only a **handful** of people were invited to the party.*

handicap **handicaps**
NOUN **1** a physical or mental disability
2 a disadvantage, or anything that makes it more difficult to do something
handicapped ADJECTIVE

handicraft **handicrafts**
NOUN an activity that involves making things with your hands, such as pottery or knitting

handkerchief **handkerchiefs**
NOUN a small square of fabric used for blowing your nose

handle **handles, handling, handled**
NOUN **1** the part of a tool, bag, cup or other object that you hold in order to pick it up or use it • *door **handle***
VERB **2** If you **handle** an object, you hold it or touch it with your hands.
3 If you **handle** something, you deal with it successfully. • *She **handled** the stress of the examination very well.*

handlebars
PLURAL NOUN the bars with handles that are used to steer a bicycle

handset **handsets**
NOUN The **handset** of a telephone is the part that you speak into and listen with.

handsome
ADJECTIVE very attractive in appearance

handstand **handstands**
NOUN the act of balancing upside down on your hands, with your feet in the air

handwriting
NOUN Someone's **handwriting** is their style of writing with a pen or pencil.

handy **handier, handiest**
ADJECTIVE If something is **handy**, it is useful or conveniently near.

hang **hangs, hanging, hung** or **hanged**
VERB **1** If you **hang** something on a hook, nail or line, or if it **hangs** there, it is attached so that it does not touch the ground. • *His jacket **hung** from a hook on the door.*

2 To **hang** someone means to kill them by suspending them by a rope around the neck.

When *hang* means to kill someone by suspending them by a rope, the past tense and past participle are **hanged**.

hang about or **hang around**
VERB INFORMAL If you **hang about** *or* **hang around** somewhere, you stay or wait there. • *Although he had left, he still **hung around** outside his old school.*

hang on
VERB **1** If you **hang on** to something, you hold it tightly or keep it.
2 INFORMAL If you **hang on**, you wait.

hang up
VERB If you **hang up** when you are speaking on the phone, you put down the receiver and end the call.

hangar **hangars**
NOUN a large building where aircraft are kept

hanger **hangers**
NOUN a piece of shaped wood, plastic or wire for hanging up clothes

hang-glider **hang-gliders**
NOUN a glider that is made for one or two people who hang below the frame in a harness

Hanukkah or **Chanukah**
NOUN an eight-day Jewish festival of lights

haphazard
ADJECTIVE not organized or planned • *He piled the books up in a **haphazard** way.*
haphazardly ADVERB

happen **happens, happening, happened**
VERB **1** When something **happens**, it occurs or takes place.
2 If you **happen** to do something, you do it by chance. • *I **happened** to notice he'd dropped his glove.*

happiness
NOUN a feeling of great contentment or pleasure

happy **happier, happiest**
ADJECTIVE **1** full of contentment or joy
ANTONYMS: miserable, sad
2 If you are **happy** with something, you are satisfied with it.
ANTONYM: dissatisfied
3 If you are **happy** to do something, you are willing to do it.
ANTONYM: reluctant
happily ADVERB

harass **harasses, harassing, harassed**
VERB If someone **harasses** you, they annoy or trouble you continually.
harassed ADJECTIVE

harbour **harbours**
NOUN a protected area of deep water where boats can be moored

hard **harder, hardest**
ADJECTIVE OR ADVERB **1** requiring a lot of effort • *The sponsored walk was **hard** work.*
2 with a lot of force • *I kicked the ball very **hard**.*
ADJECTIVE **3** difficult
4 not easy to bend or break

hard disk **hard disks**
NOUN a part of a computer that holds a large amount of information

harden **hardens, hardening, hardened**
VERB If something **hardens** it becomes hard or gets harder. • *The glue took a long time to **harden**.*

hardly
ADVERB only just • *I could **hardly** believe it.*

hardship
NOUN a time or situation of suffering and difficulty

hardware
NOUN **1** tools and equipment for use in the home and garden
2 computer machinery rather than computer programs

hardy **hardier, hardiest**
ADJECTIVE tough and able to bear cold and difficult conditions

A B C D E F G H I J K L M N O P Q R S T U V W X Y Z

hare **hares**
NOUN an animal like a large rabbit, but with longer ears and legs

harm **harms, harming, harmed**
VERB **1** If someone **harms** someone or something, they injure or damage them.
SYNONYM: hurt
NOUN **2** injury or damage
SYNONYM: hurt

harmful
ADJECTIVE having a bad effect on something • *Too much sun can be **harmful** to your skin.*
harmfully ADVERB

harmless
ADJECTIVE safe to use or be near
harmlessly ADVERB

harmonica **harmonicas**
NOUN a small musical instrument played by moving it across the lips and blowing and sucking air through it. Also called a mouth organ.

harmony **harmonies**
NOUN **1** a state of peaceful agreement and cooperation • *The neighbours lived in **harmony**.*
2 In music, **harmony** is the pleasant combination of two or more notes played at the same time.

harness **harnesses, harnessing, harnessed**
NOUN **1** a set of straps fastened round an animal to control it or attach it to something, such as a horse to a cart
VERB **2** If you **harness** an animal, you put a harness on it.
3 If someone **harnesses** something, they control it so that they can use it. • *The windmills **harnessed** the power of the wind.*

harp **harps**
NOUN a musical instrument consisting of a triangular frame with vertical strings that you pluck with your fingers
harpist NOUN

harpoon **harpoons**
NOUN a barbed spear attached to a rope, thrown or fired from a gun and used for catching whales or large fish

harsh **harsher, harshest**
ADJECTIVE **1** **Harsh** living conditions or climates are rough and unpleasant.
SYNONYMS: hard, severe, tough
2 **Harsh** actions or remarks are unkind and show no sympathy.
harshly ADVERB **harshness** NOUN

harvest **harvests**
NOUN the act of gathering a crop, or the time when this is done
[from Old German *herbist* meaning autumn]

has
VERB part of the verb *have*

hasn't
VERB a contraction of *has not*

hassle **hassles, hassling, hassled**
NOUN **1** INFORMAL Something that is a **hassle** is difficult or causes trouble. • *Organizing the school trip is always a **hassle**.*
VERB **2** If you **hassle** someone, you annoy them by repeatedly asking them to do something.

hasty **hastier, hastiest**
ADJECTIVE done quickly and without preparation • *Do not give a **hasty** answer.*

hat **hats**
NOUN a covering for the head

hatch **hatches, hatching, hatched**
VERB **1** When an egg **hatches**, or when a bird or a reptile **hatches** from an egg, the shell breaks open and the young bird or reptile comes out.
NOUN **2** an opening in a wall where food can be passed through

hatchback **hatchbacks**
NOUN a car with a door at the back that opens upwards

hatchet **hatchets**
NOUN a small axe

hate **hates, hating, hated**
VERB If you **hate** someone or something, you dislike them very much.

hateful
ADJECTIVE very nasty and detestable

hatred
NOUN an extremely strong feeling of dislike

haul **hauls, hauling, hauled**
VERB If you **haul** something somewhere, you pull it with great effort.

haunt **haunts, haunting, haunted**
VERB If a ghost **haunts** a place, it is seen or heard there regularly.
haunting ADJECTIVE

haunted
ADJECTIVE Somewhere that is **haunted** is visited often by a ghost. • *People believe that the house on the hill is **haunted**.*

have **has, having, had**
VERB **1** If you **have** something, it belongs to you or you possess it.
2 If you **have** something such as a cold or an accident, you feel or experience it.
3 If you **have** something such as lunch or a letter, you take or get it.
4 If you **have** something such as a haircut, you cause it to be done.
PHRASE **5** If you **have to** do something, you must do it. • *I **have to** clean my room before I go out.*
VERB **6** **Have** can be used with other verbs to form the past tense. • *I **have** already read that book.*

haven't
VERB a contraction of *have not*

havoc
NOUN disorder and confusion • *The bad weather played **havoc** with our plans.*

hawk **hawks**
NOUN a bird of prey with short, rounded wings and a long tail

hay
NOUN grass that has been cut and dried and is used to feed animals

hay fever
NOUN an allergy to pollen and grass, causing sneezing and watering eyes

haystack **haystacks**
NOUN a large, firmly-built pile of hay, usually covered and left out in the open

hazard **hazards**
NOUN something that could be dangerous to you • *The pollution in the city centre is a health **hazard**.*

haze
NOUN If there is a **haze**, it is difficult to see clearly because there is moisture or smoke in the air.

hazel **hazels**
NOUN **1** a small tree with edible nuts
ADJECTIVE **2** a green-brown colour • *He has **hazel** eyes.*

hazy **hazier, haziest**
ADJECTIVE dim or vague • ***hazy** sunshine* • *a **hazy** memory*

he
PRONOUN **He** is used to refer to a man, boy or male animal that has already been mentioned.

head **heads, heading, headed**
NOUN **1** the part of your body that has your eyes, brain and mouth in it
2 the top or front of something, or the most important end of it • *We went to the **head** of the queue.*
3 When you toss a coin, the side called **heads** is the one with the **head** on it.
4 In an organization or group of people, the **head** is the main person in charge.
VERB **5** If you **head** something, you lead it. • *She **headed** the expedition to the North Pole.*
6 If you **head** somewhere, you go in that direction or towards something. • *We **headed** to the canteen for lunch.*
7 If you **head** a ball, you hit it with your head. • *He **headed** the ball into the goal.*

headache **headaches**
NOUN a pain in your head

heading **headings**
NOUN a piece of writing that is written or printed at the top of a page

headlight **headlights**
NOUN the large, powerful lights on the front of a motor vehicle

headline **headlines**
NOUN The **headline** of a newspaper is the heading printed in big, bold letters on the front page at the top of an article.

a b c d e f g h i j k l m n o p q r s t u v w x y z

A B C D E F G H I J K L M N O P Q R S T U V W X Y Z

headphones
NOUN a pair of small speakers that you wear over your ears to listen to a radio, a television or a stereo without other people hearing

headquarters
NOUN the main place from which an organization is run

head teacher **head teachers**
NOUN the teacher who is in charge of a school

heal **heals, healing, healed**
VERB If a cut or a wound **heals**, it gets better. • *The cut on my leg **healed** quickly.*

health
NOUN the condition of someone's body and mind • *I felt in very good **health** after our holiday.*

healthy **healthier, healthiest**
ADJECTIVE **1** Someone who is **healthy** is fit and well, and is not suffering from any illness. • *She goes to the gym to stay **healthy**.*
2 Something that is **healthy** is good for you. • *You should try and eat a **healthy** diet.*

heap **heaps, heaping, heaped**
NOUN **1** an untidy pile of things
VERB **2** If you **heap** things, you pile them up.

hear **hears, hearing, heard**
VERB **1** When you **hear** sounds, you are aware of them because they reach your ears. • *We could **hear** the waves crashing on the beach.*
2 When you **hear** from someone, they write to you or phone you.

hearing
NOUN **1** the ability to hear
2 If someone gives you a **hearing**, they let you give your point of view and listen to you.

hearse **hearses**
NOUN a large car that carries the coffin at a funeral

heart **hearts**
NOUN **1** the organ in your chest that pumps the blood around your body

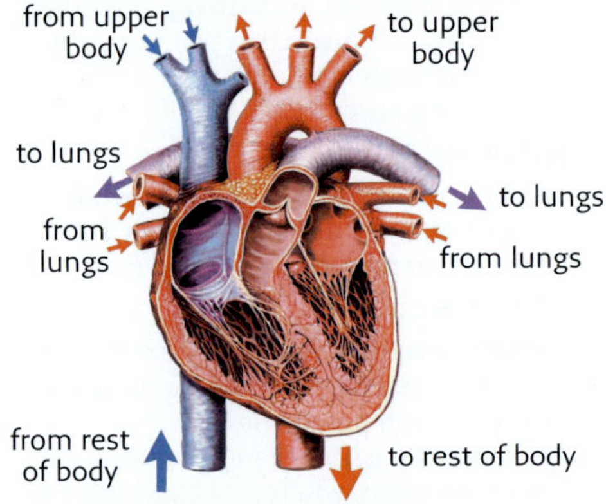

2 Your **heart** is also thought of as the centre of your emotions and feelings.
• *When his hamster died it broke his **heart**.*
3 the most central or important part of something • *It is always busy in the **heart** of the city.*
4 courage
5 a curved shape like this ♥, or a playing card with this shape on it
PHRASE **6** If you learn something **by heart**, you learn it so that you know it from memory.

heart attack **heart attacks**
NOUN a serious medical condition in which someone's heart suddenly beats irregularly or stops completely

hearth **hearths**
Said "**harth**" NOUN the floor of a fireplace

heat **heats, heating, heated**
NOUN **1** warmth or the quality of being hot
• *the fierce **heat** of the sun*
2 a contest or race in a competition that decides who will compete in the final
VERB **3** When you **heat** something, you warm it.

heater **heaters**
NOUN a device used to produce heat in order to warm a place, such as a room or a car

heath
NOUN a large open area of land covered in rough grass or heather, with very few trees

heather
NOUN a plant with small purple or white flowers that grows wild on hills and moorland

heave **heaves, heaving, heaved**
VERB If you **heave** something, you lift, push or throw it with a lot of effort.

heaven
NOUN In some religions, **heaven** is the place where God lives and where good people go when they die.

heavy **heavier, heaviest**
ADJECTIVE **1** Something that is **heavy** weighs a lot.
2 You use **heavy** to talk about how much something weighs. • *How **heavy** is the baby?*

Hebrew
Said "**hee**-broo" NOUN an ancient language that is now spoken in Israel by the Jewish people

hectare **hectares**
NOUN a unit for measuring an area of land, equal to 10,000 square metres or about 2.471 acres

hectic
ADJECTIVE involving a lot of rushed activity • *She leads a very **hectic** life.*

he'd
a contraction of *he had* or *he would*

hedge **hedges**
NOUN a row of bushes along the edge of a garden, field or road

hedgehog **hedgehogs**
NOUN a small, brown mammal with sharp spikes covering its back

heel **heels**
NOUN **1** the back part of your foot, below your ankle
2 the part on the bottom at the back of a shoe or sock

heifer **heifers**
NOUN a young cow that has not yet had calves

height **heights**
NOUN **1** a measurement from the bottom to the top of someone or something
2 a high position or place • *He's afraid of **heights**.*
3 the highest or most important part of something • *He's at the **height** of his success.*

heir **heirs**
NOUN the person who is entitled to inherit someone's property or title • *the **heir** to the throne*

held
VERB the past tense of **hold**

helicopter **helicopters**
NOUN an aircraft with rotating blades instead of wings, that enable it to take off vertically

helium
NOUN a gas that is lighter than air. It is sometimes used to fill party balloons.

he'll
a contraction of *he will* or *he shall*

hell
NOUN **1** In some religions, **hell** is the place where the Devil lives and where wicked people are sent to be punished when they die.
2 INFORMAL If you say that something is **hell**, you mean that it is very unpleasant.

hello
EXCLAMATION OR GREETING You say **hello** when you meet someone or answer the telephone.

helmet **helmets**
NOUN a hard hat that you wear to protect your head

help **helps, helping, helped**
VERB **1** If you **help** someone, you make something easier or better for them.
NOUN **2** assistance • *Thanks for your **help**.*

a b c d e f g h i j k l m n o p q r s t u v w x y z

A B C D E F G H I J K L M N O P Q R S T U V W X Y Z

helpful
ADJECTIVE If you are **helpful**, you cooperate with others and support them.
helpfully ADVERB

helping **helpings**
NOUN a portion of food at a meal

helpless
ADJECTIVE If you are **helpless**, you are unable to protect yourself or do anything useful.
helplessly ADVERB

hem **hems, hemming, hemmed**
NOUN **1** The **hem** of a garment is the edge of it that has been folded up and stitched in place.
VERB **2** If you **hem** a garment, you make a hem on it.

hemisphere **hemispheres**
NOUN one half of the earth or a sphere

hen **hens**
NOUN **1** a female chicken
2 any female bird

heptagon **heptagons**
NOUN a flat shape with seven flat sides

her
PRONOUN OR ADJECTIVE **1** refers to a woman, girl or female animal that has already been mentioned • *I like Amy. I often play with **her**.*
2 shows that something belongs to a particular female • *Mum is going to wear **her** blue jumper.*

heraldry
NOUN the study of coats of arms

herb **herbs**
NOUN a plant whose leaves are used as a medicine or to flavour food

herbivore **herbivores**
NOUN an animal that eats only plants
herbivorous ADJECTIVE

herd **herds, herding, herded**
NOUN **1** a large group of animals grazing together • *a **herd** of cattle*
VERB **2** If you **herd** animals or people, you make them move together as a group.
• *The teachers **herded** the children on to the bus.*

here
ADVERB at, to or in the place where you are

hereditary
ADJECTIVE passed on to a child from a parent

heritage
NOUN The **heritage** of a country is all its traditions, customs and art that have been passed from one generation to another.

hermit **hermits**
NOUN someone who prefers to live a simple life alone and far from other people, often for religious reasons

hero **heroes**
NOUN **1** the main male character in a book, film or play
2 a person who is admired because they have done something brave or good

heroine **heroines**
NOUN the main female character in a book, play or film

heron **herons**
NOUN a wading bird with very long legs and a long beak and neck

herring **herrings**
NOUN a silvery fish that lives in large shoals in northern seas

hers
PRONOUN refers to something that belongs or relates to a woman, girl or other female animal

herself
PRONOUN refers to the same woman, girl or female animal who does an action and is affected by it • *She pulled **herself** up.*

he's
a contraction of *he is* or *he has*

hesitate **hesitates, hesitating, hesitated**
VERB If you **hesitate**, you pause or show uncertainty.

hexagon **hexagons**
NOUN a flat shape with six straight sides
hexagonal ADJECTIVE

hibernate **hibernates, hibernating, hibernated**
VERB Animals that **hibernate** spend the winter in a state like a deep sleep.
hibernation NOUN

hiccup **hiccups, hiccupping, hiccupped**; also spelt **hiccough**
NOUN **1** short, uncontrolled sounds in your throat
VERB **2** When you **hiccup**, you suffer from hiccups.

hide **hides, hiding, hid, hidden**
VERB **1** If you **hide** something, you put it where it cannot be seen, or prevent it from being discovered. • *He **hid** his disappointment.*
2 If you **hide**, you go somewhere where you cannot be seen or found easily.

hideous
ADJECTIVE extremely ugly or unpleasant
hideously ADVERB

hieroglyphics
Said "hy-ro-**gliff**-iks" PLURAL NOUN ancient Egyptian writing that uses pictures instead of words. It involves over 700 picture signs.

high **higher, highest**
ADJECTIVE **1** **High** refers to how much something measures from the bottom to the top. • *The statue was three metres **high**.*
ADJECTIVE OR ADVERB **2** a long way above the ground • *He jumped **high** into the air.*
3 great in degree, quantity or intensity • *There were **high** winds before the storm.*

highlight **highlights, highlighting, highlighted**
NOUN **1** the most interesting part of something • *The **highlight** of the week was our trip to the cinema.*
VERB **2** If you **highlight** a point or a problem, you emphasize it.

high-rise
ADJECTIVE **High-rise** buildings are very tall.

highway **highways**
NOUN a main road

hijab **hijabs**; also spelt **hejab**
Said "hi-**jab**" NOUN a veil worn by some Muslim women in public, covering the hair and the chest

hijack **hijacks, hijacking, hijacked**
VERB If someone **hijacks** a plane or other vehicle, they take control of it unlawfully and by force.
hijacker NOUN

hike **hikes, hiking, hiked**
VERB **1** If you **hike**, you go for a long walk across country.
NOUN **2** a long and demanding walk

hilarious
ADJECTIVE very funny

hill **hills**
NOUN a high, rounded piece of ground

hilt **hilts**
NOUN the handle of a knife or sword

him
PRONOUN refers to a man, boy or male animal that has already been mentioned • *Let's invite Ben. I really like **him**.*

himself
PRONOUN refers to the same man, boy or male animal that does an action and is affected by it • *He pushed **himself** to the front of the crowd.*

hind **hinds**
NOUN **1** a female deer
ADJECTIVE **2** The **hind** legs of an animal are its back legs.

hinder **hinders, hindering, hindered**
VERB If you **hinder** someone or something, you get in their way and make it difficult for them to do what they want to do.

Hindu **Hindus**
NOUN a person who believes in Hinduism, an Indian religion that has many gods and involves the belief that people have another life on earth after death

hinge **hinges**
NOUN the movable joint that attaches a door or window to its frame

hint **hints, hinting, hinted**
NOUN **1** an indirect suggestion • *He dropped **hints** about his birthday present.*
2 a helpful piece of advice
VERB **3** If you **hint** that something is true, you suggest it indirectly. • *The teacher **hinted** that they had all done well in the tests.*

hip **hips**
NOUN Your **hips** are the joints and the bony parts at the top of your thigh and below your waist.

hippopotamus **hippopotamuses** or **hippopotami**
NOUN a large, African mammal with thick, wrinkled skin and short legs, that lives near rivers

hire **hires, hiring, hired**
VERB **1** If you **hire** something, you pay money to use it for a period of time.
PHRASE **2** Something that is **for hire** is available for people to hire. • *There are bicycles **for hire** down by the beach.*

his
PRONOUN refers to something that belongs or relates to a man, boy or other male animal

hiss **hisses, hissing, hissed**
VERB If someone or something **hisses**, they make a long *s* sound.

historic
ADJECTIVE important in the past, or likely to be seen as important in the future

historical
ADJECTIVE occurring in the past, or relating to the study of the past

history **histories**
NOUN **1** the study of the past
2 the set of facts that are known about a place or subject • *There was a leaflet on the **history** of the stately home.*
[from Greek *historein* meaning to narrate a story]

hit **hits, hitting, hit**
VERB **1** If you **hit** someone or something, you strike or knock them with force.
2 If something **hits** you, it affects you suddenly and forcefully. • *The answer suddenly **hit** me.*
NOUN **3** If someone or something is a big **hit**, they are a great success.
4 the action of hitting something

hitch **hitches, hitching, hitched**
VERB **1** If you **hitch** something, you tie it up using a loop.
2 INFORMAL If you **hitch** somewhere, you travel by getting lifts from passing vehicles.
NOUN **3** a slight problem of difficulty • *Their plans went ahead without a **hitch**.*

hitchhike **hitchhikes, hitchhiking, hitchhiked**
VERB to travel by getting lifts from passing vehicles

hive **hives**
NOUN **1** a beehive
2 A place that is a **hive** of activity is very busy.

hoard **hoards, hoarding, hoarded**
VERB **1** If you **hoard** things, you save them even though they may no longer be useful.
NOUN **2** a store of things that has been saved or hidden

hoarse **hoarser, hoarsest**
ADJECTIVE A **hoarse** voice sounds rough and unclear.
hoarsely ADVERB

hoax **hoaxes**
NOUN a trick or an attempt to deceive someone • *The bomb scare was a **hoax**.*

hobby **hobbies**
NOUN something that you do for enjoyment in your spare time

hockey
NOUN a game in which two teams use long sticks with curved ends to try to hit a small ball into the other team's goal

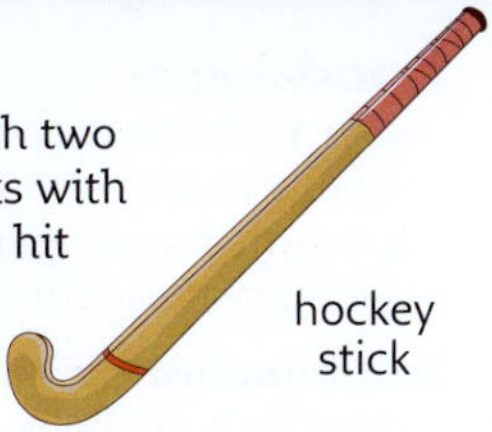
hockey stick

hoe **hoes**
NOUN a long-handled gardening tool with a small, square blade, used to remove weeds and break up the soil

Hogmanay
NOUN New Year's Eve and its celebrations in Scotland

hoist **hoists, hoisting, hoisted**
VERB If someone **hoists** something, they lift it, especially using ropes and pulleys, a crane or other machinery.

hold **holds, holding, held**
VERB **1** If you **hold** something, you carry it or keep it in place, usually with your hands or arms.
2 If you **hold** a meeting or a party, you arrange it and cause it to happen.
3 If you **hold** someone responsible for something, you decide that they did it.
4 If something **holds** a certain amount, it can contain that amount. • *This jug **holds** a litre of water.*
5 If you **hold** something, you possess it. • *She **holds** the world long jump record.*
NOUN **6** the part of a ship or aircraft where cargo or luggage is stored
7 If someone has a **hold** over you, they have power over you.
8 If you keep a **hold** on something, you hold it securely.

hole **holes**
NOUN an opening or hollow space in something

Holi
NOUN a Hindu festival celebrated in spring

holiday **holidays**
NOUN **1** a period of time spent away from home for enjoyment
2 a day when people do not go to work or school because of a national festival • *In Britain, Christmas Day is always a **holiday**.*

hollow **hollows, hollowing, hollowed**
ADJECTIVE **1** Something that is **hollow** has a hole or space inside it.
ANTONYM: solid
NOUN **2** a small valley or sunken place
VERB **3** If you **hollow** something out, you make it hollow. • *We **hollowed** out the pumpkin to make a lantern for Halloween.*

holly
NOUN an evergreen tree or shrub with spiky leaves. It often has red berries in winter.

hologram **holograms**
NOUN a three-dimensional picture made by laser beams

holster **holsters**
NOUN a holder for a hand gun, worn at the side of the body or under the arm

holy **holier, holiest**
ADJECTIVE Something that is **holy** relates to God or to a particular religion.

home **homes**
NOUN **1** the building or place in which you live
2 A nursing **home** is a building in which elderly or ill people live and are looked after.
3 the place where you feel you belong

homeless
ADJECTIVE Someone who is **homeless** has nowhere to live.
homelessness NOUN

home page **home pages**
NOUN the first page you see on a website, which tells you about the site and has links to the information or services provided

homesick
ADJECTIVE If you are **homesick**, you are unhappy because you are away from your home and family. • *I enjoyed my exchange trip to Germany, but I did feel **homesick** sometimes.*

homework
NOUN school work given to pupils to be done at home

homograph **homographs**
NOUN one of a group of words spelt in the same way but with different meanings, such as *saw* (meaning a tool for cutting) and *saw* (the past tense of *see*)

homonym **homonyms**
NOUN one of a group of words that are pronounced or spelt in the same way but have different meanings; for example *eight* and *ate*, or *bank* (meaning a slope) and *bank* (meaning a place where you keep your money)

homophone **homophones**
NOUN one of a group of words with different meanings that are pronounced in the same way but spelt differently. *Write* and *right* are **homophones**.

honest
NOUN If you are **honest**, you can be trusted to tell the truth.
SYNONYMS: trustworthy, truthful
honestly ADVERB

honey
NOUN a sweet, edible, sticky substance made by bees

honeycomb
honeycombs
NOUN a wax structure made with six-sided cells by bees for storing honey

honeymoon **honeymoons**
NOUN a holiday for a newly married couple after their wedding

honour **honours, honouring, honoured**
NOUN **1** An **honour** is an award given to someone for something they have done.
2 If you feel that it is an **honour** to do something, you feel proud or privileged to do it.
VERB **3** If you **honour** someone, you give them special praise or attention, or an award.

hood **hoods**
NOUN **1** a loose covering for the head, usually part of a coat or jacket
2 In American English, the **hood** of a car is the cover over the engine at the front.

hoof **hooves** or **hoofs**
NOUN the hard, bony part of the feet of horses, cattle and deer

hook **hooks, hooking, hooked**
NOUN **1** a curved piece of metal or plastic that is used for catching things or for holding things up
VERB **2** If you **hook** one thing on to another, you attach it there using a hook.
• *He **hooked** the caravan to the car.*

hooligan **hooligans**
NOUN a destructive and violent young person
hooliganism NOUN

hoop **hoops**
NOUN a large wooden, metal or plastic ring

hoot **hoots, hooting, hooted**
VERB **1** If a car horn **hoots**, it makes a loud, honking noise.
2 If someone **hoots**, they make a long *oo* sound like an owl or a car horn.
• *We all **hooted** with laughter at his joke.*

hop **hops, hopping, hopped**
VERB **1** If you **hop**, you jump on one foot.
2 When animals such as kangaroos, birds or insects **hop**, they jump with two or more feet together.

hope **hopes, hoping, hoped**
VERB **1** If you **hope** that something will happen, you want or expect it to happen.
NOUN **2** the wish or expectation that things will go well in the future

hopeful
ADJECTIVE If you are **hopeful** about something, you hope it will turn out well.
hopefully ADVERB

hopeless
ADJECTIVE **1** You say something is **hopeless** when it is very bad and you do not feel it can get any better.
2 unable to do something well • *I'm **hopeless** at art.*
hopelessly ADVERB

horde **hordes**
NOUN a large group or number of people or other animals

horizon **horizons**
NOUN the distant line where the sky seems to touch the land or sea

horizontal
ADJECTIVE flat and level with, or parallel to the ground
horizontally ADVERB

horn **horns**
NOUN **1** a warning device on a vehicle that makes a loud noise
2 one of the hard, pointed things that grow from the head of a cow or goat

hornet **hornets**
NOUN **1** a type of very large wasp
PHRASE **2** A situation described as **a hornet's nest** is very difficult to deal with and likely to cause trouble.

horoscope **horoscopes**
NOUN a prediction about what is going to happen to someone, based on the position of the stars when they were born

horrible
ADJECTIVE disagreeable and unpleasant

horrific
ADJECTIVE If something is **horrific**, it horrifies people.

horrify **horrifies, horrifying, horrified**
VERB If someone or something **horrifies** you, they make you feel disgusted and shocked.

horror
NOUN a strong feeling of alarm caused by something very unpleasant

horse **horses**
NOUN a large mammal with a mane and tail, that people can ride

horse chestnut **horse chestnuts**
NOUN a large tree with flowers and shiny, brown nuts known as conkers

horsepower
NOUN a unit used for measuring how powerful an engine is

horseshoe **horseshoes**
NOUN a U-shaped piece of iron that is nailed to the bottom of a horse's hoof to protect it

hose **hoses**
NOUN a long, flexible tube through which liquid or gas can be passed • *a garden **hose***

hospitable
ADJECTIVE If you are **hospitable**, you are friendly, welcoming and generous to others.

hospital **hospitals**
NOUN a place where sick people are looked after by doctors and nurses

host **hosts, hosting, hosted**
NOUN **1** the person who gives a party or organizes an event, and who welcomes and looks after the guests
2 a large number of things • *There was a **host** of things to do at the fair.*
VERB **3** If you **host** an event, you organize it and act as the host.

hostage **hostages**
NOUN a person who is illegally held prisoner and threatened with injury or death unless certain demands are met by other people

hostel **hostels**
NOUN a large house where people can stay cheaply for a short time • *a youth **hostel***

hostile
ADJECTIVE If someone is **hostile** to you, they behave in an unfriendly aggressive way towards you.

hot **hotter, hottest**
ADJECTIVE **1** having a high temperature
2 having a burning taste caused by spices

hotel **hotels**
NOUN a building where people stay, paying for their room and meals

hound **hounds**
NOUN a dog, especially one used for hunting or racing

hour **hours**
NOUN a period of 60 minutes
[from Greek *hora* meaning season or time of day]

A B C D E F G H I J K L M N O P Q R S T U V W X Y Z

house houses
NOUN a building where people live

household households
NOUN 1 all the people who live as a group in a house or flat
PHRASE 2 Someone who is **a household name** is very well known.
householder NOUN

housewife housewives
NOUN a married woman who does not have a paid job, but instead looks after her home and children

housework
NOUN all the work done in the home, like the cleaning and cooking

hover hovers, hovering, hovered
VERB When a bird, insect or aircraft **hovers**, it stays in the same position in the air.

hovercraft hovercraft or hovercrafts
NOUN a vehicle that can travel over water or land supported by a cushion of air

how
ADVERB used to ask about, explain or refer to the way something is done • ***How** did you get so dirty?*

however
ADVERB 1 You use **however** when you are adding a comment that contrasts with what has just been said. • *He is very chatty and seems confident. **However**, he is quite shy.*
2 You use **however** to say that something makes no difference to a situation. • ***However** hard she tried, nothing seemed to work.*

howl howls, howling, howled
VERB 1 If someone or something **howls**, they make a long, loud wailing noise such as that made by a dog or a baby when it is upset.
NOUN 2 a long, loud wailing noise

hub hubs
NOUN 1 the centre part of a wheel
2 the most important or active part of a place or organization

huddle huddles, huddling, huddled
VERB 1 If you **huddle** up, or are **huddled**, you are curled up with your arms and legs close to your body.
2 When people or animals **huddle** together, they sit or stand close to each other, often for warmth.

hug hugs, hugging, hugged
VERB If you **hug** someone, you put your arms round them and hold them close to you, usually to comfort them or to show affection.

huge
ADJECTIVE extremely large in amount, size or degree • *The party was a **huge** success.*
SYNONYMS: enormous, gigantic, vast

hull hulls
NOUN The **hull** of a ship is the main part of its body that sits in the water.

hum hums, humming, hummed
VERB 1 If something **hums**, it makes a continuous, low noise.
2 If you **hum**, you sing with your lips closed.
NOUN 3 a continuous, low noise

human humans
ADJECTIVE 1 relating to or concerning people • *We are all part of the **human** race.*
NOUN 2 a person
[from Latin *homo* meaning man]

human being human beings
NOUN a person

humane
ADJECTIVE showing kindness and sympathy towards others
humaneness NOUN **humanely** ADVERB

humanity
NOUN 1 the human race
2 Someone who shows **humanity** is kind and sympathetic.

humble humbler, humblest
ADJECTIVE A **humble** person is modest and thinks that they have very little value.
humbly ADVERB

humid
ADJECTIVE If the weather is **humid**, the air feels damp, heavy and warm.
humidity NOUN

humiliate **humiliates, humiliating, humiliated**
VERB If you **humiliate** someone, you make them feel ashamed or appear stupid to other people.
humiliation NOUN

humour **humours, humouring, humoured**
NOUN **1** the quality of being funny
2 the ability to be amused by certain things • *She's got a peculiar sense of* ***humour****.*
VERB **3** If you **humour** someone, you try to please them, so that they will not become upset.

hump **humps**
NOUN a small, rounded lump or mound • *a camel's* ***hump***

hunch **hunches, hunching, hunched**
VERB **1** If you **hunch** your shoulders, you raise them and push them forward, bending forward slightly.
2 If you have a **hunch** about something, you have an idea that something will happen.

hundred **hundreds**
NOUN A **hundred** is the number 100.
hundredth NOUN OR ADJECTIVE

hung
VERB the past tense and past participle of **hang**

hunger
NOUN the need or desire to eat

hungry **hungrier, hungriest**
ADJECTIVE If you are **hungry**, you need or want food.
hungrily ADVERB

hunt **hunts, hunting, hunted**
VERB **1** If you **hunt** for something, you search for it.
2 When people **hunt**, they chase and kill wild animals for food or sport.
NOUN **3** the act of searching for something • *The neighbours joined in the* ***hunt*** *for the missing cat.*

hurdle **hurdles**
NOUN **1** one of the frames or barriers that you jump over in an athletics race called **hurdles** • *She knocked over the last* ***hurdle****, but still managed to win the race.*
2 a problem or difficulty • *Several* ***hurdles*** *had to be overcome before the school play could go ahead.*

hurl **hurls, hurling, hurled**
VERB If you **hurl** something, you throw it with great force.

hurricane **hurricanes**
NOUN a very violent storm with strong winds

The sun heats the ocean making a spiral of clouds and wind. The centre of a hurricane is called the eye.

a b c d e f g h i j k l m n o p q r s t u v w x y z

A B C D E F G H I J K L M N O P Q R S T U V W X Y Z

hurry **hurries, hurrying, hurried**
VERB **1** If you **hurry** somewhere, you go there quickly.
2 If you **hurry** someone or something, or if you tell someone to **hurry** up, you try to make something happen more quickly.
PHRASE **3** If you are **in a hurry** to do something, you want to do it quickly. If you do something **in a hurry**, you do it quickly.

hurt **hurts, hurting, hurt**
VERB **1** If you **hurt** yourself or someone else, you injure or cause physical pain to yourself or someone else.
2 If a part of your body **hurts**, you feel pain there.
3 If you **hurt** someone, or **hurt** their feelings, you upset them by being unkind towards them.
ADJECTIVE **4** If you are **hurt**, you are injured.
5 If you feel **hurt**, you are upset because of someone's unkindness towards you.
• *She was **hurt** that they did not invite her to the party.*
[from Old French *hurter* meaning to knock against]

hurtle **hurtles, hurtling, hurtled**
VERB If someone or something **hurtles**, they move along very fast in an uncontrolled way. • *The car **hurtled** along the bumpy road.*

husband **husbands**
NOUN A woman's **husband** is the man she is married to.

hustle **hustles, hustling, hustled**
VERB **1** If you **hustle** someone, you make them move by pushing and jostling them.
2 hurry

hut **huts**
NOUN a small house or shelter

hutch **hutches**
NOUN a wooden box with wire mesh at one side, in which small pets can be kept

hydrant **hydrants**
NOUN a pipe connected to the main water supply of a town and used for emergencies

hydraulic
ADJECTIVE operated by water or other fluid that is under pressure

hydroelectric
ADJECTIVE **Hydroelectric** power is electricity produced from the energy of moving water.

hydrogen
NOUN a colourless gas that is the lightest and most common element in the world. **Hydrogen**-filled balloons explode because this gas is very flammable.

hyena **hyenas**; also spelt **hyaena**
Said "high-**ee**-na" NOUN a wild, dog-like animal found in Africa and Asia, that hunts in packs
[from Greek *huaina* meaning hog]

hygiene
Said "**hy**-jeen" NOUN the state of being clean and free of germs

hymn **hymns**
NOUN a Christian song in praise of God

hyphen **hyphens**
NOUN a punctuation mark (-) used to join together words or parts of words, as in *left-handed*

hypocrite **hypocrites**
NOUN someone who pretends to have certain views and beliefs that are different from their actual views and beliefs
hypocritical ADJECTIVE **hypocrisy** NOUN

hypothermia
NOUN a condition in which a person is very ill because their body has been extremely cold for a long time • *After spending the night stuck on the mountain, the climbers had **hypothermia**.*

Ii

I
PRONOUN A speaker or writer uses **I** to refer to themselves.

ice
NOUN water that has frozen solid

iceberg **icebergs**
NOUN a large mass of ice floating in the sea [from Dutch *ijsberg* meaning ice mountain]

ice cream **ice creams**
NOUN a very cold, sweet, creamy food

ice skate **ice skates**
NOUN a boot with a metal blade on the bottom, that you wear to move around on ice
ice-skate VERB

icicle **icicles**
NOUN a piece of ice shaped like a pointed stick, that hangs down from a surface

icing
NOUN a sweet covering for a cake or biscuits

icon **icons**
NOUN **1** a picture on a computer screen representing a program that can be activated by moving the cursor over it
2 a holy picture of Christ, the Virgin Mary or a saint

ICT
NOUN an abbreviation of *Information and Communication Technology*. **ICT** is the use of computers, telephones, television and radio to store, organize and give out information.

icy **icier, iciest**
ADJECTIVE **1** Something that is **icy** is very cold. • *We tried to shelter from the **icy** wind.*
2 An **icy** road has ice on it.
icily ADVERB

I'd
a contraction of *I had* or *I would*

idea **ideas**
NOUN **1** a plan or possible course of action
2 an opinion or belief
3 If you have an **idea** of something, you have a general but not a detailed knowledge of it. • *Could you give me an **idea** of the cost?*

ideal
ADJECTIVE The **ideal** person or thing for a particular purpose is the best possible one.

identical
ADJECTIVE exactly the same • *They are **identical** twins.*

identification
NOUN a document, such as a driving licence or passport, that states who you are

identify **identifies, identifying, identified**
VERB If you **identify** someone or something, you recognise and name them.
identifiable ADJECTIVE

identity **identities**
NOUN the things that make you who you are

idiom **idioms**
NOUN a group of words that, when used together, mean something different from when the words are used individually. For example, *It rained cats and dogs.*

a b c d e f g h i j k l m n o p q r s t u v w x y z

idiot **idiots**
NOUN someone who is stupid or foolish

idiotic
ADJECTIVE very stupid
idiotically ADVERB

idle **idler, idlest**
ADJECTIVE **1** If you are **idle**, you are doing nothing.
2 Machines or factories that are **idle** are not being used.
3 lazy
idleness NOUN **idly** ADVERB

idol **idols**
NOUN a famous person who is loved and admired by fans

i.e.
i.e. means *that is.* • *Please meet me in three days' time,* ***i.e.*** *on Sunday.*
[from Latin *id est* meaning that is]

if
CONJUNCTION **1** on condition that • *You can watch TV* ***if*** *you do your homework first.*
2 whether • *I asked him* ***if*** *he could come to the party.*

igloo **igloos**
NOUN a dome-shaped house built out of blocks of snow by the Inuit or Eskimo people
[from *igdlu*, an Inuit word meaning house]

ignite **ignites, igniting, ignited**
VERB If you **ignite** something, or it **ignites**, you set it on fire or it catches fire.
[from Latin *ignis* meaning fire]

ignorant
ADJECTIVE If you are **ignorant** of something, you do not know about it.

ignore **ignores, ignoring, ignored**
VERB If you **ignore** someone or something, you do not take any notice of them.

iguana **iguanas**
NOUN a large, tropical lizard

il-
PREFIX You add **il-** to the beginning of a word to mean that it is not something. For example, **il**legal means not legal, and **il**legible means not legible.

I'll
a contraction of *I will* or *I shall*

ill
ADJECTIVE unhealthy or sick
SYNONYM: unwell
[from Norse *illr* meaning bad]

illegal
ADJECTIVE If something is **illegal** it is forbidden by the law.
SYNONYMS: criminal, unlawful
illegally ADVERB

illegible
ADJECTIVE Writing that is **illegible** is unclear and very difficult to read.
ANTONYM: legible
illegibly ADVERB

illegitimate
ADJECTIVE If something is **illegitimate** it is not allowed by law, or is not accepted as fair by most people.
illegitimacy NOUN

illiterate
ADJECTIVE unable to read or write
ANTONYM: literate

illness **illnesses**
NOUN **1** the state or experience of being ill
2 a particular disease • *Flu is a common* ***illness*** *during the winter months.*

illogical
ADJECTIVE An **illogical** feeling or action is not reasonable or sensible.
ANTONYM: logical
illogically ADVERB

illuminate **illuminates, illuminating, illuminated**
VERB If you **illuminate** something, you shine light on to it so that it is easier to see, or you decorate it with lights.

illumination **illuminations**
NOUN one of the coloured lights put up to decorate a town, especially at Christmas

illusion **illusions**
NOUN **1** an idea that you think is true, but is not • *We were under the **illusion** that this was going to be an easy project.*
2 something that seems to be there but does not really exist

illustrate **illustrates, illustrating, illustrated**
VERB **1** If you **illustrate** a book, you help to explain its meaning by putting in pictures and diagrams.
2 If you **illustrate** a point when you are speaking, you make its meaning clearer, often by giving examples.

illustration **illustrations**
NOUN a picture or a diagram that helps to explain something

illustrator **illustrators**
NOUN someone who produces the pictures that go into books

I'm
a contraction of *I am*

im-
PREFIX You add **im-** to the beginning of a word to mean not something. For example, something that is **im**movable cannot be moved, and something that is **im**perfect is not perfect.

image **images**
NOUN a picture or photograph

imagery
NOUN The **imagery** of a poem or book is the words that are used to produce a picture in the mind of the reader.

imaginary
ADJECTIVE Something that is **imaginary** exists only in your mind, not in real life.
ANTONYM: real

imagination **imaginations**
NOUN If you show **imagination**, you have the ability to form ideas and pictures in your mind.

imaginative
ADJECTIVE If you are **imaginative**, you find it easy to create new and exciting ideas in your mind.
ANTONYM: unimaginative
imaginatively ADVERB

imagine **imagines, imagining, imagined**
VERB If you **imagine** something or someone, you create a picture of them in your mind.

imam
NOUN a person who leads a group in prayer in a mosque

imitate **imitates, imitating, imitated**
VERB If you **imitate** someone or something, you copy them.
SYNONYM: mimic

imitation **imitations**
NOUN a copy of something else

immature
ADJECTIVE **1** Something that is **immature** is not fully grown or developed.
ANTONYM: mature
2 An **immature** person does not behave in a sensible way.
ANTONYM: mature
immaturely ADVERB **immaturity** NOUN

immediately
ADVERB If something happens **immediately**, it happens at once.

immense
ADJECTIVE very large
SYNONYMS: huge, vast
immensely ADVERB **immensity** NOUN

immerse **immerses, immersing, immersed**
VERB **1** If you **immerse** something, you cover it completely with liquid.
2 If you **immerse** yourself in an activity, you become completely occupied with it.
immersion NOUN

immigrant **immigrants**
NOUN someone who has come to live in a country from another country

immigrate **immigrates, immigrating, immigrated**
VERB If someone **immigrates**, they come

to live permanently in a country that is not their own.
ANTONYM: emigrate

immobile
ADJECTIVE If something or someone is **immobile**, they are not moving.
immobility NOUN

immoral
ADJECTIVE If someone is **immoral**, they do not follow most people's standards of acceptable behaviour.
immorality NOUN

immortal
ADJECTIVE **1** Someone or something that is **immortal** is famous and will be remembered for a long time.
2 Something that is **immortal** will last forever.
immortality NOUN

immune
ADJECTIVE If you are **immune** to a particular disease, you cannot catch it.
immunity NOUN

immunize **immunizes, immunizing, immunized**
VERB If a doctor **immunizes** you against a disease, they give you an injection so that you are protected from the disease.
immunization NOUN

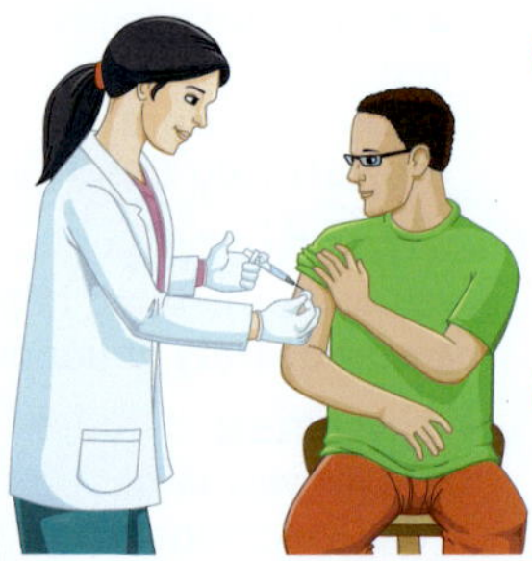

impact **impacts**
NOUN **1** The **impact** of one object on another is the force with which it hits it.
2 If something has an **impact** on a situation or person, it has a strong effect on them.
[from Latin *impactus* meaning pushed against]

impartial
ADJECTIVE If you are **impartial** about something, you are fair and unbiased.
ANTONYM: partial
impartially ADVERB

impatient
ADJECTIVE If you are **impatient**, you become annoyed easily because you do not want to wait for someone or something.
ANTONYM: patient
impatiently ADVERB **impatience** NOUN

imperfect
ADJECTIVE Something that is **imperfect** has faults.
imperfectly ADVERB **imperfection** NOUN

imperial
ADJECTIVE **1** relating to an empire, emperor or empress
2 The **imperial** system of measurement is a system that uses inches, feet and yards, ounces and pounds, and pints and gallons.

impersonal
ADJECTIVE Something that is **impersonal** makes you feel that individuals and their feelings do not matter.
impersonally ADVERB

impersonate **impersonates, impersonating, impersonated**
VERB If you **impersonate** someone, you pretend to be that person.
impersonation NOUN
impersonator NOUN

impertinent
ADJECTIVE If you are **impertinent**, you are disrespectful and rude to someone.

import **imports, importing, imported**
Said "im-**port**" VERB **1** If someone **imports** something, they buy it or bring it in from another country.
ANTONYM: export
Said "**im**-port" NOUN **2** **Imports** are goods brought into one country from another country.
ANTONYM: export

important
ADJECTIVE **1** Something that is **important** is very valuable, necessary or significant.
2 An **important** person has a lot of influence or power.

impose **imposes, imposing, imposed**
VERB If someone **imposes** something on someone, they force it on them.

imposing
ADJECTIVE If someone or something is **imposing**, they look impressive and important.

impossible
ADJECTIVE Something that is **impossible** cannot happen or cannot be done.
impossibly ADVERB **impossibility** NOUN

imposter **imposters**
NOUN An **imposter** is someone who pretends to be someone else, usually for devious reasons.

impractical
ADJECTIVE If someone or something is **impractical**, they are not sensible or realistic. • *It is **impractical** to camp in this wet weather.*
ANTONYM: practical

impress **impresses, impressing, impressed**
VERB **1** If you **impress** someone, you cause them to admire or respect you.
2 If you **impress** something on someone, you make sure that they understand it and remember it.

impression **impressions**
NOUN **1** An **impression** of someone or something is a vague idea or feeling that you have about them. • *I have the **impression** that I've met you before.*
2 a mark made by pressing • *You leave an **impression** when you press a coin into Plasticine then take it away.*
3 an imitation of a person, animal or thing

impressive
ADJECTIVE If someone or something is **impressive**, it causes you to admire or respect it.
impressively ADVERB

imprison **imprisons, imprisoning, imprisoned**
VERB If someone **imprisons** another person, they put them in prison or lock them up somewhere.
imprisonment NOUN

improbable
ADJECTIVE not probable or likely to happen
ANTONYM: probable
improbably ADVERB **improbability** NOUN

improve **improves, improving, improved**
VERB If something **improves**, or if you **improve** it, it gets better.
improvement NOUN

improvise **improvises, improvising, improvised**
VERB **1** If you **improvise** something, you make or do something without planning it in advance, and with whatever materials are available. • *In order to save money the children **improvised** their costumes for the school play.*
2 When musicians or actors **improvise**, they make up the music or words as they go along.
improvised ADJECTIVE **improvisation** NOUN

impudent
ADJECTIVE If you are **impudent**, you are rude and insolent.
impudently ADVERB **impudence** NOUN

impulse **impulses**
NOUN If you have an **impulse** to do something, you have a strong urge to do it immediately.
impulsive ADJECTIVE

in
PREPOSITION OR ADVERB **1** at or inside • *The cow was **in** the field.*
2 into • *They went **in** the house.*
3 during • *It snows **in** winter.*

in-
PREFIX You add **in-** to the beginning of a word to mean not something. For example, **in**accurate means not accurate, and **in**accessible means not accessible.

inability **inabilities**
NOUN If you have an **inability** to do something, you cannot do it.
ANTONYM: ability

inaccessible
ADJECTIVE If something is **inaccessible**, it is very difficult or impossible to reach.
ANTONYM: accessible

inaccurate
ADJECTIVE If something is **inaccurate**, it is incorrect.
ANTONYM: accurate

inadequate
ADJECTIVE If something is **inadequate**, there is not enough of it, or it is not good enough for a particular purpose.
ANTONYM: adequate

inanimate
ADJECTIVE not alive. For example, rocks and furniture are **inanimate**.

inaudible
ADJECTIVE If something is **inaudible**, it cannot be heard.
ANTONYM: audible

incapable
ADJECTIVE Someone who is **incapable** of doing something is not able to do it.
ANTONYM: capable

incendiary
ADJECTIVE An **incendiary** device is designed to set fire to things.

incense
NOUN a spicy substance that gives off a sweet smell when it is burned

incessant
ADJECTIVE If something is **incessant**, it continues without stopping. • *The sound of the rain on the windows was **incessant**.*
incessantly ADVERB

inch **inches**
NOUN a unit of length equal to about 2.54 centimetres
[from Latin *uncia* meaning twelfth part; there are twelve inches in a foot]

incident **incidents**
NOUN an event or occurrence, especially an unusual one

incidentally
ADVERB If something happens **incidentally**, it happens along with something else, as a minor part of it.

incinerate **incinerates, incinerating, incinerated**
VERB If you **incinerate** something, you burn it until only ashes are left.
incineration NOUN

incisor **incisors**
NOUN Your **incisors** are the sharp teeth at the front of your mouth, used for biting and cutting food.

inclination **inclinations**
NOUN If you have an **inclination** to do something, you want to do it.

incline **inclines, inclining, inclined**
Said "in-**klyn**" VERB **1** If you are **inclined** to do something, you often do it or you would like to do it.
Said "**in**-klyn" NOUN **2** a slope

include **includes, including, included**
VERB If one thing **includes** another, the second thing is part of the first thing.
• *Meals are **included** in the price at this hotel.*
ANTONYM: exclude

inclusive
ADJECTIVE When something is **inclusive**, it includes everything and nothing is left out. • *The price for the meal was **inclusive**, so Gran had nothing extra to pay for our milkshakes.*

incognito
ADVERB If someone is **incognito**, they are in disguise.
[from Latin *in* + *cognitus* meaning not known]

income **incomes**
NOUN the money a person earns

incomplete
ADJECTIVE Something that is **incomplete** is not complete or finished.
ANTONYM: complete

incongruous
ADJECTIVE If something is **incongruous** in a particular place or situation, it seems unsuitable and out of place.
incongruously ADVERB

inconsiderate
ADJECTIVE If you are **inconsiderate**, you do not consider the needs or feelings of others.
ANTONYM: considerate

inconspicuous
ADJECTIVE If someone or something is **inconspicuous**, they are not noticeable or obvious, and cannot easily be seen.
ANTONYM: conspicuous
inconspicuously ADVERB

inconvenient
ADJECTIVE If something is **inconvenient**, it is awkward and causes difficulties. • *an **inconvenient** time to call*
ANTONYM: convenient
inconveniently ADVERB

incorporate **incorporates, incorporating, incorporated**
VERB If someone **incorporates** one thing into another thing, they include the first thing so that it becomes part of the second.

incorrect
ADJECTIVE Something that is **incorrect** is wrong or untrue.
ANTONYM: correct

increase **increases, increasing, increased**
VERB **1** If something **increases**, or if you **increase** it, it becomes larger in number, level or amount. • *Her dad **increased** her pocket money.*
ANTONYM: decrease
NOUN **2** a rise in the number, level or amount of something • *There has been an **increase** in the number of children walking to school.*
ANTONYM: decrease

incredible
ADJECTIVE totally amazing or impossible to believe
SYNONYM: unbelievable

incubate **incubates, incubating, incubated**
Said "**in**-kyoo-bayt" VERB When eggs **incubate**, or a bird **incubates** them, they are kept warm until they hatch.

incubator **incubators**
NOUN a piece of hospital equipment in which sick or weak newborn babies are kept warm and safe

incurable
ADJECTIVE If someone has an **incurable** disease, they cannot be cured.
ANTONYM: curable

indebted
ADJECTIVE If you are **indebted** to someone, you are very grateful to them.

indecent
ADJECTIVE Something that is **indecent** is shocking or rude.
ANTONYM: decent
indecently ADVERB **indecency** NOUN

indecisive
ADJECTIVE If someone is **indecisive**, they find it difficult to make up their mind.
ANTONYM: decisive

indeed
ADVERB **1** You use **indeed** to emphasize a point that you are making. • *The cake was very good **indeed**.*
2 You use **indeed** to show that you agree with something. • *"Are you going to the party?" "**Indeed** I am."*

indefinite
ADJECTIVE If something is **indefinite**, it is vague and unclear.
ANTONYM: definite

indefinitely
ADVERB If something goes on **indefinitely**, there is no clear time when it will finish and it can go on for an unlimited time.

indent **indents, indenting, indented**
VERB If you **indent** a paragraph when you write, you start the first line further to the right, away from the margin.

independent
ADJECTIVE **1** If you are **independent**, you are able to do things yourself and do not need help from other people.
2 free and not controlled by anyone
independently ADVERB
independence NOUN

indestructible
ADJECTIVE If something is **indestructible**, it cannot be destroyed.

a b c d e f g h i j k l m n o p q r s t u v w x y z

A B C D E F G H I J K L M N O P Q R S T U V W X Y Z

indicate **indicates, indicating, indicated**
VERB **1** If you **indicate** something to someone, you point it out or show it to them.
2 If the driver of a vehicle **indicates**, they give a signal to show which way they are going to move or turn. • *The cyclist* ***indicated*** *that he was turning right.*

indicator **indicators**
NOUN **1** something that tells you what something is like or what is happening
2 A car's **indicators** are the lights at the front and back that are used to show when it is turning left or right.

indifferent
ADJECTIVE If you are **indifferent** to something, you have no interest in it.
indifferently ADVERB **indifference** NOUN

indigestion
NOUN a pain you get when you have difficulty digesting food

indignant
ADJECTIVE If you are **indignant** about something, you are angry about it because you think it is unfair.
indignantly ADVERB

indigo
ADJECTIVE deep blue or violet

indirect
ADJECTIVE If something happens in an **indirect** way, it does not happen in a straightforward way.
ANTONYM: direct
indirectly ADVERB

indispensable
ADJECTIVE absolutely necessary; essential

indistinct
ADJECTIVE not clear
ANTONYM: distinct
indistinctly ADVERB

individual **individuals**
ADJECTIVE **1** relating to one particular person or thing • *Each child in the class gets* ***individual*** *attention.*
2 single or separate • *Each sweet in the packet comes in an* ***individual*** *wrapper.*
NOUN **3** a person, different from any other person • *We should treat people as* ***individuals****.*

indoor
ADJECTIVE happening inside a building • *The hotel has an* ***indoor*** *swimming pool.*

indoors
ADVERB If something happens **indoors**, it takes place inside a building.

indulge **indulges, indulging, indulged**
VERB **1** If you **indulge** in something, you allow yourself to do it because you enjoy it.
2 If you **indulge** someone, you allow them to have or do what they want.
indulgence NOUN

industrial
ADJECTIVE to do with the work and processes involved in making things in factories

industrious
ADJECTIVE If you are **industrious**, you work hard.
industriously ADVERB

industry **industries**
NOUN **1** the work involved in making things in factories
2 all the people and processes involved in manufacturing a particular thing • *My dad works in the computer* ***industry****.*
[from Latin *industria* meaning diligence or hard work]

inedible
ADJECTIVE If something is **inedible**, it is too unpleasant or poisonous to eat.

inefficient
ADJECTIVE badly organized, wasteful and slow
inefficiently ADVERB **inefficiency** NOUN

inevitable
ADJECTIVE certain to happen

inexpensive
ADJECTIVE not costing much

inexplicable
ADJECTIVE If something is **inexplicable**,

you cannot explain it.
inexplicably ADVERB

infamous
Said "**in**-fum-uss" ADJECTIVE Someone or something that is **infamous** is well known for their bad qualities.
SYNONYM: notorious

infant **infants**
NOUN a baby or very young child
[from Latin *infans* meaning unable to speak]

infantry
NOUN In an army, the **infantry** are soldiers who fight on foot rather than in tanks or on horses.

infatuated
ADJECTIVE If you are **infatuated** with someone, you are so much in love with them that you cannot think reasonably about them.
infatuation NOUN

infect **infects, infecting, infected**
VERB If someone or something **infects** another person or animal, they pass a disease on to them.

infection **infections**
NOUN an illness caused by germs

infectious
ADJECTIVE Something that is **infectious** spreads from one person to another.
• *Measles is an **infectious** disease.*

infer **infers, inferring, inferred**
VERB If you **infer** that something is happening or is correct, you work it out from the details you already have.
inference NOUN

inferior
ADJECTIVE Something that is **inferior** is not as good as something else of a similar kind. • *The trainers were of **inferior** quality.*
inferiority NOUN

inferno **infernos**
NOUN a huge and fierce fire

infertile
ADJECTIVE **1** **Infertile** soil is of poor quality and plants cannot grow well in it.
2 A person, animal or plant that is **infertile** is unable to reproduce.

infested
ADJECTIVE If something is **infested**, it is full of pests, like insects, rats or fleas.

infinite
ADJECTIVE If something is **infinite**, it is endless and without limits.
infinitely ADVERB

infinitive **infinitives**
NOUN the base form of a verb. An **infinitive** often has "to" in front of it, for example *to be* or *to see.*

infirm
ADJECTIVE If someone is **infirm**, they are weak because they are ill or old.
infirmity NOUN

infirmary **infirmaries**
NOUN a hospital

inflammable
ADJECTIVE An **inflammable** material burns easily.

inflammation
NOUN painful redness or swelling of a part of the body

inflate **inflates, inflating, inflated**
VERB If you **inflate** something, you put air or a gas such as helium into it to make it swell.
inflatable ADJECTIVE

inflation
NOUN a general increase in the price of goods and services in a country

inflexible
ADJECTIVE If someone or something is **inflexible**, they cannot be bent or altered.

A B C D E F G H I J K L M N O P Q R S T U V W X Y Z

inflict **inflicts, inflicting, inflicted**
VERB If you **inflict** something unpleasant on someone, you make them suffer it.

influence **influences, influencing, influenced**
VERB If you **influence** someone or something, you have an effect on what they do or what happens.

influential
ADJECTIVE Someone who is **influential** is important and can influence people or events.
[from Latin *influentia* meaning power flowing from the stars]

influenza
NOUN FORMAL flu

inform **informs, informing, informed**
VERB If you **inform** somebody about something, you let them know about it.

informal
ADJECTIVE relaxed and casual
informally ADVERB

information
NOUN knowledge about something • *He used the encyclopedia to find more **information**.*

information technology
NOUN the storage and communication of information using computers

informative
ADJECTIVE Something that is **informative** gives you information.

infuriate **infuriates, infuriating, infuriated**
VERB If someone or something **infuriates** you, they make you very angry.
infuriating ADJECTIVE

ingenious
Said "in-**jeen**-yuss" ADJECTIVE Something that is **ingenious** is clever and involves new ideas.
ingeniously ADVERB

ingratitude
NOUN If you show **ingratitude**, you show a lack of care or thanks for something that has been done for you.
ANTONYM: gratitude

ingredient **ingredients**
NOUN **Ingredients** are the things that something is made from, especially in cookery.

inhabit **inhabits, inhabiting, inhabited**
VERB If you **inhabit** a place, you live there.

inhabitant **inhabitants**
NOUN If you are an **inhabitant** of a place, you live there.

inhale **inhales, inhaling, inhaled**
VERB When you **inhale** something, you breathe it in.
inhalation NOUN

inherit **inherits, inheriting, inherited**
VERB **1** If you **inherit** money or property, you receive it from someone who has died.
2 If you **inherit** a feature or quality from a parent or ancestor, you are born with it.
• *Her children have **inherited** her love of sport.*
inheritance NOUN **inheritor** NOUN

inhospitable
ADJECTIVE **1** If you are **inhospitable**, you are unwelcoming to people who visit you.
2 An **inhospitable** place is an unpleasant and difficult place to live in.

inhuman
ADJECTIVE **1** not human or not behaving like a human
2 extremely cruel

initial **initials**
Said "in-**nish**-ul" NOUN **1** one of the capital letters that begin each word of a name
ADJECTIVE **2** first or at the beginning
initially ADVERB

initiative
Said "in-**nish**-ut-iv" NOUN If you show **initiative**, you have the ability to see what needs to be done and do it, without relying on others.

inject **injects, injecting, injected**
VERB If a doctor or nurse **injects** you, they use a needle and syringe to put medicine into your body.
[from Latin *in* + *jacere* meaning to throw into]

injure **injures, injuring, injured**
VERB If you **injure** someone, you hurt or harm them in some way.

injury **injuries**
NOUN damage to part of a person's or animal's body

injustice
NOUN If someone suffers **injustice**, they are treated unfairly.

ink
NOUN the coloured liquid used for writing or printing

inland
ADJECTIVE OR ADVERB If a place is **inland**, it is away from the coast.

inlet **inlets**
NOUN a narrow bay or channel of water that goes inland from the sea, a lake or a river

inmate **inmates**
NOUN someone who lives in an institution, such as a prison

inn **inns**
NOUN a small, old country pub or hotel

inner
ADJECTIVE contained inside a place or object • *The **inner** tube of my front tyre has a puncture.*

innings
NOUN In cricket, an **innings** is a period of time when a particular team is batting.

innocent
ADJECTIVE not guilty of a crime or of doing something wrong
ANTONYM: guilty
innocently ADVERB **innocence** NOUN

innovation **innovations**
NOUN a completely new idea, product or way of doing things

inoculate **inoculates, inoculating, inoculated**
VERB If a doctor or nurse **inoculates** you, they give you an injection to protect you from catching a particular disease.
inoculation NOUN

input **inputs, inputting, input**
NOUN **1** Your **input** is your contribution and what you put into something. • *The class project requires **input** from everyone.*
2 In computing, **input** is information that is fed into a computer.
VERB **3** To **input** information into a computer means to feed it in.

inquest **inquests**
NOUN an official inquiry to find out what caused a person's death

inquire **inquires, inquired, inquiring**; also spelt **enquire**
VERB If you **inquire** about something, you ask for information about it.

inquiry **inquiries**
NOUN **1** an official investigation
2 a question or a request for information

inquisitive
ADJECTIVE Someone who is **inquisitive** is keen to find out about things.
inquisitively ADVERB **inquisitiveness** NOUN

insane
ADJECTIVE Someone or something **insane** is mad.
insanely ADVERB **insanity** NOUN

inscription **inscriptions**
NOUN the words that are carved or engraved on something such as a monument, gravestone or coin, or written in the front of a book

insect **insects**
NOUN a small animal with six legs and no backbone, with its skeleton on the outside. **Insects** often have wings, for example beetles, butterflies and grasshoppers.
[from Latin *insectum* meaning animal that has been cut into, because the bodies of many insects are divided into parts]

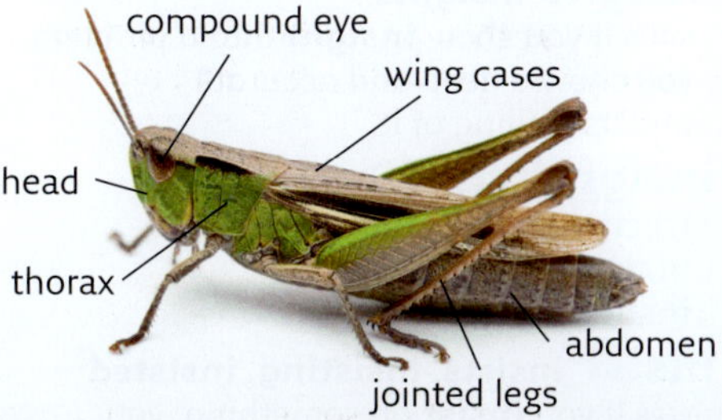

a b c d e f g h i j k l m n o p q r s t u v w x y z

A B C D E F G H I J K L M N O P Q R S T U V W X Y Z

insecticide **insecticides**
NOUN a poisonous chemical used to kill insects

insecure
ADJECTIVE **1** If you feel **insecure**, you lack confidence and feel worried.
2 If something is **insecure**, it is not fixed properly.
insecurity NOUN

inseparable
ADJECTIVE **1** If people are **inseparable**, they are always together. • *The three of them are such good friends, they're **inseparable**.*
2 If things are **inseparable**, they cannot be parted.

insert **inserts, inserting, inserted**
VERB If you **insert** an object into something, you put it inside. • *He **inserted** the key into the lock.*

inside **insides**
ADVERB, PREPOSITION OR ADJECTIVE **1** **Inside** means in something. • *an **inside** pocket* • *I waited **inside** the house.*
ANTONYM: outside
NOUN **2** The **inside** of something is the part that is surrounded by the main part, and is often hidden. • *I painted the **inside** of the shed.*
ANTONYM: outside
PHRASE **3** **Inside out** means with the inside part facing outwards. • *Her umbrella blew **inside out**.*
PLURAL NOUN **4** Your **insides** are the parts within your body that cannot be seen.

> Do not use *of* after *inside* when it is a preposition. It is correct to say *I waited inside the shop*, not *I waited inside of the shop*.

insight **insights**
NOUN If you show **insight** into a problem, you show a deep and accurate understanding of it.

insignificant
ADJECTIVE small and unimportant
insignificantly ADVERB
insignificance NOUN

insist **insists, insisting, insisted**
VERB If you **insist** on something, you demand it forcefully. • *As it was already dark, she **insisted** on giving us a lift home.*

insistent
ADJECTIVE If you are **insistent**, you insist on having or doing something.
insistence NOUN

insolent
ADJECTIVE very rude and showing no respect
insolently ADVERB **insolence** NOUN

insoluble
ADJECTIVE **1** impossible to solve
2 unable to dissolve

insomnia
NOUN difficulty in sleeping
insomniac NOUN

inspect **inspects, inspecting, inspected**
VERB If you **inspect** something, you examine or check it carefully.

inspector **inspectors**
NOUN **1** someone in authority whose job it is to inspect things
2 a rank of police officer

inspire **inspires, inspiring, inspired**
VERB If someone or something **inspires** you, they give you new ideas, confidence and enthusiasm.
inspired ADJECTIVE **inspiration** NOUN

install **installs, installing, installed**
VERB If you **install** something, you put it in place so that it is ready to be used.
installation NOUN

instalment **instalments**
NOUN **1** If you pay for something in **instalments**, you pay small amounts of money regularly over a period of time.
2 one of the parts of a story or television series

instance **instances**
NOUN **1** a particular example or occurrence of something
PHRASE **2** You use **for instance** to give an example of something you are talking about. • *In some countries, **for instance** in Spain, many shops are closed at lunchtime.*

instant **instants**
NOUN **1** a moment or short period of time

ADJECTIVE **2** immediate and without delay • *The book was an* ***instant*** *success.*
instantly ADVERB

instead
ADVERB If you do one thing **instead** of another, you do the first thing and not the second thing. • *They took the stairs* ***instead*** *of the lift.*

instinct **instincts**
NOUN a natural tendency to do something in a particular way • *Her* ***instincts*** *told her to run away as quickly as possible.*

institute **institutes**
NOUN an organization set up for a purpose, such as teaching or research

institution **institutions**
NOUN a large, important organization, such as a university or bank

instruct **instructs, instructing, instructed**
VERB **1** If you **instruct** someone to do something, you tell them to do it.
2 If someone **instructs** you in a subject or skill, they teach you about it.
instructor NOUN **instructive** ADJECTIVE

instruction **instructions**
NOUN If you follow an **instruction**, you do what someone tells you to do.

instrument **instruments**
NOUN **1** a tool that is used to do a particular job
2 an object, such as a piano or guitar, that you play to make music

insufficient
ADJECTIVE not enough for a particular purpose • *There is* ***insufficient*** *flour to make two cakes.*

insulate **insulates, insulating, insulated**
VERB If you **insulate** something, you cover it with materials such as foam or plastic to stop heat or electricity passing out of it.
insulation NOUN **insulator** NOUN

insulin
NOUN a substance that controls the level of sugar in your blood

insult **insults, insulting, insulted**
Said "in-**sult**" VERB **1** If you **insult** someone, you offend them by being rude to them.
Said "**in**-sult" NOUN **2** a rude remark that offends someone
insulting ADJECTIVE

insurance
NOUN an amount of money paid on a regular basis to a company that, in return, will pay you money if you have an accident or need medical treatment

intact
ADJECTIVE If something is **intact**, it is complete and undamaged.

integer **integers**
NOUN a whole number. For example, 2 is an **integer** but $2^1/_2$ is not.

integrate **integrates, integrating, integrated**
VERB If a person **integrates** into a group, they become a part of it.

integrity
NOUN the quality of being honest and trustworthy

intellectual
ADJECTIVE involving thought, ideas and understanding • *an* ***intellectual*** *exercise, like learning French*

intelligence
NOUN Your **intelligence** is your ability to understand and learn things.

intelligent
ADJECTIVE clever and able to understand things easily
intelligently ADVERB

intend **intends, intending, intended**
VERB If you **intend** to do something, you decide or plan to do it.

intense
ADJECTIVE very great in strength or amount • ***intense*** *heat*
intensely ADVERB **intensity** NOUN

intensive
ADJECTIVE If something is **intensive**, it

involves a lot of energy or effort over a short time.
intensively ADVERB

intention **intentions**
NOUN an idea or a plan of what you mean to do • *He had every* ***intention*** *of working hard that day.*

intentional
ADJECTIVE If something is **intentional**, it is done on purpose.
intentionally ADVERB

inter-
PREFIX You add **inter-** to a word to mean between or among two or more people or things. • ***inter****-school competitions*
• ***inter****national travel*

interactive
ADJECTIVE If a computer is **interactive**, it allows two-way communication between itself and the person using it, so that information can pass in both directions.

intercept **intercepts, intercepting, intercepted**
VERB If you **intercept** someone or something as they move from one place to another, you stop them reaching their destination.
interception NOUN

intercom **intercoms**
NOUN a device that people use to communicate with each other if they are in different rooms

interest **interests, interesting, interested**
NOUN **1** a thing you enjoy doing
2 **Interest** is an extra payment that you receive if you have invested money, or an extra payment that you make if you have borrowed money.
VERB **3** If something **interests** you, you want to know more about it.

interfere **interferes, interfering, interfered**
VERB **1** If you **interfere** in a situation, you try to influence it, although it does not concern you.
2 If you **interfere** with a plan, you get in the way of it.

interior **interiors**
NOUN **1** the inside part of something
• *the* ***interior*** *of the building*
ADJECTIVE **2** inside • *the* ***interior*** *walls*

interjection **interjections**
NOUN a word or phrase spoken suddenly to expresses an emotion, such as surprise, excitement or anger. For example, *Help!* is an **interjection**.

intermediate
ADJECTIVE An **intermediate** stage occurs in the middle, between two others. • *This dance class is for beginners. The next one is at* ***intermediate*** *level.*

internal
ADJECTIVE happening on, or part of, the inside of something • *Your lungs are* ***internal*** *organs.*

international
ADJECTIVE involving different countries
• *This is an important* ***international*** *match.*

internet or **Internet**
NOUN a worldwide system where people communicate using computers

interpret **interprets, interpreting, interpreted**
VERB **1** If you **interpret** something, you decide what it means. • *I tried to* ***interpret*** *his painting.*
2 If you **interpret** what someone is saying, you immediately translate it into another language.
interpretation NOUN **interpreter** NOUN

interrogate **interrogates, interrogating, interrogated**
VERB If you **interrogate** someone, you question them in great detail.
interrogation NOUN **interrogator** NOUN

interrupt **interrupts, interrupting, interrupted**
VERB If you **interrupt** someone, you start talking while they are talking.
interruption NOUN

intersect **intersects, intersecting, intersected**
VERB When two roads **intersect**, they cross each other.

intersection **intersections**
NOUN **1** a point where two roads cross over each other
2 the point where lines, arcs or sets cross each other

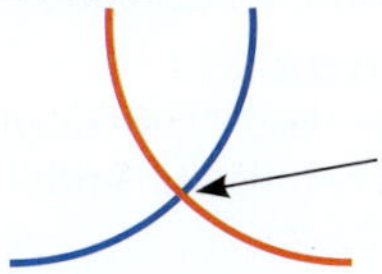

interval **intervals**
NOUN a short break during a play, concert or performance

intervene **intervenes, intervening, intervened**
VERB If you **intervene** in a situation, you step in, usually to sort out an argument or quarrel.
intervention NOUN

interview **interviews, interviewing, interviewed**
NOUN **1** a formal meeting where someone is asked questions
VERB **2** When someone **interviews** you, they ask you questions, usually in order to find out if you are suitable for something in particular.

intestine **intestines**
NOUN the part of your digestive system that carries food from your stomach. Your **intestines** are long tubes folded up inside your abdomen.
intestinal ADJECTIVE

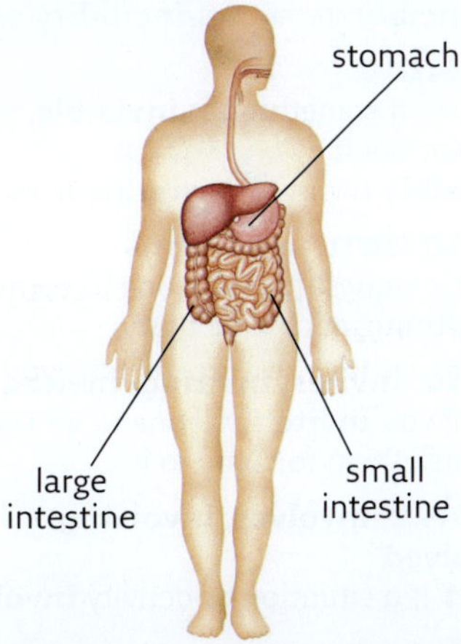

intimate
ADJECTIVE **1** If you are **intimate** with someone, you are very friendly with them.
2 **Intimate** details or thoughts are personal or private.

intimidate **intimidates, intimidating, intimidated**
VERB If you **intimidate** someone, you frighten them in a threatening way.
[from Latin *timidus* meaning fearful]
intimidated ADJECTIVE
intimidating ADJECTIVE
intimidation NOUN

into
PREPOSITION **1** If you go **into** something, you go inside it. • *Come **into** the house.*
2 If you bump or crash **into** something, you bump or crash against it.

intrepid
ADJECTIVE brave and fearless
intrepidly ADVERB

intricate
ADJECTIVE detailed and complicated
intricately ADVERB

intrigue **intrigues, intriguing, intrigued**
VERB If something **intrigues** you, you are fascinated by it and curious about it.
intrigue NOUN **intriguing** ADJECTIVE

introduce **introduces, introducing, introduced**
VERB **1** If you **introduce** one person to another, you tell them each other's name so that they can get to know each other.
2 If you **introduce** someone to something, they learn about it for the first time from you. • *My friend **introduced** me to water-skiing on holiday.*

introduction **introductions**
NOUN a piece of writing at the beginning of a book, that tells you what the book is about
introductory ADJECTIVE

intrude **intrudes, intruding, intruded**
VERB If you **intrude** on someone or something, you disturb them.
intrusion NOUN **intrusive** ADJECTIVE

intruder **intruders**
NOUN a person who forces their way into someone else's property without their consent • *The security guard caught an* ***intruder*** *last night.*

intuition **intuitions**
NOUN the ability to know about something without thinking about it or being able to explain it
intuitive ADJECTIVE **intuitively** ADVERB

Inuit **Inuits**
NOUN an Eskimo who comes from North America or Greenland

invade **invades, invading, invaded**
VERB If an army **invades** a country, it enters it by force.

invalid **invalids**
Said "**in**-va-lid" NOUN **1** someone who is so ill that they need to be looked after by someone else
Said "in-**val**-id" ADJECTIVE **2** If something is **invalid**, it cannot be accepted because there is something wrong with it. • *Your ticket is* ***invalid*** *for this train service.*

invaluable
ADJECTIVE extremely useful

invasion **invasions**
NOUN the forceful entering or attacking of a place • *At the end of the match, there was an* ***invasion*** *of the pitch by fans.*

invent **invents, inventing, invented**
VERB **1** If you **invent** something, you are the first person to think of it or make it.
2 If you **invent** a story or an excuse, you make it up.
inventor NOUN **invention** NOUN
inventive ADJECTIVE **inventiveness** NOUN

inverse
NOUN FORMAL In mathematics, if you turn something upside down or back to front, you have its **inverse**. • *The* ***inverse*** *of 23 is 32.*

invert **inverts, inverting, inverted**
VERB **1** If you **invert** something, you turn it upside down.
2 If you **invert** a fraction, the top number changes places with the bottom number.

invertebrate **invertebrates**
NOUN an animal without a backbone

inverted commas
NOUN punctuation marks (" ") are used to show where speech begins and ends
• *"Good morning!" she cried.*

invest **invests, investing, invested**
VERB If you **invest** money in something, you try to increase its value, for example by putting it into a bank or building society so that it will gain interest.
investor NOUN **investment** NOUN

investigate **investigates, investigating, investigated**
VERB If someone **investigates** something, they try to find out all the facts about it. • *Police are still* ***investigating*** *the accident.*
SYNONYMS: examine, look into, study
investigator NOUN

investigation **investigations**
NOUN If you conduct an **investigation** into something, you examine it carefully and try to find out the facts about it.
• *The disappearance of the money was under* ***investigation****.*

invincible
ADJECTIVE If something is **invincible**, it cannot be defeated.
invincibly ADVERB **invincibility** NOUN

invisible
ADJECTIVE If something is **invisible**, you cannot see it.
invisibly ADVERB **invisibility** NOUN

invitation **invitations**
NOUN a request for someone to come to something, such as a party

invite **invites, inviting, invited**
VERB If you **invite** someone to an event, you ask them to come to it.

involve **involves, involving, involved**
VERB **1** If a situation or activity **involves**

something, that thing is a necessary part of it. • *Being president **involves** a lot of responsibility.*
2 If you **involve** yourself in something, you take part in it. • *I'm **involved** in the production of the school play.*

ir-
PREFIX a variation of in-, meaning not. For example, **ir**relevant means not relevant, and **ir**replaceable means not replaceable.

irate
ADJECTIVE very angry
irately ADVERB

iris **irises**
NOUN the coloured part of your eye
[from Greek *iris* meaning rainbow or coloured circle]

iron **irons, ironing, ironed**
NOUN **1** a hard, dark metal used to make steel
2 an appliance you heat up and press on clothes to remove creases
VERB **3** If you **iron** clothes, you use a hot iron to remove creases from them.
ironing NOUN

irony
NOUN When you use **irony**, you use words, often in a humorous way, to say the opposite of what you really mean.
ironic ADJECTIVE **ironically** ADVERB

irrational
ADJECTIVE If you act in an **irrational** way, you show no reason or logic in what you do.
irrationally ADVERB

irregular
ADJECTIVE **1** Something that is **irregular** is not smooth or straight, or does not make a regular pattern.
2 Irregular verbs do not follow the usual rules.
irregularly ADVERB **irregularity** NOUN

irrelevant
ADJECTIVE If something is **irrelevant**, it has nothing to do with what is being said or discussed.
irrelevance NOUN

irresistible
ADJECTIVE **1** If something is **irresistible**, it cannot be controlled. • *I had an **irresistible** urge to laugh.*
2 If someone is **irresistible**, they are very attractive.

irresponsible
ADJECTIVE If you do something in an **irresponsible** way, you act thoughtlessly and carelessly.
SYNONYMS: careless, thoughtless
irresponsibly ADVERB
irresponsibility NOUN

irreversible
ADJECTIVE If something is **irreversible**, it cannot be reversed or changed back to the way it was before.
irreversibly ADVERB

irrigate **irrigates, irrigating, irrigated**
VERB To **irrigate** land is to supply it with water brought through pipes or ditches.
• *In hot, dry countries the land is **irrigated**.*
[from Latin *rigare* meaning to moisten]
irrigated ADJECTIVE **irrigation** NOUN

irritable
ADJECTIVE If you are **irritable**, you are easily annoyed.
irritably ADVERB

irritate **irritates, irritating, irritated**
VERB If something **irritates** you, it annoys you.
irritation NOUN

is
VERB a present tense of **be**

Islam
NOUN the Muslim religion, which teaches that there is only one God, Allah, and Mohammed is his prophet

island **islands**
NOUN a piece of land surrounded by water

isle **isles**
NOUN a literary word for an island

isn't
VERB a contraction of *is not*

a b c d e f g h i j k l m n o p q r s t u v w x y z

isolate **isolates, isolating, isolated**
VERB **1** If you **isolate** yourself, you separate yourself from other people.
• *I **isolated** myself in my room.*
2 To **isolate** a sick person or animal means to keep them away from others so that the disease does not spread.
isolated ADJECTIVE **isolation** NOUN

isosceles
ADJECTIVE An **isosceles** triangle has two sides of the same length and two equal angles.

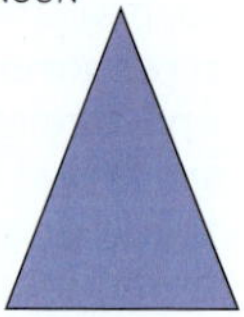

ISP **ISPs**
NOUN a business that provides access to the internet. **ISP** is an abbreviation for *internet service provider.*

issue **issues**
NOUN **1** an important subject that people are talking about • *The **issue** of homeless people is important to many people.*
2 a particular newspaper or magazine
• *this week's **issue** of the local paper*

it
PRONOUN **1** used to refer to something that has already been mentioned. **It** can also refer to babies or other animals whose gender is not known. • *I like that dog. **It** is very friendly.*
2 You use **it** to talk about the weather, time or date. • ***It**'s been raining all day.*

IT
NOUN an abbreviation of *Information Technology*

italics
PLURAL NOUN letters printed in a particular sloping way. They are often used for emphasis. • *This writing is in **italics**.*

itch **itches, itching, itched**
VERB **1** When a part of your body **itches**, you have an unpleasant feeling that makes you want to scratch it.
NOUN **2** an unpleasant feeling on your skin that makes you want to scratch it

item **items**
NOUN one of a collection or list of objects
• *Milk is the most important **item** on my shopping list.*

itinerary **itineraries**
NOUN The **itinerary** of a journey is a detailed plan of where to go and what to see along the route.

it's
a contraction of *it is* or *it has*

Do not confuse *it's* with *its*.

its
ADJECTIVE OR PRONOUN **Its** is used to refer to something belonging to things, children or animals that have already been mentioned. • *The cat won't eat. **Its** bowl needs cleaning.*

Do not confuse *its* with *it's*.

I've
a contraction of *I have*

ivory
NOUN **1** the valuable, creamy-white bone that forms the tusk of an elephant. It is used to make ornaments.
NOUN OR ADJECTIVE **2** creamy-white

ivy
NOUN an evergreen plant that creeps along the ground and up walls

Jj

jab **jabs, jabbing, jabbed**
VERB **1** If you **jab** something, you poke at it roughly.
NOUN **2** a sharp, sudden poke • *a **jab** in the ribs*
3 INFORMAL an injection • *a measles **jab***

jack **jacks**
NOUN **1** a piece of equipment for lifting heavy objects, especially for lifting a car when changing a wheel
2 In a pack of cards, a **jack** is a card whose value is between a ten and a queen.

jackal **jackals**
NOUN a wild animal related to the dog

jacket **jackets**
NOUN **1** a short coat
2 the paper cover of a book

jackpot **jackpots**
NOUN the top prize in a gambling game • *He was excited to hear he had won the **jackpot** in the lottery.*

jagged
ADJECTIVE A **jagged** rock has a rough, uneven shape with sharp edges.

jail **jails, jailing, jailed** or **gaol**
NOUN **1** a building where people convicted of a crime are locked up
VERB **2** To **jail** someone means to lock them up in a jail.

jam **jams, jamming, jammed**
NOUN **1** a food made by boiling fruit with sugar
2 a situation where there are so many people or things that it is difficult to move • *There is often a traffic **jam** at that junction.*
VERB **3** If you **jam** something into a place, you squeeze it in. • *He **jammed** his clothes into the suitcase.*
4 If you **jam** something, or if it **jams**, it becomes stuck. • *The coin was **jammed** in the slot.*

January
NOUN the first month of the year. **January** has 31 days.

jar **jars, jarring, jarred**
NOUN **1** a glass container used for storing food
VERB **2** If something **jars**, you find it unpleasant or annoying.

jargon
NOUN language containing lots of technical words, used by particular groups of people • *Doctors often use **jargon**.*

jaundice
NOUN an illness of the liver, where the skin and the whites of the eyes become yellow

javelin **javelins**
NOUN a long spear that is thrown in sports competitions

jaw **jaws**
NOUN **1** the bone in which teeth are set
2 the mouth and teeth of a person or animal

jazz
NOUN a style of popular music with a strong rhythm

jealous
ADJECTIVE If you are **jealous**, you feel envious of others, wanting to have what they have or wanting to be like them.
jealously ADVERB **jealousy** NOUN

jeans
PLURAL NOUN cotton trousers, often made of denim

jeep **jeeps**
NOUN TRADEMARK a four-wheeled motor vehicle designed for driving over rough ground

jeer **jeers, jeering, jeered**
VERB **1** If you **jeer** at someone, you insult them in a loud, unpleasant way.
NOUN **2** **Jeers** are rude and insulting remarks.
jeering ADJECTIVE

A B C D E F G H I J K L M N O P Q R S T U V W X Y Z

jelly **jellies**
NOUN **1** a clear, sweet food eaten as a dessert
2 a type of clear, set jam • *I like mint **jelly** with lamb.*

jellyfish **jellyfishes**
NOUN a sea creature with a clear, soft body and tentacles that may sting

jerk **jerks, jerking, jerked**
VERB **1** If you **jerk** something, you give it a sudden, sharp pull.
2 If something **jerks**, it moves suddenly and sharply.

jersey **jerseys**
NOUN a knitted garment for the upper half of the body

jet **jets**
NOUN **1** an aeroplane that can fly very fast
2 a rush of air, steam or liquid that is forced out under pressure

jetty **jetties**
NOUN a wide stone wall or wooden platform at the edge of the sea or a river, where boats can be moored

Jew **Jews**
NOUN a person who practises the religion of Judaism or who is of Hebrew descent
Jewish ADJECTIVE

jewel **jewels**
NOUN a precious stone, often used to decorate valuable items such as rings or necklaces
jewelled ADJECTIVE

jeweller **jewellers**
NOUN a person who makes or sells jewellery

jewellery
NOUN the ornaments that people wear, like rings and necklaces

jigsaw **jigsaws**
NOUN a puzzle that is made up of odd-shaped pieces that must be fitted together to make a picture

jingle **jingles**
NOUN **1** a short, catchy phrase or rhyme with music, used to advertise something on radio or television
2 a gentle ringing sound

job **jobs**
NOUN **1** the work that someone does to earn money
2 anything that has to be done

jockey **jockeys**
NOUN someone who rides a horse in a race

joey **joeys**
NOUN a young kangaroo

jog **jogs, jogging, jogged**
VERB **1** If you **jog**, you run slowly, often for exercise.
2 If you **jog** something, you knock it slightly so that it shakes or moves.
• *My pen slipped when he **jogged** my arm.*
jogger NOUN **jogging** NOUN

join **joins, joining, joined**
VERB **1** If you **join** a club, you become a member of it.
2 When two things **join**, or when one thing **joins** another, they come together.
• *The two streams **join** and form a river.*
SYNONYMS: connect, link

join in
VERB If you **join in** an activity, you take part in it.

joiner **joiners**
NOUN a person who makes wooden window frames, doors and furniture

joint **joints**
ADJECTIVE **1** shared by or belonging to two or more people • *The project was a **joint** effort.*
NOUN **2** a part of your body, such as your elbow or knee, where two bones meet and are able to move together

joke **jokes, joking, joked**
NOUN **1** something that you say to make people laugh
VERB **2** If you **joke**, you say something amusing or tell a funny story.

jolly **jollier, jolliest**
ADJECTIVE If you are **jolly**, you are happy and cheerful.

jolt **jolts, jolting, jolted**
VERB **1** If something **jolts**, it moves or shakes roughly and violently. • *The bus **jolted** along the bumpy road.*
2 If something or someone **jolts** you, they bump into you clumsily.
NOUN **3** a sudden, jerky movement
4 an unpleasant shock or surprise

jostle **jostles, jostling, jostled**
VERB If people or animals **jostle**, they push and bump into each other roughly, usually because they are in a crowd.

jot **jots, jotting, jotted**
VERB If you **jot** something down, you write a quick, brief note.

journal **journals**
NOUN **1** a magazine that deals with a particular interest
2 a diary where you write what happens each day

journalist **journalists**
NOUN a person whose job is to gather news and write about it for a newspaper or magazine, or present it on television or radio

journey **journeys**
NOUN the act of travelling from one place to another

joy **joys**
NOUN **1** a feeling of great happiness or pleasure
2 something that makes you happy or gives you pleasure • *It was a **joy** to see my friend again.*

joystick **joysticks**
NOUN **1** a lever in a plane that the pilot uses to control height and direction
2 a lever that controls the cursor on a computer screen, especially in computer games

jubilee **jubilees**
NOUN a special anniversary of an event such as a coronation • *Queen Elizabeth's Silver **Jubilee** was in 1977.*
[from Hebrew *yobhel* meaning ram's horn, blown during festivals and celebrations to mark the freedom of Hebrew slaves each 50th year, known as the jubilee]

Judaism
NOUN the religion of the Jewish people. It is based on a belief in one God, and draws its laws from the Old Testament.
Judaic ADJECTIVE

judge **judges, judging, judged**
NOUN **1** the person in a law court who decides how criminals should be punished according to the law
2 the person who chooses the winner of a competition
VERB **3** If a person **judges** someone or something, they act as a judge.
4 If you **judge** someone or something, you decide what they are like.

judgment **judgments**; also spelt **judgement**
NOUN an opinion that you have after thinking carefully about something

judo
NOUN a sport in which two people try to force each other to the ground using special throwing techniques. It originated in Japan as a form of self-defence.
[from Japanese *ju do* meaning gentleness art]

jug **jugs**
NOUN a container with a handle and a lip, used for holding and pouring liquids

juggernaut **juggernauts**
NOUN a large, heavy lorry
[from Hindi *Jagannath*, the name of a huge idol of the god Krishna, which is wheeled through the streets of Puri in India every year]

juggle **juggles, juggling, juggled**
VERB When someone **juggles** they throw different objects into the air, keeping more than one object in the air at the same time without dropping them.
juggler NOUN

a
b
c
d
e
f
g
h
i
j
k
l
m
n
o
p
q
r
s
t
u
v
w
x
y
z

A B C D E F G H I J K L M N O P Q R S T U V W X Y Z

juice **juices**
NOUN the liquid that can be obtained from fruit, vegetables and other food • *orange* ***juice***

juicy **juicier, juiciest**
ADJECTIVE having a great deal of juice • *The orange was very* ***juicy****.*

July
NOUN the seventh month of the year. **July** has 31 days.

jumble **jumbles, jumbling, jumbled**
NOUN **1** an untidy muddle of things
2 articles for a **jumble** sale
VERB **3** If you **jumble** things, you mix them up untidily.

jumble sale **jumble sales**
NOUN an event where second-hand items are sold to raise money cheaply, often for charity

jump **jumps, jumping, jumped**
VERB **1** When you **jump**, you spring off the ground using the muscles in your legs.
2 If someone **jumps**, they make a sudden, sharp movement because they are surprised.

jumper **jumpers**
NOUN a warm piece of clothing that covers the top part of your body

junction **junctions**
NOUN a place where roads or railway lines meet or cross

June
NOUN the sixth month of the year. **June** has 30 days.

jungle **jungles**
NOUN a dense, tropical forest where many trees and other plants grow close together
[from Hindi *jangal* meaning wasteland]

junior
ADJECTIVE **1** A **junior** official or employee holds a lower position in an organization. • *She will be a* ***junior*** *doctor after finishing her training.*
2 younger • *He is the* ***junior*** *of the two brothers.*

junk **junks**
NOUN **1** old, unwanted or worthless things that are sold cheaply or thrown away
2 a Chinese sailing boat that has a flat bottom and wide sails

junk food
NOUN food that is easy and quick to prepare, or bought ready to eat, but is not always very good for you

jury **juries**
NOUN a group of people in a court of law who are chosen to listen to the facts about a crime and then decide whether the accused person is guilty or not

just
ADJECTIVE **1** Someone who is **just** is fair.
ADVERB **2** If something has **just** happened, it happened a very short time ago.
3 If you **just** do something, you almost don't do it. • *He* ***just*** *managed to climb the fence.*
4 If something is **just** what you want, it is exactly what you want.

justice
NOUN **1** fairness in the way that people are treated
2 the system of laws created by a community

justify **justifies, justifying, justified**
VERB If you **justify** what you are doing or saying, you prove or explain why it is reasonable or necessary.
justification NOUN **justifiable** ADJECTIVE

jut **juts, jutting, jutted**
VERB If something **juts** out, it sticks out beyond a surface or an edge. • *The pier* ***jutted*** *out into the sea.*

juvenile **juveniles**
ADJECTIVE **1** suitable for or to do with young people
2 childish and rather silly
NOUN **3** a young person not old enough to be considered an adult

Kk

kaleidoscope **kaleidoscopes**
NOUN a toy made of a tube with a hole at one end. When you look through the hole and twist the other end of the tube, you can see a changing pattern of colours.

kangaroo **kangaroos**
NOUN a large, Australian marsupial with very strong back legs that it uses for jumping

karate
NOUN a sport in which people fight each other using only their hands, elbows, feet and legs
[from Japanese *kara* + *te* meaning empty hand]

kayak **kayaks**
NOUN a covered canoe with a small opening for the person sitting in it, originally used by Inuit people

kebab **kebabs**
NOUN pieces of meat or vegetable grilled on a stick
[from Arabic *kabab* meaning roast meat]

keen **keener, keenest**
ADJECTIVE **1** If you are **keen** to do something, or for something to happen, you want very much to do it or for it to happen. • *I was **keen** to meet my cousins from Australia.*
2 If you are **keen** on something or someone, you are fond of them or attracted to them.
3 If your senses are **keen**, you are able to see, hear, taste and smell things very clearly or strongly.

keep **keeps, keeping, kept**
VERB **1** If you **keep** something, you have it and don't give it away. • *I will **keep** this book forever.*
2 If you **keep** an animal, you look after it. • *He **keeps** rabbits.*
3 If you **keep** something somewhere, you store it there. • *I **keep** my bicycle in the garage.*
4 If you **keep** doing something, you do it again and again.
5 If something **keeps** you a certain way, you stay that way because of it. • *The duvet **keeps** me warm.*
6 If you **keep** a promise, you do what you have said you will do.
7 If you **keep** a secret, you do not tell it to anyone else.
NOUN **8** the main tower inside the walls of a castle

keeper **keepers**
NOUN **1** a person whose job is to look after the animals in a zoo
2 a goalkeeper in soccer or hockey • *The **keeper** managed to stop the ball and save the penalty.*

kennel **kennels**
NOUN **1** a small hut for a dog to sleep in
2 A **kennels** is a place where dogs are bred and trained, or looked after when their owners are away.

kept
VERB the past tense and past participle of **keep**

kerb **kerbs**
NOUN the raised edge of a pavement, that separates it from the road • *You must look both ways for traffic before stepping off the **kerb**.*

kernel **kernels**
NOUN the part of a nut that is inside the shell

kestrel **kestrels**
NOUN a type of small hawk

ketchup
NOUN a cold sauce, usually made from tomatoes

kettle **kettles**
NOUN a covered container with a spout, in which you boil water

key **keys**
NOUN **1** a specially shaped piece of metal that fits in a lock, and is turned in order to open the lock
2 The **keys** on a piano or a computer are the buttons that you press in order to operate it.
ADJECTIVE **3** **Key** words or sentences are the important ones in a piece of text.
NOUN **4** information arranged in a way that can be used to identify animals, plants and materials. You can use a **key** to help you name an unknown animal, plant or material.

keyboard **keyboards**
NOUN a set of keys on a piano, typewriter or computer

keyhole **keyholes**
NOUN the hole in a lock where you put a key

khaki
NOUN OR ADJECTIVE yellowish-brown. Soldiers' uniforms are often made of **khaki** material.
[from Urdu *kaki* meaning dusty]

kick **kicks, kicking, kicked**
VERB **1** If you **kick** someone or something, you hit them with your foot.
NOUN **2** If you give something a **kick**, you hit it with your foot.
3 INFORMAL If you get a **kick** out of something, you enjoy it very much.

kick off
VERB When a soccer or rugby team **kicks off**, they begin playing.

kid **kids, kidding, kidded**
NOUN **1** INFORMAL a child
2 a young goat
VERB **3** If you **kid** someone, you tease them and try to make them believe something that isn't true.
SYNONYM: tease

kidnap **kidnaps, kidnapping, kidnapped**
VERB If someone **kidnaps** someone else, they take them away by force and demand something in exchange for returning them.
[from *kid* + *nap* meaning child stealing; in the 17th century children were kidnapped to work on American plantations]

kidney **kidneys**
NOUN one of the two organs in your body that remove waste products from your blood

kill **kills, killing, killed**
VERB If someone **kills** a person, animal or plant, they make them die.

kiln **kilns**
NOUN an oven for baking china or pottery until it becomes hard and dry

kilo **kilos**
NOUN a kilogram

kilogram **kilograms**
NOUN a unit of mass and weight (kg) equal to 1000 grams

kilohertz
NOUN a unit of measurement of radio waves (kHz) equal to 1000 hertz

kilometre **kilometres**
NOUN a unit of distance (km) equal to 1000 metres

kilowatt **kilowatts**
NOUN a unit of power (kW) equal to 1000 watts

kilt **kilts**
NOUN a tartan skirt worn by men as part of Scottish Highland dress

kimono **kimonos**
NOUN a long, loose garment with wide sleeves and a sash, worn in Japan

kin
PLURAL NOUN Your **kin** are your relatives.

kind **kinder, kindest; kinds**
ADJECTIVE **1** Someone who is **kind** behaves in a caring and helpful way towards other people.
SYNONYM: considerate
NOUN **2** a particular thing of the same type as other things • *I do not like this **kind** of bread.*
SYNONYMS: sort, class
kindly ADVERB **kindness** NOUN

king **kings**
NOUN a man who is the head of state in a country, and who inherited his position from his parents

kingdom **kingdoms**
NOUN a country that is governed by a king or queen

kingfisher **kingfishers**
NOUN a brightly-coloured bird that lives near water and feeds on fish

kiosk **kiosks**
NOUN a small shop or hut where you can buy newspapers, snacks, and sweets

kipper **kippers**
NOUN a herring that has been dried in smoke to preserve it and give it a special taste

kiss **kisses, kissing, kissed**
VERB **1** When you **kiss** someone, you touch them with your lips in order to show your affection.
NOUN **2** When you give someone a **kiss**, you kiss them.

kit **kits**
NOUN **1** a collection of equipment and clothing that you use for a sport or other activity • *football **kit***
2 a set of parts that you fit together to make something • *I got a model aeroplane **kit** for my birthday.*

kitchen **kitchens**
NOUN a room used for cooking and preparing food

kite **kites**
NOUN a light frame covered with paper or cloth, that you fly in the air at the end of a long string

kitten **kittens**
NOUN a very young cat

kiwi **kiwi** or **kiwis**
NOUN **1** a type of bird found in New Zealand. **Kiwis** cannot fly.
2 INFORMAL Someone who comes from New Zealand is called a **kiwi**.
[A Maori word]

kiwi fruit **kiwi fruits**
NOUN a fruit with a brown, hairy skin and green flesh

knack
NOUN an ability to do something easily

knead **kneads, kneading, kneaded**
VERB If you **knead** dough, you press it and squeeze it with your hands before baking it.

knee **knees**
NOUN the joint in your leg between your ankle and your hip

kneel **kneels, kneeling, knelt**
VERB When you **kneel**, or **kneel down**, you bend your legs and lower your body so that one or both knees are touching the ground.

knew
VERB the past tense of **know**

knickers
PLURAL NOUN underpants worn by women and girls

knife **knives**
NOUN a sharp, metal tool used for cutting things

knight **knights, knighting, knighted**
NOUN **1** In medieval times, a **knight** was a nobleman who served his king or lord in battle. • *King Arthur and the **Knights** of the Round Table*
VERB **2** If a king or queen **knights** a man, they give him the title *Sir* before his name.
[from Old English *cniht* meaning servant]

knit **knits, knitting, knitted**
VERB If you **knit** a piece of clothing, you

A B C D E F G H I J K L M N O P Q R S T U V W X Y Z

make it from wool, using knitting needles or a knitting machine.

knob **knobs**
NOUN a round handle or switch on doors, furniture and machinery

knock **knocks, knocking, knocked**
VERB **1** If you **knock** on something, you hit it hard with your hand to make a noise. • *I **knocked** on the door when I arrived.*
2 If you **knock** against something, you bump into it.

knocker **knockers**
NOUN a metal lever attached to a door, that you use to knock on the door

knot **knots, knotting, knotted**
NOUN **1** a fastening made by passing one end of a piece of string or fabric through a loop and pulling it tight • *The **knot** in my laces was so tight that I could not undo it.*

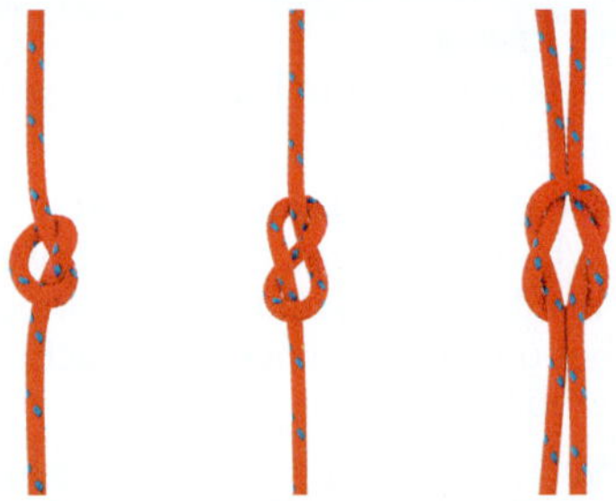

Overhand knot — Figure 8 knot — Square or reef knot

2 a hard, round spot on a piece of wood, where a branch grew on the tree
3 a unit for measuring the speed of ships and aircraft
VERB **4** If you **knot** a piece of string, you tie a knot in it.

know **knows, knowing, knew, known**
VERB **1** If you **know** something, you have it clearly in your mind and you do not need to learn it. • *I **know** how to swim.*
2 If you **know** a person, place or thing, you are familiar with them. • *I've **known** him for five years.*

knowledge
NOUN all the information and facts that you know • *general **knowledge***

knuckle **knuckles**
NOUN one of the joints in your fingers

koala **koalas**
NOUN an Australian marsupial with grey fur and small, tufted ears. **Koalas** live in trees and eat eucalyptus leaves.

Koran or **Qur'an**
NOUN the holy book of Islam
[from Arabic *kara'a* meaning to read]

kosher
ADJECTIVE **Kosher** food has been specially prepared to be eaten according to Jewish law.

Ll

label **labels, labelling, labelled**
NOUN **1** a piece of paper or plastic attached to something and giving information about it • *The **label** on the bottle told him when to have his medicine.*
VERB **2** If you **label** something, you put a label on it.

laboratory **laboratories**
NOUN a place where scientific experiments are carried out

labour
NOUN **1** hard work
2 In Britain, **Labour**, or the **Labour** Party, is one of the main political parties.

Labrador **Labradors**
NOUN a large dog with short black, golden or chocolate brown hair

labyrinth **labyrinths**
NOUN a complicated series of paths or passages that are difficult to find your way around

lace **laces, lacing, laced**
NOUN **1** a fine, decorated cloth, with a pattern of many holes in it
2 one of the thin pieces of material that are used to fasten shoes
VERB **3** When you **lace** something up, you fix it together by tying a lace.

lack **lacks, lacking, lacked**
NOUN **1** If there is a **lack** of something, there is not enough of it or there is none of it. • *Despite his **lack** of training, he won the race.*
VERB **2** If someone or something **lacks** something, they do not have it.

lacquer **lacquers**
NOUN thin, clear paint that you put on wood to protect it and make it shiny

ladder **ladders**
NOUN a wooden or metal frame consisting of two long poles with short bars in between. **Ladders** are used for climbing up and down things.

ladle **ladles**
NOUN a long-handled spoon with a deep, round bowl, which you use to serve soup

lady **ladies**
NOUN **1** a polite word for woman
2 In Britain, **Lady** is the title of the wife of a knight or a lord.

ladybird **ladybirds**
NOUN a small, flying beetle with a round body, usually red, patterned with black spots

lag **lags, lagging, lagged**
VERB **1** If a person or a thing **lags** behind, they make slower progress than other people or other things and do not keep up. • *Don't **lag** behind, or you'll get lost!*
2 If you **lag** pipes or water tanks, you cover them with insulating material to stop heat escaping and prevent freezing.

lager **lagers**
NOUN a kind of light beer

lagoon **lagoons**
NOUN an area of water separated from the sea by reefs or sand

laid
VERB the past tense of **lay**

lain
VERB the past participle of some meanings of *lie* • *It must have **lain** there for days.*

lair **lairs**
NOUN a place where a wild animal lives

a b c d e f g h i j k l m n o p q r s t u v w x y z

A B C D E F G H I J K L M N O P Q R S T U V W X Y Z

lake **lakes**
NOUN a large area of fresh water surrounded by land

lamb **lambs**
NOUN **1** a young sheep
2 the meat from a lamb

lame
ADJECTIVE **1** Someone who is **lame** has an injured leg and cannot walk easily.
2 A **lame** excuse is unconvincing.
lamely ADVERB **lameness** NOUN

lamp **lamps**
NOUN a device that produces light • *Please turn on the table **lamp** now that it is getting dark.*

lamppost **lampposts**
NOUN a tall column in a street, with a lamp at the top

lance **lances**
NOUN a long spear that was used in the past by soldiers on horseback

land **lands, landing, landed**
NOUN **1** an area of ground • *We camped on the **land** surrounding the castle.*
2 the parts of the earth's surface that are not covered by water
VERB **3** When someone or something **lands** somewhere, they reach the ground after moving through the air.
4 When you **land** somewhere on a plane or a ship, you arrive there.

landing **landings**
NOUN the flat area at the top of a flight of stairs in a building

landlady **landladies**
NOUN a woman who owns a house or small hotel and who lets rooms to people

landlord **landlords**
NOUN **1** a man who owns a house or small hotel and who lets rooms to people
2 a person who looks after a public house
3 someone who owns a large amount of land or houses and lets some of it out in return for rent

landmark **landmarks**
NOUN a noticeable feature in a landscape, that you can use to check your position • *The tower on the hill is a local **landmark**.*

landscape **landscapes**
NOUN everything you can see when you look across an area of land

lane **lanes**
NOUN **1** a narrow road, especially in the country
2 one of the parallel strips into which a road, a race track or a swimming pool is divided

language **languages**
NOUN a system of words used by a particular group of people to communicate with each other

lantern **lanterns**
NOUN a lamp in a metal frame with glass sides

lap **laps, lapping, lapped**
NOUN **1** the flat area formed by your thighs when you are sitting down
2 one circuit of a running track or racecourse
VERB **3** When water **laps** against something, it gently moves against it in little waves.
4 When an animal **laps** a drink, it uses its tongue to flick the liquid into its mouth.

lapel **lapels**
NOUN the part of the collar that folds back over the front of a jacket or coat

lapse **lapses, lapsing, lapsed**
NOUN **1** a moment of bad behaviour by someone who usually behaves well
2 a period of time that has passed
VERB **3** If you **lapse** into a different way of behaving, you start behaving that way. • *The class **lapsed** into silence.*
4 If something such as a promise or an agreement **lapses**, it is no longer valid.

laptop **laptops**
NOUN a portable computer small enough to fit on your lap, which is especially useful if you are travelling

lard
NOUN fat from a pig, used in cooking

larder **larders**
NOUN a room in which you store food, often next to a kitchen

large **larger, largest**
ADJECTIVE bigger than usual

largely
ADVERB to a great extent • *It was **largely** a party for his birthday, but we celebrated his sister's exam results too.*

lark **larks, larking, larked**
NOUN **1** a small, brown bird with a very pleasant song
2 If you do something for a **lark**, you do it in a high-spirited or mischievous way for fun.
VERB **3** If you **lark** about, you enjoy yourself in a high-spirited way.

larva **larvae**
NOUN an insect after it has hatched from its egg, and before it becomes an adult. A caterpillar is the **larva** of a butterfly.

lasagne
NOUN an Italian dish made with wide, flat sheets of pasta, meat or vegetables and cheese sauce
[from Latin *lasanum* meaning cooking pot]

laser **lasers**
NOUN **1** a narrow beam of concentrated light produced by a special machine. It is used to cut very hard materials and in some kinds of surgery.
2 the machine that produces the beam of light
[from the first letters of *Light Amplification by Stimulated Emission of Radiation*]

lash **lashes, lashing, lashed**
NOUN **1** Your **lashes** are the hairs growing on the edge of your eyelids.
VERB **2** If rain **lashes** down, it beats down strongly.
3 If you **lash** things together, you tie them together firmly.

lash out
VERB If you **lash out** at someone you speak to them or strike them harshly.

lasso **lassoes** or **lassos, lassoing, lassoed**
NOUN **1** a length of rope looped at one end with a slip-knot, used by cowboys to catch cattle and horses
VERB **2** If you **lasso** an animal, you catch it by throwing the loop of a lasso around its neck.

last **lasts, lasting, lasted**
ADJECTIVE **1** The **last** person or thing is the one that comes after all the others of the same kind. • *I was the **last** person to arrive.*
2 The **last** one of a group of things is the only one that remains after all the others have gone. • *No one wanted the **last** piece of pizza.*
3 The **last** thing or event is the most recent one. • *The **last** time we went to the beach it rained.*
VERB **4** If something **lasts**, it continues to exist or happen. • *The sunny weather seems to have **lasted** for ages.*
5 If something **lasts** for a particular time, it remains in good condition for that time.
PHRASE **6** **At last** means after a long time.
• *The bus arrived **at last**.*

late **later, latest**
ADVERB OR ADJECTIVE **1** If something or someone is **late**, they arrive after the time that was arranged or expected.
2 If something happens **late**, it happens near the end of something. • *In the summer it doesn't get dark until **late** in the evening.*

lately
ADVERB If something happened **lately**, it happened recently. • *We've had a lot of homework **lately**.*

lather
NOUN the frothy foam that you get when you rub soap in water

Latin
NOUN **1** the language of ancient Rome
ADJECTIVE **2** **Latin** peoples and cultures are those of countries such as France, Italy, Spain and Portugal, whose languages developed from Latin.

A B C D E F G H I J K L M N O P Q R S T U V W X Y Z

latitude **latitudes**
NOUN The **latitude** of a place is its distance north or south of the equator measured in degrees.

latter
ADJECTIVE OR NOUN **1** You use **latter** to refer to the second of two things you have just mentioned. • *They were eating sandwiches and cakes (the **latter** bought from Mrs Paul's bakery).*
ADJECTIVE **2** The **latter** part of something is the second or later part of it. • *the **latter** stages of the race*

laugh **laughs, laughing, laughed**
VERB **1** When you **laugh**, you make a noise that shows that you are amused or happy.
NOUN **2** the sound you make when you laugh

laughter
NOUN laughing or the sound of people laughing

launch **launches, launching, launched**
VERB **1** When someone **launches** a ship, they put it into water for the first time.
2 When someone **launches** a rocket, they send it into space.

laundry **laundries**
NOUN **1** dirty clothes and sheets that are being washed or waiting to be washed
2 a business that washes and irons clothes and sheets

lava
NOUN the very hot, liquid rock that shoots out of a volcano when it erupts, and becomes solid as it cools

lavatory **lavatories**
NOUN a toilet

lavender
NOUN a small bush with blue flowers that have a strong, pleasant scent

lavish
ADJECTIVE If you are **lavish**, you are very generous with your time, money or gifts.

law **laws**
NOUN **1** the system of rules developed by the government of a country, that tells people what they are allowed to do
2 one of the rules established by a government, that tells people what they are allowed to do
lawful ADJECTIVE **lawfully** ADVERB

lawn **lawns**
NOUN a piece of well-kept grass, usually in a park or garden

lawnmower **lawnmowers**
NOUN a machine for cutting grass

lawyer **lawyers**
NOUN someone who is trained in the law and who speaks for people in court

lay **lays, laying, laid**
VERB **1** When you **lay** something somewhere, you place it there.
2 If you **lay** the table, you put things such as knives and forks on the table ready for a meal.
3 When a bird **lays** an egg, an egg comes out of its body.

layer **layers**
NOUN a single thickness of something underneath or above something else • *There was a thin **layer** of snow on the ground.*

layout **layouts**
NOUN the pattern in which something is arranged • *The clear **layout** of this book makes it a lot easier to use.*

lazy **lazier, laziest**
ADJECTIVE If you are **lazy**, you are idle and are unwilling to work.
lazily ADVERB

lead **leads, leading, led**
Said "**leed**" VERB **1** If you **lead** someone somewhere, you go in front of them in order to show them the way.
2 If a road or door **leads** somewhere, you can get to that place by following the road or going through the door.
3 If you **lead** in a race or competition, you are at the front.
4 Someone who **leads** a group of people is in charge of them.

NOUN **5** If you take the **lead** in a race or competition, or if you are in the **lead**, you are winning.
6 a length of leather or chain attached to an animal's collar, used for controlling the animal • *Put the dog on the **lead** when you take him for a walk.*
7 an electric cable for connecting an electrical appliance to a battery or the mains
Said "**led**" NOUN **8** a soft, grey, heavy metal
9 the **lead** in a pencil is the part that makes marks on paper

leader **leaders**
NOUN **1** If you are the **leader** of a group, you are in charge of it.
2 If you are the **leader** in a race or a competition, you are winning.

leaf **leaves**
NOUN **1** a flat structure growing from the stem of a plant. Most plants have green **leaves**.

2 one of the sheets of paper in a book
leafy ADJECTIVE

leaflet **leaflets**
NOUN a piece of paper or thin booklet with information or advertisements

league **leagues**
NOUN a group of people, clubs or countries that have joined together for a particular purpose or because they share a common interest

leak **leaks, leaking, leaked**
VERB **1** If a container or other object **leaks**, it has a hole through which gas or liquid escapes.
NOUN **2** If a container or other object has a **leak**, it has a hole through which gas or liquid escapes.

lean **leans, leaning, leant** or **leaned; leaner, leanest**
VERB **1** When you **lean** in a particular direction, you bend your body in that direction. • *She **leant** out of the window.*
2 When you **lean** on something, you rest your body against it for support. • *He was **leaning** on the railing.*
3 If you **lean** something somewhere, you place it there so that its weight is supported. • *He **leaned** his bike against the wall.*
ADJECTIVE **4** If meat is **lean**, it does not have much fat.

> You can write either *leant* or *leaned* as the past form of *lean*.

leap **leaps, leaping, leapt** or **leaped**
VERB **1** If you **leap** somewhere, you jump a long distance or high in the air.
NOUN **2** a jump over a long distance or high in the air

leap year **leap years**
NOUN A **leap year** has 366 days instead of 365, with an extra day in February. It occurs every four years.

learn **learns, learning, learnt** or **learned**
VERB When you **learn** something, you gain knowledge or a skill by practice or by being taught. • *He's **learning** to play the piano.*

> You can write either *learnt* or *learned* as the past form of *learn*.

lease **leases**
NOUN A **lease** is an agreement that lets someone use a house or a flat in return for rent.

least
NOUN **1** the smallest possible amount of something
ADJECTIVE OR ADVERB **2** a superlative form of *little* • *He ate the **least** amount of food because he felt ill.*
PHRASE **3** You use **at least** to show that you are referring to the minimum amount of something, and that the true amount may be greater. • *There were **at least** 500 people at the concert.*

A B C D E F G H I J K L M N O P Q R S T U V W X Y Z

leather
NOUN animal skin that has been specially treated so that it can be used to make shoes, clothes, bags and other things

leave **leaves, leaving, left**
VERB **1** When you **leave** a place or person, you go away from them.
2 If you **leave** something somewhere, you let it stay there, or put it there before you go away. • *I* ***left*** *my bags in the car.*
3 If you **leave** a job or a school, you stop being a part of it.
4 In arithmetic, when you take one number from another, it **leaves** a third number. For example, if you take 2 from 12, it **leaves** 10.
NOUN **5** holiday time • *I'm going to use my* ***leave*** *to go abroad this year.*

lecture **lectures**
NOUN a formal talk intended to teach people about a particular subject

led
VERB the past tense of **lead**

ledge **ledges**
NOUN a narrow shelf on the side of a cliff or rock face, or on the outside of a building, directly under a window

leek **leeks**
NOUN a long vegetable of the onion family, that is white at one end and has green leaves at the other

left
VERB **1** the past tense of **leave**
NOUN **2** one of the two opposite directions, sides or positions. The **left** is the side of a page that you begin reading on in English.
ANTONYM: right
ADJECTIVE OR ADVERB **3** on or towards the **left** of something • *a cut over his* ***left*** *eye*
ANTONYM: right
ADJECTIVE **4** If a certain amount of something is **left** *or* **left over**, it remains when the rest has gone. • *They have two games* ***left*** *to play.*

leftovers
PLURAL NOUN the bits of uneaten food that are left at the end of a meal

leg **legs**

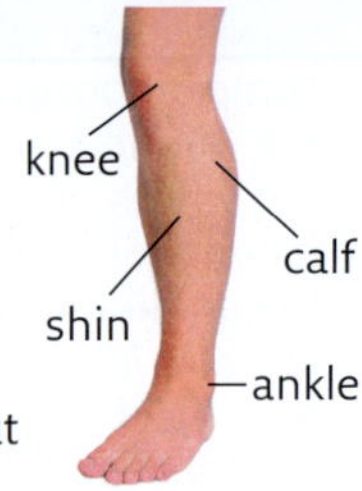

NOUN **1** one of the long parts of a human or other animal's body that they stand on and walk with
2 The **legs** of a pair of trousers are the parts that cover your legs.
3 The **legs** of a table or chair are the parts that rest on the floor and support it.
4 A **leg** of a journey or a sports match is one part of it. • *The first* ***leg*** *of the race was very hard work.*

legacy **legacies**
NOUN property or money that is given to someone in the will of a person who has died

legal
ADJECTIVE relating to the law

legend **legends**
NOUN a very old and popular story

legible
ADJECTIVE Writing that is **legible** is clear enough to be read.
ANTONYM: illegible
legibly ADVERB **legibility** NOUN

legislation
NOUN a law or group of laws made by a government

legitimate
ADJECTIVE If something is **legitimate** it is allowed by law, or is accepted as fair by most people.
legitimately ADVERB

leisure
NOUN time when you do not have to work and can do things that you enjoy

lemon **lemons**
NOUN a yellow citrus fruit with a sour taste

lemonade
NOUN a clear, sweet drink made from lemons, water and sugar. **Lemonade** is often fizzy.

lend **lends, lending, lent**
VERB **1** If you **lend** something to someone, you let them have it for a period of time.
2 If a person or bank **lends** you money, they give you money and you agree to pay it back later, usually with interest.

length **lengths**
NOUN **1** The **length** of something is the distance from one end to the other.
• *We walked the* ***length*** *of the street.*
2 The **length** of an event or activity is the amount of time it continues. • *The film is over two hours in* ***length****.*

lengthen **lengthens, lengthening, lengthened**
VERB If you **lengthen** something, you make it longer.
ANTONYM: shorten

lengthy **lengthier, lengthiest**
ADJECTIVE Something that is **lengthy** lasts for a long time. • *The speech was rather* ***lengthy****.*

lens **lenses**
NOUN a thin, curved piece of glass, plastic or other transparent material that makes things appear larger or clearer • *a camera* ***lens***

lent
VERB the past tense and past participle of **lend**

Lent
NOUN the forty-day period before Easter when some Christians fast or give up something that they enjoy

lentil **lentils**
NOUN **Lentils** are small, dried, red or brown seeds that are cooked and eaten in soups, stews and curries.

leopard **leopards**
NOUN a large wild cat, with yellow fur and black or brown spots, found in Africa and Asia

leotard **leotards**
Said "**lee**-uh-tard" NOUN a tight-fitting garment that covers the body rather like a swimming costume, which is worn for dancing or exercise

less
ADJECTIVE OR ADVERB **1** a smaller amount of something, or to a smaller extent • *It is* ***less*** *than three weeks until we go back to school.*
ANTONYM: more
2 a comparative form of *little*
PREPOSITION **3** You use **less** to show that one number or amount is to be subtracted from another. • *You can have your pocket money,* ***less*** *the money you borrowed last week.*

Use *less* to talk about things that can't be counted and *fewer* for things that can be counted: *less time; fewer apples.*

lesson **lessons**
NOUN **1** a fixed period of time during which people are taught something by a teacher
2 an experience that makes you understand something important

let **lets, letting, let**
VERB **1** If you **let** someone do something, you allow them to do it.
2 If someone **lets** a house or flat that they own, they allow others to use it in return for payment.

lethal
ADJECTIVE Something that is **lethal** can kill you. • *A gun is a* ***lethal*** *weapon.*
[from Latin *letum* meaning death]

let's
VERB a contraction of *let us*

letter **letters**
NOUN **1** a message written on paper and sent to someone, usually through the post
2 one of the written symbols that go together to make words

letter box **letter boxes**; also spelt **letter-box**
NOUN **1** an oblong gap in a front door, through which letters are delivered
2 a large, metal container in the street or at a post office, for posting letters

A B C D E F G H I J K L M N O P Q R S T U V W X Y Z

lettering
NOUN You use **lettering** to describe writing that is done in a certain way. • *The poster had large black **lettering**.*

lettuce **lettuces**
NOUN a vegetable with large, green leaves that you eat in salads

leukaemia; also spelt **leukemia**
Said "loo-**kee**-mee-a" NOUN a serious illness that affects the blood
[from Greek *leukos* meaning white and *haima* meaning blood]

level **levels, levelling, levelled**
NOUN **1** the height, position or amount of something • *This is the lowest **level** of rainfall for years.*
2 a standard or grade of achievement • *Now that I have passed this piano exam, I will move on to the next **level**.*
SYNONYMS: grade, stage
ADJECTIVE **3** A surface that is **level** is completely flat.
4 If one thing is **level** with another, it is at the same height or position.
VERB **5** If you **level** something, you make it flat.

level crossing **level crossings**
NOUN a place where traffic is allowed to drive across a railway track

lever **levers**
NOUN **1** a handle on a machine that you pull in order to make the machine work
2 a bar that you wedge underneath a heavy object and press down on to make the object move

liable
ADJECTIVE **1** Something that is **liable** to happen will probably happen. • *Britain is **liable** to be cold in January.*
2 If someone is **liable** for something such as a crime or a debt, they are legally responsible for it.
liability NOUN

liar **liars**
NOUN a person who tells lies

liberal
ADJECTIVE **1** If someone is **liberal**, they are tolerant of other people's behaviour and opinions.
2 If you are **liberal** with something, you are generous with it.
liberally ADVERB

liberty
NOUN the freedom to do what you want to do and go where you want to go

librarian **librarians**
NOUN a person who works in, or is in charge of, a library

library **libraries**
NOUN a building in which books are kept, especially a public building from which people can borrow books

> There is an *r* after the *b* in *library*.

licence **licences**
NOUN an official document that gives you permission to do, use or own something • *You have to pass a test before you receive a full driving **licence**.*

> The noun *licence* ends in *ce*.

license **licenses, licensing, licensed**
VERB If someone **licenses** an activity, they give official permission for it to be carried out.

> The verb *license* ends in *se*.

lichen **lichens**
Said "**lie**-kun" NOUN a green or greeny-grey mossy growth, found on rocks, trees and walls

lick **licks, licking, licked**
VERB If you **lick** something, you move your tongue over it. • *I **licked** the stamp and stuck it to the envelope.*

lid **lids**
NOUN a cover for a box, jar or other container

lie[1] **lies, lying, lay, lain**
VERB **1** If someone or something **lies** somewhere, they rest there in a flat position.
2 You use **lie** to say where something is or what its position is. • *The village **lies** to the east of the river.*

The past tense of this verb *lie* is *lay*. Do not confuse it with the verb *lay* meaning 'put'.

lie² **lies, lying, lied**
VERB **1** If you **lie**, you say something that you know is not true. • *He **lied** about his age.*
NOUN **2** something you say that you know is not true

lieutenant **lieutenants**
Said "lef-**ten**-ant" NOUN a junior officer in the army or navy

life **lives**
NOUN **1** the state of being alive that makes people, animals and plants different from objects
2 your existence from the time you are born until the time you die

lifeboat **lifeboats**
NOUN a boat used for rescuing people who are in danger at sea

life cycle **life cycles**
NOUN the series of changes and developments in the life of a living thing • *There are several stages in the **life cycle** of a butterfly.*

lifeguard **lifeguards**
NOUN a person whose job is to rescue people who are in difficulty in the sea or in a swimming pool

life jacket **life jackets**
NOUN a sleeveless, inflatable jacket that keeps you afloat in water

lifelike
ADJECTIVE A picture or a sculpture that is **lifelike** looks very real, almost as if it is alive.
SYNONYM: realistic

lifeline **lifelines**
NOUN something that helps you to survive or helps an activity to continue • *His help was a real **lifeline** to me after I had so many difficulties.*

lifetime **lifetimes**
NOUN the period of time during which you are alive

lift **lifts, lifting, lifted**
VERB **1** If you **lift** something, you move it to a higher position.
NOUN **2** a device that carries people or goods from one floor to another in a building

light **lights, lighting, lighted** or **lit; lighter, lightest**
NOUN **1** the brightness from the sun, moon, fire or lamps, that lets you see things

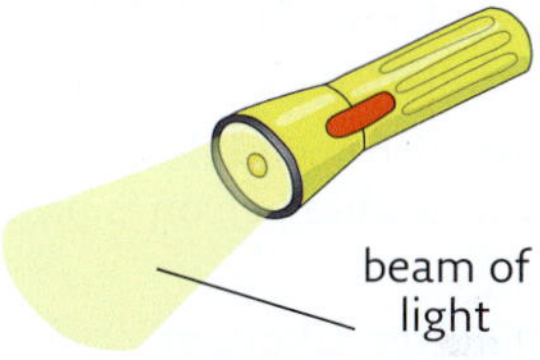

2 a lamp or other device that gives out brightness
ADJECTIVE **3** If it is **light**, there is enough light from the sun to see things.
ANTONYM: dark
4 A **light** colour is pale.
5 A **light** object does not weigh much.
ANTONYM: heavy
VERB **6** If you **light** a fire, you make it start burning.

lighten **lightens, lightening, lightened**
VERB **1** When something **lightens**, it becomes brighter and less dark. • *After the storm the sky **lightened**.*
2 If you **lighten** a load, you make it less heavy. • *My case was too heavy, so I **lightened** it by taking out three books.*

lighter **lighters**
NOUN a device for lighting something, such as a fire or a cigarette

lighthouse **lighthouses**
NOUN a tower by the sea, that shines a powerful light to guide ships and warn them of danger

lighting
NOUN The **lighting** in a room or building is the way it is lit.

lightning
NOUN very bright flashes of light you see in the sky, usually during a thunderstorm.

a b c d e f g h i j k l m n o p q r s t u v w x y z

Lightning is caused by electrical activity in the atmosphere.

light year **light years**
NOUN the distance that light travels in a year, which is about 6 million miles or 9.5 million kilometres

like **likes, liking, liked**
VERB **1** If you **like** someone or something, you find them pleasing.
PREPOSITION **2** If one thing is **like** another, they are similar.

likeable; also spelt **likable**
ADJECTIVE A **likeable** person is pleasant and friendly.

likely **likelier, likeliest**
ADJECTIVE If something is **likely**, it will probably happen or is probably true.

lilac **lilacs**
NOUN **1** a small tree with sweet-smelling clusters of mauve, pink or white flowers
2 a pale mauve colour

lily **lilies**
NOUN a plant with trumpet-shaped flowers of various colours

limb **limbs**
NOUN Your **limbs** are your arms and legs.

lime **limes**
NOUN **1** a small, green, citrus fruit, rather like a lemon
2 a bright green colour
3 a chemical substance used in cement or as a fertiliser

limerick **limericks**
NOUN an amusing nonsense poem of five lines

limit **limits, limiting, limited**
NOUN **1** the largest or smallest amount of something that is possible or allowed
• *The speed **limit** on this road is 30 mph.*
VERB **2** If you **limit** something, you restrict it to a certain amount or number. • *The children were **limited** to two biscuits each.*
limited ADJECTIVE

limousine **limousines**
NOUN a large, luxurious car, usually driven by a chauffeur

limp **limps, limping, limped; limper, limpest**
VERB **1** If you **limp**, you walk in an uneven way because you have hurt your leg or foot.
NOUN **2** an uneven way of walking • *While her leg was in plaster she walked with a **limp**.*
ADJECTIVE **3** Something that is **limp** is soft or weak.

limpet **limpets**
NOUN a small shellfish with a pointed shell, that attaches itself very firmly to rocks

line **lines, lining, lined**
NOUN **1** a long, thin mark
2 a number of people or things that are arranged in a row
3 a long piece of string or wire • *a washing **line***
4 a number of words together, for example the **lines** in a play are the words that an actor has to speak • *This is my favourite **line** in the poem.*
5 a railway or railway track
VERB **6** If people or things **line** something, they make a border or edge along it.
• *Crowds **lined** the streets to see the Queen.*

linen
NOUN **1** a type of cloth made from a plant called flax
2 household goods made of cloth, such as sheets and tablecloths

liner **liners**
NOUN a large passenger ship that makes long sea journeys

linesman **linesmen**
NOUN an official at a sports match who watches the lines of the field or court and decides if the ball has gone outside them

linger **lingers, lingering, lingered**
VERB If someone or something **lingers**, they stay for a long time. • *The smell **lingered** in the kitchen.*
lingering ADJECTIVE

linguist **linguists**
NOUN someone who studies foreign languages and can speak them well

lining **linings**
NOUN any material that is used to line the inside of something • *There is a fleece **lining** in this jacket.*

link **links, linking, linked**
NOUN **1** one of the rings in a chain
2 a relationship or connection between two things • *There is a **link** between the weather and the clothes we wear.*
3 a physical connection between two things or places • *There is a rail **link** between the two cities.*
VERB **4** If someone or something **links** people, places, or things, they join them together. • *They want to **link** the village to the town with a better road.*

lion **lions**
NOUN a large member of the cat family that is found in Africa. Male **lions** have long hair on their head and neck, called a mane.

lioness **lionesses**
NOUN a female lion

lip **lips**
NOUN Your **lips** are the two outer edges of your mouth.

lipstick **lipsticks**
NOUN a cosmetic for colouring the lips, usually in the form of a small stick

liquid **liquids**
NOUN a substance such as water, which is neither a gas nor a solid and which can be poured. A **liquid** always takes the shape of the container it is in.

liquidizer **liquidizers**
NOUN an electric machine used for making food into liquid • *Dad put strawberries, bananas and milk in the **liquidizer** and mixed us a delicious milkshake.*

liquorice or **licorice**
NOUN **1** a root used to flavour sweets
2 sweets flavoured with liquorice

lisp **lisps, lisping, lisped**
NOUN **1** Someone who has a **lisp** pronounces the sounds *s* and *z* like *th*.
VERB **2** If someone **lisps**, they speak with a lisp.

list **lists, listing, listed**
NOUN **1** a set of words or items written one after the other • *a shopping **list***
VERB **2** If you **list** a number of things, you write them or say them one after another.

listen **listens, listening, listened**
VERB **1** If you **listen** to someone, you pay attention to what they are saying.
2 If you **listen** to something, you pay attention to its sound. • *She enjoys **listening** to music.*

lit
VERB the past tense and past participle of **light**

literacy
NOUN the ability to read and write

literally
ADVERB You use **literally** to emphasize that what you are saying is actually true, even though it seems unlikely. • *We **literally** almost died of thirst.*

literate
ADJECTIVE If you are **literate**, you are able to read and write.
literacy NOUN

literature
NOUN Novels, plays and poetry are referred to as **literature**.
[from Latin *litteratura* meaning writing]

litre **litres**
NOUN a unit for measuring liquid (l) equal to 1000 millilitres or about 1.76 pints

litter **litters, littering, littered**
NOUN **1** rubbish in the street and other public places
2 baby animals born at the same time to the same mother
VERB **3** If things **litter** a place, they are scattered all over it. • *Paper **littered** the pavement.*

little **less, lesser, least**
ADJECTIVE **1** small in size or amount • *Stay a **little** longer.*
ANTONYMS: big, large
ADVERB OR PRONOUN **2** not much • *I had very **little** money left.*

A B C D E F G H I J K L M N O P Q R S T U V W X Y Z

NOUN **3** A **little** is a small amount or degree of something. • *He showed me a **little** of his work.*

live **lives, living, lived**
Rhymes with "give" VERB **1** If someone or something **lives**, they are alive.
2 If you **live** in a place, that is where your home is. • *He **lives** with his parents.*
3 The way someone **lives** is the kind of life they have. • *We **live** quite simply.*
Rhymes with "five" ADJECTIVE **4** **Live** television or radio is broadcast while the event is taking place.
5 **Live** animals or plants are alive, rather than dead or artificial.

lively **livelier, liveliest**
ADJECTIVE full of energy and enthusiasm

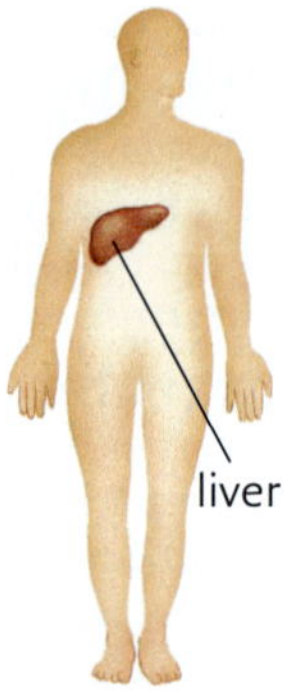

liver **livers**
NOUN a large organ in your body that cleans your blood and stores substances such as vitamins and minerals

living
ADJECTIVE **1** If someone or something is **living**, they are alive.
NOUN **2** Someone who works for a **living**, works to earn the money needed in order to live. • *He makes a **living** by selling cars.*

living room **living rooms**
NOUN a room in a house where you sit and relax, doing such things as watching television and reading

lizard **lizards**
NOUN a reptile with short legs and a tail

llama **llamas**
NOUN a South American animal that looks rather like a small camel with thick hair and no hump

load **loads, loading, loaded**
VERB **1** If you **load** a vehicle or container, you put things into it.
2 When you **load** a camera, you put film into it.
NOUN **3** something large or heavy that is being carried • *a tractor with a big **load** of hay*
4 INFORMAL A **load** of something, or **loads** of something, means a lot of it. • *He's got **loads** of CDs.*

loaf **loaves**
NOUN a large piece of bread in a shape that can be cut into slices

loan **loans, loaning, loaned**
NOUN **1** a sum of money that you borrow
VERB **2** If you **loan** something to someone, you lend it to them.

loathe **loathes, loathing, loathed**
VERB If you **loathe** someone or something, you feel a very strong dislike for them.
loathing NOUN **loathsome** ADJECTIVE

lobster **lobsters**
NOUN an edible shellfish with two front claws and eight legs

local **locals**
ADJECTIVE **1** existing in or belonging to the area where you live • *the **local** newspaper*
NOUN **2** someone who lives in and comes from a particular area

locality **localities**
NOUN a small area of a country or a city • *Golden eagles can be seen in certain **localities** in Scotland.*

locate **locates, locating, located**
VERB **1** If you **locate** someone or something, you find out where they are.
2 If something is **located** in a place, it is in that place.

location **locations**
NOUN the place where something is found or where something happens • *She couldn't remember the exact **location** of the church.*

loch **lochs**
NOUN In Scottish English, a **loch** is a lake. • *They say there is a monster in **Loch** Ness.*

lock **locks, locking, locked**
VERB **1** If you **lock** something, you fasten it with a key.

2 If you **lock** something in a place, you put it there and fasten the lock. • *They **locked** the money in the safe.*
NOUN **3** a device that prevents something from being opened except with a key • *He heard a key in the **lock**.*

locker **lockers**
NOUN a small cupboard for someone's personal belongings, for example in a changing room

locket **lockets**
NOUN a small piece of jewellery worn on a chain around the neck, which opens so that you can put a small photograph inside

locomotive **locomotives**
NOUN a railway engine

locust **locusts**
NOUN an insect like a large grasshopper, that travels in huge swarms and eats crops

loft **lofts**
NOUN the space immediately under the roof of a house, often used for storing things

log **logs**
NOUN **1** a thick piece of wood from a branch or trunk of a tree, that has fallen or been cut off
2 an official written account of what happens each day • *The captain wrote each day's events in the ship's **log**.*

logic
NOUN a way of reasoning that makes sense
logical ADJECTIVE **logically** ADVERB

logo **logos**
NOUN the special design that is put on all the products of an organization

loiter **loiters, loitering, loitered**
VERB If you **loiter** in a place, you stand around without going very far or doing very much. • *After school they **loitered** round the shops.*

lollipop **lollipops**
NOUN a hard sweet on the end of a stick [from Romani *lolli* meaning red and *pobbel* meaning apple]

lolly **lollies**
NOUN **1** a lollipop
2 a flavoured ice or ice cream on a stick

lonely **lonelier, loneliest**
ADJECTIVE **1** If you are **lonely**, you are unhappy because you are alone.
2 A **lonely** place is one that very few people visit.

long **longer, longest; longs, longing, longed**
ADJECTIVE **1** continuing for a great amount of time • *There had been no rain for a **long** time.*
ADVERB **2** You use **long** to talk about amounts of time. • *How **long** is the film?*
ADJECTIVE **3** great in length or distance • *It's a **long** way home.*
4 You use **long** to talk about the distance that something measures from one end to the other.
PHRASE **5** If something **no longer** happens, it used to happen but does not happen now.
VERB **6** If you **long** for something to happen, or if you **long** to do it, you want it to happen very much.

long division **long divisions**
NOUN a method of dividing one large number by another one, where you write out all the stages instead of doing them in your head or on a calculator

longitude **longitudes**
NOUN a position measured in degrees east or west of an imaginary line passing through Greenwich in London

look **looks, looking, looked**
VERB **1** If you **look** at something, you turn your eyes towards it so that you can see it.
2 If you **look** for someone or something, you try to find them.
3 If you describe the way that something **looks**, you are describing its appearance. • *He **looked** a bit pale.*
NOUN **4** If you take a **look** at something, you look at it. • *Lucy took a last **look** in the mirror.*
SYNONYM: glance
5 The **look** on your face is the expression on it.

a b c d e f g h i j k l m n o p q r s t u v w x y z

A B C D E F G H I J K L M N O P Q R S T U V W X Y Z

look after
VERB If you **look after** someone or something, you take care of them.

look forward
VERB If you **look forward** to something, you want it to happen because you think you will enjoy it.

look out
PHRASE You say **look out** to warn someone of danger. • ***Look out**! There's a car coming.*

lookout **lookouts**
NOUN **1** someone who is watching for danger, or a place where someone watches for danger
PHRASE **2** If you are **on the lookout** for something, you are watching or waiting for it to happen.

loom **looms, looming, loomed**
NOUN **1** a machine for weaving cloth
VERB **2** If something **looms** in front of you, it suddenly appears as a tall, unclear and sometimes frightening shape. • *A monster **loomed** out of the darkness.*
3 If a situation or event is **looming**, it is likely to happen soon and is rather worrying. • *A storm is **looming** on the horizon.*

loop **loops, looping, looped**
NOUN **1** a curved or circular shape in something such as a piece of string or wire
VERB **2** If you **loop** rope or string around an object, you place it in a loop around the object. • *He **looped** the rope over the horse's neck.*

loose **looser, loosest**
Said "**looss**" ADJECTIVE **1** not firmly held or fixed in place • *a **loose** tooth*
2 not tight • *a **loose** jacket*
ADVERB **3** If people or animals break **loose**, or are set **loose**, they are released after they have been held back or tied up.

> Do not confuse *loose* with *lose*.

loot **loots, looting, looted**
VERB **1** If someone **loots** shops and houses, they steal goods from them, especially during a riot or war.
NOUN **2** stolen money or goods

lopsided
ADJECTIVE Something that is **lopsided** is uneven because one side is different from the other, for example one side is heavier or larger.

lord **lords**
NOUN In Britain, **Lord** is a title used in front of the names of some men.

lorry **lorries**
NOUN a large vehicle for transporting goods by road

lose **loses, losing, lost**
Said "**looz**" VERB **1** If you **lose** something, you cannot find it, or you no longer have it because it has been taken from you. • *He **lost** his place in the team.*
2 If you **lose** a fight or an argument, you are beaten.

> Do not confuse *lose* with *loose*.

loss **losses**
NOUN The **loss** of something is the fact of having lost it or of having less of it.

lost
VERB **1** the past tense and past participle of **lose**
ADJECTIVE **2** If you are **lost**, you do not know where you are.
3 If something is **lost**, you cannot find it.

lot **lots**
NOUN **1** a large amount of something • *a **lot** of children*
2 very much or very often • *I miss him a **lot**.*
3 the whole of something • *He had a whole packet of biscuits and ate the **lot**.*

lotion **lotions**
NOUN a liquid that you put on your skin to protect or soften it • *suntan **lotion***

lottery **lotteries**
NOUN a way of raising money by selling tickets and giving prizes to people who have winning tickets, which are selected at random

loud **louder, loudest**
ADJECTIVE A **loud** noise produces a lot of sound.
loudly ADVERB

loudspeaker **loudspeakers**
NOUN a piece of electrical equipment that produces the sound in things such as radios, telephones and CD players

lounge **lounges, lounging, lounged**
NOUN **1** a room in a house, hotel or airport where people can sit and relax
VERB **2** If you **lounge** around, you lean against something or lie around in a lazy way.

louse **lice**
NOUN a small insect that lives on people's bodies

lout **louts**
NOUN a young man who behaves in a rude or aggressive way
loutish ADJECTIVE

love **loves, loving, loved**
VERB **1** If you **love** someone or something, you have strong feelings of affection for them.
2 If you would **love** to do something, you want very much to do it.
NOUN **3** a strong feeling of affection for someone or something
PHRASE **4** If you are **in love** with someone, you feel strongly attracted to them romantically.

lovely **lovelier, loveliest**
ADJECTIVE very beautiful, attractive, pleasant or enjoyable • *We had a **lovely** day out.*

low **lower, lowest**
ADJECTIVE OR ADVERB **1** Something that is **low** is close to the ground.
ANTONYM: high
ADJECTIVE **2** below average in value or amount • *The temperature was **low** for the time of year.*
ANTONYM: high

lower **lowers, lowering, lowered**
VERB **1** If you **lower** something, you move it downwards. • *She **lowered** the bucket into the well.*
ADJECTIVE **2** The **lower** of two things is the bottom one. • *the **lower** deck of the bus*

lower-case
ADJECTIVE **Lower-case** letters are small letters, not capital letters.

loyal
ADJECTIVE If you are **loyal**, you are firm in your friendship or support for someone or something.

lozenge **lozenges**
NOUN **1** a small sweet with medicine in it, that you can suck if you have a sore throat or a cough
2 a diamond shape, like a rhombus
See **rhombus**

lubricate **lubricates, lubricating, lubricated**
VERB If someone **lubricates** something like a machine, they put oil or grease on to it so that it moves smoothly.
[from Latin *lubricus* meaning slippery]
lubrication NOUN **lubricant** NOUN

luck
NOUN **1** something that happens by chance • *We had good **luck** with the weather.* • *It was bad **luck** that I lost the game of Monopoly.*
PHRASE **2** You say **good luck** to someone when you are wishing them success.

lucky **luckier, luckiest**
ADJECTIVE Someone who is **lucky** has a lot of good luck.
luckily ADVERB

luggage
NOUN Your **luggage** is the bags and suitcases that you take with you when you travel.

lukewarm
ADJECTIVE slightly warm

lull **lulls, lulling, lulled**
NOUN **1** a pause in something, or a short time when it is quiet and calm

VERB **2** If you **lull** someone, you calm them and make them feel safe.

lullaby **lullabies**
NOUN a song used for sending a baby or child to sleep

lumber **lumbers, lumbering, lumbered**
NOUN **1** wood that has been roughly cut up
VERB **2** If you **lumber** around, you move heavily and clumsily.

luminous
ADJECTIVE Something that is **luminous** glows in the dark without being hot.
luminously ADVERB **luminosity** NOUN

lump **lumps**
NOUN a solid piece of something

lunar
ADJECTIVE relating to the moon • *The **lunar** module landed safely on the moon.*
[from Latin *luna* meaning moon]

lunch **lunches**
NOUN a meal eaten in the middle of the day

lung **lungs**
NOUN Your **lungs** are the two organs inside your chest that you breathe with.

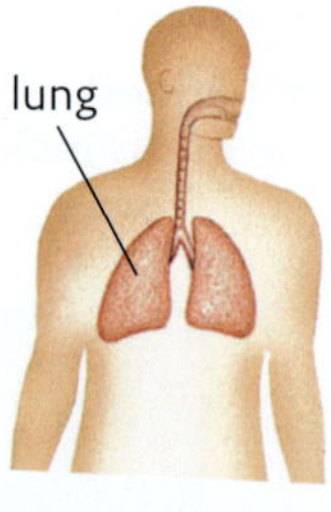

lurch **lurches, lurching, lurched**
VERB **1** If someone or something **lurches**, they make a sudden, jerky movement.
PHRASE **2** If someone leaves you **in the lurch**, they leave you in a difficult or dangerous situation, instead of helping you.

lure **lures, luring, lured**
VERB If you **lure** someone or something, you tempt them into going somewhere or doing something. • *He **lured** the cat back into the house with some milk.*

lurk **lurks, lurking, lurked**
VERB If someone **lurks** somewhere, they hide there and wait.

lush **lusher, lushest**
ADJECTIVE In a **lush** field or garden, the grass or plants are healthy and growing thickly.

lute **lutes**
NOUN an old-fashioned, stringed musical instrument that is plucked like a guitar

luxury **luxuries**
NOUN **1** great comfort, especially among expensive and beautiful surroundings
2 A **luxury** is something that you would like to have but do not need, and is usually expensive.

lying
VERB the present participle of **lie**

lyrics
PLURAL NOUN The **lyrics** of a song are the words.

Mm

macaroni
NOUN short, hollow tubes of pasta
[an Italian word; from Greek *makaria* meaning food made from barley]

machine **machines**
NOUN a piece of equipment designed to do a particular job. It is usually powered by an engine or by electricity. • *a washing* ***machine***

machine gun **machine guns**
NOUN a gun that works automatically, firing a continuous stream of bullets very quickly

machinery
NOUN machines in general • *farm* ***machinery*** • *factory* ***machinery***

mackintosh **mackintoshes**
NOUN a raincoat made from waterproof cloth

mad **madder, maddest**
ADJECTIVE **1** Someone who is **mad** has a mental illness that causes them to behave in strange ways.
2 If you describe someone as **mad**, you mean that they are very foolish.
3 INFORMAL Someone who is **mad** is angry.
PHRASE **4** If you are **mad about** someone or something, you like them very much.
• *She had always been* ***mad about*** *football.*
madly ADVERB **madness** NOUN

made
VERB the past tense and past participle of **make**

magazine **magazines**
NOUN a weekly or monthly publication containing articles and photographs

maggot **maggots**
NOUN the larva of some kinds of fly. **Maggots** look like small, fat worms.
maggoty ADJECTIVE

magic
NOUN **1** In fairy stories, **magic** is a special power that can make impossible things happen.
2 the art of performing tricks to entertain people
magical ADJECTIVE

magician **magicians**
NOUN **1** a person who performs tricks that seem like magic to entertain people
2 In fairy stories, a **magician** is a man with magic powers.

magistrate **magistrates**
NOUN an official who acts as a judge in a law court that deals with less serious crimes

magnet **magnets**
NOUN a piece of iron or steel that attracts other objects made of iron or steel towards it. **Magnets** can also push away, or repel, other **magnets**.

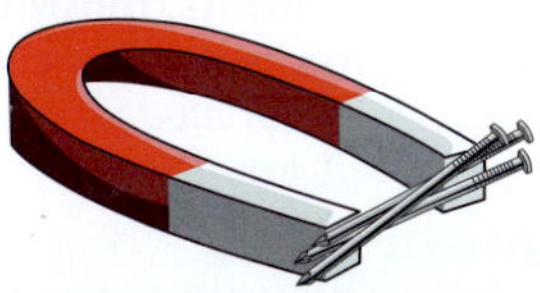

magnetic
ADJECTIVE Something that is **magnetic** is attracted towards a magnet. Only iron, steel, nickel and cobalt are **magnetic**.

magnificent
ADJECTIVE extremely beautiful or impressive
SYNONYMS: imposing, splendid
[from Latin *magnificus* meaning great in deeds]

magnify **magnifies, magnifying, magnified**
VERB When a microscope or lens **magnifies** something, it makes it appear bigger than it actually is.
magnification NOUN

magnifying glass **magnifying glasses**
NOUN a glass lens that magnifies things, making them appear bigger than they really are

magpie **magpies**
NOUN a large, black-and-white bird with a long tail

mahogany
NOUN a hard, reddish-brown wood used for making furniture

maid **maids**
NOUN a female servant

maiden name **maiden names**
NOUN the surname a woman had before she married

mail **mails, mailing, mailed**
NOUN **1** the letters and parcels delivered to you by the post office
2 same as **e-mail**
VERB **3** If you **mail** a letter, you send it by post.
4 If you **mail** someone, you send them an e-mail.
[from Old French *male* meaning bag]

maim **maims, maiming, maimed**
VERB To **maim** someone is to injure them very badly for life.
maimed ADJECTIVE

main **mains**
ADJECTIVE **1** most important or largest • *My **main** interest is music.*
SYNONYMS: chief, major, principal
NOUN **2** The **mains** are the large pipes or cables that carry gas, water or electricity to a building.

mainland
NOUN the main part of a country or continent, not including the islands around it

mainly
ADVERB mostly, chiefly or usually • *We eat **mainly** vegetarian food.*

maintain **maintains, maintaining, maintained**
VERB **1** If you **maintain** something, you keep it going at a particular rate or level. • *You will need to **maintain** this level of fitness if you want to take part in the finals.*
2 If you **maintain** a machine or a building, you keep it in good condition.
3 If you **maintain** a belief or an opinion, you have it and state it clearly.

maize
NOUN a tall plant that produces sweetcorn

majesty **majesties**
NOUN **1** You say **His Majesty** when you are talking about a king, and **Her Majesty** when you are talking about a queen.
2 the quality of being dignified and impressive
majestic ADJECTIVE

major **majors**
ADJECTIVE **1** more important or more serious than other things • *She has a **major** role in the school play.*
ANTONYM: minor
NOUN **2** an army officer of the rank immediately above captain

majority **majorities**
NOUN more than half of a group • *The **majority** of the passengers became ill.*

make **makes, making, made**
VERB **1** If you **make** something, you create or produce it. • *This is the cake I **made** yesterday.*
2 If you **make** someone or something do something, you force them to do it or cause it to happen. • *Her mother **made** her do her homework every night.*
3 If you **make** a promise to do something, you say you will definitely do it.
4 Two amounts added together **make** a sum. • *3 and 5 **make** 8.*
5 If you **make** a phone call, you use the telephone to speak to someone.
NOUN **6** the name of the product of a particular manufacturer • *What **make** is your bicycle?*

make-believe
NOUN a fantasy of pretend or imaginary things

make-up
NOUN coloured creams and powders that women and actors put on their faces

malaria
NOUN a serious tropical disease, caught from mosquitoes, that causes fever and shivering

male **males**
NOUN **1** a person or animal belonging to the gender that cannot have babies
ANTONYM: female
ADJECTIVE **2** concerning or affecting men rather than women
ANTONYM: female

malevolent
Said "mal-**lev**-oh-lent" ADJECTIVE
1 **Malevolent** people want to cause harm or do evil things.
2 A **malevolent** act is cruel and spiteful.

malfunction **malfunctions, malfunctioning, malfunctioned**
VERB If a machine **malfunctions**, it fails to work properly.

malicious
ADJECTIVE **Malicious** talk or behaviour is intended to harm someone.

mall **malls**
NOUN a sheltered place with cafés, shops and restaurants • *a shopping* ***mall***

mallet **mallets**
NOUN a wooden hammer with a square head

malnutrition
NOUN a condition resulting from not eating enough healthy food or not having enough to eat

mammal **mammals**
NOUN an animal that gives birth to live babies and feeds its young with milk from the mother's body. Human beings, dogs and whales are all **mammals**.
[from Latin *mamma* meaning breast]
mammalian ADJECTIVE

mammoth **mammoths**
ADJECTIVE **1** very large indeed
NOUN **2** a huge animal that looked like a hairy elephant with long tusks. **Mammoths** became extinct a long time ago.

man **men; mans, manning, manned**
NOUN **1** an adult, male human being
ANTONYM: woman
2 Human beings, both male and female, are sometimes referred to as **man**.
• *Primitive* ***man*** *lived in caves.*
VERB **3** If you **man** something, you are in charge of it or you operate it. • *Can you* ***man*** *the bookstall?*

manage **manages, managing, managed**
VERB **1** If you **manage** to do something, you succeed in doing it even if it is difficult.
• *We* ***managed*** *to find somewhere to sit.*
2 If someone **manages** an organization or business, they are responsible for controlling it.

management
NOUN **1** the controlling and organizing of a business
2 the people who control an organization

manager **managers**
NOUN a man or woman who is responsible for running a business or organization

mane **manes**
NOUN long hair growing from the neck of a lion or a horse

manger **mangers**
NOUN a feeding box in a barn or stable

mangle **mangles, mangling, mangled**
VERB **1** If you **mangle** something, you crush or twist it out of shape.
NOUN **2** an old-fashioned piece of equipment consisting of two large rollers, for squeezing water out of wet clothes

mango **mangoes** or **mangos**
NOUN a sweet yellow fruit that grows in tropical climates

mankind
NOUN used to refer to all human beings
• *Pollution is a threat to* ***mankind***.

manner **manners**
NOUN **1** the way you do something or behave
PLURAL NOUN **2** If you have good **manners**, you behave very politely.

A B C D E F G H I J K L M N O P Q R S T U V W X Y Z

manoeuvre manoeuvres, manoeuvring, manoeuvred
Said "man-**noo**-ver" VERB **1** If you **manoeuvre** something into place, you move it there skilfully. • *Mum **manoeuvred** the car into the small parking space.*
NOUN **2** A **manoeuvre** is a clever thing that you do or say in order to make something happen the way you want it to.

manor manors
NOUN a large country house with land, especially one that was built in the Middle Ages

mansion mansions
NOUN a very large house

manslaughter
NOUN the accidental killing of a person

mantelpiece mantelpieces
NOUN a shelf over a fireplace

manual manuals
ADJECTIVE **1** **Manual** work involves physical strength or skill with your hands, rather than mental skill.
2 **Manual** equipment is operated by hand rather than being automatic or operated by electricity or a motor. • *a **manual** whisk*
NOUN **3** a book that tells you how to use a machine • *an instruction **manual***
[from Latin *manus* meaning hand]
manually ADVERB

manufacture manufactures, manufacturing, manufactured
VERB **1** If someone **manufactures** goods, they make them in a factory.
NOUN **2** The **manufacture** of goods is the making of them in a factory.

manure
NOUN animal dung used to improve the soil

manuscript manuscripts
NOUN a handwritten or typed copy of a book, play, or piece of music before it is printed
[from Latin *manus* meaning hand and *scribere* meaning to write]

many
ADJECTIVE OR PRONOUN **1** If there are **many** people or things, there are a large number of them.
2 You use **many** to talk about how great a number or quantity is. • *How **many** tickets do you need?*

map maps
NOUN a detailed drawing of an area of land, showing its shape and features as it would appear if you saw it from above

maple maples
NOUN a tree that has large leaves with five points

marathon marathons
NOUN a race in which people run 26 miles along roads
[named after *Marathon*, a place from which a messenger ran more than 20 miles to Athens, bringing news of a victory in 490 BC]

marble
NOUN a very hard, cold stone that is often polished to show the coloured patterns in it

march marches, marching, marched
NOUN **1** an organized protest in which a large group of people walk somewhere together
VERB **2** When soldiers **march**, they walk with quick regular steps as a group.
NOUN **3** music with a strong beat for marching to

March
NOUN the third month of the year. **March** has 31 days.
[from Latin *Martius* month of Mars, the Roman god of war]

mare mares
NOUN an adult female horse

margarine
NOUN a soft substance made from vegetable oil and animal fats, and used like butter

margin **margins**
NOUN **1** the blank space at the top and bottom and on each side of a written or printed page
2 If you win a race or a competition by a large or small **margin**, you win it by a large or small amount.

marina **marinas**
NOUN a harbour for pleasure boats and yachts

marine **marines**
NOUN **1** a soldier who is trained for duties at sea
ADJECTIVE **2** relating to or involving the sea, and the animals and plants that live in the sea

mark **marks, marking, marked**
NOUN **1** a small stain or damaged area on a surface
2 a score given to a student for homework or for an exam
3 a written or printed symbol
VERB **4** If something **marks** a surface, it stains or damages it in some way.
5 When a teacher **marks** a student's work, they decide how good it is and give it a mark.
6 If you **mark** the opposing player in a team game such as hockey or netball, you stay close to them and prevent them from getting the ball.

market **markets, marketing, marketed**
NOUN **1** a place where goods are bought and sold, usually outdoors
VERB **2** If someone **markets** a product, they sell it in an organized way.

marmalade
NOUN a type of jam made from oranges or lemons

maroon
NOUN OR ADJECTIVE dark reddish-purple

marquee **marquees**
NOUN a very large tent used at a fair, a wedding or other outdoor events
[from French, meaning awning]

marriage **marriages**
NOUN **1** the relationship between two people who are married
2 a wedding ceremony

married
VERB **1** the past tense and past participle of **marry**
ADJECTIVE **2** If someone is **married**, they have a husband or a wife.

marrow **marrows**
NOUN a long, thick, green vegetable with cream-coloured flesh

marry **marries, marrying, married**
VERB When two people **marry**, they become partners in a special ceremony.

marsh **marshes**
NOUN an area of land that is permanently wet

marshmallow **marshmallows**
NOUN a soft, spongy sweet, usually pink or white

marsupials **marsupials**
NOUN an animal that carries its young in a pouch. Koalas, kangaroos and wallabies are **marsupials**.
[from Greek *marsupion* meaning purse]

kangaroo

martial
Said "**mar**-shul" ADJECTIVE **Martial** describes anything to do with military matters, war and soldiers.

martial arts
PLURAL NOUN The **martial arts** are techniques of self-defence, such as judo and karate, that come from the Far East.

martyr **martyrs**
NOUN someone who suffers or is killed for their beliefs
martyrdom NOUN

a b c d e f g h i j k l m n o p q r s t u v w x y z

A B C D E F G H I J K L M N O P Q R S T U V W X Y Z

marvel **marvels, marvelling, marvelled**
VERB **1** If you **marvel** at something, you are filled with amazement and admiration for it. • *We **marvelled** at the sight of people swimming with the dolphins.*
NOUN **2** something that fills you with surprise and admiration

marvellous
ADJECTIVE wonderful or excellent

marzipan
NOUN a paste made of almonds, sugar and egg. It is put on top of cakes or used to make small sweets.

mascot **mascots**
NOUN a person, animal or toy that is thought to bring good luck

masculine
ADJECTIVE typical of men, rather than women
ANTONYM: feminine

mask **masks, masking, masked**
NOUN **1** something you wear over your face for protection or as a disguise
VERB **2** If you **mask** something, you cover it so that it is protected or disguised.

mass **masses**
NOUN **1** a large amount or heap of something
2 In science, **mass** is the amount of matter in an object. **Mass** is measured in grams (g).
3 A **Mass** is a communion service in a Roman Catholic church.
ADJECTIVE **4** involving or affecting a large number of people

massacre **massacres, massacring, massacred**
NOUN **1** the killing of a very large number of people in a violent and cruel way
VERB **2** To **massacre** a group of people means to kill them in large numbers in a violent and cruel way.

massage **massages, massaging, massaged**
VERB **1** If you **massage** someone, you rub parts of their body in order to help them relax or to relieve pain.
NOUN **2** treatment that involves rubbing parts of the body

massive
ADJECTIVE extremely large
SYNONYMS: huge, vast, enormous

mast **masts**
NOUN the tall, upright pole that supports the sails of a boat

master **masters, mastering, mastered**
VERB **1** If you **master** a skill, you learn how to do it well.
NOUN **2** someone who is very skilled at something • *a **master** of disguise*
3 a male teacher

masterpiece **masterpieces**
NOUN an excellent painting, novel, film or other work of art that has been made with great skill • *The 'Mona Lisa' is considered a **masterpiece**.*

mat **mats**
NOUN **1** a small piece of carpet or other material that is put on floors for protection or decoration
2 a small piece of cloth or other material that is put on a table or other surface to protect it

match **matches, matching, matched**
NOUN **1** an organized game of football, cricket or some other sport
2 a small, thin wooden stick tipped with a chemical that produces a flame when you strike it against a rough surface. **Matches** are used to light things.
VERB **3** If colours **match**, they go well together. • *My dress **matched** my shoes.*
4 If you **match** one thing with another, you find the connection between them.

mate **mates, mating, mated**
NOUN **1** INFORMAL Your **mates** are your friends.
2 The first **mate** on a ship is second in importance after the captain.
VERB **3** When a pair of animals **mate**, they come together in order to breed.

material materials
NOUN **1** cloth
2 anything from which something else can be made • *artists' **materials***

maternal
ADJECTIVE **1** used to describe things relating to a mother • *My **maternal** grandfather was Welsh.*
2 A woman who is **maternal** has strong motherly feelings.

maternity
ADJECTIVE relating to or involving pregnant women and childbirth • *The baby was born in the **maternity** wing of the hospital.*

mathematics
NOUN the study of numbers, quantities and shapes
mathematical ADJECTIVE
mathematically ADVERB
mathematician NOUN

maths
NOUN an abbreviation of *mathematics*

matinee matinees
Said "**mat**-i-nay" NOUN an afternoon performance at a theatre or cinema

matrix matrices
Said "**may**-trix, **may**-tri-sees" NOUN In mathematics, a **matrix** is a set of numbers or letters set out in rows and columns.

matt
ADJECTIVE dull rather than shiny • *Mum painted the front door **matt** green.*

matter matters, mattering, mattered
NOUN **1** a task or situation that you have to attend to • *We will have to discuss the **matter** with the head teacher.*
SYNONYMS: affair, business, subject
2 any substance • *The scientists explored how **matter** behaves at high temperatures.*
VERB **3** If something **matters**, it is important.
PHRASE **4** If you ask **What's the matter?**, you want to know what is wrong.

mattress mattresses
NOUN a large, flat, spongy pad that is put on a bed to make it comfortable to sleep on

mature matures, maturing, matured
VERB **1** When a child or other young animal **matures**, it becomes an adult.
ADJECTIVE **2** fully grown or developed
maturely ADVERB **maturity** NOUN

maul mauls, mauling, mauled
VERB If an animal **mauls** someone, they savagely attack and badly injure them.

mauve
Rhymes with "stove" NOUN OR ADJECTIVE a light purple colour

maximum
ADJECTIVE **1** The **maximum** amount is the most that is possible or allowed. • *The **maximum** score for this question is five marks.*
ANTONYM: minimum
NOUN **2** the most that is possible or allowed • *Pupils are allowed a **maximum** of two pounds to spend on the school trip.*
ANTONYM: minimum

may
VERB **1** If something **may** happen, it is possible that it will happen.
2 If you **may** do something, you are allowed to do it.

May
NOUN the fifth month of the year. **May** has 31 days.
[probably from the Roman goddess *Maia*]

maybe
ADVERB If you think there is a possibility that something will happen, but you are not sure, you use **maybe**. • ***Maybe** we will be allowed to go to the cinema tonight.*

mayonnaise
NOUN a thick salad dressing made with egg yolks and oil

mayor mayors
NOUN someone who has been elected to represent the people of a town at official functions

maze mazes
NOUN a system of complicated passages which it is difficult to find your way through

a b c d e f g h i j k l m n o p q r s t u v w x y z

A B C D E F G H I J K L M N O P Q R S T U V W X Y Z

me
PRONOUN A speaker or writer uses **me** to refer to himself or herself.

meadow **meadows**
NOUN a field of grass

meagre
ADJECTIVE very small and poor • ***meagre*** *portions*

meal **meals**
NOUN **1** an occasion when people eat
2 the food people eat at meal times

mean **means, meaning, meant; meaner, meanest**
VERB **1** If you ask someone what something **means**, you want them to explain it to you.
2 If you **mean** to do something, you intend to do it.
SYNONYMS: aim, plan
3 If something **means** a lot to you, it is important to you.
ADJECTIVE **4** unkind
5 Someone who is **mean** is unwilling to share with others.
NOUN **6** In mathematics, the **mean** is the average of a set of numbers.

meander **meanders, meandering, meandered**
Said "mee-**and**-er" VERB If a road or river **meanders**, it has a lot of bends in it.
[from *Maiandros*, the name of a Greek river]

meaning **meanings**
NOUN The **meaning** of a word, expression or gesture is what it refers to or expresses. • *Do you know the* ***meaning*** *of the proverb "more haste, less speed"?*

meanwhile
ADVERB If something happens, and **meanwhile** something else is happening, the two things are happening at the same time.

measles
NOUN an infectious illness that causes a high temperature and red spots on the skin
[from Germanic *masele* meaning spot on the skin]

measure **measures, measuring, measured**
VERB **1** If you **measure** something, you find out the size or amount of it.
NOUN **2** a unit used to measure something
3 a container or an instrument, such as a ruler or a measuring jug, that you use to measure something
4 an action that you take to achieve something

measurement **measurements**
NOUN the result you obtain when you measure something

meat **meats**
NOUN the flesh of animals that people cook and eat

mechanic **mechanics**
NOUN someone whose job is to repair and maintain machines and engines

mechanical
ADJECTIVE **1** to do with machinery. Anything **mechanical** is worked by machinery.
2 If you do something in a **mechanical** way, you do it without thinking about it.
mechanically ADVERB

medal **medals**
NOUN a small piece of decorative metal, often shaped like a large coin and attached to a ribbon, given as an award for bravery or as a prize in sport

meddle **meddles, meddling, meddled**
VERB If you **meddle**, you interfere and try to change things without being asked.

media
PLURAL NOUN You can refer to the television, radio and newspapers as the **media**.

> *Media* is the plural of *medium* but it is becoming more common for it to be used as a singular noun: *The media is obsessed with celebrities.*

median **medians**
NOUN In mathematics, the **median** of a set of numbers is the middle number once the numbers have been arranged in order of size. • *The* ***median*** *of 4, 0, 1, 2, 3 is 2, as 2 is in the middle once they are organized in order.*

medical
ADJECTIVE to do with the treatment of people who are ill

medication **medications**
NOUN a substance that is used to treat illness

medicine **medicines**
NOUN **1** a substance that you take to help cure an illness
2 the care and treatment of ill people

medieval; also spelt **mediaeval**
ADJECTIVE relating to the period between about 1100 AD and 1500 AD, especially in Europe

mediocre
Said "mee-dee-**oh**-ker" ADJECTIVE
Something that is **mediocre** is of average or poor quality or standard. • *We were disappointed by the film – it was **mediocre**.*
mediocrity NOUN

Mediterranean
NOUN **1** the large sea between southern Europe and northern Africa
ADJECTIVE **2** relating to the Mediterranean or the countries adjoining it

medium **mediums** or **media**
ADJECTIVE **1** If something is of **medium** size, it is neither large nor small.
NOUN **2** a means of communicating or expressing something

meek **meeker, meekest**
ADJECTIVE A **meek** person is timid and does what other people say.
meekly ADVERB **meekness** NOUN

meet **meets, meeting, met**
VERB **1** If you **meet** someone, you make an arrangement to go to the same place at the same time as they do. • *Let's **meet** at your house before we go out.*
2 If you **meet** someone, you come face-to-face with them or are introduced to them for the first time. • *We **met** on our first day at school.*

meeting **meetings**
NOUN **1** an event at which people discuss things or make decisions
2 an occasion when you meet someone by arrangement

megabyte **megabytes**
NOUN a unit of storage in a computer, equal to 1,048,576 bytes

melancholy
ADJECTIVE OR NOUN If you feel **melancholy**, you feel very sad.

melodramatic
ADJECTIVE behaving in an exaggerated, emotional way

melody **melodies**
NOUN a tune
[from Greek *meloidia* meaning singing]

melon **melons**
NOUN a large, juicy fruit with a green or yellow skin and many seeds inside

melt **melts, melting, melted**
VERB When something **melts**, or when you **melt** it, it changes from a solid to a liquid because it has been heated.

member **members**
NOUN one of the people or things belonging to a group

membrane **membranes**
NOUN a very thin skin

memorable
ADJECTIVE **Memorable** things or people are likely to be remembered because they are special or unusual.

memorial **memorials**
NOUN a structure built to remind people of a famous person or event • *a war **memorial***

a b c d e f g h i j k l m n o p q r s t u v w x y z

A B C D E F G H I J K L M N O P Q R S T U V W X Y Z

memorize **memorizes, memorizing, memorized**
VERB If you **memorize** something, you learn it so well that you remember it and can repeat it exactly. • *She **memorized** all the times tables from 2 to 12 in one week.*

memory **memories**
NOUN **1** your ability to remember things
2 A computer's **memory** is its capacity to store information.

men
PLURAL NOUN the plural of **man**

menace **menaces, menacing, menaced**
NOUN **1** someone or something that is likely to cause harm • *That dog is a **menace**.*
VERB **2** If someone or something **menaces** you, they threaten to harm you.
menacing ADJECTIVE **menacingly** ADVERB

mend **mends, mending, mended**
VERB If you **mend** something that is broken, you repair or fix it.

menstruate **menstruates, menstruating, menstruated**
VERB When a woman **menstruates**, blood comes from her womb. This normally happens once a month.
menstruation NOUN **menstrual** ADJECTIVE

mental
ADJECTIVE relating to the mind and the process of thinking • ***mental** arithmetic*

mention **mentions, mentioning, mentioned**
VERB **1** If you **mention** something, you speak or write briefly about it.
NOUN **2** a brief comment about someone or something

menu **menus**
NOUN **1** a list of the food and drink you can buy in a restaurant or café
2 a list of options shown on a computer screen, which the user must choose from

mercenary **mercenaries**
ADJECTIVE **1** Someone who is **mercenary** is mainly interested in getting money.
NOUN **2** a soldier who is paid to fight for a foreign country

merchandise
NOUN goods for buying and selling
• *The market stalls were full of all kinds of **merchandise**.*

merchant **merchants**
NOUN a trader who imports and exports goods

mercury
NOUN a silver-coloured metallic element that is liquid at room temperature. **Mercury** is used in some thermometers.

mercy **mercies**
NOUN If you show **mercy**, you show kindness and forgiveness instead of punishing someone.

merge **merges, merging, merged**
VERB When two things **merge**, they combine or join together to make one thing. • *The two roads **merged** at the junction.*

meridian **meridians**
NOUN one of the lines on maps or globes, drawn from the North Pole to the South Pole, that help to describe the position of a place

merit **merits, meriting, merited**
NOUN **1** If something has **merit**, it is good or worthwhile.
2 The **merits** of something are its advantages or good qualities. • *I can see now the **merits** of working hard.*
VERB **3** If something or someone **merits** a particular treatment, they deserve that treatment. • *He **merits** a place in the team.*

mermaid **mermaids**
NOUN a creature in stories, with a woman's body and a fish's tail instead of legs

merry **merrier, merriest**
ADJECTIVE happy and cheerful
merrily ADVERB

mesh
NOUN threads of wire, plastic or other material twisted together like a net

mess **messes, messing, messed**
NOUN **1** something dirty or untidy
2 something full of problems

mess about or **mess around**
VERB If you **mess about** or **mess around**, you spend time doing silly or casual things. • *Stop **messing about** and get on with your work.*

mess up
VERB If you **mess up** something, you make it untidy, spoil it or do it badly. • *He'd already **messed up** one piece of paper.*

message **messages**
NOUN a piece of information or a request from one person to another

messenger **messengers**
NOUN someone who takes a message

messy **messier, messiest**
ADJECTIVE **1** dirty or untidy
2 complicated or confused • *He's got himself into a **messy** situation.*

met
VERB the past tense and past participle of **meet**

metal **metals**
NOUN a hard substance such as iron, steel, copper or lead. **Metals** are good conductors of heat and electricity.
metallic ADJECTIVE

metaphor **metaphors**
NOUN an imaginative way of describing one thing as another thing. For example, if a person is shy and timid, you could describe them as a mouse.

meteor **meteors**
NOUN a piece of rock or metal moving rapidly through space, that burns very briefly and brightly when it enters the earth's atmosphere

meteorite **meteorites**
NOUN a piece of rock from space that has landed on earth

meteorology
NOUN the study of the weather
meteorologist NOUN

meter **meters**
NOUN a device that measures and records something, such as a gas **meter** that records how much gas a household has used

method **methods**
NOUN a particular way of doing something • *Use the **method** I showed you to work out the sum.*

methodical
ADJECTIVE **Methodical** people do things in a careful and organized way.
methodically ADVERB

metre **metres**
NOUN a unit of length (m) equal to 100 centimetres

metric
ADJECTIVE relating to the system of measurement that uses metres, grams and litres

mew **mews, mewing, mewed**
VERB When a cat **mews**, it makes a short, high-pitched noise.

miaow **miaows, miaowing, miaowed**
NOUN **1** the noise a cat makes
VERB **2** When a cat **miaows**, it makes a crying sound.

mice
PLURAL NOUN the plural of **mouse**

micro-
PREFIX added to some words to mean very small. For example, a **micro**computer is a very small computer.

microbe **microbes**
NOUN a very small, living thing that can only be seen through a microscope. **Microbes** can feed, grow and reproduce.

microchip **microchips**
NOUN a small piece of silicon that has electronic circuits printed on it, and is used in computers and electronic equipment

micro-organism **micro-organisms**
NOUN a very small organism that can only be seen under a powerful microscope. Some **micro-organisms** are harmful and cause disease. Others, such as yeast, are helpful. Microbes, germs and viruses are sometimes called **micro-organisms**.

microphone **microphones**
NOUN a device that is used to record sounds or make them louder

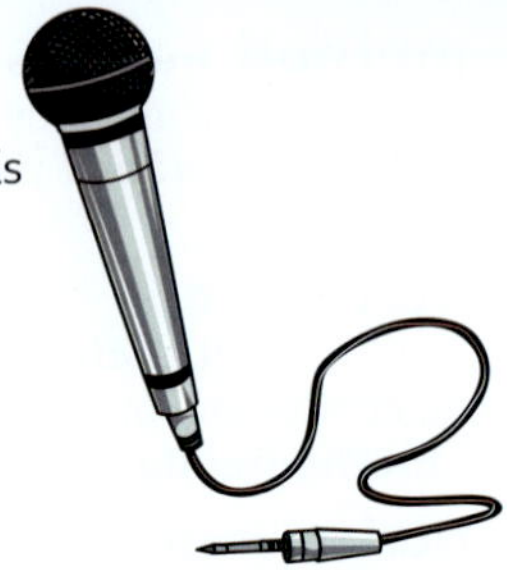

microscope **microscopes**
NOUN a piece of equipment that magnifies very small objects so that you can study them • *When the class looked at a leaf through the **microscope**, they could see the small veins that they had not been able to see before.*

microscopic
ADJECTIVE too small to be seen without using a microscope

microwave **microwaves**
NOUN a type of oven that cooks food very quickly by radiation

mid-
PREFIX used to form words that refer to the middle part of a place or a period of time • *We had a break **mid**morning.*

midday
NOUN twelve o'clock in the middle of the day

middle **middles**
NOUN **1** The **middle** of something is the part furthest from the edges, ends or surface. • *He stood in the **middle** of the room.*
2 The **middle** of an event is the part that comes after the first part and before the last part. • *There was an interval in the **middle** of the play.*
ADJECTIVE **3** The **middle** thing in a series is the one with an equal number of things on each side. • *M and N are the **middle** letters in the alphabet.*

Middle Ages
NOUN In European history, the **Middle Ages** were the period between about 1100 AD and 1500 AD.

midnight
NOUN twelve o'clock at night

midwife **midwives**
NOUN a nurse who is trained to help women during pregnancy and at the birth of their baby
midwifery NOUN

might
VERB **1** You use **might** to say that something will possibly happen or is possibly true. • *I **might** not be back until tomorrow.*
NOUN **2** If you do something with all your **might**, you do it with all your strength and energy.

migraine **migraines**
NOUN a severe headache that makes you feel very ill

migrant **migrants**
NOUN **1** a person who moves from one place to another, usually to find work • ***Migrants** arrived for the fruit-picking season.*
2 a bird, fish or animal that migrates from one part of the world to another • *The spotted flycatcher, a **migrant** from Africa, arrives in Britain in May.*

migrate **migrates, migrating, migrated**
VERB **1** If people **migrate**, they move from one place to another, especially to find work.
2 When birds or animals **migrate**, they move at a particular season to a different place, usually to breed or to find new feeding grounds.
migration NOUN **migratory** ADJECTIVE

mild **milder, mildest**
ADJECTIVE Something that is **mild** is gentle, and not very strong or severe. • ***mild** weather*
mildly ADVERB

mildew
NOUN a soft, white fungus that grows on things when they are warm and damp
mildewed ADJECTIVE

mile **miles**
NOUN a unit of distance equal to about 1.6 kilometres

[from Latin *milia passuum* meaning a thousand paces]

mileage **mileages**
NOUN the distance you have travelled, measured in miles • *The **mileage** from home to the hotel was 120 miles.*

military
ADJECTIVE to do with the armed forces of a country

milk **milks, milking, milked**
NOUN **1** the white liquid produced by mammals to feed their young. People drink cows' and goats' milk and make it into butter, cheese and yogurt.
VERB **2** When someone **milks** a cow or other animal, they get milk from it by pulling its udders.

milkman **milkmen**
NOUN a man who delivers milk to your house

mill **mills**
NOUN **1** a building where grain is crushed to make flour
2 a factory for making materials such as steel, wool or cotton • *a cotton **mill***
3 a small device for grinding something. For example, a pepper **mill** grinds peppercorns.

millennium **millennia** or **millenniums**
NOUN a period of 1000 years

milligram **milligrams**
NOUN a unit of weight (mg). There are 1000 **milligrams** in a gram.

millilitre **millilitres**
NOUN a unit for measuring liquid (ml). There are 1000 **millilitres** in a litre.

millimetre **millimetres**
NOUN a unit of length (mm). There are 10 **millimetres** in a centimetre.

million **millions**
NOUN A **million** is the number 1,000,000.
millionth NOUN OR ADJECTIVE

millionaire **millionaires**
NOUN someone who has money or property worth at least a million pounds or dollars

mime **mimes, miming, mimed**
NOUN **1** the use of movements and gestures to express something or to tell a story without using speech
VERB **2** If you **mime** something, you describe or express it using mime.

mimic **mimics, mimicking, mimicked**
VERB **1** If you **mimic** someone's actions or voice, you imitate them in an amusing way.
NOUN **2** a person who can imitate other people

minaret **minarets**
NOUN a tall, thin tower on a mosque

mince **minces, mincing, minced**
NOUN **1** meat that has been ground into very small pieces
VERB **2** If you **mince** meat, you grind it into very small pieces.

mincemeat
NOUN a sweet mixture of dried fruits used, for example, in mince pies

mind **minds, minding, minded**
NOUN **1** Your **mind** is your ability to think, together with your memory and all the thoughts you have. • *He could still see her face in his **mind**.*
PHRASE **2** If you **change your mind**, you change a decision that you have made or an opinion that you have.
VERB **3** If you do not **mind** what happens or what something is like, you do not have a strong preference about it. • *I don't **mind** where we go.*
4 If you tell someone to **mind** something,

A B C D E F G H I J K L M N O P Q R S T U V W X Y Z

you are warning them to be careful. • ***Mind** that plate, it's hot.*
5 If you **mind** something for someone, you look after it for a while.

mindless

ADJECTIVE **1 Mindless** behaviour is stupid and destructive.
2 A **mindless** job or activity is so simple, or repeated so often, that you do not need to think about it at all.
SYNONYM: repetitive

mine mines

PRONOUN **1** something belonging or relating to the person who is speaking or writing • *He's a good friend of **mine**.*
NOUN **2** a place where deep holes or tunnels are dug under the ground in order to extract minerals • *a coal **mine***
3 a bomb hidden in the ground or underwater, that explodes when people or things touch it

minefield minefields

NOUN an area of land or water where explosive mines have been laid

miner miners

NOUN a person who works underground in mines to find and dig out coal, diamonds, gold and other minerals • *a coal **miner***

mineral minerals

NOUN small particles that make up different rocks. For example, quartz and diamonds are **minerals**.

mineral water

NOUN water that comes from a natural spring

mingle mingles, mingling, mingled

VERB If things **mingle**, they become mixed together.

mini-

PREFIX used with another word to describe something shorter or smaller than the usual size • *a **mini**skirt*

miniature

ADJECTIVE a tiny copy of something much larger • *I bought a **miniature** version of the Eiffel Tower as a souvenir.*

minibus minibuses

NOUN a van with seats in the back, that is used as a small bus

minimum

ADJECTIVE **1** A **minimum** amount of something is the smallest amount that is possible, allowed or needed.
ANTONYM: maximum
NOUN **2** the smallest amount of something that is possible, allowed or needed
ANTONYM: maximum

minister ministers

NOUN **1** a person who is in charge of a particular government department
2 a member of the clergy, especially in a Protestant church
[from Latin *minister* meaning servant]

ministry ministries

NOUN a government department that deals with a particular area of work • *the **Ministry** of Education*

mink minks

NOUN a small wild mammal with valuable brown fur

minnow minnows

NOUN a very small, freshwater fish

minor

ADJECTIVE less important or serious than other things • *He had a **minor** part in the play.*
ANTONYM: major

minority minorities

NOUN less than half of a group of people or things

minstrel minstrels

NOUN a singer and entertainer in medieval times

mint mints

NOUN **1** a plant with strong-smelling leaves used as flavouring in cooking
2 a sweet flavoured with these leaves
3 the place where the official coins of a country are made
ADJECTIVE **4** If something is in **mint** condition, it is like new.

minus
PREPOSITION **1** You use **minus** (–) to show that one number is being subtracted from another. • *Ten **minus** six equals four (10 – 6 = 4).*
ADJECTIVE **2** **Minus** before a number means that the number is less than zero. • *There are sometimes temperatures of **minus** 65 °C (–65 °C) in the Arctic.*

minute **minutes**
Said "**min**-nit" NOUN **1** a unit of time equal to sixty seconds
2 a short period of time • *See you in a **minute**.*
Said "my-**nyoot**" ADJECTIVE **3** extremely small • *A **minute** amount of milk is needed.*

miracle **miracles**
NOUN a surprising and wonderful event, especially one believed to have been caused by God
[from Latin *mirari* meaning to wonder at]

mirage **mirages**
Said "mi-**rarzh**" NOUN an image that you can see in the distance in very hot weather, but that does not actually exist

mirror
mirrors
NOUN an object made of glass in which you can see your reflection

mis-
PREFIX added to some words to mean badly or wrongly. For example, **mis**behave means to behave badly, and **mis**calculate means to calculate wrongly.

misbehave **misbehaves, misbehaving, misbehaved**
VERB If someone **misbehaves**, they are naughty or behave badly.
misbehaviour NOUN

miscarriage **miscarriages**
NOUN **1** If a woman has a **miscarriage**, she gives birth to a baby too early, before it is able to survive in the outside world.
2 A **miscarriage** of justice is a wrong decision made by a court, which results in an innocent person being punished.

miscellaneous
Said "miss-uh-**lay**-nee-uss" ADJECTIVE
A **miscellaneous** group is made up of a mixture of people or things that are different from each other.

mischief
NOUN naughty behaviour, teasing people or playing tricks

mischievous
ADJECTIVE If you are **mischievous**, you enjoy being naughty by teasing or playing tricks on people.
mischievously ADVERB

miser **misers**
NOUN a mean person who enjoys hoarding money, but hates spending it
miserly ADVERB

miserable
ADJECTIVE If you are **miserable**, you are very unhappy.

misery **miseries**
NOUN great unhappiness
SYNONYM: grief

misfire **misfires, misfiring, misfired**
VERB If a plan **misfires**, it goes wrong.

misfit **misfits**
NOUN a person who cannot get on with other people or fit into a group

misfortune **misfortunes**
NOUN an unpleasant occurrence that is regarded as bad luck • *I had the **misfortune** to fall off my bike.*

mishap **mishaps**
Said "**miss**-hap" NOUN an accidental or unfortunate happening that is not very serious • *Grandma had a small **mishap** when her hat blew away.*

misjudge **misjudges, misjudging, misjudged**
VERB If you **misjudge** someone or something, you form a wrong or unfair opinion of them.

mislay **mislays, mislaying, mislaid**
VERB If you **mislay** something, you cannot remember where you put it.

mislead **misleads, misleading, misled**
VERB If you **mislead** someone, you make them believe something that is not true.

misprint **misprints**
NOUN a mistake such as a spelling mistake in something that has been printed

miss **misses, missing, missed**
VERB **1** If you **miss** someone or something, you feel sad because they are no longer with you.
2 If you **miss** a bus, plane or train, you arrive too late to catch it.
3 If you **miss** an event or activity, you fail to attend it. • *I had to **miss** my piano lesson.*
4 If you **miss** something that you are aiming at, you fail to hit it. • *The arrow **missed** the target.*
NOUN **5** **Miss** is used before the name of a girl or unmarried woman. • *My teacher this year is **Miss** Weston.*

missile **missiles**
NOUN **1** a weapon that moves long distances through the air and explodes when it reaches its target • *nuclear **missiles***
2 any object thrown to harm someone or something

missing
ADJECTIVE Something that is **missing** is lost or not in its usual place. • *One of my shoes is **missing**.*

mission **missions**
NOUN **1** a journey made by a military aeroplane or space rocket to carry out a task
2 an important task that has to be done

missionary **missionaries**
NOUN a Christian who has been sent to a foreign country to work for the Church

misspell **misspells, misspelling, misspelt** or **misspelled**
VERB If you **misspell** a word, you spell it wrongly.

mist **mists**
NOUN many tiny drops of water in the air that make it hard to see clearly

mistake **mistakes, mistaking, mistook, mistaken**
NOUN **1** If you make a **mistake**, you do something wrong without intending to. • *There are some spelling **mistakes** in your homework.*
VERB **2** If you **mistake** someone or something for another person or thing, you wrongly think that they are the other person or thing. • *I **mistook** him for his brother.*

mistletoe
NOUN a plant that grows on trees and has white berries on it

mistook
VERB the past tense of **mistake**

mistreat **mistreats, mistreating, mistreated**
VERB If you **mistreat** a person or an animal, you treat them badly and make them suffer.

mistress **mistresses**
NOUN **1** a woman schoolteacher • *There is a new French **mistress**.*
2 a woman who is in charge of something or someone • *The dog had run away from its **mistress**.*

mistrust **mistrusts, mistrusting, mistrusted**
VERB **1** If you **mistrust** someone, you feel that that they are not to be trusted.
ANTONYM: trust
NOUN **2** the feeling of not being able to trust someone or something
ANTONYM: trust

misunderstand **misunderstands, misunderstanding, misunderstood**
VERB If you **misunderstand** someone, you do not properly understand what they say or do. • *He **misunderstood** the instructions and took the wrong turning.*

misunderstanding **misunderstandings**
NOUN If people have a **misunderstanding**,

they have a disagreement or a slight quarrel about something.

misuse **misuses, misusing, misused**
NOUN **1** The **misuse** of something is the incorrect or dishonest use of it.
VERB **2** If you **misuse** something, you use it wrongly or dishonestly.

mix **mixes, mixing, mixed**
VERB If you **mix** things, you combine them.
mixed up ADJECTIVE

mix up
VERB If you **mix up** things, you get confused.

mixture **mixtures**
NOUN **1** two or more things mixed together • *They felt a **mixture** of fear and excitement as they climbed the wall.*
2 a substance consisting of two or more other substances that have been mixed together

moan **moans, moaning, moaned**
VERB **1** If you **moan**, you make a low, miserable sound because you are in pain or unhappy.
2 If you **moan** about something, you complain about it.
NOUN **3** a low cry of pain or unhappiness

moat **moats**
NOUN a wide, deep ditch around a castle, usually filled with water, to help defend the building

mob **mobs, mobbing, mobbed**
NOUN **1** a large, disorganized crowd of people
VERB **2** If a group **mobs** someone, they gather closely around them in a disorderly way. • *The fans **mobbed** the band.*

mobile **mobiles**
ADJECTIVE **1** able to move or be moved easily • *He's much more **mobile** since getting his new wheelchair.*
NOUN **2** short for **mobile phone**
3 an ornament made up of several parts that hang from threads and move in the breeze

mobile phone **mobile phones**
NOUN a small telephone that you can carry around with you

mock **mocks, mocking, mocked**
VERB **1** If you **mock** someone, you tease them or try to make them look foolish.
SYNONYMS: laugh at, make fun of
ADJECTIVE **2** not genuine • *The ring is made of **mock** diamonds.*

mode **modes**
NOUN **1** a particular way of behaving or of doing something
2 In mathematics, the mode is the most popular or most frequently occurring value. • *Of the following numbers – 5, 5, 6, 7, 7, 7, 8 – 7 is the **mode**.*

model **models**
NOUN OR ADJECTIVE **1** a smaller copy of something that shows what it looks like or how it works in real life • *Mark has a **model** railway in his bedroom.*
NOUN **2** a type or version of a product • *Which **model** of computer did you choose?*
3 a person who wears clothes that are being displayed to possible buyers, or who poses for a photographer or artist
ADJECTIVE **4** A **model** student is an excellent example of a student who is worth copying.

modem **modems**
NOUN a piece of equipment that links a computer to the telephone system so that data can be sent from one computer to another

moderate **moderates, moderating, moderated**
Said "**mod**-er-ut" ADJECTIVE **1** A **moderate** amount of something is not too much or too little of it.
2 **Moderate** ideas and opinions are not extreme.
Said "**mod**-er-ayt" VERB **3** If something **moderates** or is **moderated**, it becomes less extreme. • *He should **moderate** his temper.*
moderately ADVERB

modern
ADJECTIVE new and involving the latest ideas or equipment
[from Latin *modo* meaning just recently]

modest
ADJECTIVE **1** quite small in size or amount • *He inherited a **modest** amount of money.*

2 Modest people do not boast about how clever or how rich they are.
ANTONYM: boastful
modesty NOUN **modestly** ADVERB

modify **modifies, modifying, modified**
VERB If you **modify** something, you change it slightly to improve it. • *When he had **modified** his bike, it went much faster.*

module **modules**
NOUN **1** one of the parts which, when put together, form a whole unit or object
2 a part of a spacecraft that can do certain things away from the main body
• *the lunar **module***

moist **moister, moistest**
ADJECTIVE slightly wet, damp

moisten **moistens, moistening, moistened**
VERB If you **moisten** something, you make it slightly wet.

moisture
NOUN tiny drops of water in the air or on the ground

molar **molars**
NOUN Your **molars** are the large teeth at the back of your mouth.

mole **moles**
NOUN **1** a small animal with black fur. **Moles** live in tunnels underground.
2 a dark, slightly-raised spot on your skin

molecule **molecules**
NOUN A **molecule** is made up of two or more atoms held together.
molecular ADJECTIVE

mollusc **molluscs**
NOUN an animal with a soft body and no backbone. Snails, slugs, clams and mussels are all **molluscs**.

molten
ADJECTIVE **Molten** rock or metal has been heated to a very high temperature and has melted to become a thick liquid.
• *When the volcano erupted, **molten** lava flowed down the mountainside.*

moment **moments**
NOUN **1** a very short period of time
• *I paused for a **moment**.*
SYNONYMS: instant, second
2 the point at which something happens • *At that **moment**, the doorbell rang.*
PHRASE **3** If something is happening **at the moment**, it is happening now.

momentum
NOUN the ability that an object has to continue moving as a result of its mass and the speed at which it is already moving

monarchy **monarchies**
NOUN a system in which a queen or king reigns in a country

monastery **monasteries**
NOUN a place where monks live and work [from Latin *monasterium* meaning to live alone]
monastic ADJECTIVE

Monday **Mondays**
NOUN the second day of the week, coming between Sunday and Tuesday
[from Old English *Monandæg* meaning moon's day]

money
NOUN the coins and banknotes that you use to buy things

mongrel **mongrels**
NOUN a dog with parents of different breeds

monitor **monitors, monitoring, monitored**
VERB **1** If you **monitor** something, you regularly check its condition and progress.
NOUN **2** a machine used to check or record things
3 the visual display unit of a computer

4 a school pupil chosen to do special duties by the teacher

monk **monks**
NOUN a member of a male religious community

monkey **monkeys**
NOUN an agile animal that has a long tail and climbs trees

mono-
PREFIX having one of something, for example a **mono**rail is a single rail, and a sound that is **mono**tone has only one tone

monologue **monologues**
NOUN a long speech by one person during a play or conversation

monotonous
ADJECTIVE having a regular pattern that is very dull and boring • *a **monotonous** voice*
monotony NOUN **monotonously** ADVERB

monsoon **monsoons**
NOUN the season of very heavy rain in South-east Asia

monster **monsters**
NOUN **1** a large, imaginary creature that looks very frightening
2 a cruel and frightening person
ADJECTIVE **3** extremely large • *She gave him a **monster** TV set for his birthday.*
[from Latin *monstrum* meaning omen or warning]

month **months**
NOUN one of the twelve periods that a year is divided into

monthly
ADJECTIVE OR ADVERB happening or appearing once every month

monument **monuments**
NOUN a large structure built to remind people of a famous person or event
[from Latin *monere* meaning to remind]

moo **moos, mooing, mooed**
VERB **1** When cows **moo**, they make a long, deep sound.
NOUN **2** the long, deep sound that cows make

mood **moods**
NOUN the way you are feeling at a particular time

moody **moodier, moodiest**
ADJECTIVE **1** **Moody** people change their mood often and very quickly, seemingly for no reason.
2 depressed and miserable
moodily ADVERB

moon **moons**
NOUN an object that moves round the earth once every four weeks. You see the **moon** as a shining circle or crescent in the sky at night. Some other planets have **moons**.

moonlight
NOUN the light that comes from the moon at night

moor **moors, mooring, moored**
NOUN **1** a high area of open land • *The farmer had flocks of sheep grazing on the **moors**.*
VERB **2** If you **moor** a boat, you attach it to the land with a rope.

moose
NOUN a North American deer or elk, with large, flat antlers

> The plural of *moose* is *moose*.

mop **mops, mopping, mopped**
NOUN **1** a tool for washing floors. It has a string or a sponge head at the end of a long handle.
VERB **2** If you **mop** something, you wipe it or clean it up with a mop or a cloth.

mope **mopes, moping, moped**
VERB If you **mope**, you feel miserable and sorry for yourself.

moral **morals**
PLURAL NOUN **1** **Morals** are values based on beliefs that are acceptable to a particular society.
ADJECTIVE **2** relating to beliefs about what is right and wrong • ***moral** values*
NOUN **3** the lesson taught by a story, that usually tells you that good behaviour is best
morality NOUN **morally** ADVERB

morale
NOUN Your **morale** is the amount of confidence and optimism you feel. • *The **morale** of the school was high.*

morbid
ADJECTIVE If you are **morbid**, you have a great interest in unpleasant things, especially death and illness.
[from Latin *morbus* meaning illness]

more
ADJECTIVE OR PRONOUN **1** a greater number or extent than something else • ***More** than 1500 schools took part in the event.*
ANTONYMS: fewer, less
2 an additional thing or amount of something • *I would like some **more** orange juice.*
ADVERB **3** **More** means to a greater degree or extent. • *We can talk **more** later.*
4 You use **more** to show that something is repeated. • *Repeat the exercise once **more**.*
5 You use **more** in front of adjectives and adverbs to form comparatives. • *He did it **more** carefully the second time.*

morning **mornings**
NOUN **1** the early part of the day, before noon
2 the part of the day between midnight and midday

Morse code
NOUN a code for sending messages by radio signals. Each letter is represented by a series of dots (short sounds) and dashes (longer sounds).

morsel **morsels**
NOUN a small piece of food

mortal **mortals**
ADJECTIVE **1** a **mortal** wound causes death
2 unable to live forever and certain to die
NOUN **3** an ordinary person

mortar **mortars**
NOUN **1** a mixture of sand, water and cement used to hold bricks firmly together
2 a short cannon that fires missiles high into the air

mortgage **mortgages**
NOUN a loan that people get from a bank or building society in order to buy a house

mortuary **mortuaries**
NOUN a special room in a hospital where dead bodies are kept before being buried or cremated

mosaic **mosaics**
NOUN a design made of small, coloured stones, tiles or pieces of coloured glass set into concrete or plaster

Moslem
NOUN OR ADJECTIVE another spelling of **Muslim**

mosque **mosques**
NOUN a building where Muslims go to worship
[from Arabic *masjid* meaning temple]

mosquito **mosquitoes** or **mosquitos**
NOUN a small, flying insect that bites people and animals in order to suck their blood

moss **mosses**
NOUN a soft, small, green plant that grows on damp soil or stone
mossy ADJECTIVE

most
ADJECTIVE OR PRONOUN **1** **Most** of a group of things or people means nearly all of them. • ***Most** people prefer sunny weather.*
2 a larger amount than anyone or anything else • *She has the **most** points.*
ADVERB **3** You use **most** in front of adjectives or adverbs to form superlatives. • *the **most** breathtaking scenery in the world*

motel **motels**
NOUN a hotel for people who are travelling by car, with parking spaces close to the rooms

moth **moths**
NOUN an insect like a butterfly that usually flies at night

mother **mothers**
NOUN Your **mother** is your female parent.

mother-in-law **mothers-in-law**
NOUN the mother of someone's husband or wife

motion **motions**
NOUN movement

motionless
ADJECTIVE If someone or something is **motionless**, they are not moving at all.

motivate **motivates, motivating, motivated**
VERB If you **motivate** someone, you make them determined to do or achieve something.
motivated ADJECTIVE **motivation** NOUN

motive **motives**
NOUN a reason or purpose for doing something

motor **motors**
NOUN a part of a vehicle or machine. The **motor** uses fuel to make the vehicle or machine work
SYNONYM: engine

motorbike **motorbikes**
NOUN a heavy two-wheeled vehicle that is driven by an engine

motorcycle **motorcycles**
NOUN another word for **motorbike**

motorist **motorists**
NOUN a person who drives a car or rides a motorbike

motorway **motorways**
NOUN a wide road built for fast travel over long distances

motto **mottoes** or **mottos**
NOUN a short sentence or phrase that is a rule for good or sensible behaviour. For example, *everything in moderation*.

mould **moulds, moulding, moulded**
VERB **1** If you **mould** a substance, you make it into a particular shape. • ***Mould** the dough into balls.*
NOUN **2** a container used to make something into a particular shape • *a jelly **mould***
3 a soft, grey or green growth that forms on old food or damp walls

mouldy **mouldier, mouldiest**
ADJECTIVE Something that is **mouldy** is covered with mould. • *This old bread had gone **mouldy**.*

moult **moults, moulting, moulted**
VERB When an animal or bird **moults**, it loses its hair or feathers so that new ones can grow.

mound **mounds**
NOUN **1** a small, man-made hill
2 a large, untidy pile

mount **mounts, mounting, mounted**
VERB **1** If you **mount** a horse or bicycle, you climb onto it.
2 If something **mounts**, it increases in amount. • *The contributions for the tombola were mounting.*
3 If you **mount** a picture or a photograph, you put it in a frame or an album to display it.
NOUN **4** a mountain, especially as part of the name • ***Mount** Everest is the highest mountain in the world.*

mountain **mountains**
NOUN a very high piece of land with steep sides

mountaineer **mountaineer**
NOUN a person who climbs mountains

mourn **mourns, mourning, mourned**
VERB If you **mourn** for someone who has died, you feel sad and think about them a lot.

mouse **mice**
NOUN **1** a small, furry rodent with a long tail
2 a computer device that you move by hand to control the position of a cursor on the screen

A B C D E F G H I J K L M N O P Q R S T U V W X Y Z

moustache **moustaches**
NOUN the hair that grows on a man's upper lip

mouth **mouths**
NOUN **1** your lips, or the space behind them where your tongue and teeth are
2 the entrance to a cave or a hole
3 the place where a river flows into the sea

mouthful **mouthfuls**
NOUN the amount of food you put in your mouth • *Don't take such huge **mouthfuls**!*

movable
ADJECTIVE Something that is **movable** can be moved from one place to another.

move **moves, moving, moved**
VERB **1** When you **move** something, or when it **moves**, its position changes. • *The train began to **move** out of the station.*
2 If you **move** or **move house**, you go to live in a different place.
3 If something **moves** you, it causes you to feel a deep emotion. • *The film **moved** us to tears.*
NOUN **4** a change from one place or position to another, especially in a game • *It's your **move**.*

movement **movements**
NOUN **1** the action of changing position or moving from one place to another
2 a group of people who act together to try and make something happen • *the animal rights **movement***
3 one of the main parts of a piece of classical music

movie **movies**
NOUN another name for **film**

moving
ADJECTIVE Something that is **moving** makes you feel deep sadness or emotion. • *a **moving** story*

mow **mows, mowing, mowed, mown**
VERB If you **mow** grass, you cut it with a lawnmower.

MP **MPs**
NOUN someone who has been elected by the people of an area to represent them in Parliament. **MP** is an abbreviation for *Member of Parliament*.

MP3 player **MP3 players**
NOUN a device that plays audio and video files, used for listening to music

Mr
Said "**miss**-ter" NOUN **Mr** is used before a man's name when you are speaking to him or talking about him. • *My teacher is called **Mr** Jones.*

Mrs
Said "**miss**-izz" NOUN **Mrs** is used before the name of a married woman when you are speaking or referring to her. • *"Good morning, **Mrs** Green."*

Ms
Said "**miz**" NOUN **Ms** is used before a woman's name when you are speaking or referring to her. **Ms** does not show whether the woman is married or not.

much
ADVERB **1** You use **much** to indicate the great size, extent or intensity of something. • *He's **much** taller than you.*
2 If something does not happen **much**, it does not happen often. • *He doesn't talk **much**.*
ADJECTIVE OR PRONOUN **3** You use **much** to talk about the size or amount of something. • *There isn't **much** left.*

mud
NOUN wet, sticky earth
muddy ADJECTIVE

muddle **muddles, muddling, muddled**
NOUN **1** a state of disorder or untidiness
VERB **2** If you **muddle** things, you mix them up.
[from Dutch *moddelen* meaning to make muddy]
muddled ADJECTIVE

muesli
NOUN a mixture of cereal flakes, chopped nuts and dried fruit that you can eat with milk for breakfast

muffled
ADJECTIVE A sound that is **muffled** is low or difficult to hear.

mug **mugs, mugging, mugged**
NOUN **1** a large, deep cup

VERB **2** INFORMAL If someone **mugs** you, they attack you in the street in order to steal your money.

mule **mules**
NOUN the offspring of a female horse and a male donkey

multiple **multiples**
ADJECTIVE **1** consisting of many parts or having many uses
NOUN **2** a number that can be divided exactly by another number • *2, 4, 6, 8, 10 and 12 are all **multiples** of 2.*

multiplication
NOUN the process of multiplying one number by another

multiply **multiplies, multiplying, multiplied**
VERB **1** When you **multiply** one number by another, you calculate the total you would get if you added the first number to itself the number of times shown by the second number. • *Six **multiplied** by three is 18 (6 × 3 = 18), because 6 + 6 + 6 = 18.*
2 When something **multiplies**, it increases greatly in number or amount.

multitude **multitudes**
NOUN FORMAL a very large number of people or things

mum **mums**
NOUN INFORMAL mother

mumble **mumbles, mumbling, mumbled**
VERB If you **mumble**, you speak very quietly and indistinctly.

mummy **mummies**
NOUN **1** INFORMAL Your **mummy** is your mother.
2 a dead body that was preserved long ago by being rubbed with special oils and wrapped in cloth • ***Mummies** have been found in tombs in Egypt.*
[(sense 2) from Persian *mum* meaning wax]

a mummy's coffin from Ancient Egypt

mumps
NOUN a disease that causes painful swelling in the neck

munch **munches, munching, munched**
VERB If you **munch** something, you chew it steadily and thoroughly.

mural **murals**
NOUN a picture painted on a wall

murder **murders, murdering, murdered**
NOUN **1** the deliberate killing of a person
VERB **2** To **murder** someone means to kill them deliberately.
murderer NOUN

murky **murkier, murkiest**
ADJECTIVE dark or dirty and hard to see through • ***murky** water*
[from Old Norse *myrkr* meaning darkness]
murk NOUN

murmur **murmurs, murmuring, murmured**
VERB **1** If you **murmur** something, you say it very quietly.
NOUN **2** something someone says that can hardly be heard • *They spoke in low **murmurs**.*

muscle **muscles**
NOUN Your **muscles** are the bundles of fibres connected to your bones, that enable you to move.
[from Latin *musculus* meaning little mouse, because muscles were thought to look like mice]

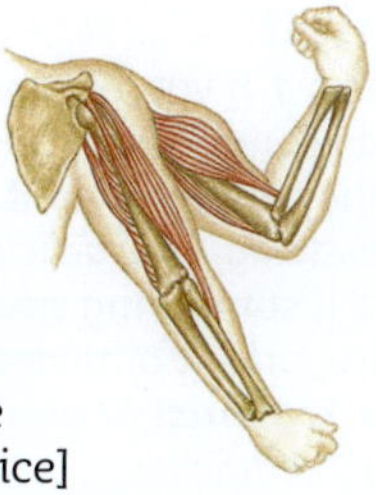

muscular
Said "**musk**-yoo-lar" ADJECTIVE
1 **Muscular** people have strong, well-developed muscles.
2 involving or affecting your muscles
• ***muscular** pain*

museum **museums**
NOUN a public building where interesting or valuable objects are kept and displayed

A B C D E F G H I J K L M N O P Q R S T U V W X Y Z

mushroom **mushrooms**
NOUN a fungus with a short stem and a round top. Some types of **mushroom** are edible.

music
NOUN **1** the pattern of sounds performed by people singing or playing instruments
2 the written symbols that represent musical sounds

musical **musicals**
ADJECTIVE **1** relating to playing or studying music • *She has considerable **musical** talent.*
NOUN **2** a play or a film that uses songs and dance to tell the story
musically ADVERB

musician **musicians**
NOUN a person who plays a musical instrument well

Muslim **Muslims**; also spelt **Moslem**
NOUN **1** a person who believes in the Islamic religion and lives according to its rules
ADJECTIVE **2** relating to Islam

mussel **mussels**
NOUN a small, edible shellfish with a black shell

must
VERB **1** If you tell someone that they **must** do something, you make them feel that they ought to do it. • *You **must** try this pudding – it's delicious.*
2 If something **must** happen, it is very important or necessary that it happens. • *You **must** be over 15 to see a film with a 15 certificate.*
3 If you think something is very likely, you think it **must** be so. • *You **must** be Sam's brother.*

mustard
NOUN a spicy-tasting yellow or brown paste made from seeds

mute
ADJECTIVE People or animals that are **mute** do not or cannot speak or make a sound.

mutilate **mutilates, mutilating, mutilated**
VERB **1** If you **mutilate** something, you damage or spoil it.
2 If someone is **mutilated**, they have been very badly cut and injured.

mutiny **mutinies, mutinying, mutinied**
VERB **1** If a group of sailors or soldiers **mutiny**, they rebel against their officers.
NOUN **2** a rebellion against someone in authority
mutineer NOUN

mutter **mutters, muttering, muttered**
VERB If you **mutter**, or if you **mutter** something, you speak very quietly so that it is difficult for people to hear you.

mutton
NOUN the meat of an adult sheep

mutual
Said "**mew**-choo-ul" ADJECTIVE **Mutual** is used to describe something that two or more people give to each other or share. • *My dad and my brother have a **mutual** love of football.*

muzzle **muzzles, muzzling, muzzled**
NOUN **1** the nose and mouth of an animal
2 a cover or a strap for a dog's nose and mouth to prevent it from biting
3 the open end of a gun where the bullets come out
VERB **4** If you **muzzle** a dog, you put a muzzle on it.

my
ADJECTIVE **My** refers to something belonging to the person who is speaking or writing. • *I ride **my** bicycle to school every day.*

myself
PRONOUN You use **myself** when you are speaking about yourself. • *I was cross with **myself** for being so mean.*

mysterious
ADJECTIVE **1** strange and puzzling • *They heard **mysterious** noises in the night.*
2 If someone is being **mysterious**, they

are being secretive about something. • *Mum is being very **mysterious** about my birthday present.*

mysteriously ADVERB

mystery **mysteries**
NOUN something that is not understood or known about • *The identity of the burglar remains a **mystery**.*

mystify **mystifies, mystifying, mystified**
VERB If something **mystifies** you, you find it impossible to understand. • *I am **mystified** by the disappearance of my sweater.*

myth **myths**
NOUN a story that was made up long ago to explain natural events and people's religious beliefs

Nn

nag **nags, nagging, nagged**
VERB If you **nag** someone, you keep complaining to them or pestering them about something.

nail **nails, nailing, nailed**
NOUN **1** Your **nails** are the thin, hard areas covering the ends of your fingers and toes.
2 a small piece of metal with a sharp point at one end, that you hammer into objects to hold them together
VERB **3** If you **nail** something somewhere, you fix it there using a nail.

naïve
Said "ny-**eeve**" ADJECTIVE If you are **naïve**, you believe that things are easier or less complicated than they really are, usually because of your lack of experience.

naïvely ADVERB

naked
ADJECTIVE not wearing any clothes

name **names, naming, named**
NOUN **1** a word that you use to identify a person, animal, place or thing
VERB **2** When you **name** someone or something, you give them a name.

nameless
ADJECTIVE not having a name or not identified • *a **nameless** terror*

nanny **nannies**
NOUN a person whose job is to look after young children

nap **naps, napping, napped**
NOUN **1** a short sleep
VERB **2** When you **nap**, you have a short sleep.

napkin **napkins**
NOUN a small piece of cloth or paper used

A B C D E F G H I J K L M N O P Q R S T U V W X Y Z

to wipe your hands and mouth after eating

nappy **nappies**
NOUN a piece of towelling or paper padding worn round a baby's bottom

narrate **narrates, narrating, narrated**
VERB If you **narrate** a story, you tell it.

narrative **narratives**
NOUN a story or an account of events

narrator **narrators**
NOUN the person in a book or a film or in a radio or television broadcast, who tells the story or explains what is happening

narrow **narrower, narrowest; narrows, narrowing, narrowed**
ADJECTIVE **1** Something that is **narrow** measures a small distance from one side to the other. • *We walked down a **narrow** passageway.*
VERB **2** If something **narrows**, it becomes less wide. • *The track **narrowed** ahead.*

nasty **nastier, nastiest**
ADJECTIVE very unpleasant
SYNONYMS: unkind, rude, disgusting

nation **nations**
NOUN a country and all the people who live there

national
ADJECTIVE relating to a country or the whole country • *He was dressed in the **national** costume.*

national anthem **national anthems**
NOUN the official song of a country

nationality **nationalities**
NOUN the fact of being a citizen of a particular nation

native **natives**
ADJECTIVE **1** Your **native** country is the country where you were born.
2 Your **native** language is the language that you first learned to speak.
NOUN **3** A **native** of a place is someone who was born there.

Nativity
NOUN In Christianity, the **Nativity** is the birth of Christ, or the festival celebrating this.

natural
ADJECTIVE **1** normal and to be expected • *It's **natural** to want to do well.*
2 existing or happening in nature, rather than caused or made by people • *Wool is a **natural** material.*
3 If you have a **natural** ability, you are born with it. • *She has a **natural** flair for mathematics.*
naturally ADVERB

natural history
NOUN the study of animals and plants

nature **natures**
NOUN **1** animals, plants and all the other things in the world that are not made by people
2 the basic quality or character of a person or thing • *They liked his warm, generous **nature**.*

naughty **naughtier, naughtiest**
ADJECTIVE A child who is **naughty** behaves badly.
naughtiness NOUN

nausea
NOUN a feeling that you are going to be sick
nauseous ADJECTIVE

nautical
ADJECTIVE relating to ships or navigation

naval
ADJECTIVE relating to a navy

navel **navels**
NOUN the small hollow on the front of your body, just below your waist

navigate **navigates, navigating, navigated**
VERB When someone **navigates**, they work out the direction in which a ship, plane or car should go, using maps and sometimes instruments.
navigation NOUN **navigator** NOUN

navy **navies**
NOUN the part of a country's armed forces that fights at sea

near **nearer, nearest; nears, nearing, neared**
PREPOSITION OR ADVERB **1** If something is **near** a place, it is a short distance from it. • *They live in a cottage **near** the river.*
VERB **2** When you are **nearing** a particular place or time, you are approaching it and will soon reach it. • *The dog began to bark as the visitor **neared** the door.*

nearby
ADJECTIVE OR ADVERB a short distance away

nearly
ADVERB not completely, but almost • *I've **nearly** finished my homework.*

neat **neater, neatest**
ADJECTIVE tidy and smart
neatly ADVERB **neatness** NOUN

necessary
ADJECTIVE Something that is **necessary** is needed or must be done. • *It might be **necessary** to leave quickly.*

Necessary has one *c* and two *ss*.

necessity **necessities**
NOUN **1** the need to do something
2 something that is needed • *Water is a basic **necessity** of life.*

neck **necks**
NOUN **1** the part of your body that joins your head to the rest of your body
2 the long, narrow part at one end of a bottle or guitar

necklace **necklaces**
NOUN a piece of jewellery that a person wears around their neck

nectar
NOUN a sweet liquid produced by flowers and collected by insects

need **needs, needing, needed**
VERB **1** If you **need** something, you cannot achieve what you want without having it or doing it. • *I **need** some help with my homework.*
PLURAL NOUN **2** Your **needs** are the things that you need to have.
SYNONYMS: necessities, requirements

needle **needles**
NOUN **1** a small, thin piece of metal with a hole at one end and a sharp point at the other, used for sewing
2 **Needles** are long, thin pieces of steel or plastic, used for knitting.
3 the sharp part of a syringe that goes into your skin when you have an injection
4 the thin pointer on a dial or compass that moves to show a measurement or bearing
5 Pine **needles** are the sharp, pointed leaves of a pine tree.

needlework
NOUN sewing or embroidery that is done by hand

negative **negatives**
ADJECTIVE **1** A **negative** answer means no.
ANTONYM: positive
2 A **negative** number is less than zero.
ANTONYM: positive
NOUN **3** the image that is first produced when you take a photograph

neglect **neglects, neglecting, neglected**
VERB **1** If you **neglect** someone or something, you do not look after them properly. • *Ben **neglected** his hamster.*
NOUN **2** failure to look after someone or something properly • *Most of her plants died from **neglect**.*

negotiate **negotiates, negotiating, negotiated**
VERB When people **negotiate**, they talk about a situation in order to reach an agreement about it.

neigh **neighs, neighing, neighed**
Said "**nay**" VERB **1** When a horse **neighs**, it makes a loud, high-pitched sound through its nose.
NOUN **2** A **neigh** is a loud, high-pitched sound made by a horse.

neighbour **neighbours**
NOUN someone who lives next door to you or near you

A B C D E F G H I J K L M N O P Q R S T U V W X Y Z

neighbourhood **neighbourhoods**
NOUN Your **neighbourhood** is the area where you live.

neither
CONJUNCTION, ADJECTIVE OR PRONOUN You use **neither** in front of two alternatives to mean not one and not the other. • *He spoke **neither** English nor German.*

neon
NOUN a gas used in glass tubes to make light sources and signs

nephew **nephews**
NOUN Someone's **nephew** is the son of their sister or brother.

nerve **nerves**
NOUN **1** long, thin fibres that send messages between your brain and other parts of your body
2 courage and calm in a difficult situation
3 INFORMAL rudeness or cheek • *She had the **nerve** to answer back to the head teacher.*

nervous
ADJECTIVE easily worried and agitated
nervously ADVERB

nest **nests**
NOUN a structure that birds, insects and other animals make, in which to lay eggs or rear their young

nestle **nestles, nestling, nestled**
Said "**ness**-sl" VERB If you **nestle** somewhere, you settle there comfortably, often very close to someone or something else. • *My kitten loves to **nestle** in my lap.*

net **nets**
NOUN **1** short for **internet**
2 material made from threads woven together with small spaces in between
3 a piece of this material used for a particular purpose, for example a fishing **net**

netball
NOUN a game in which two teams of seven players each try to score goals by throwing a ball through a net at the top of a pole

nettle **nettles**
NOUN a wild plant covered with little hairs that sting

network **networks**
NOUN **1** a large number of lines or roads that cross each other at many points
2 a group of computers connected to each other

neutral
ADJECTIVE People who are **neutral** do not support either side in a disagreement or war.

never
ADVERB at no time in the past, present or future • *I've **never** met such a lovely person.*

nevertheless
ADVERB in spite of what has just been said • *I know you're home safely, but **nevertheless** I want you to ring for a lift in future.*

new **newer, newest**
ADJECTIVE **1** recently made, created or discovered • *She's got a **new** film out.*
2 different • *We've got a **new** maths teacher.*

news
NOUN up-to-date information about things that have happened

newsagent **newsagents**
NOUN a person or shop that sells newspapers and magazines

newspaper **newspapers**
NOUN a publication, on large sheets of folded paper, that is produced regularly and contains news and articles

newt **newts**
NOUN a small, amphibious creature with a moist skin, short legs and a long tail

newton **newtons**
NOUN a unit for measuring force (N)
[named after Sir Isaac *Newton*]

New Year
NOUN the time when people celebrate the start of a year

next
ADJECTIVE **1** The **next** thing, person or event is the one that comes immediately after the present one. • *We'll catch the **next** train.*
ADVERB **2** You use **next** to refer to an action that follows immediately after the present one. • *What shall we do **next**?*
3 The **next** place or person is the one nearest to you. • *She lives in the **next** street.*
PHRASE **4** If one thing is **next to** another, it is at the side of it. • *She sat down **next to** him.*

nib **nibs**
NOUN the pointed end of a pen, where the ink comes out

nibble **nibbles, nibbling, nibbled**
VERB **1** When you **nibble** something, you take small bites of it.
NOUN **2** a small bite of something

nice **nicer, nicest**
ADJECTIVE pleasant or kind
nicely ADVERB

nickname **nicknames**
NOUN an informal name for someone or something • *Red got his **nickname** because of his ginger hair.*
[from Middle English *an ekename* meaning an additional name]

nicotine
NOUN an addictive substance found in tobacco
[named after Jacques *Nicot*, who first brought tobacco to France]

niece **nieces**
NOUN Someone's **niece** is the daughter of their sister or brother.

night **nights**
NOUN the time between sunset and sunrise, when it is dark

nightdress **nightdresses**
NOUN a loose dress that a woman or girl wears to sleep in

nightfall
NOUN the time of day when it starts to get dark

nightingale **nightingales**
NOUN a small, brown European bird, the male of which sings very beautifully, especially at night

nightmare **nightmares**
NOUN **1** a frightening dream
2 an unpleasant or frightening situation • *The whole journey was a **nightmare**.*

nil
NOUN zero or nothing, especially in sports scores • *At half-time the score was still **nil-nil**.*

nimble **nimbler, nimblest**
ADJECTIVE able to move quickly and easily
nimbly ADVERB

nine
NOUN **Nine** is the number 9.
ninth NOUN OR ADJECTIVE

nineteen
NOUN **Nineteen** is the number 19.
nineteenth NOUN OR ADJECTIVE

ninety
NOUN **Ninety** is the number 90.
ninetieth NOUN OR ADJECTIVE

nip **nips, nipping, nipped**
VERB **1** If you **nip** someone or something, you give them a slight pinch or bite.

2 If you **nip** somewhere, you go there quickly. • *I have to* ***nip*** *to the shop for some milk.*
NOUN **3** A **nip** is small bite or pinch.

niqab **niqabs**
Said "ni-**kab**" NOUN a veil worn by some Muslim women in public, covering all the face except the eyes

nitrogen
NOUN a chemical element, usually found as a colourless gas. **Nitrogen** makes up about 78% of the earth's atmosphere.

no
EXCLAMATION **1** You say **no** when you do not want something or do not agree.
ANTONYM: yes
ADJECTIVE OR ADVERB **2** none at all or not at all • *He has* ***no*** *excuse for his behaviour.*

noble **nobler, noblest**
ADJECTIVE If someone is **noble**, they are honest and brave, and deserve admiration.

nobody
PRONOUN not a single person • *For a long time* ***nobody*** *spoke.*

Nobody and *no one* mean the same thing.

nocturnal
ADJECTIVE happening or active at night • *The hedgehog is a* ***nocturnal*** *animal.*

nod **nods, nodding, nodded**
VERB When you **nod** your head, you move it up and down, usually to say yes.

noise **noises**
NOUN a sound, especially one that is loud or unpleasant

noisy **noisier, noisiest**
ADJECTIVE making a lot of noise, or full of noise

nomad **nomads**
NOUN a person who travels from place to place rather than staying in just one • *The Bedouin people in Arabia are* ***nomads****.*
[from Latin *nomas* meaning wandering shepherd]
nomadic ADJECTIVE

nominate **nominates, nominating, nominated**
VERB If a person **nominates** someone for a job or position, they formally suggest that they have it.
nomination NOUN

non-
PREFIX not, for example something that is **non**existent does not exist

none
PRONOUN not a single thing or person, or not even a small amount of something • *They asked me for my ideas, but I had* ***none****.*

non-fiction
NOUN writing dealing with facts and events rather than imaginative storytelling
ANTONYM: fiction

nonsense
NOUN foolish or meaningless words or behaviour

nonsmoking
ADJECTIVE A **nonsmoking** area is a place where smoking is forbidden.

nonstop
ADJECTIVE OR ADVERB continuing without any pauses or breaks
SYNONYM: continuous

noodle **noodles**
NOUN a kind of pasta shaped into long, thin pieces

noon
NOUN midday

no one or **no-one**
PRONOUN not a single person • ***No one*** *goes to that play park any more.*
SYNONYM: nobody

noose **nooses**
NOUN a loop at the end of a piece of rope, with a knot that tightens when the rope is pulled

nor
CONJUNCTION used after *neither*, or to add emphasis • ***Neither*** *you* ***nor*** *I know the answer.* • *I couldn't afford to go to the fair, and* ***nor*** *could my friends.*

normal
ADJECTIVE usual and ordinary

north
NOUN one of the four main points of the compass. If you face the point where the sun rises, **north** is on your left. The abbreviation for **north** is N.

north-east
NOUN, ADVERB OR ADJECTIVE halfway between north and east

northern
ADJECTIVE in or from the north • *The mountains of **northern** Spain are very beautiful.*

north-west
NOUN, ADVERB OR ADJECTIVE halfway between north and west

nose **noses**
NOUN the part of your face above your mouth, that you use for smelling and breathing

nostalgia
NOUN a feeling of affection for the past, and sadness that things have changed
nostalgic ADJECTIVE **nostalgically** ADVERB

nostril **nostrils**
NOUN Your **nostrils** are the two openings in your nose that you breathe through.

nosy **nosier, nosiest**; also spelt **nosey**
ADJECTIVE **Nosy** people always want to know about other people's business, and like to interfere where they are not wanted.

not
ADVERB used to make a sentence mean the opposite • *I am **not** very happy.*

note **notes**
NOUN **1** a short letter
2 You take **notes** to help you remember what has been said.
3 In music, a **note** is a musical sound of a particular pitch, or a written symbol that represents this sound.
4 a piece of paper money • *a ten-pound **note***

notebook **notebooks**
NOUN a small book for writing notes in

nothing
PRONOUN not a single thing, or not a single part of something

notice **notices, noticing, noticed**
VERB **1** If you **notice** something, you become aware of it. • *She **noticed** a bird sitting on the fence.*
NOUN **2** a written announcement
PHRASE **3** If you **take notice of** something, you pay attention to it.

noticeable
ADJECTIVE obvious and easy to see

notify **notifies, notifying, notified**
VERB If you **notify** someone of something, you officially inform them of it. • *You must **notify** us of any change of address.*
notification NOUN

notorious
ADJECTIVE well known for something bad • *a **notorious** criminal*

nought **noughts**
NOUN the number 0, zero

noun **nouns**
NOUN a word that refers to a person, thing or idea. Examples of **nouns** are *table*, *happiness* and *John*.

nourish **nourishes, nourishing, nourished**
VERB If you **nourish** people or animals, you give them plenty of food.
nourishing ADJECTIVE

nourishment
NOUN the food that your body needs to grow and stay healthy, including vitamins and minerals • *"Eat your vegetables, they're full of **nourishment**."*

novel **novels**
NOUN **1** a book that tells a long story about imaginary people and events
ADJECTIVE **2** new and interesting • *This whole trip has been a **novel** experience.*

novelty **novelties**
NOUN **1** the quality of being new and interesting

a b c d e f g h i j k l m n o p q r s t u v w x y z

2 something new and interesting
3 a small object sold as a gift or souvenir

November
NOUN the eleventh month of the year. **November** has 30 days.
[from Latin *November* meaning the ninth month]

novice **novices**
NOUN someone who is not yet experienced at something • *Most of the group are* ***novices*** *at horse riding.*

now
ADVERB **1** at the present time or moment
CONJUNCTION **2** as a result or consequence of a particular fact • *Your writing will improve* ***now*** *you have a new pen.*

nowhere
ADVERB not anywhere • *There was* ***nowhere*** *to hide.*

nozzle **nozzles**
NOUN a spout fitted onto the end of a pipe or hose to control the flow of liquid or gas

nuclear
ADJECTIVE relating to the energy produced when atoms are split • *We live near a* ***nuclear*** *power station.*

nucleus **nuclei**
Said "**nyoo**-clee-us" *and* "**nyoo**-clee-eye"
NOUN **1** the central part of an atom or a cell

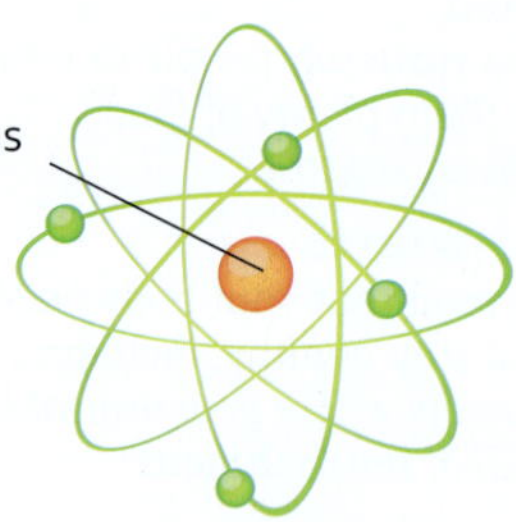

an atom

2 the important or central part of something • *We still have the* ***nucleus*** *of the team.*

nude **nudes**
ADJECTIVE **1** If someone is **nude**, they are naked.
NOUN **2** A **nude** is a picture or statue of a naked person.

nudge **nudges, nudging, nudged**
VERB **1** If you **nudge** someone, you push them gently with your elbow to get their attention or to make them move.
NOUN **2** a gentle push with your elbow

nugget **nuggets**
NOUN a small rough lump of something, especially gold

nuisance **nuisances**
NOUN someone or something that is annoying or causing problems

numb
ADJECTIVE unable to feel anything • *I was so cold my hands and feet felt* ***numb****.*
[from Middle English *nomen* meaning paralysed]

number **numbers, numbering, numbered**
NOUN **1** a word or symbol used for counting or calculating
2 the series of numbers that you dial when you telephone someone
VERB **3** If you **number** something, you give it a number, usually in a sequence.
• *Please* ***number*** *each page you write on.*

numeracy
NOUN the ability to do arithmetic

numeral **numerals**
NOUN a symbol that is used to represent a number

numerator **numerators**
NOUN the top number of a fraction. It tells you the number of pieces or parts you are dealing with.

numerical
ADJECTIVE expressed in numbers or relating to numbers • *Please put these pages in* ***numerical*** *order.*

numerous
ADJECTIVE Things that are **numerous** exist or happen in large numbers. • *There are* ***numerous*** *things to do in a large city.*

nun **nuns**
NOUN a woman who has taken religious

vows and is a member of a religious community

nurse **nurses, nursing, nursed**
NOUN **1** a person whose job is to look after people who are ill
VERB **2** If you **nurse** someone, you look after them when they are ill. • *I helped dad to **nurse** mum when she had flu.*

nursery **nurseries**
NOUN **1** a place where young children are looked after when their parents are working
2 a place where plants are grown and sold

nursery rhyme **nursery rhymes**
NOUN a short poem or song for young children, such as *Little Miss Muffet* and *Jack and Jill*

nursery school **nursery schools**
NOUN a school for children aged three to five years old

nut **nuts**
NOUN **1** a fruit with a hard shell that grows on certain trees and bushes

brazil nut

almond

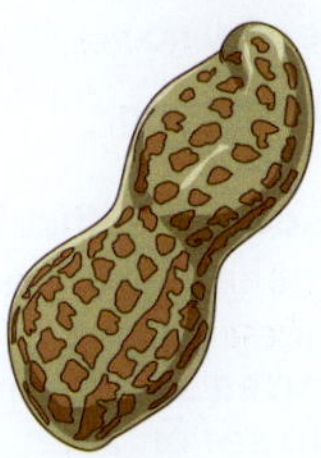
peanut

walnut

2 a piece of metal with a hole in the middle that a bolt screws into

nutrient **nutrients**
Said "**new**-tree-unt" NOUN one of the substances that help plants and animals to grow • *Very heavy rainfall washes valuable **nutrients** from the soil.*

nutrition
Said "new-**trish**-un" NOUN the food that you eat that helps you to grow and keeps you healthy • *Good **nutrition** is vital for healthy development.*

nutritious
ADJECTIVE If food is **nutritious** it helps you to grow and remain healthy. • *Spinach is a very **nutritious** vegetable.*

nylon
NOUN a type of strong, artificial fibre used for making, for example, clothes, ropes and brushes • *The rock climbers used brightly coloured ropes made of **nylon** to abseil down the rock face.*

Oo

oak **oaks**
NOUN a large tree that produces acorns. The **oak** has a hard wood that is often used to make furniture.

oar **oars**
NOUN a pole with a flat end used to row a boat through water

oasis **oases**
NOUN a small area in a desert where water and plants are found

oath **oaths**
NOUN a formal promise, especially a promise to tell the truth in a court of law

oats
PLURAL NOUN a type of grain

obedient
ADJECTIVE If you are **obedient**, you do as you are told.
ANTONYM: disobedient
obediently ADVERB **obedience** NOUN

obey **obeys, obeying, obeyed**
VERB If you **obey** a person or an order, you do what you are told to do.

obituary **obituaries**
NOUN a piece of writing about the life and achievements of someone who has just died

object **objects, objecting, objected**
Said "**ob**-jekt" NOUN **1** anything solid that you can touch or see, and that is not alive • *This painting is an* ***object*** *of beauty.*
2 an aim or purpose • *The* ***object*** *of the marathon is to raise money.*
Said "ob-**jekt**" VERB **3** If you **object** to something, you dislike it, disagree with it or disapprove of it.

objection **objections**
NOUN If you have an **objection** to something, you dislike it or disagree with it.

oblige **obliges, obliging, obliged**
VERB **1** If you are **obliged** to do something, you have to do it.
2 If you **oblige** someone, you help them. • *He* ***obliged*** *us by showing the way.*
3 If you are **obliged** to someone, you are grateful to them. • *I would be much* ***obliged*** *if you could show me where this street is.*
obliging ADJECTIVE

oblique
ADJECTIVE An **oblique** line slopes at an angle.

oblong **oblongs**
NOUN **1** a four-sided shape with four right angles, similar to a square but with two sides longer than the other two
ADJECTIVE **2** shaped like an oblong

obnoxious
ADJECTIVE extremely unpleasant
SYNONYMS: hateful, odious

oboe **oboes**
NOUN a woodwind instrument that makes a high-pitched sound
[from French *haut bois* meaning literally high wood, a reference to the instrument's pitch]
oboist NOUN

obscene
ADJECTIVE very rude and likely to upset people
obscenely ADVERB **obscenity** NOUN

obscure **obscures, obscuring, obscured**
ADJECTIVE **1** Something **obscure** is difficult to see or to understand.
ANTONYMS: obvious, clear
VERB **2** If something **obscures** something else, it makes it difficult to see or understand. • *The moon* ***obscured*** *the sun during the eclipse.*

observant
ADJECTIVE An **observant** person notices things that are not usually noticed.

observation **observations**
NOUN the act of watching something closely • *You will need to make careful* ***observations*** *of the experiment before you do the writing.*
[from Latin *observare* meaning to watch]

observe **observes, observing, observed**
VERB If you **observe** someone or something, you watch them carefully.
observer NOUN

obsession **obsessions**
NOUN If someone has an **obsession** about something or someone, they cannot stop thinking about them.
obsessional ADJECTIVE **obsessed** ADJECTIVE
obsessive ADJECTIVE

obsolete
ADJECTIVE out of date and no longer used

obstacle **obstacles**
NOUN something that is in your way and makes it difficult for you to do something

obstinate
ADJECTIVE Someone who is **obstinate** is stubborn and unwilling to change their mind.

obstruct **obstructs, obstructing, obstructed**
VERB If something **obstructs** a road or path, it blocks it.

obtain **obtains, obtaining, obtained**
VERB If you **obtain** something, you get it.

obtuse
ADJECTIVE An **obtuse** angle is an angle between 90° and 180°.

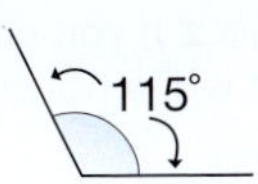

obvious
ADJECTIVE easy to see or understand • *It was* ***obvious*** *that he didn't know the answer.*
obviously ADVERB

occasion **occasions**
NOUN a time when something happens
• *I met her on several* ***occasions****.*

There are two *c*s but only one *s* in *occasion.*

occasional
ADJECTIVE happening sometimes, but not often • *We go for an* ***occasional*** *walk in the woods.*
occasionally ADVERB

occupant **occupants**
NOUN the people who live or work in a building

occupation **occupations**
NOUN a job or profession

occupy **occupies, occupying, occupied**
VERB **1** The people who **occupy** a building are the people who live or work there.
2 If something **occupies** you, you spend your time doing it or thinking about it.

occur **occurs, occurring, occurred**
VERB If something **occurs**, it happens.

occur to
VERB If something **occurs to** you, you suddenly think of it or realize it.

ocean **oceans**
NOUN one of the five very large areas of sea in the world

o'clock
ADVERB You use **o'clock** after the number of the hour to say what the time is.
• *We have to be at school by eight* ***o'clock****.*

octagon **octagons**
NOUN a flat shape with eight straight sides
octagonal ADJECTIVE

octahedron **octahedrons**
NOUN a solid figure with eight identical flat surfaces

octave **octaves**
NOUN the difference in pitch between the first note and the eighth note of a musical scale

October
NOUN the tenth month of the year. **October** has 31 days.
[from Latin *October* meaning the eighth month, as it was the eighth month in the Roman calendar]

octopus **octopuses**
NOUN a sea creature with eight long tentacles that it uses to catch food

odd **odder, oddest**
ADJECTIVE **1** strange or unusual
2 **Odd** things do not match each other.
• *She always ended up with **odd** socks.*
3 **Odd** numbers cannot be divided exactly by two. Three and seven are examples of **odd** numbers.
ANTONYM: even

odour **odours**
NOUN FORMAL a strong smell

of
PREPOSITION **1** consisting of or containing
• *a cup **of** tea*
2 used when talking about things that are characteristic of something
• *a woman **of** great importance*
3 belonging to or connected with
• *a friend **of** Eve*

off
PREPOSITION OR ADVERB **1** used to show movement away from or out of a place
• *They got **off** the bus.*
2 used to show separation or distance from a place • *There are several islands **off** the coast of Britain.*
ADVERB **3** not at work • *He took a day **off**.*
ADVERB OR ADJECTIVE **4** not switched on
• *The television was **off**.*
ADJECTIVE **5** cancelled or postponed
• *The match is **off**.*
6 Food that is **off** is no longer fresh enough to eat, usually tastes unpleasant, and may make you ill.

> Do not use *of* after *off*. It is correct to say *I got off the bus*, not *I got off of the bus*.

offence **offences**
NOUN **1** a crime • *Burglary is a serious **offence**.*
PHRASE **2** If you **cause offence**, you embarrass or upset someone.
3 If you **take offence**, you feel that someone has been rude or hurtful to you.

offend **offends, offending, offended**
VERB **1** If you **offend** someone, you upset them.
2 If someone **offends**, they break the law.
offender NOUN

offensive
ADJECTIVE If something is **offensive**, it is rude and upsetting.

offer **offers, offering, offered**
VERB **1** If you **offer** something to someone, you ask them if they would like it, or say that you are willing to do it. • *I **offered** to wash the car.*
NOUN **2** something that someone says they will give you or do for you

office **offices**
NOUN **1** a room where people work at desks
2 a place where people can go for information, tickets or other services

officer **officers**
NOUN a person with a position of authority in the armed forces, the police or a government organization

official
ADJECTIVE approved by the government or by someone in authority
officially ADVERB

offline
ADJECTIVE **1** If a computer is **offline**, it is not connected to the internet.
ADVERB **2** If you do something **offline**, you do it while not connected to the internet.

often
ADVERB happening many times or a lot of the time • *He **often** goes swimming on Sunday.*

ogre **ogres**
NOUN a cruel, frightening giant in fairy stories

oil **oils, oiling, oiled**
NOUN **1** a thick, sticky liquid found under rocks that is used for fuel, lubrication and for making plastics and chemicals

2 a thick, greasy liquid made from plants or animal fat • *cooking **oil***
VERB **3** If you **oil** something, you put oil in it or on it to make it work better. • *This squeaky hinge needs to be **oiled**.*

oily **oilier, oiliest**
ADJECTIVE Something that is **oily** is covered with or contains oil.

ointment **ointments**
NOUN a smooth, thick substance that you put on sore skin to heal it

OK or **okay**
ADJECTIVE all right; fine • *She slipped on the ice but she was **OK**.*

old **older, oldest**
ADJECTIVE **1** having lived or existed for a long time
2 Old is used to give the age of someone or something. • *The baby is six months **old**.*
3 You can use **old** to talk about something that is no longer used or has been replaced by something else. • *I bumped into my teacher from my **old** primary school.*

old-fashioned
ADJECTIVE **1** Something **old-fashioned** is out of date and no longer fashionable.
ANTONYM: fashionable
2 If someone is **old-fashioned**, they believe in the values and standards of the past.

olive **olives**
NOUN **1** a small green or black fruit containing a stone. **Olives** are usually pickled and eaten as a snack, or crushed to produce oil for cooking.
ADJECTIVE OR NOUN **2** dark yellowish-green

Olympic Games
Said "ul-**lim**-pic games" NOUN a series of international sporting contests held in a different country every four years
[The word *Olympic* comes from *Olympia* in Greece, where games were held in ancient times]

omelette **omelettes**
NOUN a dish made by beating eggs together and cooking them in a flat pan

omit **omits, omitting, omitted**
VERB If you **omit** something, you do not include it. • *She **omitted** to mention that her mother could not come.*

omni-
PREFIX added to some words to mean all or everywhere, for example **omni**potent means all-powerful, and **omni**present means present everywhere

omnibus **omnibuses**
NOUN **1** a book containing a collection of stories or articles by the same author or about the same subject
ADJECTIVE **2** An **omnibus** edition of a radio or television series contains two or more episodes that were originally shown separately.

omnivore **omnivores**
NOUN an animal that eats all kinds of food, including meat and plants
omnivorous ADJECTIVE

on
PREPOSITION **1** touching something or attached to it • *We sat **on** the seat.*
2 If you are **on** a bus, a plane or a train, you are inside it.
3 If something happens **on** a particular day, that is when it happens.
4 If something is done **on** an instrument or a machine, it is done using it.
5 A book or a talk **on** a particular subject is about that subject.
ADVERB **6** If someone has a piece of clothing **on**, they are wearing it.
ADJECTIVE OR ADVERB **7** If a machine or a switch is **on**, it is working or is in action. • *"Please would you switch the radio **on**?"*

once
ADVERB **1** If something happens **once**, it happens one time only.
2 If something was **once** true, it was true in the past, but is no longer true. • *That ground was **once** covered by trees.*
CONJUNCTION **3** If something happens **once** another thing has happened, it happens immediately afterwards. • *I'll do my homework **once** I've finished my tea.*
PHRASE **4** If you do something **at once**, you

A B C D E F G H I J K L M N O P Q R S T U V W X Y Z

do it immediately. • *We must go home **at once**.*
5 If several things happen **at once**, they all happen at the same time. • *He tried to hold three glasses **at once**.*

one
NOUN **1 One** is the number 1.
ADJECTIVE **2** When you refer to **one** person or **one** thing, you mean a single person or thing. • *We have **one** main holiday a year.*
PRONOUN **3 One** refers to a particular person or thing. • *This book was the best **one** she had read for ages.*

onion **onions**
NOUN a small, round vegetable with a very strong taste

online
ADJECTIVE **1** If a computer is **online**, it is connected to the internet.
ADVERB **2** If you do something **online**, you do it while connected to the internet.

only
ADVERB **1** You use **only** to show the one thing or person involved. • ***Only** one girl was able to complete the race.*
2 You use **only** to make a condition that must happen before something else can happen. • *You will be allowed in **only** if you have a ticket.*
3 You use **only** to emphasize that something is unimportant or small. • *He's **only** very young.*
ADJECTIVE **4** If you talk about the **only** thing or person, you mean that there are no others. For example, if you are an **only** child, you have no brothers or sisters.
CONJUNCTION **5** You can use **only** to mean but or except. • *He was very much like you, **only** with blond hair.*

onomatopoeia
Said "on-uh-mat-uh-**pee**-a" NOUN the use of words that sound like the thing that they represent. *Hiss* and *buzz* are examples of **onomatopoeia**.

onto or on to
PREPOSITION If you put something **onto** an object, you put it on it. • *He threw the pillow **onto** the bed.*

ooze **oozes, oozing, oozed**
VERB When a thick liquid **oozes**, it flows slowly. • *The cold mud **oozed** over her toes.* [from Old English *wos* meaning juice]

opaque
ADJECTIVE If something is **opaque**, it does not let light through, so you cannot see through it. • ***opaque** glass windows*
ANTONYM: clear

open **opens, opening, opened**
ADJECTIVE **1** Something that is **open** is not closed or fastened, allowing things to pass through. • *A light breeze came through the **open** window.*
2 not enclosed or covered • *At last we were out in the **open** countryside.*
VERB **3** When you **open** something, or when it **opens**, it is moved so that it is no longer closed. • *She **opened** the box of chocolates.*
4 When a shop or office **opens**, people are allowed to go in to do business.
5 If you **open** a book, you turn back the cover so that you can read it.
6 If something **opens**, it starts or begins.
ADJECTIVE **7** Someone who is **open** is honest and not secretive.
openly ADVERB

opening **openings**
NOUN **1** a hole or gap • *There was a small **opening** in the fence.*
ADJECTIVE **2** coming first • *He sang the **opening** song in the concert.*
NOUN **3** the first part of a book or film • *I love the **opening** of that book.*

opera **operas**
NOUN a play in which the words are sung rather than spoken

operate **operates, operating, operated**
VERB **1** When you **operate** a machine, you make it work. • *I know how to **operate** the computer.*
2 When surgeons **operate**, they cut open a person's body to remove or repair a damaged part.

operation **operations**
NOUN **1** a form of medical treatment in

which a surgeon cuts open a patient's body to remove or repair a damaged part **2** a complex, planned event • *Moving house is going to be quite a difficult **operation**.*

opinion **opinions**
NOUN a belief or view

opponent **opponents**
NOUN someone who is against you in an argument or a contest

opportunity **opportunities**
NOUN a chance to do something

oppose **opposes, opposing, opposed**
VERB If you **oppose** something or someone, you disagree with them and are against them.

opposing
ADJECTIVE **Opposing** means opposite or very different. • *We managed to be friends even though we had **opposing** points of view.*

opposite **opposites**
PREPOSITION OR ADVERB **1** If one thing is **opposite** another, it is facing it. • *Our house is **opposite** the park.*
NOUN **2** If people or things are **opposites**, they are completely different from each other.

opposition
NOUN **1** If there is **opposition** to something, there is resistance to it and people oppose it. • *There is a lot of **opposition** to the building of a new road.*
2 In a games or sports event, the **opposition** is the person or team that you are competing against.

opt **opts, opting, opted**
VERB **1** If you **opt** for something, you choose to do it. • *I **opted** to go to the Gym Club.*
2 If you **opt** out of something, you choose not to do it or be involved with it. • *I **opted** out of football practice.*

optical
ADJECTIVE concerned with vision, light or images

optician **opticians**
NOUN someone who tests people's eyesight, and makes and sells glasses and contact lenses

optimist **optimists**
NOUN An **optimist** is a person who is always hopeful that everything will turn out well in the future.
ANTONYM: pessimist
optimism NOUN **optimistic** ADJECTIVE

option **options**
NOUN a choice between two or more things

optional
ADJECTIVE If something is **optional**, you can choose whether to do it or not. • *Tennis is **optional** at our school.*
ANTONYM: compulsory

or
CONJUNCTION used to link two alternatives or choices • *You need to decide whether to stay **or** leave.*

oral
ADJECTIVE **1** spoken rather than written • *Tomorrow we have our French **oral** examination.*
2 to do with your mouth or using your mouth • ***Oral** hygiene is vital for healthy teeth.*
orally ADVERB

orange **oranges**
NOUN **1** a round citrus fruit that is juicy and sweet and has a thick reddish-yellow skin
ADJECTIVE OR NOUN **2** reddish-yellow
[from Sanskrit *naranga* meaning orange]

orang-utan **orang-utans**; also spelt **orang-utang**
NOUN a large ape with reddish-brown hair

orbit **orbits, orbiting, orbited**
NOUN **1** the curved path followed by an object going round a planet or the sun
VERB **2** If something **orbits** a planet or the sun, it goes round and round it.
• *Our moon **orbits** the earth.*

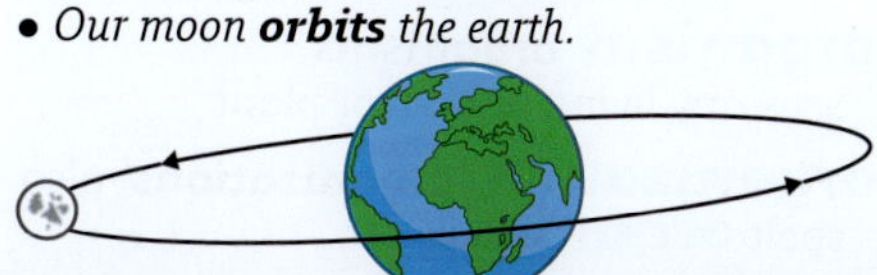

A B C D E F G H I J K L M N O P Q R S T U V W X Y Z

orchard **orchards**
NOUN a piece of land where fruit trees are grown

orchestra **orchestras**
NOUN a large group of musicians who play musical instruments together

orchid **orchids**
NOUN a type of plant with beautiful and unusual flowers

ordeal **ordeals**
NOUN a very difficult and unpleasant experience

order **orders, ordering, ordered**
NOUN **1** a command given by someone in authority
2 If things are arranged or done in a particular **order**, they are arranged or done in that sequence. • *alphabetical **order***
VERB **3** If you **order** someone to do something, you tell them firmly to do it.
4 When you **order** something, you ask for it to be brought or sent to you.

ordinary
ADJECTIVE not special or different in any way

ore **ores**
NOUN rock or earth from which metal can be obtained

organ **organs**
NOUN **1** Your **organs** are parts of your body that have a particular purpose, for example your lungs are the **organs** with which you breathe.
2 a large musical instrument with a keyboard and windpipes through which air is forced to produce a sound

organic
ADJECTIVE **1** **Organic** food is produced without the use of artificial fertilizers or pesticides.
2 produced or found in living things
organically ADVERB

organism **organisms**
NOUN any living animal or plant

organization **organizations**; also spelt **organisation**
NOUN **1** any business or group of people working together for a purpose
2 the act of planning and arranging something

organize **organizes, organizing, organized**; also spelt **organise**
VERB If you **organize** something, you plan and arrange it.

oriental
ADJECTIVE Something that is **oriental** comes from the Far East, which includes countries such as India, China and Japan. • *I like **oriental** food.*

orienteering
NOUN a sport in which people find their way from one place to another in the countryside, using a map and compass

origin **origins**
NOUN the beginning or cause of something • *The **origins** of man have been written about in many books.*

original **originals**
ADJECTIVE **1** the first or earliest • *The **original** owner of this house made lots of alterations.*
2 imaginative and clever • *His paintings are highly **original**.*
NOUN **3** a work of art or a document that is the one that was produced first, and is not a copy
originally ADVERB

ornament **ornaments**
NOUN a small, attractive object that you display in your home or that you wear in order to look attractive

ornithology
NOUN the study of birds
ornithologist NOUN

orphan **orphans**
NOUN a child whose parents are dead

orphanage **orphanages**
NOUN a place where orphans are looked after

ostrich **ostriches**
NOUN the largest bird in the world. **Ostriches** can run fast but cannot fly.

other **others**
PRONOUN **1** The **other** can mean the second of two things. • *One of the rooms is empty, but the **other** is not.*
ADJECTIVE **2 Other** people or things are different from those already mentioned.
3 The **other** day means a few days ago.

otherwise
ADVERB **1** or else
2 apart from the thing mentioned • *The food was good, but **otherwise** the party was awful.*

otter **otters**
NOUN a small, furry animal with a long tail, that lives near water. **Otters** swim well and eat fish.

ought
VERB **1** If you say that someone **ought** to do something, you mean they should do it.
2 If you say that something **ought** to be the case, you mean that you expect it to be the case. • *He **ought** to be here by now.*

ounce **ounces**
NOUN a unit of weight equal to one-sixteenth of a pound or about 28.35 grams

our
ADJECTIVE belonging to us • ***Our** cat is black.*

ours
PRONOUN belonging to us • *That cat is **ours**.*

ourselves
PRONOUN **Ourselves** is used when talking about a group of people that includes the speaker or writer. • *We didn't hurt **ourselves** too badly.*

out
ADVERB **1** towards the outside of a place or thing • *Take the ice cream **out** of the freezer.*
ADJECTIVE **2** not at home

outbreak **outbreaks**
NOUN If there is an **outbreak** of something unpleasant, such as war, it suddenly occurs. • *The **outbreak** of the disease made many people unwell.*

outburst **outbursts**
NOUN a sudden strong expression of emotion, especially anger or violent action • *He apologized for his angry **outburst**.*

outcome **outcomes**
NOUN a result

outdoor
ADJECTIVE happening or used outside

outdoors
ADVERB If something happens **outdoors**, it takes place outside in the open air.

outer
ADJECTIVE The **outer** parts of something are the parts furthest from the centre. • *the **outer** doors*

outer space
NOUN everything beyond the earth's atmosphere

outfit **outfits**
NOUN a set of clothes • *I bought a new **outfit** for the party.*

outgoing
ADJECTIVE Someone who is **outgoing** is friendly and not shy. • *She is always fun to be with as she has such an **outgoing** personality.*

outgrow **outgrows, outgrowing, outgrew, outgrown**
VERB **1** If you **outgrow** a piece of clothing, you grow too big to wear it. • *I've already **outgrown** my best jeans.*
2 If you **outgrow** a way of behaving, you stop behaving that way because you are older and more mature.

outing **outings**
NOUN a trip made for pleasure

outlaw **outlaws, outlawing, outlawed**
VERB **1** If someone **outlaws** something, they ban it.
NOUN **2** In the past, an **outlaw** was a criminal.

outlet **outlets**
NOUN **1** a hole or pipe through which water or air can flow away

2 a shop that sells goods made by a particular manufacturer

outline **outlines, outlining, outlined**
NOUN **1** The **outline** of something is its shape.
VERB **2** If you **outline** a plan or idea, you give brief details of it.

outlook **outlooks**
NOUN **1** Your **outlook** is your general attitude towards life. • *His **outlook** on life is always positive.*
2 The **outlook** of a situation is the way it is likely to develop. • *The **outlook** for the weather over the next few days is not very good.*

outnumber **outnumbers, outnumbering, outnumbered**
VERB If there is more of one group than of another, the first group **outnumbers** the second. • *Boys **outnumber** girls in our class.*

outpatient **outpatients**
NOUN someone who receives treatment in hospital without staying overnight

output **outputs**
NOUN **1** the amount of something produced by a person or organization
2 The **output** of a computer is the information that it produces.

outrage **outrages, outraging, outraged**
VERB **1** If something **outrages** you, it angers and shocks you.
NOUN **2** a feeling of anger and shock
3 something very shocking or violent
outrageous ADJECTIVE **outrageously** ADVERB

outright
ADJECTIVE **1** total and complete • *She made an **outright** refusal to come with us.*
ADVERB **2** completely, totally • *Smoking in the building has been banned **outright**.*

outside
NOUN **1** The **outside** of something is the part that surrounds or encloses the rest of it. • *We wandered around the **outside** of the house.*
ADVERB, ADJECTIVE OR PREPOSITION **2** not inside
NOUN **3** not included in something • *The building will be closed **outside** school hours.*

> Do not use *of* after *outside* when it is a preposition. It is correct to say *I met her outside the school*, not *I met her outside of the school.*

outskirts
PLURAL NOUN the parts around the edge of a city or town • *Our home is on the **outskirts** of a large town.*

outspoken
ADJECTIVE **Outspoken** people give their opinions openly, even if they shock other people.

outstanding
ADJECTIVE extremely good

outwit **outwits, outwitting, outwitted**
VERB If you **outwit** someone, you use your intelligence or a clever trick to defeat them or get the better of them.

oval **ovals**
NOUN **1** a shape similar to a circle, but wider in one direction than the other

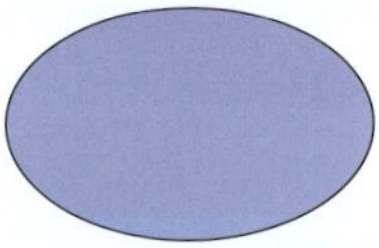

ADJECTIVE **2** shaped like an oval
[from Latin *ovalis* meaning egg-shaped]

oven **ovens**
NOUN the part of a cooker that you use for baking or roasting food

over **overs**
PREPOSITION **1** directly above something or covering it • *She hung the picture **over** the fireplace.* • *He put his hands **over** his eyes.*
2 A view **over** an area is a view across it. • *I love the view **over** the lake to the mountains.*
3 If something happens **over** a period of time, it happens during that period. • *I went to New Zealand **over** Christmas.*
ADVERB **4** If an amount of something is left **over**, that amount remains.
5 If you lean **over**, you bend your body in a particular direction. • *He leant **over** to*

open the door of the car.
6 If something rolls or turns **over**, it moves so that its other side is facing upwards.
ADJECTIVE **7** Something that is **over** is completely finished.
NOUN **8** In cricket, an **over** is a series of six balls bowled by one bowler.

over-
PREFIX too much, or to too great an extent. For example, if fruit is **over**ripe, it is too ripe, and if someone **over**eats, they eat too much.

overall
ADJECTIVE OR ADVERB taking into account all the parts or aspects of something • ***Overall**, the project has been a success.*

overalls
PLURAL NOUN a piece of clothing that you wear to protect your other clothes when you are working

overboard
ADVERB If you fall **overboard**, you fall over the side of a ship into the water.

overcast
ADJECTIVE When the sky is **overcast**, it is covered by thick cloud.

overcoat **overcoats**
NOUN a thick, warm coat

overcome **overcomes, overcoming, overcame, overcome**
VERB **1** If you **overcome** a problem or a feeling, you manage to deal with it or control it.
2 If you are **overcome**, you are affected by strong emotions. • *They were **overcome** with happiness.*
3 If you are **overcome** by fumes, gas or smoke, for example, you are made unconscious by them.

overcrowded
ADJECTIVE If a place is **overcrowded**, there are too many things or people in it.

overdue
ADJECTIVE If someone or something is **overdue**, they are late. • *The train is now **overdue**.*

overflow **overflows, overflowing, overflowed**
VERB If a liquid **overflows**, it spills over the edge of its container. If a river **overflows**, it flows over its banks.

overgrown
ADJECTIVE If a place is **overgrown**, it is thickly covered with plants and weeds.

overhaul **overhauls, overhauling, overhauled**
VERB **1** If you **overhaul** something, you examine and check it carefully, and repair any faults.
NOUN **2** An **overhaul** is a careful and detailed examination of something in order to repair its faults.

overhead
ADVERB OR ADJECTIVE above your head, or in the sky • *Seagulls flew **overhead**.* • *The **overhead** wires were being repaired.*

overhear **overhears, overhearing, overheard**
VERB If you **overhear** someone's conversation, you hear what they are saying to someone else.

overlap **overlaps, overlapping, overlapped**
VERB If one thing **overlaps** another, it covers part of the other thing.

overload **overloads, overloading, overloaded**
VERB If you **overload** someone or something, you give them too much to do or to carry.

overlook **overlooks, overlooking, overlooked**
VERB **1** If a building or window **overlooks** a place, it has a view of it from above.
2 If you **overlook** something, you ignore it or do not notice it.

overnight
ADVERB OR ADJECTIVE **1** during the night • *We took an **overnight** flight.*
2 sudden or suddenly • *He seemed to become such a good player **overnight**.*

overseas
ADJECTIVE OR ADVERB abroad • *We have some **overseas** students visiting the school.* • *My brother is going **overseas** for a year.*

oversleep **oversleeps, oversleeping, overslept**
VERB If you **oversleep**, you sleep on past the time you intended to wake up.

overtake **overtakes, overtaking, overtook, overtaken**
VERB If you **overtake** someone or something, you pass them because you are moving faster than they are.

overtime
NOUN time that someone works in addition to their normal working hours

overture **overtures**
NOUN the opening piece of music at a concert, show or ballet

overweight
ADJECTIVE People or animals that are **overweight** are too heavy for their size.

overwhelm **overwhelms, overwhelming, overwhelmed**
VERB **1** If something **overwhelms** you, it affects you very strongly.
2 If one group of people **overwhelms** another, they completely defeat them.
3 If you **overwhelm** someone with something, you load them with too much of it. • *He was **overwhelmed** with work.*

owe **owes, owing, owed**
VERB **1** If you **owe** someone money, they have lent it to you and you have not yet paid it back.
2 If you **owe** a quality or skill to someone, you only have it because of them. • *He **owes** his success as a tennis player to his coach.*

owl **owls**
NOUN a bird of prey that hunts at night. **Owls** have large eyes and short, hooked beaks.

own **owns, owning, owned**
ADJECTIVE OR PRONOUN **1** If something is your **own**, it belongs to you or is associated with you. • *She now has her **own** bedroom.*
VERB **2** If you **own** something, it belongs to you.
PHRASE **3 On your own** means alone.

owner **owners**
NOUN the person to whom something belongs

ox **oxen**
NOUN **Oxen** are cattle used for carrying or pulling things.

oxygen
NOUN a colourless gas that makes up about 21% of the earth's atmosphere. All animals and plants need **oxygen** to live, and fires need it to burn.

oyster **oysters**
NOUN a large, flat shellfish. Some **oysters** can be eaten, and others produce pearls.

ozone
NOUN a form of oxygen that is poisonous and has a strong smell
[from Greek *ozein* meaning smell]

ozone layer
NOUN a layer of the earth's atmosphere that protects living things from the harmful radiation of the sun

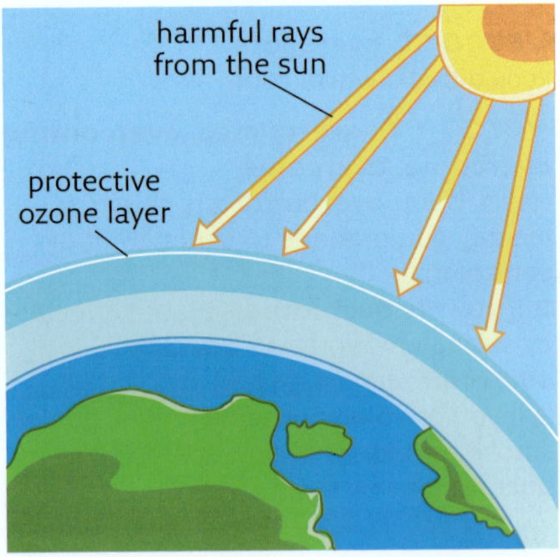

Pp

pace **paces, pacing, paced**
NOUN **1** the distance you move when you take one step
2 Your **pace** is the speed at which you are walking or running.
VERB **3** If you **pace**, you walk up and down, usually because you are anxious or impatient.

Pacific
NOUN the ocean separating North and South America from Asia and Australia

pacifist **pacifists**
NOUN someone who is opposed to all violence and war
pacifism NOUN

pacify **pacifies, pacifying, pacified**
VERB If you **pacify** someone who is angry, you calm them.
pacifier NOUN

pack **packs, packing, packed**
VERB **1** If you **pack** things, you put them neatly into a container, bag or box.
NOUN **2** a complete set of playing cards
3 a group of wolves or dogs

package **packages**
NOUN a small parcel

packet **packets**
NOUN a small box or bag in which something is sold

pact **pacts**
NOUN a formal agreement or treaty

pad **pads**
NOUN **1** a set of sheets of paper glued together at one end
2 a thick, soft piece of material
3 one of the soft parts under an animal's paws

paddle **paddles, paddling, paddled**
NOUN **1** a short pole with a broad blade at one or both ends, used to move a small boat or a canoe
VERB **2** If someone **paddles** a boat, they move it using a paddle.
3 If you **paddle**, you walk in shallow water with bare feet.

paddock **paddocks**
NOUN a small field where horses are kept

padlock **padlocks, padlocking, padlocked**
NOUN **1** a special kind of metal lock used to fasten two things together
VERB **2** If you **padlock** something, you lock it with a padlock.

pagan **pagans**
NOUN **1** someone who does not believe in any of the main religions of the world
ADJECTIVE **2** involving beliefs and worship outside the main religions of the world
• ***pagan*** *myths and cults*
paganism NOUN

page **pages**
NOUN **1** one side of a sheet of paper in a book or magazine • *Turn to* ***page*** *four.*
2 a single sheet of paper

pagoda **pagodas**
NOUN a tall, elaborately decorated Buddhist or Hindu temple

paid
VERB past tense and past participle of **pay**

pail **pails**
NOUN a bucket

pain **pains**
NOUN **1** a feeling of discomfort and hurt in your body, caused by an illness or injury

a b c d e f g h i j k l m n o p q r s t u v w x y z

A B C D E F G H I J K L M N O P Q R S T U V W X Y Z

PHRASE **2** If you are **in pain** you are hurting.
[from Latin *poena* meaning punishment]

painful
ADJECTIVE causing emotional or physical pain

painkiller **painkillers**
NOUN a drug that reduces or stops pain

painless
ADJECTIVE Something that is **painless** causes no pain.

paint **paints, painting, painted**
NOUN **1** a coloured liquid used to decorate buildings and make pictures
VERB **2** If you **paint** a picture of something, you make a picture of it using paint.
3 If you **paint** something such as a wall, you cover it with paint.

painting **paintings**
NOUN **1** a picture that someone has created using paints
2 the activity of painting pictures

pair **pairs**
NOUN **1** two things of the same type that are meant to be used together • *a **pair** of socks*
2 objects that have two main parts of the same size and shape • *a **pair** of scissors*

Do not confuse *pair* with *pear*.

pal **pals**
NOUN INFORMAL a friend
[from the Romani for brother]

palace **palaces**
NOUN a large, grand house, especially the home of a king or queen

pale **paler, palest**
ADJECTIVE not strong or bright in colour

palette **palettes**
NOUN a board on which an artist mixes colours

palm **palms**
NOUN **1** a tropical tree with no branches and broad, long leaves at the top of its trunk. **Palm** trees often produce fruit, such as coconuts or dates.
2 the flat area on the inside of your hand

pamper **pampers, pampering, pampered**
VERB If you **pamper** someone, you give them a lot of kindness and comfort.

pamphlet **pamphlets**
NOUN a very thin book in paper covers, giving information about something

pan **pans**
NOUN a round metal container with a long handle, used for cooking things

pancake **pancakes**
NOUN a thin, flat piece of fried batter that can be served with savoury or sweet fillings

panda **pandas**
NOUN a large animal, rather like a bear, that lives in China. A giant **panda** has black fur with large patches of white.

pane **panes**
NOUN a sheet of glass in a window or door

panel **panels**
NOUN **1** a group of people who are chosen to discuss or decide something
2 a flat piece of wood, metal or other material that is part of a larger object, such as a door or a wall

panic **panics, panicking, panicked**
NOUN **1** a sudden strong feeling of fear or anxiety
VERB **2** If you **panic**, you become so afraid or anxious that you cannot act sensibly.

panorama **panoramas**
NOUN an extensive view over a wide area of land
panoramic ADJECTIVE

pant **pants, panting, panted**
VERB If you **pant**, you take short, quick breaths through your mouth.

panther **panthers**
NOUN a large wild animal belonging to the cat family, especially the black leopard

pantomime **pantomimes**
NOUN a funny musical play, usually based on a fairy story and performed at Christmas

pants
PLURAL NOUN **1** underpants or knickers
2 another word for **trousers**

paper **papers**
NOUN **1** a material that you write on or wrap things with
2 a newspaper
[from *papyrus*, the plant from which paper was made in ancient Egypt, Greece and Rome]

paperback **paperbacks**
NOUN a book with a thin cardboard cover

papier-mâché
Said "pap-yey **mash**-ay" NOUN a mixture of mashed wet paper and glue that can be moulded into shapes, then dried and decorated to make bowls, ornaments and other objects
[from French, meaning chewed paper]

parable **parables**
NOUN a short story that makes a moral or religious point

parachute **parachutes**
NOUN a large umbrella-like piece of fabric attached by lines to a person or package so that it can fall safely to the ground from an aircraft
parachuting NOUN

parade **parades, parading, paraded**
NOUN **1** a line of people or vehicles moving together through a public place in order to celebrate something
VERB **2** When people **parade**, they walk together in a group, usually in front of spectators.
3 When soldiers **parade**, they gather together for inspection.

paradise
NOUN **1** According to some religions, **paradise** is a wonderful place where good people go when they die.
2 Somewhere very beautiful and wonderful in real life can be called **paradise**. • *Some of the beaches we went to on holiday were **paradise**.*

paraffin
NOUN a strong-smelling liquid used as a fuel

paragraph **paragraphs**
NOUN a section of a piece of writing. **Paragraphs** begin on a new line.

parallel
ADJECTIVE If two lines or objects are **parallel**, they are the same distance apart along the whole of their length.

parallel lines

parallelogram **parallelograms**
NOUN a four-sided shape, each side of which is parallel to the opposite side

paralysed
ADJECTIVE If a part of your body is **paralysed**, you cannot move it. • *Since the accident my uncle has been **paralysed** from the waist down.*
paralyse VERB **paralysis** NOUN

paramedic **paramedics**
NOUN a person who does some types of medical work, for example for the ambulance service

parasite **parasites**
NOUN a small animal or plant that lives on or inside a larger animal or plant
[from Greek *parasitos* meaning someone who eats at someone else's table]
parasitic ADJECTIVE

paratroops or **paratroopers**
PLURAL NOUN soldiers trained to be dropped from aircraft by parachute

A B C D E F G H I J K L M N O P Q R S T U V W X Y Z

parcel **parcels**
NOUN something wrapped up in paper

parched
ADJECTIVE **1** very dry and in need of water • *The earth was **parched** during the drought.*
2 very thirsty • *I was **parched** after the race.*

pardon **pardons, pardoning, pardoned**
PHRASE **1** You say **pardon** or **I beg your pardon** when you want someone to repeat something they have said.
VERB **2** If you **pardon** someone, you forgive or excuse them for something they have done wrong.

parent **parents**
NOUN Your **parents** are your father and mother.

parish **parishes**
NOUN an area with its own church and clergyman

park **parks, parking, parked**
VERB **1** When someone **parks** a vehicle, they drive it into a position where it can be left.
NOUN **2** a public area with grass and trees

parliament **parliaments**
NOUN the group of people who make or change the laws of a country

parole
NOUN When prisoners are given **parole**, they are released early on condition that they behave well.

parrot **parrots**
NOUN a brightly coloured tropical bird with a curved beak

parsley
NOUN a herb with curly leaves used for flavouring in cooking

parsnip **parsnips**
NOUN a long, pointed, cream-coloured root vegetable

part **parts, parting, parted**
NOUN **1** a piece of something, and not all of it
2 If you have a **part** in a play, you have a role in it.
VERB **3** If you **part** people or things, you separate them.

partial
ADJECTIVE **1** not complete or whole
PHRASE **2** If you are **partial to** someone or something, you like them.
partially ADVERB

participate **participates, participating, participated**
VERB If you **participate** in an activity, you take part in it or join in with other people.

participle **participles**
NOUN a word that is formed from a verb and used as part of the verb or as an adjective. For example, *eating* is the present **participle** of *eat*, and *loaded* is the past **participle** of *load*.

particle **particles**
NOUN a very small piece of something • *There were **particles** of dust floating in the air.*

particular
ADJECTIVE **1** to do with only one person or thing • *That **particular** recipe is very easy to make.*
2 If you are **particular**, you are fussy and pay attention to detail.
particularly ADVERB

partition **partitions**
NOUN a screen separating one part of a room or vehicle from another

partly
ADVERB to some extent, but not completely • *It's **partly** my fault.*

partner **partners**
NOUN **1** Someone's **partner** is the person they are married to or living with.
2 one of two people who do something together, such as dancing or running a business

part of speech **parts of speech**
NOUN one of the groups that words are divided into in grammar, such as a noun or an adjective

partridge **partridges**
NOUN a brown game bird with a round body and a short tail

part-time
ADJECTIVE OR ADVERB involving work for only a part of each normal working day or week

party **parties**
NOUN **1** a social occasion when people meet to enjoy themselves, often in order to celebrate something
2 a group of people who are doing something together • *A* ***party*** *of school children visited the museum.*

pass **passes, passing, passed**
VERB **1** If you **pass** someone or something, you go past them without stopping.
2 If you **pass** something to someone, you give it to them.
3 If you **pass** an examination, you are successful in it.

passage **passages**
NOUN **1** a long, narrow corridor or space that connects two places • *There was a* ***passage*** *from the front garden through to the back garden.*
2 a section of a book or piece of music

passenger **passengers**
NOUN a person travelling in a vehicle, aircraft or ship

passion **passions**
NOUN a very strong feeling

passive
ADJECTIVE **1** Someone who is **passive** does not take action or react strongly to things.
NOUN **2** In grammar, the **passive**, or **passive** voice, is the form of the verb in which the person or thing to which an action is being done is the subject of the sentence. For example, the sentence *The burglar was seen by the police* is in the **passive**. For the active, or active voice, the subject of the sentence is the person or thing doing the activity: *The police saw the burglar.*

Passover
NOUN an eight-day Jewish festival held in spring

passport **passports**
NOUN an official document showing your identity and nationality, that you need to show when you enter or leave a country

password **passwords**
NOUN **1** a secret word known to only a few people. It allows people on the same side to recognize a friend.
2 a word you need to know to get into some computer files

past
NOUN **1** the period of time before the present
ADJECTIVE **2** **Past** events are ones that happened or existed before the present.
PREPOSITION OR ADVERB **3** You use **past** to tell the time when it is thirty minutes or less after a particular hour. • *It's ten* ***past*** *eleven.*
4 If you go **past** something, you move towards it and continue until you are on the other side. • *An ambulance drove* ***past****.*
PREPOSITION **5** Something that is **past** a place is situated on the other side of it. • *The farm is just* ***past*** *the next village.*

pasta
NOUN a dried mixture of flour, eggs and water, formed into different shapes [an Italian word meaning flour mixture]

paste **pastes, pasting, pasted**
NOUN **1** a soft, sticky mixture that can be spread easily
VERB **2** If you **paste** something somewhere, you stick it there with glue.

pasteurized; also spelt **pasteurised**
Said "**past**-yoor-ized" ADJECTIVE
Pasteurized milk has been heated by a special process to kill bacteria.
[after the French chemist Louis *Pasteur* who invented the process]

pastime **pastimes**
NOUN something that you enjoy doing in your spare time

pastry **pastries**
NOUN **1** a mixture of flour, fat and water that is used for making pies

2 a small cake • *There is a selection of* ***pastries*** *for tea.*

pasture **pastures**
NOUN an area of grass where cows, horses and sheep can graze

pasty **pasties; pastier, pastiest**
Rhymes with "nasty" NOUN **1** a small pie containing meat and vegetables
Rhymes with "tasty" ADJECTIVE **2** Someone who is **pasty** looks pale and unhealthy.

pat **pats, patting, patted**
VERB If you **pat** someone or something, you tap them lightly with an open hand.

patch **patches, patching, patched**
NOUN **1** a piece of material used to cover a hole in something • *She put a* ***patch*** *over the hole in her jeans.*
2 an area of a surface that is different in appearance from the rest • *We want to grow vegetables on that* ***patch*** *of ground.*
VERB **3** If you **patch** something that has a hole in it, you mend it by fixing something over the hole.

patchy **patchier, patchiest**
ADJECTIVE uneven in quantity, quality or both • *We drove through* ***patchy*** *fog.*

pâté **pâtés**
Said "**pa**-tay" NOUN a paste made from meat, fish or vegetables, and spread on toast or biscuits
[from the French word for paste]

patent **patents**
NOUN the official right given to someone to make something they have invented. It stops others from copying it.

paternal
ADJECTIVE relating to or like a father
[from Latin *pater* meaning father]

path **paths**
NOUN **1** a strip of ground for people to walk or ride along
2 the direction in which something travels • *The trail of smoke showed the* ***path*** *of the plane.*

pathetic
ADJECTIVE **1** If something is **pathetic**, it makes you feel pity.
2 very poor or unsuccessful • *He made a* ***pathetic*** *attempt to swim.*
[from Greek *pathetikos* meaning sensitive]
pathetically ADVERB

patience
NOUN the ability to stay calm in a difficult or irritating situation

patient **patients**
ADJECTIVE **1** If you are **patient**, you stay calm in a difficult or irritating situation.
NOUN **2** a person receiving treatment from a doctor
patiently ADVERB

patio **patios**
NOUN a paved area close to a house

patriot **patriots**
NOUN someone who loves their own country and is very loyal to it
patriotic ADJECTIVE **patriotism** NOUN

patrol **patrols, patrolling, patrolled**
VERB **1** When soldiers, police or guards **patrol** an area, they walk or drive around it to make sure there is no trouble.
NOUN **2** a group of people patrolling an area

patter **patters, pattering, pattered**
VERB **1** If something **patters** on a surface, it makes quick, light, tapping sounds.
• *The rain* ***pattered*** *against the window.*
NOUN **2** a series of light, tapping sounds
• *We could hear the* ***patter*** *of light rain.*

pattern **patterns**
NOUN **1** a design of shapes repeated at regular intervals
2 a drawing that can be copied to make something else, such as clothes

pause **pauses, pausing, paused**
VERB **1** If you **pause**, you stop speaking or doing something for a short time.
NOUN **2** a period when something stops for a short time before continuing

pavement **pavements**
NOUN a raised pathway with a hard surface along the side of a road
[from Latin *pavimentum* meaning hard floor]

pavilion **pavilions**
NOUN a building at a sports ground, especially a cricket pitch, where players can change

paw **paws**
NOUN the foot of an animal that has claws and pads

pawn **pawns, pawning, pawned**
VERB **1** If you **pawn** something, you leave it with someone called a pawnbroker who lends you money. When you repay the money, the pawnbroker will give back the item you **pawned**.
NOUN **2** the smallest and least valuable piece in the game of chess

pay **pays, paying, paid**
VERB **1** If you **pay** someone, you give them money in exchange for something.
PHRASE **2** If you **pay attention**, you listen carefully to what is being said.

payment **payments**
NOUN If you make a **payment** for something, you give someone money in exchange for goods or a service.

PC **PCs**
NOUN **1** the abbreviation of *personal computer*
2 In Britain, **PC** is also the abbreviation of *police constable*.

PE
NOUN an abbreviation of *physical education*, which is the sports that you do at school

pea **peas**
NOUN a small, round green seed that is eaten as a vegetable

peace
Said "**peess**" NOUN **1** a state of undisturbed calm and quiet
2 If a country is at **peace**, it is not at war.

Do not confuse *peace* with *piece*.

peaceful
ADJECTIVE quiet and calm

peach **peaches**
NOUN a soft, round fruit with yellow flesh and a yellow and red skin

peacock **peacocks**
NOUN a large male bird with very long green and blue tail feathers that it can spread out in a fan. The female is called a peahen.

peak **peaks**
NOUN **1** the highest point of a mountain
2 The **peak** of an activity or process is the point at which it is strongest or most successful.
3 the part of a cap that sticks out over your eyes

peal **peals**
NOUN the loud musical sound made by bells ringing one after another

peanut **peanuts**
NOUN a small nut that grows under the ground

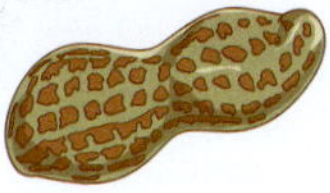

pear **pears**
NOUN a green or yellow fruit that is narrow at the top and wider at the bottom

Do not confuse *pear* with *pair*.

pearl **pearls**
NOUN a hard, round, creamy-white ball used in jewellery. **Pearls** grow inside the shell of an oyster.

peasant **peasants**
NOUN a person who works on the land, earning little money

peat
NOUN dark-brown decaying plant material found in cool, wet regions. Dried **peat** can be used as fuel or fertilizer.

pebble **pebbles**
NOUN a smooth, round stone often found on the beach

peck **pecks, pecking, pecked**
VERB If a bird **pecks** something, it bites at it quickly with its beak. • *The birds* ***pecked*** *at the seeds on the ground.*

peculiar
ADJECTIVE strange and unusual • *She thought the food tasted* ***peculiar****.*
peculiarly ADVERB **peculiarity** NOUN

pedal **pedals, pedalling, pedalled**
VERB **1** When you **pedal** a bicycle, you push the pedals around with your feet to make it move.
NOUN **2** a control lever that you press with your foot to make a machine or vehicle work

pedestrian **pedestrians**
NOUN someone who is walking • *Only **pedestrians** are allowed down this street.*

pedigree **pedigrees**
ADJECTIVE **1** A **pedigree** animal is bred from a single breed and its ancestors are known and recorded.
NOUN **2** a list of a person's or an animal's ancestors

peek **peeks, peeking, peeked**
VERB **1** If you **peek** at something, you have a quick look at it.
NOUN **2** a quick look at something

peel **peels, peeling, peeled**
NOUN **1** the skin of a fruit or vegetable
VERB **2** When you **peel** fruit or vegetables, you remove the skin.
3 If a layer of something **peels**, it comes off a surface. • *Paint was **peeling** off the walls.*

peep **peeps, peeping, peeped**
VERB **1** If you **peep** at something, you have a quick, secretive look at it, or you look at it through a small opening.
NOUN **2** a quick look at something

peer **peers, peering, peered**
VERB **1** If you **peer** at something, you look at it very hard. • *He **peered** into the dark room.*
NOUN **2** Your **peers** are your equals in age, interests and background.

peg **pegs**
NOUN **1** a plastic or wooden clip for attaching clothes to a washing line
2 a hook where you can hang things

pelican **pelicans**
NOUN a large water bird with a pouch beneath its beak in which it stores fish

pellet **pellets**
NOUN a small ball of food, paper, lead or other material

pelt **pelts, pelting, pelted**
NOUN **1** the skin and fur of an animal, especially when it is used for making clothes
VERB **2** If you **pelt** someone with something, you throw it at them very hard.
3 If rain **pelts** down, it rains very hard.

pen **pens**
NOUN **1** an instrument with a pointed end used for writing with ink
2 a small, fenced area where farm animals are kept • *a sheep **pen***

penalty **penalties**
NOUN **1** a punishment
2 In sport, a **penalty** is an advantage or point given to one team when their opponents break the rules.

pence
NOUN a plural form of **penny**

pencil **pencils**
NOUN a small stick of wood with a type of soft mineral called graphite in the centre, used for drawing or writing
[from Latin *pencillus* meaning painter's brush]

pendant **pendants**
NOUN a piece of jewellery attached to a chain and worn round the neck

penetrate **penetrates, penetrating, penetrated**
VERB If someone or something **penetrates** an object or area, they succeed in getting into or through it. • *Eventually they **penetrated** the forest and found the cabin.*

pen friend **pen friends**
NOUN someone living in a different place or country whom you write to regularly, although you may never have met each other

penguin **penguins**
NOUN a black and white bird with webbed feet and small wings like flippers. **Penguins** are found mainly in the Antarctic.

penicillin
NOUN a powerful antibiotic obtained from fungus and used to treat infections

peninsula **peninsulas**
NOUN an area of land almost surrounded by water
[from Latin *paene* + *insula* meaning almost an island]

penis **penises**
NOUN A man's **penis** is the part of the body he uses when urinating.

penknife **penknives**
NOUN a small folding knife

penny **pennies** or **pence**
NOUN a unit of currency in Britain and some other countries. In Britain, there are 100 **pennies** in a pound.

pension **pensions**
NOUN a regular sum of money paid to a retired, widowed or disabled person

pentagon **pentagons**
NOUN a flat shape with five straight sides
pentagonal ADJECTIVE

pentathlon **pentathlons**
NOUN a sports contest in which athletes compete in five different events
[from Greek *pente* meaning five and *athlon* meaning contest]

people
PLURAL NOUN human beings – men, women and children

pepper **peppers**
NOUN **1** a hot-tasting powdered spice used for flavouring in cooking
2 a hollow green, red or yellow vegetable, with sweet-flavoured flesh

peppermint **peppermints**
NOUN **1** a plant with a strong taste. It is used for making sweets and in medicine.
2 a sweet flavoured with peppermint

per
PREPOSITION **Per** means *for each* and is used when speaking about prices, measurements, rates and ratios
• *60 kilometres* ***per*** *hour* • *three times* ***per*** *year* • *90p* ***per*** *kilo*

perceive **perceives, perceiving, perceived**
VERB If you **perceive** something, you see, notice or understand it.

per cent
PHRASE You use **per cent** to show amounts out of a hundred. The symbol for per cent is %. • *She got 98* ***per cent*** *(98%) for her maths test.*
[from Latin **per** meaning each and **centum** meaning hundred]

percentage **percentages**
NOUN an amount or rate expressed as a number of hundredths

perceptive
ADJECTIVE Someone who is **perceptive** notices and understands things more quickly than other people.
SYNONYMS: observant, sharp
perceptively ADVERB

perch **perches, perching, perched**
VERB **1** If you **perch** on something, you sit on the edge of it.
2 When a bird **perches** on something, it stands on it.
NOUN **3** a short rod for a bird to stand on
4 an edible freshwater fish

percussion
NOUN OR ADJECTIVE musical instruments that you hit or shake to produce sounds, such as drums and tambourines
percussionist NOUN

perennial
ADJECTIVE occurring or lasting for many years

perfect **perfects, perfecting, perfected**
Said "**pur**-fikt" ADJECTIVE **1** Something that is **perfect** is as good as it possibly can be.

a b c d e f g h i j k l m n o p q r s t u v w x y z

Said "pur-**fekt**" VERB **2** If you **perfect** something, you make it as good as it possibly can be.

perform **performs, performing, performed**
VERB **1** If you **perform** a play or piece of music, you do a show of it in front of an audience.
2 If you **perform** a task or action, you do it.
performer NOUN

performance **performances**
NOUN an entertainment provided for an audience • *The orchestra gave an excellent **performance**.*

perfume **perfumes**
NOUN **1** a pleasant-smelling liquid that people put on their skin
2 a pleasant smell • *These roses have a lovely **perfume**.*

perhaps
ADVERB You use **perhaps** when you are not sure if something is true or possible. • ***Perhaps** we could see you tomorrow?*

peril **perils**
NOUN FORMAL great danger
perilous ADJECTIVE **perilously** ADVERB

perimeter **perimeters**
NOUN **1** the distance all the way round the edge of an area
2 the edge or boundary of something

period **periods**
NOUN **1** a particular length of time • *We will be away for a **period** of a few months.*
2 A woman's **period** is the monthly bleeding from her womb.
3 In American English, a **period** is a full stop.

periodical **periodicals**
NOUN a magazine that is published regularly

periscope **periscopes**
NOUN a tube with mirrors placed in it so that you can see things that are otherwise out of sight. **Periscopes** are used for seeing out of submarines.

perish **perishes, perishing, perished**
VERB **1** If fruit, rubber or fabric **perishes**, it rots.
2 FORMAL If someone or something **perishes**, they die or are destroyed.
perishable ADJECTIVE

perm **perms**
NOUN If someone has a **perm**, their hair is curled and treated with chemicals to keep the curls for several months.

permanent
ADJECTIVE lasting forever or present all the time

permission
NOUN If you have **permission** to do something, you are allowed to do it.

permit **permits, permitting, permitted**
Said "pur-**mit**" VERB **1** If someone or something **permits** you to do something, they allow it or make it possible. • *We **permit** children to ride bicycles to school.*
SYNONYM: give permission
Said "**pur**-mit" NOUN **2** an official document that says that you are allowed to do something

perpendicular
ADJECTIVE A line that is **perpendicular** to another one meets it at a right angle (90°).

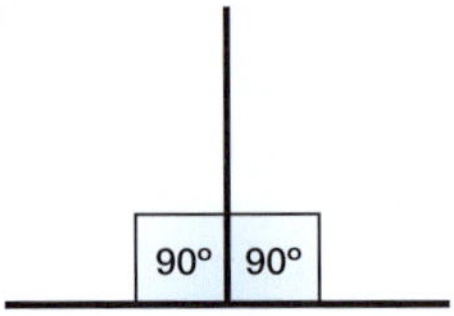

perpetual
ADJECTIVE never ending
perpetually ADVERB

perplexed
ADJECTIVE If you are **perplexed**, you are puzzled and do not know what to do.
SYNONYM: confused

persecute **persecutes, persecuting, persecuted**
VERB If someone **persecutes** another person, they continually treat them with cruelty and unfairness, often because of their religious beliefs.
persecution NOUN **persecutor** NOUN

persevere **perseveres, persevering, persevered**
VERB If you **persevere**, you keep trying to do something and do not give up.
perseverance NOUN

persist **persists, persisting, persisted**
VERB **1** If something **persists**, it continues and will not stop. • *The rain* ***persisted*** *all day.*
2 If you **persist** in doing something, you continue with it in spite of difficulties or opposition.

person **people** or **persons**
NOUN **1** a man, woman or child
SYNONYMS: human being, individual
2 In grammar, the first **person** is the speaker (I), the second **person** is the person being spoken to (you), and the third **person** is anyone else being referred to (he, she, they).
PHRASE **3** If you do something **in person**, you do it yourself rather than letting someone else do it for you.
[from Latin *persona* meaning actor's mask]

The usual plural of *person* is *people*. *Persons* is much less common, and is used only in formal English.

personal
ADJECTIVE **1** belonging or relating to a particular person
SYNONYMS: individual, own
2 Personal matters are personal things that you may not wish to discuss with other people. • *I cannot tell you for* ***personal*** *reasons.*

personality **personalities**
NOUN Your **personality** is your character and nature. • *She's got a very lively* ***personality***.

personally
ADVERB **1** in person • *He came to school to thank us* ***personally*** *for the money we raised for the charity.*
2 You use **personally** to express your own opinion of something. • ***Personally***, *I don't mind where we go.*

personnel
Said "per-son-**nell**" PLURAL NOUN the people who work for an organization

perspective **perspectives**
NOUN **1** the impression of distance and depth in a picture or a drawing
2 a particular way of thinking about something or looking at something
• *What is your* ***perspective*** *on discipline?*

perspire **perspires, perspiring, perspired**
VERB When people **perspire**, they sweat.
perspiration NOUN

persuade **persuades, persuading, persuaded**
VERB If you **persuade** someone to do something, or **persuade** them that something is true, you make them do it or believe it by giving them good reasons.
persuasion NOUN **persuasive** ADJECTIVE

pessimism
NOUN the feeling that bad things will always happen

pessimist **pessimists**
NOUN If you are a **pessimist**, you expect the worst to happen.
ANTONYM: optimist
pessimistic ADJECTIVE
pessimistically ADVERB

pest **pests**
NOUN **1** an insect or other small animal that damages plants or food supplies
2 someone who keeps bothering or annoying you

pester **pesters, pestering, pestered**
VERB If you **pester** someone, you keep bothering them or asking them to do something.

pesticide **pesticides**
NOUN a chemical sprayed onto plants to kill insects and grubs

pet **pets**
NOUN **1** a tame animal kept at home
2 a person who is treated as a favourite

petal **petals**
NOUN one of the coloured outer parts of a flower that attract insects. Some **petals** are perfumed.

petition **petitions**
NOUN a written document, signed by a lot of people, requesting official action be taken on something

petrified
ADJECTIVE If you are **petrified**, you are very frightened.
SYNONYM: terrified

petrol
NOUN a liquid that is used as a fuel for motor vehicles

petty **pettier, pettiest**
ADJECTIVE trivial and unimportant • *We should not argue over **petty** things.*

pew **pews**
NOUN a long wooden seat with a back, that people sit on in church

pH
NOUN The **pH** of a solution or of the soil is a measurement of how acid or alkaline it is. Substances with a **pH** above 7 are alkaline and substances with a **pH** below 7 are acid.

phantom **phantoms**
NOUN **1** a ghost
ADJECTIVE **2** imagined or unreal

pharmacy **pharmacies**
NOUN a shop where medicines are sold
SYNONYM: chemists

phase **phases**
NOUN a particular stage in the development of something

pheasant **pheasants**
NOUN a large, long-tailed game bird

phenomenon **phenomena**
NOUN something that happens or exists, especially something extraordinary or remarkable • *The eclipse was a fascinating **phenomenon**.*
phenomenal ADJECTIVE
phenomenally ADVERB

philosophy **philosophies**
NOUN **1** the study or creation of ideas about humans, their relationship to the universe and beliefs
2 a set of beliefs a person has

phobia **phobias**
NOUN a deep fear or dislike of something
phobic ADJECTIVE

phoenix **phoenixes**
Said "**fee**-niks" NOUN an imaginary bird that, according to myth, sets fire to itself every five hundred years, and rises from the ashes

phone **phones, phoning, phoned**
NOUN OR VERB an abbreviation of **telephone**

phoney **phonier, phoniest**; also spelt **phony**
ADJECTIVE false, not genuine, and meant to trick • *He had a **phoney** passport.*
ANTONYM: genuine

photo **photos**
NOUN an abbreviation of **photograph**

photocopier **photocopiers**
NOUN a machine that makes instant copies of documents

photocopy **photocopies, photocopying, photocopied**
VERB **1** If you **photocopy** a document, you make a copy of it using a photocopier.
NOUN **2** a copy of a document made using a photocopier

photograph **photographs, photographing, photographed**
NOUN **1** a picture taken with a camera and then printed on special paper
VERB **2** If you **photograph** someone or something, you use a camera to take a picture of them.

photography
Said "fo-**tog**-raff-ee" NOUN the job or hobby of taking photographs
photographer NOUN

photosynthesis
Said "fo-toh-**sin**-th-sis" NOUN the process by which green plants make their own food from carbon dioxide and water in the presence of sunlight

phrase **phrases**
NOUN a short group of words or musical notes

physical
ADJECTIVE concerning the body rather than the mind
[from Greek *phusis* meaning nature]

physical education
NOUN physical exercise and sports that you do at school

physics
NOUN the scientific study of the forces and properties of matter, such as heat, light, sound and electricity

pianist **pianists**
NOUN someone who plays the piano

piano **pianos**
NOUN a large musical instrument with a row of black and white keys. When the keys are pressed, little hammers hit wires to produce different notes.

piccolo **piccolos**
NOUN a high-pitched wind instrument like a small flute

pick **picks, picking, picked**
VERB **1** If you **pick** someone or something, you choose them. • *I **picked** Hannah for my partner.*
2 If you **pick** a flower or a fruit, you break it off from where it is growing.
3 If someone **picks** a lock, they open it with a piece of wire instead of a key.

pick on
VERB If you **pick on** someone, you treat them unkindly and unfairly.

pick up
VERB **1** If you **pick up** someone or something, you lift them.
2 If you **pick up** someone or something from a place, you collect them from there.

picket **pickets, picketing, picketed**
VERB **1** When a group of people **picket** a place of work during a strike, they stand outside and try to persuade other workers not to go in to work.
NOUN **2** someone who is picketing a place

pickle **pickles**
NOUN **Pickles** are vegetables or fruit preserved in vinegar or salt water.

pickpocket **pickpockets**
NOUN a thief who steals things from pockets or bags

picnic **picnics**
NOUN a meal eaten outdoors

pictogram **pictograms**
NOUN a type of graph that uses small pictures to show information

pictorial
ADJECTIVE relating to or using pictures

picture **pictures**
NOUN a drawing, painting, photograph or television image of someone or something

picturesque
ADJECTIVE A place that is **picturesque** is very attractive and unspoiled.
[from Italian *pittoresco* meaning in the style of a painter]

pie **pies**
NOUN a dish of meat, vegetables or fruit covered with pastry

piece **pieces**
Said "**peess**" NOUN **1** a portion or part of something
2 an individual thing of a particular kind • *This is a good **piece** of work.*
3 a coin • *a 50 pence **piece***

Do not confuse *piece* with *peace.*

pie chart **pie charts**
NOUN a circular diagram that is divided into segments to show how a quantity or an amount of something is shared

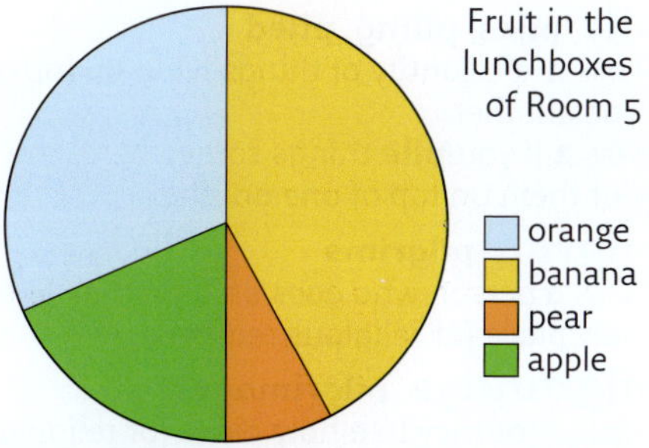

pier **piers**
NOUN a large structure at the seaside, with a platform built from the shore out into the sea, that people can walk along

pierce **pierces, piercing, pierced**
VERB If a sharp object **pierces** something, it goes through it, making a hole.

piercing
ADJECTIVE **1** a **piercing** sound is high pitched and sharp, and it hurts your ears
SYNONYM: shrill
2 Someone with **piercing** eyes seems to stare at you intensely.

pig **pigs**
NOUN a farm animal with pink or black skin, a curly tail and a snout, that is kept for its meat. Pork, ham and bacon all come from **pigs**.

pigeon **pigeons**
NOUN a grey bird with a small head and large chest, often found in towns and cities

piglet **piglets**
NOUN a young pig

pigsty **pigsties**
NOUN **1** a small shelter with an enclosed area where pigs are kept
2 If you say a place is like a **pigsty**, you mean that it is very dirty and untidy.

pigtail **pigtails**
NOUN a plait of hair • *She wore her hair in **pigtails**.*

pike **pikes**
NOUN **1** a large freshwater fish with strong, sharp teeth
2 a weapon used in medieval times. A **pike** was a long pole with a spike on the end.

pile **piles, piling, piled**
NOUN **1** a quantity of things lying on top of one another
VERB **2** If you **pile** things somewhere, you put them on top of one another.

pilgrim **pilgrims**
NOUN a person who goes on a journey to a holy place for religious reasons

pilgrimage **pilgrimages**
NOUN a journey to a holy place for religious reasons

pill **pills**
NOUN a small, round tablet of medicine that you swallow

pillar **pillars**
NOUN a tall, solid structure like a large post, often made of stone and usually supporting part of a building

pillow **pillows**
NOUN a large cushion that you rest your head on when you are in bed

pilot **pilots**
NOUN **1** a person who is trained to fly an aircraft
2 the person who guides a ship into port

pimple **pimples**
NOUN a small spot on the skin
pimply ADJECTIVE

pin **pins, pinning, pinned**
NOUN **1** a thin, pointed piece of metal, used to fasten things like paper or cloth together
VERB **2** If you **pin** something, you attach it with a pin.

pincers
PLURAL NOUN **1** The **pincers** of a crab or a lobster are its large front claws.
2 a tool consisting of two pieces of metal hinged in the middle, used for gripping and pulling things

pinch **pinches, pinching, pinched**
VERB **1** If you **pinch** something, you squeeze it between your thumb and first finger.
2 INFORMAL If someone **pinches** something, they steal it.
NOUN **3** A **pinch** of something is the amount that you can hold between your thumb and first finger. • *Add a **pinch** of salt to the soup.*

pine **pines, pining, pined**
NOUN **1** an evergreen tree with very thin leaves called needles

VERB **2** If you **pine** for something or someone, you feel sad because they are not there.

pineapple **pineapples**
NOUN a large, oval tropical fruit with sweet, yellow flesh and thick, woody skin

pink **pinker, pinkest**
ADJECTIVE pale reddish-white

pint **pints**
NOUN a unit of measurement for liquids equal to about 0.568 litres

pioneer **pioneers**
NOUN one of the first people to go to a place or to do something new

pip **pips**
NOUN **1** the hard seeds in a fruit
2 a short, high-pitched sound

pipe **pipes, piping, piped**
NOUN **1** a long, hollow tube through which liquid or gas can flow
2 an object that is used for smoking tobacco, consisting of a small hollow bowl attached to a thin tube
3 a tube-shaped musical instrument
VERB **4** If liquid or gas is **piped** somewhere, it is transferred there through a pipe.

pipeline **pipelines**
NOUN **1** a large underground pipe that carries oil or gas over a long distance
PHRASE **2** If something is **in the pipeline**, it is already planned or has begun.

pirate **pirates**
NOUN a sailor who attacks and robs other ships

pistol **pistols**
NOUN a small gun held in the hand

pit **pits**
NOUN **1** a large hole in the ground
2 a coal mine

pitch **pitches, pitching, pitched**
NOUN **1** an area of ground marked out for playing a game such as football or cricket
2 The **pitch** of a sound is how high or low it is.
3 a black substance painted onto roofs and boat bottoms to make them waterproof
VERB **4** If you **pitch** something somewhere, you throw it there with a lot of force.
5 If you **pitch** a tent, you put it up.

pitcher **pitchers**
NOUN a large jug

pitchfork **pitchforks**
NOUN a long-handled fork with two large prongs, used for lifting and moving hay

pitfall **pitfalls**
NOUN one of the difficulties or dangers of a situation

pitta **pittas**
NOUN a flat disc of bread with a hollow inside, that can be filled with food [from Greek, meaning a cake]

pity **pities, pitying, pitied**
VERB **1** If you **pity** someone, you feel sorry for them.
NOUN **2** a feeling of sadness and concern for someone
3 If you say that something is a **pity**, you mean it is disappointing. • *It's a **pity** we couldn't play tennis.*

pivot **pivots, pivoting, pivoted**
VERB **1** If something **pivots**, it balances or turns on a central point.
NOUN **2** the central point on which something balances or turns
pivotal ADJECTIVE

pizza **pizzas**
Said "**peet**-sa" NOUN a flat piece of dough usually covered with cheese, tomato and other savoury food and baked in an oven [an Italian word]

placard **placards**
NOUN a large notice carried at a demonstration or displayed in a public place • *The man carried a **placard** advertising the furniture sale.*

place **places, placing, placed**
NOUN **1** a particular point, position, building or area • *They found a good **place** to camp.*
2 a particular position in a race,

competition, or series • *Last year she finished in third **place**.*
3 If you have a **place** in a team or on a course, you are allowed to join the team or course. • *I eventually got a **place** at the new school.*
VERB **4** If you **place** something somewhere, you put it there. • *She **placed** her hand gently on my shoulder.*
PHRASE **5** When something **takes place**, it happens. • *The competition will **take place** next month.*

placid
ADJECTIVE calm and not easily excited or upset
SYNONYMS: even-tempered, unexcitable
placidly ADVERB

plague **plagues, plaguing, plagued**
Said "**playg**" NOUN **1** a very infectious disease that kills large numbers of people
2 A **plague** of unpleasant things is a large number of them occurring at the same time.
VERB **3** If you **plague** someone, you keep pestering them.
4 If problems **plague** you, they keep causing you trouble.

plaice
NOUN an edible European flat fish

plaid **plaids**
Said "**plad**" NOUN woven material with a tartan design

plain **plainer, plainest; plains**
ADJECTIVE **1** very simple in style, with no pattern or decoration
2 obvious or easy to understand
NOUN **3** a large, flat area of land with very few trees

plait **plaits, plaiting, plaited**
Said "**plat**" VERB **1** If you **plait** hair or rope, you twist three lengths together in turn to make one thick length.
NOUN **2** a length of hair that has been plaited

plan **plans, planning, planned**
NOUN **1** a method of achieving something that has been worked out beforehand
VERB **2** If you **plan** something, you decide in detail what you are going to do.
3 If you **plan** to do something, you intend to do it.

plane **planes**
NOUN **1** an abbreviation of *aeroplane*
2 a tool for smoothing wood
ADJECTIVE **3** A **plane** shape has a flat, level surface. A **plane** mirror is flat and not curved.

planet **planets**
NOUN a large sphere in space that orbits a sun. The Earth and Mars are both **planets** that revolve around our sun.

plank **planks**
NOUN a long rectangular piece of wood

plankton
NOUN a layer of tiny plants and animals that live just below the surface of a sea or lake

plant **plants, planting, planted**
NOUN **1** a living thing that grows in the earth and has a stem, leaves, and roots.
VERB **2** If you **plant** things such as flowers or trees, you put them in the ground so that they will grow.

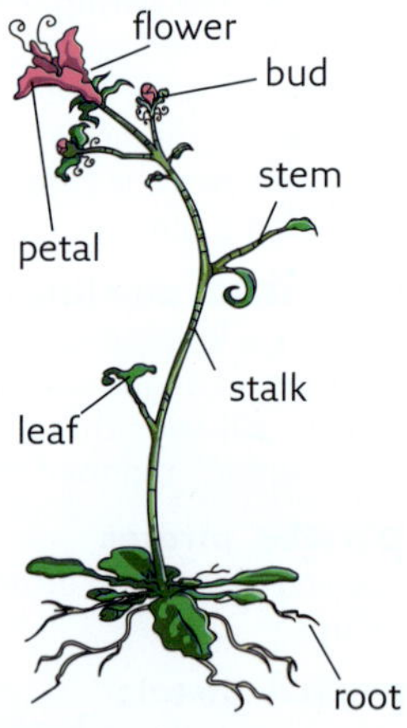

plantation **plantations**
NOUN **1** a large area of land where crops such as tea, cotton or sugar are grown
2 a large number of trees planted together

plaque **plaques**
Said "**plak**" NOUN **1** a flat piece of metal or porcelain, fixed to a wall, with an inscription on it in memory of a famous person or event

2 a substance that forms around your teeth. It is made up of bacteria, saliva and food.

plaster **plasters**
NOUN **1** a paste made of sand, lime and water, that is used to form a smooth surface for inside walls and ceilings
2 a strip of sticky material with a small pad, used for covering cuts on your body
3 **Plaster** of Paris is a white powder mixed with water, that becomes hard when it dries. It is used for making moulds and for holding broken bones in place while they heal.
plasterer NOUN

plastic **plastics**
NOUN **1** a light synthetic material made from oil by a chemical process. **Plastics** can be moulded into different shapes for many different uses.
ADJECTIVE **2** made of plastic

Plasticine
NOUN TRADEMARK a soft, coloured material like clay, used for making models

plate **plates**
NOUN **1** a flat dish used to hold food
2 a flat piece of hard material such as glass or metal

plateau **plateaus** or **plateaux**
NOUN a large area of high and fairly flat land
[from Old French *platel* meaning a flat piece of metal]

platform **platforms**
NOUN **1** a raised structure on which someone or something can stand
2 the raised area in a railway station where passengers get on and off trains

platinum
NOUN a valuable silver-coloured metal

platypus **platypuses**
NOUN an Australian mammal that lives in rivers. It has brown fur, webbed feet, and a beak like a duck.
[from Greek *platus* meaning flat and *pous* meaning foot]

play **plays, playing, played**
VERB **1** When children **play**, they take part in games or use toys for fun.
2 When you **play** a sport or game, you take part in it.
3 If an actor **plays** a character in a play or film, they perform that role.
4 If you **play** a musical instrument, you produce music from it.
NOUN **5** **Play** is the activity of playing a game or sport.
6 a story acted out in the theatre, on the radio or on television
player NOUN

playground **playgrounds**
NOUN a special area for children to play in

playgroup **playgroups**
NOUN an informal group of very young children who play together, supervised by adults

playtime **playtimes**
NOUN the time in a school day when children go out to play

playwright **playwrights**
NOUN a person who writes plays

plea **pleas**
Said "**plee**" NOUN **1** If you make a **plea**, you make an urgent request or an appeal for something.
2 In a law court, a **plea** is someone's statement that they are guilty or not guilty.

plead **pleads, pleading, pleaded**
VERB **1** If you **plead** with someone, you beg them for something. • *She came to* ***plead*** *for help.*
2 In a law court, when a person **pleads** guilty or not guilty, they state that they are guilty or not guilty.

pleasant
ADJECTIVE nice, pleasing, enjoyable or attractive in some way

please **pleases, pleasing, pleased**
1 You say **please** when you are asking someone politely to do something. • *Can you help me,* ***please****?*
VERB **2** If something **pleases** you, it makes you feel happy and satisfied.

pleasure **pleasures**
NOUN a feeling of happiness, satisfaction or enjoyment

pleat **pleats**
NOUN a permanent fold in fabric, made by folding one part over another

pledge **pledges, pledging, pledged**
NOUN **1** a solemn promise
VERB **2** If you **pledge** something, you promise that you will do it or give it.

plenty
NOUN OR PRONOUN If you have **plenty** of something, you have more than enough for your needs. • *We've got **plenty** of time.*

pliable
ADJECTIVE If something is **pliable**, you can bend it without breaking it. • *This **pliable** material will be easier to work with.*
SYNONYM: flexible

pliers
PLURAL NOUN a small tool with metal jaws for gripping small objects such as nails and bending wire

plight **plights**
NOUN a difficult or dangerous situation • *the **plight** of the homeless*

plod **plods, plodding, plodded**
VERB If you **plod**, you walk slowly and heavily. • *We **plodded** home through the mud.*

plop **plops, plopping, plopped**
NOUN **1** a gentle sound of something lightweight dropping into a liquid
VERB **2** If something **plops** into a liquid, it drops into it with a gentle sound.

plot **plots, plotting, plotted**
NOUN **1** a secret plan made by a group of people
2 The **plot** of a film, novel or play is the story.
VERB **3** If people **plot** to do something, they plan it secretly.

plough **ploughs, ploughing, ploughed**
NOUN **1** a large farming tool that is pulled across a field to turn the soil over before planting seeds
VERB **2** When farmers **plough** land, they use a plough to turn over the soil.

pluck **plucks, plucking, plucked**
VERB **1** If you **pluck** a fruit or flower, you remove it with a sharp pull.
2 If you **pluck** a dead bird, such as a chicken or a turkey, you pull the feathers off it before cooking it.
3 When you **pluck** a stringed instrument, you pull the strings and let them go.

plug **plugs, plugging, plugged**
NOUN **1** a device that connects a piece of electrical equipment to an electric socket
2 a thick circular piece of rubber or plastic that you use to block the hole in a sink or bath

plug in
VERB If you **plug in** a piece of electrical equipment, you push its plug into an electric socket.

plum **plums**
NOUN a small fruit with a smooth red or yellow skin and a stone in the middle

plumage
NOUN a bird's feathers

plumber **plumbers**
NOUN a person who connects and repairs water pipes

plump **plumper, plumpest**
ADJECTIVE rounded, or slightly fat

plunge **plunges, plunging, plunged**
VERB If you **plunge** somewhere, especially into water, you fall or rush there.
SYNONYMS: dive, drop, fall

plural **plurals**
NOUN the form of a word that is used when referring to more than one person or thing • *The usual **plural** of person is people.*

plus
PREPOSITION **1** You use **plus** to show that one number is being added to another. • *Two **plus** two equals four.*
2 You can use **plus** when you mention an additional item. • *She gave us our coats, **plus** a blanket.*

plywood
NOUN wooden board made from several thin sheets of wood glued together under pressure

p.m.
used to show times between 12 noon and 12 midnight • *I go to bed at 8* ***p.m.*** *on schooldays and 9* ***p.m.*** *at weekends.*
[from Latin *post meridiem* meaning after noon]

pneumatic
ADJECTIVE operated by or filled with compressed air • *a* ***pneumatic*** *drill*

pneumonia
NOUN a serious disease that affects a person's lungs and makes breathing difficult

poach **poaches, poaching, poached**
VERB **1** If someone **poaches** animals, they hunt them illegally on someone else's land.
2 When you **poach** food, especially fish, or an egg taken out of its shell, you cook it gently in hot liquid.
poacher NOUN

pocket **pockets**
NOUN a small pouch for keeping things in, that forms part of a piece of clothing

pocket money
NOUN an amount of money given regularly to children by their parents

pod **pods**
NOUN a long, narrow seed container that grows on plants such as peas or beans

podcast **podcasts**
NOUN a file similar to a radio broadcast that can be downloaded for listening to on a computer or MP3 player

poem **poems**
NOUN a piece of writing, usually arranged in short rhythmic lines, with words chosen for their sound or impact

poet **poets**
NOUN a person who writes poems

poetry
NOUN poems, considered a form of literature

point **points, pointing, pointed**
VERB **1** If you **point** at or to something, you hold out your finger towards it to show where it is.
NOUN **2** the thin, sharp end of something such as a needle or knife
3 a particular place or time • *At some* ***point*** *during the night, the storm began.*
4 a single mark in a competition • *They won by 21* ***points*** *to 18.*
5 the purpose or the most important part of something • *What do you think is the* ***point*** *of this exercise?*
6 an opinion or fact expressed by someone • *That's a very good* ***point****.*
7 In mathematics, the decimal **point** in a number is marked by a dot, as in 5.2.
8 one of the 32 marks on the circumference of a compass to show direction

pointed
ADJECTIVE A **pointed** object has a thin, sharp end.

pointless
ADJECTIVE Something that is **pointless** has no purpose.

point of view **points of view**
NOUN Your **point of view** is your opinion about something or your attitude towards it.

poised
ADJECTIVE If you are **poised** to do something, you are ready to do it at any moment.

poison **poisons, poisoning, poisoned**
NOUN **1** a substance that harms or kills you if you swallow it or absorb it
VERB **2** To **poison** someone means to harm them by giving them poison.

poke **pokes, poking, poked**
VERB If you **poke** someone or something, you give them a push with your finger or a sharp object.

poke out
VERB If something **pokes out** from behind or from underneath another thing, it

shows. • *The label **poked out** from the back of his anorak.*

polar
ADJECTIVE relating to the area around the North Pole or the South Pole • *the **polar** regions*

polar bear **polar bears**
NOUN a large white bear that lives in the area around the North Pole

pole **poles**
NOUN **1** a long, slender, rounded piece of wood or metal
2 The earth has two **poles** at the opposite ends of its imaginary axis.
• *the North and South **Pole***

pole vault
NOUN an athletics event in which contestants jump over a high bar using a long, flexible pole to lift themselves into the air

police
PLURAL NOUN the official organization responsible for making sure that people obey the law

police officer **police officers**
NOUN a member of the police force

policy **policies**
NOUN a set of plans and ideas, especially in politics or business • *What is their **policy** on education?*

polish **polishes, polishing, polished**
NOUN **1** a substance that you put on an object to clean it and make it shine
VERB **2** If you **polish** something, you put polish on it or rub it with a cloth to make it shine.

polite
ADJECTIVE Someone who is **polite** has good manners and is not rude to other people.
SYNONYM: courteous

political
ADJECTIVE to do with politics and politicians

politician **politicians**
NOUN a person who is involved in the government of a country

politics
NOUN the activity of governing a country

poll **polls**
NOUN a survey in which people are asked their opinions about something

pollen
NOUN a fine yellow or orange powder produced by the male part of a flowering plant

pollinate **pollinates, pollinating, pollinated**
VERB A plant is **pollinated** when pollen from the male part of another plant lands on its female part. This leads to fertilization and the formation of seeds.

pollination
NOUN the process by which plants are fertilized with pollen

pollute **pollutes, polluting, polluted**
VERB If water, air or land is **polluted**, it is dirty and dangerous to use or live in.

polo
NOUN a game played between two teams of players on horseback. The players use wooden hammers with long handles to hit a ball.

poltergeist **poltergeists**
NOUN a noisy, mischievous ghost that moves or throws things around in a house

poly-
PREFIX added to some words to mean many, for example **poly**gons and **poly**hedrons are many-sided shapes

polyester
NOUN a man-made fibre, especially used to make clothes

A B C D E F G H I J K L M N O P Q R S T U V W X Y Z

polygon **polygons**
NOUN any two-dimensional shape whose sides are all straight

polyhedron **polyhedra**
NOUN a solid shape with many faces

polystyrene
NOUN a very light plastic, especially used as insulating material or to make containers

polythene
NOUN a type of plastic that is used to make thin sheets or bags

pompous
ADJECTIVE Someone who is **pompous** behaves in a way that is too serious and self-important.
pomposity NOUN

pond **ponds**
NOUN a small area of water enclosed by land

ponder **ponders, pondering, pondered**
VERB If you **ponder**, you think carefully and seriously about something.

pony **ponies**
NOUN a small horse

ponytail **ponytails**
NOUN a hairstyle in which long hair is scooped up and tied at the back of the head so that it hangs down like a tail

pool **pools**
NOUN **1** a small area of still water, such as a pond or a puddle
2 an abbreviation of *swimming pool*

poor **poorer, poorest**
ADJECTIVE **1** having very little money
2 of a low quality or standard

poorly
ADJECTIVE **1** If you are **poorly**, you feel ill.
ADVERB **2** If something is done **poorly**, it is not done well.

pop **pops, popping, popped**
NOUN **1** modern music, played and enjoyed especially by young people
2 a short, sharp, explosive sound
3 a fizzy, non-alcoholic drink
VERB **4** If you **pop** somewhere, you go there quickly for a short while. • *I will **pop** in to see you before tea.*

popcorn
NOUN a snack food made from grains of maize that are heated until they puff up and burst

Pope **Popes**
NOUN the head of the Roman Catholic Church

poplar **poplars**
NOUN a type of tall, slender tree

poppadom **poppadoms**
NOUN thin, round, crisp bread, fried or roasted and served with Indian food
[from Tamil *pappadam* meaning lentil cake]

poppy **poppies**
NOUN a plant with a large red flower on a hairy stem, that often grows in cornfields and meadows

popular
ADJECTIVE liked or approved of by a lot of people

populated
ADJECTIVE If a place is **populated**, people or animals live there.

population **populations**
NOUN **1** the people who live in a place
2 the number of people living in a place

porch **porches**
NOUN a covered area at the entrance to a building

porcupine **porcupines**
NOUN a large rodent with long spines covering its body
[from Old French *porc d'espins* meaning pig with spines]

pore **pores, poring, pored**
NOUN **1** The **pores** in your skin or on the surface of a plant are very small holes that allow moisture to pass through.
VERB **2** If you **pore** over a piece of writing or a diagram, you study it carefully.

pork
NOUN meat from a pig

A B C D E F G H I J K L M N O P Q R S T U V W X Y Z

porous
ADJECTIVE If something is **porous**, it lets water through.

porpoise porpoises
NOUN a sea mammal related to the dolphin
[from Latin *porcus* meaning pig and *piscis* meaning fish]

porridge
NOUN a thick, sticky food made from oats cooked in water or milk

port ports
NOUN **1** a town or area that has a harbour or docks
ADJECTIVE **2** The **port** side of a ship is the left side when you are facing the front.

portable
ADJECTIVE designed to be easily carried

porter porters
NOUN a person employed to carry luggage and other goods at a railway station or in a hotel

porthole portholes
NOUN a small window in the side of a ship or aircraft

portion portions
NOUN **1** a part of something
SYNONYMS: bit, piece
2 an amount of food sufficient for one person

portrait portraits
NOUN a picture or photograph of someone, often of only their head and shoulders

pose poses, posing, posed
NOUN **1** a way of standing, sitting or lying for a photograph to be taken, or a drawing or painting to be made of you
• *Try to hold this **pose** while the others draw it.*
VERB **2** If you **pose** for a photograph or painting, you stay in a particular position so that someone can photograph or paint you.
3 If you **pose** as someone or something, you pretend to be someone or something you are not.
4 If something **poses** a problem or danger, it causes it. • *This polluted water could **pose** a threat to their health.*

position positions, positioning, positioned
NOUN **1** When someone or something is in a particular **position**, they are sitting or lying in that way. • *I raised myself to a sitting **position**.*
2 The **position** that you are in is the situation that you are in. • *Your request puts me in a difficult **position**.*
PHRASE **3** If you are **in position** at the beginning of a race, you are ready to start.
VERB **4** If you **position** something, you put it in place.

positive
ADJECTIVE **1** If something is **positive**, it is certain.
2 If someone is **positive**, they are confident and hopeful.

possession possessions
NOUN a thing that you own, or that you have with you

possessive
ADJECTIVE **1** A **possessive** person wants to keep things for themselves.
NOUN **2** In grammar, the **possessive** is the form of a noun or pronoun used to show possession, for example, *my, his, theirs, Harry's*.

possible
ADJECTIVE If something is **possible**, it can be done or can happen.
possibility NOUN

possum possums
NOUN a nocturnal marsupial with thick fur and a long tail that lives in trees

post posts, posting, posted
NOUN **1** the system by which letters and parcels are collected and delivered
2 letters and parcels that are delivered to you
3 an upright pole fixed into the ground
VERB **4** If you **post** a letter, you send it to someone through the post.

postage
NOUN the money that you pay to send letters and parcels by post • *You will need to send extra money for* ***postage*** *and packing.*

post box **post boxes**
NOUN a box into which you put letters that are to be sent by post

postcard **postcards**
NOUN a card, often with a picture on one side, that you write on and send to someone without an envelope

postcode **postcodes**
NOUN a short sequence of letters and numbers at the end of an address

poster **posters**
NOUN a large notice, picture or advertisement that you stick on a wall

postman or **postwoman**
postmen or **postwomen**
NOUN someone who collects and delivers parcels and letters

post office **post offices**
NOUN a building where you can buy stamps and post letters and parcels

postpone **postpones, postponing, postponed**
VERB If you **postpone** an event, you arrange for it to take place at a later time than was originally planned.

potato **potatoes**
NOUN a round, white, root vegetable that has a brown or red skin and grows beneath the ground

potential
ADJECTIVE **1** capable of happening or of becoming a particular kind of person or thing • *He's a* ***potential*** *world champion.*
NOUN **2** If someone or something has **potential**, they are capable of being successful or useful in the future.

pothole **potholes**
NOUN **1** a hole in the surface of a road caused by bad weather or traffic
2 a deep, natural hole in the ground that often leads to an underground cavern

potion **potions**
NOUN a drink containing medicine, poison or supposed magical powers
[from Latin *potio* meaning a drink]

potter **potters, pottering, pottered**
NOUN **1** a person who makes pottery
VERB **2** If you **potter** about, you pass the time doing pleasant, unimportant things.

pottery
NOUN **1** pots, dishes and other items made from clay and fired in a kiln
2 the craft of making pottery

pouch **pouches**
NOUN **1** a small, soft container with a fold-over top, like a bag or a pocket
2 a pocket of skin in which marsupials carry their young

poultry
NOUN chicken, turkeys and other birds that are kept for their meat or eggs

pounce **pounces, pouncing, pounced**
VERB If a person or other animal **pounces** on something, they jump on it suddenly.

pound **pounds, pounding, pounded**
NOUN **1** the main unit of currency in Britain
2 a unit of weight equal to 16 ounces, or about 0.454 kilograms
VERB **3** If you **pound** something, or **pound** on it, you hit it repeatedly or crush it.
4 If your heart **pounds**, it beats very fast and strongly.
5 If you **pound** somewhere, you run there with loud, heavy footsteps.

pour **pours, pouring, poured**
VERB **1** If you **pour** liquid out of a container, you tip the container until the liquid flows out.
2 If something **pours** somewhere, it flows there quickly and in large quantities.
3 If it is **pouring** with rain, it is raining very heavily.

pout **pouts, pouting, pouted**
VERB If you **pout**, you stick out your lips, or

A B C D E F G H I J K L M N O P Q R S T U V W X Y Z

your bottom lip, because you are cross or annoyed.

poverty
NOUN the state of being very poor

powder **powders**
NOUN many tiny particles of a solid, dry substance, such as flour

power **powers**
NOUN **1** control over people and events
2 physical strength
3 the rate at which energy is changed from one form to another, such as electrical energy changed into light or heat

powerful
ADJECTIVE **Powerful** people or organizations have a great deal of power or influence.
powerfully ADVERB

powerless
ADJECTIVE If you are **powerless**, you are unable to control or influence events.
powerlessly ADVERB

power station **power stations**
NOUN a building where electricity is produced

practical
ADJECTIVE **1** Someone who is **practical** is efficient and sensible, and good at getting things done.
2 Something that is **practical** is sensible and useful.
3 involving real situations and doing things, rather than ideas or theories • *We will do some **practical** experiments in Science today.*
[from Greek *praktikos* meaning concerned with action]

practical joke **practical jokes**
NOUN a trick you play on someone

practice **practices**
NOUN **1** regular training or exercise that you do to improve your skill at something
2 A doctor's or lawyer's **practice** is their business.

The noun *practice* ends in *ce*.

practise **practises, practising, practised**
VERB **1** If you **practise** something, you do it regularly in order to do it better.
• *She **practises** every day on the piano.*
2 When people **practise** a religion, custom or craft, they regularly take part in the activities associated with it. • *a custom still **practised** in some areas*
3 If you **practise** medicine or law, you work as a doctor or lawyer.

The verb *practise* ends in *se*.

prairie **prairies**
NOUN a large area of flat, grassy land in North America

praise **praises, praising, praised**
VERB **1** If you **praise** someone or something, you say good things about them, or tell them they have done well.
NOUN **2** what you say or write when you praise someone or something

pram **prams**
NOUN a small carriage, like a baby's cot on wheels, for pushing a baby around in

prank **pranks**
NOUN a childish trick

prawn **prawns**
NOUN a small, edible shellfish with a long tail

pray **prays, praying, prayed**
VERB When someone **prays**, they speak to God, to give thanks or to ask for help.

prayer **prayers**
NOUN the activity of praying or the words said when someone prays

pre-
PREFIX added to some words to mean before a particular time or event, for example **pre**school, **pre**war, **pre**history

preach **preaches, preaching, preached**
VERB When someone **preaches**, they give a short talk on a religious or moral subject.
preacher NOUN

precarious
ADJECTIVE **1** Someone or something in a **precarious** position is not very safe or secure, and they may fall or fail at any time. • *Her position was* ***precarious*** *because she needed only one point to win.*
2 Something that is **precarious** is likely to fall because it is not well balanced or secured.
precariously ADVERB

precaution **precautions**
NOUN an action that is intended to prevent something unwanted or unpleasant from happening

precede **precedes, preceding, preceded**
VERB **1** If one event **precedes** another, it happens before it. • *A short film* ***preceded*** *the talk about elephants.*
2 If you **precede** someone, you go in front of them.

precinct **precincts**
NOUN a pedestrian shopping area

precious
ADJECTIVE Something that is **precious** is valuable or important and should be looked after or used carefully.
[from Latin *pretiosus* meaning valuable]

precipice **precipices**
NOUN a very steep rock face or sheer cliff

precise
ADJECTIVE very accurate • *We will never know the* ***precise*** *details of what happened.*
SYNONYM: exact

predator **predators**
NOUN an animal that kills and eats other animals
predatory ADJECTIVE

predecessor **predecessors**
NOUN Someone's **predecessor** is the person who used to do their job before them.

predicament **predicaments**
NOUN a difficult or awkward situation

predict **predicts, predicting, predicted**
VERB If you **predict** something, you say what you think will happen in the future.

preen **preens, preening, preened**
VERB When a bird **preens**, it cleans and tidies its feathers using its beak.

preface **prefaces**
NOUN an introduction at the beginning of a book, explaining what it is about or why it was written

prefect **prefects**
NOUN a pupil who has special duties at a school
[from Latin *praefectus* meaning someone put in charge]

prefer **prefers, preferring, preferred**
VERB If you **prefer** one thing to another, you like it better than the other thing.

preferable
ADJECTIVE Something that is **preferable** to something else, is more suitable or you like it better than the other thing. • *We thought that going to the cinema was* ***preferable*** *to watching TV.*

prefix **prefixes**
NOUN a letter or group of letters added to the beginning of a word to make a new word, for example *dis-*, *pre-* and *un-*

pregnant
ADJECTIVE A woman or other female animal who is **pregnant** has a baby developing in their womb.

prehistoric
ADJECTIVE existing at a time in the past before anything was written down

prejudice **prejudices**
NOUN an unreasonable and unfair dislike of or preference for a particular person or thing
prejudiced ADJECTIVE

A B C D E F G H I J K L M N O P Q R S T U V W X Y Z

preliminary
ADJECTIVE **Preliminary** activities take place before something starts and in preparation for it. • *They lost in the **preliminary** rounds of the competition.*

prelude **preludes**
NOUN **1** something that happens before an event and prepares you for it
2 a short piece of music

premature
ADJECTIVE happening too early, or earlier than expected • *The **premature** baby had to spend time in hospital to gain weight.*
prematurely ADVERB

premier **premiers**
Said "**prem**-mee-uh" NOUN **1** The leader of a government is sometimes referred to as the **premier**.
2 In Australia, the leader of a State government is called the **Premier**.
ADJECTIVE **3** considered to be the best or most important • *the **premier** department store*
[from Latin *primarius* meaning principal]

premiere **premieres**
Said "**prem**-mee-er" NOUN the first public performance of a new play or film • *The **premiere** of the new film is in London next week.*
[from French *premier* meaning first]

premises
Said "**prem**-is-iz" PLURAL NOUN buildings and land belonging to an organization

premium **premiums**
Said "**pree**-mee-um" NOUN **1** an extra sum of money that has to be paid for something
2 money paid regularly to an insurance company

premonition **premonitions**
NOUN a feeling that something unpleasant is going to happen

preoccupied
ADJECTIVE If you are **preoccupied**, you are deep in thought or totally involved with something, and you do not notice anything else. • *It is difficult to talk to him as he seems so **preoccupied**.*

preparation **preparations**
NOUN **1** **Preparation** is the act of getting things ready.
2 **Preparations** are all the things you do and the arrangements you make before an event can happen. • *We started making **preparations** for the party by buying some decorations.*

prepare **prepares, preparing, prepared**
VERB If you **prepare** something, or **prepare** for something, you get it ready or get ready for it.

preposition **prepositions**
NOUN a word that is used before a noun or pronoun to show how it is connected to other words. For example, in the sentence *I put the book on the table*, the word *on* is the **preposition**.

prescribe **prescribes, prescribing, prescribed**
VERB If a doctor **prescribes** a medicine for a patient, he or she tells the patient what medicine they need and gives them a prescription.

prescription **prescriptions**
NOUN a written instruction from a doctor to a chemist, to provide a person with a particular medicine

presence
NOUN the **presence** of a person in a place is the fact that they are there

present **presents, presenting, presented**
Said "**prez**-ent" ADJECTIVE **1** If someone is **present** at a place or an event, they are there.
2 happening now
SYNONYMS: contemporary, current
NOUN **3** the period of time that is taking place now
4 something that you give to someone for them to keep, especially on their birthday or at Christmas, or on some other special occasion
SYNONYM: gift
Said "pri-**zent**" VERB **5** If you **present** someone with something, or if you

present it to them, you formally give it to them.

presentation **presentations**
NOUN **1** a talk or a lecture showing or describing something
2 a ceremony where awards or prizes are given
3 The **presentation** of something is the way it looks. • *My teacher was pleased with the **presentation** of my project.*

presently
ADVERB If something will happen **presently**, it will happen soon. • *I'll finish the job **presently**.*

preservative **preservatives**
NOUN a substance or a chemical that stops things such as food from going bad

preserve **preserves, preserving, preserved**
VERB If you **preserve** something, you make sure that it stays as it is and does not change or end.

president **presidents**
NOUN The **president** of a country that has no king or queen is the leader of the country. • *the **President** of the United States*

press **presses, pressing, pressed**
VERB **1** If you **press** something, you push it or hold it firmly against something else.
2 If you **press** clothes, you iron them.
3 If you **press** someone to do something, you try to make them do it.
NOUN **4** a machine for printing
5 The **press** is a term used for all the newspapers and the journalists who work for them.

pressure **pressures**
NOUN **1** the amount of force that is pushing on a particular area
2 If there is **pressure** on you to do something, someone is trying to persuade or force you do it.

presume **presumes, presuming, presumed**
VERB If you **presume** something, you think that it is probably true without knowing for certain.
SYNONYMS: believe, suppose
presumption NOUN

pretend **pretends, pretending, pretended**
VERB If you **pretend** that something is the case, you try to make people believe that it is true when it is not.

pretty **prettier, prettiest**
ADJECTIVE **1** attractive and pleasant
ADVERB **2** INFORMAL quite or rather • *He spoke **pretty** good English.*

prevent **prevents, preventing, prevented**
VERB If you **prevent** something, you stop it happening.

preview **previews**
NOUN a showing of something like a film, play or exhibition before it is shown to the general public

previous
ADJECTIVE A **previous** time or thing is one that occurred before the present one. • *I'm happier in this class than I was in the **previous** one.*
previously ADVERB

prey **preys, preying, preyed**
NOUN **1** an animal that is hunted and eaten by another animal
VERB **2** An animal that **preys** on another animal lives by hunting and eating it.

price **prices**
NOUN the amount of money that you pay to buy something • *The **price** of bread has increased significantly.*

priceless
ADJECTIVE Something that is **priceless** is so valuable that it is difficult to work out how much it is worth.

prick **pricks, pricking, pricked**
VERB If you **prick** something, you stick a sharp object into it.

prickle **prickles, prickling, prickled**
NOUN **1** a small sharp point or thorn growing on a plant

A B C D E F G H I J K L M N O P Q R S T U V W X Y Z

VERB **2** If your skin **prickles**, it feels as if a lot of sharp points are being stuck into it.
prickly ADJECTIVE

pride **prides**
NOUN **1** a feeling of satisfaction and pleasure you have when you, or people close to you, have done something well
2 a feeling of dignity and self-respect
3 a group of lions that live together

priest **priests**
NOUN **1** a member of the clergy in some Christian Churches
2 someone who performs religious ceremonies in non-Christian religions

prim **primmer, primmest**
ADJECTIVE Someone who is **prim** always behaves very correctly and is easily shocked by anything rude.

primary
ADJECTIVE extremely important or most important

primary colour **primary colours**
NOUN The **primary colours** are red, yellow and blue. From these all the other colours can be made.

primary school **primary schools**
NOUN a school for children between the ages of 5 and 11

prime
ADJECTIVE **1** main or most important
2 of the best quality
[from Latin *primus* meaning first]

prime minister **prime ministers**
NOUN the leader of the government

primitive
ADJECTIVE **1** connected with a society in which people live very simply
2 very simple, basic or old-fashioned
• *Their accommodation was **primitive**, but they still enjoyed their trip.*

primrose **primroses**
NOUN a small plant that has pale yellow flowers in spring
[from Latin *prima rosa* meaning first rose]

prince **princes**
NOUN a male member of a royal family, especially the son of a king or queen

princess **princesses**
NOUN a female member of a royal family, especially the daughter of a king or queen, or the wife of a prince

principal **principals**
ADJECTIVE **1** main or most important • *He had the **principal** role in the play.*
NOUN **2** the person in charge of a school or college

> Do not confuse *principal* with *principle*.

principle **principles**
NOUN **1** a general rule or law about how something works
2 a belief that you have about the way you should behave • *I try to help others as a matter of **principle**.*

> Do not confuse *principle* with *principal*.

print **prints, printing, printed**
VERB **1** When words or pictures are **printed**, they are put onto paper in large numbers by a printing machine, for example to make books or newspapers.
2 If you **print** your name, or some other writing, you write letters that are not joined up.
NOUN **3** The letters and numbers on the pages of a book or newspaper are referred to as the **print**. • *The columns of tiny **print** were difficult to read.*

printer **printers**
NOUN **1** a person who prints books and newspapers
2 a machine that prints the data from a computer onto paper

print-out **print-outs**
NOUN a printed copy of information from a computer

priority **priorities**
NOUN something that needs to be dealt with first because it is more urgent or important than other things • *He needed to make his homework a **priority**.*

prism **prisms**
NOUN **1** In mathematics, a **prism** is any three- dimensional shape that has the same size and shape of face at each end. A **prism** is the same size and shape along its length.
2 a solid piece of clear glass or plastic with flat sides, that can be used to separate light passing through it into the colours of the rainbow

prison **prisons**
NOUN a building where people who have broken the law are locked up as a punishment

prisoner **prisoners**
NOUN someone who is kept in prison or held in captivity

privacy
NOUN If you have **privacy**, you have somewhere private where you can be alone without being disturbed.

private **privates**
ADJECTIVE **1** for the use of only one person or group of people, rather than for the general public • *The hotel had a* ***private*** *beach.*
2 meant to be kept secret
NOUN **3** a soldier of the lowest rank

privilege **privileges**
NOUN a special right or advantage that is given to a person or group

prize **prizes**
NOUN a reward given to the winner of a competition or game

pro-
PREFIX supporting or being in favour of • *a* ***pro-****animal rights march*
ANTONYM: anti-

probability
NOUN the measure of how likely an event is

probable
ADJECTIVE likely to happen or likely to be true

probably
ADVERB likely but not certainly • *I am* ***probably*** *having a party for my birthday.*

probation
NOUN **1** a period of time during which a person convicted of a crime is supervised by a social worker called a **probation** officer, instead of being sent to prison
2 a period of time when someone is tried out to see if they are suitable for a particular job

probe **probes, probing, probed**
VERB **1** If you **probe**, you investigate something, often by asking a lot of questions to discover the facts about it.
2 If you **probe** something, you gently push a long, thin instrument into it, usually to find something.
NOUN **3** a long, thin instrument used to look closely at something
[from Latin *probare* meaning to test]

problem **problems**
NOUN **1** an unsatisfactory situation that causes difficulties
SYNONYMS: difficulty, predicament
2 a puzzle or question that you solve using logical thought or mathematics

procedure **procedures**
NOUN a way of doing something, especially the correct or usual way • *The entire* ***procedure*** *takes about 15 minutes.*

proceed **proceeds, proceeding, proceeded**
Said "pro-**seed**" VERB **1** If you **proceed** to do something, you do it after doing something else. • *He then* ***proceeded*** *to tell us the story.*

A B C D E F G H I J K L M N O P Q R S T U V W X Y Z

2 If you **proceed**, you move in a particular direction. • *We* ***proceeded*** *along the corridor.*
Said "**pro**-seedz" PLURAL NOUN **3** The **proceeds** of an event are the money that is obtained from it. • *The* ***proceeds*** *from the concert will go towards famine relief.*
[from Latin *pro* + *cedere* meaning to go onward]

process **processes, processing, processed**
NOUN **1** a series of actions or events that have a particular result
PHRASE **2** If you are **in the process** of doing something, you have started doing it but have not yet finished.
VERB **3** You **process** something when you put it through a series of actions in order to have a particular result. For example, you **process** milk to pasteurize it.

procession **processions**
NOUN a group of people or vehicles moving together in a line, often as part of a ceremony • *There was a* ***procession*** *of musicians along the high street on Sunday.*

proclaim **proclaims, proclaiming, proclaimed**
VERB If someone **proclaims** something, they announce it or make it known publicly.
proclamation NOUN

prod **prods, prodding, prodded**
VERB If you **prod** something or somebody, you give them a poke with your finger.

produce **produces, producing, produced**
Said "pro-**dewss**" VERB **1** If someone or something **produces** something, they make it or cause it to happen.
2 If you **produce** something from somewhere, you bring it out so that it can be seen. • *The magician* ***produced*** *a rabbit out of the hat.*
3 If you **produce** a film, play or other form of entertainment, you are in charge of organizing it.
Said "**prod**-yooss" NOUN **4** food that is grown to be sold

producer **producers**
NOUN The **producer** of a record, film, play or programme is the person in charge of making it or putting it on. • *a television* ***producer***

product **products**
NOUN **1** something that is made or produced to be sold
2 The **product** is the answer to a multiplication sum. • *The* ***product*** *of 4 and 6 is 24.*

production **productions**
NOUN **1** the process of manufacturing or growing something in large quantities
2 a version of something such as a play or a film

profession **professions**
NOUN a job for which you need special training and education • *the medical* ***profession*** • *the teaching* ***profession***

professional **professionals**
ADJECTIVE **1** **Professional** is used to describe activities that are done to earn money rather than as a hobby.
• *He earns a lot of money as a* ***professional*** *footballer.*
2 You can use **professional** to describe work that is of a very high standard.
NOUN **3** someone who does a particular type of work to earn money

professor **professors**
NOUN the most senior teacher in a department of a British university, or a teacher at an American college or university

proficient
ADJECTIVE If you are **proficient** at something, you can do it well. • *I am pleased to see how* ***proficient*** *you are in reading.*
proficiency NOUN

profile **profiles**
NOUN the outline of a face seen from the side
[from Italian *profilare* meaning to sketch lightly]

profit **profits, profiting, profited**
NOUN **1** an amount of money that you gain when you are paid more for something than it cost to buy or make
VERB **2** If you **profit** from something, you gain or benefit from it. • *I think you will **profit** from some extra lessons.*

profound
ADJECTIVE **1** very deep or intense • *discoveries that have a **profound** effect on life today*
2 showing or needing deep thought or understanding • *He asked a **profound** question for someone of his age.*

program **programs, programming, programmed**
NOUN **1** a set of instructions that a computer follows in order to perform particular tasks
VERB **2** When someone **programs** a computer, they prepare a program and put it into the computer.

programme **programmes**
NOUN **1** something that is broadcast on television or radio
2 a planned series of events
3 a booklet giving information about a play, concert or show

progress **progresses, progressing, progressed**
Said "**proh**-gress" NOUN **1** the process of gradually improving or getting near to achieving something
Said "pro-**gress**" VERB **2** If you **progress**, you become more advanced or skilful at something.
3 to continue or move forward • *As the trip **progressed**, I began to feel sick.*

prohibit **prohibits, prohibiting, prohibited**
VERB If someone **prohibits** something, they forbid it or make it illegal. • *Visitors are prohibited from smoking.*

project **projects, projecting, projected**
Said "**proj**-ekt" NOUN **1** a carefully planned task that requires a lot of time or effort
Said "pro-**jekt**" VERB **2** If you **project** an image onto a screen, you make it appear there using a projector.
3 If something **projects**, it sticks out.

projector **projectors**
NOUN a piece of equipment that produces a large image on a screen by shining light through a photographic slide or film strip

prologue **prologues**
Said "**pro**-log" NOUN a short piece of writing at the beginning of a book, or a speech that introduces a play

prolong **prolongs, prolonging, prolonged**
VERB If you **prolong** something, you make it last longer. • *We **prolonged** the holiday.*

promenade **promenades**
Said "prom-un-**ahd**" NOUN a path or road by the sea for walking along

prominent
ADJECTIVE **1** A **prominent** person is important or well known.
2 very noticeable • *The church is a **prominent** landmark.*
[from Latin *prominere* meaning to stick out]

promise **promises, promising, promised**
VERB **1** If you **promise** to do something, you say that you will definitely do it.
NOUN **2** a statement made by someone that they will definitely do something
3 Someone or something that shows **promise** seems likely to be successful in the future.

promising
ADJECTIVE likely to be successful or good

promote **promotes, promoting, promoted**
VERB **1** If someone **promotes** something, they try to make it happen, or become more popular or successful.
2 If someone is **promoted**, they are given a more important job at work.

prompt **prompts, prompting, prompted**
VERB **1** If something or someone **prompts** you to do something, they encourage you or make you decide to do it.

A B C D E F G H I J K L M N O P Q R S T U V W X Y Z

2 If you **prompt** an actor, you remind them of their lines in a play if they forget them.
ADJECTIVE **3** A **prompt** action is done immediately, without any delay.

prone

ADJECTIVE **1** If you are **prone** to something, you have a tendency to be affected by it or to do it. • *I am **prone** to catching colds in the winter.*
2 If you are **prone**, you are lying flat and face downwards.

prong **prongs**

NOUN The **prongs** of a fork are the long pointed parts.

pronoun **pronouns**

NOUN a word that is used to replace a noun. **Pronouns** are used instead of naming a person or a thing. *He*, *she* and *them* are all examples of **pronouns**.

pronounce **pronounces, pronouncing, pronounced**

VERB **1** When you **pronounce** a word, you say it.
2 When someone **pronounces** something, they state or announce it formally.

pronunciation **pronunciations**

NOUN the way a word is usually said

proof

NOUN If you have **proof** of something, you have evidence which shows that it is true or exists.
SYNONYM: confirmation

prop **props, propping, propped**

VERB **1** If you **prop** an object somewhere, you lean it against something for support.
NOUN **2** an object, such as a piece of wood or metal, used to support something
3 an object or piece of furniture used on stage in the theatre, or on a film set

propaganda

NOUN information, sometimes untrue and often exaggerated, that is used by political groups to influence people

propel **propels, propelling, propelled**

VERB To **propel** something is to push it forward.

propeller

propellers
NOUN a device on a boat or aircraft with rotating blades, that makes the boat or aircraft move

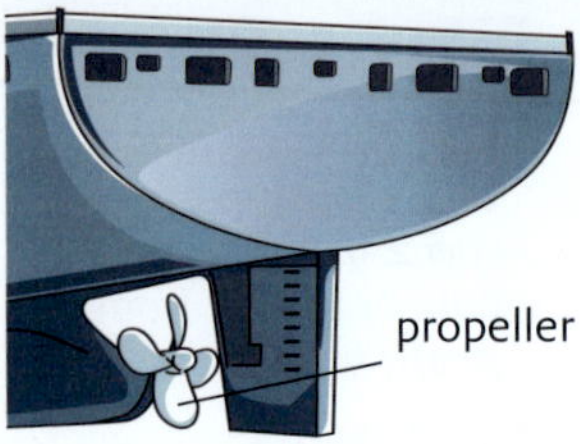

proper

ADJECTIVE If you do something in the **proper** way, you do it correctly.

properly

ADVERB If something is done **properly**, it is done correctly and to the right standard.

proper noun **proper nouns**

NOUN A proper noun is the name of a person, place or institution, and usually starts with a capital letter. For example, *Mary*, *London* and the *Statue of Liberty* are all **proper nouns**.
See **noun**

property **properties**

NOUN **1** A person's **property** is something, or all the things, that belong to them.
2 A **property** is a building and the land around it.
3 a characteristic that something has • *A **property** of mint is its strong smell.*
[from Latin *proprietas* meaning something personal]

prophet **prophets**

NOUN a person who predicts what will happen in the future

proportion **proportions**

NOUN **1** part of an amount or group
2 The **proportion** of one amount to another is its size in relation to the whole amount, usually expressed as a fraction or percentage. • *The **proportion** of boys in the school is 58%.*

propose **proposes, proposing, proposed**

VERB **1** If you **propose** a plan or idea, you suggest it.
2 If you **propose** to someone, you ask them to marry you.

proprietor **proprietors**
NOUN the owner of a shop or business

prose
NOUN ordinary written language, rather than poetry

prosecute **prosecutes, prosecuting, prosecuted**
VERB If someone is **prosecuted**, they are charged with a crime and put on trial.

prospect **prospects, prospecting, prospected**
NOUN **1** something that may happen in the future
2 Your **prospects** are your chances of being successful in the future. • *If she works hard at school, her **prospects** are good.*
VERB **3** When people **prospect** for gold, oil or other minerals, they search for them.
prospector NOUN

prosper **prospers, prospering, prospered**
VERB When people or businesses **prosper**, they are successful and make money.
prosperous ADJECTIVE **prosperity** NOUN

protect **protects, protecting, protected**
VERB If you **protect** someone or something, you prevent them from being harmed.

protein **proteins**
NOUN a substance that is found in meat, eggs and milk. It is needed by your body to make you grow and keep you healthy.

protest **protests, protesting, protested**
Said "pro-**test**" VERB **1** If you **protest**, you say or do something to show that you strongly disapprove of something.
Said "**pro**-test" NOUN **2** a demonstration or statement to show that you strongly disapprove of something

Protestant **Protestants**
NOUN someone who belongs to the branch of the Christian Church that separated from the Catholic Church in the sixteenth century

protractor **protractors**
NOUN a flat, semicircular instrument used for measuring angles

protrude **protrudes, protruding, protruded**
VERB FORMAL If something **protrudes** from a surface or edge, it sticks out. • *The handle of his racket **protruded** from his sports bag.*
protrusion NOUN

proud **prouder, proudest**
ADJECTIVE **1** If you are **proud** of something, you feel satisfaction and pleasure because of something you own or have achieved.
2 Someone who is **proud** has a lot of dignity and self-respect.

prove **proves, proving, proved** or **proven**
VERB If you **prove** that something is true, you show by means of argument or evidence that it is definitely true.
SYNONYMS: confirm, verify

proverb **proverbs**
NOUN a short, well-known saying that gives advice or makes a comment about life. For example, *A stitch in time saves nine.*
proverbial ADJECTIVE

provide **provides, providing, provided**
VERB If you **provide** something for someone, you give it to them or make it available to them.

province **provinces**
NOUN one of the areas into which some large countries are divided • *Each **province** has its own administration.*

provision **provisions**
NOUN the act of supplying or making something available to people

provisional
ADJECTIVE A **provisional** arrangement is one that has been agreed on for the time being, but has not yet been made definite.

provisions
PLURAL NOUN supplies of food and drink

provoke **provokes, provoking, provoked**
VERB **1** If you **provoke** someone, you deliberately try to make them angry.
2 If something **provokes** a reaction or feeling, it causes it.
provocation NOUN **provocative** ADJECTIVE

prow **prows**
NOUN the front part of a boat or ship

prowl **prowls, prowling, prowled**
VERB If a person or animal **prowls** around, they move around quietly and secretly, as if hunting.

proximity
NOUN FORMAL nearness to someone or something • *I lost my bag in the **proximity** of the swimming pool.*

prune **prunes, pruning, pruned**
NOUN **1** a dried plum
VERB **2** When someone **prunes** a tree or shrub, they cut back some of the branches to make it grow well.

pry **pries, prying, pried**
VERB If someone **pries**, they try to find out about something secret or private.

PS
PS is written at the end of a letter to give an extra message. It is an abbreviation of *postscript*.
[from Latin *postscribere* meaning to write (*scribere*) after (*post*)]

psalm **psalms**
NOUN one of the 150 songs, poems and prayers that form the Book of **Psalms** in the Bible
[from Greek *psalmos* meaning song accompanied on the harp]

pseudonym **pseudonyms**
NOUN a false name an author uses rather than using their real name

psychiatry
Said "sy-**ky**-a-tree" NOUN the branch of medicine concerned with mental illness
[from Greek *psukhē* meaning mind and *iatros* meaning healer]
psychiatrist NOUN **psychiatric** ADJECTIVE

psychic
ADJECTIVE having unusual mental powers, such as the ability to read people's minds or predict the future

psychology
NOUN the scientific study of the mind and of the reasons for people's behaviour

PTO
an abbreviation of *please turn over*. **PTO** is written at the bottom of a page to show that there is more writing on the other side.

pub **pubs**
NOUN a place where people go to buy and drink alcoholic and other drinks, and to talk to their friends. **Pub** is an abbreviation of *public house*.

puberty
NOUN the stage when a person's body changes from that of a child into that of an adult

public
NOUN **1** You can refer to people in general as the **public**. • *The castle is open to the **public** on Sundays.*
ADJECTIVE **2** relating to people in general • ***public** opinion*
3 provided for everyone to use • *We try to use **public** transport whenever possible.*

publication **publications**
NOUN **1** The **publication** of a book is the act of printing it and making it available.
2 a book, newspaper or magazine

publicity
NOUN information or advertisements about an item or event to attract attention to it

public school **public schools**
NOUN **1** In England and Wales, a **public school** is a private secondary school that charges fees.
2 In Scotland and America, a **public school** is a state school.

publish **publishes, publishing, published**
VERB **1** When a company **publishes** a

book, newspaper or magazine, they print copies of it and distribute it.
2 When a newspaper or magazine **publishes** an article or photograph, they print it.

pudding **puddings**
NOUN **1** a cooked sweet food, often made with flour and eggs, and usually served hot
2 You can refer to the sweet course of a meal as the **pudding**.

puddle **puddles**
NOUN a small shallow pool of rain water or other liquid

puff **puffs, puffing, puffed**
VERB **1** If you are **puffing**, you are breathing loudly and quickly with your mouth open.
2 If something **puffs out** *or* **puffs up**, it swells and becomes larger and rounder.
NOUN **3** a small blast of air, smoke or steam • *The car let out a* ***puff*** *of smoke before it sped away.*

pull **pulls, pulling, pulled**
VERB **1** If you **pull** something, you get hold of it and move it towards you with force.
2 If a vehicle or an animal **pulls** something, they move it along behind them.
3 When you **pull** the curtains, you move them across a window.
4 If you **pull** a muscle, you damage it temporarily by stretching it too much.
5 If someone **pulls down** a building, they demolish it.
6 If you **pull out** of an activity, you decide not to do it.

pulley **pulleys**
NOUN a piece of machinery with a wheel and chain or rope over it, used for lifting heavy things

pullover **pullovers**
NOUN a knitted piece of clothing, put on over your head, that covers the top part of your body

pulpit **pulpits**
NOUN the small raised platform in a church or cathedral where a member of the clergy stands to preach

pulse **pulses**
NOUN **1** the regular beating of your heart as it pumps blood through your body. You can feel your **pulse** at your wrists and some other places on your body.
2 Your **pulse** rate is a measure of how fast your heart is beating.

pump **pumps, pumping, pumped**
NOUN **1** a machine that is used to force a liquid or gas to move in a particular direction
VERB **2** If someone or something **pumps** a liquid or gas somewhere, they force it to flow in that direction, using a pump.

pumpkin **pumpkins**
NOUN a very large, round, orange vegetable

pun **puns**
NOUN a clever and amusing use of words so that what you say has two different meanings

punch **punches, punching, punched**
VERB **1** If you **punch** someone or something, you hit them hard with your fist.
NOUN **2** a hard blow with the fist

punchline **punchlines**
NOUN The **punchline** of a joke or a story is the last part, that makes it funny.

punctual
ADJECTIVE arriving at the correct time
SYNONYMS: on time, prompt
punctually ADVERB **punctuality** NOUN

punctuation
NOUN the marks in writing that make it easier to understand, such as full stops, question marks and commas

puncture **punctures**
NOUN a small hole in a car or bicycle tyre, made by a sharp object

pungent
ADJECTIVE having a strong, unpleasant smell or taste
pungency NOUN

A B C D E F G H I J K L M N O P Q R S T U V W X Y Z

punish **punishes, punishing, punished**
VERB To **punish** someone means to make them suffer for doing wrong.
punishment NOUN

puny **punier, puniest**
ADJECTIVE very small and weak

pupa **pupae**
NOUN an insect at the stage of development between a larva and a fully grown adult
SYNONYM: chrysalis

pupil **pupils**
NOUN **1** The **pupils** at a school are the children who attend it.
2 Your **pupils** are the small, round, black holes in the centre of your eyes.

puppet **puppets**
NOUN a doll that can be moved by pulling strings or by putting your hand inside its body

puppy **puppies**
NOUN a young dog

purchase **purchases, purchasing, purchased**
VERB **1** When you **purchase** something, you buy it.
NOUN **2** something that you have bought

pure **purer, purest**
ADJECTIVE **1** Something that is **pure** is not mixed with anything else.
2 clean and free from harmful substances

purify **purifies, purifying, purified**
VERB If someone **purifies** something, they remove all dirty or harmful substances from it.
purification NOUN

purple
ADJECTIVE OR NOUN reddish-blue

purpose **purposes**
NOUN **1** the reason for something
2 the thing that you want to achieve
PHRASE **3** If you do something **on purpose**, you do it deliberately.

purr **purrs, purring, purred**
VERB When a cat **purrs**, it makes a low vibrating sound because it is contented.

purse **purses**
NOUN **1** a container, usually made of leather, plastic or fabric and like a very small bag, for carrying money and credit cards
2 In American English, a **purse** is a handbag.

pursue **pursues, pursuing, pursued**
VERB **1** If you **pursue** someone, you follow them in order to catch them.
2 If you **pursue** an activity or plan, you try to achieve it.

pus
NOUN a thick yellowish liquid that forms in an infected wound or a boil

push **pushes, pushing, pushed**
VERB If you **push** someone or something, you use force to move them away from you.

pushchair **pushchairs**
NOUN a small folding chair on wheels in which a baby or a toddler can be pushed along

put **puts, putting, put**
VERB **1** If you **put** something somewhere, you move it into that position.
2 If you **put** an idea in a particular way, you express it.
PHRASE **3** If you **put off** doing something, you delay it.
4 If you **put out** the light, you switch it off.
5 If you **put up** with something, you let it happen without complaining.

putt **putts**
NOUN In golf, a **putt** is a gentle stroke made when the ball is near the hole.

putty
NOUN a paste used to fix panes of glass into frames

puzzle **puzzles, puzzling, puzzled**
VERB **1** If something **puzzles** you, it confuses you and you do not understand it.

NOUN **2** a game or question that requires a lot of thought to complete or solve

PVC
NOUN a plastic material used for making various things, including clothing, drainpipes and tiles. **PVC** is an abbreviation of *polyvinyl chloride*.

pyjamas
PLURAL NOUN loose trousers and a loose jacket that you wear in bed
[from Persian *pay jama* meaning leg clothing]

pylon **pylons**
NOUN a tall metal structure that carries overhead electricity cables

pyramid **pyramids**
NOUN **1** a three-dimensional shape with a flat base and flat triangular sides sloping upwards to a point
2 an ancient stone structure in this shape, built over the tombs of Egyptian kings and queens

python **pythons**
NOUN a large snake that kills other animals by squeezing them with its body
[from Greek *Puthon*, a huge mythical serpent]

Qq

quack **quacks, quacking, quacked**
VERB **1** When a duck **quacks**, it makes a loud harsh sound.
NOUN **2** A **quack** is the sound made by a duck.

quadrangle **quadrangles**
NOUN **1** a courtyard with buildings all round it
2 In geometry, a **quadrangle** is a four-sided shape.

quadrant **quadrants**
NOUN a quarter of a circle

quadrilateral **quadrilaterals**
NOUN a plane shape with four straight sides

quadruplet **quadruplets**
NOUN one of four children born at the same time to the same mother

quail **quails**
NOUN a type of small game bird with a round body and a short tail

quaint **quainter, quaintest**
ADJECTIVE If something is **quaint**, it is attractive and charming in an old-fashioned or unusual way. • *The **quaint** little village was filled with thatched cottages.*

quake **quakes, quaking, quaked**
VERB **1** If you **quake**, you tremble because you are very frightened.
2 If the ground **quakes**, it moves, usually because of an earthquake.
NOUN **3** an abbreviation of *earthquake*

Quaker **Quakers**
NOUN a member of a Christian group called the Society of Friends, that gathers together for peaceful thought and prayer

qualification **qualifications**
NOUN Your **qualifications** are your skills and achievements. You gain **qualifications** by passing tests and examinations.

qualify **qualifies, qualifying, qualified**
VERB If you **qualify**, you pass examinations and gain qualifications, often for a particular job. • *After many years of study and training, she* ***qualified*** *as a doctor.*

quality
NOUN The **quality** of something is how good it is.

quantity **quantities**
NOUN an amount that you can measure or count

quarantine
Said "**kwo**-ran-teen" NOUN a period of time that a person or animal has to spend apart from others to prevent the possible spread of disease
[from Italian *quarantina* meaning forty days]

quarrel **quarrels, quarrelling, quarrelled**
NOUN **1** an angry argument
VERB **2** If people **quarrel**, they have an angry argument.

quarry **quarries**
NOUN a place where stone is removed from the ground by digging or blasting

quart **quarts**
Said "**kwort**" NOUN a unit of liquid volume equal to two pints or about 1.136 litres

quarter **quarters**
NOUN **1** one of four equal parts of something
2 When you are telling the time, **quarter** means fifteen minutes before or after the hour. • *The programme starts at a* ***quarter*** *to six, and finishes at a* ***quarter*** *past.*
3 an American or Canadian coin worth 25 cents, which is a **quarter** of a dollar

quartet **quartets**
NOUN **1** a group of four musicians who sing or play together
2 a piece of music written for four instruments or singers

quartz
NOUN a type of hard, shiny crystal used in making very accurate watches and clocks

quay **quays**
NOUN a place where boats are tied up and loaded or unloaded

queasy **queasier, queasiest**
ADJECTIVE If you feel **queasy**, you feel slightly sick.

queen **queens**
NOUN a female monarch or a woman married to a king

queer **queerer, queerest**
ADJECTIVE very strange

quench **quenches, quenching, quenched**
VERB If you **quench** your thirst, you have a drink so that you are no longer thirsty.

query **queries**
NOUN a question • *I cannot answer your* ***query****.*

quest **quests**
NOUN a long search for something

question **questions, questioning, questioned**
NOUN **1** a sentence that asks for information
VERB **2** If you **question** someone, you ask them questions.
PHRASE **3** If something is **out of the question**, it is impossible and not worth considering.

question mark **question marks**
NOUN a punctuation mark (?) used at the end of a question

questionnaire **questionnaires**
NOUN a list of questions that people fill in as part of a survey

queue **queues, queuing** or **queueing, queued**
NOUN **1** a line of people or vehicles that are waiting for something
VERB **2** When people **queue**, or **queue up**, they stand in a line waiting for something.

> *Queuing* and *queueing* are both correct spellings.

quibble **quibbles, quibbling, quibbled**
VERB If you **quibble** about something, you argue about something that is not very important.

quiche **quiches**
Said "**keesh**" NOUN a tart with a savoury filling made of eggs

quick **quicker, quickest**
ADJECTIVE If you are **quick**, you move or do things with great speed.

quicksand **quicksands**
NOUN an area of deep, wet sand that you sink into if you walk on it

quid
NOUN INFORMAL In British English, a **quid** is a pound in money.

quiet **quieter, quietest**
ADJECTIVE **1** If someone or something is **quiet**, they are not making much noise, or they are not making any noise at all.
2 A **quiet** place, time or situation is calm and peaceful.
NOUN **3** silence

quill **quills**
NOUN **1** a pen made from a feather
2 A bird's **quills** are the large feathers on its wings and tail.
3 A porcupine's **quills** are its spines.

quilt **quilts**
NOUN a thick, soft, warm cover for a bed, usually padded

quit **quits, quitting, quit**
VERB If you **quit** something, you leave it or stop doing it.

quite
ADVERB fairly but not very • *She's **quite** old, but not as old as my grandma.*

quiver **quivers, quivering, quivered**
VERB **1** If something **quivers**, it trembles. • *The leaves on the trees **quivered** in the breeze.*
NOUN **2** a container for carrying arrows

quiz **quizzes**
NOUN a game in which someone tests your knowledge by asking you questions

quota **quotas**
NOUN a number or quantity of something that is allowed by the rules • *We have already had our **quota** of class outings for this term.*
[from Latin *quot* meaning how many]

quotation **quotations**
NOUN a small part of a piece of writing taken from a book or speech

quotation marks
PLURAL NOUN the punctuation marks (" " ' ') that show where written speech or quotations begin and end

quote **quotes, quoting, quoted**
VERB If you **quote** something that someone has written or said, you repeat their words.

quotient **quotients**
NOUN the number of times one number can be divided into another. For example, in 42 ÷ 6 = 7, 7 is the **quotient**.

Qur'an
NOUN another spelling of **Koran**

Rr

rabbi **rabbis**
NOUN a Jewish religious leader

rabbit **rabbits**
NOUN a small furry rodent with long ears

rabies
NOUN a disease that causes humans and some other animals, especially dogs, to go mad and die

race **races, racing, raced**
NOUN **1** a competition to see who is fastest at something
2 a large group of people who look alike in some way. Different **races** have, for example, different skin colour or differently shaped eyes.
VERB **3** If you **race**, you take part in a race. • *She has **raced** against some of the best in the world.*
4 If you **race** somewhere, you go there as quickly as possible. • *He **raced** after the others.*

racehorse **racehorses**
NOUN a horse that is trained to run fast for races

racial
ADJECTIVE to do with the different races that people belong to
racially ADVERB

racism
Said "**ray**-sizm" NOUN **1** hostility shown by one race of people to another
2 believing that one race of people is better than all others
racist NOUN OR ADJECTIVE

rack **racks**
NOUN a piece of equipment for holding things or hanging things on

racket **rackets**
NOUN **1** a bat with an oval frame and strings across and down it, used in games like tennis
2 If someone is making a **racket**, they are making a lot of noise.

radar
NOUN a way of discovering the position or speed of objects, such as ships or aircraft, by using radio signals
[an abbreviation for *radio detecting and ranging*]

radiant
ADJECTIVE **1** shining or sparkling
2 Someone who is **radiant** looks beautiful because they are so happy.

radiate **radiates, radiating, radiated**
VERB **1** Things that **radiate** from something come out in lines from a central point, like the spokes of a wheel or the sun's rays.
2 When a fire or a light **radiates** heat or light, it gives them out.

radiation
NOUN **1** very small particles given out by radioactive substances
2 the heat and light energy given out from a source such as the sun

radiator **radiators**
NOUN **1** a hollow metal device filled with hot water for heating a room
2 the part of a car that is filled with water to cool the engine

radio **radios**
NOUN **1** a system of sending sound over a distance by transmitting electrical signals
2 the broadcasting of programmes for the public to listen to by radio
3 a piece of equipment for listening to radio programmes • *They are in daily **radio** contact with the expedition.*
4 a piece of equipment for sending and receiving **radio** messages • *A policeman raised the alarm on his **radio**.*

radioactive
ADJECTIVE **Radioactive** substances give out energy in the form of powerful and harmful rays.

radish **radishes**
NOUN a small salad vegetable with a red skin and white flesh, and with a hot taste

radius **radii**
NOUN **1** a straight line going from the centre of a circle to the outside edge
2 the length of a straight line going from the centre of a circle to the outside edge

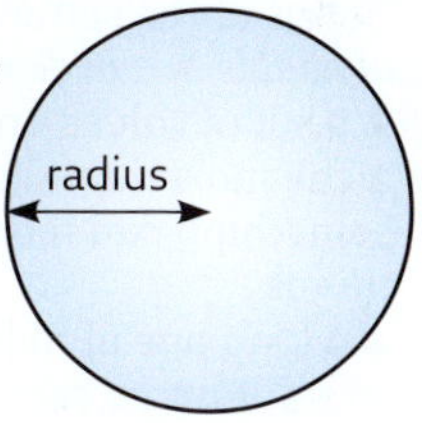

raffle **raffles, raffling, raffled**
NOUN **1** a competition in which people buy numbered tickets and win a prize if their ticket is chosen
VERB **2** If you **raffle** something, you give it as a prize in a raffle.

raft **rafts**
NOUN a floating platform made from long pieces of wood tied together

rafter **rafters**
NOUN the sloping pieces of wood that support a roof

rag **rags**
NOUN **1** a piece of old cloth used to wipe or clean things
2 If someone is dressed in **rags**, they are wearing very old, torn clothes.

rage **rages, raging, raged**
NOUN **1** strong, uncontrollable anger
SYNONYMS: anger, fury, wrath
VERB **2** If something such as a storm or battle **rages**, it continues with great force or violence.

ragged
ADJECTIVE torn or frayed, with rough edges

raid **raids, raiding, raided**
VERB **1** When people **raid** a place, they enter it by force in order to attack it or to look for something or someone.
NOUN **2** a sudden, surprise attack

rail **rails**
NOUN **1** a fixed bar that you can hang things on
2 one of the heavy metal bars that trains run along

railings
PLURAL NOUN a series of metal bars that make up a fence

railway **railways**
NOUN a route along which trains travel on metal tracks

rain **rains, raining, rained**
NOUN **1** water falling from the clouds in small drops
VERB **2** When it **rains**, small drops of water fall from clouds in the sky.

Do not confuse *rain* with *rein* or *reign*.

rainbow **rainbows**
NOUN an arch of different colours that sometimes appears in the sky after it has been raining

raincoat **raincoats**
NOUN a waterproof coat

rainfall
NOUN the amount of rain that falls in one place during a particular period of time

rainforest **rainforests**
NOUN a dense forest of tall trees that grows in a tropical area where there is a lot of rain

raise **raises, raising, raised**
VERB **1** If you **raise** something, you make it higher. • *He **raised** his hand.*
2 If you **raise** your voice, you speak more loudly.
3 If you **raise** money for something, you get people to give money towards it.

raisin **raisins**
NOUN a dried grape

rake **rakes**
NOUN a garden tool with a row of metal teeth and a long handle, for collecting together dead leaves or cut grass

rally **rallies**
NOUN **1** a competition in which vehicles race along public roads
2 a large public meeting

A B C D E F G H I J K L M N O P Q R S T U V W X Y Z

3 In tennis or squash, a **rally** is a continuous series of shots exchanged by the players.

ram **rams, ramming, rammed**
VERB **1** If you **ram** something somewhere, you push it there firmly. • *She* ***rammed*** *her purse into her bag as she ran for the bus.*
2 If one vehicle **rams** another, it crashes into it.
NOUN **3** an adult male sheep

Ramadan
NOUN the ninth month of the Muslim year, during which Muslims eat and drink nothing during daylight
[from Arabic *Ramadan* meaning be hot, as the fasting takes place during a hot month]

ramble **rambles, rambling, rambled**
NOUN **1** a long walk in the countryside
VERB **2** to go for a ramble
3 If you **ramble**, you talk in a confused way.
rambler NOUN

ramp **ramps**
NOUN a sloping surface linking two places that are at different levels

rampage **rampages, rampaging, rampaged**
VERB If you **rampage**, you rush about wildly, causing damage.

rampart **ramparts**
NOUN an earth bank, often with a wall on top, built to protect a castle or city

ramshackle
ADJECTIVE A **ramshackle** building is in very poor condition.

ran
VERB the past tense of **run**

ranch **ranches**
NOUN a large farm where cattle or horses are reared, especially in the USA

random
ADJECTIVE OR NOUN Something that is done in a **random** way, or at **random**, is done by chance or without a definite plan.
SYNONYMS: chance, haphazard

rang
VERB the past tense of **ring**

range **ranges, ranging, ranged**
NOUN **1** a selection or choice of different things of the same kind • *This top is available in a wide* ***range*** *of colours.*
2 a set of values on a scale
3 the maximum distance over which something can reach things or detect things
4 a long line of hills or mountains
VERB **5** When a set of things **ranges** between two points, they vary within these points on a scale.

ranger **rangers**
NOUN someone whose job is to look after a forest or park

rank **ranks**
NOUN **1** a position or grade that someone holds in an organization
2 a row of people or things • *We went to the taxi* ***rank*** *outside the station to catch a taxi home.*

ransack **ransacks, ransacking, ransacked**
VERB If you **ransack** a place, you disturb everything in order to search for or steal something, and leave it in a mess.

ransom **ransoms**
NOUN money that is demanded by kidnappers to free someone they have taken hostage

rap **raps, rapping, rapped**
NOUN **1** a quick knock or blow on something • *There was a sharp* ***rap*** *on the door.*
2 a type of music in which the words are spoken in a rapid, rhythmic way
VERB **3** If you **rap** something, or **rap** on it, you hit it with a series of quick blows.

rapid
ADJECTIVE happening or moving very quickly

rapier **rapiers**
NOUN a long thin sword with a sharp point

rare **rarer, rarest**
ADJECTIVE **1** Something that is **rare** is not common or does not often happen.
2 Meat that is **rare** is cooked very lightly.

rascal **rascals**
NOUN someone who does naughty or mischievous things

rash **rashes**
NOUN **1** an area of red spots that appear on your skin when you are ill or have an allergy
ADJECTIVE **2** If you are **rash**, you do something without thinking properly about it.

rasher **rashers**
NOUN a thin slice of bacon

raspberry **raspberries**
NOUN a small soft red fruit that grows on a bush

rat **rats**
NOUN a rodent with a long tail, that looks like a large mouse

rate **rates**
NOUN how quickly or slowly, or how often something happens

rather
ADVERB **1** fairly, or to a certain extent • ***rather*** *large*
2 If you would **rather** do one thing than another, you would prefer to do it. • *I don't want to go out. I'd* ***rather*** *stay here.*

ratio **ratios**
NOUN The **ratio** between two things shows how many times one is bigger than another. A **ratio** is used to compare two or more quantities, for example, if a class has 15 boys and 10 girls, the **ratio** of boys to girls is 15 to 10.

ration **rations, rationing, rationed**
NOUN **1** the amount of something you are allowed to have
VERB **2** When something is **rationed**, you are only allowed a limited amount of it because there is a shortage.
rationing NOUN

rational
Said "**rash**-un-ul" ADJECTIVE well thought out, sensible and reasonable • *It was a* ***rational*** *decision.*
ANTONYM: irrational

rattle **rattles, rattling, rattled**
VERB When something **rattles**, or when you **rattle** it, it makes short, regular knocking sounds, for example because it is shaking.

rattlesnake **rattlesnakes**
NOUN a poisonous American snake that can rattle its tail

rave **raves, raving, raved**
VERB **1** If someone **raves**, they talk in an excited and uncontrolled way.
2 INFORMAL If you **rave** about something, you talk about it very enthusiastically.
NOUN **3** INFORMAL a large dance event with electronic music

raven **ravens**
NOUN **1** a large black bird with a deep, harsh call
ADJECTIVE **2** **Raven** hair is black and shiny.

ravenous
ADJECTIVE very hungry
ravenously ADVERB

ravine **ravines**
NOUN a deep, narrow valley with steep sides

ravioli
NOUN an Italian dish made of small squares of pasta filled with meat or vegetable paste and served with sauce

raw
ADJECTIVE **1** **Raw** food is uncooked.
2 If part of your body is **raw**, the skin has been rubbed or scraped away.
3 A **raw** substance is in its natural state before being processed.

raw material **raw materials**
NOUN natural substances used to make things

A B C D E F G H I J K L M N O P Q R S T U V W X Y Z

ray **rays**
NOUN a beam of light • *the sun's* ***rays***

razor **razors**
NOUN an instrument that people use for shaving

re-
PREFIX used to form words that show something is being done again. For example, if you **re**use something you use it again, if you read something again you **re**read it, and if you marry for a second time you **re**marry.

reach **reaches, reaching, reached**
VERB **1** When you **reach** a place, you arrive there.
2 When you **reach** for something, you stretch out your arm to touch or get hold of it. • *I can't* ***reach*** *that shelf.*

react **reacts, reacting, reacted**
VERB When you **react** to something, you behave in a particular way because of it.

reaction **reactions**
NOUN Your **reaction** to something is what you say, do or feel because of it.

reactor **reactors**
NOUN a device used to produce nuclear energy

read **reads, reading, read**
VERB When you **read** something that is written, you look at it and understand or say aloud the words that are there.

reader **readers**
NOUN The **readers** of a newspaper or magazine are the people who read it regularly.

readily
Said "**red**-ily" ADVERB **1** willingly or eagerly • *They* ***readily*** *tidied their bedrooms.*
2 easily or quickly • *Help was* ***readily*** *available.*

reading **readings**
NOUN **1** the act of reading books, newspapers or magazines
2 The **reading** on a meter, gauge or other measuring instrument is the amount it shows.

ready
ADJECTIVE If someone or something is **ready**, they are prepared for doing something. • *Your glasses will be* ***ready*** *in a fortnight.*

real
ADJECTIVE **1** actually true and not imagined
2 genuine and not artificial

realistic
ADJECTIVE **1** A **realistic** painting, story or film shows things in a way that is like real life.
2 If you are **realistic** about a situation, you recognize and accept that it is true.

reality
NOUN **1** what is real, and not imagined or invented
SYNONYMS: fact, truth
2 If something has become a **reality**, it has happened. • *Her dream of being a dancer had become a* ***reality***.

realize **realizes, realizing, realized**; also spelt **realise**
VERB If you **realize** something, you become aware of it or understand it.

really
ADVERB **1** You use **really** to emphasize a point. • *It is a* ***really*** *good film.*
2 You use **really** when you are talking about the true facts about something. • *What was* ***really*** *going on?*

reap **reaps, reaping, reaped**
VERB When someone **reaps** a crop, such as corn, they cut and gather it.
reaper NOUN

reappear **reappears, reappearing, reappeared**
VERB When people or things **reappear**, they can be seen again after they have been out of sight.

rear **rears, rearing, reared**
NOUN **1** The **rear** of something is the part at the back.
VERB **2** To **rear** children or other young animals means to bring them up until they are able to look after themselves.
3 When a horse **rears**, it raises the front part of its body, so that its front legs are in the air.

rearrange **rearranges, rearranging, rearranged**
VERB If you **rearrange** something, you organize it or arrange it in a different way.

reason **reasons, reasoning, reasoned**
NOUN **1** the fact that explains why something happens
VERB **2** to think in a logical way and draw conclusions
3 If you **reason** with someone, you discuss something with them in a sensible way.

reasonable
ADJECTIVE **1** fair and sensible
2 A **reasonable** amount is a fairly large amount.

reassure **reassures, reassuring, reassured**
VERB If you **reassure** someone, you say or do things to calm their fears or stop them from worrying.

rebel **rebels, rebelling, rebelled**
Said "**reb**-el" NOUN **1** someone who does not agree with rules, and behaves differently from other people
2 one of a group of people who are fighting against their own country's army in order to change how it is ruled
Said "rib-**el**" VERB **3** When someone **rebels**, they refuse to obey rules, and they behave differently from other people.

rebellious
ADJECTIVE Someone who is **rebellious** breaks rules and refuses to obey orders.
rebellion NOUN

rebound **rebounds, rebounding, rebounded**
VERB If something **rebounds**, it bounces back after hitting something.

rebuild **rebuilds, rebuilding, rebuilt**
VERB When something is **rebuilt**, it is built again after being damaged or destroyed.

rebuke **rebukes, rebuking, rebuked**
VERB If you **rebuke** someone, you tell them off for something wrong that they have done.

recall **recalls, recalling, recalled**
VERB When you **recall** something, you remember it.

recede **recedes, receding, receded**
VERB **1** When something **recedes**, it moves away into the distance. • *We watched the tide* ***receding****.*
2 When a man's hair **recedes**, he starts to go bald from the front of his head.

receipt **receipts**
NOUN a piece of paper given to you as proof that you have paid for something or delivered something

receive **receives, receiving, received**
VERB When you **receive** something, you get it after someone has given or sent it to you.

receiver **receivers**
NOUN the part of a telephone that you hold near to your ear and your mouth

recent
ADJECTIVE A **recent** event is something that happened a short time ago.

reception **receptions**
NOUN **1** the place near the entrance of a hotel or office where appointments and enquiries are dealt with
2 a formal party

receptionist **receptionists**
NOUN In a hotel or office, the **receptionist** is the person who receives and welcomes visitors as they arrive, answers the telephone and arranges appointments.

recipe **recipes**
NOUN a list of ingredients and instructions for cooking or preparing a particular dish
• *My grandma gave me her* ***recipe*** *for Yorkshire pudding.*

recital **recitals**
NOUN a performance of poetry or music, usually by one person

recite **recites, reciting, recited**
VERB If you **recite** something such as a poem, you say it aloud.
recitation NOUN

a b c d e f g h i j k l m n o p q r s t u v w x y z

A B C D E F G H I J K L M N O P Q R S T U V W X Y Z

reckless
ADJECTIVE If you are **reckless**, you do not care about any danger or damage you cause.

reckon **reckons, reckoning, reckoned**
VERB **1** If you **reckon** an amount, you calculate it.
2 If you **reckon** something is true, you think it is true.

reclaim **reclaims, reclaiming, reclaimed**
VERB **1** When you **reclaim** something, you fetch it after losing it or leaving it somewhere.
2 If land is **reclaimed**, it is made useable again, for example by draining water from it.

recline **reclines, reclining, reclined**
VERB to lean or lie back • *We* ***reclined*** *on deckchairs in the sun.*

recognize **recognizes, recognizing, recognized**; also spelt **recognise**
VERB When you **recognize** someone or something, you realize you know who or what they are.

recoil **recoils, recoiling, recoiled**
VERB If you **recoil**, you suddenly back away from something, usually because it shocks or horrifies you. • *I* ***recoiled*** *from the huge spider.*

recollect **recollects, recollecting, recollected**
VERB If you **recollect** something, you remember it.
recollection NOUN

recommend **recommends, recommending, recommended**
VERB If you **recommend** something to someone, you suggest that they try it because you think it is good.

reconcile **reconciles, reconciling, reconciled**
VERB When people are **reconciled**, they become friendly again after a quarrel.
reconciliation NOUN

reconstruct **reconstructs, reconstructing, reconstructed**
VERB To **reconstruct** something that has been damaged means to build it again.
reconstruction NOUN

record **records, recording, recorded**
Said "**rek**-ord" NOUN **1** a written account of something
2 a round, flat piece of plastic on which music has been recorded
3 an achievement that is the best of its type • *He holds the world* ***record*** *for the high jump.*
Said "ri-**kord**" VERB **4** If you **record** information, you write it down so that it can be referred to later.
5 If you **record** sounds and pictures, you copy them onto a tape or disc so that they can be listened to or watched again.

recorder **recorders**
NOUN **1** a small woodwind instrument

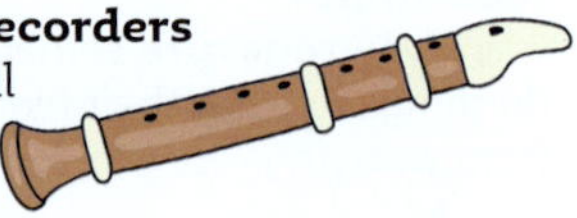

2 a machine for copying sounds and pictures, such as a tape **recorder** or a video **recorder**

recount **recounts, recounting, recounted**
Said "ri-**count**" VERB **1** If you **recount** a story, you tell it.
Said "**ree**-count" VERB **2** If you **recount** something such as votes, you count them for a second time.

recover **recovers, recovering, recovered**
VERB **1** When you **recover**, you get better after being ill.
2 If you **recover** something that has been lost or stolen, you get it back.

recreation **recreations**
NOUN the things you do for enjoyment in your spare time

recruit **recruits, recruiting, recruited**
VERB **1** If you **recruit** people, you persuade them to join a group or help with something.
NOUN **2** someone who has joined the

army or some other organization
recruitment NOUN

rectangle **rectangles**
NOUN a four-sided shape with four right angles
rectangular ADJECTIVE

recuperate **recuperates, recuperating, recuperated**
VERB When you **recuperate**, you gradually recover after being ill or injured.
recuperation NOUN

recur **recurs, recurring, recurred**
VERB If something **recurs**, it happens again.

recycle **recycles, recycling, recycled**
VERB When you **recycle** something, you use it again for a different purpose.

red **redder, reddest; reds**
NOUN OR ADJECTIVE **1** the colour of blood or of a ripe tomato
ADJECTIVE **2** **Red** hair is between orange and brown in colour.

redden **reddens, reddening, reddened**
VERB If something **reddens**, it becomes red. • *His face **reddened** with embarrassment.*

red-handed
ADJECTIVE If you catch someone **red-handed**, you catch them while they are doing something wrong.

redraft **redrafts, redrafting, redrafted**
VERB If you **redraft** a piece of writing, you rewrite it to improve or change it.

reduce **reduces, reducing, reduced**
VERB If you **reduce** something, you make it smaller in size or amount.
SYNONYMS: cut, decrease

reduction **reductions**
NOUN If there is a **reduction** in something, it becomes smaller or less. • *There are great **reductions** in prices during the sales.*

redundant
ADJECTIVE **1** When people are made **redundant**, they lose their jobs because there is no more work for them.
2 If something becomes **redundant**, it is no longer needed or useful.

reed **reeds**
NOUN **1** a hollow-stemmed plant that grows in shallow water or on wet ground
2 a thin piece of cane or metal inside some wind instruments, that vibrates and makes a sound when air is blown over it

reef **reefs**
NOUN a long line of rocks or coral close to the surface of the sea

reek **reeks, reeking, reeked**
VERB **1** If something **reeks**, it has a strong, unpleasant smell.
NOUN **2** a strong, unpleasant smell

reel **reels, reeling, reeled**
NOUN **1** a cylindrical object around which you wrap something such as a fishing line, a film or thread
2 a fast Scottish dance
VERB **3** If you **reel**, you stagger and look as if you will fall.

refer **refers, referring, referred**
VERB **1** If you **refer** to someone or something, you mention them when you are speaking or writing.
2 If you **refer** to a book or other source of information, you look at it in order to find something out.
3 If someone **refers** a problem or a question to someone else, they pass it on to them to deal with.

referee **referees**
NOUN the official who controls a sports match and makes sure that the rules are not broken

A B C D E F G H I J K L M N O P Q R S T U V W X Y Z

reference **references**
NOUN **1** a mention of someone or something in a speech or a piece of writing
2 a document written by someone who knows you, that describes your character and abilities, usually when you are applying for a job

reference book **reference books**
NOUN a book that you use to get information

referendum **referendums** or **referenda**
NOUN a vote in which all the people of voting age in a country are asked to say if they agree with a particular government policy or not

refill **refills, refilling, refilled**
VERB **1** If you **refill** something, you fill it again.
NOUN **2** a container of something to replace something that is used up • *I need a **refill** for my pen.*

refine **refines, refining, refined**
VERB If substances such as oil or sugar are **refined**, all the impurities are taken out of them.

refined
ADJECTIVE Someone who is **refined** is very polite and well mannered.

refinery **refineries**
NOUN a factory where sugar or oil are refined

reflect **reflects, reflecting, reflected**
VERB **1** When rays of heat or light **reflect** off something, they bounce back from it.
2 When something smooth and shiny, such as a mirror, **reflects** something, it shows an image of it.
3 When you **reflect** on something, you think about it carefully.

reflection **reflections**
NOUN the image you see when you look in a mirror or in very clear, still water

reflex **reflexes**
NOUN **1** a sudden uncontrollable movement that you make as a result of pressure or a blow to a particular nerve
2 If you have good **reflexes**, you respond very quickly when something unexpected happens.

reform **reforms, reforming, reformed**
VERB **1** When organizations or laws are **reformed**, changes are made to them to improve them.
2 When people **reform**, they stop doing bad things such as committing crimes.

refrain **refrains, refraining, refrained**
VERB **1** FORMAL If you **refrain** from doing something, you do not do it.
NOUN **2** a short, simple part of a song that is repeated
SYNONYM: chorus

refresh **refreshes, refreshing, refreshed**
VERB If something **refreshes** you, it makes you feel less tired or less thirsty.

refreshing
ADJECTIVE If something is **refreshing**, it makes you cool or less tired after you have been hot or busy. • *We went for a **refreshing** swim after walking along the beach.*

refreshments
PLURAL NOUN drinks and snacks

refrigerator **refrigerators**
NOUN an electrically cooled container for putting food in to keep it fresh

refuel **refuels, refuelling, refuelled**
VERB When an aircraft or vehicle is **refuelled**, it is filled with more fuel.

refuge **refuges**
NOUN a place where you go for safety and protection
SYNONYMS: haven, sanctuary, shelter
[from Latin *refugere* meaning to flee]

refugee **refugees**
NOUN a person who has been forced to leave their country and live elsewhere, for example because of war, famine or persecution

refund **refunds, refunding, refunded**
NOUN **1** a sum of money that is paid back to you, for example because you have returned goods to a shop
VERB **2** If someone **refunds** your money, they pay it back to you.

refuse **refuses, refusing, refused**
Said "ri-**fyooz**" VERB **1** If you **refuse** something, you say no to it, or decide firmly that you will not do it or do not accept it.
Said "**ref**-yooss" NOUN **2** rubbish or waste

regal
ADJECTIVE very grand and suitable for a king or queen

regard **regards, regarding, regarded**
VERB **1** To **regard** someone or something in a certain way is to think of them in that way. • *We **regarded** him as a friend.*
2 to look closely at someone or something
NOUN **3** If you have a high **regard** for someone, you have a very good opinion of them.

regarding
PREPOSITION on the subject of • *"I will now answer any questions **regarding** your homework," said the teacher.*

regardless
PREPOSITION OR ADVERB If you do something **regardless** of what may happen as a result, you do it anyway.

regards
PLURAL NOUN kind wishes or friendly feelings for someone, usually sent in a message • *Give him my **regards** when you see him.*

regatta **regattas**
NOUN a race meeting for sailing or rowing boats

reggae
NOUN a type of music with a strong beat, originally from the West Indies

regiment **regiments**
NOUN a large group of soldiers commanded by a colonel
regimental ADJECTIVE

region **regions**
NOUN a large area of a country or of the world

register **registers, registering, registered**
NOUN **1** an official list that is used to keep a record of things that happen or people who attend an event
VERB **2** When something is **registered**, it is recorded on an official list.

regret **regrets, regretting, regretted**
VERB **1** If you **regret** something, you wish that it had not happened or you had not done it.
2 You can use **regret** to say you are sorry about something. • *We **regret** any inconvenience caused to passengers by the delay.*

regretful
ADJECTIVE If you are **regretful**, you are sorry or sad about something.

regular
ADJECTIVE **1** **Regular** events happen at equal or frequent intervals.
2 If you are a **regular** visitor somewhere, you go there often.

regulate **regulates, regulating, regulated**
VERB If someone or something **regulates** something, they control it. • *My grandad takes tablets to **regulate** his blood pressure.*

regulation **regulations**
NOUN an official rule

rehearse **rehearses, rehearsing, rehearsed**
VERB When people **rehearse** a performance, they practise it in preparation for the actual event.

A B C D E F G H I J K L M N O P Q R S T U V W X Y Z

reign **reigns, reigning, reigned**
VERB **1** When a king or queen **reigns**, he or she is the leader of the country.
NOUN **2** The **reign** of a king or queen is the period when they reign.

> Do not confuse *reign* with *rain* or *rein*.

rein **reins**
NOUN one of the thin leather straps that you hold when you are riding a horse

> Do not confuse *rein* with *rain* or *reign*.

reindeer
NOUN a deer with large antlers, that lives in northern regions of the world

reinforce **reinforces, reinforcing, reinforced**
VERB If you **reinforce** something, you strengthen it.

reject **rejects, rejecting, rejected**
VERB If you **reject** something, you throw it away or refuse to accept it.

rejoice **rejoices, rejoicing, rejoiced**
VERB If you **rejoice**, you celebrate because you are very pleased about something.

relate **relates, relating, related**
VERB **1** If one thing **relates** to another, it is concerned or connected with it in some way, or can be compared with it.
2 If you **relate** a story, you tell it.

related
ADJECTIVE If people, animals or plants are **related**, they belong to the same family groups or species.

relation **relations**
NOUN **1** one of the people who are related to you, such as aunts, uncles and grandparents
2 the way that one thing is connected or compared with another

relationship **relationships**
NOUN **1** The **relationship** between two people or groups is the way they feel and behave towards each other.
2 a close friendship, especially one involving romantic feelings

relative **relatives**
ADJECTIVE **1** compared with other things or people of the same kind
NOUN **2** a member of your family

relax **relaxes, relaxing, relaxed**
VERB **1** When you **relax**, or when something **relaxes** you, you become calm and less worried or tense. • *Massage is used to **relax** muscles.*
2 If you **relax**, you stop work and rest or enjoy your free time.
SYNONYMS: take it easy, unwind

relay **relays, relaying, relayed**
VERB **1** If you **relay** something, such as a message, you pass it from one person to the next.
NOUN **2** a race between teams, in which each team member runs one part of the race

release **releases, releasing, released**
VERB If you **release** someone or something, you set them free or unfasten them.

relent **relents, relenting, relented**
VERB If someone **relents**, they give in and allow something that they refused to allow before. • *Dad **relented** and allowed us to stay up late.*

relevant
ADJECTIVE connected with what is being discussed or dealt with

reliable
ADJECTIVE **Reliable** people and things can be trusted and depended upon.

relic **relics**
NOUN **1** an object or custom that has survived from an earlier time
2 an object regarded as holy because it is thought to be connected with a saint

relief
NOUN If you feel **relief**, you feel glad because something unpleasant is over or has been avoided.

relieve **relieves, relieving, relieved**
VERB If something **relieves** an unpleasant feeling, it makes it less unpleasant.

relieved

ADJECTIVE If you are **relieved**, you are thankful that something worrying or unpleasant has stopped. • *I was **relieved** when the exams were over.*

religion religions

NOUN **1** belief in a god or gods
2 a particular set of religious beliefs
• *the Christian **religion***

religious

ADJECTIVE to do with religion

relish relishes, relishing, relished

VERB **1** If you **relish** something, you enjoy it very much. • *He **relished** the thought of chocolate cake for tea.*
NOUN **2** enjoyment • *"I'm allowed to stay up as long as like," she said with **relish**.*
3 a savoury pickle

reluctant

ADJECTIVE If you are **reluctant** to do something, you do not want to do it.

rely relies, relying, relied

VERB If you **rely** on someone or something, you trust and depend on them. • *I **relied** on my friends to help me.*

remain remains, remaining, remained

VERB **1** If you **remain** in a particular place, you stay there.
PLURAL NOUN **2** The **remains** of something are the parts that are left after most of it has been destroyed or used.

remainder

NOUN **1** the part of something that is left
2 In arithmetic, the **remainder** is the amount left over when one number cannot be divided exactly by another.

remark remarks, remarking, remarked

VERB **1** If you **remark** on something, you mention it or comment on it.
NOUN **2** a comment you make or something you say

remarkable

ADJECTIVE impressive and noticeable • *Her tennis skills were **remarkable**.*

remedy remedies, remedying, remedied

NOUN **1** a cure for something
2 a way of dealing with a problem
VERB **3** If you **remedy** a problem, you put it right.

remember remembers, remembering, remembered

VERB **1** If you **remember** someone or something from the past, you still have an idea of them and you are able to think about them.
2 If you **remember** to do something, you do it when you intended to.
3 If you **remember** something, it suddenly comes into your mind again.

remind reminds, reminding, reminded

VERB **1** If someone **reminds** you of something, they help you remember it.
2 If someone or something **reminds** you of another person or thing, they are similar to the other person or thing and make you think of them.

remnant remnants

NOUN a small part of something that is left after the rest has been used or destroyed

remorse

NOUN FORMAL a strong feeling of guilt and regret
remorseful ADJECTIVE

remote remoter, remotest

ADJECTIVE **1** far away from where most people live
2 far away in time

remote control

NOUN **1** a system of controlling a machine or vehicle from a distance, using radio or electronic signals
2 a hand-held device for controlling a machine or vehicle from a distance
• *a TV **remote control***

removal removals

NOUN **1** the act of taking something away
• *The house felt very bare after the **removal** of the furniture.*
ADJECTIVE **2** A **removal** company moves furniture from one building to another.

A B C D E F G H I J K L M N O P Q R S T U V W X Y Z

remove **removes, removing, removed**
VERB If you **remove** something, you take it away.

rendezvous
Said "**ron**-day-voo" NOUN a meeting or meeting place
[a French word, meaning present yourselves!]

renew **renews, renewing, renewed**
VERB **1** If you **renew** something such as a piece of equipment, you replace it or parts of it with a new one or new parts.
2 If you **renew** an activity or relationship, you begin it again.

renewable
ADJECTIVE **1** able to be renewed • *a good source of **renewable** energy*
NOUN **2** a renewable form of energy, such as wind power or solar power
• *Our energy mix needs more **renewables**.*

renovate **renovates, renovating, renovated**
VERB If you **renovate** something old, you repair it and restore it to good condition.
renovation NOUN

renowned
ADJECTIVE well known, especially for something good • *She's **renowned** for her kindness.*

rent **rents, renting, rented**
VERB **1** If you **rent** something, you pay the owner a regular sum of money to use it.
NOUN **2** the amount of money you pay regularly to use something that belongs to someone else

rental **rentals**
NOUN **1** the amount paid as rent
ADJECTIVE **2** to do with rent

repair **repairs, repairing, repaired**
NOUN **1** something that you do to mend something that is damaged
VERB **2** If you **repair** something that is damaged, you mend it.

repay **repays, repaying, repaid**
VERB **1** When you **repay** money, you give it back to the person who lent it to you.
2 If you **repay** a favour, you do something to help the person who helped you.
repayment NOUN

repeat **repeats, repeating, repeated**
VERB **1** If you **repeat** something, you say, write or do it again.
NOUN **2** something that is done again or happens again

repeatedly
ADVERB again and again, several times
• *He knocked **repeatedly** on the door, but nobody answered.*

repel **repels, repelling, repelled**
VERB **1** If something **repels** you, it disgusts you.
2 If someone **repels** an attack, they defend themselves successfully against it.
3 If someone or something **repels** something, they push it away. • *True magnets can **repel** other magnets.*
repellent ADJECTIVE

repetition
NOUN If there is a **repetition** of something, it happens again or is repeated.

repetitive
ADJECTIVE Something that is **repetitive** is repeated over and over again, and can be extremely boring. • *Fruit picking is a **repetitive** job.*

replace **replaces, replacing, replaced**
VERB **1** If you **replace** something, you put it back.
2 If you **replace** something old, broken or missing, you put another one or a new one in its place. • *Ben **replaced** Tina in the team.*

replay **replays, replaying, replayed**
VERB **1** If you **replay** a tape or a film, you play it again.
NOUN **2** a sports match that is played for a second time

replica **replicas**
NOUN an accurate copy of something

reply **replies, replying, replied**
VERB **1** If you **reply** to something, you say or write something as an answer to it.
NOUN **2** what you say or write when you answer someone

report **reports, reporting, reported**
VERB **1** If you **report** that something has happened, you inform someone about it.
NOUN **2** an account of an event or situation

reporter **reporters**
NOUN someone who writes news articles or broadcasts news reports

represent **represents, representing, represented**
VERB If someone **represents** you, they act on your behalf.

representative **representatives**
NOUN a person who acts on behalf of another person or group of people

reprieve **reprieves**
NOUN a cancellation or postponement of a punishment, especially the death penalty

reprimand **reprimands, reprimanding, reprimanded**
VERB If you **reprimand** someone, you officially tell them that they should not have done something.

reproach **reproaches, reproaching, reproached**
VERB **1** If you **reproach** someone, you blame them for something, or criticize them.
NOUN **2** the act of reproaching someone

reproduce **reproduces, reproducing, reproduced**
VERB **1** If you **reproduce** something, you make a copy of it.
2 When living things **reproduce**, they produce more of their own kind. • *Rats **reproduce** up to five times every year.*

reproduction
NOUN the process by which each living thing produces young
reproductive ADJECTIVE

reptile **reptiles**
NOUN an animal such as a snake, turtle or lizard that has scales on its skin, lays eggs, and is cold-blooded
[from Latin *reptilis* meaning creeping]

republic **republics**
NOUN a country that has a president rather than a king or queen

repulsion
NOUN the force pushing two magnets away from each other

repulsive
ADJECTIVE horrible and disgusting

reputation **reputations**
NOUN the opinion that people have of someone or something

request **requests, requesting, requested**
VERB **1** If you **request** something, you ask for it politely or formally.
NOUN **2** If you make a **request** for something, you ask for it.

require **requires, requiring, required**
VERB **1** If you **require** something, you need it.
2 If you are **required** to do something, you have to do it. • *You are **required** to report to the office at 9 a.m.*

requirement **requirements**
NOUN something you must have or must do

rescue **rescues, rescuing, rescued**
VERB **1** If you **rescue** someone, you save them from a dangerous or unpleasant situation.
NOUN **2** an attempt to save someone from a dangerous or unpleasant situation

a b c d e f g h i j k l m n o p q r s t u v w x y z

A B C D E F G H I J K L M N O P Q R S T U V W X Y Z

research **researches, researching, researched**
NOUN **1** detailed study to discover facts about something
VERB **2** If you **research** something, you study it carefully to discover facts about it.

resemble **resembles, resembling, resembled**
VERB If one thing or person **resembles** another, they are similar to each other.

resent **resents, resenting, resented**
VERB If you **resent** something, you feel bitter and angry about it.

reserve **reserves, reserving, reserved**
VERB **1** If you **reserve** something, you ask for it to be kept aside or ordered for you, or you keep it for a particular purpose. • *We have **reserved** this table for someone else.*
NOUN **2** an area of land where animals, birds or plants are officially protected and can safely breed
3 If you are a **reserve** in a team, you play if one of the other team members cannot.

reserved
ADJECTIVE **1** kept for someone • *All of these tables are **reserved**.*
2 People who are **reserved** are quiet and shy.

reservoir **reservoirs**
Said "**rez**-uh-vwar" NOUN a lake, often artificial, used for storing water before it is supplied to people

residence **residences**
NOUN FORMAL Your **residence** is your home.

resident **residents**
NOUN A **resident** of a house or area is someone who lives there.

resign **resigns, resigning, resigned**
VERB **1** If you **resign** from your job, you give it up.
2 If you **resign** yourself to an unpleasant situation, you accept it without complaining.
resignation NOUN

resist **resists, resisting, resisted**
VERB **1** If you **resist** something, you refuse to accept it and try to stop it happening.
2 If you **resist** an attack, you fight back.

resistance
NOUN fighting or taking action against something or someone • *Her body's **resistance** to disease helped her to get well.*

resolute
Said "**rez**-ul-loot" ADJECTIVE If you are **resolute**, you are determined not to change your mind.
resolutely ADVERB

resolution **resolutions**
Said "rez-ul-**loo**-shun" NOUN
1 determination
2 If you make a **resolution**, you promise yourself that you will do something.
3 a decision made at a meeting • *The **resolution** to improve the play area was agreed.*

resolve **resolves, resolving, resolved**
VERB **1** If you **resolve** a problem, you find a way of sorting it out.
2 If you **resolve** to do something, you make up your mind firmly to do it.
NOUN **3** determination to do something

resort **resorts, resorting, resorted**
NOUN **1** a place where a lot of people spend their holidays, especially by the sea
VERB **2** If you **resort** to doing something, you do it because everything else has failed and you have no alternative.
PHRASE **3** If you do something **as a last resort**, you do it because you can find no other way of solving a problem.

resource **resources**
NOUN The **resources** of a country, organization or person are the materials, money or skills they have and can use.

resourceful
ADJECTIVE A **resourceful** person is good at solving problems and finding ways to do things.

respect **respects, respecting, respected**
VERB **1** If you **respect** someone, you admire and like them.
2 If you **respect** someone's feelings or wishes, you treat them with consideration.
NOUN **3** a feeling of admiration for someone's good qualities or achievements
4 consideration for other people

respectable
ADJECTIVE Someone who is **respectable** behaves in a way that is approved of in the society where they live.

respiration
NOUN breathing • *His **respiration** was affected by his cold.*

respond **responds, responding, responded**
VERB If you **respond** to someone or something, you react to them by doing or saying something.

response **responses**
NOUN a reply or a reaction to something

responsible
ADJECTIVE **1** If you are **responsible** for something, you are in charge of it and must take the blame if it goes wrong. • *If we get a pet, you will be **responsible** for looking after it.*
2 A **responsible** person is sensible, trustworthy and reliable.
3 If you are **responsible** for something, you are the cause of it. • *She was **responsible** for the accident.*
responsibility NOUN

rest **rests, resting, rested**
VERB **1** If you **rest**, you take a break from what you are doing and relax for a while.
2 If you **rest** something against something else, you lean it there.
NOUN **3** The **rest** of something is all the parts that are left or have not been mentioned.
4 If you have a **rest**, you do not do anything active for a while.
5 an object that supports something else, such as a headrest or a footrest

restaurant **restaurants**
NOUN a place where you can buy and eat a meal • *an Italian **restaurant***

restless
ADJECTIVE If you are **restless**, you find it hard to stay still or relaxed because you are bored or impatient.
restlessness NOUN **restlessly** ADVERB

restore **restores, restoring, restored**
VERB If you **restore** something, you get it back to its original state.

restrain **restrains, restraining, restrained**
VERB If you **restrain** someone or something, you hold them back or stop them from doing what they want to.

restrict **restricts, restricting, restricted**
VERB To **restrict** someone or something means to set limits on them. • *The police **restricted** parking outside the school.*

result **results, resulting, resulted**
NOUN **1** The **result** of an action or situation is what happens because of it.
2 The **result** of a contest, calculation or exam is the final score, figure or mark at the end of it.
VERB **3** If something **results** from a particular event, it is caused by that event.

resume **resumes, resuming, resumed**
VERB If you **resume** something, you start doing it again after a break. • *After dinner, Dad **resumed** his work on the car.*

retail
NOUN the activity of selling goods to the public, usually in small amounts
ANTONYM: wholesale
retailer NOUN

A B C D E F G H I J K L M N O P Q R S T U V W X Y Z

retain **retains, retaining, retained**
VERB If you **retain** something, you keep it.

retaliate **retaliates, retaliating, retaliated**
VERB If you **retaliate**, you do something to harm or upset someone because they have harmed or upset you.
retaliation NOUN

retire **retires, retiring, retired**
VERB **1** When older people **retire**, they leave their job and stop working.
2 If you **retire** from a race, you withdraw from it.

retort **retorts, retorting, retorted**
VERB **1** If you **retort**, you reply angrily.
NOUN **2** a short, angry reply

retrace **retraces, retracing, retraced**
VERB If you **retrace** your steps, you go back exactly the same way you came.

retreat **retreats, retreating, retreated**
VERB If you **retreat** from someone or something unpleasant or dangerous, you move away from them.

retrieve **retrieves, retrieving, retrieved**
VERB If you **retrieve** something, you get it back or find it again.

return **returns, returning, returned**
VERB **1** If you **return** to a place, you go back there.
2 If you **return** something to someone, you give it back to them.
NOUN **3** the act of giving or putting something back
4 a ticket for a journey to a place and back again

reunion **reunions**
NOUN a meeting or a party at which people who have not seen each other for a long time get together
reunite VERB

rev **revs, revving, revved**
VERB **1** When someone **revs** an engine, they press the accelerator to increase its speed.
NOUN **2** The speed of an engine is measured in **revs**, which is an abbreviation of *revolutions per minute*.

reveal **reveals, revealing, revealed**
VERB **1** If you **reveal** something, you tell people about it.
2 If you **reveal** something that has been hidden, you uncover it.

revel **revels, revelling, revelled**
VERB If you **revel** in a situation, you enjoy it very much.
reveller NOUN **revelry** NOUN

revenge
NOUN the act of hurting someone who has hurt you

revenue **revenues**
NOUN money that a government, company or organization receives

Reverend
NOUN a title used before the name of a member of the clergy

reverse **reverses, reversing, reversed**
VERB **1** If you **reverse** the order of things, you arrange them in the opposite order.
2 When someone **reverses** a car, they drive it backwards.

reversible
ADJECTIVE **Reversible** clothing can be worn with either side on the outside.

review **reviews, reviewing, reviewed**
NOUN **1** an article in a magazine or newspaper, or a talk on television or radio, giving an opinion of a new book, play, or film
VERB **2** When someone **reviews** a book, play or film, they write an account or have a discussion expressing their opinion of it.

revise **revises, revising, revised**
VERB If you **revise** for an exam, you go over your work to make sure you know it properly.

revive **revives, reviving, revived**

VERB When you **revive** someone who has fainted, they become conscious again.

revolt **revolts, revolting, revolted**
NOUN **1** a violent uprising or rebellion against authority
VERB **2** When people **revolt**, they rebel against the system that governs them.
3 If something **revolts** you, it disgusts you.

revolting
ADJECTIVE horrible and disgusting

revolution **revolutions**
NOUN a violent attempt by a large number of people to change the way their country is run

revolutionize **revolutionizes, revolutionizing, revolutionized**
VERB If something is **revolutionized**, it is changed completely, usually for the better. • *Science and technology have **revolutionized** the way we live.*

revolve **revolves, revolving, revolved**
VERB When something **revolves**, it turns in a circle around a central point.
revolving ADJECTIVE

revolver **revolvers**
NOUN a small gun held in the hand

reward **rewards, rewarding, rewarded**
NOUN **1** something you are given because you have done something good
VERB **2** If you **reward** someone, you give them a reward.

rewarding
ADJECTIVE Something that is **rewarding** gives you a lot of satisfaction. • *Nursing is a **rewarding** job.*

rewind **rewinds, rewinding, rewound**
VERB If you **rewind** a cassette or video tape, you wind it back to the beginning.

rewrite **rewrites, rewriting, rewrote, rewritten**
VERB If you **rewrite** something you have written, you write it again to make changes to it and improve it.
SYNONYM: redraft

rhetorical
ADJECTIVE A question that is **rhetorical** is asked in order to make a statement, rather than to get an answer. For example, *What's the world coming to?*

rheumatism
NOUN an illness that makes your joints and muscles stiff and painful
rheumatic ADJECTIVE

rhinoceros **rhinoceroses**
NOUN a large African or Asian mammal with one or two horns on its nose [from Greek *rhin* meaning of the nose and *keras* meaning horn]

rhombus **rhombuses** or **rhombi**
NOUN a plane shape like a diamond, with four equal sides and no right angles

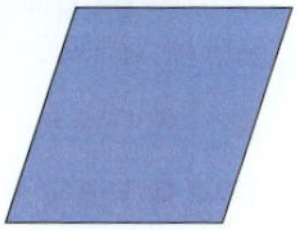

rhubarb
NOUN a plant with long red stems that can be cooked with sugar and eaten

rhyme **rhymes, rhyming, rhymed**
VERB **1** If one word **rhymes** with another, both words have a very similar sound in their final syllable. For example, *Sally* rhymes with *valley*.
NOUN **2** a word that rhymes with another • *He couldn't find a **rhyme** for "orange".*

There is an *h* before the *y* in *rhyme* and *rhythm*.

rhythm **rhythms**
NOUN a regular series of sounds, movements or actions • *The poem was easy to learn because it had a strong **rhythm**.*

rib **ribs**
NOUN Your **ribs** are the curved bones that go from your spine to your chest.

ribbon **ribbons**
NOUN a long, narrow piece of cloth used as a fastening or decoration

rice
NOUN white or brown grains taken from a cereal plant and used for food

rich **richer, richest; riches**
ADJECTIVE **1** Someone who is **rich** has a lot of money or possessions.

2 Something that is **rich** in something contains a large amount of it. • *Fruit is **rich** in vitamins.*
3 Rich food contains a large amount of fat, oil or sugar.
PLURAL NOUN **4 Riches** are valuable possessions or large amounts of money.

rickshaw **rickshaws**
NOUN a two-wheeled, hand-pulled cart used in Asia for carrying passengers

ricochet **ricochets, ricocheting** or **ricochetting, ricocheted** or **ricochetted**
Said "**rik**-oh-shay" VERB When an object **ricochets**, it hits a surface and then bounces away from it.

rid
PHRASE When you **get rid of** something you do not want, you throw it away.

riddle **riddles**
NOUN an amusing or puzzling question, sometimes in rhyme, to which you must find an answer

ride **rides, riding, rode, ridden**
VERB **1** When you **ride** a horse or a bicycle, you sit on it and control it as it moves along.
2 When you **ride** in a car, you travel in it.
NOUN **3** a journey on a horse or bicycle or in a vehicle

ridge **ridges**
NOUN a long, narrow piece of high land

ridicule **ridicules, ridiculing, ridiculed**
VERB **1** If you **ridicule** someone, you make fun of them in an unkind way.
NOUN **2** unkind laughter or teasing

ridiculous
ADJECTIVE very foolish

rifle **rifles**
NOUN a gun with a long barrel

rig **rigs, rigging, rigged**
NOUN **1** a large structure used for taking oil or gas from the ground or the sea bed • *an oil **rig***
VERB **2** When someone **rigs** a boat, they fit it with ropes and sails.

right **rights**
NOUN **1** correct behaviour • *At least he knew **right** from wrong.*
ANTONYM: wrong
2 If you have a **right** to do something, you are allowed to do it.
3 one of two opposite directions, sides or positions. If you are facing north and you turn to the **right**, you will be facing east.
ANTONYM: left
ADJECTIVE OR ADVERB **4** If something is **right**, it is correct.
ANTONYM: wrong
5 on or towards the right of something
ANTONYM: left

right angle **right angles**
NOUN an angle of 90°

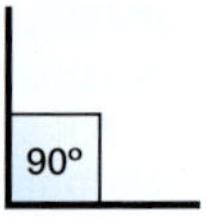

rigid
ADJECTIVE A **rigid** object is stiff and does not bend easily.
rigidly ADVERB

rim **rims**
NOUN the outer edge of something such as a bowl or wheel

rind **rinds**
NOUN the skin on bacon, cheese and some fruits

ring **rings, ringing, rang, rung**
VERB **1** If you **ring** someone, you phone them.
2 When a telephone or bell **rings**, it makes a clear, loud sound.
NOUN **3** a small circle of metal that you wear on your finger

ringleader **ringleaders**
NOUN the leader of a group, who leads the others into mischief or crime

rink **rinks**
NOUN a large indoor area for ice skating or roller skating

rinse **rinses, rinsing, rinsed**
VERB When you **rinse** something, you wash it in clean water, without soap.

riot **riots, rioting, rioted**
NOUN **1** When there is a **riot**, a crowd of people behave violently in a public place.
VERB **2** When people **riot**, they behave violently in a public place.

rip **rips, ripping, ripped**
VERB If you **rip** something, you tear it.

ripe **riper, ripest**
ADJECTIVE **Ripe** fruit or grain is fully developed and ready to be eaten.

ripple **ripples, rippling, rippled**
NOUN **1** a little wave on the surface of calm water
2 If there is a **ripple** of laughter or applause, people laugh or clap their hands gently for a short time.
VERB **3** When the surface of water **ripples**, little waves appear on it.

rise **rises, rising, rose, risen**
VERB **1** If something **rises**, it moves upwards. • *Wilson watched the smoke **rise** from the fire.*
2 When the sun or moon **rises**, it appears from below the horizon.
NOUN **3** When something goes up, it is called a **rise**, for example a **rise** in the land or a **rise** in prices.
VERB **4** When you **rise**, you get out of bed.
5 If something such as a sound, or the level of a liquid or prices **rise**, they become higher.

risk **risks, risking, risked**
NOUN **1** If there is a **risk** of something unpleasant, it might happen.
2 Someone or something that is a **risk** is likely to cause harm or have bad results.
VERB **3** If you **risk** something, you do something knowing that an unpleasant thing might happen as a result. • *If he doesn't play, he **risks** losing his place in the team.*

ritual **rituals**
NOUN **1** a traditional ceremony
ADJECTIVE **2** **Ritual** activities happen as part of a tradition or ritual.

rival **rivals**
NOUN Someone's **rival** is the person they are competing with.

river **rivers**
NOUN a large, continuous stretch of fresh water flowing in a channel across land, to a larger **river**, a lake or the sea

road **roads**
NOUN a long stretch of hard ground built between two places so that people can travel along it easily

roam **roams, roaming, roamed**
VERB If you **roam** around, you wander around without any particular reason.

roar **roars, roaring, roared**
VERB **1** If something **roars**, it makes a very loud noise.
NOUN **2** a very loud noise

roast **roasts, roasting, roasted**
VERB **1** When you **roast** meat or other food, you cook it in an oven or over a fire.
ADJECTIVE **2** **Roast** meat or vegetables have been roasted.

rob **robs, robbing, robbed**
VERB If someone **robs** a person or place, they steal money or property from them.

robe **robes**
NOUN a long, loose piece of clothing that covers the body

robin **robins**
NOUN a small bird with a red breast

robot **robots**
NOUN a machine that moves and does things automatically
[from Czech *robota* meaning work]

rock **rocks, rocking, rocked**
NOUN **1** **Rock** is made up of small pieces of one or more minerals. The earth's surface is made up of **rock**.
2 A **rock** is a piece of rock.
3 music with a strong beat, usually involving electric guitars and drums
4 a hard sweet, usually brightly coloured and shaped like a long stick
VERB **5** When something **rocks**, or when you **rock** it, it moves regularly backwards and forwards or from side to side.

rocket **rockets**
NOUN **1** a space vehicle, usually shaped like a long pointed tube
2 an explosive missile

rod **rods**
NOUN a long, thin pole or bar

rode
VERB the past tense of **ride**

rodent **rodents**
NOUN a small mammal with sharp front teeth that it uses for gnawing. Rabbits and mice are **rodents**.
[from Latin *rodere* meaning to gnaw]

rogue **rogues**
NOUN a dishonest or mischievous person

role **roles**
NOUN An actor's **role** is the character that he or she plays in a play or film.

roll **rolls, rolling, rolled**
VERB **1** If something **rolls**, or if you **roll** it, it moves along a surface, turning over many times.
2 If you **roll** something, or **roll it up**, you wrap it around itself so that it has a rounded shape.
NOUN **3** A **roll** of paper or cloth is a long piece of it that has been rolled into a tube.
4 a small, circular loaf of bread

roller coaster **roller coasters**
NOUN a pleasure ride at a fun fair, consisting of a small railway that goes up and down steep slopes and around bends

roller skate **roller skates**
NOUN **Roller skates** are shoes or boots with four small wheels underneath.
roller-skate VERB

ROM
NOUN a computer storage device that holds information that cannot be changed by the programmer. **ROM** is an abbreviation for *read only memory*.

Roman Catholic **Roman Catholics**
NOUN someone who belongs to the branch of the Christian Church that has the Pope in Rome as its leader

romance **romances**
NOUN **1** a love story
2 If two people have a **romance**, they have a romantic relationship.

Romani; also spelt **Romany**
NOUN the language of the Gypsies

Roman numerals
PLURAL NOUN numbers written in the form of letters and used by ancient Romans. For example, I = 1, V = 5, X = 10, L = 50, C = 100, D = 500, M = 1000.

romantic
ADJECTIVE **1** to do with romance and love
2 A **romantic** person is rather emotional and not very realistic about life and love.

roof **roofs**
NOUN the covering on top of a building or vehicle

rook **rooks**
NOUN **1** a large black bird
2 a chess piece that can move any number of squares in a straight but not diagonal line. It is also called a castle.

room **rooms**
NOUN **1** a separate section in a building, divided from other **rooms** by walls
2 If there is **room** for something, there is enough space for it.

roost **roosts, roosting, roosted**
NOUN **1** a place where birds rest or build their nests

VERB **2** When birds **roost**, they settle somewhere for the night.

root **roots**
NOUN **Roots** are the parts of a plant that usually grow underground. They anchor the plant and carry water from the soil.

root word **root words**
NOUN a word that you can add a prefix or a suffix to in order to make other words. For example, in the words *unclear*, *clearly* and *cleared*, the **root word** is *clear*.

rope **ropes, roping, roped**
NOUN **1** a thick, strong cord made by twisting together several thinner cords
VERB **2** If you **rope** one thing to another, you tie them together with rope.

rosary **rosaries**
NOUN a string of beads that Catholics use for counting prayers

rose **roses**
NOUN **1** a flower that has a pleasant smell and grows on a bush with thorns
VERB **2** the past tense of **rise**

rosette **rosettes**
NOUN a large circular badge of coloured ribbons worn as a prize in a competition or to support a political party

Rosh Hashanah; also spelt **Rosh Hashana**
NOUN the festival celebrating the Jewish New Year

rosy **rosier, rosiest**
ADJECTIVE **1** reddish-pink • *Our cheeks were **rosy** after our walk on the windy beach.*
2 hopeful and positive • *He always has a **rosy** outlook on life.*

rot **rots, rotting, rotted**
VERB When food, wood or other substances **rot**, or when something **rots** them, they decay and fall apart.
SYNONYM: decompose

rotary
ADJECTIVE moving or able to move in a circular direction around a fixed point

rotate **rotates, rotating, rotated**
VERB When something **rotates**, it turns with a circular movement, like a wheel.

rotation **rotations**
NOUN **1** a complete circular movement • *the **rotation** of a wheel* • *the **rotation** of the earth*
PHRASE **2** If you do things **in rotation**, you do them one after the other, and when you finish you start all over again.

rotor **rotors**
NOUN **1** the part of a machine that turns
2 The **rotors**, or **rotor** blades, of a helicopter are the four long, flat pieces of metal on top of it, that rotate and lift it off the ground.

rotten
ADJECTIVE **1** Something that is **rotten** has decayed.
2 INFORMAL bad, unpleasant or unfair • *I think it's a **rotten** idea.*

rough **rougher, roughest**
ADJECTIVE **1** uneven and not smooth • *His hands were hard and **rough**.*
ANTONYM: smooth
2 using too much force • *Don't be so **rough** with that toy or you'll break it.*
ANTONYM: gentle
3 approximate • *At a **rough** guess, it is five o'clock.*
ANTONYMS: exact, precise

roughly
ADVERB **1** almost or approximately • *There are **roughly** 100 marbles in that box.*
2 If you treat someone or something **roughly**, you treat them clumsily or violently.

round **rounder, roundest; rounds**
ADJECTIVE **1** Something **round** is shaped like a ball or a circle.
PREPOSITION OR ADVERB **2** If something is **round** something else, it surrounds it.
3 If something goes **round**, it moves in a circle. • *The sails of the windmill went **round**.*
PREPOSITION **4** If you go **round** something, you go to the other side of it. • *Suddenly a car came **round** the corner.*

ADVERB **5** If you turn or look **round**, you turn or look in a different direction.
6 If you move things **round**, you move them so that they are in different places.
7 If you go **round** to someone's house, you visit them.
NOUN **8** one of a series of events, especially in a competition
9 a series of calls or deliveries • *Our house is the last one on the milkman's **round**.*
10 a whole slice of bread, or a sandwich made of two slices
11 a type of song in which people sing the same words but start at different times
rounded ADJECTIVE

roundabout **roundabouts**
NOUN **1** a meeting point of several roads with a circle in the centre that vehicles have to travel around
2 a circular platform that goes round and that children can ride on in a playground
3 a large, circular platform with horses or cars on it, for children to ride on as it goes round and round
SYNONYM: merry-go-round

rounders
NOUN a team game in which players hit a ball with a bat and run round a circuit

rouse **rouses, rousing, roused**
VERB **1** If you **rouse** someone, you wake them up.
2 If you **rouse** yourself, you make yourself get up and do something.
3 If something **rouses** your emotions, it makes you feel those emotions.

rousing
ADJECTIVE Something that is **rousing**, such as a game, speech or song, makes you feel excited and emotional.

route **routes**
NOUN a way from one place to another
• *the most direct **route** to the town centre*

routine **routines**
ADJECTIVE **1** **Routine** activities are done regularly.
NOUN **2** the usual way or order in which you do things

row **rows, rowing, rowed**
Rhymes with "snow" VERB **1** When you **row** a boat, you use oars to make it move through the water.

NOUN **2** several objects or people in a line
Rhymes with "cow" NOUN **3** an argument
4 a lot of noise

rowdy **rowdier, rowdiest**
ADJECTIVE rough and noisy
rowdily ADVERB

royal
ADJECTIVE belonging to or involving a queen, a king, or a member of their family

RSVP
RSVP written at the end of a letter or an invitation means please reply.
[an abbreviation for the French expression *Répondez s'il vous plaît* meaning please reply]

rub **rubs, rubbing, rubbed**
VERB If you **rub** something, you move your hand, or a cloth, very firmly backwards and forwards over it.

rubber **rubbers**
NOUN **1** a strong, elastic substance used for making tyres, boots and other products
2 a small piece of rubber or plastic that you use to remove mistakes when writing or drawing with a pencil

rubbish
NOUN **1** unwanted things or waste material
SYNONYMS: garbage, refuse, trash
2 something foolish
3 something of very poor quality

rubble
NOUN bits of old brick and stone

ruby **rubies**
NOUN a type of red jewel

A B C D E F G H I J K L M N O P Q R S T U V W X Y Z

rucksack **rucksacks**
NOUN a bag with shoulder straps for carrying things on your back

rudder **rudders**
NOUN a piece of wood or metal at the back of a boat or plane that is moved to make the boat or plane turn

rude **ruder, rudest**
ADJECTIVE **1** not polite
2 embarrassing or offensive because of reference to body parts or bodily functions

ruff **ruffs**
NOUN a stiff circular collar with many pleats in it. These collars were very popular in the 16th century.

ruffle **ruffles, ruffling, ruffled**
VERB **1** If you **ruffle** someone's hair, you move your hand quickly backwards and forwards over their head.
2 If something **ruffles** you, it makes you annoyed or upset.
NOUN **3** **Ruffles** are small folds made in a piece of material for decoration.

rug **rugs**
NOUN **1** a small thick carpet
2 a warm covering for your knees or for sitting on outdoors

rugby
NOUN a game played by two teams, who try to kick or throw an oval ball past a line at their opponents' end of the pitch [named after *Rugby* School where it was first played]

rugged
ADJECTIVE **1** Somewhere **rugged** is rocky, wild and unsheltered.
2 Someone **rugged** is strong and tough.

ruin **ruins, ruining, ruined**
VERB **1** If you **ruin** something, you destroy or spoil it completely.
NOUN **2** the part that is left after something has been severely damaged

rule **rules, ruling, ruled**
NOUN **1** **Rules** are instructions that tell you what you must do.
VERB **2** When someone **rules** a country or a group of people, they govern it and are in charge of its affairs.

ruler **rulers**
NOUN **1** a person who rules a country
2 a long, flat object with straight edges, marked with a scale, used for measuring things or drawing straight lines

rum **rums**
NOUN a strong alcoholic drink made from sugar cane juice

rumble **rumbles, rumbling, rumbles**
VERB **1** If something **rumbles**, it makes a continuous low sound. • *My stomach is **rumbling** because I am hungry.*
NOUN **2** a continuous deep sound • *There was a **rumble** of thunder.*

rumour **rumours**
NOUN a piece of information or a story that people are talking about, but which may not be true

run **runs, running, ran**
VERB **1** When you **run**, you move quickly, with both feet leaving the ground at each stride.
2 If you **run** water, you turn on the tap to let the water flow out.
3 If your nose is **running**, a lot of liquid is coming out of it.
4 If you **run** an activity or a place such as a school or shop, you are in charge of it.
5 If you **run away** from a place, you leave it suddenly and secretly.

run out
VERB If you **run out** of something, you have no more left.

rung **rungs**
NOUN one of the bars that form the steps of a ladder

runner **runners**
NOUN **1** a person who runs as a sport, especially in competitions
2 a person who takes messages or runs errands
3 A **runner** on a plant such as a strawberry is a long shoot from which a new plant develops.

A B C D E F G H I J K L M N O P Q R S T U V W X Y Z

runny **runnier, runniest**
ADJECTIVE flowing or moving like liquid

runway **runways**
NOUN a long strip of ground used by aeroplanes for taking off and landing

rural
ADJECTIVE to do with the countryside

rush **rushes, rushing, rushed**
VERB **1** If you **rush** somewhere, or if you are **rushed** there, you go there quickly.
2 If you **rush** something, or if you are **rushed** into something, you do it too quickly.
NOUN **3** a type of plant that grows in or beside fresh water, such as rivers, ponds and lakes

rust **rusts, rusting, rusted**
NOUN **1** a reddish-brown substance that forms on metal when it is exposed to water and the oxygen in the air
VERB **2** When metal **rusts**, it corrodes and a reddish-brown substance is formed. **Rusting** occurs when iron or steel is exposed to water and the oxygen in the air.

rustle **rustles, rustling, rustled**
VERB If something **rustles**, it makes a soft, crisp sound as it moves, like the sound of dry leaves moving.

rusty **rustier, rustiest**
ADJECTIVE **1** covered with rust • *The old bicycle was **rusty**.*
2 not as good as it once was because of lack of practice • *Dad's maths is a bit **rusty**.*

rut **ruts**
NOUN a deep, narrow groove in the ground made by the wheels of a vehicle

ruthless
ADJECTIVE very harsh or cruel, and without any pity

rye
NOUN a cereal crop that produces light-brown grain used to make flour

Ss

Sabbath **Sabbaths**
NOUN the day of the week that some religious groups, such as Jews and Christians, use for rest and prayer
[from Hebrew *shabbath* meaning to rest]

sabotage **sabotages, sabotaging, sabotaged**
NOUN **1** the deliberate damaging of machinery and equipment such as railway lines
VERB **2** If something is **sabotaged**, it is deliberately damaged.
saboteur NOUN

sabre **sabres**
NOUN **1** a heavy curved sword
2 a light sword used in fencing

sachet **sachets**
NOUN a small packet containing something like sugar or shampoo

sack **sacks**
NOUN **1** a large bag made of rough material, for carrying such things as potatoes and grain • *a **sack** of potatoes*
PHRASE **2** INFORMAL If someone **gets the sack**, they are dismissed from their job by their employer.

sacred
ADJECTIVE holy, or connected with religion or religious ceremonies

sacrifice **sacrifices, sacrificing, sacrificed**
VERB If you **sacrifice** something valuable or important, you give it up.

sad **sadder, saddest**
ADJECTIVE If you are **sad**, you feel unhappy.

sadden **saddens, saddening, saddened**
VERB If something **saddens** you,

it makes you feel sad.
saddening ADJECTIVE

saddle **saddles, saddling, saddled**
NOUN **1** a leather seat strapped to an animal's back, for the rider to sit on
2 the seat on a bicycle
VERB **3** If you **saddle** a horse, you put a saddle on it.

safari **safaris**
NOUN an expedition for hunting or observing wild animals
[from Swahili *safari* meaning journey]

safari park **safari parks**
NOUN a large park where wild animals such as lions, giraffes and elephants are free to roam

safe **safer, safest; safes**
ADJECTIVE **1** If you are **safe**, you are not in any danger.
2 Something that is **safe** does not cause harm or danger.
NOUN **3** a strong metal box with special locks, in which you can keep valuable things

safeguard **safeguards, safeguarding, safeguarded**
VERB **1** If you **safeguard** something, you protect it.
NOUN **2** a law or a rule to help protect people or things from harm

safety
NOUN protection, being safe • *child* ***safety*** • *We should have* ***safety*** *in our homes.*

saga **sagas**
NOUN a very long story, usually telling of many different adventures

said
VERB the past tense and past participle of **say**

sail **sails, sailing, sailed**
VERB **1** When a ship **sails**, it moves across water.
2 If you **sail** somewhere, you go there by ship.
NOUN **3** one of the large pieces of material attached to a ship's mast. The wind blows against the **sail** and moves the ship.
4 The arm of a windmill is called a **sail**.

sailor **sailors**
NOUN **1** a member of a ship's crew
2 someone who sails

saint **saints**
NOUN a person who is given a special honour by a Christian Church, after they have died, because they lived a very holy life

sake **sakes**
PHRASE If you do something for someone's **sake**, you do it to help or please them.

salad **salads**
NOUN a mixture of foods eaten cold or warm, and often raw

salami
NOUN a kind of spicy sausage
[Italian plural of *salame*, from *salare* meaning to salt]

salary **salaries**
NOUN a payment made each month to an employee

sale **sales**
NOUN **1** The **sale** of goods is the selling of them.
2 an occasion when a shop sells things at reduced prices

saliva
NOUN the watery liquid in your mouth that softens food, which helps you chew and digest it

salmon **salmons** or **salmon**
NOUN a large, edible, silver-coloured fish with pink flesh

salt
NOUN a white substance used to flavour and preserve food

salute **salutes, saluting, saluted**
NOUN **1** a formal sign of respect. Soldiers give a **salute** by raising their right hand to their forehead.
VERB **2** If you **salute** someone, you give them a salute.

salvage **salvages, salvaging, salvaged**
VERB If you **salvage** things, you save them from, for example, a wrecked ship or a destroyed building.

same
ADJECTIVE **1** If two things are the **same**, they are like one another.
2 just one thing and not two different ones • *They were born in the **same** town.*

sample **samples, sampling, sampled**
NOUN **1** a small amount of something that you can try or test, for example for quality or to find out more about it
VERB **2** If you **sample** something, you try it. • *I **sampled** his cooking.*

sanctuary **sanctuaries**
NOUN **1** a place where you are safe from harm or danger
2 a place where wildlife is protected

sand **sands**
NOUN a substance consisting of tiny pieces of stone. Beaches are made of **sand**.

sandal **sandals**
NOUN **Sandals** are light shoes with straps, worn in warm weather.

sandwich **sandwiches**
NOUN two slices of bread with a filling between them

sandy **sandier, sandiest**
ADJECTIVE **1** A **sandy** area is covered with sand.
2 **Sandy** hair is a light orange-brown colour.

sane **saner, sanest**
ADJECTIVE If someone is **sane**, they have a healthy mind.

sang
VERB the past tense of **sing**

sank
VERB the past tense of **sink**

sap **saps, sapping, sapped**
NOUN **1** the juice found in the stems of plants
VERB **2** If something such as an illness **saps** your energy or your strength, it gradually weakens you.

sapling **saplings**
NOUN a young tree

sapphire **sapphires**
NOUN a blue precious stone

sarcastic
ADJECTIVE If someone is **sarcastic**, they say the opposite of what they really mean in order to mock or insult someone.

sardine **sardines**
NOUN a small edible sea fish

sari **saris**
NOUN a piece of clothing consisting of a long piece of material folded around the body, worn especially by Indian women [a Hindi word]

sash **sashes**
NOUN a long piece of cloth worn round the waist or over one shoulder

sat
VERB the past tense and past participle of **sit**

satchel **satchels**
NOUN a leather or cloth bag with a long strap, especially used for carrying books to and from school

satellite **satellites**
NOUN **1** a spacecraft sent into space to orbit the earth, to collect information, or as part of a communications system

2 a natural object in space that moves round another, larger object, such as a planet or star

satellite dish **satellite dishes**
NOUN a dish-shaped aerial that receives television signals sent by satellite

satellite television
NOUN television programmes received by signals from artificial satellites

satin **satins**
NOUN a kind of smooth, shiny fabric often made from silk

satisfactory
ADJECTIVE acceptable or adequate
satisfactorily ADVERB

satisfy **satisfies, satisfying, satisfied**
VERB If you **satisfy** someone, you do something or give them something to make them pleased or contented.

saturated
ADJECTIVE soaking wet

Saturday **Saturdays**
NOUN the seventh day of the week, coming between Friday and Sunday

sauce **sauces**
NOUN a liquid eaten with food to add flavour • *It's pasta with tomato **sauce** for dinner.*

saucepan **saucepans**
NOUN a deep metal pan with a handle and a lid used for cooking

saucer **saucers**
NOUN a small curved plate for a cup to stand on

sauna **saunas**
Said "**saw** -nah" NOUN If you have a **sauna**, you go into a very hot room in order to sweat, then have a cold bath or shower.
[a Finnish word]

saunter **saunters, sauntering, sauntered**
VERB If you **saunter** somewhere, you walk there slowly and casually.

sausage **sausages**
NOUN a mixture of minced meat and herbs formed into a tubular shape and served cooked

savage **savages, savaging, savaged**
ADJECTIVE **1** cruel and violent
SYNONYMS: brutal, vicious
NOUN **2** If you call someone a **savage**, you mean that they are violent and uncivilized.
VERB **3** If an animal **savages** you, it attacks you and bites you.

savannah **savannahs**
NOUN a grassy plain with few trees in a hot country

save **saves, saving, saved**
VERB **1** If you **save** someone, you rescue them or help to keep them safe.
2 If you **save** something, you keep it so that you can use it later.
3 If you **save** time, money or effort, you stop it from being wasted.

savings
PLURAL NOUN Your **savings** are money you have saved.

saviour **saviours**
NOUN **1** a person who saves others from danger or loss
PROPER NOUN **2** In Christianity, the **Saviour** is Jesus Christ.

savoury
ADJECTIVE salty or spicy • *Salt and vinegar crisps are my favourite **savoury** snack.*

saw **saws, sawing, sawed, sawn**
NOUN **1** a tool that has a blade with sharp teeth along one edge for cutting wood
VERB **2** If you **saw** something, you cut it with a saw.
3 the past tense of **see**

sawdust
NOUN the fine powder produced when you saw wood

saxophone **saxophones**
NOUN a curved metal wind instrument often played in jazz bands
[named after Adolphe *Sax* (1814–1894), who invented the instrument]

say **says, saying, said**
VERB If you **say** something, you speak words.

saying **sayings**
NOUN a well-known sentence or phrase that tells you something about life

scab **scabs**
NOUN a hard, dry covering that forms over a wound while it is healing

a b c d e f g h i j k l m n o p q r s t u v w x y z

A B C D E F G H I J K L M N O P Q R S T U V W X Y Z

scaffolding
NOUN a framework of poles and boards that is used by workmen to stand on while they are working on the outside of a building

scald **scalds, scalding, scalded**
VERB **1** If you **scald** yourself, you burn yourself with very hot liquid or steam.
NOUN **2** a burn caused by very hot liquid or steam

scale **scales**
NOUN **1** the size or extent of something • *The **scale** of the building was enormous.*
2 a set of marks or numbers used for measuring something
3 The **scale** of something like a map, a plan or a model shows the relationship between the measurements represented and those in the real world. For example, a **scale** of 1:10 tells you that one centimetre on a model represents 10 centimetres in real life.
4 one of the small, hard pieces of skin covering the body of a fish or a reptile
5 a series of musical notes going upwards or downwards in a particular order
PLURAL NOUN **6** **Scales** are a piece of equipment used for weighing things or people.

scalene
ADJECTIVE A **scalene** triangle has sides of different lengths.

scalp **scalps**
NOUN the skin under the hair on your head

scamper **scampers, scampering, scampered**
VERB If you **scamper**, you run quickly and lightly.

scampi
PLURAL NOUN large prawns, often eaten fried in breadcrumbs

scan **scans, scanning, scanned**
VERB **1** If you **scan** something, you look at every part of it carefully.
2 If you **scan** a piece of writing, you look at it quickly but not in detail.
3 If a machine **scans** something, it examines it with a beam of light or X-rays.
NOUN **4** an examination of part of the body with X-ray or laser equipment

scandal **scandals**
NOUN **1** a situation or event that people think is shocking and immoral
2 gossip about bad things that can ruin a person's reputation
scandalous ADJECTIVE

scanner **scanners**
NOUN a machine that is used to examine, identify or record things by using a beam of light or an X-ray

scapegoat **scapegoats**
NOUN If someone is made a **scapegoat**, they are blamed for something, although it may not be their fault.

scar **scars, scarring, scarred**
NOUN **1** a mark left on your skin after a wound has healed
VERB **2** If an injury **scars** you, it leaves a mark on your skin for ever.

scarce **scarcer, scarcest**
ADJECTIVE If something is **scarce**, there is not very much of it.

scare **scares, scaring, scared**
VERB **1** If something **scares** you, it frightens you.
NOUN **2** something that gives you a fright

scarecrow **scarecrows**
NOUN an object shaped like a person and put in a field to scare birds away from the crops

scarf **scarfs** or **scarves**
NOUN a piece of cloth worn round your neck or head to keep you warm

scarlet
NOUN OR ADJECTIVE bright red

scary **scarier, scariest**
ADJECTIVE INFORMAL frightening • *The film was so **scary** I hid behind the sofa.*

scatter **scatters, scattering, scattered**
VERB **1** When you **scatter** things, you throw or drop them so they spread over a large area.

2 If a group of people or animals **scatter**, they suddenly move off in different directions.

scavenge **scavenges, scavenging, scavenged**
VERB If a human or other animal **scavenges** for things, they search for them among waste and rubbish.
scavenger NOUN

scene **scenes**
NOUN part of a play or film in which a series of events happen in one place

scenery
NOUN **1** In the countryside, you can refer to everything you see as the **scenery**.
2 In a theatre, the **scenery** is the painted cloth on the stage that makes it seem like a particular place.

scent **scents**
NOUN a smell, especially a pleasant one

sceptic **sceptics**
Said "**skep**-tik" NOUN someone who does not believe things easily

schedule **schedules**
NOUN a list of events or things you have to do, and the times at which each thing should be done or will happen

scheme **schemes, scheming, schemed**
NOUN **1** a plan or arrangement
VERB **2** When people **scheme**, they make secret plans.

scholar **scholars**
NOUN **1** a person who studies an academic subject and knows a lot about it
2 In South African English, a **scholar** is a school pupil.

scholarship **scholarships**
NOUN If you win a **scholarship** to a school or university, your studies are paid for by the school or university, or by some other organization.

school **schools**
NOUN a place where children are educated

science **sciences**
NOUN the study of living things, materials and physical processes such as forces, electricity, sound and light

science fiction
NOUN stories about travelling through space, and imaginary events happening in the future or in other worlds

scientist **scientists**
NOUN someone who studies science or is an expert in science

scissors
PLURAL NOUN a cutting tool with two sharp blades

scold **scolds, scolding, scolded**
VERB If you **scold** someone, you tell them off.

scone **scones**
NOUN a small cake made from flour and fat, and usually eaten with cream and jam

scoop **scoops, scooping, scooped**
VERB **1** If you **scoop** something up, you pick it up using a spoon or the palm of your hand.
NOUN **2** an object like a large spoon that is used for picking up food such as ice cream

scooter **scooters**
NOUN **1** a small, light motorcycle
2 a simple cycle that a child rides, with two wheels and a narrow platform for standing on while pushing the ground with one foot

scope
NOUN **1** the opportunity or freedom to do something
2 the extent of something • *That subject is beyond the **scope** of this lesson.*

scorch **scorches, scorching, scorched**
VERB If you **scorch** something, you burn it slightly.

score **scores, scoring, scored**
VERB **1** If you **score** in a game, you get a goal, a run or a point.
NOUN **2** the number of goals, runs or points obtained by the two opponents in a game

scornful
ADJECTIVE If you are **scornful** of something or someone, you think very little of them and show very little respect for them.

scorpion **scorpions**
NOUN an animal that looks like a small lobster. It has a long tail with a poisonous sting on the end.

scour **scours, scouring, scoured**
VERB **1** If you **scour** a place, you look all over it in order to find something.
2 If you **scour** something like a pan, you clean it by rubbing it hard with something rough.

scout **scouts, scouting, scouted**
NOUN **1** A **Scout** is a boy who is a member of the **Scout** Association, an organization for boys that aims to develop character and responsibility.
2 someone who is sent on ahead to get information about something
VERB **3** If you **scout** around for something, you look around for it.

scowl **scowls, scowling, scowled**
VERB **1** If you **scowl**, you frown because you are angry.
NOUN **2** an angry expression

scrabble **scrabbles, scrabbling, scrabbled**
VERB If you **scrabble** at something, you scrape at it with your hands.

scramble **scrambles, scrambling, scrambled**
VERB **1** If you **scramble** over something, you climb over it using your hands to help you.
2 When you **scramble** eggs, you mix them up and cook them in a pan.
NOUN **3** a motorcycle race over rough ground

scrap **scraps, scrapping, scrapped**
NOUN **1** a very small piece of something
2 unwanted or waste material
3 INFORMAL If you get into a **scrap**, you get into a fight.
VERB **4** If you **scrap** something, you get rid of it.

scrapbook **scrapbooks**
NOUN a book with blank pages that you can fill with photographs or cuttings that interest you

scrape **scrapes, scraping, scraped**
VERB **1** If you **scrape** something off a surface, you remove it by pulling a rough or sharp object over it.
2 If you **scrape** past something, you pass very close to it.

scratch **scratches, scratching, scratched**
VERB **1** If you **scratch** something, you make a small cut or mark on it with something sharp.
2 If you **scratch**, you rub your skin with your nails because it is itching.
NOUN **3** a small cut or mark on the surface of something

scrawl **scrawls, scrawling, scrawled**
VERB **1** If you **scrawl** something, you write it in a careless and untidy way.
NOUN **2** careless and untidy writing

scream **screams, screaming, screamed**
VERB **1** If you **scream**, you shout or cry in a loud, high-pitched voice.
NOUN **2** a loud, high-pitched cry

screech **screeches, screeching, screeched**
VERB **1** If a person, animal or machine **screeches**, they make an unpleasant, high-pitched noise.
NOUN **2** an unpleasant, high-pitched noise

screen **screens, screening, screened**
NOUN **1** a vertical surface on which a picture can be shown, such as a television **screen**
2 a panel used to separate different parts of a room, or to protect or hide something
VERB **3** If a doctor **screens** you for a disease, they test to see if you have it.

screenplay **screenplays**
NOUN the script of a film

screw **screws, screwing, screwed**
NOUN **1** a small, sharp piece of metal with

a spiral groove cut into it, used for fixing things together or for fixing something to a wall using a twisting action
VERB **2** If you **screw** something onto something else, you fix it there by twisting it round and round, or by using a screw. • *He **screwed** the top on the ink bottle.*

screw up
VERB If you **screw up** paper or cloth, you twist it or squeeze it into a tight ball.

screwdriver **screwdrivers**
NOUN a tool for putting in or taking out screws

scribble **scribbles, scribbling, scribbled**
VERB **1** If you **scribble** something, you write it quickly and untidily.
2 To **scribble** also means to make meaningless marks. • *When Caroline was three she **scribbled** on a wall.*

script **scripts**
NOUN the written version of a play or film

scripture **scriptures**
NOUN sacred writings, especially the Bible

scroll **scrolls, scrolling, scrolled**
NOUN **1** a long roll of paper or parchment with writing on it
VERB **2** When you **scroll** text on a computer screen, you move it up or down to see the text that is not visible on the screen.

scrounge **scrounges, scrounging, scrounged**
VERB INFORMAL If you **scrounge** something, you get it by asking for it rather than by earning or buying it.

scrub **scrubs, scrubbing, scrubbed**
VERB **1** If you **scrub** something, you clean it by rubbing it very hard, especially with a brush and water.
NOUN **2** ground covered with bushes and small trees

scruffy **scruffier, scruffiest**
ADJECTIVE untidy

scrum **scrums**
NOUN When rugby players form a **scrum**, they form a group and push against each other with their heads down in an attempt to get the ball.

scuba diving
NOUN the sport of swimming underwater with special breathing equipment [an abbreviation for *self-contained underwater breathing apparatus*]

scuffle **scuffles, scuffling, scuffled**
VERB **1** When people **scuffle**, they have a short, rough fight.
NOUN **2** a short, rough fight

sculptor **sculptors**
NOUN someone who makes sculptures

sculpture **sculptures**
NOUN a work of art made by shaping or carving stone, clay or wood

scum
NOUN a layer of dirty froth on the surface of a liquid

scurry **scurries, scurrying, scurried**
VERB If you **scurry**, you run with quick, short steps.

scuttle **scuttles, scuttling, scuttled**
VERB **1** If a person or an animal **scuttles**, they run with short, quick steps.
2 To **scuttle** a ship means to sink it deliberately by making holes in the bottom.
NOUN **3** a container for coal

scythe **scythes**
NOUN a tool with a long handle and a curved blade used for cutting grass or grain

sea **seas**
NOUN one of the areas of salty water that cover much of the earth's surface

seafood
PLURAL NOUN fish or shellfish from the sea eaten as food

seagull **seagulls**
NOUN a common, white, grey and black bird that lives near the sea

A B C D E F G H I J K L M N O P Q R S T U V W X Y Z

seahorse **seahorses**
NOUN a small fish that swims upright, with a head that looks rather like a horse's head

seal **seals, sealing, sealed**
NOUN **1** a fish-eating mammal with flippers, that lives partly on land and partly in the sea
2 something fixed over the opening of a container that prevents anything getting in or out, and which must be broken before the container can be opened
VERB **3** If you **seal** an envelope, you stick down the flap.

seam **seams**
NOUN **1** a line of stitches joining two pieces of cloth
2 a long, narrow layer of coal beneath the ground

search **searches, searching, searched**
VERB **1** If you **search** for something, you look for it very thoroughly.
2 If a person is **searched**, their body and clothing are examined to see if they are hiding anything.
NOUN **3** an attempt to find something
• *I found my purse after a long **search**.*

search engine **search engines**
NOUN a service on the internet which lets you search for information

searchlight **searchlights**
NOUN a light with a powerful beam that can be turned in different directions

seashore
NOUN the land along the edge of the sea

seasick
ADJECTIVE feeling sick because of the movement of a boat
seasickness NOUN

seaside
NOUN a place by the sea, especially where people go on holiday

season **seasons, seasoning, seasoned**
NOUN **1** one of the periods into which a year is divided and which have their own typical weather conditions. The **seasons** are spring, summer, autumn and winter.
2 a period of the year when something usually happens
VERB **3** If you **season** food, you add salt, pepper, herbs or spices to it.

seasoning **seasonings**
NOUN something with a strong taste, like salt, pepper or spices used to add flavour to food

seat **seats**
NOUN something you can sit on

seat belt **seat belts**
NOUN a strap that you put around your body for safety when you are travelling in a car, coach or aircraft

seaweed
NOUN plants that grow in the sea

secluded
ADJECTIVE quiet and hidden from view
• *We found a lovely **secluded** beach.*

second **seconds**
NOUN OR ADJECTIVE **1** The **second** or the **second** thing in a series is the one counted as number two.
NOUN **2** one of the sixty parts that a minute is divided into

secondary
ADJECTIVE **1** Something **secondary** is less important than something else.
2 **Secondary** education is education for pupils between the ages of 11 and 18.

secondary school **secondary schools**
NOUN a school for pupils aged between 11 and 18

second-hand
ADJECTIVE OR ADVERB Something that is **second-hand** has already been owned by someone else. • *My brother has a **second-hand** car.*

second person
NOUN In grammar, you use the **second person** *you* when you speak or write to someone directly, for example, *you said*, *you are*.

secret **secrets**
ADJECTIVE **1** Something that is **secret** is known to only a small number of people and hidden from everyone else. • *a **secret** meeting*
NOUN **2** something known to only a small number of people and hidden from everyone else

secretary **secretaries**
NOUN a person employed by an organization to keep records, write letters and do office work

secretive
ADJECTIVE **Secretive** people tend to hide their feelings and intentions, and like to keep things secret.

sect **sects**
NOUN a group of people who have special or unusual religious beliefs

section **sections**
NOUN one of the parts that something is divided into

secure **secures, securing, secured**
VERB **1** If you **secure** something, you make it safe or fix it firmly.
ADJECTIVE **2** If something is **secure**, it is safe from harm.

security
NOUN OR ADJECTIVE all the things you do to make sure that you and your property are safe

see **sees, seeing, saw, seen**
VERB **1** If you **see** something, you look at it or notice it with your eyes.
2 If you **see** something, you understand it or realize what it means. • *I **see** what you mean.*
3 If you **see** that something happens, you make sure that it is done.

seed **seeds**
NOUN the part of a plant that can grow into a new plant of the same type

seek **seeks, seeking, sought**
VERB FORMAL If you **seek** something, you try and find it.

seem **seems, seeming, seemed**
VERB If something **seems** to be the case, it appears to be the case, or you think it is the case.

seen
VERB the past participle of **see**

seep **seeps, seeping, seeped**
VERB If a liquid or gas **seeps**, it flows very slowly.

seesaw **seesaws**
NOUN a long plank supported in the middle, so that one person can sit on either end and each can move up and down

seethe **seethes, seething, seethed**
VERB **1** When a liquid **seethes**, it boils or bubbles.
ADJECTIVE **2** If you are **seething**, you are very angry.

segment **segments**
NOUN **1** one part of something
2 The **segments** of an orange or grapefruit are the sections you can divide it into.

segregate **segregates, segregating, segregated**
VERB To **segregate** two groups of people means to keep them apart from each other.

seize **seizes, seizing, seized**
VERB If you **seize** something, you grab it firmly.

seldom
ADVERB not very often • *They **seldom** watch television.*

select **selects, selecting, selected**
VERB If you **select** something, you choose it.

self **selves**
NOUN your own personality or nature that makes you different from anyone else

a b c d e f g h i j k l m n o p q r s t u v w x y z

self-conscious
ADJECTIVE Someone who is **self-conscious** is easily embarrassed, and worried about what other people think of them. • *She was **self-conscious** when the teacher asked her to read her poem.*

self-defence
NOUN the use of special physical techniques to protect yourself when someone attacks you

selfie **selfies**
NOUN INFORMAL a photograph taken by pointing a camera at yourself

selfish
ADJECTIVE caring only about yourself, and not about other people

self-service
ADJECTIVE A **self-service** shop or restaurant is one where you serve yourself.

sell **sells, selling, sold**
VERB If you **sell** something, you let someone have it in return for money.

Sellotape
NOUN TRADEMARK a transparent sticky tape

semaphore
NOUN a system of signalling by holding flags out with your arms in different positions to show letters of the alphabet

semi-
PREFIX You add **semi-** to the beginning of a word to mean half or partly. For example, a **semi**circle is half of a circle.

semicircle **semicircles**
NOUN a half of a circle, or something with this shape
semicircular ADJECTIVE

semicolon **semicolons**
NOUN the punctuation mark (;) is used to separate different parts of a sentence or to show a pause

semidetached
ADJECTIVE A **semidetached** house is joined to another house on one side.

semifinal **semifinals**
NOUN one of the two matches or races in a competition that are held to decide who will compete in the final

send **sends, sending, sent**
VERB **1** When you **send** something to someone, you arrange for it to be delivered to them.
2 If a person **sends** someone somewhere, they tell them to go there.

senile
ADJECTIVE If old people become **senile**, they become confused and cannot look after themselves.

senior **seniors**
ADJECTIVE **1** A **senior** official or employee has one of the highest and most important jobs in an organization.
NOUN **2** If you are someone's **senior**, you are older than they are, or in a more important position.

senior citizen **senior citizens**
NOUN an elderly person, especially one receiving a pension

sensation **sensations**
NOUN **1** a feeling that you have
2 If something causes a **sensation**, it causes great interest and excitement.

sensational
ADJECTIVE **1** INFORMAL extremely good • *The concert was **sensational**.*
2 causing great excitement or interest

sense **senses**
NOUN **1** the physical abilities of sight, hearing, smell, touch and taste • *I have a good **sense** of smell.*
2 a feeling • *a **sense** of guilt*
3 the ability to think and behave sensibly
PHRASE **4** If something **makes sense**, you can understand it or it seems sensible.

senseless
ADJECTIVE **1** Something **senseless** has no reason to it. • *The violence of the hooligans was **senseless**.*
2 If someone is **senseless**, they are unconscious.

sensible
ADJECTIVE showing good sense and judgment

sensitive
ADJECTIVE **1** If you are **sensitive**, you understand other people's feelings.
SYNONYM: perceptive
2 If you are **sensitive** about something, you are easily worried or upset about it.
SYNONYM: touchy
3 easily affected or harmed by something • *My skin is **sensitive** to the sun.*

sent
VERB the past tense and past participle of **send**

sentence **sentences, sentencing, sentenced**
NOUN **1** a group of words that make a statement, question or command. When written down, a **sentence** begins with a capital letter and ends with a full stop.
2 In a law court, a **sentence** is a punishment given to someone who has been found guilty.
VERB **3** When a guilty person is **sentenced**, they are told officially what their punishment will be.

sentimental
ADJECTIVE **1** having an exaggerated feeling of tenderness or sadness
2 having something to do with a person's feelings

sentry **sentries**
NOUN a soldier who keeps watch and guards a camp or building

separate **separates, separating, separated**
ADJECTIVE **1** If something is **separate** from something else, the two things are not connected.
VERB **2** If you **separate** people or things, you cause them to be apart from each other.
3 If people or things **separate**, they move away from each other.

There are two *a*s in *separate*.

September
NOUN the ninth month of the year. **September** has 30 days.
[from the Latin word *septem* meaning seven, because it was the seventh month of the Roman calendar]

septic
ADJECTIVE If a wound becomes **septic**, it becomes infected by harmful bacteria.

sequel **sequels**
NOUN A **sequel** to a book or film is another book or film that continues the story.

sequence **sequences**
NOUN **1** a number of events coming one after the other
2 the order in which things are arranged or happen • *Put the pictures in **sequence** to tell the story.*

serene
ADJECTIVE peaceful and calm

sergeant **sergeants**
NOUN a rank in the police force, the army or the air force

serial **serials**
NOUN a story that is broadcast or published in a number of parts over a period of time

series
NOUN **1** a number of things coming one after the other
2 A radio or television **series** is a set of programmes with the same title.

serious
ADJECTIVE **1** A **serious** problem or situation is very bad and worrying.
2 **Serious** matters are important and should be thought about carefully.
3 If you are **serious** about something, you really mean it.
4 People who are **serious** are thoughtful, quiet and do not laugh much.

sermon **sermons**
NOUN a talk on a religious or moral subject given as part of a church service

serpent **serpents**
NOUN LITERARY a snake

servant **servants**
NOUN someone who is employed to work in another person's house

serve **serves, serving, served**
VERB **1** If you **serve** food or drink to people, you give it to them.
2 When someone **serves** customers in a shop, bar or restaurant, they help them and supply them with what they want. • *The shop was very busy so we had to wait for the assistant to* ***serve*** *us.*
3 In some games, such as tennis, when you **serve** you start the game by hitting the ball to your opponent.

service **services**
NOUN **1** a system organized to provide something for the public • *The bus* ***service*** *from our village into town is very good.*
2 Motorway **services** consist of a petrol station, toilets, a shop and a restaurant.
3 If your car has a **service**, it is checked over and repaired if it is broken or damaged.
4 a religious ceremony

session **sessions**
NOUN the period during which an activity takes place

set **sets, setting, set**
VERB **1** When something such as jelly or concrete **sets**, it changes from a liquid into a solid.
NOUN **2** a group of things that go together
3 In mathematics, a **set** is a collection of numbers that are treated as a group.
4 In tennis, a **set** is a group of six or more games.
VERB **5** If you **set** your watch or clock, you adjust it for a particular time.
ADJECTIVE **6** If you do something at a **set** time, it is fixed at that time and does not change.

settee **settees**
NOUN a long comfortable seat for two or three people to sit on
SYNONYM: sofa

setting **settings**
NOUN The **setting** of something like a play or a story is its surroundings, and where it happens.

settle **settles, settling, settled**
VERB **1** If you **settle** something, you decide on it or sort it out. • *Let's* ***settle*** *this argument as quickly as possible.*
2 If you **settle** in a place, you make it your home.
3 If you **settle**, or **settle** down, you relax and make yourself comfortable.
4 If snow or dust **settles**, it sinks slowly down and comes to rest.

settlement **settlements**
NOUN a place where people have settled and made their homes

seven
NOUN **Seven** is the number 7.
seventh NOUN OR ADJECTIVE

seventeen
NOUN **Seventeen** is the number 17.
seventeenth NOUN OR ADJECTIVE

seventy
NOUN **Seventy** is the number 70.
seventieth NOUN OR ADJECTIVE

sever **severs, severing, severed**
Rhymes with "never" VERB If you **sever** something, you cut it off or cut right through it.

several
ADJECTIVE OR PRONOUN a small number of people or things

severe
Said "suh-**veer**" ADJECTIVE **1** extremely bad or serious
2 strict or harsh

sew **sews, sewing, sewed, sewn**
VERB When you **sew** something, you use a needle and thread to make or mend it.

sewage
NOUN dirty water and waste that is carried away in drains from buildings

sewer **sewers**
NOUN a series of pipes and drains that carries away dirty water and waste from buildings

sex **sexes**
NOUN **1** one of the two groups, male and female, into which animals, including humans, are divided

2 the physical activity by which people and animals produce young
sexual ADJECTIVE

sexism
NOUN the belief that one gender is less intelligent or less able than the other, or in some way not as good as the other
sexist ADJECTIVE OR NOUN

shabby **shabbier, shabbiest**
ADJECTIVE Something or someone who is **shabby** looks old and ragged.

shack **shacks**
NOUN a small, roughly built hut

shade **shades, shading, shaded**
NOUN **1** an area of darkness and coolness that sunshine does not reach
2 the different forms of a colour. For example, olive green is a **shade** of green.
3 an object that decreases or shuts out light, such as a lampshade
VERB **4** If you **shade** a person or a thing, you protect them from the sun's heat or light.

shadow **shadows, shadowing, shadowed**
NOUN **1** the dark shape formed when an opaque object stops light from reaching a surface

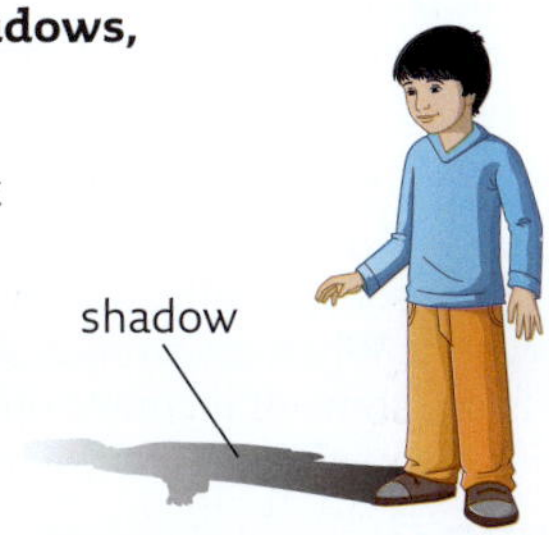

VERB **2** When you **shadow** someone, you follow them and watch them closely.

shady **shadier, shadiest**
ADJECTIVE A **shady** place is sheltered from the sunlight by trees or buildings.

shaft **shafts**
NOUN **1** A **shaft** in a mine or for a lift is a passage that goes straight down.
2 a beam of light
3 In a machine, the **shaft** is a rod that turns in order to transmit power or movement.

shaggy **shaggier, shaggiest**
ADJECTIVE covered with thick, long, untidy hair

shake **shakes, shaking, shook, shaken**
VERB **1** If you **shake** something, you move it quickly from side to side or up and down.
2 If something **shakes**, it moves from side to side or up and down with small, quick movements.
3 When you **shake** your head, you move it from side to side in order to say no.
NOUN **4** If you give something a **shake**, you shake it.
PHRASE **5** When you **shake hands** with someone, you grasp their hand in yours as a way of greeting them.

shaky **shakier, shakiest**
ADJECTIVE rather weak, shaking and unsteady • *The foal got up on **shaky** legs.*

shall **should**
VERB used with *I* and *we* to refer to the future • *I **shall** go shopping tomorrow.* • *I **should** wait till next week to open my birthday present.*

shallow **shallower, shallowest**
ADJECTIVE not deep • *The water here is quite **shallow**.*

shame
NOUN **1** the feeling of guilt or embarrassment you get when you know you have done something wrong or foolish
2 If you say something is a **shame**, you mean you are sorry about it. • *It's a **shame** you can't come round to tea.*

shampoo **shampoos**
NOUN a soapy liquid used for washing your hair

shamrock **shamrocks**
NOUN a plant with three round leaves on each stem, which is the national emblem of Ireland
[from Irish Gaelic *seamrog* meaning little clover]

shanty **shanties**
NOUN **1** a small, rough hut
2 A sea **shanty** is a song sailors used to sing.

shape **shapes**
NOUN **1** The **shape** of something is the form or pattern of its outline, for example whether it is round or square. • *The chocolates came in a box in the **shape** of a heart.*
2 something with a definite form, for example a circle or square

share **shares, sharing, shared**
VERB **1** If two people **share** something, they both use it, do it, or have it. • *We **shared** a bar of chocolate.*
NOUN **2** A **share** of something is a portion of it. • *I want a fair **share** of the cake.*

share out
VERB If you **share out** something, you give it out equally among a group of people. • *They **shared out** the food between them.*

shark **sharks**
NOUN a large, powerful fish, usually with two fins on its back and rows of sharp teeth

sharp **sharper, sharpest**
ADJECTIVE **1** A **sharp** object has an edge or point that is good for cutting or piercing things.
2 A **sharp** change is sudden and noticeable. • *There was a **sharp** rise in temperature after the sun came up.*
3 A **sharp** taste is sour.
4 Someone who is **sharp** can pick up ideas very quickly.
5 A **sharp** pain is strong and sudden.

sharpen **sharpens, sharpening, sharpened**
VERB If you **sharpen** an object such as a knife, you make its edge or point sharper.

shatter **shatters, shattering, shattered**
VERB If something **shatters**, it breaks into a lot of small pieces. • *The windows **shattered** in the explosion.*

shave **shaves, shaving, shaved**
VERB When someone **shaves**, they remove hair with a razor from part of their body.

shavings
PLURAL NOUN small, fine pieces of wood that have been cut off a larger piece

shawl **shawls**
NOUN a large piece of cloth worn round a woman's head or shoulders, or used to wrap a baby in

she
PRONOUN **She** is used to refer to a woman or girl who has already been mentioned.

sheaf **sheaves**
NOUN **1** a bundle of papers
2 a bundle of ripe corn

shear **shears, shearing, sheared, shorn**
VERB When someone **shears** a sheep, they cut the wool off it.

shears
PLURAL NOUN **Shears** are a tool like a large pair of scissors, used especially for cutting hedges.

sheath **sheaths**
NOUN a cover for the blade of a knife or a sword

shed **sheds, shedding, shed**
NOUN **1** a small building used for storing things, especially in a garden
VERB **2** When an animal **sheds** hair or skin, some of it comes off.
3 If you **shed** tears, you cry.

she'd
a contraction of *she had* or *she would*

sheen
NOUN a gentle shine on the surface of something

sheep
NOUN a mammal kept on farms for its meat and wool

The plural of *sheep* is *sheep*.

sheepdog **sheepdogs**
NOUN a breed of dog often used for controlling sheep

sheepish
ADJECTIVE If you look **sheepish**, you look shy or embarrassed.

sheer **sheerer, sheerest**
ADJECTIVE **1** A **sheer** cliff or drop is vertical.
2 complete and total • ***sheer*** *exhaustion*
3 **Sheer** fabrics are very light and delicate.

sheet **sheets**
NOUN **1** a large rectangular piece of cloth used to cover a bed
2 a rectangular piece of paper

sheikh **sheikhs**
Rhymes with "make" NOUN an Arab chief or ruler
[from Arabic *shaykh* meaning old man]

shelf **shelves**
NOUN a flat piece of wood, metal or glass fixed to a wall or a cabinet or cupboard and used for putting things on

shell **shells**
NOUN **1** the hard covering of an egg or nut
2 the hard, protective covering on the back of a tortoise, snail or crab

she'll
a contraction of *she will* or *she shall*

shellfish **shellfish** or **shellfishes**
NOUN a small sea creature with a shell

shelter **shelters, sheltering, sheltered**
NOUN **1** a small building made to protect people from bad weather or danger • *We waited in the bus* ***shelter****.*
2 If a place gives **shelter**, it protects you from bad weather or danger.
VERB **3** If you **shelter** in a place, you stay there and are safe and protected.
4 To **shelter** someone or something means to protect them from bad weather or danger.

shepherd **shepherds**
NOUN a person who looks after sheep

sheriff **sheriffs**
NOUN **1** in America, a person elected to enforce the law in a county
2 in Scotland, the senior judge of a county or district
3 in Australia, an officer of the Supreme Court who does certain paperwork

sherry **sherries**
NOUN a kind of strong wine

she's
a contraction of *she is* or *she has*

shield **shields, shielding, shielded**
NOUN **1** a large piece of a strong material like metal or plastic that soldiers or policemen carry to protect themselves
VERB **2** If you **shield** someone or something, you protect them from something. • *He* ***shielded*** *his eyes from the sun with his hand.*

shift **shifts, shifting, shifted**
VERB **1** If you **shift** something, you move it.
2 If something **shifts**, it moves.
NOUN **3** a set period during which people work • *the night* ***shift***

shilling **shillings**
NOUN a coin that was once used in Britain, Australia and New Zealand. There were 20 **shillings** in a pound.

shimmer **shimmers, shimmering, shimmered**
VERB **1** If something **shimmers**, it shines with a faint, flickering light.
NOUN **2** a faint, flickering light

shin **shins**
NOUN the front part of your leg between your knee and your ankle

shine **shines, shining, shone** or **shined**
VERB **1** When something **shines**, it is bright because it gives out or reflects light.
2 If you **shine** a torch or lamp somewhere, you point it there so that it becomes light.
3 If you **shine** your shoes, you polish them.

shingle
NOUN small pebbles on the seashore

shingles
PLURAL NOUN a disease that causes a painful red rash, especially around the waist

shiny **shinier, shiniest**
ADJECTIVE **Shiny** things are bright and look as if they have been polished.

ship **ships, shipping, shipped**
NOUN **1** a large boat that carries passengers or cargo
VERB **2** If people or things are **shipped** somewhere, they are transported there by ship.

shipwreck **shipwrecks; shipwrecked**
NOUN **1** When there is a **shipwreck**, a ship is destroyed in a storm or an accident at sea.
2 the remains of a ship that has been damaged or sunk
ADJECTIVE **3** If someone is **shipwrecked**, they survive a shipwreck and manage to reach land.

shipyard **shipyards**
NOUN a place where ships are built and repaired

shirk **shirks, shirking, shirked**
VERB If you **shirk** a task, you try to avoid doing it.

shirt **shirts**
NOUN a piece of clothing with a collar, sleeves and buttons down the front, worn on the upper part of the body

shiver **shivers, shivering, shivered**
VERB When you **shiver**, you tremble slightly because you are cold or scared.

shoal **shoals**
NOUN a large group of fish swimming together

shock **shocks, shocking, shocked**
NOUN **1** a sudden upsetting experience
VERB **2** If something **shocks** you, it upsets you because it is unpleasant and unexpected.

shocking
ADJECTIVE **1** Something that shocks people is **shocking**.
2 INFORMAL very bad • *The weather has been **shocking**.*

shoddy **shoddier, shoddiest**
ADJECTIVE badly made or done

shoe **shoes**
NOUN a strong covering for each of your feet. **Shoes** cover most of your foot, but not your ankle.

shoelace **shoelaces**
NOUN a cord for fastening a shoe

shone
VERB the past tense and past participle of **shine**

shook
VERB the past tense of **shake**

shoot **shoots, shooting, shot**
VERB **1** If someone **shoots** a person or an animal, they injure or kill them by firing a gun at them.
2 When a film is **shot**, it is filmed.

shooting star **shooting stars**
NOUN a meteor

shop **shops, shopping, shopped**
NOUN **1** a place where things are sold
2 a place where a particular type of work is done • *a bicycle repair **shop***
VERB **3** When you **shop**, you go to the shops to buy things.

shopkeeper **shopkeepers**
NOUN someone who owns or manages a small shop

shopping
NOUN Your **shopping** is the goods you have bought in a shop.

shore **shores**
NOUN the land along the edge of a sea, lake or wide river

short **shorter, shortest**
ADJECTIVE **1** not lasting very long
2 small in length, distance or height
3 If you are **short** of something, you do not have enough of it.

4 If a name is **short** for another name, it is a quick way of saying it. • *her friend Kes (**short** for Kesewa)*

shortage **shortages**
NOUN If there is a **shortage** of something, there is not enough of it.

shortcut **shortcuts**
NOUN **1** a quicker way of getting somewhere than the usual route
2 a quicker way of doing something than the usual way

shorten **shortens, shortening, shortened**
VERB If you **shorten** something, you make it shorter.

shorthand
NOUN a way of writing in which signs represent words or syllables. It is used to write down quickly what someone is saying.

shortly
ADVERB soon • *I'll be there **shortly**.*

shorts
PLURAL NOUN trousers with legs that stop at or above the knee

short-sighted
ADJECTIVE If you are **short-sighted**, you cannot see things clearly when they are far away.

shot **shots**
VERB **1** the past tense of **shoot**
NOUN **2** the act of firing a gun
3 In football, golf, tennis and other ball games, a **shot** is the act of kicking or hitting the ball.
4 a photograph or short film sequence

should
VERB **1** You use **should** to say that something ought to happen. • *Kylie **should** have done better.*
2 You also use **should** to say that you expect something to happen. • *We **should** have heard by now.*
3 **Should** is used in questions where you are asking someone for advice about what to do. • ***Should** we tell her about it?*

shoulder **shoulders**
NOUN Your **shoulders** are the parts of your body between your neck and the tops of your arms.

shouldn't
VERB a contraction of *should not*

shout **shouts, shouting, shouted**
NOUN **1** a loud call or cry
VERB **2** If you **shout** something, you say it very loudly.

shove **shoves, shoving, shoved**
VERB **1** If you **shove** someone or something, you push them roughly.
NOUN **2** a rough push

shovel **shovels, shovelling, shovelled**
NOUN **1** a tool like a spade, with the sides curved up, used for moving earth or snow
VERB **2** If you **shovel** earth or snow, you move it with a shovel.

show **shows, showing, showed, shown**
VERB **1** If you **show** someone something, you let them see it.
2 If you **show** someone how to do something, you demonstrate it to them. • *Jake **showed** me how to make a chocolate cake.*
3 If something **shows**, you can see it.
4 If you **show** someone to a room or seat, you lead them there.
NOUN **5** a form of entertainment at the theatre or on television • *My favourite talk **show** is on TV tonight.*
6 a display or exhibition • *a flower **show***

show off
VERB INFORMAL If someone is **showing off**, they are trying to impress people.

shower **showers, showering, showered**
NOUN **1** a device that sprays you with water so that you can wash yourself
2 If you have a **shower**, you wash yourself by standing under a **shower**.
3 a short period of rain

VERB **4** If you are **showered** with a lot of things, they fall on you like rain.

showroom **showrooms**
NOUN a shop where goods such as cars or electrical items are displayed for customers to look at

shrank
VERB the past tense of **shrink**

shrapnel
NOUN small pieces of metal scattered from an exploding shell
[named after General Henry *Shrapnel* (1761–1842), who invented it]

shred **shreds, shredding, shredded**
VERB **1** If you **shred** something, you cut or tear it into very small pieces.
NOUN **2** a small, narrow piece of paper or material

shrew **shrews**
NOUN a small mouse-like mammal with a long pointed nose

shrewd **shrewder, shrewdest**
ADJECTIVE Someone who is **shrewd** makes good judgments and uses their common sense.

shriek **shrieks, shrieking, shrieked**
NOUN **1** a high-pitched cry or scream
VERB **2** If you **shriek**, you make a high-pitched cry or scream.

shrill **shriller, shrillest**
ADJECTIVE A **shrill** sound is unpleasantly high-pitched and piercing.
shrilly ADVERB

shrimp **shrimps**
NOUN a small edible shellfish with a long tail and many legs

shrine **shrines**
NOUN a place of worship connected with a sacred person or object

shrink **shrinks, shrinking, shrank, shrunk**
VERB If something **shrinks**, it becomes smaller.

shrinkage
NOUN the amount by which something shrinks

shrivel **shrivels, shrivelling, shrivelled**
VERB When something **shrivels**, it becomes dry and withered.

shrub **shrubs**
NOUN a bushy plant with woody stems

shrug **shrugs, shrugging, shrugged**
VERB If you **shrug** your shoulders, you raise them slightly as a sign that you do not know or do not care about something.

shrunk
VERB the past participle of **shrink**

shudder **shudders, shuddering, shuddered**
VERB **1** If you **shudder**, you tremble with fear or horror.
2 If a machine or vehicle **shudders**, it shakes violently.
NOUN **3** a shiver of fear or horror

shuffle **shuffles, shuffling, shuffled**
VERB **1** If you **shuffle**, you walk without lifting your feet off the ground properly, so that they drag.
2 If you **shuffle** a pack of cards, you mix them up before you begin a game.

shut **shuts, shutting, shut**
VERB **1** If you **shut** something, you close it.
ADJECTIVE **2** If something is **shut**, it is closed.

shutter **shutters**
NOUN **1** a screen that can be closed over a window
2 the device in a camera that opens and closes to let light onto the film

shuttle **shuttles**
ADJECTIVE **1** A **shuttle** service is an air, bus or train service that makes frequent journeys between two places.
NOUN **2** a type of American spacecraft

shuttlecock **shuttlecocks**
NOUN the feathered object that players hit over the net in the game of badminton

shy **shyer, shyest**
ADJECTIVE A **shy** person is quiet and uncomfortable in the company of other people.

sibling **siblings**
NOUN FORMAL Your **siblings** are your brothers and sisters.
[from Old English *sibling* meaning relative]

sick **sicker, sickest**
ADJECTIVE **1** If you are **sick**, you are ill.
2 If you feel **sick**, you feel as if you are going to vomit.
3 If you are **sick**, you vomit.

sickness **sicknesses**
NOUN an illness or disease

side **sides, siding, sided**
NOUN **1** a position to the left or right of something • *There were trees on both* ***sides*** *of the road.*
2 The **sides** of something are its outside surfaces, or edges, that are not at the top, bottom, front or back. • *There is a label on the* ***side*** *of the box.*
3 The **sides** of an area, surface or object are its different surfaces or edges. • *Write on one* ***side*** *of the paper.*
4 Your **sides** are the parts of your body from your armpits down to your hips.
5 The two **sides** in a war, argument or relationship are the two people or groups involved. • *Whose* ***side*** *are you on?*
ADJECTIVE **6** situated on a side of a building or vehicle • *the* ***side*** *door*
VERB **7** If you **side** with someone, you support them in a quarrel or an argument.

sideways
ADVERB moving or facing towards one side • *I took a step* ***sideways****.*

siding **sidings**
NOUN a short railway track beside the main tracks, where engines and carriages are left when not in use

siege **sieges**
NOUN a military operation in which an army surrounds a place to stop food or help from reaching the people inside

sieve **sieves, sieving, sieved**
NOUN **1** a tool made of mesh, used for sifting or straining things
VERB **2** If you **sieve** a powder or liquid, you pass it through a sieve to get rid of lumps and make it smooth.

sift **sifts, sifting, sifted**
VERB If you **sift** a powdery substance like flower or sugar, you pass it through a sieve to remove lumps.

sigh **sighs, sighing, sighed**
VERB When you **sigh**, you let out a deep breath, usually because you are tired, sad or relieved.

sight **sights**
NOUN **1** being able to see
2 something you see • *The sunset was a beautiful* ***sight****.*
PLURAL NOUN **3** **Sights** are interesting places that tourists visit.

sightseeing
NOUN visiting the interesting places that tourists usually visit

sign **signs, signing, signed**
NOUN **1** a mark or symbol that always has a particular meaning, for example in mathematics or music • *a plus* ***sign***
2 a board or notice with words, a picture or a symbol on it, giving information or a warning • *a stop* ***sign***
VERB **3** If you **sign** a document, you write your name on it by hand, in the way you usually write it.

signal **signals**
NOUN **1** a gesture, sound or action that is meant to give a message to someone
2 A railway **signal** is a piece of equipment beside the track that tells train drivers whether or not to stop.

signature **signatures**
NOUN If you write your **signature**, you write your name by hand in the way you usually write it.

significant
ADJECTIVE **1** A **significant** amount is large enough to be noticed and to matter. • *A* ***significant*** *number of people can't read.*

A B C D E F G H I J K L M N O P Q R S T U V W X Y Z

2 Something that is **significant** is important and means something.

sign language
NOUN a way of communicating using your hands, used especially by deaf people

signpost **signposts**
NOUN a road sign with information on it, such as the name of a town and how far away it is

Sikh **Sikhs**
NOUN a person who believes in Sikhism, an Indian religion that separated from Hinduism in the 16th century and which teaches that there is only one God

silence
NOUN When there is **silence**, there is no sound.
SYNONYM: quietness

silent
ADJECTIVE **1** If you are **silent**, you are not saying anything.
2 When something is **silent**, it makes no noise.

silhouette **silhouettes**
NOUN the dark outline of a shape against a light background
silhouetted ADJECTIVE

silicon
NOUN an element found in sand, clay and stone. It is used to make glass and parts of computers.

silk **silks**
NOUN fine, soft cloth made from threads produced from silkworm cocoons

sill **sills**
NOUN a strip of stone, wood or metal underneath a window or a door

silly **sillier, silliest**
ADJECTIVE foolish or childish

silver
NOUN a valuable greyish-white metal used for making jewellery and ornaments

similar
ADJECTIVE If one thing is **similar** to another, they are quite like each other.

simile **similes**
NOUN an expression in which a person or thing is described as being similar to someone or something else. Examples of **similes** are *she runs like a deer* and *he's as white as a sheet.*

simmer **simmers, simmering, simmered**
VERB When food **simmers**, it cooks gently, just below boiling point.

simple **simpler, simplest**
ADJECTIVE **1** Something that is **simple** is easy to understand or do.
2 plain in style

simplify **simplifies, simplifying, simplified**
VERB If you **simplify** something, you make it simple or easy to understand.

simply
ADVERB in a simple way

simultaneous
ADJECTIVE Things that are **simultaneous** happen at the same time.
simultaneously ADVERB

sin **sins, sinning, sinned**
NOUN **1** wicked behaviour, particularly if it breaks a religious or moral law
VERB **2** To **sin** means to do something wicked.

since
PREPOSITION, CONJUNCTION OR ADVERB **1** from a particular time until now • *I've been waiting **since** half past three.*
2 because • *I had a drink, **since** I was feeling thirsty.*

sincere
ADJECTIVE If you are **sincere**, you are genuine and truly mean what you say.

sing **sings, singing, sang, sung**
VERB **1** When you **sing**, you make musical sounds with your voice, usually with words that fit a tune.
2 When birds or insects **sing**, they make pleasant and tuneful sounds.

singe **singes, singeing, singed**
VERB If you **singe** something, you burn it

slightly so that it goes brown but does not catch fire.

single **singles**
ADJECTIVE **1** only one and not more • *A **single** shot was fired.*
2 People who are **single** are not married.
3 A **single** bed or bedroom is for one person.
NOUN **4** A **single**, or a **single** ticket, is a ticket for a journey to a place but not back again.
5 a recording of one or two short pieces of music on a small record, CD or cassette

singular
NOUN In grammar, the **singular** is the form of a word that means just one person or thing.
ANTONYM: plural

sinister
ADJECTIVE Something or someone **sinister** seems harmful or evil.
[from Latin *sinister* meaning left-hand side, because the left side was considered unlucky]

sink **sinks, sinking, sank, sunk**
NOUN **1** a fixed basin with taps supplying water, usually in a kitchen or bathroom
VERB **2** If something **sinks**, it moves downwards, especially through water.

sip **sips, sipping, sipped**
VERB If you **sip** a drink, you take small mouthfuls.

sir
NOUN **1** FORMAL a polite way to address a man
2 Sir is the title of a knight or baronet.

siren **sirens**
NOUN a warning device, for example on an ambulance, that makes a loud, wailing noise • *The fire engines switched on their **sirens** as they raced to the fire.*

sister **sisters**
NOUN Your **sister** is a girl or woman who has the same parents as you.

sister-in-law **sisters-in-law**
NOUN Someone's **sister-in-law** is the wife of their brother, the sister of their husband or wife, or the woman married to their wife's or husband's brother.

sit **sits, sitting, sat**
VERB When you **sit**, you rest your bottom on something such as a chair or the floor.
• *We **sat** on the bench at the bus stop.*

site **sites**
NOUN a piece of ground where something happens or will happen • *the **site** for the fairground*

sitting room **sitting rooms**
NOUN a room with comfortable chairs for relaxing in

situated
ADJECTIVE in a particular place • *The cottage was **situated** on the edge of a forest.*

situation **situations**
NOUN **1** what is happening in a particular place at a particular time
2 The **situation** of a town or a building is its surroundings and its position.

six
NOUN **Six** is the number 6.
sixth NOUN OR ADJECTIVE

sixteen
NOUN **Sixteen** is the number 16.
sixteenth NOUN OR ADJECTIVE

sixty
NOUN **Sixty** is the number 60.
sixtieth NOUN OR ADJECTIVE

size **sizes**
NOUN **1** The **size** of something is how big it is.
2 a standard measurement for clothes, shoes and other objects

sizzle **sizzles, sizzling, sizzled**
VERB If something **sizzles**, it makes a hissing sound. • *The sausages **sizzled** in the frying pan.*

skate **skates, skating, skated**
NOUN **1 Skates** are ice **skates** or roller **skates**.
VERB **2** If you **skate**, you move about wearing skates.

skateboard **skateboards**
NOUN a narrow board on wheels, that you stand on and ride for fun
skateboarder NOUN **skateboarding** NOUN

skeleton **skeletons**
NOUN the framework of bones in your body

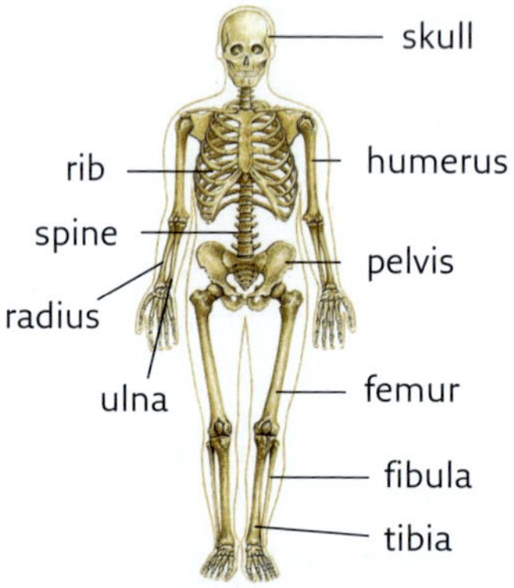

sketch **sketches, sketching, sketched**
NOUN **1** a quick, rough drawing
VERB **2** If you **sketch** something, you draw it quickly and roughly.

sketchy **sketchier, sketchiest**
ADJECTIVE If something is **sketchy**, it has little detail. • *The map showing how to get to the new house was **sketchy**.*

ski **skis, skiing, skied**
NOUN **1** **Skis** are long pieces of wood, metal or plastic that you fasten to special boots so you can move easily on snow.
VERB **2** When you **ski**, you move on snow wearing skis, especially as a sport.
[from Old Norse *skith* meaning snowshoes]

skid **skids, skidding, skidded**
VERB **1** If someone or something **skids**, they slide accidentally.
NOUN **2** a skidding movement

skilful
ADJECTIVE having a lot of skill
skilfully ADVERB

skill **skills**
NOUN **1** the knowledge and ability that enable you to do something well
2 a type of work or technique that needs special training and knowledge • *I would like to learn some new **skills**.*

skim **skims, skimming, skimmed**
VERB **1** If you **skim** something from the surface of a liquid, you remove it.
2 If something **skims** a surface, it moves lightly, smoothly and quickly over it.
• *seagulls **skimming** the waves*

skin **skins**
NOUN **1** the natural covering of a person or animal
2 the outer covering a fruit or vegetable

skinny **skinnier, skinniest**
ADJECTIVE thin

skip **skips, skipping, skipped**
VERB **1** When you **skip**, you jump lightly from one foot to the other, often over a rope.
2 If you **skip** something, you miss it out.
• *Amy **skipped** the part with the long words.*

skipper **skippers**
NOUN INFORMAL the captain of a ship or boat

skirt **skirts**
NOUN a piece of clothing that fastens at a woman's or girl's waist and hangs down over her legs

skittle **skittles**
NOUN **1** a wooden or plastic object, shaped like a bottle, that people try to knock down with a ball
2 **Skittles** is a game in which players roll a ball and try to knock down objects called skittles.

skull **skulls**
NOUN the bony part of your head that surrounds your brain

skunk **skunks**
NOUN a small black and white animal from North America that gives off an unpleasant smell if it is frightened

sky **skies**
NOUN the space around the earth that you can see when you look upwards

skyscraper **skyscrapers**
NOUN a very tall building

slab **slabs**
NOUN a thick, flat piece of something, such as stone

slack **slacker, slackest**
ADJECTIVE Something that is **slack** is loose and not firmly stretched or pulled tight.

slam **slams, slamming, slammed**
VERB If you **slam** something, such as a door, or if it **slams**, it shuts with a loud bang.

slang
NOUN very informal words and expressions

slant **slants, slanting, slanted**
VERB **1** If something **slants**, it slopes.
NOUN **2** a slope or a leaning position

slap **slaps, slapping, slapped**
VERB **1** If you **slap** someone, you hit them with the palm of your hand.
NOUN **2** If you give someone a **slap**, you slap them.

slash **slashes, slashing, slashed**
VERB **1** If someone **slashes** something, they make a long, deep cut in it.
NOUN **2** a long, deep cut

slate **slates**
NOUN **1** a dark grey rock that splits easily into thin layers
2 **Slates** are small, flat pieces of slate used for covering roofs.

slaughter **slaughters, slaughtering, slaughtered**
VERB **1** To **slaughter** farm animals means to kill them for meat.
2 To **slaughter** animals or people means to kill a large number of them unjustly or cruelly.
NOUN **3** the killing of many people or animals

slave **slaves, slaving, slaved**
NOUN **1** someone who is owned by another person and must work for them
VERB **2** If you **slave** over something, you work very hard at it.

slay **slays, slaying, slew, slain**
VERB LITERARY To **slay** someone means to kill them.

sledge
sledges
NOUN a vehicle on runners used for travelling over snow

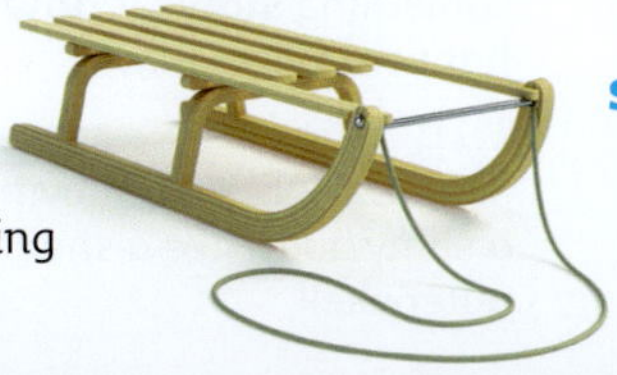

sledgehammer **sledgehammers**
NOUN a large, heavy hammer

sleek **sleeker, sleekest**
ADJECTIVE If something such as hair is **sleek**, it is smooth and shiny.

sleep **sleeps, sleeping, slept**
VERB When you **sleep**, you close your eyes and your whole body rests.

sleepless
ADJECTIVE unable to sleep or without sleep
• *I had a **sleepless** night last night.*

sleepy **sleepier, sleepiest**
ADJECTIVE tired and feeling like sleeping
sleepily ADVERB **sleepiness** NOUN

sleet
NOUN a mixture of rain and snow

sleeve **sleeves**
NOUN The **sleeves** of a piece of clothing are the parts that cover your arms.
• *a shirt with long **sleeves***

sleigh **sleighs**
NOUN a sledge pulled by animals

slender
ADJECTIVE slim

slept
VERB the past tense and past participle of **sleep**

slice **slices, slicing, sliced**
NOUN **1** A **slice** of cake, bread or other food is a piece of it cut from a larger piece.
VERB **2** If you **slice** food, you cut it into thin pieces.
3 To **slice** through something means to cut or move through it quickly, like a knife. • *The ship **sliced** through the water.*

slick **slicker, slickest; slicks**
ADJECTIVE **1** A **slick** action is done quickly and smoothly.
NOUN **2** An oil **slick** is a layer of oil floating on the surface of the sea or a lake.

slide **slides, sliding, slid**
VERB When something **slides**, it moves smoothly over or against something else.
• *She **slid** the door open.*

A B C D E F G H I J K L M N O P Q R S T U V W X Y Z

slight **slighter, slightest**
ADJECTIVE **1** small in amount • *a **slight** dent in the car*
2 A **slight** person has a slim, small body.

slim **slimmer, slimmest**
ADJECTIVE **1** A **slim** person is thin.
2 A **slim** object is fairly thin. • *a **slim** book*
3 If there is only a **slim** chance that something will happen, there is only a small chance that it will happen.

slime
NOUN an unpleasant, thick, slippery substance

sling **slings, slinging, slung**
VERB **1** INFORMAL If you **sling** something somewhere, you throw it there.
2 If you **sling** a rope between two points, you attach it so that it hangs loosely between them.
NOUN **3** a piece of cloth tied round a person's neck to support a broken or injured arm

slip **slips, slipping, slipped**
VERB **1** If you **slip**, you accidentally lose your balance.
2 If you **slip** somewhere, you go there quickly and quietly.
NOUN **3** a small mistake
4 a small piece of paper

slipper **slippers**
NOUN **Slippers** are loose, soft shoes that you wear indoors.

slippery
ADJECTIVE smooth, wet or greasy, and difficult to hold or walk on

slit **slits**
NOUN a long cut or narrow opening

slither **slithers, slithering, slithered**
VERB To **slither** somewhere means to move there by sliding along the ground in an uneven way. • *The snake **slithered** into the water.*

sliver **slivers**
NOUN a small, thin piece of something

slog **slogs, slogging, slogged**
VERB **1** If you **slog** at something, you work hard at it.
NOUN **2** a piece of hard work or effort

slogan **slogans**
NOUN a short, easily-remembered phrase used in advertising or by a political party
SYNONYMS: catch phrase, motto

slope **slopes, sloping, sloped**
NOUN **1** a flat surface that is at an angle, so that one end is higher than the other
VERB **2** If a surface **slopes**, it is at an angle.

sloppy **sloppier, sloppiest**
ADJECTIVE **1** liquid and spilling easily
2 careless or badly done
3 sentimental
sloppily ADVERB **sloppiness** NOUN

slot **slots**
NOUN a narrow opening in a machine or container for pushing something into
• *She put the coin in the **slot**.*

sloth **sloths**
NOUN **1** a South and Central American animal that moves very slowly and hangs upside down from the branches of trees
2 FORMAL laziness
slothful ADJECTIVE

slouch **slouches, slouching, slouched**
VERB If you **slouch**, you stand or sit with your shoulders and head drooping forwards.

slow **slower, slowest; slows, slowing, slowed**
ADJECTIVE **1** moving, happening or doing something with very little speed
2 If a clock or watch is **slow**, it shows a time earlier than the correct one.
VERB **3** If something **slows**, or you **slow** it, it moves or happens more slowly.

slow down
VERB If something **slows down** or something **slows** it **down**, it moves or happens more slowly.

slug **slugs**
NOUN a small, slow-moving animal with a slimy body, like a snail without an outer shell

sluggish
ADJECTIVE moving slowly and without much energy

slum **slums**
NOUN a poor, run-down area of a city or town

slumber **slumbers, slumbering, slumbered**
NOUN **1** LITERARY sleep
VERB **2** LITERARY When you **slumber**, you sleep.

slump **slumps, slumping, slumped**
VERB If you **slump** somewhere, you fall or sit down heavily.

slush
NOUN melting snow

sly **slyer** or **slier**, **slyest** or **sliest**
ADJECTIVE **1** A **sly** person is cunning and good at deceiving people.
2 A **sly** expression or remark shows that you know something other people do not know.

smack **smacks, smacking, smacked**
VERB **1** If you **smack** someone, you hit them with your open hand.
NOUN **2** If you give someone a **smack**, you smack them.

small **smaller, smallest**
ADJECTIVE not large in size, number or amount

smart **smarter, smartest**
ADJECTIVE **1** A **smart** person is clean and neatly dressed.
2 clever • *That's a **smart** idea.*

smartphone **smartphones**
NOUN a mobile phone that can send e-mails and access the internet

smash **smashes, smashing, smashed**
VERB **1** If you **smash** something, you break it into a lot of pieces by hitting it or dropping it.
2 If someone or something **smashes** through something, such as a fence, they go through it by breaking it.
3 To **smash** against something means to hit it with great force. • *A huge wave **smashed** against the boat.*

smear **smears, smearing, smeared**
NOUN **1** a dirty, greasy mark on a surface
VERB **2** If something **smears** something else, it leaves a dirty or greasy mark by rubbing against it.

smell **smells, smelling, smelled** or **smelt**
VERB **1** When you **smell** something, you notice it with your nose.
2 If something **smells**, it gives out an odour that people notice.
NOUN **3** Your sense of **smell** is your ability to smell things.
4 an odour or scent, especially an unpleasant one

You can write either *smelled* or *smelt* as the past form of *smell.*

smile **smiles, smiling, smiled**
VERB When you **smile**, you are happy. Your lips curve upwards at the edges and open a little.

smirk **smirks, smirking, smirked**
VERB When you **smirk**, you smile in a sneering, unpleasant way.

smog
NOUN a mixture of smoke and fog that occurs in some industrial cities
[from a combination of *smoke* and *fog*]

smoke **smokes, smoking, smoked**
NOUN **1** a mixture of gases and small bits of solid material sent into the air when something burns
VERB **2** If something is **smoking**, smoke is coming from it.
3 When someone **smokes** a cigarette, cigar or pipe, they suck smoke from it into their mouth and blow it out again.

smooth **smoother, smoothest; smooths, smoothing, smoothed**
ADJECTIVE **1** A **smooth** surface has no roughness and no holes in it.
2 A **smooth** liquid or mixture has no lumps in it.
VERB **3** If you **smooth** something, you move your hands over it to make it smooth and flat.

smother **smothers, smothering, smothered**
VERB **1** If you **smother** a fire, you cover it with something to put it out.
2 To **smother** a person means to cover their face with something so that they cannot breathe.

smoulder **smoulders, smouldering, smouldered**
VERB When something **smoulders**, it burns slowly, producing smoke but no flames.

smudge **smudges, smudging, smudged**
NOUN **1** a dirty or blurred mark or a smear on something
VERB **2** If you **smudge** something, you make it dirty or messy by touching it or rubbing it.

smug **smugger, smuggest**
ADJECTIVE Someone who is **smug** is very pleased with how good or clever they are, and is self-satisfied in an unpleasant way.
smugly ADVERB

smuggle **smuggles, smuggling, smuggled**
VERB To **smuggle** goods means to take them in or out of a country secretly and against the law.

snack **snacks**
NOUN **1** a small, quick meal
2 something eaten between meals

snag **snags, snagging, snagged**
NOUN **1** a small problem
VERB **2** If you **snag** your clothes, you catch them on something sharp.

snail **snails**
NOUN a small, slow-moving animal with a long, shiny body and a shell on its back

snake **snakes**
NOUN a long, thin reptile with scales and no legs

snap **snaps, snapping, snapped**
VERB **1** If something **snaps**, it breaks suddenly with a sharp noise.
2 If an animal **snaps** at you, it shuts its jaws together quickly as if it is going to bite you.
NOUN **3** an informal photograph

snare **snares, snaring, snared**
NOUN **1** a trap for catching birds or small animals
VERB **2** To **snare** an animal or bird means to catch it using a snare.

snarl **snarls, snarling, snarled**
VERB **1** When an animal **snarls**, it bares its teeth and makes a fierce, growling noise.
2 If you **snarl**, you say something in a fierce, angry way.
NOUN **3** the noise an animal makes when it snarls

snatch **snatches, snatching, snatched**
VERB **1** If you **snatch** something, you reach out for it quickly and grab it.
NOUN **2** A **snatch** of conversation or song is a very small piece of it.

sneak **sneaks, sneaking, sneaked**
VERB If you **sneak** somewhere, you go there quietly, trying not to be seen or heard.

sneaky **sneakier, sneakiest**
ADJECTIVE dishonest or deceitful

sneer **sneers, sneering, sneered**
VERB If you **sneer** at someone or something, you show by what you say that you think they are stupid or inferior.

sneeze **sneezes, sneezing, sneezed**
VERB **1** When you **sneeze**, you suddenly take a breath and blow it noisily down your nose, because there is a tickle in your nose or you have a cold.
NOUN **2** the action or sound of sneezing

sniff **sniffs, sniffing, sniffed**
VERB When you **sniff**, you breathe in air through your nose hard enough to make a sound.

snigger **sniggers, sniggering, sniggered**
VERB If you **snigger**, you laugh quietly and disrespectfully.

snip **snips, snipping, snipped**
VERB If you **snip** something, you make small, quick cuts in it or through it.

sniper **snipers**
NOUN a person who shoots at people from a hiding place

snivel **snivels, snivelling, snivelled**
VERB When someone **snivels**, they cry and sniff in an irritating way.

snob **snobs**
NOUN **1** someone who admires people considered to be socially superior and looks down on people considered to be socially inferior
2 someone who believes that they are better than other people
snobbery NOUN

snooker
NOUN a game played on a large table covered with smooth, green cloth. Players score points by hitting differently coloured balls into pockets using a long stick called a cue.

snoop **snoops, snooping, snooped**
VERB INFORMAL If you **snoop**, you secretly look round a place to find out things.

snooze **snoozes, snoozing, snoozed**
VERB **1** INFORMAL If you **snooze**, you sleep lightly for a short time, especially during the day.
NOUN **2** INFORMAL a short, light sleep

snore **snores, snoring, snored**
VERB When a sleeping person **snores**, they make a loud noise each time they breathe.

snorkel **snorkels, snorkelling, snorkelled**
NOUN **1** a tube you can breathe through when you are swimming just under the surface of the sea
VERB **2** If you **snorkel**, you swim underwater using a snorkel.
snorkelling NOUN

snout **snouts**
NOUN An animal's **snout** is its nose.

snow **snows, snowing, snowed**
NOUN **1** soft, white flakes of ice that fall from the sky in cold weather
VERB **2** When it **snows**, snow falls from the sky.

snowball **snowballs**
NOUN a ball of snow for throwing

snowboard **snowboards**
NOUN a board you stand on to slide across snow
snowboarding NOUN

snowflake **snowflakes**
NOUN a flake of snow

snowman **snowmen**
NOUN a pile of snow shaped like a person

snowstorm **snowstorms**
NOUN a storm with snow falling

snub **snubs, snubbing, snubbed**
VERB **1** If you **snub** someone, you behave rudely towards them, especially by making an insulting remark or ignoring them.
ADJECTIVE **2** A **snub** nose is short and turned-up.

snug
ADJECTIVE **1** A **snug** place is warm and comfortable.
2 If you are **snug**, you are warm and comfortable.
3 If something is a **snug** fit, it fits very closely.
snugly ADVERB

snuggle **snuggles, snuggling, snuggled**
VERB If you **snuggle** somewhere, you cuddle up more closely to something or someone.

so
ADVERB **1** also • *She laughed, and **so** did the teacher.*
2 very • *You are **so** funny.*
CONJUNCTION **3** therefore, for that reason • *I was cold, **so** I put on a coat.*

soak **soaks, soaking, soaked**
VERB **1** If you **soak** something, or leave it to **soak**, you put it in a liquid and leave it there for some time.
2 When a liquid **soaks** something, it makes it very wet.
3 When something **soaks** up a liquid,

a b c d e f g h i j k l m n o p q r s t u v w x y z

the liquid is drawn up into it. • *The cloth **soaked** up the spilt milk.*

soap **soaps**
NOUN a substance used with water for washing yourself • *a bar of **soap***

soap opera **soap operas**
NOUN a popular television drama serial about people's daily lives
[so called because soap manufacturers were often sponsors of these]

soar **soars, soaring, soared**
VERB If something **soars** into the air, it rises high into it.
soaring ADJECTIVE

sob **sobs, sobbing, sobbed**
VERB When someone **sobs**, they cry noisily, gulping in short breaths.

sober **soberer, soberest**
ADJECTIVE **1** not drunk
2 serious and thoughtful

soccer
NOUN a game played by two teams of eleven players kicking a ball in an attempt to score goals

sociable
ADJECTIVE **Sociable** people are friendly and enjoy talking to other people.
SYNONYM: friendly

social
ADJECTIVE **1** to do with society or life within a society • *women from similar **social** backgrounds*
2 to do with leisure activities that involve meeting other people • *We should organize more **social** events.*

social networking site **social networking sites**
NOUN a website that lets people connect, chat and share photographs, videos, etc

society **societies**
NOUN **1** the community of people in a particular country or region
2 an organization for people who have the same interests

sock **socks**
NOUN a piece of clothing that covers your foot and ankle

socket **sockets**
NOUN **1** a place on a wall or on a piece of electrical equipment into which you can put a plug or bulb
2 any hollow part of something, or an opening into which another part fits • *eye **sockets***

sofa **sofas**
NOUN a long comfortable seat, with a back and arms, for two or more people
[from Arabic *suffah* meaning an upholstered raised platform]

soft **softer, softest**
ADJECTIVE **1** not hard, stiff or firm • *a **soft** towel*
2 very gentle • *a **soft** breeze*

soften **softens, softening, softened**
VERB When you **soften** something, you make it softer.

software
NOUN computer programs

soggy **soggier, soggiest**
ADJECTIVE unpleasantly wet

soil **soils, soiling, soiled**
NOUN **1** the top layer of the land surface of the earth, in which plants can grow
VERB **2** If you **soil** something, you make it dirty.

solar
ADJECTIVE to do with the sun • ***solar** energy*

solar system
NOUN the sun and all the planets, comets and asteroids that orbit round it

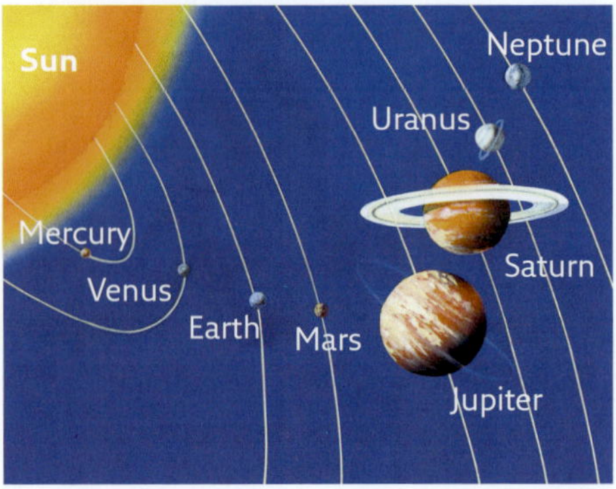

A B C D E F G H I J K L M N O P Q R S T U V W X Y Z

sold
VERB the past tense and past participle of **sell**

soldier **soldiers**
NOUN a person in an army

sole **soles**
NOUN The **sole** of your foot or shoe is the underneath part.

solemn
ADJECTIVE serious rather than cheerful

solicitor **solicitors**
NOUN a lawyer who gives legal advice and prepares legal documents and cases

solid **solids**
NOUN **1** a substance that is not a liquid or gas
2 an object that is hard or firm
ADJECTIVE **3** You say that something is **solid** when it does not have any space in it. • *a **solid** steel bar*
4 A **solid** shape is a three-dimensional shape such as a cylinder or a cone.

solidify **solidifies, solidifying, solidified**
VERB If something **solidifies**, it changes from a liquid into a solid.

solitary
ADJECTIVE alone

solo **solos**
NOUN **1** a piece of music played or sung by one person alone
ADJECTIVE **2** A **solo** performance or activity is done by one person alone.
ADVERB **3** alone • *to sail **solo** around the world*

solstice **solstices**
NOUN one of two times in the year when the sun is at its furthest point south or north of the equator

soluble
ADJECTIVE able to be dissolved in a liquid
• ***soluble** aspirin*

solution **solutions**
NOUN **1** a way of dealing with a problem or difficult situation
2 the answer to a riddle or a puzzle
3 a liquid in which a solid substance has been dissolved

solve **solves, solving, solved**
VERB If you **solve** a problem or a question, you find a solution or answer to it.
SYNONYM: work out

sombre
ADJECTIVE **1** **Sombre** colours are dark and dull.
2 A **sombre** person is serious, sad or gloomy.

some
ADJECTIVE OR PRONOUN You use **some** to refer to a quantity or number when you are not stating the exact quantity or number.
• *There's **some** money on the table.*

somebody
PRONOUN some person
See **someone**

somehow
ADVERB **1** You use **somehow** to say that you do not know how something was done or will be done. • *You'll find a way of doing it **somehow**.*
2 You use **somehow** to say that you do not know the reason for something.
• ***Somehow** it didn't feel quite right.*

someone
PRONOUN You use **someone** to refer to a person without saying exactly who you mean. • *I need **someone** to help me.*

somersault **somersaults, somersaulting, somersaulted**
NOUN **1** a forwards or backwards roll in which the head is placed on the ground and the body is brought over it
VERB **2** If you **somersault**, you perform a somersault.

something
PRONOUN You use **something** to refer to anything that is not a person, without saying exactly what it is. • *There was **something** wrong.*

sometimes
ADVERB occasionally, rather than always or never

A B C D E F G H I J K L M N O P Q R S T U V W X Y Z

somewhere
ADVERB **1 Somewhere** is used to refer to a place without stating exactly where it is. • *a flat **somewhere** in the city*
2 Somewhere is used when giving an approximate amount, number or time. • *It was **somewhere** between four and five o'clock.*

son **sons**
NOUN a person's male child

song **songs**
NOUN **1** a piece of music with words that are sung to the music
2 singing • *I was woken by the bird **song** early in the morning.*

sonnet **sonnets**
NOUN a poem with 14 lines that rhyme according to fixed patterns

soon **sooner, soonest**
ADVERB If something is going to happen **soon**, it will happen in a very short time.

soot
NOUN black powder that rises in the smoke from a fire
sooty ADJECTIVE

soothe **soothes, soothing, soothed**
VERB **1** If you **soothe** someone who is angry or upset, you make them calmer.
2 Something that **soothes** pain makes the pain less severe.

sophisticated
ADJECTIVE **1** A **sophisticated** person is experienced in social situations and able to talk easily about anything.
SYNONYMS: cultured, urbane
2 Something **sophisticated** is made using advanced and complicated methods, or is able to do advanced and complicated things. • *a **sophisticated** new telescope*
SYNONYM: highly developed

sorcerer **sorcerers**
NOUN someone in stories who performs magic by using the power of evil spirits

sore **sorer, sorest; sores**
ADJECTIVE **1** If part of your body is **sore**, it causes you pain and is uncomfortable. • *I have a cough and a **sore** throat.*
SYNONYMS: painful, sensitive, tender
NOUN **2** a painful place where your skin has become infected

sorrow **sorrows**
NOUN deep sadness or regret

sorry **sorrier, sorriest**
ADJECTIVE If you are **sorry** about something, you feel sadness, regret or sympathy because of it.

sort **sorts, sorting, sorted**
NOUN **1** Different **sorts** of something are different types of it.
SYNONYM: kind
VERB **2** If you **sort** things, you arrange them into different groups.

sort out
VERB If you **sort out** a problem or misunderstanding, you find a solution to it.

SOS
NOUN a signal appealing urgently for help from someone whose life is in danger. **SOS** stands for Save Our Souls.

sought
VERB the past tense and past participle of **seek**

soul **souls**
NOUN the spiritual part of a person that some people think continues after the body is dead

sound **sounds, sounding, sounded**
NOUN **1 Sound** is everything that can be heard.
2 something particular that you hear • *the **sound** of a door opening*
VERB **3** If something **sounds**, or if you **sound** it, it makes a noise. • *He **sounded** his horn to warn them.*

sound effect **sound effects**
NOUN **Sound effects** are added to films or plays to make them sound more life-like.

soundproof **soundproofs, soundproofing, soundproofed**
ADJECTIVE **1** If a room is **soundproof**,

sound cannot get into it or out of it.
VERB **2** To **soundproof** something means to make it soundproof.

soup **soups**
NOUN liquid food made by boiling meat, fish or vegetables in water

sour
ADJECTIVE **1** If something is **sour**, it has a sharp, acid taste like lemons or vinegar.
2 If milk is **sour**, it is no longer fresh.

source **sources**
NOUN The **source** of something is the person, place or thing that it originally comes from. • *the **source** of the river*

south
NOUN one of the four main points of the compass. If you face the point where the sun rises, **south** is on your right. The abbreviation for **south** is S.

south-east
NOUN, ADJECTIVE OR ADVERB midway between south and east. The abbreviation for **south-east** is SE.

southern
ADJECTIVE in or from the south

south-west
NOUN, ADJECTIVE OR ADVERB midway between south and west. The abbreviation for **south-west** is SW.

souvenir **souvenirs**
NOUN something you keep to remind you of a holiday, place or event

sovereign **sovereigns**
NOUN **1** a king, queen or royal ruler of a country
2 In the past, a **sovereign** was a British gold coin worth one pound.

sow **sows, sowing, sowed, sown**
Rhymes with "cow" NOUN **1** a female pig
Rhymes with "go" VERB **2** If you **sow** seeds, you put them in the ground so they can grow.

soya
NOUN a protein derived from **soya** beans. **Soya** beans are used to make **soya** flour, margarine, oil and milk.

space **spaces**
NOUN **1** the area that is empty or available in a place, building or container
2 the area beyond the earth's atmosphere surrounding the stars and planets
3 a gap between two things

spacecraft **spacecraft**
NOUN a vehicle for travelling in outer space

spaceship **spaceships**
NOUN a spacecraft

spacesuit **spacesuits**
NOUN protective clothing that astronauts wear in outer space

spacious
ADJECTIVE having or providing a lot of space

spade **spades**
NOUN **1** a tool with a flat metal blade and a long handle used for digging
2 **Spades** is one of the four suits in a pack of playing cards. It is marked by a black symbol in the shape of a heart-shaped leaf with a stem.

spaghetti
NOUN long, thin pieces of pasta
[the plural of the Italian word *spaghetto* meaning string]

span **spans, spanning, spanned**
NOUN **1** a period of time • *looking back over a **span** of 40 years*
2 the total length of something from one end to the other • *Seagulls have a large wing **span**.*
3 Your **span** is the distance from the top of your thumb to the top of your little finger when your hand is stretched.
VERB **4** If something **spans** a particular length of time, a distance or a gap, it stretches across it. • *The bridge **spanned** the width of the river.*

spaniel **spaniels**
NOUN a breed of dog with long ears and silky fur

spank **spanks, spanking, spanked**
VERB If a child is **spanked**, it is punished by being slapped, usually on the leg or bottom.

spanner **spanners**
NOUN a tool with a specially shaped end that fits round a nut to turn it

spare **spares, sparing, spared**
ADJECTIVE **1** extra, or kept to be used when it is needed • *There is a **spare** tyre in the boot of the car.*
VERB **2** If you **spare** something for a particular purpose, you make it available. • *Can you **spare** the time to help me later?*
3 If someone is **spared** an unpleasant experience, they are prevented from suffering it.

spark **sparks**
NOUN a tiny, bright piece of burning material thrown up by a fire

sparkle **sparkles, sparkling, sparkled**
VERB If something **sparkles**, it shines with a lot of small, bright points of light.
SYNONYMS: glitter, twinkle

sparrow **sparrows**
NOUN a common, small bird with brown and grey feathers

sparse **sparser, sparsest**
ADJECTIVE small in number or amount and spread out over an area

spatter **spatters, spattering, spattered**
VERB If something **spatters** a surface, it covers it with small drops of liquid.

spawn **spawns, spawning, spawned**
NOUN **1** a jelly-like substance containing the eggs of fish or amphibians
VERB **2** When fish or amphibians **spawn**, they lay their eggs.

speak **speaks, speaking, spoke, spoken**
VERB **1** When you **speak**, you use your voice to say words.
SYNONYMS: say, talk, utter
2 If you **speak** a foreign language, you know it and can use it.

speaker **speakers**
NOUN **1** a person who is speaking or making a speech
2 the part of a radio or stereo system from which the sound comes

spear **spears, spearing, speared**
NOUN **1** a weapon consisting of a long pole with a sharp point
VERB **2** To **spear** something means to pierce it with a spear or other pointed object.

special
ADJECTIVE Someone or something **special** is different from other people or things, often in a way that makes it more important or better than others.

specialist **specialists**
NOUN an expert in a particular subject

species
NOUN a group of plants or animals that have the same main features and are able to breed with each other

The plural of *species* is *species*.

specimen **specimens**
NOUN an example or small amount of something that gives an idea of what the whole is like • *a **specimen** of your writing*

speck **specks**
NOUN **1** a very small stain
2 a very small amount of something

speckled
ADJECTIVE Something that is **speckled** is covered in small marks or spots.

spectacle **spectacles**
NOUN **1** a grand and impressive event or performance
PLURAL NOUN **2** Someone's **spectacles** are their glasses.

spectacular
ADJECTIVE very impressive or dramatic

spectator **spectators**
NOUN a person who watches an event or a show

spectrum **spectra** or **spectrums**
NOUN the range of different colours

produced when light passes through a prism or a drop of water. A rainbow shows the colours in a **spectrum**.

speech **speeches**
NOUN **1** the ability to speak or the act of speaking
2 a formal talk given to an audience

speech bubble **speech bubbles**
NOUN a line around words, used in comic strips or cartoons to show what characters are saying

speechless
ADJECTIVE unable to speak

speech marks
PLURAL NOUN punctuation marks (“ ” ‘ ’) used in written texts to show when someone is speaking

speed **speeds, speeding, sped** or **speeded**
NOUN **1** the rate at which something moves or happens
2 very fast movement or travel
VERB **3** If you **speed** somewhere, you move or travel there quickly.
4 Someone who is **speeding** is driving a vehicle faster than the legal speed limit.

speedboat **speedboats**
NOUN a fast motorboat

spell **spells, spelling, spelt** or **spelled**
VERB **1** When you **spell** a word, you name or write its letters in order.
NOUN **2** a short period of something
• *We expect a **spell** of good weather.*
3 words or rhymes used to perform magic

> You can write either *spelt* or *spelled* as the past form of *spell*.

spellbound
ADJECTIVE If you are **spellbound**, you are so fascinated by something that you cannot think of anything else.

spellcheck **spellchecks, spellchecking, spellchecked**
VERB If you **spellcheck** a document, you run a program over it to find any words that have not been spelt correctly.

spelling **spellings**
NOUN the correct order of letters in a word

spend **spends, spending, spent**
VERB **1** When you **spend** money, you buy things with it.
2 If you **spend** time or energy, you use it.

sphere **spheres**
NOUN a perfectly round object, such as a ball

sphinx **sphinxes**
NOUN In mythology, the **sphinx** was a monster with a person's head and a lion's body.

spice **spices**
NOUN a substance obtained from a plant, often in the form of a powder or a seed, and added to food to give it flavour

spicy **spicier, spiciest**
ADJECTIVE strongly flavoured with spices

spider **spiders**
NOUN a small animal with eight legs. Some **spiders** spin webs to catch insects for food, others hunt.

spike **spikes**
NOUN something long and sharply pointed. Runners often have **spikes** on the soles of their shoes to stop them slipping.

spill **spills, spilling, spilled** or **spilt**
VERB If you **spill** something, or if it **spills**, it accidentally falls or runs out of a container.

> You can write either *spilled* or *spilt* as the past form of *spill*.

spin **spins, spinning, spun**
VERB **1** If someone or something **spins**, it turns quickly around a central point.
• *The earth **spins** on its own axis.*
NOUN **2** a rapid turn around a central point

spinach
NOUN a vegetable with large green leaves

spine **spines**
NOUN **1** the row of bones down the middle of your back
SYNONYM: backbone
2 a spike on a plant or an animal

• *Porcupines are covered in **spines**.*
3 the part of a book where the pages are joined together

spiral **spirals**
NOUN **1** a continuous curve that winds round and round, with each curve moving further out or further up
ADJECTIVE **2** in the shape of a spiral

spire **spires**
NOUN the pointed structure on top of a steeple

spirit **spirits**
NOUN **1** the part of you that is not physical and that is connected with the way you are
2 a ghost or supernatural being
3 liveliness, energy and self-confidence

spiritual
ADJECTIVE **1** to do with people's thoughts and beliefs, rather than their bodies and physical surroundings
2 to do with people's religious beliefs

spit **spits, spitting, spat**
VERB **1** If you **spit**, you forcefully send saliva out of your mouth.
NOUN **2** saliva
3 a long piece of metal or wood that you push through meat so that it can be hung over a fire to cook
4 a long, flat, narrow piece of land sticking out into the sea

spite
NOUN **1** the desire to deliberately hurt or upset somebody
PHRASE **2** **In spite of** is used to begin a statement that makes the rest of what you are saying seem surprising. • ***In spite of** the rain, they watched the fireworks outside.*

spiteful
ADJECTIVE A **spiteful** person does or says nasty things to people to hurt them.
spitefully ADVERB

splash **splashes, splashing, splashed**
VERB **1** If you **splash** around in water, you make the water fly around in a noisy way.
NOUN **2** the sound made when something hits or falls into water

splendid
ADJECTIVE very good or very impressive

splint **splints**
NOUN a straight piece of metal or wood that is tied to a broken arm or leg to stop it moving

splinter **splinters, splintering, splintered**
NOUN **1** a thin, sharp piece of wood or glass that has broken off a larger piece
VERB **2** If something **splinters**, it breaks into thin, sharp pieces.

split **splits, splitting, split**
VERB If something **splits**, or if you **split** it, it divides into two or more parts.

split second **split seconds**
NOUN an extremely short period of time

splutter **splutters, spluttering, spluttered**
VERB **1** If you **splutter**, you speak in a confused way because you are embarrassed or angry.
2 If someone or something **splutters**, they make a series of short, coughing, spitting noises.

spoil **spoils, spoiling, spoiled** or **spoilt**
VERB **1** To **spoil** something means to damage it or stop it being successful or satisfactory. • *My holiday was **spoiled** by rain.*
2 To **spoil** children means to give them everything they want, making them selfish.

> You can write either *spoiled* or *spoilt* as the past form of *spoil*.

spoilsport **spoilsports**
NOUN someone who spoils other people's fun

spoke **spokes**
NOUN **1** The **spokes** of a wheel are the

bars that connect the hub to the rim.
VERB **2** the past tense of **speak**

spoken
VERB the past participle of **speak**

sponge **sponges**
NOUN **1** a soft, natural or man-made material with lots of small holes, used for washing yourself
2 an animal found in the sea that has a body made up of many cells
3 a soft, light cake or pudding
spongy ADJECTIVE

sponsor **sponsors, sponsoring, sponsored**
VERB **1** If an organization **sponsors** something, such as an event or someone's training, it gives money to pay for it.
2 If you **sponsor** someone who is doing something for charity, you agree to give them a sum of money for the charity if they manage to do it.
NOUN **3** a person or organization that sponsors something or someone

spontaneous
ADJECTIVE something that is not planned or arranged
spontaneously ADVERB

spooky **spookier, spookiest**
ADJECTIVE frightening and creepy

spoon **spoons**
NOUN an object shaped like a small shallow bowl with a long handle, used for eating, stirring and serving food

sport **sports**
NOUN games and other enjoyable activities that need physical effort and skill

spot **spots, spotting, spotted**
NOUN **1** a small, round, coloured area on a surface
2 a pimple on a person's skin
3 a small amount of something
4 a particular place
VERB **5** If you **spot** something, you suddenly see it.
PHRASE **6** If you do something **on the spot**, you do it immediately.

spotless
ADJECTIVE perfectly clean

spotlight **spotlights**
NOUN a powerful light that can be directed to light up a small area • *stage* ***spotlights***

spotty **spottier, spottiest**
ADJECTIVE marked with spots

spouse **spouses**
NOUN Someone's **spouse** is the person they are married to.

spout **spouts, spouting, spouted**
VERB **1** When liquid or flame **spouts** out of something, it shoots out in a long stream.
NOUN **2** a tube or opening from which liquid can pour
VERB **3** When someone **spouts** what they have learned, they say it in a boring way.

sprain **sprains, spraining, sprained**
VERB **1** If you **sprain** a joint, you accidentally damage it by twisting it violently.
NOUN **2** the injury caused by spraining a joint

sprang
VERB the past tense of **spring**

sprawl **sprawls, sprawling, sprawled**
VERB **1** If you **sprawl** somewhere, you sit or lie there with your legs and arms spread out. • *She* ***sprawled*** *on the bed reading her book.*
2 A place that **sprawls** is spread out over a large area.

spray **sprays, spraying, sprayed**
NOUN **1** many small drops of liquid splashed or forced into the air
2 a liquid kept under pressure in a container
VERB **3** If you **spray** a liquid over something, you cover it with drops of the liquid. • *We* ***sprayed*** *the dry lawn with water from the hose pipe.*

spread **spreads, spreading, spread**
VERB **1** If you **spread** a substance on a surface, you put a thin layer of it on the surface. • ***Spread*** *the butter on the bread before you make the sandwich.*

a b c d e f g h i j k l m n o p q r s t u v w x y z

2 If you **spread** something out, you open it out or arrange it so that it can be seen or used easily. • *He **spread** the map out on his knees.*
3 If something **spreads**, it gradually reaches more people. • *The news **spread** quickly.*

sprightly **sprightlier, sprightliest**
ADJECTIVE lively and active

spring **springs, springing, sprang, sprung**
NOUN **1** the season between winter and summer, when most plants start to grow
2 a coil of wire that returns to its original shape after being pressed or pulled
3 a place where water naturally comes up through the ground
VERB **4** If you **spring**, you jump upwards or forwards.

springboard **springboards**
NOUN a springy board on which a gymnast or diver jumps to gain height

springbok **springboks**
NOUN a small South African antelope that moves in leaps

sprinkle **sprinkles, sprinkling, sprinkled**
VERB If you **sprinkle** a liquid or powder over something, you scatter it over it.

sprint **sprints, sprinting, sprinted**
NOUN **1** a short, fast race
VERB **2** If you **sprint**, you run fast over a short distance.

sprout **sprouts, sprouting, sprouted**
VERB **1** When something **sprouts**, it starts to grow.
2 If things **sprout** up, they appear very quickly.
NOUN **3** an abbreviation of *Brussels sprout*

sprung
VERB the past participle of **spring**

spun
VERB the past tense and past participle of **spin**

spur **spurs, spurring, spurred**
VERB **1** If you **spur** someone on, you encourage them.
NOUN **2** a sharp device worn on the heel of a rider's boot to urge the horse to go faster

spurt **spurts, spurting, spurted**
NOUN **1** a jet of liquid or flame
2 a sudden increase in speed
VERB **3** If a liquid **spurts**, it gushes in a sudden stream. • *Water **spurted** out of the hose.*

spy **spies, spying, spied**
NOUN **1** a person sent to find out secret information about a country or organization
VERB **2** Someone who **spies** tries to find out secret information about another country or organization.
3 If you **spy** on someone, you watch them secretly.

squabble **squabbles, squabbling, squabbled**
VERB **1** When people **squabble**, they quarrel about something unimportant.
NOUN **2** a quarrel

squad **squads**
NOUN a small group of people chosen to do a particular activity

squadron **squadrons**
NOUN a section of one of the armed forces, especially the air force
[from Italian *squadrone* meaning soldiers drawn up in a square formation]

squalid
ADJECTIVE dirty, untidy and in bad condition

squander **squanders, squandering, squandered**
VERB If you **squander** money or resources, you waste them.

square **squares**
NOUN **1** a plane shape with four equal sides and four right angles
2 In a town or city, a **square** is a flat, open area with buildings or streets around the edge.
ADJECTIVE **3** shaped like a **square**
[from Latin *quadra* meaning square]

squash **squashes, squashing, squashed**
VERB If you **squash** something, you press it so that it becomes flat or loses its shape.

squat **squats, squatting, squatted; squatter, squattest**
VERB **1** If you **squat** down, you crouch, balancing on your feet with your legs bent.
2 A person who **squats** in an unused building lives there without permission and without paying.
ADJECTIVE **3** short and thick

squawk **squawks, squawking, squawked**
VERB **1** When a bird **squawks**, it makes a loud, harsh noise.
NOUN **2** a loud, harsh noise made by a bird

squeak **squeaks, squeaking, squeaked**
VERB **1** If something or someone **squeaks**, they make a short, high-pitched sound.
NOUN **2** a short, high-pitched sound

squeal **squeals, squealing, squealed**
VERB **1** When things or people **squeal**, they make long, high-pitched sounds.
NOUN **2** a long, high-pitched sound

squeamish
ADJECTIVE easily upset by unpleasant sights or situations

squeeze **squeezes, squeezing, squeezed**
VERB **1** When you **squeeze** something, you press it firmly from two sides.
2 If you **squeeze** somewhere, you force yourself into a small space or through a gap.
3 If you **squeeze** something somewhere, you force it into a small space.

squelch **squelches, squelching, squelched**
VERB If something **squelches**, it makes a wet, sucking sound.

squid **squids**
NOUN an animal that lives in the sea, with a long, soft body and ten limbs

squiggle **squiggles**
NOUN a wiggly line

squint **squints, squinting, squinted**
VERB **1** If you **squint**, you screw up your eyes to look at something.
NOUN **2** If someone has a **squint**, their eyes look in different directions from each other.

squirm **squirms, squirming, squirmed**
VERB If you **squirm**, you wriggle and twist your body about, usually because you are nervous or embarrassed.

squirrel **squirrels**
NOUN a small, furry rodent with a long, bushy tail

squirt **squirts, squirting, squirted**
VERB **1** If a liquid **squirts**, or you **squirt** it, it comes out of a narrow opening in a thin, fast stream.
NOUN **2** a thin, fast stream of liquid

stab **stabs, stabbing, stabbed**
VERB To **stab** someone means to wound them by pushing a knife into their body.

stable **stables**
NOUN **1** a building in which horses are kept
ADJECTIVE **2** Something that is **stable** cannot be moved or shaken.
3 If someone is **stable**, they are level-headed and dependable.

stack **stacks, stacking, stacked**
NOUN **1** a pile of things, one on top of the other
VERB **2** If you **stack** items, you pile them up neatly.

stadium **stadiums**
NOUN a sports ground with rows of seats around it for spectators

A B C D E F G H I J K L M N O P Q R S T U V W X Y Z

staff staffs
NOUN the people who work for an organization

stag stags
NOUN an adult male deer

stage stages, staging, staged
NOUN **1** In a theatre, the **stage** is the raised platform where the actors or entertainers perform.
VERB **2** If someone **stages** a play or event, they organize it or present it.

stagger staggers, staggering, staggered
VERB **1** If you **stagger**, you walk unsteadily, for example because you are ill.
2 If something **staggers** you, it amazes you.
3 If events are **staggered**, they are arranged so that they do not all happen at the same time.

stagnant
ADJECTIVE **Stagnant** water is still rather than flowing, and is often smelly and dirty.

stain stains
NOUN a mark on something that is difficult or impossible to clean off

stair stairs
NOUN one of a set of steps, usually inside a building going from one floor to another

staircase staircases
NOUN a set of stairs

stake stakes, staking, staked
PHRASE **1** If something is **at stake**, it might be lost or damaged if something else is not successful. • *The cup was **at stake** if he missed the goal.*
VERB **2** If you say you would **stake** your money, life or reputation on the result of something, you mean you would risk it.

stalactite stalactites
NOUN a stony spike hanging down like an icicle from the ceiling of a cave

stalagmite stalagmites
NOUN a pointed piece of rock standing on the floor of a cave

stalactites and stalagmites in a cave

stale staler, stalest
ADJECTIVE **Stale** food or air is no longer fresh.
SYNONYMS: fusty, musty, old

stalk stalks, stalking, stalked
NOUN **1** The **stalk** of a flower or leaf is its stem.
VERB **2** To **stalk** a person or an animal means to follow them quietly in order to catch, kill or observe them. • *The cat is **stalking** the bird in the garden.*

stall stalls, stalling, stalled
NOUN **1** a large table displaying goods for sale or information
PLURAL NOUN **2** In a theatre, the **stalls** are the seats at the lowest level, in front of the stage.
VERB **3** When a vehicle **stalls**, the engine suddenly stops.

stallion stallions
NOUN an adult male horse that can be used for breeding

stamen stamens
NOUN the part of a flower that produces pollen

stamina
NOUN the physical or mental energy needed to do something for a very long time • *Running a marathon takes determination and **stamina**.*

stammer **stammers, stammering, stammered**
VERB **1** When someone **stammers**, they speak with difficulty, repeating words and sounds and hesitating.
NOUN **2** Someone who has a **stammer** tends to stammer when they speak.

stamp **stamps, stamping, stamped**
NOUN **1** a small piece of paper that you stick on a letter or parcel before posting it, to prove that you have paid the postage
VERB **2** To **stamp** a piece of paper means to make a mark on it using a small block with a pattern cut into it. • *He* ***stamped*** *her passport.*
3 If you **stamp**, you lift your foot and put it down hard on the ground.

stamp out
VERB To **stamp out** something means to put an end to it. • *We must try to* ***stamp out*** *this kind of behaviour.*

stampede **stampedes, stampeding, stampeded**
VERB **1** When a group of animals **stampede**, they rush forward in a wild, uncontrolled way.
NOUN **2** a group of animals stampeding

stand **stands, standing, stood**
VERB **1** If you are **standing**, you are upright with your weight on your feet.
2 If something **stands** somewhere, that is where it is. • *The house* ***stands*** *on top of a hill.*
3 If you cannot **stand** someone or something, you do not like them at all.
4 If you **stand** in an election, you are a candidate.
NOUN **5** A **stand** at a sports ground is a building where people can watch what is happening.

stand up
VERB When you **stand up**, you get into a standing position.

standard **standards**
NOUN **1** how good something is
2 an officially agreed level against which things can be measured or judged

standstill
NOUN a complete stop

stank
VERB the past tense of **stink**

stanza **stanzas**
NOUN a verse of a poem

staple **staples, stapling, stapled**
NOUN **1** a small piece of wire that holds sheets of paper firmly together. You insert it with a device called a stapler.
VERB **2** If you **staple** sheets of paper, you fasten them together with staples.

star **stars**
NOUN **1** a large ball of burning gases in space that appears as a point of light in the sky at night. Our sun is a **star**.
2 a shape with several points, usually five or six, sticking out in a regular pattern
3 a famous actor, sports player or musician

starboard
ADJECTIVE OR NOUN The **starboard** side of a ship is the right-hand side when you are facing the front.

starch **starches**
NOUN **1** a substance found in foods such as bread, rice, pasta and potatoes that gives you energy
2 a substance used for stiffening fabric

stare **stares, staring, stared**
VERB **1** If you **stare** at something, you look at it for a long time.
NOUN **2** a long, fixed look at something

starfish **starfishes** or **starfish**
NOUN a star-shaped animal found in the sea that has five pointed limbs

starling **starlings**
NOUN a common European bird with shiny dark feathers

start **starts, starting, started**
VERB **1** If you **start** something, you begin it.
NOUN **2** The **start** of something is the point or time at which it begins.

A B C D E F G H I J K L M N O P Q R S T U V W X Y Z

startle **startles, startling, startled**
VERB If something sudden and unexpected **startles** you, it surprises you and give you a slight fright.

starve **starves, starving, starved**
VERB If people are **starving**, they are suffering from a serious lack of food and are likely to die.

state **states, stating, stated**
NOUN **1** The **state** of something or someone is their condition, or how they are.
2 Some countries are divided into regions called **states** that make some of their own laws.
3 You can call the government and the officials of a country the **state**. • *Carmen received a pension from the **state**.*
VERB **4** If you **state** something, you say it or write it clearly, especially in a formal way. • *Please **state** your name and address.*

statement **statements**
NOUN something you say or write that gives information in a formal way

static
ADJECTIVE **1** never moving or changing • *The temperature is fairly **static**.*
NOUN **2** an electrical charge caused by friction

station **stations**
NOUN **1** a building where trains or buses stop to let passengers on and off
2 A building that is used by people such as the police and fire brigade. • *police **station***

stationary
ADJECTIVE not moving • *a **stationary** car*
SYNONYM: motionless

stationery
NOUN paper, pens and other writing equipment

statistics
PLURAL NOUN facts worked out by looking at information that is given in numbers • *They gathered **statistics** about journeys to school.*

statue **statues**
NOUN a sculpture, often of a person

stay **stays, staying, stayed**
VERB **1** If you **stay** in one place, you do not move away from it.
2 If you **stay** with a friend, you spend time with them as a visitor.

steady **steadier, steadiest**
ADJECTIVE firm and not moving about • *She made sure the ladder was **steady** before she climbed up it.*
SYNONYMS: firm, secure, stable

steak **steaks**
NOUN a large, good-quality piece of beef or fish

steal **steals, stealing, stole, stolen**
VERB If someone **steals** something, they take it without permission and without meaning to return it.

steam
NOUN the hot vapour formed when water boils

steam-engine **steam-engines**
NOUN any engine that is powered by steam

steel
NOUN a very strong metal made mainly from iron

steel band **steel bands**
NOUN a group of people who play music on special metal drums

steep **steeper, steepest**
ADJECTIVE A **steep** slope rises sharply and is difficult to go up.

steeple **steeples**
NOUN a tall, pointed structure above a church roof

steer **steers, steering, steered**
VERB When someone **steers** a vehicle or boat, they control it so that it goes in the direction they want.

stem **stems**
NOUN the thin, usually upright, part of a plant that grows above the ground and on which the leaves and flowers grow

stencil **stencils, stencilling, stencilled**
NOUN **1** a thin sheet of card, metal or plastic with a pattern cut out of it. The pattern can be copied onto another surface by painting over the **stencil**.
VERB **2** If you **stencil** a design onto a surface, you create it using a stencil.

step **steps, stepping, stepped**
NOUN **1** the movement of lifting your foot and putting it down again when you are walking, running or dancing
2 one of the places at different levels that you put your feet on when you go up and down a ladder or stairs
VERB **3** If you **step** in a particular direction, you take a step there.

stepbrother **stepbrothers**
NOUN the son of someone's stepmother or stepfather

stepchild **stepchildren**
NOUN a stepdaughter or stepson

stepdaughter **stepdaughters**
NOUN someone's daughter by their wife's or husband's previous marriage

stepfather **stepfathers**
NOUN a man who is married to your mother but who is not your natural father

stepmother **stepmothers**
NOUN a woman who is married to your father but who is not your natural mother

stepsister **stepsisters**
NOUN the daughter of someone's stepmother or stepfather

stepson **stepsons**
NOUN someone's son by their wife's or husband's previous marriage

stereo **stereos**
NOUN a piece of equipment that reproduces sound from records, tapes or CDs, directing the sound through two speakers

stereotype **stereotypes**
NOUN a simplified way people think of a particular type of person or thing
• *the **stereotype** of the polite, industrious Japanese*

sterile
ADJECTIVE **1** clean and free from germs
2 unable to have children or reproduce
sterility NOUN

sterling
NOUN the money system of Great Britain

stern **sterner, sternest**
ADJECTIVE very serious and strict

stethoscope **stethoscopes**
NOUN a device used by doctors to listen to a patient's heart and breathing, made of earpieces connected to a hollow tube and a small disc

stew **stews, stewing, stewed**
NOUN **1** a dish of small pieces of savoury food cooked together slowly in a liquid
VERB **2** If you **stew** meat, vegetables or fruit, you cook them slowly in a liquid.
[from Middle English *stuen* meaning to take a very hot bath]

steward **stewards**
NOUN **1** a person who works on a ship or plane looking after passengers and serving meals
2 a person who helps to direct the public at events such as a race or a concert

stick **sticks, sticking, stuck**
NOUN **1** a long, thin piece of wood

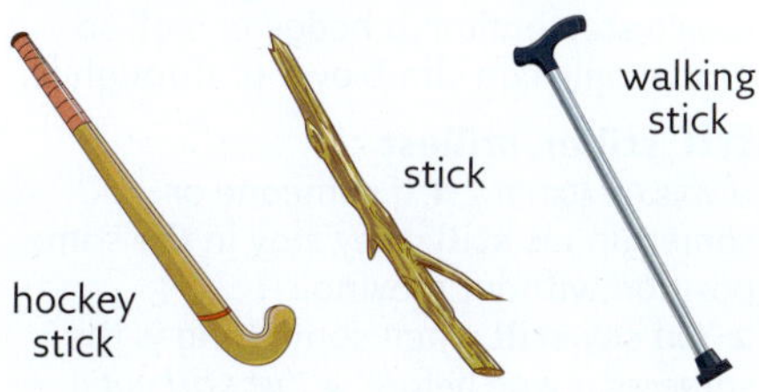

VERB **2** If you **stick** a long or pointed object into something, you push it in.
3 If you **stick** one thing to another, you attach it with glue or tape.
4 If something **sticks**, it becomes fixed or jammed.

stick out
VERB If something **sticks out**, it projects from something else.

a b c d e f g h i j k l m n o p q r s t u v w x y z

stick up for
VERB INFORMAL If you **stick up for** someone or something, you support or defend them.

sticker **stickers**
NOUN a label with words or pictures on it for sticking on something

sticky **stickier, stickiest**
ADJECTIVE If something is **sticky**, it is covered with a substance that can stick to other things.

stiff **stiffer, stiffest**
ADJECTIVE **1** Something that is **stiff** is firm and not easily bent. • *a **stiff** piece of card*
2 If you feel **stiff**, your muscles or joints ache when you move.
3 **Stiff** behaviour is formal, and not friendly or relaxed.
4 difficult or severe • *It was a **stiff** competition.*

stifle **stifles, stifling, stifled**
VERB **1** If you feel **stifled**, you feel you cannot breathe properly.
2 If you **stifle** something, you stop it happening. • *She **stifled** a yawn.*
ADJECTIVE **3** **Stifling** heat is very hot and makes it difficult to breathe. • *The atmosphere in the greenhouse was **stifling**.*

stile **stiles**
NOUN a step built in a hedge or wall so that people can climb over or through it

still **stiller, stillest**
ADVERB OR ADJECTIVE **1** If someone or something is **still**, they stay in the same position without moving.
2 You say **still** when something is the same as it was before. • *I've **still** got a headache.*
3 When the air is **still**, there is no wind.
4 A **still** drink is not fizzy.
5 even then • *I've worked all day and there's **still** more to do.*

stilts
PLURAL NOUN **1** long poles on which people balance or walk
2 long poles on which houses are sometimes built

stimulate **stimulates, stimulating, stimulated**
VERB **1** To **stimulate** something means to encourage it to begin or develop.
• *to **stimulate** interest*
SYNONYM: inspire
2 If something **stimulates** you, it interests and excites you.
SYNONYM: inspire

sting **stings, stinging, stung**
VERB **1** If an animal or plant **stings** you, it pricks your skin and hurts.
2 If a part of your body **stings**, you feel a sharp, tingling pain there.

stink **stinks, stinking, stank, stunk**
VERB **1** Something that **stinks** smells very unpleasant.
NOUN **2** a very unpleasant smell

stir **stirs, stirring, stirred**
VERB **1** When you **stir** a liquid, you move it around using a spoon or a stick.
2 If someone **stirs**, they move slightly, or start to move after sleeping or being still.
• *It was very noisy but the baby didn't **stir**.*

stirrup **stirrups**
NOUN one of the two metal loops hanging by leather straps from a horse's saddle, that you put your feet in when riding

stitch **stitches, stitching, stitched**
VERB **1** When you **stitch** pieces of material together, you use a needle and thread to sew them together.
NOUN **2** one of the pieces of thread that can be seen where material has been sewn
3 one of the pieces of thread that can be seen where skin has been sewn together to heal a wound • *He had eleven **stitches** in his lip.*
4 a sharp pain you feel in your side after running

stoat **stoats**
NOUN a small wild mammal with a long body, brown fur and a black-tipped tail

stock **stocks**
NOUN **1** the total amount of goods a shop has for sale
2 If you have a **stock** of things, you have a supply ready for use.

stocking stockings
NOUN one of a pair of long pieces of fine, stretchy fabric that cover a woman's leg and foot

stole stoles
VERB **1** the past tense of **steal**
NOUN **2** a shawl to cover a woman's shoulders

stolen
VERB the past participle of **steal**

stomach stomachs
NOUN **1** the organ inside your body where food is digested

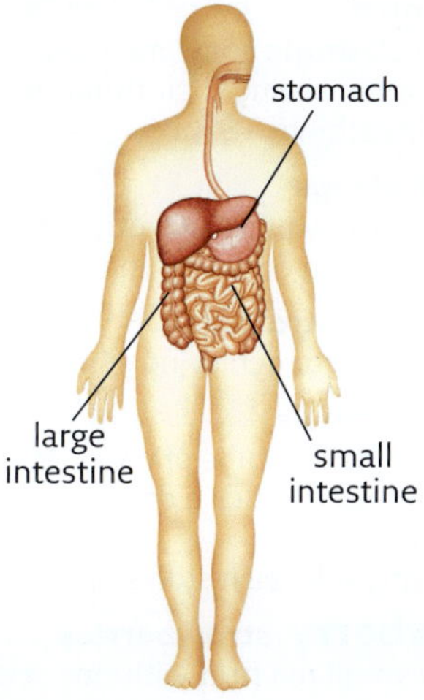

2 the front part of your body below your waist

stone stones
NOUN **1** the hard solid substance found in the ground and used for building
2 a small piece of rock
3 a unit of weight equal to 14 pounds or about 6.35 kilograms

stony stonier, stoniest
ADJECTIVE **Stony** ground has many stones in it.

stood
VERB the past tense and past participle of **stand**

stool stools
NOUN a seat with legs but no back or arms

stoop stoops, stooping, stooped
VERB **1** If you **stoop**, you bend your body forwards.
2 If you would not **stoop** to something, you would not disgrace yourself by doing it.

stop stops, stopping, stopped
VERB **1** If you **stop** doing something, you no longer do it.
2 If an activity **stops**, it comes to an end.
3 If you **stop** something, you prevent it from happening or continuing.
4 If people or things that are moving **stop**, they no longer move.
NOUN **5** a place where a bus, train or other vehicle stops to let passengers on and off

stopwatch stopwatches
NOUN a watch that can be started and stopped, that is used to time things such as races

storage
NOUN the keeping of something somewhere until it is needed

store stores, storing, stored
NOUN **1** a shop
2 a supply of something that is kept until it is needed
3 a place where things are kept while they are not used
VERB **4** When you **store** something somewhere, you keep it there until it is needed.

storey storeys
NOUN one of the floors or levels of a building

stork storks
NOUN a very large white and black bird with long red legs and a long bill. **Storks** live mainly near water in Eastern Europe and Africa.

storm storms, storming, stormed
NOUN **1** a period of bad weather, when there is heavy rain, a strong wind and often thunder and lightning
VERB **2** If soldiers **storm** a defended place, they make a surprise attack on it.
NOUN **3** If there is a **storm** of protest, many people complain loudly.

A B C D E F G H I J K L M N O P Q R S T U V W X Y Z

story **stories**
NOUN a telling of events, real or imaginary, spoken or written

stout **stouter, stoutest**
ADJECTIVE **1** rather fat
2 thick, strong and sturdy • ***stout** walking shoes*

stove **stoves**
NOUN a piece of equipment for heating a room or for cooking • *She warmed the milk on the **stove**.*

straddle **straddles, straddling, straddled**
VERB If you **straddle** something, you stand or sit with your legs either side of it.

straight **straighter, straightest**
ADJECTIVE OR ADVERB **1** continuing in the same direction without curving or bending
2 honest and direct • *a **straight** answer*
ADVERB **3** immediately and directly • *We will go **straight** to school.*
4 If you stand up **straight**, you stand upright.

straighten **straightens, straightening, straightened**
VERB If you **straighten** something, you make it straight.

straightforward
ADJECTIVE **1** easy to understand
2 honest and truthful

strain **strains, straining, strained**
ADJECTIVE **1** If you feel **strained**, you feel tense and anxious.
NOUN **2** If a **strain** is put on something, it is affected by a strong force that may damage it.
VERB **3** If you **strain** a muscle, you use it too much and injure it so that it is painful.
4 If you **strain** food or a mixture, you separate the solid parts from the liquid parts, for example by putting it through a sieve.

strait **straits**
NOUN a narrow strip of sea between two pieces of land, that connects two larger areas of sea

stranded
ADJECTIVE If someone or something is **stranded**, they are stuck somewhere and cannot leave. • ***stranded** on the rocks*

strange **stranger, strangest**
ADJECTIVE **1** unusual or unexpected • *a **strange** dream*
2 not known, seen or experienced before • *She was all alone in a **strange** country.*

stranger **strangers**
NOUN someone you have never met before

strangle **strangles, strangling, strangled**
VERB To **strangle** someone means to kill them by squeezing their throat to stop them breathing.

strap **straps**
NOUN a narrow piece of leather or cloth, used to fasten or hold things together

strategy **strategies**
NOUN a plan for achieving something

straw **straws**
NOUN **1** a hollow tube of paper or plastic that you use to suck a drink into your mouth
2 the dry, yellowish stalks of some crops

strawberry **strawberries**
NOUN a small red fruit with tiny seeds in its skin

stray **strays, straying, strayed**
VERB **1** When people or animals **stray**, they wander away from where they should be.
2 If your thoughts **stray**, you stop concentrating.
ADJECTIVE **3** A **stray** dog or cat is one that has wandered away from its home.
NOUN **4** a stray dog or cat

streak **streaks**
NOUN a long, narrow mark or stain

stream **streams, streaming, streamed**
NOUN **1** a small river
2 You can refer to a steady flow of something as a **stream**. • *a constant **stream** of children*

VERB **3** If something **streams**, it flows fast, without stopping. • *Rain **streamed** down the windscreen.*

streamer **streamers**
NOUN a long piece of paper or ribbon used as a decoration

street **streets**
NOUN a road in a town or village, usually with buildings along it

strength
NOUN how strong or powerful someone or something is
SYNONYMS: might, force, power

strenuous
ADJECTIVE involving a lot of effort or energy

stress **stresses, stressing, stressed**
NOUN **1** worry and nervous tension
SYNONYMS: anxiety, pressure, strain
VERB **2** If you **stress** a point, you emphasize it and draw attention to how important it is.

stretch **stretches, stretching, stretched**
VERB **1** If you **stretch** something soft or elastic, you pull it to make it longer or bigger.
2 Something that **stretches** over an area covers the whole of that area. • *Forests **stretched** the length of the valley.*
3 When you **stretch**, you move part of your body as far away from you as you can.
NOUN **4** an area of something • *This is a quiet **stretch** of beach.*

stretcher **stretchers**
NOUN a long piece of material with a pole along each side, used to carry an injured person

strict **stricter, strictest**
ADJECTIVE **1** Someone who is **strict** controls other people very firmly.
2 exact or complete • *We were given **strict** instructions.*

stride **strides, striding, strode, stridden**
VERB **1** If you **stride** along, you walk quickly with long steps.
NOUN **2** a long step

strike **strikes, striking, struck**
VERB **1** If you **strike** something, you hit it with a lot of force.
2 If workers **strike**, they refuse to work because they want better working conditions or more money.
3 If you **strike** a match, you make a flame by rubbing it against something rough.

striking
ADJECTIVE very noticeable because of being unusual or attractive

string **strings**
NOUN **1** thin rope made of twisted threads
2 a row or series of similar things • *a **string** of islands*

strip **strips, stripping, stripped**
NOUN **1** a long, narrow piece of something
VERB **2** If you **strip**, you take off all your clothes.

stripe **stripes**
NOUN a long, thin line of colour

strode
VERB the past tense of **stride**

stroke **strokes, stroking, stroked**
VERB **1** If you **stroke** something, you move your hand smoothly and gently over it.
NOUN **2** The **strokes** of a brush or pen are the movements that you make with it.
3 If someone has a **stroke**, a blood vessel in the brain bursts or gets blocked, possibly causing death or paralysis.
4 a style of swimming • *My best **stroke** is the front crawl.*

stroll **strolls, strolling, strolled**
VERB **1** If you **stroll** along, you walk slowly in a relaxed way.
SYNONYMS: amble, saunter
NOUN **2** a slow, pleasurable walk
SYNONYMS: amble, saunter

strong **stronger, strongest**
ADJECTIVE **1** Someone who is **strong** has a lot of physical power.
2 You also say that someone is **strong**

when they are confident and have courage.
3 Strong objects are able to withstand rough treatment, and are not easily damaged.
4 great or intense • *a **strong** wind*

struck
VERB the past tense and past participle of **strike**

structure **structures**
NOUN **1** The **structure** of something is the way it is made, built or organized.
2 something that has been built or put together

struggle **struggles, struggling, struggled**
VERB **1** If you **struggle** to do something difficult, you try hard to do it.
2 When people **struggle**, they twist and move violently to get free of something or someone.
NOUN **3** Something that is a **struggle** is difficult to achieve and takes a lot of effort.

stubble
NOUN **1** the short stalks remaining in the ground after a crop is harvested
2 If a man has **stubble** on his face, he has very short hair growing there because he has not shaved recently.

stubborn
ADJECTIVE Someone who is **stubborn** is determined not to change the way they think or how they do things.
SYNONYM: obstinate

stuck
ADJECTIVE **1** If something or someone is **stuck**, they cannot be moved.
2 If you are **stuck**, you cannot go on with your work because you are finding it too difficult.
VERB **3** the past tense and past participle of **stick**

stud **studs**
NOUN **1** a small piece of metal, or other material, fixed into something • *Rachel wore gold **studs** in her ears.*
2 A male horse or other animal that is kept for **stud** is kept for breeding purposes.
3 a place where horses are kept and bred

student **students**
NOUN a person studying at a university, college or school

studio **studios**
NOUN **1** a room where an artist works
2 a room containing special equipment where records, films, or radio or television programmes are made

studious
ADJECTIVE Someone who is **studious** studies hard or is fond of studying.

study **studies, studying, studied**
VERB **1** If you **study** a particular subject, you spend time learning about it.
2 If you **study** something, you look at it carefully.
NOUN **3** a room for studying or working in

stuff **stuffs, stuffing, stuffed**
NOUN **1** You can refer to a substance or a group of things as **stuff**. • *She spread out her **stuff** on top of the table.*
VERB **2** If you **stuff** something somewhere, you push it there quickly and carelessly.
3 If you **stuff** something, you fill it with something else. • *Mum **stuffed** the turkey.*

stuffy **stuffier, stuffiest**
ADJECTIVE **1** If it is **stuffy** in a room, there is not enough fresh air.
2 boring and old-fashioned

stumble **stumbles, stumbling, stumbled**
VERB **1** If you **stumble** while you are walking or running, you trip and nearly fall.
2 If you **stumble** when you are speaking, you hesitate or make mistakes.

stump **stumps, stumping, stumped**
NOUN **1** a small part of something that is left when the rest has gone • *a tree **stump***
2 In cricket, the **stumps** are the three upright wooden sticks that support the bails, forming the wicket.
VERB **3** If a question or problem **stumps** you, you cannot think of an answer or solution.

stun **stuns, stunning, stunned**
VERB **1** If you are **stunned**, or something **stuns** you, you are very shocked by it.
2 If something **stuns** a person or an animal, it knocks them unconscious.

stung
VERB the past tense and past participle of **sting**

stunk
VERB the past participle of **stink**

stunt **stunts**
NOUN an unusual or dangerous and exciting thing that someone does to get publicity or as part of a performance

stupid **stupider, stupidest**
ADJECTIVE If you are **stupid**, you are not sensible and do not make wise decisions.

sturdy **sturdier, sturdiest**
ADJECTIVE strong, firm and well built

stutter **stutters, stuttering, stuttered**
NOUN **1** Someone who has a **stutter** finds it difficult to speak smoothly and often repeats the beginning of words.
VERB **2** When someone **stutters**, they hesitate or repeat sounds when speaking.

sty **sties**
NOUN a hut with a yard where pigs are kept on a farm

style **styles**
NOUN **1** how something is done, made, said or written • *The food was cooked in Cantonese **style**.*
2 A person or place that has **style** is smart, elegant and fashionable.

sub-
PREFIX You add **sub-**to the beginning of a word to mean below or beneath. For example, something that is **sub**standard is below the required standard, and a **sub**heading comes somewhere below a main heading.

subheading **subheadings**
NOUN a title to a part of a larger section of a book. A chapter may have several sections in it, each with a **subheading**.

subject **subjects, subjecting, subjected**
Said "**sub**-jekt" NOUN **1** The **subject** of a book, programme or conversation is the thing or person it is about. • *Horses are the **subject** of this book.*
2 something that you learn about • *Maths is my favourite **subject**.*
3 The **subjects** of a country are the people who live there.
4 In grammar, the **subject** is the word or words representing the person or thing doing the action. For example, in the sentence *My cat keeps catching birds*, *my cat* is the **subject**.
Said "sub-**jekt**" VERB **5** If you **subject** someone to something, you make them experience it.

submarine **submarines**
NOUN a type of ship that can travel beneath the surface of the sea

submerge **submerges, submerging, submerged**
VERB To **submerge** means to go beneath the surface of a liquid, or to push something beneath the surface of a liquid.

submit **submits, submitting, submitted**
VERB **1** If you **submit** to something or someone, you give in to them.
2 If you **submit** something like a report or an essay, you hand it in.

subscribe **subscribes, subscribing, subscribed**
VERB If you **subscribe** to something, you regularly pay a sum of money to be a member of something or to receive a magazine.

subside **subsides, subsiding, subsided**
VERB **1** If something **subsides**, it sinks.
2 To **subside** is to become quiet or back to normal after a fuss.

a b c d e f g h i j k l m n o p q r s t u v w x y z

A B C D E F G H I J K L M N O P Q R S T U V W X Y Z

substance **substances**
NOUN anything that is a solid, a powder, a liquid or a paste
SYNONYM: material

substantial
ADJECTIVE **1** very large in degree or amount
2 large and strongly built

substitute **substitutes, substituting, substituted**
VERB **1** If you **substitute** one thing for another, you use it instead of the other thing.
NOUN **2** If one thing is a **substitute** for another, it is used instead of it or put in its place.
SYNONYMS: alternative, replacement

subtitle **subtitles**
NOUN A film or television programme with **subtitles** has the speech, or a translation of it, printed at the bottom of the screen.

subtle **subtler, subtlest**
ADJECTIVE very fine, delicate or small in degree

subtract **subtracts, subtracting, subtracted**
VERB If you **subtract** one number from another, you take away the first number from the second.

suburban
ADJECTIVE to do with the outskirts of a town or city

subway **subways**
NOUN **1** a footpath that goes underneath a road
2 an underground railway

succeed **succeeds, succeeding, succeeded**
VERB **1** If you **succeed**, you manage to do what you are trying to do.
2 If one person **succeeds** another, they come after them and take their place.

success **successes**
NOUN the achievement of something you have been trying to do

successful
ADJECTIVE having success

succession **successions**
NOUN **1** a number of things happening one after the other
2 When someone becomes the next person to have an important position, you can call this event their **succession**.

such
ADVERB **1** You can use **such** to emphasize something. • *He's **such** a nice boy.*
ADJECTIVE **2** the same kind or similar • *I have never seen **such** flowers.*
PHRASE **3** You can use **such as** to introduce examples of something. • *There were trees **such as** oak, ash and elm.*

suck **sucks, sucking, sucked**
VERB If you **suck** something, you hold it in your mouth and pull at it with your cheeks and tongue, usually to get liquid out of it.

sudden
ADJECTIVE happening quickly and unexpectedly • *We heard a **sudden** cry.*

sue **sues, suing, sued**
VERB To **sue** someone means to start a legal case against them, usually to claim money from them.

suede
NOUN a thin, soft leather with a velvety surface

suffer **suffers, suffering, suffered**
VERB If you **suffer**, you feel pain or sadness.

sufficient
ADJECTIVE If an amount is **sufficient**, there is enough of it available.

suffix **suffixes**
NOUN a group of letters that is added to the end of a word to form a new word, for example *-ness* or *-ship*, which would make *good* into *goodness* and *friend* into *friendship*

suffocate **suffocates, suffocating, suffocated**
VERB If someone **suffocates**, they die because they have no air to breathe.

sugar
NOUN a sweet substance obtained from some plants and used to sweeten food and drinks

suggest **suggests, suggesting, suggested**
VERB When you **suggest** something, you offer it as an idea.

suicide
NOUN People who commit **suicide** deliberately kill themselves.

suit **suits, suiting, suited**
NOUN **1** a matching jacket and trousers or skirt
VERB **2** If an arrangement **suits** you, it is convenient and suitable for you.
3 If a piece of clothing or a colour **suits** you, you look good when you are wearing it.
NOUN **4** A **suit** in a pack of cards is one of the sets of diamonds, clubs, hearts or spades.

suitable
ADJECTIVE right or acceptable for a certain person, occasion, time or place • *Many roads are not **suitable** for cycling.*

suitcase **suitcases**
NOUN a case in which you carry your belongings when you are travelling

suite **suites**
NOUN **1** a set of rooms in a hotel
2 a set of matching furniture or bathroom fittings

sulk **sulks, sulking, sulked**
VERB If you **sulk**, you show your annoyance by being silent and moody.

sullen
ADJECTIVE behaving in a bad-tempered and disagreeably silent way

sulphur
NOUN a yellow chemical used in industry and medicine. **Sulphur** burns with a very unpleasant smell.

sultana **sultanas**
NOUN a dried, seedless grape

sum **sums**
NOUN **1** an amount of money
2 the total of numbers added together

summarize **summarizes, summarizing, summarized**; also spelt **summarise**
VERB If you **summarize** something, you give a short account of its main points.

summary **summaries**
NOUN a short account of the main points of something said or written

summer **summers**
NOUN the warmest season of the year, between spring and autumn

summit **summits**
NOUN the top of a mountain • *The view from the **summit** was spectacular.*

summon **summons, summoning, summoned**
VERB If someone **summons** you, they order you to go to them.

sun
NOUN **1** the star in our solar system around which the earth and other planets travel, and that gives us heat and light
2 the heat and light from the sun

sunbathe **sunbathes, sunbathing, sunbathed**
VERB When you **sunbathe**, you sit in the sun to get brown.

A B C D E F G H I J K L M N O P Q R S T U V W X Y Z

sunburn
NOUN sore red skin due to being in the sun for too long

Sunday **Sundays**
NOUN the first day of the week, coming before Monday

sunflower **sunflowers**
NOUN a tall flower with a very large, round yellow head

sung
VERB the past participle of **sing**

sunglasses
PLURAL NOUN dark glasses worn to protect your eyes from the sun

sunk
VERB the past participle of **sink**

sunlight
NOUN the light from the sun

sunny **sunnier, sunniest**
ADJECTIVE having lots of sunshine

sunrise **sunrises**
NOUN the time in the day when the sun first appears

sunset **sunsets**
NOUN the time when the sun goes down

sunshine
NOUN warmth and light that come from the sun

super
ADJECTIVE excellent, very good

superb
ADJECTIVE very good indeed

superficial
ADJECTIVE only on the surface

superior
ADJECTIVE **1** better or of higher quality than other similar things
2 in a more important position than another person

superlative **superlatives**
ADJECTIVE **1** of the highest quality, the best
NOUN **2** the form of an adverb or adjective that expresses *most*. For example, the **superlative** of *hot* is *hottest*, and the **superlative** of *easy* is *easiest*.

supermarket **supermarkets**
NOUN a very large self-service shop that sells food and household goods

supernatural
ADJECTIVE Something that is **supernatural**, such as ghosts or witchcraft, cannot be explained by natural, scientific laws.

supersonic
ADJECTIVE faster than the speed of sound [from Latin *super* + *sonus* meaning above sound]

superstar **superstars**
NOUN a very famous entertainer or sportsperson

superstitious
ADJECTIVE People who are **superstitious** believe in things like magic and powers that bring good or bad luck.

supervise **supervises, supervising, supervised**
VERB If you **supervise** someone, you check what they are doing to make sure that they do it correctly.

supper **suppers**
NOUN a meal eaten in the evening or a snack eaten before you go to bed

supple
ADJECTIVE able to bend and move easily
• *Gymnasts are usually very **supple**.*

supplement **supplements, supplementing, supplemented**
VERB **1** To **supplement** something means to add something to it to improve it.
• *Many villagers **supplemented** their food supply by fishing for salmon.*
NOUN **2** something that is added to something else to improve it

supply **supplies, supplying, supplied**
VERB **1** If you **supply** someone with something, you provide them with it.
PLURAL NOUN **2** **Supplies** are food and equipment for a special purpose. • *His medical **supplies** were running low.*

support **supports, supporting, supported**
VERB **1** If something **supports** an object, it is underneath it and holding it up.
2 If you **support** a sports team, you are a fan.
3 If you **support** someone, you give them money, help or encouragement.
NOUN **4** If you give **support** to someone, you are kind, encouraging and helpful to them.
5 something that supports an object

suppose **supposes, supposing, supposed**
VERB If you **suppose** that something is so, you think that it is likely.

suppress **suppresses, suppressing, suppressed**
VERB If an army or government **suppresses** something, it stops people doing it.

supreme
ADJECTIVE greatest, best or most important

sure **surer, surest**
ADJECTIVE **1** If you are **sure** about something, you know you are right.
2 If something is **sure** to happen, it will definitely happen.

surf **surfs, surfing, surfed**
NOUN **1** the white foam that forms on the top of waves when they break near the shore
VERB **2** When you **surf**, you ride towards the shore on top of a wave, on a special board called a surfboard.

3 When you **surf** the Internet, you go from website to website reading the information.

surface **surfaces**
NOUN the top or outside area of something • *The wind ruffled the **surface** of the lake.*

surge **surges, surging, surged**
NOUN **1** a sudden great increase in the amount of something • *After the rain there was a **surge** of water down the river.*
VERB **2** If someone or something **surges**, they move suddenly and powerfully.
• *The crowd **surged** forward.*

surgeon **surgeons**
NOUN a doctor who performs operations

surgery **surgeries**
NOUN **1** medical treatment in which part of the patient's body is cut open • *He had to have **surgery** to repair his knee.*
2 a room where doctors or dentists see their patients

surname **surnames**
NOUN your last name. Members of the same family usually have the same **surname**.

surplus **surpluses**
NOUN If there is a **surplus** of something, there is more of it than is needed.

surprise **surprises, surprising, surprised**
NOUN **1** an unexpected event
2 the feeling caused when something unexpected happens
VERB **3** If something **surprises** you, it gives you a feeling of surprise.

surrender **surrenders, surrendering, surrendered**
VERB If someone **surrenders**, they admit that they are defeated.

surround **surrounds, surrounding, surrounded**
VERB To **surround** someone or something means to be situated all around them.
• *The house is **surrounded** by a high fence.*

surroundings
PLURAL NOUN the things and conditions around a person or place

survey **surveys, surveying, surveyed**
Said "sur-**vey**" VERB **1** If you **survey** something, you look carefully at the whole of it. • *They stood back and **surveyed** the scene.*
2 to make a detailed inspection of something
Said "**sur**-vey" NOUN **3** A **survey** of something, such as people's habits, is a detailed examination of it, often in a report.

survive **survives, surviving, survived**
VERB To **survive** means to continue to live or exist in spite of danger or difficulties.

suspect **suspects, suspecting, suspected**
Said "sus-**spekt**" VERB **1** If you **suspect** something, you think that it might be true.
2 If you **suspect** someone of doing something wrong, you think that they have done it.
Said "**suss**-pekt" NOUN **3** someone who is thought to be guilty of a crime

suspend **suspends, suspending, suspended**
VERB **1** to hang something up
2 to delay something for a time

suspense
NOUN the feeling of excitement or fear when you are waiting for something to happen

suspicion **suspicions**
NOUN the feeling of not trusting someone or that something is wrong

suspicious
ADJECTIVE **1** If you are **suspicious** of someone, you do not trust them.
2 If something is **suspicious**, it causes suspicion.

swallow **swallows, swallowing, swallowed**
VERB If you **swallow** something, you make it go down your throat and into your stomach.

swam
VERB the past tense of **swim**

swamp **swamps, swamping, swamped**
NOUN **1** an area of permanently wet land
VERB **2** If something is **swamped**, it is covered or filled with water.
3 If you are **swamped** by things, you have more than you can manage.

swan **swans**
NOUN a large, usually white, bird with a long neck that lives on rivers or lakes

swap **swaps, swapping, swapped**
Rhymes with "stop" VERB If you **swap** one thing for another, you replace the first thing with the second.
SYNONYM: exchange

swarm **swarms, swarming, swarmed**
NOUN **1** a large group of insects flying together
VERB **2** When bees or other insects **swarm**, they fly together in a large group.
3 If a place is **swarming** with people, it is crowded with people.

swat **swats, swatting, swatted**
VERB If you **swat** an insect, you hit it quickly to kill it.

sway **sways, swaying, swayed**
VERB If something or someone **sways**, they lean or swing slowly from side to side.

swear **swears, swearing, swore, sworn**
VERB **1** If you **swear**, you use very rude words.
2 If you **swear** to do something, you promise that you will do it.

sweat **sweats, sweating, sweated**
NOUN **1** the salty liquid that comes through your skin when you are hot or afraid
VERB **2** When you **sweat**, sweat comes through your skin.

sweater **sweaters**
NOUN a knitted piece of clothing covering your upper body and arms

sweatshirt **sweatshirts**
NOUN a piece of clothing made of thick cotton, covering your upper body and arms

swede **swedes**
NOUN a large round root vegetable with yellow flesh and a brownish-purple skin

sweep **sweeps, sweeping, swept**
VERB **1** If you **sweep** the floor, you use a brush to gather up dust or rubbish from it.
2 If you **sweep** things off a surface, you push them all off with a quick, smooth movement.
3 If something **sweeps** from one place to another, it moves there very quickly.
• *The boat* ***swept*** *down the river with the outgoing tide.*

sweet **sweeter, sweetest; sweets**
ADJECTIVE **1** tasting of sugar or honey
2 A **sweet** sound is gentle and tuneful.
3 attractive and delightful • *He's such a* ***sweet*** *little baby.*
NOUN **4** small pieces of sweet food, such as toffees, chocolates and mints
5 something sweet that you eat at the end of a meal
SYNONYM: dessert

sweetcorn
NOUN a long stalk covered with juicy yellow seeds that can be eaten as a vegetable

sweetheart **sweethearts**
NOUN You can call someone you are very fond of **sweetheart**.

swell **swells, swelling, swelled, swollen**
VERB If something **swells**, it becomes larger and rounder.

sweltering
ADJECTIVE If the weather is **sweltering**, it is very hot.

swept
VERB the past tense and past participle of **sweep**

swerve **swerves, swerving, swerved**
VERB If someone or something **swerves**, they suddenly change direction to avoid colliding with something.

swift **swifter, swiftest; swifts**
ADJECTIVE **1** happening or moving very quickly
NOUN **2** a bird with narrow crescent-shaped wings

swim **swims, swimming, swam, swum**
VERB When you **swim**, you move through water by making movements with your arms and legs.

swimming
NOUN the act of moving through water using your arms and legs

swimming costume **swimming costumes**
NOUN a garment you wear while swimming

swimming pool **swimming pools**
NOUN an area of water made for swimming, usually a large hole that has been tiled and filled with water

swimsuit **swimsuits**
NOUN a one-piece swimming costume

swindle **swindles, swindling, swindled**
VERB **1** If someone **swindles** someone else, they trick them to obtain money or property.
NOUN **2** a trick in which someone is cheated out of money or property

swine **swine**
NOUN OLD-FASHIONED a pig

The plural of *swine* is *swine*.

swing **swings, swinging, swung**
VERB **1** If something **swings**, or if you **swing** it, it moves repeatedly from side to side or backwards and forwards from a fixed point.
NOUN **2** a seat hanging from a frame or a branch, that moves backwards and forwards when you sit on it

a b c d e f g h i j k l m n o p q r s t u v w x y z

swipe **swipes, swiping, swiped**
VERB **1** If you **swipe** at something, you try to hit it with a curved swinging movement.
2 If a credit card is **swiped**, it is put though an electronic machine to read it when paying.
3 INFORMAL If someone **swipes** something, they steal it.

switch **switches, switching, switched**
NOUN **1** a device used to control an electrical device or machine. When the **switch** is on, or closed, it completes the circuit and electricity can flow.
2 a change
VERB **3** To **switch** to a different task or topic means to change to it.

switch off
VERB If you **switch off** a light or a machine, you stop it working by pressing a switch.

switch on
VERB If you **switch on** a light or a machine, you start it working by pressing a switch.

switchboard **switchboards**
NOUN a panel with switches on for connecting telephone lines

swivel **swivels, swivelling, swivelled**
VERB **1** to turn round on a central point
ADJECTIVE **2** A **swivel** chair or lamp is made so that you can move the main part of it while the base remains in a fixed position.

swollen
ADJECTIVE **1** Something that is **swollen** has swelled up.
SYNONYMS: enlarged, puffed up
VERB **2** the past participle of **swell**

swoop **swoops, swooping, swooped**
VERB To **swoop** is to move downwards through the air in a fast curving movement.

swop **swops, swopping, swopped**
VERB to swap

sword **swords**
NOUN a weapon consisting of a very long blade with a short handle

swum
VERB the past participle of **swim**

swung
VERB the past tense and past participle of **swing**

sycamore **sycamores**
NOUN a tree that has large leaves with five points, and winged seed cases

syllable **syllables**
NOUN a part of a word that contains a single vowel sound and is said as one unit • *"Book" has one **syllable** and "reading" has two.*

syllabus **syllabuses** or **syllabi**
NOUN the subjects that are studied for a particular course or examination

symbol **symbols**
NOUN a shape, design or idea that is used to represent something • *Apple blossom is a Chinese **symbol** of peace and beauty.*

symmetrical
ADJECTIVE **Symmetrical** objects can be divided in half so that both halves match, with one half like a reflection of the other.

a symmetrical pattern

symmetry
NOUN If something has **symmetry**, it is the same in both halves.

sympathetic
ADJECTIVE feeling sympathy or understanding for someone

sympathy
NOUN an understanding of people's feelings and opinions, especially someone who is in difficulties

SYNONYM: compassion

symphony **symphonies**
NOUN a piece of music for an orchestra, usually in four parts called movements

symptom **symptoms**
NOUN something wrong with your body that is a sign of illness

synagogue **synagogues**
NOUN a building where Jewish people meet for worship and religious instruction

synonym **synonyms**
NOUN two words that have the same or a very similar meaning • *Speak is a* ***synonym*** *for talk.*

synthetic
ADJECTIVE made from artificial substances rather than natural ones

syringe **syringes**
NOUN a hollow tube with a plunger, used for drawing up or pushing out liquids. Doctors and vets use them to give injections.

syrup **syrups**
NOUN a thick, sweet liquid made by boiling sugar with water
[from Arabic *sharab* meaning drink]

system **systems**
NOUN an organized way of doing or arranging something according to a fixed plan or set of rules

Tt

tab **tabs**
NOUN a small extra piece that is attached to something and sticks out, for example a sticky marker that you put in a book to mark your place

table **tables**
NOUN **1** a piece of furniture with a flat top supported by one or more legs
2 a set of facts or figures arranged in rows or columns

tablecloth **tablecloths**
NOUN a cloth used to cover a table and to keep it clean

tablespoon **tablespoons**
NOUN **1** a large spoon used for serving food
2 the amount that a **tablespoon** contains • *For this recipe you need two* ***tablespoons*** *of caster sugar.*

tablet **tablets**
NOUN **1** medicine in a small, solid lump that you swallow
SYNONYM: pill
2 a flat piece of stone with words carved on it
3 a small mobile personal computer with a screen that you tap or swipe

table tennis
NOUN a game for two or four people who use bats to hit a small ball over a net across the middle of the table

tabloid **tabloids**
NOUN a newspaper with small pages, short news stories, and lots of photographs

tack **tacks, tacking, tacked**
NOUN **1** a short nail with a flat top
2 If you change **tack**, you find a different way of doing something.
VERB **3** If you **tack** something to a surface, you fix it there with a tack.

A B C D E F G H I J K L M N O P Q R S T U V W X Y Z

4 If you **tack** in a boat, you sail in a zigzag course to catch the wind.
5 If you **tack** a piece of fabric, you sew it with long, loose stitches.
NOUN **6** equipment for horses, such as bridles, saddles and harnesses

tackle **tackles, tackling, tackled**
VERB **1** If you **tackle** a difficult task, you start dealing with it.
2 If you **tackle** someone in a game such as hockey or soccer, you try to get the ball away from them.
NOUN **3** an attempt to get the ball away from your opponent in certain sports

tact
NOUN the ability to deal with people without upsetting or offending them
tactless ADJECTIVE **tactlessly** ADVERB

tactful
ADJECTIVE Someone who is **tactful** has the ability to deal with people without upsetting or offending them.
tactfully ADVERB

tactic **tactics**
NOUN one of the methods you use in order to achieve what you want

tadpole **tadpoles**
NOUN a young frog or toad. **Tadpoles** are black with round heads and long tails, and live in water.
[Middle English *tadde* meaning toad and *pol* meaning head]

tag **tags, tagging, tagged**
NOUN **1** a small label made of cloth
2 a game in which one person chases the other people who are playing
VERB **3** If you **tag along** behind someone, you follow and try to keep up.

tail **tails**
NOUN **1** The **tail** of an animal is the part extending beyond the end of its body. For example, a fox has a bushy **tail**.
2 the end part of something
ADJECTIVE OR ADVERB **3** When you toss a coin, the **tails** side is the one that does not have a person's head on it.

> Do not confuse *tail* with *tale*.

tailor **tailors**
NOUN a person who makes, alters and repairs clothes, especially for men

take **takes, taking, took, taken**
VERB **1** If you **take** someone or something to a place, you get them there. • *She **took** the cat to the vet.*
2 **Take** is used to show what activity is being done. • *Sam **took** a shower.*
3 If you **take** a pill or some medicine, you swallow it.
4 When you **take** one number from another, you subtract it.
5 If you **take** a photograph, you use a camera to produce it.

take after
VERB If you **take after** a member of your family, you are like them in some way.

take off
VERB When a plane **takes off**, it goes into the air.

takeaway **takeaways**
NOUN **1** a shop or restaurant that sells hot, cooked food to be taken away and eaten elsewhere
2 a hot cooked meal bought from a takeaway restaurant

talcum powder
NOUN a soft, perfumed powder to put on the skin to dry it

tale **tales**
NOUN a story

> Do not confuse *tale* with *tail*.

talent **talents**
NOUN the ability to do something very well

talk **talks, talking, talked**
VERB **1** When you **talk**, you say things to someone.
NOUN **2** a conversation or discussion
3 an informal speech about something

talkative
ADJECTIVE If you are **talkative**, you talk a lot.
SYNONYM: chatty

tall **taller, tallest**
ADJECTIVE **1** If you are **tall**, you are more than the average height.
2 having a particular height • *How **tall** are you?*

tally **tallies**
NOUN an informal record that you keep as you count objects

Talmud
NOUN a collection of books of the ancient Jewish ceremonies and laws

talon **talons**
NOUN a sharp, hooked claw, especially of a bird of prey

tambourine **tambourines**
NOUN a percussion instrument made of a skin stretched tightly over a circular frame. It has small round pieces of metal around the edge that jangle when the **tambourine** is beaten or shaken.
[from Old French *tambourin* meaning little drum]

tame **tamer, tamest; tames, taming, tamed**
ADJECTIVE **1** A **tame** animal is not afraid of people.
VERB **2** If you **tame** a wild animal, you train it not to be afraid of humans.

tamper **tampers, tampering, tampered**
VERB If you **tamper** with something, you interfere with it.

tan **tans, tanning, tanned**
NOUN **1** a suntan
2 a yellowish-brown colour
VERB **3** If your skin **tans**, it goes brown in the sun.
4 When an animal's skin is **tanned**, it is turned into leather by treating it with chemicals.

tang **tangs**
NOUN a strong flavour or smell

tangerine **tangerines**
NOUN **1** a type of small sweet orange that is easy to peel
NOUN OR ADJECTIVE **2** reddish-orange

tangle **tangles, tangling, tangled**
NOUN **1** a mass of things, such as hairs or fibres, that are twisted together and difficult to separate
VERB **2** If you **tangle** something, you twist it into knots.

tank **tanks**
NOUN **1** a large container for storing liquid or gas
2 an armoured military vehicle that moves on tracks and has guns or rockets

tanker **tankers**
NOUN a ship or lorry designed to carry large quantities of gas or liquid

tantrum **tantrums**
NOUN a noisy and sometimes violent outburst of bad temper, especially by a child

tap **taps, tapping, tapped**
NOUN **1** a device for controlling the flow of gas or liquid from a pipe
VERB **2** If you **tap** something, you hit it lightly and quickly.
NOUN **3** a light hit, or its sound

tape **tapes, taping, taped**
NOUN **1** a long plastic ribbon covered with a magnetic substance and used to record sounds, pictures and computer information
2 a cassette with magnetic **tape** wound round it • *video **tape***
3 a strip of sticky plastic used for sticking things together
VERB **4** If you **tape** sounds or television pictures, you record them using a tape recorder or a video recorder.

tape measure **tape measures**
NOUN a long, narrow tape marked with centimetres or inches, and used for measuring

taper **tapers, tapering, tapered**
VERB Something that **tapers** becomes thinner towards one end.

tape recorder **tape recorders**
NOUN a machine that records sounds onto a special magnetic tape that can be played back later

tapestry **tapestries**
NOUN a piece of heavy cloth with designs embroidered on it
[from Old French *tapisserie* meaning carpeting]

tar
NOUN a thick, black, sticky substance that is used in making roads

tarantula **tarantulas**
NOUN a large, hairy, poisonous spider

target **targets**
NOUN something you aim at when firing a weapon

tarmac
NOUN a mixture of tar and crushed stones, used for making road surfaces
[short for *tarmacadam*, from the name of John *McAdam*, the Scottish engineer who invented it]

tarnish **tarnishes, tarnishing, tarnished**
VERB If metal **tarnishes**, it becomes stained and loses its shine.
tarnished ADJECTIVE

tarpaulin **tarpaulins**
NOUN a sheet of heavy waterproof material used as a protective covering

tart **tarts**
NOUN **1** a pastry case, usually filled with something sweet such as fruit or jam
ADJECTIVE **2** Something **tart** has a sharp or sour taste.

tartan **tartans**
NOUN a coloured, woollen fabric from Scotland, with a special pattern of checks and stripes, depending on which clan it belongs to

task **tasks**
NOUN any piece of work that has to be done
SYNONYMS: chore, duty, job

tassel **tassels**
NOUN a tuft of loose threads tied by a knot and used for decoration

taste **tastes, tasting, tasted**
NOUN **1** Your sense of **taste** is your ability to recognize the flavour of things in your mouth.
2 The **taste** of something is its flavour.
3 your own particular choice of things such as clothes, music and food • *Jenny and I have the same **taste** in music.*
VERB **4** When you can **taste** something in your mouth, you know what its flavour is like.
5 If food or drink **tastes** of something, it has that flavour.

tasty **tastier, tastiest**
ADJECTIVE Something that is **tasty** has a pleasant flavour.

tattered
ADJECTIVE ragged and torn

tattoo **tattoos, tattooing, tattooed**
VERB **1** If someone is **tattooed**, they have a design drawn on their skin by pricking little holes and filling them with coloured dye.
NOUN **2** a picture or design tattooed on someone's body

taught
VERB the past tense and past participle of **teach**

taunt **taunts, taunting, taunted**
VERB If you **taunt** someone, you tease them about their weaknesses or failures in order to make them angry or upset.

taut
ADJECTIVE Something that is **taut** is stretched very tight.

tawny
ADJECTIVE brownish-yellow

tax **taxes, taxing, taxed**
NOUN **1** an amount of money that people

have to pay to the government so that it can provide public services such as health care and education
VERB **2** If a sum of money is **taxed**, a certain amount of it is paid to the government.
3 If something **taxes** you, it exhausts you and drains your energy.

taxi **taxis**
NOUN a car with a driver that you hire, usually for a short journey

tea **teas**
NOUN **1** the dried leaves of a shrub found in Asia
2 a drink made by soaking the leaves of the tea plant in hot water
3 a meal taken in the late afternoon or early evening

tea bag **tea bags**
NOUN a small paper packet with tea leaves in it, that you use to make a drink of tea

teach **teaches, teaching, taught**
VERB If someone **teaches** you something, they help you learn about it or show you how to do it.
SYNONYMS: educate, instruct, train

teacher **teachers**
NOUN someone who teaches at a school or college

teak
NOUN a hard wood that comes from a large Asian tree

team **teams**
NOUN a group of people who play together against another group in a sport or game

teapot **teapots**
NOUN a container in which tea is made. It has a handle, a spout and a lid.

tear **tears, tearing, tore, torn**
Rhymes with "fear" NOUN **1** a drop of liquid that comes out of your eyes when you cry
Rhymes with "hair" NOUN **2** a hole or rip that has been made in something • *There was a **tear** in the curtain.*
VERB **3** If you **tear** something, you damage it by pulling so that a hole or rip appears in it.

tearful
ADJECTIVE If you are **tearful**, you cry easily or you are crying.

tease **teases, teasing, teased**
VERB If someone **teases** you, they deliberately make fun of you or embarrass you.

teaspoon **teaspoons**
NOUN **1** a small spoon used for stirring drinks
2 the amount that a **teaspoon** holds
• *I have two **teaspoons** of sugar in my coffee.*

teat **teats**
NOUN **1** a nipple on a female animal
2 a piece of rubber or plastic that is shaped like a nipple and fitted to a baby's feeding bottle

technical
ADJECTIVE If something is **technical**, it is to do with machines, the way things work, and materials used in industry, transport and communications.

technique **techniques**
Said "tek-**neek**" NOUN a particular way of doing something

technology
NOUN practical things that have come about because of a greater understanding of science • *New **technology** has helped us develop faster computers.*

teddy bear **teddy bears**
NOUN a soft, furry toy bear

tedious
ADJECTIVE boring and lasting for a long time

teenager **teenagers**
NOUN a person aged between 13 and 19 years old

teeth
PLURAL NOUN the plural of **tooth**

tele-
PREFIX You add **tele-** to the beginning of a word to mean at or over a distance.
• ***tele**phone*
[from the Greek *tele* meaning far]

a b c d e f g h i j k l m n o p q r s t u v w x y z

A B C D E F G H I J K L M N O P Q R S T U V W X Y Z

telecommunications
NOUN the science and activity of sending signals and messages over long distances, for example by radio and telephone

telegram **telegrams**
NOUN a message sent by telegraph to an office, and then delivered by hand to a person's home • *He received many letters and* ***telegrams*** *of congratulations when he won the race.*

telegraph
NOUN a system of sending messages over long distances using electrical or radio signals

telephone **telephones, telephoning, telephoned**
NOUN **1** a piece of electrical equipment for talking directly to someone who is in a different place
VERB **2** If you **telephone** someone, you speak to them using a telephone.

telescope
telescopes
NOUN a long instrument, shaped like a tube, that contains lenses. When you look through it with one eye, distant objects appear larger and nearer.

televise **televises, televising, televised**
VERB If an event is **televised**, it is filmed and shown on television.

television **televisions**
NOUN a piece of electronic equipment that receives pictures and sounds transmitted over a distance

tell **tells, telling, told**
VERB **1** If you **tell** someone something, you let them know about it.
2 If you **tell** someone to do something, you order them to do it.

telly **tellies**
NOUN an abbreviation of *television*

temper
NOUN **1** Your **temper** is the mood you are in and the way you are feeling, whether you are irritable and angry or calm and peaceful. • *I started the day in a bad* ***temper****.*
PHRASE **2** If you **lose your temper**, you become very angry.

temperamental
ADJECTIVE Someone who is **temperamental** changes their mood often and suddenly.

temperature **temperatures**
NOUN **1** how hot or cold something is • *There was a sudden drop in* ***temperature*** *once the sun had gone down.*
2 Your **temperature** is the temperature of your body. The normal body **temperature** for humans is 37°C. • *His* ***temperature*** *continued to rise.*

temple **temples**
NOUN **1** a building used for the worship of a god in various religions
2 the part on either side of your head between your forehead and your ear

tempo **tempos** or **tempi**
NOUN TECHNICAL The **tempo** of a piece of music is its speed.

temporary
ADJECTIVE lasting for only a short time

tempt **tempts, tempting, tempted**
VERB **1** If you **tempt** someone, you try to persuade them to do something by offering them something they want.
ADJECTIVE **2** If something is **tempting**, it is attractive and difficult to resist.

ten
NOUN **Ten** is the number 10.
tenth NOUN OR ADJECTIVE

tenant **tenants**
NOUN someone who pays rent for the place they live in, or for land or buildings that they use
tenancy NOUN

tend **tends, tending, tended**
VERB **1** If something **tends** to happen, it usually happens.

2 If you **tend** something or someone, you look after them. • *Bob **tended** the plants.*

tendency **tendencies**
NOUN the way a person or a thing is likely to behave or has a habit of behaving • *She has a **tendency** to write messily.*

tender **tenderer, tenderest**
ADJECTIVE **1** Someone who is **tender** is gentle and caring.
SYNONYMS: affectionate, gentle, loving
2 **Tender** food is easy to cut and chew.
3 If a part of your body is **tender**, it is painful and sore.

tendon **tendons**
NOUN **Tendons** are like strong cords. They hold your muscles and bones together.

tennis
NOUN a game played by two or four players on a rectangular court. The players hit a ball over a central net.

tense **tenser, tensest; tenses, tensing, tensed**
ADJECTIVE **1** If you are **tense**, you feel worried and unable to relax.
NOUN **2** The **tense** of a verb shows whether it is in the past, present or future.
VERB **3** If you **tense** your muscles, you tighten them up.

tension **tensions**
NOUN the feeling of nervousness or worry that you have when something dangerous or important is happening

tent **tents**
NOUN a shelter made of fabric held up by poles and pinned down at the bottom with pegs and ropes

tentacle **tentacles**
NOUN the long, bending parts of an animal, such as an octopus, that it uses to feel and hold things

tepid
ADJECTIVE **Tepid** liquid is only slightly warm.

term **terms**
NOUN **1** one of the periods of time that each year is divided into at a school or college
2 **Terms** are words that relate to a particular subject, for example, medical **terms**, legal **terms** and scientific **terms**.
3 **Terms** are the conditions of an agreement. • *He made a list of **terms** for doing the job.*
4 If you are on good **terms** with someone, you get on well with them.

terminal **terminals**
NOUN **1** a place where vehicles, passengers or goods begin or end a journey
2 a keyboard and screen connected to a main computer
ADJECTIVE **3** A **terminal** illness or disease cannot be cured and gradually causes death.
[from Latin *terminus* meaning end]

terminate **terminates, terminating, terminated**
VERB When you **terminate** something, or it **terminates**, it stops or ends.

terrace **terraces**
NOUN **1** a row of houses joined together
2 a flat area of stone next to a building, where people can sit

terrapin **terrapins**
NOUN a small North American freshwater turtle
[an American Indian word]

terrible
ADJECTIVE **1** serious and unpleasant • *He had a **terrible** illness.*
2 very bad or of poor quality • *That is a **terrible** haircut.*

terrier **terriers**
NOUN a breed of small dog
[from Old French *chien terrier* meaning earth dog, because they were originally bred to hunt animals living in holes in the ground, such as rabbits and badgers]

terrific
ADJECTIVE **1** very pleasing or impressive • *That was a **terrific** film.*
2 very great or strong • *There is a **terrific** wind blowing down on the beach.*

terrify **terrifies, terrifying, terrified**
VERB If something **terrifies** you, it makes you feel extremely frightened.

A B C D E F G H I J K L M N O P Q R S T U V W X Y Z

territory **territories**
NOUN The **territory** of a country is the land that it controls.

terror **terrors**
NOUN great fear or panic

terrorism
NOUN the use of violence for political purposes

test **tests, testing, tested**
VERB **1** When you **test** something, you try it to find out what it is, what condition it is in, or how well it works.
2 To **test** someone means to ask them questions to find out how much they know.
NOUN **3** a set of questions or tasks given to someone to find out what they know or can do

test tube **test tubes**
NOUN a small cylindrical glass container that is used in chemical experiments

tetanus
NOUN a painful infectious disease caused by germs getting into wounds

tether **tethers, tethering, tethered**
VERB **1** If you **tether** an animal, you tie it to something such as a post.
NOUN **2** a rope for tying an animal to something such as a post

tetrahedron
tetrahedrons or **tetrahedra**
NOUN a solid shape with four triangular faces

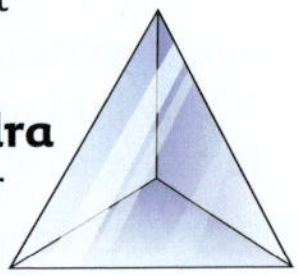

text **texts, texting, texted**
NOUN **1** the written part of a book, rather than the pictures or the index
2 short for **text message**
VERB **3** If you **text** someone, you send them a text message.

textbook **textbooks**
NOUN a book about a particular subject for students to use

textile **textiles**
NOUN a woven cloth or fabric

text message **text messages**
NOUN a written message sent using a mobile phone

texture **textures**
NOUN the way something feels when you touch it • *Silk has a very smooth, soft* ***texture****.*

than
CONJUNCTION OR PREPOSITION You use **than** when you compare one thing with another. • *She is bigger* ***than*** *her sister.*

thank **thanks, thanking, thanked**
VERB When you **thank** someone, you show that you are pleased or grateful for something that they have done for you.

thank you
EXCLAMATION You say **thank you** to show that you are grateful to someone for something.

that **those**
ADJECTIVE OR PRONOUN **1** **That** is used when you are referring to someone or something you have already mentioned.
• ***That*** *is the film I want to see.*
CONJUNCTION **2** **That** is used to introduce a fact, a statement or a result. • *His writing was so bad* ***that*** *nobody could read it.*

thaw **thaws, thawing, thawed**
VERB **1** When snow or ice **thaws**, it melts.
2 When you **thaw** frozen food, or when it **thaws**, it defrosts.

the
ADJECTIVE called the definite article. You use **the** in front of a noun when you are referring to something in particular.
• *That's* ***the*** *chair I bought yesterday.*

theatre **theatres**
NOUN **1** a building where plays and other shows are performed on a stage
2 a room in a hospital where operations are carried out

theft **thefts**
NOUN the crime of stealing
SYNONYM: robbery

their
ADJECTIVE **Their** refers to something belonging to people or things, other than

yourself or the person you are talking to, that have already been mentioned. • *The children had been playing football, and **their** shirts were dirty.*

Do not confuse *their* with *there* or *they're*.

theirs

PRONOUN **Theirs** refers to something belonging to people or things, other than yourself or the person you are talking to, that have already been mentioned. • *The children said that the ball that came over the wall was **theirs**.*

them

PRONOUN **Them** refers to things or people, other than yourself or the person you are talking to, that have already been mentioned. • *She took her gloves off and put **them** in a drawer.*

theme **themes**

NOUN a main idea in a piece of writing, painting, film or music • *The main **theme** of the book is growing up.*

themselves

PRONOUN **Themselves** is used when people, other than yourself or the person you are talking to, do an action and are affected by it. • *They enjoyed **themselves** at the fair.*

then

ADVERB after that; next • *He put on his shoes and **then** went for a walk.*

theology

NOUN the study of religion and God

theory **theories**

NOUN an idea or set of ideas that is meant to explain something

therapy

NOUN the treatment of a mental or physical illness
therapist NOUN

there

ADVERB in that place or to that place • *He's sitting over **there**.*

Do not confuse *there* with *their* or *they're*.

therefore

ADVERB as a result • *I worked hard and **therefore** I won a prize.*

thermal

ADJECTIVE **1** to do with or caused by heat
2 Thermal clothing is specially designed to keep you warm in cold weather.

thermometer **thermometers**

NOUN an instrument for measuring the temperature of a room or a person's body

Thermos

NOUN TRADEMARK a container used to keep drinks hot or cold

thermostat **thermostats**

NOUN a device used to control temperature, for example on a central heating system

thesaurus **thesauruses**

NOUN a reference book in which words with similar meanings are grouped together

these

ADJECTIVE OR PRONOUN the plural of **this**

they

PRONOUN **They** refers to people or things that have already been mentioned. • *I saw Tom and Ben. **They** were looking in a shop window.*

they'd

a contraction of *they had* or *they would*

they'll

a contraction of *they will* or *they shall*

they're

a contraction of *they are*

Do not confuse *they're* with *their* or *there*.

they've

a contraction of *they have*

thick **thicker, thickest**

ADJECTIVE **1** Something **thick** has a large distance between its two sides. • *I'd like a **thick** slice of bread and butter.*
ANTONYM: thin
2 If you want to know how **thick** something is, you want to know the measurement between its two sides.

A B C D E F G H I J K L M N O P Q R S T U V W X Y Z

• *How **thick** is this wall?*
ANTONYM: thin
3 close together and in a large number
• *She has **thick**, dark hair.*
4 Thick liquids contain little water and do not flow easily. • *The **thick** soup was very filling.*
ANTONYM: thin

thicken **thickens, thickening, thickened**
VERB If you **thicken** something, or if it **thickens**, it becomes thicker. • *Stir the custard in the pan until it **thickens**.*

thickness **thicknesses**
NOUN how thick something is

thief **thieves**
NOUN a person who steals

thigh **thighs**
NOUN the top part of your leg, between your knee and your hip

thimble **thimbles**
NOUN a small metal or plastic cap that you put on the end of your finger to protect it from the needle when you are sewing

thin **thinner, thinnest**
ADJECTIVE **1** Something that is **thin** is much narrower than it is long.
ANTONYM: thick
2 A **thin** person or animal has very little fat on their body.
3 Thin liquids contain a lot of water and flow easily.
ANTONYM: thick

thing **things**
NOUN an object rather than a plant, animal or person

think **thinks, thinking, thought**
VERB **1** When you **think** about ideas or problems, you use your mind to sort them out.
2 If you **think** something, you believe it is true. • *I **think** she's got a bike for her birthday.*
3 If you **think** of something, you remember it or it comes into your mind.
4 If you are **thinking** of doing something, you might do it.

third **thirds**
NOUN OR ADJECTIVE **1** The **third** or the **third** thing in a series is the one counted as number three.
NOUN **2** one of three equal parts into which something can be divided

third person
NOUN In grammar, the **third person** is *he*, *she*, *it* or *they*.

thirst
NOUN If you have a **thirst**, you feel the need to drink something.

thirsty **thirstier, thirstiest**
ADJECTIVE If you are **thirsty**, you feel as if you need to drink something.
thirstily ADVERB

thirteen
NOUN **Thirteen** is the number 13.
thirteenth NOUN OR ADJECTIVE

thirty
NOUN **Thirty** is the number 30.
thirtieth NOUN OR ADJECTIVE

this **those**
ADJECTIVE OR PRONOUN **This** means the one here, not a different one. • ***This** food looks nice.*

thistle **thistles**
NOUN a wild plant with prickly-edged leaves and purple flowers

thorn **thorns**
NOUN one of many sharp points growing on the stems of some plants. For example, brambles have many **thorns**.

thorough
ADJECTIVE done very carefully and completely
thoroughly ADVERB

those
ADJECTIVE OR PRONOUN the plural of **that**

though
Rhymes with "show" CONJUNCTION **1** despite the fact that • *She felt better, **though** her cough was still bad.*
2 You can use **though** to mean if.
• *Try to look as **though** you're working.*

thought **thoughts**
VERB **1** the past tense and past participle of **think**
NOUN **2** the activity of thinking • *She was lost in **thought**.*

thoughtful
ADJECTIVE **1** If you are **thoughtful**, you are quiet and serious.
2 A **thoughtful** person thinks of what other people need and what they would like.
thoughtfully ADVERB

thoughtless
ADJECTIVE A **thoughtless** person does not care or think about other people's needs.
thoughtlessness NOUN
thoughtlessly ADVERB

thousand **thousands**
NOUN A **thousand** is the number 1000.
thousandth NOUN OR ADJECTIVE

thrash **thrashes, thrashing, thrashed**
VERB **1** To **thrash** someone is to beat them by hitting them with something like a stick or a whip.
2 If you **thrash** someone in a contest or fight, you defeat them completely.
3 If you **thrash**, or **thrash** about, you move about wildly and violently.

thread **threads**
NOUN a long, fine piece of cotton, silk, nylon or wool

threadbare
ADJECTIVE Fabric or clothes that are **threadbare** are old and worn thin.

threat **threats**
NOUN **1** a warning that someone will harm you if you do not do what they want
2 a danger or something that might cause harm

threaten **threatens, threatening, threatened**
VERB If you **threaten** someone, you tell them that you intend to harm them in some way.

three
NOUN **Three** is the number 3.

three-dimensional
ADJECTIVE A **three-dimensional** object or shape is not flat, but has height or depth as well as length and width.

threw
VERB the past tense of **throw**

thrill **thrills, thrilling, thrilled**
NOUN **1** a sudden feeling of great excitement, pleasure or fear
VERB **2** If something **thrills** you, it gives you a feeling of great pleasure and excitement.
thrilled ADJECTIVE **thrilling** ADJECTIVE

thriller **thrillers**
NOUN a book, film or play that tells an exciting story about dangerous or mysterious events

thrive **thrives, thriving, throve** or **thrived**
VERB to grow strongly and healthily, or to prosper

throat **throats**
NOUN **1** the back of your mouth and the top part of the tubes inside your neck that lead to your stomach and lungs
2 the front part of your neck

throb **throbs, throbbing, throbbed**
VERB If something **throbs**, it beats or vibrates with a strong, regular rhythm. • *My finger **throbbed** after I trapped it in the door.*

throne **thrones**
NOUN a ceremonial chair used by a king or queen on important official occasions

throng **throngs, thronging, thronged**
NOUN **1** a large crowd of people • *There was a **throng** of fans waiting at the stage door.*
VERB **2** If people **throng** somewhere, or **throng** a place, they go there in great numbers. • *Hundreds of royal admirers **thronged** to see the procession.*

throttle **throttles, throttling, throttled**
VERB If a person **throttles** someone, they

A B C D E F G H I J K L M N O P Q R S T U V W X Y Z

kill or injure them by squeezing their throat.
SYNONYM: strangle

through
PREPOSITION If you move **through** something, you go from one side of it to the other. • *We followed the path **through** the woods.*

throughout
PREPOSITION OR ADVERB all the way through

throw **throws, throwing, threw, thrown**
VERB When you **throw** something you let it go with a quick movement of your arm, so that it moves through the air.
SYNONYMS: chuck, fling, toss

throw away
VERB If you **throw away** something that you do not want, you get rid of it, usually by putting it in the rubbish bin.

thrush **thrushes**
NOUN a small brown songbird

thrust **thrusts, thrusting, thrust**
VERB If you **thrust** something somewhere, you move or push it there quickly and with a lot of force.

thud **thuds, thudding, thudded**
VERB **1** to fall heavily
NOUN **2** the dull sound of something heavy falling

thug **thugs**
NOUN a very rough and violent person
[from Hindi *thag* meaning thief]

thumb **thumbs**
NOUN the short, thick, jointed part on the side of your hand, similar to a finger but lower down

thump **thumps, thumping, thumped**
VERB **1** If you **thump** someone or something, you hit them hard with your fist.
2 When your heart **thumps**, it beats strongly and quickly.
NOUN **3** a hard hit
4 a fairly loud, dull sound

thunder
NOUN the loud, rumbling noise that you hear from the sky during some storms, often after a flash of lightning

thunderstorm **thunderstorms**
NOUN a storm with thunder and lightning

Thursday
NOUN the fifth day of the week, coming between Wednesday and Friday
[from Old English *Thursdæg* meaning Thor's day; Thor was the Norse god of thunder]

tick **ticks, ticking, ticked**
NOUN **1** a written mark to show that something is correct
VERB **2** If you **tick** something written on a piece of paper, you put a tick next to it.
3 When a clock **ticks**, it makes a regular clicking noise as it works.

ticket **tickets**
NOUN a piece of paper or card which shows that you have paid for a journey or have paid to go into a place • *Don't lose your bus **ticket**.*

tickle **tickles, tickling, tickled**
VERB When you **tickle** someone, you move your fingers lightly over their body in order to make them laugh.

tide **tides**
NOUN the regular change in the level of the sea on the shore

tidy **tidier, tidiest; tidies, tidying, tidied**
ADJECTIVE **1** Something that is **tidy** is neat and arranged in an orderly way.
2 Someone who is **tidy** always keeps their things neat.
VERB **3** If you **tidy** a place, you make it neat by putting things in their proper place.

tie **ties, tying, tied**
VERB **1** If you **tie** one thing to another, you fasten it using cord of some kind.
2 If you **tie** a piece of cord or cloth, you fasten the ends together in a knot or bow.
NOUN **3** a long, narrow piece of cloth worn around the neck under a shirt collar, and tied in a knot at the front

tiger **tigers**
NOUN a large wild cat that has an orange-coloured coat with black stripes

tight **tighter, tightest**
ADJECTIVE **1** If clothes are **tight**, they fit you very closely.
ADVERB **2** If you hold **tight**, you hold on very firmly.

tighten **tightens, tightening, tightened**
VERB **1** If you **tighten** something like a rope or a chain, you pull it until it is straight and firmly stretched.
2 If you **tighten** something like a screw or a knot, you fasten or fix it more firmly.

tightrope **tightropes**
NOUN a tightly-stretched rope on which an acrobat balances and performs tricks

tights
PLURAL NOUN a piece of clothing made of thin, stretchy material that fits closely round a person's hips, legs and feet

tile **tiles, tiling, tiled**
NOUN **1** a flat, rectangular piece of something, such as slate, carpet or baked clay, that is used to cover surfaces
VERB **2** If you **tile** a surface, you fix tiles to it.

till **tills, tilling, tilled**
NOUN **1** a drawer or box in a shop where money is kept, usually in a cash register
PREPOSITION OR CONJUNCTION **2** up to a certain time • *You can stay up **till** nine o'clock.*
VERB **3** If someone **tills** the soil, they plough it.

tiller **tillers**
NOUN a handle fixed to the top of the rudder on a boat. It turns the rudder and steers the boat.

tilt **tilts, tilting, tilted**
VERB If you **tilt** an object, you move it so that one end or side is higher than the other.

timber **timbers**
NOUN **1** wood that has been cut and prepared ready for building and making furniture
2 The **timbers** of a ship or house are the large pieces of wood that have been used to build it.

time **times, timing, timed**
NOUN **1** what we measure in minutes, hours, days, weeks and years
2 a particular point in the day • *What **time** is it?*
3 a particular period in history
VERB **4** If you **time** something like a race, you measure how long it takes.

times
PLURAL NOUN multiplied by • *Two **times** three is six* (2 × 3 = 6).

timetable **timetables**
NOUN **1** a plan of the times when particular activities or jobs should be done
2 a list of the times when particular trains, boats, buses or aircraft arrive and depart

timid
ADJECTIVE If you are **timid**, you are shy and lacking in confidence.
ANTONYM: bold
timidly ADVERB

tin **tins**
NOUN **1** a soft, silvery-white metal
2 a metal container that is filled with food and then sealed in order to keep the food fresh
3 a small metal container that may have a lid

tingle **tingles, tingling, tingled**
VERB When a part of your body **tingles**, you feel a slight prickling sensation there.
tingling NOUN OR ADJECTIVE

tinkle **tinkles, tinkling, tinkled**
VERB Something that **tinkles** makes a light, ringing sound.

tinsel
NOUN long threads with strips of shiny paper attached, used as a decoration at Christmas

tint **tints**
NOUN a shade of a particular colour, particularly a pale one

A B C D E F G H I J K L M N O P Q R S T U V W X Y Z

tiny **tinier, tiniest**
ADJECTIVE extremely small

tip **tips, tipping, tipped**
NOUN **1** the point or the very end of something
2 a small gift of money given to someone like a waiter, who has done a service for you
3 a place where rubbish is left
4 a piece of useful information or advice
VERB **5** If you **tip** something, you tilt or overturn it. • *When he jumped up, he **tipped** the chair over.*
6 If you **tip** something somewhere, you pour it quickly and carelessly, or you empty it from a container. • *When they had finished the washing up, they **tipped** the water out of the bowl.*

tiptoe **tiptoes, tiptoeing, tiptoed**
VERB If you **tiptoe** somewhere, you walk there very quietly on your toes.

tire **tires, tiring, tired**
VERB **1** If something **tires** you, it makes you use a lot of energy so that you want to rest or sleep afterwards.
2 If you **tire** of something, you become bored with it.
tired ADJECTIVE **tiredness** NOUN

tissue **tissues**
NOUN a small piece of soft paper that you use as a handkerchief

title **titles**
NOUN the name of something such as a book, play, film or piece of music

to
PREPOSITION **1** towards
2 used to compare units • *There are 100 centimetres **to** a metre.*
3 compared with or rather than • *I prefer fruit **to** chocolate.*
4 used to indicate the limit of something • *I am allowed to spend up **to** an hour watching television each night.*
ADVERB **5** if you push something like a door **to**, you close it but do not shut it completely

Do not confuse *to* with *too* or *two*.

toad **toads**

NOUN an animal similar to a frog, but with drier skin and living more on land and less in the water

toadstool **toadstools**
NOUN a type of fungus similar to a mushroom and often poisonous

toast **toasts, toasting, toasted**
NOUN **1** slices of bread made brown and crisp by cooking them at a high temperature
VERB **2** If you **toast** bread, you cook it at a high temperature so that it becomes brown and crisp.

toaster **toasters**
NOUN an electrical device for toasting bread

tobacco
NOUN the dried leaves of a plant called **tobacco**. People smoke it in pipes, cigarettes and cigars.

toboggan **toboggans, tobogganing, tobogganed**
NOUN **1** a flat seat with two wooden or metal runners, used for sliding over the snow
SYNONYM: sledge
VERB **2** If you **toboggan**, you use a toboggan to slide over the snow.
SYNONYM: sledge

today
NOUN OR ADVERB the day that is happening now

toddler **toddlers**
NOUN a small child who has just learned to walk

toe **toes**
NOUN **1** one of the five movable parts at the end of your foot
2 the part of a shoe or sock that covers the end of your foot

toffee **toffees**
NOUN a sticky, chewy sweet made by boiling sugar and butter together with water

toga **togas**
NOUN a long, loose robe worn in ancient Rome

together
ADVERB **1** If people do something **together**, they do it with each other.
2 If two things happen **together**, they happen at the same time.
3 If things are joined, mixed or fixed **together**, they are put with each other.

toil **toils, toiling, toiled**
VERB **1** If you **toil**, you work very hard.
NOUN **2** very hard work

toilet **toilets**
NOUN **1** a large bowl, connected to the drains, which you use to get rid of waste from your body
SYNONYM: lavatory
2 a small room containing a toilet
SYNONYM: lavatory

token **tokens**
NOUN **1** a piece of paper or card that is worth a particular amount of money and can be exchanged for goods • *I got a book **token** for my birthday.*
2 a flat round piece of metal or plastic that can sometimes be used instead of money • *Some of the telephones only take **tokens**.*
3 a sign or symbol of something • *We bought her some flowers as a **token** of our thanks.*

told
VERB the past tense and past participle of **tell**

tolerate **tolerates, tolerating, tolerated**
VERB If you **tolerate** something, you put up with it even though you do not like it.

tomato **tomatoes**
NOUN a small, round, red fruit used as a vegetable and eaten cooked or raw

tomb **tombs**
NOUN a large grave where one or more people are buried

tomorrow
NOUN OR ADVERB the day after today

> *Tomorrow* has one *m* and two *r*s.

ton **tons**
NOUN a unit of weight equal to 2240 pounds or about 1016 kilograms

tone **tones**
NOUN **1** a particular quality that a sound has • *the clear **tone** of the bell*
2 a shade of a colour

tongs
PLURAL NOUN two long, narrow pieces of metal joined together at one end. You press the pieces together to pick up objects.

tongue **tongues**
NOUN the soft part in your mouth that you can move and use for tasting, licking and speaking

tongue twister **tongue twisters**
NOUN a sentence or a rhyme that is very difficult to say

tonight
ADVERB OR NOUN the evening or night that will come at the end of today

tonne **tonnes**
NOUN a unit of weight equal to 1000 kilograms

tonsil **tonsils**
NOUN one of the two small, soft lumps at the back of your throat

tonsillitis
NOUN a painful swelling of your tonsils caused by an infection

too
ADVERB **1** also or as well • *She was there **too**.*
2 **Too** shows that there is more of something than you want. • *I've had **too** much to eat.*

> Do not confuse *too* with *to* or *two*.

took
VERB the past tense of **take**

tool **tools**
NOUN any hand-held piece of equipment that you use to help you do a particular kind of work

tooth **teeth**
NOUN one of the hard, white bony parts in your mouth that you use for biting and chewing food

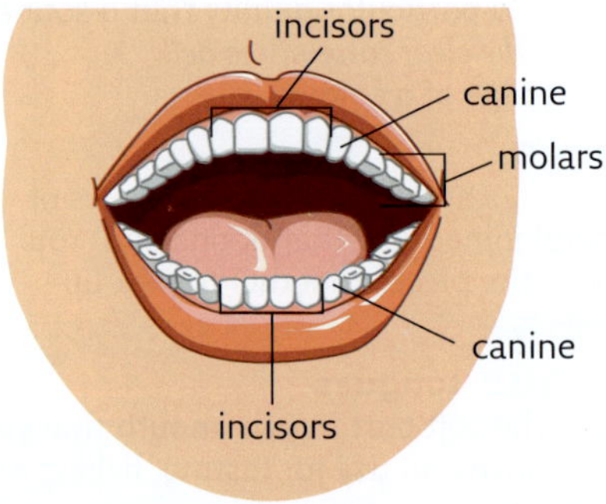

toothache
NOUN a pain in one of your teeth

toothbrush **toothbrushes**
NOUN a brush for cleaning your teeth

toothpaste
NOUN the substance that you use with a toothbrush to clean your teeth

top **tops**
NOUN **1** the highest point of something • *There was snow on the mountain **top**.*
2 the upper side of something • *There was a vase of flowers on the table **top**.*
3 a piece of clothing that you wear on the top half of your body
4 a toy that can be made to spin
ADJECTIVE **5** The **top** thing of a series of things is the highest one. • *the **top** floor of the building*

topic **topics**
NOUN a particular subject that you write about or discuss

topical
ADJECTIVE to do with things that are happening now

Torah
NOUN Jewish law and teaching

torch **torches**
NOUN a small electric light carried in the hand and powered by batteries
[from Old French *torche* meaning handful of twisted straw, which was set on fire and held up to provide light]

tore
VERB the past tense of **tear**

torment **torments, tormenting, tormented**
NOUN **1** great pain or unhappiness
VERB **2** If something **torments** you, it causes you great unhappiness.
3 If someone **torments** you, they keep deliberately annoying you.

torn
VERB the past participle of **tear**

tornado **tornadoes** or **tornados**
NOUN a violent storm with strong circular winds around a funnel-shaped cloud

torpedo **torpedoes, torpedoing, torpedoed**
NOUN **1** a tube-shaped bomb that travels underwater and explodes when it hits a target
VERB **2** If a ship is **torpedoed**, it is hit, and usually sunk, by a torpedo.

torrent **torrents**
NOUN a very strong stream or fall of water • *The rain fell in a **torrent**.*

torrential
ADJECTIVE **Torrential** rain pours down very fast and in great quantities.

tortoise **tortoises**
NOUN a slow-moving reptile with a hard shell over its body into which it can pull its head and legs for protection

torture **tortures, torturing, tortured**
VERB If someone **tortures** another person, they deliberately cause them great pain, usually as a punishment or to get information from them.

toss **tosses, tossing, tossed**
VERB **1** If you **toss** something somewhere, you throw it there lightly and carelessly.
2 If you **toss** a coin, you decide

something by throwing a coin into the air and guessing which side will face upwards when it lands.

total **totals, totalling, totalled**
NOUN **1** the number you get when you add several numbers together
VERB **2** If you **total** amounts, you add them together to find the total.
ADJECTIVE **3** complete

toucan **toucans**
NOUN a large tropical bird with a large, colourful beak

touch **touches, touching, touched**
VERB **1** If you **touch** something, you put your fingers or hand on it.
2 When two things **touch**, they come into contact.
3 If something **touches** you, it affects your emotions. • *The sad story* ***touched*** *us all.*
NOUN **4** Your sense of **touch** is your ability to feel things by touching them.

touchdown **touchdowns**
NOUN the landing of an aircraft or spacecraft

touchy **touchier, touchiest**
ADJECTIVE sensitive and easily offended

tough **tougher, toughest**
ADJECTIVE **1** A **tough** person is strong and able to put up with things that are difficult.
2 Something that is **tough** is strong and difficult to break or damage.
3 **Tough** food is difficult to cut and chew.
ANTONYM: tender

tour **tours, touring, toured**
NOUN **1** a long journey during which you visit several places
2 a short trip round a place such as a city or a famous building
VERB **3** If you **tour** a place, you go on a journey or a trip round it.

tourist **tourists**
NOUN someone who is travelling on holiday

tournament **tournaments**
NOUN a competition in which many players or teams compete in a series of games or contests

tow **tows, towing, towed**
VERB **1** If a vehicle **tows** another vehicle, it pulls it along behind it.
NOUN **2** To give a vehicle a **tow** is to pull it along behind.

towards
PREPOSITION If you go **towards** something, you move in its direction.

towel **towels**
NOUN a piece of thick, soft cloth that you use to dry yourself with

tower **towers**
NOUN a tall, narrow building, sometimes attached to a larger building such as a castle or church

town **towns**
NOUN a place with many streets and buildings where people live and work

toxic
ADJECTIVE poisonous

toy **toys**
NOUN something to play with

trace **traces, tracing, traced**
VERB **1** If you **trace** something like a drawing, you copy it by drawing on thin paper over the top, which you can see through.
2 If you **trace** something, you find it after looking for it. • *Scientists* ***traced*** *the origin of the disease.*
NOUN **3** a tiny amount of something or a small mark

track **tracks, tracking, tracked**
NOUN **1** a narrow road or path
2 a strip of ground with rails on it that a train travels along
3 a piece of ground, shaped like a ring, that horses, cars or athletes race around
VERB **4** If you **track** someone or something, you follow them by following the marks they leave as they pass.

tracksuit **tracksuits**
NOUN a loose, warm suit of trousers and a top, worn for outdoor sports

A B C D E F G H I J K L M N O P Q R S T U V W X Y Z

tractor **tractors**
NOUN a vehicle with large rear wheels, that is used on farms for pulling machinery and other heavy loads

trade **trades**
NOUN the activity of buying, selling or exchanging goods or services between people or countries
SYNONYM: business

trademark **trademarks**
NOUN a name or symbol that a manufacturer always uses on its products. **Trademarks** are usually protected by law so that no one else can use them.

trade union **trade unions**
NOUN an organization of workers that tries to improve the pay and conditions of its members

tradition **traditions**
NOUN a custom or belief that has existed for a long time and been passed down through the generations without changing [from Latin *traditio* meaning a handing down]

traditional
ADJECTIVE **1** passed down from one generation to the next
2 having existed or gone on for a long time

traffic
NOUN all the vehicles, ships, aircraft or people moving along a route at a particular time

traffic lights
PLURAL NOUN a set of lights used to control traffic at road junctions

traffic warden **traffic wardens**
NOUN an official whose job is to make sure that vehicles are not parked in the wrong place or for longer than is allowed

tragedy **tragedies**
NOUN **1** a very sad or disastrous event or situation, especially one in which people are killed
2 a serious story or play that usually ends with the death of the main character

tragic
ADJECTIVE very sad and distressing, usually involving death, destruction or disaster

trail **trails**
NOUN **1** a rough path across open country or through forests
2 a series of marks or other signs left by someone or something as they move along • *He left a **trail** of mud behind him.*

trailer **trailers**
NOUN **1** a small vehicle that can be loaded with things and pulled behind a car or lorry
2 a series of short pieces taken from a film or television programme in order to advertise it

train **trains, training, trained**
NOUN **1** a number of carriages or trucks that are pulled by a railway engine along railway lines
VERB **2** If you **train**, you learn how to do a particular job.
3 If you **train**, or someone **trains** you, for a sports match or a race, you prepare for it by doing exercises.

trainers
PLURAL NOUN special shoes worn for running and other sports

traitor **traitors**
NOUN someone who betrays their country or the group that they belong to

tram **trams**
NOUN a passenger vehicle that runs on rails along the street and is powered by electricity from an overhead wire

tramp **tramps, tramping, tramped**
NOUN **1** a person who has no home, no job, and very little money
2 a long country walk
VERB **3** If you **tramp** from one place to another, you walk with slow, heavy footsteps.

trample **tramples, trampling, trampled**
VERB If you **trample** on something, you tread heavily on it so that it is damaged.

trampoline **trampolines**
NOUN a piece of gymnastic equipment made of a large piece of strong cloth held tight by springs in a frame, on which a gymnast bounces

trance **trances**
NOUN If someone is in a **trance**, they seem to be asleep, but they can still see, hear, answer questions and obey orders.

trans-
PREFIX You add **trans-** to a word to mean across, through or beyond. For example, **trans**atlantic means across or beyond the Atlantic Ocean.

transaction **transactions**
NOUN a business deal that involves buying and selling something

transatlantic
ADJECTIVE used to describe something that crosses the Atlantic Ocean or is on the other side of it

transfer **transfers, transferring, transferred**
VERB **1** If you **transfer** something from one place to another, you move it there.
NOUN **2** a piece of paper with a design or drawing on one side that can be ironed or pressed onto another surface, such as cloth, paper or china

transform **transforms, transforming, transformed**
VERB If you **transform** something, or it **transforms**, it changes completely.

transfusion **transfusions**
NOUN a process in which blood donated by a healthy person is injected into the body of another person who needs it because they are badly injured or ill

transistor **transistors**
NOUN **1** a small electrical device in something such as a television or radio, which is used to control electric currents
2 a small portable radio

translate **translates, translating, translated**
VERB If you **translate** something that someone has said or written, you say it or write it in a different language.

translucent
ADJECTIVE If something is **translucent**, it allows the light to shine through and appears to glow.

transmit **transmits, transmitting, transmitted**
VERB **1** When a message or an electronic signal is **transmitted**, it is sent by radio waves.
2 If you **transmit** something, you send it to a different place.
3 If you **transmit** a disease, you pass it on to other people.

transmitter **transmitters**
NOUN a device for sending radio messages

transparent
ADJECTIVE If an object or substance is **transparent**, you can see through it.
SYNONYMS: clear, see-through

transplant **transplants, transplanting, transplanted**
VERB **1** To **transplant** something living, like a plant or an organ, means to remove it from one place and put it in another.
NOUN **2** an operation where an organ, such as a heart or a kidney, is taken from one person and put into another

transport **transports, transporting, transported**
VERB **1** If you **transport** someone or something, you take them from one place to another.
NOUN **2** the name for vehicles you travel in
• *Cars and planes are forms of **transport**.*

A B C D E F G H I J K L M N O P Q R S T U V W X Y Z

trap **traps, trapping, trapped**
NOUN **1** a piece of equipment or a hole that is dug to catch animals
2 a plan to trick, capture or cheat a person
VERB **3** If you **trap** animals, you catch them using a trap.
4 If you **trap** someone, you trick, capture or cheat them.

trapeze **trapezes**
NOUN a bar hanging from two ropes on which acrobats and gymnasts swing and perform skilful movements

trash
NOUN rubbish

traumatic
ADJECTIVE A **traumatic** experience is very upsetting and causes great stress.

travel **travels, travelling, travelled**
VERB **1** If you **travel**, you go from one place to another.
NOUN **2** the journeys that people make

trawler **trawlers**
NOUN a fishing boat that pulls a wide net behind it to catch fish

tray **trays**
NOUN a flat piece of wood, metal or plastic used for carrying things on

treacherous
ADJECTIVE **1** disloyal and untrustworthy
2 dangerous or unreliable

treacle
NOUN a thick, sweet syrup used to make cakes and toffee

tread **treads, treading, trod, trodden**
VERB **1** If you **tread** on something, you walk on it or step on it.
NOUN **2** The **tread** of a tyre or shoe is the pattern of ridges on it that stops it slipping.
3 the part of a staircase or ladder that you put your foot on

treason
NOUN the crime of betraying your country, for example by helping its enemies

treasure **treasures, treasuring, treasured**
NOUN **1** a collection of gold, silver, jewels or other precious objects, especially one that has been hidden
2 a valuable object, such as a work of art
VERB **3** If you **treasure** something, you look after it carefully because it is important to you. • *She **treasured** the shells she had collected on her holiday.*

treasury **treasuries**
NOUN **1** a place where treasure is stored
2 The **Treasury** is the government department that looks after a country's finances.

treat **treats, treating, treated**
NOUN **1** If you give someone a **treat**, you buy or arrange something special for them that they will enjoy.
VERB **2** When a doctor **treats** a patient or an illness, he or she gives them medical care and attention.
3 If you **treat** someone or something in a particular way, you behave that way towards them.

treaty **treaties**
NOUN a written agreement between countries, in which they agree to do something or to help each other

treble **trebles, trebling, trebled**
VERB **1** If something **trebles**, or is **trebled**, it becomes three times greater in number or amount.
NOUN **2** **Treble** the amount of something is three times the amount.

tree **trees**
NOUN a large plant with a hard trunk, branches and leaves

trek **treks, trekking, trekked**
VERB **1** If you **trek** somewhere, you go on a long and difficult journey to get there.
NOUN **2** a long and difficult journey, especially one made on foot
[an Afrikaans word]

tremble **trembles, trembling, trembled**
VERB If you **tremble**, you shake slightly,

usually because you are frightened or cold.

tremendous
ADJECTIVE **1** large or impressive • *It was a **tremendous** performance.*
2 INFORMAL very good or pleasing • *The game was **tremendous** fun.*

tremor **tremors**
NOUN **1** a small earthquake
2 a slight, uncontrollable shaking movement

trench **trenches**
NOUN a long narrow channel or ditch dug into the ground

trend **trends**
NOUN **1** a general direction in which something is moving
2 a fashion

trendy **trendier, trendiest**
ADJECTIVE INFORMAL fashionable

trespass **trespasses, trespassing, trespassed**
VERB If you **trespass** on someone's land or property, you go onto it without their permission.

trial **trials**
NOUN **1** a legal process in which a court listens to evidence to decide whether a person is innocent or guilty of a crime
2 a type of experiment in which someone or something is tested to see how well they perform

triangle **triangles**

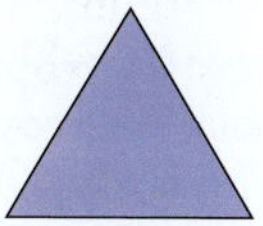

NOUN **1** a plane shape with three straight sides
2 a percussion instrument consisting of a thin steel bar bent in the shape of a triangle. It produces a note when struck with a small metal rod.
triangular ADJECTIVE

tribe **tribes**
NOUN a group of people of the same race, who have the same customs, religion, beliefs, language or land
tribal ADJECTIVE

tributary **tributaries**
NOUN a stream or river that flows into a larger river

tribute **tributes**
NOUN something said or done to show admiration and respect for someone

trick **tricks, tricking, tricked**
VERB **1** If someone **tricks** you, they deceive you.
NOUN **2** an action done to deceive someone
3 a clever or skilful action that is done in order to entertain people • *a card **trick***

trickle **trickles, trickling, trickled**
VERB When a liquid **trickles**, it flows slowly in a thin stream.

tricky **trickier, trickiest**
ADJECTIVE difficult to do or deal with

tricycle **tricycles**
NOUN a vehicle similar to a bicycle but with three wheels, two at the back and one at the front

tried
VERB the past tense and past participle of **try**

trifle **trifles**
NOUN **1** a cold pudding made of layers of sponge cake, fruit, jelly and custard
2 something unimportant or of little value

trigger **triggers**
NOUN the small lever on a gun that is pulled in order to fire it

trim **trims, trimming, trimmed; trimmer, trimmest**
VERB **1** If you **trim** something, you cut small amounts off it to make it more tidy.
ADJECTIVE **2** neat and tidy
NOUN **3** If something is given a **trim**, it is cut a little.
4 a decoration along the edges of something • *a coat with a velvet **trim***

trinket **trinkets**
NOUN a cheap ornament or piece of jewellery

trio **trios**
NOUN **1** a group of three musicians who sing or play together
2 a piece of music written for three instruments or singers

trip **trips, tripping, tripped**
NOUN **1** a journey made to a place
VERB **2** If you **trip**, or **trip over**, you catch your foot on something and fall over.
3 If you **trip** someone, or **trip** them up, you make them fall over by making them catch their foot on something.

triple **triples, tripling, tripled**
ADJECTIVE **1** made of three things or three parts
VERB **2** If you **triple** something, or if it **triples**, it becomes three times greater in number or size.

triplet **triplets**
NOUN one of three children born at the same time to the same mother

tripod **tripods**
NOUN a stand with three legs used to support something like a camera or telescope

triumph **triumphs, triumphing, triumphed**
NOUN **1** a great success or achievement
2 a feeling of great satisfaction when you win or achieve something
VERB **3** If you **triumph**, you win a victory or succeed in overcoming something.

triumphant
ADJECTIVE If you are **triumphant**, you feel very happy because you have won a victory or achieved something.

trivial
ADJECTIVE unimportant

trod
VERB the past tense of **tread**

trodden
VERB the past participle of **tread**

troll **trolls**
NOUN an imaginary creature in Scandinavian mythology, that is either a dwarf or a giant and lives in caves or mountains

trolley **trolleys**
NOUN **1** a basket or cart on wheels, in which you can carry your shopping or luggage
2 a small table on wheels, used to serve food and drink

trombone **trombones**
NOUN a brass wind instrument with a U-shaped tube that you slide to produce different notes

troop **troops, trooping, trooped**
PLURAL NOUN **1** **Troops** are soldiers.
NOUN **2** A **troop** of people or animals is a group of them.
VERB **3** If people **troop** somewhere, they go there in a group.

trophy **trophies**
NOUN a cup or shield given as a prize to the winner of a competition

tropic **tropics**
NOUN The **tropics** are the hottest regions of the world, that lie on either side of the equator.

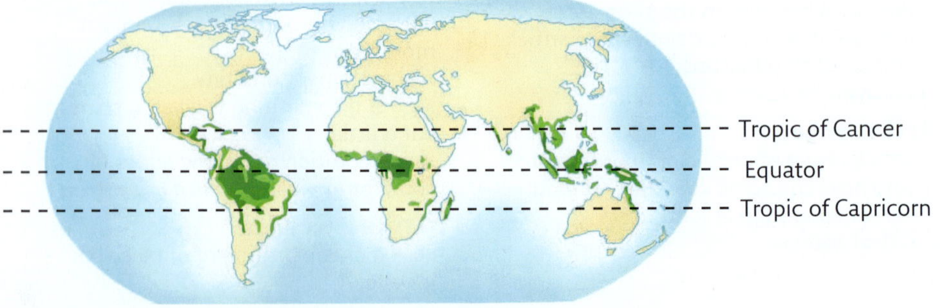

tropical
ADJECTIVE belonging to or typical of the tropics

trot **trots, trotting, trotted**
VERB **1** When a horse **trots**, it runs with short steps, lifting its feet quite high off the ground.
2 If you **trot**, you run slowly with small steps.

trouble **troubles, troubling, troubled**
NOUN **1** a difficulty or problem
SYNONYM: worry
PHRASE **2** If you are **in trouble**, someone is angry with you because of something you have done wrong.
VERB **3** If something **troubles** you, it worries or bothers you.
4 If you **trouble** someone, you worry or bother them.

trough **troughs**
NOUN a long, narrow container from which animals drink or feed

trousers
PLURAL NOUN a piece of clothing for the lower half of your body, from the waist down, covering each leg separately

trout
NOUN a type of edible freshwater fish

trowel **trowels**
NOUN **1** a garden tool like a small spade, used for planting or weeding
2 a small, flat spade used by builders for spreading cement and mortar

truant **truants**
NOUN a child who stays away from school without permission

truce **truces**
NOUN an agreement between two people or groups to stop fighting for a short time

truck **trucks**
NOUN a large motor vehicle used for carrying heavy loads

trudge **trudges, trudging, trudged**
VERB **1** If you **trudge**, you walk with slow, heavy steps.
NOUN **2** a slow, tiring walk

true **truer, truest**
ADJECTIVE **1** A **true** story or statement is based on facts and is not invented.
SYNONYMS: accurate, correct, factual
PHRASE **2** If something **comes true**, it actually happens. • *I hope your wish* ***comes true****.*

trumpet **trumpets**
NOUN a wind instrument made of a narrow brass tube that widens at the end into a bell-like shape

truncheon **truncheons**
NOUN a short, thick stick that policemen carry as a weapon

trunk **trunks**
NOUN **1** the main stem of a tree from which the branches and roots grow
2 the long, flexible nose of an elephant
3 a large, strong case or box with a hinged lid, used for storing things
4 In American English, the **trunk** of a car is the boot, a covered space at the back or front that is used for luggage.
5 the main part of your body, excluding your arms, legs and head
PLURAL NOUN **6** A man's **trunks** are his bathing pants or shorts.

trust **trusts, trusting, trusted**
VERB **1** If you **trust** someone, you believe that they are honest and reliable, and will treat you fairly.
2 If you **trust** someone to do something, you believe they will do it.
NOUN **3** the feeling that someone can be trusted
4 the responsibility you have to people who trust you

trustworthy
ADJECTIVE A **trustworthy** person is responsible and reliable, and you know that they will do what they say they will do.

truth **truths**
NOUN the facts about something, rather than things that are imagined or invented

truthful
ADJECTIVE A **truthful** person is honest and tells the truth.

try **tries, trying, tried**
VERB **1** If you **try** to do something, you make an effort to do it.
2 If you **try** something, you use it, taste it or experiment with it to see how good or suitable it is.
3 When a court **tries** a person, they listen to evidence to decide if that person is guilty of a crime.
4 A person who **tries** your patience is extremely irritating and difficult.
NOUN **5** an attempt to do something
6 A **try** in rugby is when a player scores by carrying the ball over the opponents' goal line and putting it on the ground.

try on
VERB If you **try on** a piece of clothing, you wear it to see if it fits you or if it looks nice.

T-shirt **T-shirts**; also spelt **tee shirt**
NOUN a simple short-sleeved cotton shirt with no collar

tub **tubs**
NOUN a wide, circular container

tuba **tubas**
NOUN a large brass musical instrument that can produce very low notes

tube **tubes**
NOUN a hollow cylinder made of metal, plastic, rubber or other material

tuck **tucks, tucking, tucked**
VERB **1** If you **tuck** a piece of fabric into or under something, you push the loose ends inside or under it to make it tidy.
2 If you **tuck** into a meal, you eat eagerly and with pleasure.
3 If you **tuck** someone up in bed, you put the bedclothes snugly round them.

Tuesday
NOUN the third day of the week, coming between Monday and Wednesday
[an Anglo-Saxon name honouring the god of war called *Tiw*, said *tue*]

tuft **tufts**
NOUN A **tuft** of something, such as hair or grass, is a bunch of it growing closely together.

tug **tugs, tugging, tugged**
VERB **1** If you **tug** something, you give it a quick, hard pull.
NOUN **2** a small, powerful boat that tows large ships

tulip **tulips**
NOUN a brightly coloured spring flower
[from Turkish *tulbend* meaning turban, because of the flower's shape]

tumble **tumbles, tumbling, tumbled**
VERB If you **tumble**, you fall with a rolling or bouncing movement.

tumbler **tumblers**
NOUN **1** a drinking glass with no handle or stem
2 an acrobat

tumour **tumours**
NOUN an abnormal growth in the body

tuna
NOUN a large, edible fish that lives in warm seas

tune **tunes**
NOUN a series of musical notes arranged in a particular way

tunnel **tunnels**
NOUN a long underground passage
• *a railway* ***tunnel***

turban **turbans**
NOUN a long piece of cloth worn wound round the head, especially by a Hindu, Muslim or Sikh man

turbine **turbines**
NOUN a machine or engine powered by a stream of air, gas, water or steam
[from Latin *turbo* meaning whirlwind]

turf
NOUN short, thick, even grass and the layer of soil beneath it

turkey **turkeys**
NOUN a large bird kept for its meat

turn **turns, turning, turned**
VERB **1** When you **turn**, you move so that you are facing or going in a different direction.
2 When you **turn** something, or when it **turns**, it moves so that it faces in a different direction or is in a different position. • *She **turned** the key in the lock.*
3 When something **turns**, or **turns into** something else, it becomes something different, or has a different appearance or quality. • *The leaves **turned** brown in autumn.*
NOUN **4** If it is your **turn** to do something, you do it next.
VERB **5** If you **turn down** something, you refuse it. • *I was not hungry, so I **turned down** the chips.*
6 If you **turn up** the television, for example, you increase the volume.
7 If someone **turns up**, they arrive.

turnip **turnips**
NOUN a round root vegetable with a white or yellow skin

turquoise
NOUN **1** light bluish-green
2 A light bluish-green stone used in jewellery.

turret **turrets**
NOUN a small, narrow tower on top of a larger tower or other building, such as a castle

turtle **turtles**
NOUN a large reptile with flippers for swimming and a thick shell covering its body. It lays its eggs on land but lives the rest of its life in the sea.
See **reptile**

tusk **tusks**
NOUN one of the pair of long, curving, pointed teeth of an elephant, wild boar or walrus

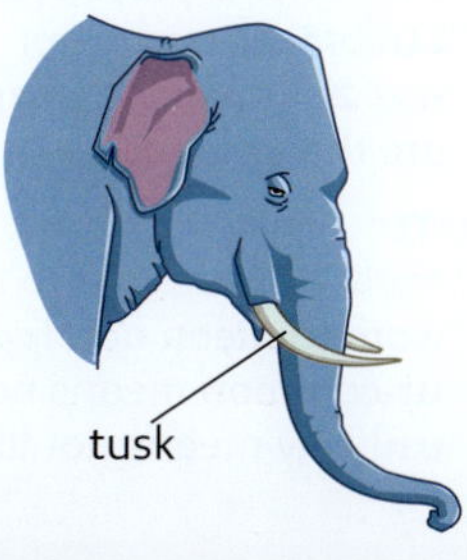

tutor **tutors**
NOUN a private teacher or a teacher at a college or university

TV
NOUN an abbreviation of *television*

tweed **tweeds**
NOUN a thick woollen cloth. Someone wearing **tweeds** is wearing a **tweed** suit.

tweezers
PLURAL NOUN a small tool with two arms that can be closed together to grip something. **Tweezers** are used for pulling out hairs or picking up small objects.

twelve
NOUN **Twelve** is the number 12.
twelfth NOUN OR ADJECTIVE

twenty
NOUN **Twenty** is the number 20.
twentieth NOUN OR ADJECTIVE

twice
ADVERB two times

twiddle **twiddles, twiddling, twiddled**
VERB If you **twiddle** something, you turn it quickly round and round or over and over.

twig **twigs**
NOUN a small branch on a tree or bush

twilight
NOUN the time after sunset when it is just getting dark

twin **twins**
NOUN If two people are **twins**, they have the same mother and were born on the same day.

twinkle **twinkles, twinkling, twinkled**
VERB Something that **twinkles** shines with little flashes of light.
SYNONYMS: glitter, sparkle

twirl **twirls, twirling, twirled**
VERB If you **twirl** something, you make it spin round quickly.

twist **twists, twisting, twisted**
VERB **1** When you **twist** something, you

turn the two ends in opposite directions. **2** If you **twist** part of your body, you injure it by turning it too sharply or in an odd direction.

two
NOUN **Two** is the number 2.

Do not confuse *two* with *to* or *too.*

two-dimensional
ADJECTIVE A **two-dimensional** object or shape is flat.

tying
VERB the present participle of **tie**

type **types, typing, typed**
NOUN **1** If something is the same **type** as something else, they belong to the same group and have many things in common.
SYNONYMS: kind, sort
VERB **2** If you **type** something, you use a typewriter or computer to write it.

typewriter **typewriters**
NOUN a machine with keys that are pressed to write numbers and letters on a page

typhoon **typhoons**
NOUN a very violent tropical storm [from Chinese *tai fung* meaning great wind]

typical
ADJECTIVE Something that is **typical** of a person or animal is usual and what is to be expected of them.

tyrannosaurus **tyrannosauruses**
NOUN a very large meat-eating dinosaur that walked upright on its back legs

tyrant **tyrants**
NOUN a person who treats the people they have power over with cruelty

tyre **tyres**
NOUN a thick ring of rubber fitted round each wheel of a vehicle and filled with air

Uu

udder **udders**
NOUN the bag-like part of a cow, goat or ewe from which milk comes

UFO **UFOs**
NOUN an abbreviation of *unidentified flying object*. **UFOs** are objects seen in the skies, which some people believe come from other planets because they cannot be identified.

ugly **uglier, ugliest**
ADJECTIVE very unattractive or unpleasant

ulcer **ulcers**
NOUN a sore area on the skin or inside the body, that can take a long time to heal

ultimate
ADJECTIVE **1** final
NOUN **2** the best example of something

ultraviolet light
NOUN **Ultraviolet light** is not visible to the human eye. It is a form of radiation that causes your skin to tan in sunlight.

umbrella **umbrellas**
NOUN a folding frame covered in fabric and attached to a long stick, which you can open over you to protect you from the rain

umpire **umpires, umpiring, umpired**
NOUN **1** The **umpire** in a cricket or tennis match is the person who makes sure that the game is played fairly and the rules are not broken.
VERB **2** If a person **umpires** a game, they are the umpire.

un-
PREFIX You add **un-** to the beginning of a word to mean not. For example, **un**common means not common, and **un**likely means not likely.

unable
ADJECTIVE If you are **unable** to do something, you cannot do it.

unanimous
Said "yoo-**nan**-nim-mus" ADJECTIVE A **unanimous** decision or vote has the agreement of everyone involved.

unaware
ADJECTIVE not aware

unbearable
ADJECTIVE Something **unbearable** is so painful or upsetting that you feel that you cannot bear or endure it.

unbelievable
ADJECTIVE **1** very surprising or wonderful
2 so unlikely that it is hard to believe

uncanny
ADJECTIVE strange and mysterious

uncertain
ADJECTIVE If you are **uncertain** about something, you are not sure about it.
SYNONYM: doubtful
uncertainty NOUN

uncle **uncles**
NOUN the brother of your mother or father, or the husband of your aunt
[from Latin *avunculus* meaning mother's brother]

uncomfortable
ADJECTIVE **1** If you are **uncomfortable**, your body is not relaxed or comfortable.
2 If something like a chair or a piece of clothing is **uncomfortable**, it is not comfortable to sit in or to wear.
3 If you feel **uncomfortable** in a situation, you feel worried or nervous.

uncommon
ADJECTIVE not common

unconscious
ADJECTIVE If someone is **unconscious**, they are unable to see, feel or hear anything that is going on. This is usually because they have fainted or been badly injured.

uncover **uncovers, uncovering, uncovered**
VERB **1** to take the cover off something
2 to find out a secret or discover something

under
PREPOSITION **1** below or beneath
2 less than • *children* ***under*** *the age of 14*
3 controlled or ruled by • *The soldiers were* ***under*** *his command.*
4 If something like a building is **under** construction, or **under** repair, it is in the process of being built or repaired.

under-
PREFIX You add **under-** at the beginning of a word to mean beneath or below. For example, if you **under**estimate an amount, you estimate it below what it really is.

undercarriage **undercarriages**
NOUN the part of an aircraft, including the wheels, that supports the aircraft when it is on the ground

underestimate **underestimates, underestimating, underestimated**
VERB **1** If you **underestimate** someone, you do not realize how much they can do.
2 If you **underestimate** something, you do not realize how big it is or how long it will take.

undergo **undergoes, undergoing, underwent, undergone**
VERB If you **undergo** something, you experience it or are subjected to it.
• *She* ***underwent*** *an operation to remove her tonsils.*

underground
ADJECTIVE **1** below the surface of the ground
NOUN **2** a railway system in which trains travel in tunnels below the ground

undergrowth
NOUN small plants growing under trees

underline **underlines, underlining, underlined**
VERB If you **underline** a word or sentence, you draw a line under it.

undermine **undermines, undermining, undermined**
VERB **1** If you **undermine** a person's efforts or plans, you weaken them.
2 To **undermine** something is to make a hollow or tunnel beneath it. When the sea **undermines** a cliff, for example, it gradually wears away the base and weakens it.

underneath
PREPOSITION OR ADVERB below or beneath

underpants
PLURAL NOUN a piece of men's underwear worn under trousers

underpass **underpasses**
NOUN a place where one road or path goes under another

underprivileged
ADJECTIVE **Underprivileged** people have less money and fewer opportunities than other people.

understand **understands, understanding, understood**
VERB **1** If you **understand** what someone says, or what you read, you know what it means.
2 If you **understand** how something works, you know how it works.
3 If you **understand** someone, you know them well and think you know why they behave the way they do.

understudy **understudies**
NOUN someone who has learnt the lines of a part in a play, and plays the part when the main actor or actress cannot perform

undertake **undertakes, undertaking, undertook, undertaken**
VERB If you **undertake** to do something, you agree to do it.

undertaker **undertakers**
NOUN someone whose job is to prepare bodies for burial and arrange funerals

underwater
ADVERB OR ADJECTIVE below the surface of the water

underwear
NOUN Your **underwear** is the clothing you wear next to your skin under your other clothes.

undo **undoes, undoing, undid, undone**
VERB **1** If you **undo** something like a knot, you loosen or unfasten it.
2 If you **undo** something that has been done, you reverse or remove the effects of it.

undress **undresses, undressing, undressed**
VERB If you **undress**, you take your clothes off.

unearth **unearths, unearthing, unearthed**
VERB If you **unearth** something, you dig it up or discover it.

uneasy **uneasier, uneasiest**
ADJECTIVE anxious or worried

unemployed
ADJECTIVE An **unemployed** person has no job.

uneven
ADJECTIVE An **uneven** surface is not level or smooth.

unexpected
ADJECTIVE Something **unexpected** is surprising because it was not thought likely to happen.

unfair
ADJECTIVE Something **unfair** does not seem right, reasonable or fair.

unfold **unfolds, unfolding, unfolded**
VERB **1** If you **unfold** something that is folded, such as a map, you open it out.
2 When a story **unfolds**, it gradually becomes clear.

unfortunate
ADJECTIVE unlucky

unfriendly
ADJECTIVE not friendly

ungrateful
ADJECTIVE not grateful

unhappy **unhappier, unhappiest**
ADJECTIVE sad, not happy

unhealthy
ADJECTIVE not healthy

unicorn **unicorns**
NOUN an imaginary animal that looks like a white horse with a straight horn growing from its forehead
[from Latin *unicornis* meaning having one horn]

uniform **uniforms**
NOUN a special set of clothes worn by people at work or school
[from Latin *uniformis* meaning of one kind]

unify **unifies, unifying, unified**
VERB If several things, especially countries, are **unified**, they join together to make one.

uninhabited
ADJECTIVE An **uninhabited** place is a place where nobody lives.

union **unions**
NOUN an organization of workers that aims to improve the working conditions, pay and benefits of its members

unique
ADJECTIVE Something that is **unique** is the only one of its kind.
[from Latin *unicus* meaning one and only]

unisex
ADJECTIVE designed to suit either men or women

unison
NOUN If a group of people does something in **unison**, they all do it together at the same time.
[from Latin *unisonus* meaning making the same musical sound]

unit **units**
NOUN **1** one single, complete thing
2 a term used to describe a fixed quantity or measurement • *A centimetre is a **unit** of length.*

unite **unites, uniting, united**
VERB If a number of people **unite**, they join together and act as a group.

universal
ADJECTIVE concerning or relating to everyone and everything

universe **universes**
NOUN everything that exists, including the whole of space, all the stars and the planets
[from Latin *universum* meaning whole world]

university **universities**
NOUN a place where students study for degrees

unkempt
ADJECTIVE untidy and not looked after properly
[from Old English *uncembed* meaning not combed]

unkind
ADJECTIVE rather cruel, not kind

unknown
ADJECTIVE If someone or something is **unknown**, people do not know about them or have not heard of them.

unleaded
ADJECTIVE **Unleaded** petrol does not contain any lead, and is less harmful to the atmosphere than petrol that does contain lead.

unless
CONJUNCTION You use **unless** to introduce the only circumstances in which something may or may not happen or is not true.
• *The team will play tomorrow **unless** it is raining.* • *I won't go **unless** you ask me.*

unlike
ADJECTIVE **1** If one thing is **unlike** another, the two things are different.
PREPOSITION **2** not like • ***Unlike** me, she hates chocolate.*

unlikely **unlikelier, unlikeliest**
ADJECTIVE not likely to happen or be true

A B C D E F G H I J K L M N O P Q R S T U V W X Y Z

unload **unloads, unloading, unloaded**
VERB to take things out of or off a container, a vehicle or a trailer

unlock **unlocks, unlocking, unlocked**
VERB When you **unlock** something, you open it by turning a key in the lock.

unlucky **unluckier, unluckiest**
ADJECTIVE If you are **unlucky**, you are unfortunate and have bad luck.
ANTONYMS: fortunate, lucky

unnatural
ADJECTIVE not natural or normal

unnecessary
ADJECTIVE not necessary

unoccupied
ADJECTIVE A house that is **unoccupied** has no one living in it.

unpack **unpacks, unpacking, unpacked**
VERB When you **unpack**, you take everything out of a suitcase, bag or box.

unpleasant
ADJECTIVE **1** Something **unpleasant** is not enjoyable and may make you uncomfortable or upset.
2 An **unpleasant** person is unfriendly or rude.

unplug **unplugs, unplugging, unplugged**
VERB If you **unplug** something, you take the plug out of the socket to disconnect it from the electricity supply.

unpopular
ADJECTIVE not liked very much

unravel **unravels, unravelling, unravelled**
VERB **1** If you **unravel** threads that are knitted or tangled, you undo or untangle them.
2 If you **unravel** a mystery, you solve it.

unreal
ADJECTIVE existing only in the imagination, not real

unreasonable
ADJECTIVE not reasonable or fair

unroll **unrolls, unrolling, unrolled**
VERB If you **unroll** something that has been rolled up, you open it and make it flat.

unruly
ADJECTIVE badly behaved and difficult to control

unsafe
ADJECTIVE not safe

unscrew **unscrews, unscrewing, unscrewed**
VERB If you **unscrew** something, you remove it by turning it or by removing the screws that are holding it.

unselfish
ADJECTIVE An **unselfish** person is not selfish and is concerned about other people's needs.

unsteady
ADJECTIVE If you are **unsteady**, you are not steady and have difficulty balancing.

unsuccessful
ADJECTIVE If you are **unsuccessful**, you do not manage to succeed in what you are trying to do.

unsuitable
ADJECTIVE Things that are **unsuitable** are not right or suitable for a particular purpose.

untidy **untidier, untidiest**
ADJECTIVE not tidy

untie **unties, untying, untied**
VERB If you **untie** something that has been tied, you unfasten or undo it.

until
PREPOSITION OR CONJUNCTION **1** If something happens **until** a particular time, it happens before that time and stops at that time. • *The shops stay open **until** eight o'clock on Thursdays.*
2 If something does not happen **until** a particular time, it does not happen before that time and only starts happening at that time. • *It didn't rain **until** the middle of the afternoon.*

untrue
ADJECTIVE not true

unusual
ADJECTIVE Something that is **unusual** is not usual and does not happen very often.

unwell
ADJECTIVE If you are **unwell**, you are ill.

unwilling
ADJECTIVE If you are **unwilling** to do something, you do not want to do it.
unwillingly ADVERB

unwind **unwinds, unwinding, unwound**
VERB **1** If you **unwind** something that was wound into a ball or around something else, you undo it.
2 If you **unwind** after working hard, you relax.

unwrap **unwraps, unwrapping, unwrapped**
VERB If you **unwrap** something, you take off the paper or other wrapping that is around it.

up
ADVERB OR PREPOSITION **1** towards or in a higher place • *They went **up** the stairs to bed.*
ADVERB **2** If an amount of something goes **up**, it increases.
PREPOSITION **3** If you go **up** the road, you go along it.
ADJECTIVE **4** If you are **up**, you are not in bed.

upbringing
NOUN the way you have been brought up, and how your parents have taught you to behave

upheaval **upheavals**
NOUN a sudden big change that causes a lot of disturbance

uphill
ADVERB If you go **uphill**, you go up a hill or a slope.

upholstery
NOUN the soft covering on chairs and sofas that makes them comfortable
upholstered ADJECTIVE

upload **uploads, uploading, uploaded**
VERB When you **upload** a computer file or program, you put it onto a computer or the internet.

upon
PREPOSITION on or on top of

upper
ADJECTIVE The **upper** of two things is the top or higher one. • *the **upper** deck of the bus*

upper-case
ADJECTIVE **Upper-case** letters are written as capitals. For example, A, H, L and P are all **upper-case** letters.

upright
ADJECTIVE OR ADVERB **1** Something or someone that is **upright**, is standing up straight or vertically, rather than bending or lying down.
2 An **upright** person is decent and honest.

uproar
NOUN a lot of shouting and noise, often because people are angry
SYNONYMS: commotion, pandemonium
[from Dutch *oproer* meaning revolt]

upset **upsets, upsetting, upset**
ADJECTIVE **1** unhappy and disappointed
VERB **2** If something **upsets** you, it makes you feel worried or unhappy.
3 If you **upset** something, you knock it over or spill it accidentally.
NOUN **4** A stomach **upset** is a slight stomach illness.

upside down
ADJECTIVE **1** the wrong way up • *She was **upside down** on the climbing frame.*

2 If a place is **upside down**, it is very untidy.

upstairs
ADVERB OR ADJECTIVE up to or on a higher floor

up-to-date
ADJECTIVE If something is **up-to-date**, it is modern or is the newest thing of its kind.

upwards
ADVERB going towards a higher place

uranium
NOUN a radioactive metallic element used to make nuclear energy and weapons

urban
ADJECTIVE to do with towns or cities rather than the country
[from Latin *urbs* meaning city]

urge **urges, urging, urged**
NOUN **1** If you have an **urge** to do something, you very much want to do it.
VERB **2** If you **urge** someone to do something, you try to persuade and encourage them to do it.

urgent
ADJECTIVE If something is **urgent**, it needs to be dealt with immediately.

urine
NOUN the waste liquid that you get rid of from your body when you go to the toilet

URL **URLs**
NOUN A website's **URL** is its address on the internet. **URL** is an abbreviation for *uniform resource locator.*

us
PRONOUN A speaker or writer uses **us** to mean himself or herself and one or more other people.

use **uses, using, used**
Said "**yooz**" VERB **1** If you **use** something, you do something with it that helps you to do a job or sort out a problem.
Said "**yooss**" NOUN **2** the purpose or value of something, and the way it is used

used
Said "**yoosst**" VERB **1** If something **used to** happen, it happened before but does not happen now. • *We* ***used to*** *fish in this stream.*
ADJECTIVE **2** If you are **used to** something, you are familiar with it and have often experienced it.
Said "**yoozd**" VERB **3** the past tense and past participle of **use**
ADJECTIVE **4** A **used** item has already belonged to someone else.

useful
ADJECTIVE If something is **useful**, you can use it to help you in some way.

useless
ADJECTIVE Something that is **useless** is no good for anything.

user-friendly
ADJECTIVE If something is **user-friendly**, it is easy to understand and use. • *the most* ***user-friendly*** *camera available*

usher **ushers**
NOUN a person who shows people where to sit at the theatre or cinema

usual
ADJECTIVE **1** Something **usual** is expected and happens often.
PHRASE **2** If something happens **as usual**, it happens as you would expect, and is not surprising because it often happens that way.

utensil **utensils**
NOUN a tool • *A whisk is a kitchen* ***utensil****.*

utility **utilities**
NOUN a service that is useful for everyone, such as water and gas supplies

utter **utters, uttering, uttered**
VERB **1** When you **utter** sounds, you make or say them.
ADJECTIVE **2** complete or total • *This is* ***utter*** *nonsense.*

Vv

vacant
ADJECTIVE If something is **vacant**, it is not being used or no one is in it. • *I couldn't find a **vacant** seat on the train.*

vacation vacations
NOUN a holiday

vaccinate vaccinates, vaccinating, vaccinated
Said "**vak**-si-nayt" VERB If someone **vaccinates** you, they give you an injection to protect you against a disease.

vacuum vacuums, vacuuming, vacuumed
NOUN **1** a completely empty space containing no matter, solid, liquid or gas
VERB **2** If you **vacuum** something, you clean it using a vacuum cleaner.
[from Latin *vacuum* meaning empty space]

vacuum cleaner vacuum cleaners
NOUN an electrical device that sucks up dust and dirt from the floor

vagina vaginas
NOUN A woman's **vagina** is the passage that leads from the outside of her body to her womb.

vague vaguer, vaguest
Said "**vayg**" ADJECTIVE not clear, definite or certain • *They could see the **vague** outline of the mountains in the distance.*
SYNONYM: unclear
vaguely ADVERB **vagueness** NOUN

vain vainer, vainest
ADJECTIVE **1** A **vain** person is too proud of their looks, intelligence or other good qualities.
2 A **vain** attempt to do something is an unsuccessful attempt.

valentine valentines
NOUN **1** someone you love and send a card to on Saint **Valentine's** Day, February 14th
2 a card you send to someone you love on Saint **Valentine's** Day
[Saint *Valentine* was a third-century martyr]

valiant
ADJECTIVE brave and courageous

valid
ADJECTIVE A **valid** ticket or document is legal and accepted by people in authority.

valley valleys
NOUN a long stretch of land between hills, often with a river flowing through it

valuable
ADJECTIVE of great worth or very important • *The diamond ring was very **valuable**.*

value values, valuing, valued
NOUN **1** the importance or usefulness of something
2 the amount of money that something is worth
VERB **3** If you **value** something, you think it is important and valuable.

valve valves
NOUN **1** a device attached to a pipe or tube that controls the flow of gas or liquid
2 a small flap in your heart or in a vein that controls the flow and direction of blood

vampire vampires
NOUN In horror stories, **vampires** come out of graves at night and suck people's blood.

van **vans**
NOUN a vehicle for carrying goods

vandal **vandals**
NOUN someone who deliberately damages or destroys things, particularly public property
vandalize or **vandalise** VERB
vandalism NOUN

vanilla
NOUN a flavouring used in food such as ice cream. It comes from the pod of a tropical plant.

vanish **vanishes, vanishing, vanished**
VERB If something **vanishes**, it disappears or does not exist any more.

vapour
NOUN a mass of tiny drops of water or other liquids in the air, which looks like mist
[from Latin *vapor* meaning steam]

variety **varieties**
NOUN a number of different kinds of similar things • *There was a **variety** of food from different countries on the menu.*
SYNONYMS: assortment, range

various
ADJECTIVE of several different types • *trees of **various** sorts*
SYNONYMS: different, miscellaneous

varnish **varnishes, varnishing, varnished**
NOUN **1** a liquid which, when painted onto a surface such as wood, gives it a hard, clear, shiny finish
VERB **2** If you **varnish** something, you paint it with varnish.

vary **varies, varying, varied**
VERB If something **varies**, it changes and is not always the same.

vase **vases**
NOUN a jar or other container for putting cut flowers in

vast
ADJECTIVE extremely large
vastly ADVERB **vastness** NOUN

vat **vats**
NOUN a large container used for storing liquids

VAT
NOUN an abbreviation of *value-added tax*, which is a tax you pay on things you buy

vault **vaults, vaulting, vaulted**
NOUN **1** a strong secure room where valuables are stored, often underneath a building, or where people are buried underneath a church
2 an arched roof, often found in churches
VERB **3** If you **vault** over something, you jump over it using your hands or a pole to help.

VDU
NOUN an abbreviation of *visual display unit*, which is a monitor screen for computers

veal
NOUN the meat from a calf

Veda
NOUN the collection of ancient sacred writings of the Hindu religion

vegetable **vegetables**
NOUN **Vegetables** are plants or parts of plants that can be eaten. Peas, carrots, cabbage and potatoes are **vegetables**.

vegetarian **vegetarians**
NOUN a person who does not eat meat, poultry or fish

vegetation
NOUN the plants growing in a particular area

vehicle **vehicles**
NOUN a machine, often with an engine, such as a car, bus or lorry, used for moving people or goods from one place to another

veil **veils**
NOUN a piece of thin, soft cloth that women sometimes wear over their heads and faces

vein **veins**
NOUN Your **veins** are the tubes in your body through which your blood flows to your heart.
See **artery**

velvet
NOUN a very soft material that has a thick layer of short threads on one side

vengeance
NOUN the act of harming someone because they have harmed you

venison
NOUN the meat from a deer

Venn diagram **Venn diagrams**
NOUN a diagram using circles to show how sets of things relate to each other. **Venn diagrams** are used in mathematics.

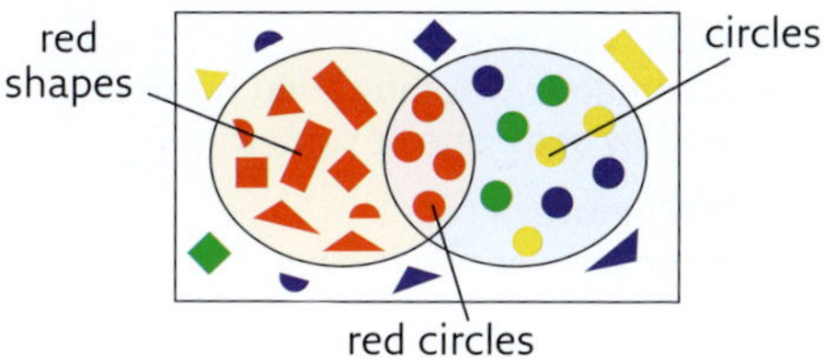

venom
NOUN the poison of a snake, scorpion or spider
[from Latin *venenum* meaning love potion or poison]
venomous ADJECTIVE **venomously** ADVERB

vent **vents**
NOUN an opening in something, especially to let out smoke or gas

ventilate **ventilates, ventilating, ventilated**
VERB If you **ventilate** a place, you allow fresh air to move freely through it.

venture **ventures, venturing, ventured**
NOUN **1** something new that you do which involves some sort of risk
VERB **2** If you **venture** somewhere that might be dangerous, you go there.

veranda **verandas**; also spelt **verandah**
NOUN a platform with a roof that is fixed to the outside wall of a house at ground level. It is often made of wood.

verb **verbs**
NOUN In grammar, a **verb** is a word that expresses actions and states, for example *be*, *become*, *take* and *run*.

verbal
ADJECTIVE spoken rather than written
verbally ADVERB

verdict **verdicts**
NOUN In a law court, a **verdict** is the decision reached by the judge or jury about whether a prisoner is guilty or not guilty.

verge **verges**
NOUN the narrow strip of grassy ground at the side of a road • *We walked along the **verge**.*

verify **verifies, verifying, verified**
VERB If you **verify** something, you check that it is true or correct.
verifiable ADJECTIVE **verification** NOUN

verruca **verrucas**
NOUN a small, hard, infectious growth that you can get on the sole of your foot

versatile
ADJECTIVE If someone or something is **versatile**, they have many different skills or uses.
versatility NOUN

verse **verses**
NOUN **1** another word for **poetry**
2 one part of a poem, song or chapter of the Bible

version **versions**
NOUN A **version** of something is a form of it that is different in some way from earlier or later forms.

versus
PREPOSITION **Versus** means against, and is used to show that two people or teams are competing against each other.

vertebra **vertebrae**
NOUN one of the bones that make up your backbone

vertebrate **vertebrates**
NOUN an animal with a backbone

A B C D E F G H I J K L M N O P Q R S T U V W X Y Z

vertex **vertices**
NOUN the highest point of a hill, or a corner of a two-dimensional or three-dimensional shape
See **apex**

vertical
ADJECTIVE Something that is **vertical** is in an upright position or points straight up.

very
ADVERB **Very** is used before words to emphasize them. • *I had a **very** bad dream.*
SYNONYMS: extremely, greatly, really

vessel **vessels**
NOUN **1** a ship or large boat
2 a container for liquids
3 one of the tubes in an animal or a plant that carries blood or other liquid around the body

vest **vests**
NOUN a piece of underwear worn on the top half of the body for warmth
[from Latin *vestis* meaning clothing]

vet **vets**
NOUN a doctor for animals. **Vet** is an abbreviation of *veterinary surgeon*.

veteran **veterans**
NOUN **1** a person with a lot of experience of something, or who has been involved in something for a long time
2 someone who has served in the armed forces, particularly during a war • *My uncle is a Gulf War **veteran**.*

via
PREPOSITION If you go to one place **via** another, you travel through that other place to get to your destination.
[from Latin *via* meaning way or road]

viaduct **viaducts**
NOUN a high bridge that carries a road or railway across a valley

vibrate **vibrates, vibrating, vibrated**
VERB If something **vibrates**, it moves a tiny amount backwards and forwards very quickly.
vibration NOUN

vicar **vicars**
NOUN a priest in the Church of England

vice **vices**
NOUN a bad habit, such as being greedy or smoking

vice versa
ADVERB the other way around

vicinity **vicinities**
NOUN an area round something • *She was seen in the **vicinity** of the school.*

vicious
ADJECTIVE cruel and violent

victim **victims**
NOUN someone who has been harmed or injured by someone or something

victor **victors**
NOUN the winner of a contest or battle

victory **victories**
NOUN a success in a battle or competition
SYNONYMS: conquest, triumph, win

video **videos, videoing, videoed**
NOUN **1** a sound and picture recording that can be played back on a television set
2 the recording and showing of films and events using a **video** recorder, tape and a television set
3 a video recorder • *Set the **video** to record a programme at eight o'clock.*
VERB **4** If you **video** something, you record it on video tape to watch later.
[from Latin *videre* meaning to see]

video game **video games**
NOUN a game that can be played by using an electronic control to move symbols on a screen

view **views**
NOUN everything you can see from a particular place

viewer **viewers**
NOUN one of the people who watch something, especially a television programme

viewpoint **viewpoints**
NOUN Your **viewpoint** is your attitude towards something.

vigilant
ADJECTIVE careful and alert to danger or trouble
vigilance NOUN **vigilantly** ADVERB

vigorous
ADJECTIVE energetic or enthusiastic
vigorously ADVERB

villa **villas**
NOUN a house, especially a pleasant holiday home in a country with a warm climate

village **villages**
NOUN a collection of houses and other buildings in the countryside
[from Old French *ville* meaning farm]

villain **villains**
NOUN someone who harms others or breaks the law
SYNONYMS: criminal, rogue

vine **vines**
NOUN a climbing plant, especially one that produces grapes

vinegar
NOUN a sharp-tasting liquid made from sour wine and used for flavouring food
[from French *vin aigre* meaning sour wine]

vineyard **vineyards**
NOUN an area of land where grapes are grown for making wine

vintage
ADJECTIVE **1** A **vintage** wine is a good quality wine made in a particular year.
2 A **vintage** car is one made between 1918 and 1930.

vinyl
NOUN a strong plastic used to make things such as furniture and floor coverings

viola **violas**
NOUN a musical instrument like a violin, but larger and with a lower pitch

violence
NOUN **1** behaviour that is intended to hurt or kill
2 force that does harm or damage • *The **violence** of the storm surprised everyone.*
violent ADJECTIVE **violently** ADVERB

violet **violets**
NOUN **1** a plant with dark purple flowers
NOUN OR ADJECTIVE **2** bluish purple

violin **violins**
NOUN a musical instrument with four strings that is held under the chin and played with a bow

VIP
NOUN an abbreviation of *very important person* • *The **VIPs** had the best seats at the concert.*

viper **vipers**
NOUN a type of poisonous snake

virtual
ADJECTIVE almost exactly the same as the real thing

virtual reality
NOUN an environment or image that has been created by a computer and looks real to the person using it

virtue **virtues**
NOUN **1** moral goodness
2 a good quality in someone's character

virus **viruses**
NOUN **1** a tiny organism that can cause disease
2 A disease caused by a virus can be called a **virus**.
3 a program that damages the information stored in a computer system

visible
ADJECTIVE able to be seen

vision **visions**
NOUN **1** the ability to see
2 a picture of something in your mind or imagination

visit **visits, visiting, visited**
VERB **1** If you **visit** someone, you go to see them and spend time with them.

2 If you **visit** a place, you go to see it.
NOUN **3** a trip to see a person or place

visor **visors**
NOUN **1** a transparent, movable shield attached to a helmet, which can be pulled down to protect the eyes or face
2 a shade to protect your eyes from the sun

visual
ADJECTIVE to do with sight and seeing

vital
ADJECTIVE necessary or very important
SYNONYM: essential

vitality
NOUN People who have **vitality** are energetic and lively.

vitamin **vitamins**
NOUN one of a group of substances you need to have in your diet in order to stay healthy. For example, **vitamin** C is found in oranges.

vivid
ADJECTIVE very bright in colour or clear in detail

vivisection
NOUN the use of living animals for medical research

vixen **vixens**
NOUN a female fox

vocabulary **vocabularies**
NOUN **1** the total number of words someone knows in a particular language
2 all the words in a language

vocal
ADJECTIVE to do with or involving the use of the human voice
vocalist NOUN **vocally** ADVERB

vocation **vocations**
NOUN **1** If you have a **vocation**, you want very much to do a particular job, especially one that involves helping other people.
2 a profession or career

voice **voices**
NOUN Your **voice** is what you hear when you speak or sing.

void **voids**
NOUN a very large empty space or deep hole

volcano **volcanoes**
NOUN a mountain with an opening at the top called a crater, from which lava, gas and ash sometimes erupt
[named after *Vulcan*, the Roman god of fire]

vole **voles**
NOUN a small mammal like a mouse with a short tail, which lives in fields and near rivers

volley **volleys**
NOUN **1** A **volley** of shots or missiles is a lot of them fired or thrown at the same time.
2 In tennis, a **volley** is a stroke in which the player hits the ball before it bounces.

volleyball
NOUN a game in which two teams hit a ball back and forth over a high net with their hands. The ball is not allowed to bounce on the ground.

volt **volts**
NOUN the unit used to measure the voltage of a battery
[named after Alessandro *Volta* who invented the electric battery]

voltage **voltages**
NOUN the measure of how much electrical current a battery can push through an electric circuit

volume **volumes**
NOUN **1** the amount of space something contains or occupies
2 The **volume** of a radio, TV or record player is how loud it is.
3 a book, or one of a series of books

voluntary
ADJECTIVE Something **voluntary** is done because you want to do it, not because you are paid or told to do it.
voluntarily ADVERB

volunteer **volunteers, volunteering, volunteered**
NOUN **1** someone who does work that they are not paid for

VERB **2** If you **volunteer** to do something, you offer to do it without expecting any reward.

vomit **vomits, vomiting, vomited**
VERB If you **vomit**, food and drink comes back up from your stomach and out through your mouth.

vote **votes, voting, voted**
NOUN **1** Someone's **vote** is their choice in an election, or at a meeting where decisions are taken.
VERB **2** When people **vote**, they show their choice or opinion, usually by writing on a piece of paper or by raising their hand.

voucher **vouchers**
NOUN a piece of paper that can be used instead of money to pay for something

vow **vows, vowing, vowed**
VERB **1** If you **vow** to do something, you make a promise to do it.
NOUN **2** a promise

vowel **vowels**
NOUN **1** a sound made without your tongue touching the roof of your mouth or your teeth
2 In the English language the letters a, e, i, o and u are **vowels**.

voyage **voyages**
NOUN a long journey on a ship or in a spacecraft

vulgar
ADJECTIVE rude or offensive

vulnerable
ADJECTIVE without protection and easily hurt or damaged
SYNONYM: defenceless

vulture **vultures**
NOUN a large bird that lives in hot countries and eats the flesh of dead animals

Ww

waddle **waddles, waddling, waddled**
VERB to walk with short, quick steps, swaying slightly from side to side • *A duck **waddled** past.*

wade **wades, wading, waded**
VERB If you **wade**, you walk through water or mud.

wafer **wafers**
NOUN a thin, crisp biscuit, often eaten with ice cream

waffle **waffles, waffling, waffled**
VERB **1** When someone **waffles**, they talk or write a lot without being clear or without saying anything of importance.
NOUN **2** a thick, crisp pancake with squares marked on it, often eaten with syrup poured over it

wag **wags, wagging, wagged**
VERB **1** When a dog **wags** its tail, it shakes it repeatedly from side to side.
2 If you **wag** your finger, you move it repeatedly up and down.

wage **wages**
NOUN the regular payment made to someone each week for the work they do

wagon **wagons**; also spelt **waggon**
NOUN a strong four-wheeled cart for carrying heavy loads. **Wagons** are usually pulled by horses or tractors.

wail **wails, wailing, wailed**
VERB If a person or an animal **wails**, they cry or moan loudly.

waist **waists**
NOUN the middle part of your body where it narrows slightly above your hips

waistcoat **waistcoats**
NOUN a sleeveless piece of clothing, usually worn over a shirt and under a jacket

wait **waits, waiting, waited**
VERB **1** If you **wait**, you spend time in a place or a situation, usually doing little or nothing, before something happens.
2 to serve people food and drinks as a waiter or waitress
NOUN **3** A **wait** is a period of time before something happens.

waiter **waiters**
NOUN a man who works in a restaurant, serving people with food and drink

waitress **waitresses**
NOUN a woman who works in a restaurant, serving people with food and drink

wake **wakes, waking, woke, woken**
VERB When you **wake**, or when something **wakes** you, you become conscious again after being asleep.

walk **walks, walking, walked**
VERB **1** When you **walk**, you move along by putting one foot in front of the other on the ground.
NOUN **2** If you go for a **walk**, you go from one place to another on foot.

wall **walls**
NOUN **1** a narrow structure of brick or stone built round a garden or building
2 one of the four sides of a room

wallaby **wallabies**
NOUN a marsupial that looks like a small kangaroo
[from *wolaba*, an Australian Aboriginal word]

wallet **wallets**
NOUN a small, flat, folding case made of leather or plastic, used for holding paper money and sometimes credit cards

wallpaper **wallpapers**
NOUN thick coloured or patterned paper that comes in rolls, for pasting onto the walls of rooms to decorate them

walnut **walnuts**
NOUN **1** a nut that you can eat. It has a wrinkled shape and a hard, round, light-brown shell.

2 the tree on which walnuts grow. The wood from these trees is often used for making expensive furniture.

walrus **walruses**
NOUN an animal that lives in the sea. It looks like a large seal with a tough skin, coarse whiskers and two tusks.

waltz **waltzes, waltzing, waltzed**
NOUN **1** a dance that has a rhythm of three beats to the bar
VERB **2** If you **waltz** with someone, you dance a waltz with them.

wand **wands**
NOUN a long, thin rod used by magicians when they perform magic tricks, and by fairies in stories

wander **wanders, wandering, wandered**
VERB If you **wander** in a place, you walk around in a casual way.

want **wants, wanting, wanted**
VERB **1** If you **want** something, you feel that you would like to have it or do it.
2 to need something

wanted
ADJECTIVE being looked for, especially by the police as a suspected criminal

war **wars**
NOUN a period of fighting between countries or states, when weapons are used and many people may be killed

ward **wards**
NOUN **1** a long room with beds in for patients in a hospital
2 a child who is looked after by a guardian rather than their parents

warden **wardens**
NOUN **1** a person in charge of a place like a park or a block of flats, or an institution like a prison or a hostel
2 an official who makes sure that certain laws or rules are obeyed

wardrobe **wardrobes**
NOUN a tall cupboard in which you can hang your clothes
[from Old French *warder* meaning to guard robes and *robes* meaning clothing]

warehouse **warehouses**
NOUN a large building where goods are stored

warm **warmer, warmest; warms, warming, warmed**
ADJECTIVE **1** Something that is **warm** has some heat, but not enough to be hot.
2 **Warm** clothes or blankets are made of material that protects you from the cold.
VERB **3** If you **warm** something, you heat it up gently so that it stops being cold.

warn **warns, warning, warned**
VERB If you **warn** someone, you tell them that they may be in danger or in trouble.

warning **warnings**
NOUN something said or written to warn someone of a possible danger or problem

warp **warps, warping, warped**
VERB If something **warps**, or is **warped**, it becomes bent and twisted, usually because of heat or dampness.

warrant **warrants**
NOUN a special document that gives someone permission to do something
• *The police had a **warrant** to search the house for evidence.*

warren **warrens**
NOUN an area of ground where there are many rabbit burrows

warrior **warriors**
NOUN a fighting man or soldier

wart **warts**
NOUN a small, hard growth on the skin

wary **warier, wariest**
ADJECTIVE If you are **wary** of something or someone, you are not sure about them, so you are cautious.

was
VERB a past tense of **be**

wash **washes, washing, washed**
VERB **1** If you **wash** something, you clean it with water and soap.
2 If you **wash**, you clean yourself using soap and water.

wash up
VERB If you **wash up**, you wash the dishes, pans and cutlery used in preparing and eating a meal.

washable
ADJECTIVE able to be washed without being damaged

washing
NOUN clothes that need to be washed or that have been washed

washing machine **washing machines**
NOUN a machine for washing clothes

washing-up
NOUN the task of washing plates, cutlery and pots after a meal

wasp **wasps**
NOUN a flying insect with yellow and black stripes across its body, which can sting

waste **wastes, wasting, wasted**
VERB **1** If you **waste** time, money or energy, you use too much of it on something that is not important or that you do not need.
NOUN **2** using more money or some other resource than you need to
3 rubbish or other material that is no longer wanted, or that is left over

watch **watches, watching, watched**
NOUN **1** a small clock, usually worn on a strap on a person's wrist
VERB **2** If you **watch** something, you look at it for some time and pay attention to what is happening.

watch out
VERB **1** If you **watch out** for something or someone, you keep alert to see if they are near you.
2 If you tell someone to **watch out**, you are warning them to be careful.

water **waters, watering, watered**
NOUN **1** a clear, colourless, tasteless liquid that falls from clouds as rain
VERB **2** If you **water** a plant, you pour water into the soil around it.
3 If your eyes or mouth **water**, they

produce tears or saliva. • *My mouth started **watering** when I smelled Mum's baking.*

watercolour **watercolours**
NOUN **1** a type of paint that is mixed with water and used for painting pictures
2 a picture that has been painted using watercolours

waterfall **waterfalls**
NOUN water from a stream or river as it flows over rocks or the edge of a steep cliff and falls to the ground below

Victoria Falls, Zimbabwe

waterlogged
ADJECTIVE Something that is **waterlogged** is so wet that it cannot soak up any more water.

watermark **watermarks**
NOUN **1** a mark showing the level of water
2 a faint design in some types of paper which you can see if you hold it up to the light

waterproof
ADJECTIVE Something that is **waterproof** does not let water pass through it.
• *We put on our **waterproof** jackets as it was raining.*

watertight
ADJECTIVE Something that is **watertight** does not allow water to pass in or out.

waterworks
NOUN the place where the public supply of water is stored and cleaned, and from where it is supplied to our homes

watt **watts**
Said "**wot**" NOUN a unit of measurement of electrical power
[Named after James *Watt* (1736–1819) who invented the steam engine]

wave **waves, waving, waved**
VERB **1** If you **wave** your hand, you move it from side to side, usually to say hello or goodbye.
2 If you **wave** something, you hold it up and move it from side to side. • *People in the crowd were **waving** flags.*
NOUN **3** a ridge of water on the surface of the sea caused by wind or by tides
4 the form in which some types of energy, such as heat, light or sound, travel

wax **waxes**
NOUN **1** a solid, slightly shiny substance made of fat or oil, that melts easily and is used to make candles and polish
2 the sticky yellow substance in your ears

way **ways**
NOUN **1** The **way** of doing something is how you do it.
2 The **way** to a place is how you get there.

WC **WCs**
NOUN an abbreviation of *water closet.* It is used on plans and signs to show where the toilet is located.

we
PRONOUN **We** refers to the person writing or talking and one or more other people.

weak **weaker, weakest**
ADJECTIVE If someone is **weak**, they do not have much strength or energy.

wealth
NOUN a large amount of money or property that someone owns

wealthy **wealthier, wealthiest**
ADJECTIVE Someone who is **wealthy** has a lot of money.

weapon **weapons**
NOUN an object used to hurt or kill people in a fight or war

wear **wears, wearing, wore, worn**
VERB When you **wear** something, such as clothes, make-up or jewellery, you have them on your body or face.

wear out
VERB When something **wears out**, or when you **wear** it **out**, it is used so much that it becomes thin, weak and no longer usable.

weary **wearier, weariest**
ADJECTIVE If you are **weary**, you are very tired.
wearily ADVERB **weariness** NOUN

weasel **weasels**
NOUN a small wild mammal with a long, thin body and short legs

weather
NOUN the conditions of sunshine, rain, wind or snow at a particular time in a particular place

weave **weaves, weaving, wove, woven**
VERB **1** If you **weave** something like cloth or a basket, you make it by crossing threads or grasses over and under each other. Cloth is often **woven** using a machine called a loom.
2 If you **weave** your way, you move from side to side past people and other obstacles.

web **webs**
NOUN a fine net of threads that a spider makes from a sticky substance that it produces in its body

Web
NOUN short for **World Wide Web**

webbed
ADJECTIVE **Webbed** feet have skin joining the toes together, like ducks' feet.

webcam **webcams**
NOUN a camera that sends pictures over the internet

website **websites**
NOUN a place on the internet where you can find out about a particular subject or person

we'd
a contraction of *we had* or *we would*

wedding **weddings**
NOUN a marriage ceremony

wedge **wedges, wedging, wedged**
VERB **1** If you **wedge** something somewhere, you make it stay there by holding it tightly, or by fixing something next to it to stop it from moving.
NOUN **2** a piece of something such as wood, metal or rubber with one thin edge and one thick edge, used to hold something still • *I put a* ***wedge*** *under the door to keep it open.*
3 a piece of something that has a thick triangular shape • *I cut a* ***wedge*** *of cheese.*

Wednesday
NOUN the fourth day of the week, coming between Tuesday and Thursday [Wednesday was the day the Anglo-Saxons honoured their god *Odin* or *Woden*]

weed **weeds, weeding, weeded**
NOUN **1** a wild plant growing somewhere it is not wanted
VERB **2** If you **weed** an area of ground, you remove the weeds from it.

week **weeks**
NOUN **1** a period of seven days, especially one beginning on a Sunday and ending on a Saturday
2 the part of a week that does not include Saturday and Sunday

weekday **weekdays**
NOUN any day except Saturday and Sunday

weekend **weekends**
NOUN Saturday and Sunday.

weekly
ADJECTIVE OR ADVERB happening or appearing once every week

weep **weeps, weeping, wept**
VERB If someone **weeps**, they cry.

weigh **weighs, weighing, weighed**
VERB **1** If something **weighs** a particular amount, that is how heavy it is.
2 If you **weigh** something, you find out how heavy it is by using scales.

weight **weights**
NOUN the heaviness of something

weir **weirs**
NOUN a low dam built across a river to raise the water level, control the flow of water, or change the direction of the water
[from Old English *wer* meaning river-dam or enclosure for fish]

weird **weirder, weirdest**
ADJECTIVE strange or odd

welcome **welcomes, welcoming, welcomed**
VERB **1** If you **welcome** a visitor, you greet them in a friendly way when they arrive.
EXCLAMATION **2 Welcome** can be said as a greeting to a visitor who has just arrived.
ADJECTIVE **3** If someone is **welcome** at a place, they will be accepted there in a friendly way.
[from Old English *wilcuma* meaning welcome guest]

weld **welds, welding, welded**
VERB If you **weld** two pieces of metal together, you join them by heating their edges and pressing them together so that when they cool they harden into one piece.
welder NOUN

welfare
NOUN The **welfare** of a person or group is their health, comfort and happiness.

welfare state
NOUN a system in which the government uses money from taxes to provide health care and education services, and to give benefits to people who are old, unemployed or sick

well **better, best; wells**
ADJECTIVE **1** If you are **well**, you are healthy.
ADVERB **2** If you do something **well**, you do it to a high standard.
NOUN **3** a hole in the ground with water or oil at the bottom

we'll
a contraction of *we will* or *we shall*

wellington **wellingtons**
NOUN a long waterproof rubber boot
[named after the Duke of *Wellington*]

went
VERB the past tense of **go**

wept
VERB a past tense and past participle of **weep**

were
VERB a past tense of **be**

we're
a contraction of *we are*

west
NOUN one of the four main points of the compass. The sun sets in the **west**. The abbreviation for **west** is W.

western **westerns**
ADJECTIVE **1** in or from the west
NOUN **2** a film or book about the west of America in the nineteenth and early twentieth centuries

wet **wetter, wettest; wets, wetting, wet** or **wetted**
ADJECTIVE **1** covered or soaked with water or other liquid
2 Wet weather is rainy.
VERB **3** If you **wet** something, you make it wet.

we've
a contraction of *we have*

whale **whales**
NOUN a very large sea mammal that breathes out water through a hole on the top of its head

wharf **wharves** or **wharfs**
NOUN a platform beside a river or the sea, where ships load and unload

what
ADJECTIVE **1 What** is used in questions.
• ***What** time is it?*

2 You use **what** to emphasize a comment. • ***What*** *excellent work!*
PHRASE **3** You use **what about** to show that you are making a suggestion or a question. • ***What about*** *the homework from last night?*
PRONOUN **4** refers to information about something • *I really have no idea* ***what*** *you mean.*

whatever
PRONOUN **1** anything or everything of a particular type
CONJUNCTION **2** You use **whatever** to mean no matter what. • *I will go* ***whatever*** *happens.*

wheat
NOUN a cereal plant grown for its grain that is used to make flour

wheel **wheels, wheeling, wheeled**
NOUN **1** a circular object that turns on a rod attached to its centre. **Wheels** are fixed underneath vehicles so that they can move along.
VERB **2** If you **wheel** something somewhere, you push it along on wheels.

wheelbarrow **wheelbarrows**
NOUN a small cart with a single wheel at the front, pushed along by two handles at the back. It is used by people such as gardeners and builders.

wheelchair **wheelchairs**
NOUN a chair with large wheels, for use by people who find walking difficult or impossible

wheeze **wheezes, wheezing, wheezed**
VERB If someone **wheezes**, they breathe with difficulty, making a whistling sound.

when
ADVERB **1** You use **when** to ask at what time something will happen or how long ago it has happened. • ***When*** *shall I see you?*
CONJUNCTION **2** You use **when** to refer to a certain time. • *I had fun* ***when*** *I was on holiday.*

whenever
CONJUNCTION at any time, or every time that something happens • *I go to the park* ***whenever*** *I can.*

where
ADVERB **1** You use **where** to ask which place something is in, is from, or is going to. • ***Where*** *are we?*
CONJUNCTION **2** You use **where** to refer to a place in which something or someone is. • *You do not know* ***where*** *we live.*

wherever
CONJUNCTION in, at or to any place or situation • *Alex heard the same thing* ***wherever*** *he went.*

whether
CONJUNCTION You use **whether** when you are talking about two or more things to choose from. • *I don't know* ***whether*** *that's true or false.*

which
ADJECTIVE OR PRONOUN **1** You use **which** to ask about alternatives. • ***Which*** *girl is your sister?*
2 Which shows the thing you are talking about or gives more detail about it. • *The book* ***which*** *is on the table is mine.*

whichever
PRONOUN OR ADJECTIVE You use **whichever** when talking about different possibilities. • *You can have cake or chocolate,* ***whichever*** *you prefer.*

whiff **whiffs**
NOUN a slight smell of something • *I caught a* ***whiff*** *of her perfume as she passed.*

while
CONJUNCTION **1** If something happens **while** something else is happening, the two things happen at the same time. • *Mum went to the café* ***while*** *I had my lesson.*
2 While can be used to mean but or although. • *I like dogs,* ***while*** *my brother prefers cats.*
NOUN **3** a period of time • *a little* ***while*** *earlier*

whim **whims**
NOUN a sudden wish or desire
SYNONYM: impulse

whimper **whimpers, whimpering, whimpered**
VERB When children or animals **whimper**, they make soft, low, unhappy sounds.

whine **whines, whining, whined**
VERB **1** If a person or an animal **whines**, they make a long, high-pitched noise, especially one that sounds sad or unpleasant.
2 If someone **whines** about something, they complain about it in an annoying way.

whip **whips, whipping, whipped**
NOUN **1** a long, thin piece of leather or rope attached to a handle, which is used for hitting people or animals
VERB **2** To **whip** a person or animal means to hit them with a whip.

whirl **whirls, whirling, whirled**
VERB When something **whirls**, or when you **whirl** it round, it turns or spins round very fast.

whirlpool **whirlpools**
NOUN a small area in a river or the sea where the water is moving quickly round and round in a circle so that objects floating near it are pulled into its centre

whirlwind **whirlwinds**
NOUN a tall column of air that spins round and round very fast

whirr **whirrs, whirring, whirred**
VERB When something like a machine **whirrs**, it makes a continuous buzzing sound.

whisk **whisks, whisking, whisked**
VERB **1** If you **whisk** eggs or cream, you stir air into them quickly.
2 If you **whisk** something somewhere, you move it there quickly.
NOUN **3** a kitchen utensil for whisking things

whisker **whiskers**
NOUN **1** The **whiskers** of an animal such as a cat are the long, stiff hairs near its mouth.
2 You can refer to the hair on a man's face, especially on his cheeks, as his **whiskers**.

whisky **whiskies**
NOUN a strong alcoholic drink made from grain such as barley

whisper **whispers, whispering, whispered**
VERB When you **whisper**, you talk very quietly and softly.

whistle **whistles, whistling, whistled**
VERB **1** When you **whistle**, you make a high-pitched sound by forcing your breath out between your lips. • *He **whistled** a tune.*
2 If something **whistles**, it makes a loud, high sound. • *The kettle **whistled**.*
NOUN **3** a small metal tube that you blow into to produce a whistling sound

white **whiter, whitest; whites**
NOUN OR ADJECTIVE **1** the lightest possible colour, like milk or fresh snow
2 **White** coffee contains milk or cream.
NOUN **3** The **white** of an egg is the clear liquid around the yolk.

whiteboard **whiteboards**
NOUN **1** a shiny white board that you can write on and then wipe clean
2 a large screen that shows computer images which can be moved or altered by a pen, a finger or a stylus

who
PRONOUN **1** You use **who** when you are asking about someone's identity. • ***Who** are you?*
2 You use **who** to refer to the person you are talking about. • *I know you are the one **who** was in trouble yesterday.*

whoever
PRONOUN **Whoever** means the person who. • ***Whoever** wants to can go on the excursion.*

whole **wholes**
NOUN OR ADJECTIVE **1** The **whole** of something is all of it.
ADVERB **2** in one piece • *He swallowed the sweet **whole**.*

wholemeal
ADJECTIVE **Wholemeal** flour is made from the whole grain of the wheat plant, including the husk.

wholesale
ADJECTIVE OR ADVERB If a shopkeeper buys his or her goods **wholesale**, he or she buys large amounts of them cheaply before selling them on to his or her customers.
ANTONYM: retail

wholesome
ADJECTIVE healthy or good for you

who's
a contraction of *who is* or *who has*

> Do not confuse *who's* with *whose*.

whose
PRONOUN **1** You use **whose** to ask who something belongs to. • ***Whose** shoe is this?*
2 **Whose** gives information about something belonging to the person or things just mentioned. • *She is the pupil **whose** poem won the prize.*

> Do not confuse *whose* with *who's*.

why
ADVERB OR PRONOUN You use **why** when you are talking about the reason for something. • ***Why** did you do that?*
• *I wondered **why** he did that.*

wick **wicks**
NOUN the cord that burns in the middle of a candle

wicked
ADJECTIVE **1** very bad
SYNONYMS: evil, sinful
2 mischievous in an amusing or attractive way
[from Old English *wicca* meaning witch]
wickedly ADVERB **wickedness** NOUN

wicker
NOUN things made of reed or cane woven together, such as baskets or furniture

wicket **wickets**
NOUN **1** one of the two sets of stumps and bails at which the bowler aims the ball in cricket
2 The grass between the **wickets** in cricket is also called the **wicket**.

wide **wider, widest**
ADJECTIVE **1** measuring a large distance from one side to the other
2 measuring a certain amount from one side to the other • *The pool is 10 metres **wide**.*
3 If there is a **wide** variety, range or selection of something, there are many different kinds of it.
ADVERB **4** If you open or spread something **wide**, you open it as far as you can.
• *Open your mouth **wide**.*

widow **widows**
NOUN a woman whose husband has died

widower **widowers**
NOUN a man whose wife has died

width **widths**
NOUN The **width** of something is how wide it is from one side to the other.

wife **wives**
NOUN A man's **wife** is the woman he is married to.

Wi-Fi
NOUN a system of accessing the internet from machines such as laptop computers that are not physically connected to a network

wig **wigs**
NOUN a covering of artificial hair worn over someone's own hair to change their appearance or to hide their baldness
[short for *periwig*, from Italian *perrucca* meaning wig]

wiggle **wiggles, wiggling, wiggled**
VERB If you **wiggle** something, you move it up and down or from side to side with small, jerky movements.
wiggly ADJECTIVE

wigwam **wigwams**
NOUN a kind of tent used by Native Americans
[from American Indian *wikwam* meaning their house]

wild **wilder, wildest; wilds**
ADJECTIVE **1** **Wild** animals and plants live and grow in natural surroundings

A B C D E F G H I J K L M N O P Q R S T U V W X Y Z

and are not looked after by people.
2 **Wild** land is natural and not used for farming.
3 **Wild** behaviour is excited and uncontrolled.
NOUN **4** a free and natural state of living • *There are very few tigers left in the* ***wild****.*

wilderness **wildernesses**
NOUN an area of natural land that is not cultivated

wildlife
NOUN wild animals and plants

wilful
ADJECTIVE **1** Someone who is **wilful** is determined to get their own way.
SYNONYMS: headstrong, stubborn
2 Something that is **wilful** is done or said deliberately. • ***wilful*** *damage*
wilfully ADVERB

will **wills**
VERB **1** You use **will** to form the future tense. • *I* ***will*** *do the washing up after dinner.*
NOUN **2** the determination to do something
3 a legal document in which people say what they want to happen to their money and property when they die
4 what you choose or want to do • *Don't make them do it against their* ***will****.*

willing
ADJECTIVE If you are **willing**, you are glad and ready to do what is wanted or needed.

willow **willows**
NOUN a tree with long, thin branches and narrow leaves that often grows near water

wilt **wilts, wilting, wilted**
VERB If a plant **wilts**, it droops because it needs more water or is dying.

wily **wilier, wiliest**
ADJECTIVE clever and cunning

wimp **wimps**
NOUN INFORMAL someone who is feeble and timid

win **wins, winning, won**
VERB **1** If you **win** a fight, game or argument, you defeat your opponent.
2 If you **win** a prize, you receive it as a reward for succeeding in something.

winch **winches, winching, winched**
NOUN **1** a machine used to lift or pull heavy objects. It consists of a cylinder or wheel around which a rope or cable is wound.
VERB **2** If you **winch** an object or person somewhere, you lift, lower or pull them using a winch.

wind **winds, winding, wound**
Rhymes with "mind" VERB **1** If a road or river **winds**, it is not straight, but twists and turns.
2 When you **wind** something round something else, you wrap it round it several times.
3 When you **wind** a clock or machine, or **wind** it up, you turn a key or handle several times to make it work.
Rhymes with "tinned" NOUN **4** a current of air that moves across the land and sea
ADJECTIVE **5** A **wind** instrument is a musical instrument that you play by blowing into it.

windmill **windmills**
NOUN a machine in a special building, for generating electricity, grinding grain or pumping water. It is powered by long arms called sails that are turned by the wind.

window **windows**
NOUN a space in a wall or roof or in the side of a vehicle, usually with glass in it so that light can pass through and people can see in or out

windpipe **windpipes**
NOUN the tube through which air travels in and out of your lungs when you breathe

windscreen **windscreens**
NOUN the glass at the front of a vehicle through which the driver looks

windsurfing
NOUN the sport of moving over the surface of the sea or a lake on a board with a sail fixed to it
windsurfer NOUN

windy **windier, windiest**
ADJECTIVE If it is **windy**, there is a lot of wind.

wine **wines**
NOUN an alcoholic drink usually made from grapes

wing **wings**
NOUN **1** A bird's or insect's **wings** are the parts of its body that it uses for flying.
2 An aeroplane's **wings** are the long, flat parts on each side that support it while it is in the air.

wink **winks, winking, winked**
VERB When you **wink**, you close and open one eye very quickly, often to show that something is a joke or a secret.

winner **winners**
NOUN someone who wins something

winter **winters**
NOUN the coldest season of the year, between autumn and spring

wipe **wipes, wiping, wiped**
VERB If you **wipe** something, you rub its surface lightly with a cloth or your hand to clear off dirt or liquid.

wire **wires, wiring, wired**
NOUN **1** long, thin, bendy metal that can be used to make or fasten things, or to conduct an electric current
VERB **2** If someone **wires** something, or **wires** it up, they connect it so that electricity can pass through it.

wireless **wirelesses**
ADJECTIVE **1** If a computer network is **wireless**, it is connected by radio signals rather than cables.
NOUN **2** OLD-FASHIONED another word for **radio**

wisdom
NOUN a person's ability to use the things they have done and learned to give good advice or make good decisions

wise **wiser, wisest**
ADJECTIVE Someone who is **wise** can use their experience and knowledge to make sensible decisions and judgements.

wish **wishes, wishing, wished**
NOUN **1** something that you want very much
2 the act of wishing for something
VERB **3** If you **wish** something for someone, you hope that they will have it.
• *I **wished** her good luck in her exams.*
4 If you **wish** to do something, you want to do it.
5 If you **wish** something was true, you would like it to be, but know it is not very likely.

wisp **wisps**
NOUN A **wisp** of something such as smoke or hair is a small, thin, streak or bunch of it. • *A **wisp** of hair fell over her eyes.*
wispy ADJECTIVE

wit **wits**
NOUN the ability to use words or ideas in an amusing and clever way

witch **witches**
NOUN a woman who claims to have magic powers and to be able to use them for good or evil. **Witches** are often characters in fairy stories.
[from Old English *wicca* meaning witch]

witchcraft
NOUN the skill or art of using magic powers, especially evil ones

with
PREPOSITION If you are **with** someone, you are in their company. • *We went **with** Mum to the shops.*

withdraw **withdraws, withdrawing, withdrew, withdrawn**
VERB **1** If you **withdraw** something, you take it out. • *He **withdrew** the money from his bank.*
2 If you **withdraw** from something, you do not continue with it. • *She **withdrew** from the race because of injury.*

wither **withers, withering, withered**
VERB If a plant **withers**, it wilts or shrivels up and dies.

within
PREPOSITION OR ADVERB **1** inside, not going outside certain limits • *Stay **within** the school grounds.*
2 before a period of time has passed • *Bring back the book **within** three weeks.*

without
PREPOSITION **1** not having, not feeling or not showing something • *They went out **without** coats as it was a warm, dry day.*
2 If you do something **without** someone else, they are not with you when you do it. • *He went **without** me.*

witness **witnesses**
NOUN **1** someone who has seen an event, such as an accident, and can describe what happened
2 someone who appears in a court of law to say what they know about a crime or other event

witty **wittier, wittiest**
ADJECTIVE amusing in a clever way

wizard **wizards**
NOUN a man in a fairy story who has magic powers

wobble **wobbles, wobbling, wobbled**
VERB If something **wobbles**, it shakes or moves from side to side because it is loose or unsteady.

wok **woks**
NOUN a large bowl-shaped pan used for Chinese cooking

woke
VERB the past tense of **wake**

woken
VERB the past participle of **wake**

wolf **wolves; wolfs, wolfing, wolfed**
NOUN **1** a wild animal related to the dog. **Wolves** hunt in packs and kill other animals for food.
VERB **2** INFORMAL If you **wolf** food, or **wolf** it down, you eat it up quickly and greedily.

woman **women**
NOUN an adult female human being

womb **wombs**
NOUN A woman's **womb** is the part inside her body where her unborn baby grows.

won
VERB the past tense and past participle of **win**

wonder **wonders, wondering, wondered**
VERB **1** If you **wonder** about something, you think about it and try to guess or understand more about it.
2 If you **wonder** at something, you are amazed by it.
NOUN **3** a feeling of amazement and admiration

wonderful
ADJECTIVE marvellous or impressive

won't
VERB a contraction of *will not*

wood **woods**
NOUN **1** the substance that forms the trunks and branches of trees
2 a large area of trees growing near each other

wooden
ADJECTIVE Something **wooden** is made of wood.

woodland **woodlands**
NOUN land that is mostly covered with trees

woodlouse **woodlice**
NOUN a small animal with seven pairs of legs, that lives in damp soil and rotten wood

woodpecker **woodpeckers**
NOUN a climbing bird with a long, sharp beak that it uses to drill holes in trees to find the insects that live in the bark

woodwind
ADJECTIVE **Woodwind** instruments are musical instruments such as flutes, oboes, clarinets and bassoons, made of wood or metal. They are played by being blown into.

woodwork
NOUN **1** the activity of making things out of wood
2 the parts of a building that are made of wood

woof **woofs**
NOUN the sound a dog makes

wool **wools**
NOUN **1** the hair that grows on sheep and some other animals
2 thread or cloth made from the wool of animals, and used to make clothes, blankets and carpets

woollen
ADJECTIVE made of wool

woolly
ADJECTIVE made of wool, or looking like wool

word **words**
NOUN **1** a single unit of language in speech or writing which has a meaning. *Bird*, *hot* and *sing* are all **words**.
PLURAL NOUN **2** The **words** of a play or song are the words you say or sing.
NOUN **3** If you give someone your **word** about something, you promise to do it.
4 If you ask for a **word** with someone, you want to say something briefly to them.

wore
VERB the past tense of **wear**

work **works, working, worked**
VERB **1** People who **work** have a job that they are paid to do.
2 When you **work**, you spend time and energy doing something useful.
3 If something **works**, it does what it is supposed to do.
PHRASE **4** If something **works its way** into a certain position, it moves itself there gradually.
5 If you **work out** an answer to a problem, you solve it.

workout **workouts**
NOUN a session of exercise or training for the body

workshop **workshops**
NOUN a room or building that has tools or machinery in it that are used for making or repairing things

world **worlds**
NOUN **1** the planet we live on
2 A person's **world** is the life they lead and the people they know.
3 a particular field of activity • *He is a top player in the rugby **world**.*
PHRASE **4** If you **think the world** of someone, you like or admire them very much.

World Wide Web
NOUN The **World Wide Web** is a system of linked documents accessed via the internet.

worm **worms**
NOUN a small, thin animal without bones or legs, especially an earthworm

worn
VERB **1** the past participle of **wear**
ADJECTIVE **2** looking old or exhausted

worry **worries, worrying, worried**
VERB **1** If you **worry**, you feel anxious about a problem or about something that might happen.
NOUN **2** a problem, or something that makes you worry

worse
ADJECTIVE OR ADVERB less good or less well. The comparative form of *bad* and *badly*. • *The team's results are **worse** this year than they were last year.*
ANTONYM: better

worship **worships, worshipping, worshipped**
VERB If you **worship** a god, you show your love and respect by praying or singing hymns.

worst
ADJECTIVE the least well or the least good. The superlative form of *bad* and *badly*. • *It was the **worst** meal I have ever eaten.*
ANTONYM: best

worth
ADJECTIVE **1** If something is **worth** a sum of money, it has that value.

2 If something is **worth** doing, it deserves to be done.

worthless

ADJECTIVE Something that is **worthless** has no use or no value.

worthwhile

ADJECTIVE If something is **worthwhile**, it is important enough to spend time or effort doing it.

would

VERB **1** the past tense of **will**. You use **would** to talk about something that was in the future the last time you were talking about it. • *We were sure it **would** be a success.*
2 You use **would** in polite questions. • ***Would** you like some lunch?*

wouldn't

VERB a contraction of *would not*

wound **wounds, wounding, wounded**

Rhymes with "sound" VERB **1** the past tense and past participle of **wind**
Said "**woond**" NOUN **2** an injury to part of a person's or an animal's body, especially a cut
VERB **3** If someone or something **wounds** a person or an animal, they injure them, especially with a cut.

wove

VERB the past tense of **weave**

woven

VERB the past participle of **weave**

wrap **wraps, wrapping, wrapped**

VERB If you **wrap** something, you fold cloth or paper around it.

wrapping **wrappings**

NOUN material used to wrap something, such as a present

wrath

NOUN great anger

wreath **wreaths**

NOUN an arrangement of flowers and leaves, often in the shape of a circle, which is put on a grave to remember someone who has died

wreck **wrecks, wrecking, wrecked**

VERB **1** To **wreck** something means to break it, destroy it or spoil it completely.
NOUN **2** a vehicle or ship that has been badly damaged, usually in an accident
wreckage NOUN

wren **wrens**

NOUN a small, brown songbird

wrench **wrenches, wrenching, wrenched**

VERB **1** If you **wrench** something, you give it a sudden and violent twist or pull.
2 If you **wrench** a limb or a joint, you twist and injure it.
NOUN **3** a wrenching movement
4 a tool for gripping or tightening nuts and bolts

wrestle **wrestles, wrestling, wrestled**

VERB If you **wrestle** someone, or **wrestle** with them, you fight them by holding or throwing them, but not hitting them.
wrestler NOUN

wretched

ADJECTIVE very unhappy or unfortunate

wriggle **wriggles, wriggling, wriggled**

VERB **1** If a person or an animal **wriggles**, they twist and turn their body in a lively and excited way.
2 If you **wriggle** out of doing something that you do not want to do, you manage to avoid doing it.

wring **wrings, wringing, wrung**

VERB When you **wring** a wet cloth, or **wring** it out, you squeeze the water out of it by twisting it.

wrinkle **wrinkles, wrinkling, wrinkled**

NOUN **1** a soft fold or crease in something, especially a person's skin as they grow older
VERB **2** If something **wrinkles**, folds or creases develop in it.

wrinkled

ADJECTIVE Something that is **wrinkled** has wrinkles in it.

wrist **wrists**
NOUN the part of your body between your hand and your arm, which bends when you move your hand

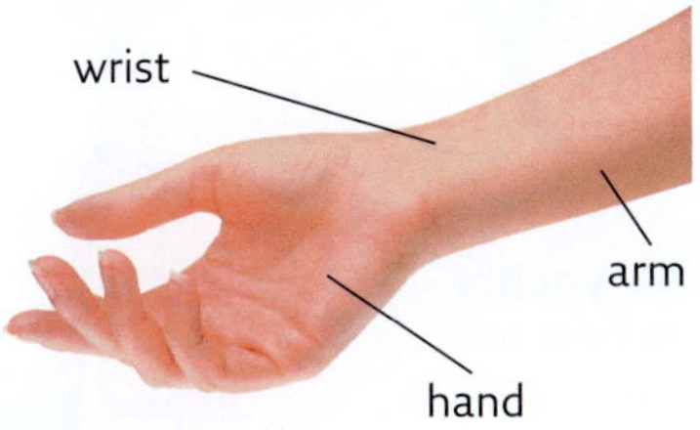

wristwatch **wristwatches**
NOUN a watch you wear on your wrist

write **writes, writing, wrote, written**
VERB **1** When you **write**, you use a pen or pencil to form letters, words or numbers on a surface. • *I have **written** my name in the front of my book.*
2 If you **write** something such as a poem, a book or a piece of music, you think of the words or notes for yourself.
3 When you **write** to someone, you send them a letter.

writer **writers**
NOUN **1** a person who writes books, stories or articles as a job
2 The **writer** of something is the person who wrote it.

writhe **writhes, writhing, writhed**
VERB If you **writhe**, you twist and turn your body, often because you are in pain.

writing **writings**
NOUN **1** something that has been written or printed
2 Your **writing** is the way you write with a pen or pencil.

written
VERB the past participle of **write**

wrong
ADJECTIVE **1** If there is something **wrong** with an object, it is not working properly or has a fault. • *There must be something **wrong** with the car as it will not start.*
2 If something is **wrong**, it is not correct or truthful.
3 An action that is **wrong** is bad or against the law.

wrote
VERB the past tense of **write**

wrung
VERB the past tense and past participle of **wring**

A B C D E F G H I J K L M N O P Q R S T U V W X Y Z

Xx

X-ray **X-rays, X-raying, X-rayed**
NOUN **1** a type of radiation that can pass through some solid materials. **X-rays** are used by doctors to examine the bones or organs inside a person's body.
2 a picture made by sending X-rays through someone's body in order to examine the inside of it
VERB **3** If someone **X-rays** something, they make a picture of the inside of it by passing X-rays through it.

xylophone **xylophones**
Said "**ziy**-lu-fohn" NOUN a musical instrument made of a row of wooden bars of different lengths. It is played by hitting the bars with special hammers.

Yy

yacht **yachts**
NOUN a boat with sails or an engine, used for racing or for pleasure trips

yak **yaks**
NOUN a type of long-haired ox with long horns, found mainly in the mountains of Tibet

yam **yams**
NOUN a root vegetable that grows in tropical regions

yard **yards**
NOUN **1** a unit of length equal to 36 inches or about 91.4 centimetres
2 a paved space with walls around it, next to a building
3 a place where certain types of work are carried out, such as a ship**yard** or a builder's **yard**

yarn **yarns**
NOUN **1** thread used for knitting or making cloth
2 INFORMAL a story that someone tells, often with invented details to make it more interesting or exciting

yawn **yawns, yawning, yawned**
VERB When you **yawn**, you open your mouth wide and take in more air than usual, often when you are tired or bored.

year **years**
NOUN **1** a period of twelve months or 365 days (366 days in a leap year), usually measured from the first of January to the thirty-first of December. It takes a **year** for the earth to orbit the sun.
2 the part of a year during which something happens or is organized
• *the school **year***

yeast
NOUN a type of fungus used in baking and in making beer

yell **yells, yelling, yelled**
VERB **1** If you **yell**, you shout loudly, usually because you are angry, excited or in pain.
NOUN **2** a loud shout

yellow **yellower, yellowest**
NOUN OR ADJECTIVE the colour of buttercups, egg yolks or lemons

yelp **yelps, yelping, yelped**
VERB **1** When people or animals **yelp**, they give a sudden cry.
NOUN **2** a sudden cry

yes
EXCLAMATION You say **yes** to agree with someone, to say that something is true or to accept something.
ANTONYM: no

yesterday
NOUN OR ADVERB the day before today

yet
ADVERB **1** If something has not happened **yet**, you expect it to happen in the future. **2** If something should not be done **yet**, it should be done later. • *Don't switch it off **yet**.*
CONJUNCTION **3** You use **yet** to introduce something that is rather surprising. • *He doesn't like maths, **yet** he always does well.*

yew **yews**
NOUN an evergreen tree with bright red berries

yodel **yodels, yodelling, yodelled**
VERB When someone **yodels**, they sing normal notes with high quick notes in between. You can hear this style of singing in the Swiss and Austrian Alps.

yoga
NOUN a Hindu form of exercise that develops the body and the mind, making you relaxed and fit

yogurt **yogurts**; also spelt **yoghurt**
NOUN a slightly sour, thick, liquid food made from milk that has had bacteria added to it

yoke **yokes**
NOUN a wooden bar laid across the necks of animals such as oxen to hold them together when they pull a plough or a cart

yolk **yolks**
NOUN the yellow part in the middle of an egg

Yom Kippur
NOUN an annual Jewish religious holiday, which is a day of fasting and prayers. It is also called the Day of Atonement.
[from Hebrew *yom* meaning day and *kippur* meaning atonement]

you
PRONOUN **You** refers to the person or people you are talking or writing to.

you'd
a contraction of *you had* or *you would*

you'll
a contraction of *you will* or *you shall*

young **younger, youngest**
ADJECTIVE **1** A **young** person, animal or plant has not lived very long and is not yet mature.
PLURAL NOUN **2** The **young** of an animal are its babies.

your
ADJECTIVE belonging to you

you're
a contraction of *you are*

yours
PRONOUN belonging to you

yourself **yourselves**
PRONOUN you and only you • *Have you hurt **yourself**?*

youth **youths**
NOUN **1** Someone's **youth** is the time of their life before they are a fully mature adult.
2 a boy or young man
3 young people in general

you've
a contraction of *you have*

yo-yo **yo-yos**
NOUN a round wooden or plastic toy attached to a string. You play by making the **yo-yo** move up and down the string.

Zz

zany **zanier, zaniest**
ADJECTIVE odd in a funny way
[from Italian *zanni* meaning clown]

zap **zaps, zapping, zapped**
VERB INFORMAL If you **zap** someone or something in a computer game, you get rid of them.

zeal
NOUN eagerness and enthusiasm

zebra **zebras**
NOUN a type of African wild horse with black and white stripes

zebra crossing **zebra crossings**
NOUN part of a road marked with broad black and white stripes, where pedestrians can cross

zero
NOUN nought. The sign for zero is 0.

zest
NOUN **1** a feeling of great enjoyment and enthusiasm
2 The **zest** of a citrus fruit such as an orange or lemon is the outside of the peel, used to flavour food and drinks.
zestful ADJECTIVE **zestfully** ADVERB

zigzag **zigzags, zigzagging, zigzagged**
NOUN **1** a line that has a series of sharp, angular bends to the right and left

VERB **2** If you **zigzag**, you move forward in a series of sharp turns to the left and right.

zinc
NOUN a bluish-white metal used to coat other metals to stop them rusting

zip **zips, zipping, zipped**
NOUN **1** a fastener used on clothes and bags, with two rows of metal or plastic interlocking teeth that separate or fasten together as you pull a small tag along them
VERB **2** When you **zip** something, or **zip** it up, you fasten it using a zip.

zodiac
NOUN a diagram used by astrologers to represent the movement of the stars. It is divided into 12 sections, each with a special name and symbol. • *"Capricorn", "Gemini", "Taurus" and "Pisces" are all signs of the* ***zodiac****.*
[from the Greek *zōidiakos kuklos* meaning "circle of signs"]

zone **zones**
NOUN an area of land or sea that is considered different from the areas around it, or is separated from the areas around it in some way

zoo **zoos**
NOUN a place where live animals are kept so that people can look at them

zoology
NOUN the scientific study of animals
zoological ADJECTIVE **zoologist** NOUN

zoom lens **zoom lenses**
NOUN A **zoom lens** on a camera helps the photographer to take close-up pictures from far away.

zucchini
PLURAL NOUN small vegetable marrows with dark green skin. They are also called courgettes.
[from Italian plural of *zucchino* meaning gourd]

Word Wizard

2D Shapes

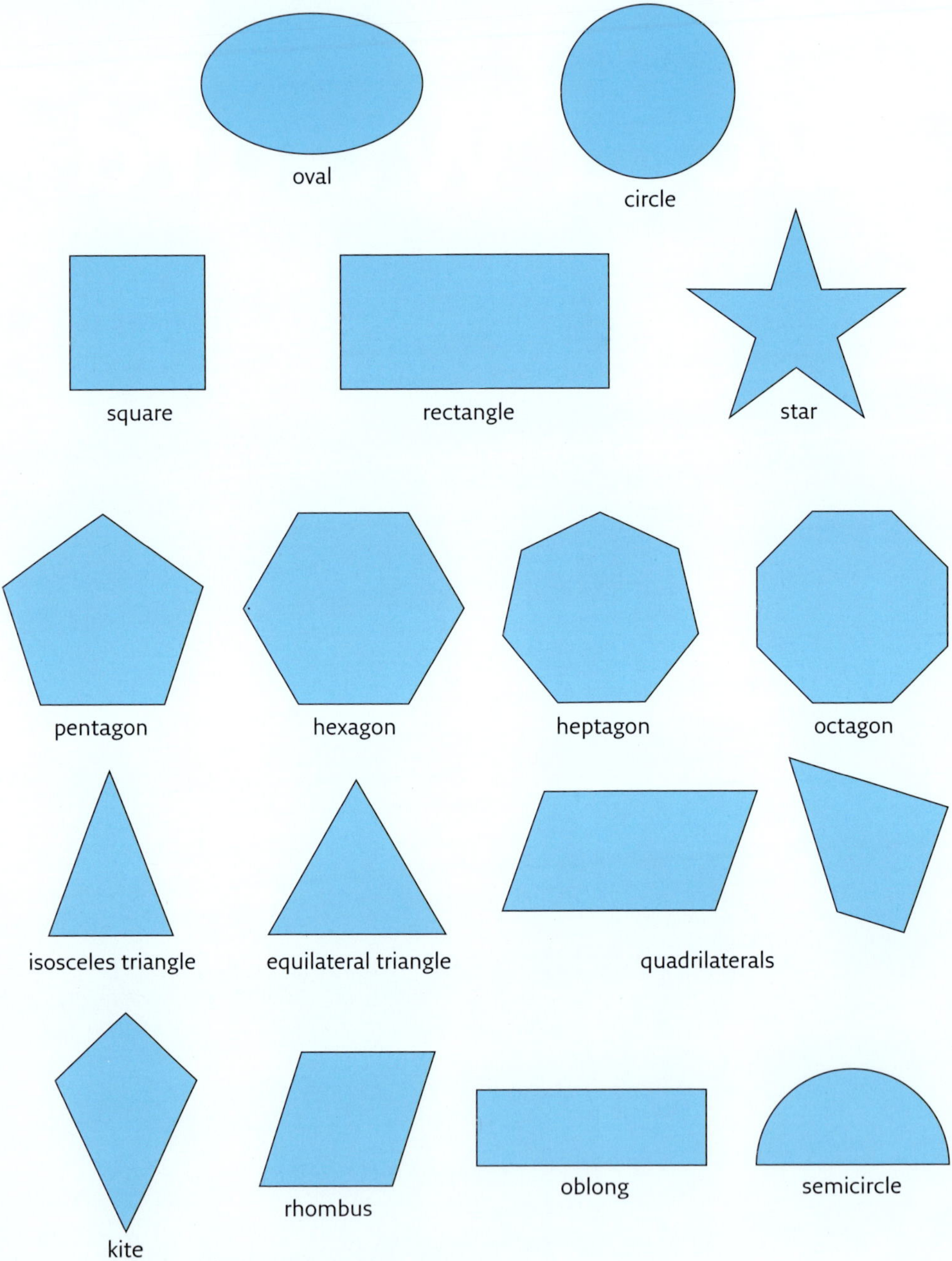
oval
circle
square
rectangle
star
pentagon
hexagon
heptagon
octagon
isosceles triangle
equilateral triangle
quadrilaterals
kite
rhombus
oblong
semicircle

3D shapes and angles

3D shapes

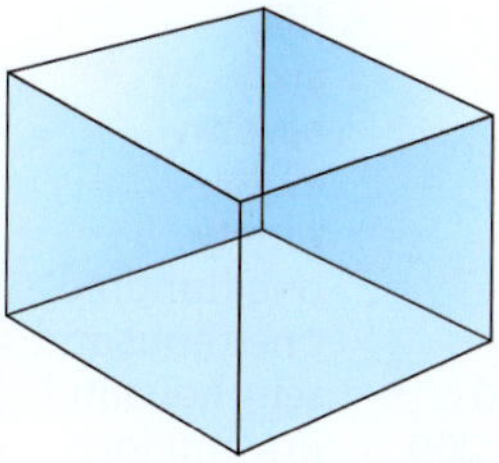
cube

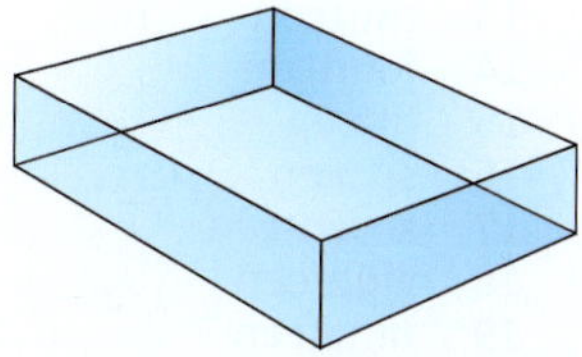
cuboid

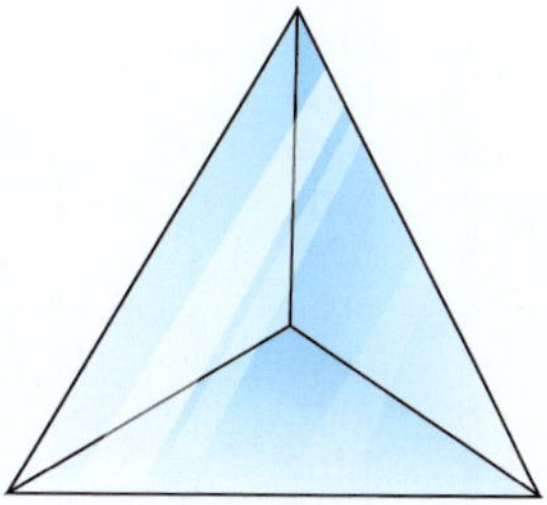
regular tetrahedron
or triangular pyramid

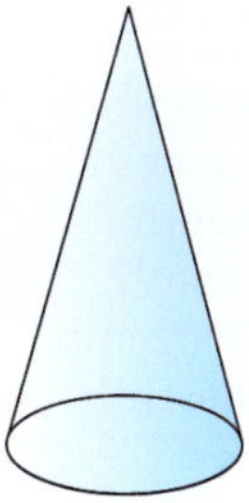
cone

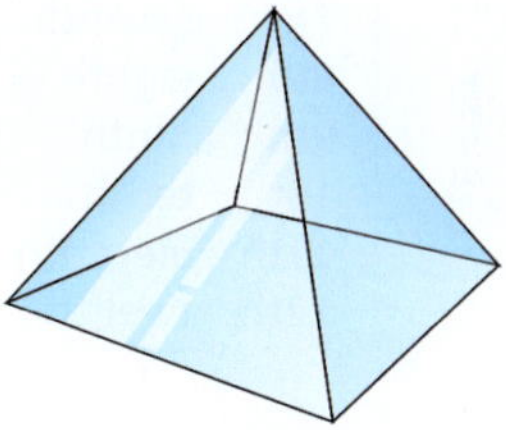
square pyramid

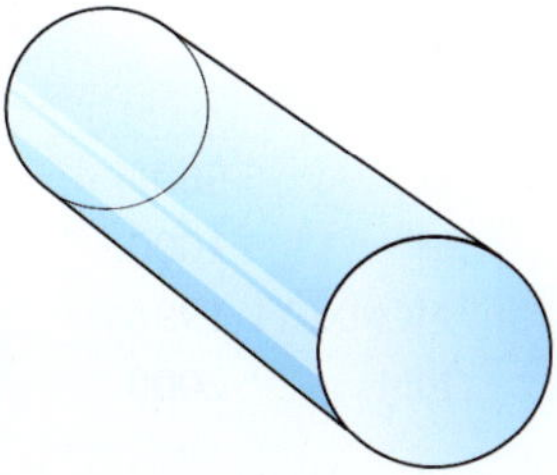
cylinder

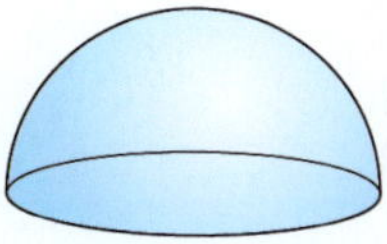
hemisphere

sphere

Angles

obtuse angle

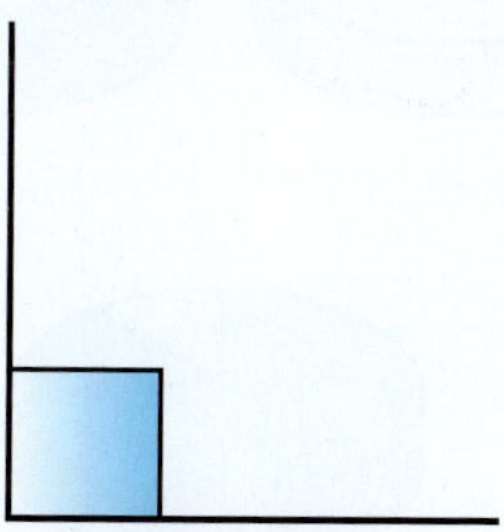
right angle (90°)

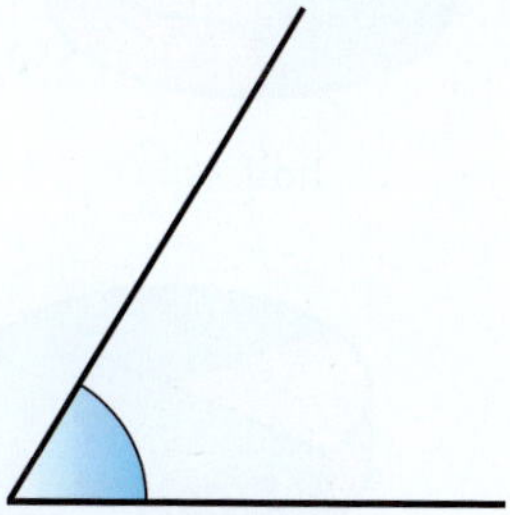
acute angle

Numbers and fractions

Numbers

1	one	12	twelve	50	fifty
2	two	13	thirteen	60	sixty
3	three	14	fourteen	70	seventy
4	four	15	fifteen	80	eighty
5	five	16	sixteen	90	ninety
6	six	17	seventeen	100	one hundred
7	seven	18	eighteen	1000	one thousand
8	eight	19	nineteen	10 000	ten thousand
9	nine	20	twenty	1 000 000	one million
10	ten	30	thirty	10 000 000	ten million
11	eleven	40	forty		

1st	first	7th	seventh	13th	thirteenth	19th	nineteenth
2nd	second	8th	eighth	14th	fourteenth	20th	twentieth
3rd	third	9th	ninth	15th	fifteenth	21st	twenty-first
4th	fourth	10th	tenth	16th	sixteenth	22nd	twenty-second
5th	fifth	11th	eleventh	17th	seventeenth		
6th	sixth	12th	twelfth	18th	eighteenth		

Roman numerals

I	1	V	5	IX	9	D	500
II	2	VI	6	X	10	M	1000
III	3	VII	7	L	50	MCMXCVI	1996
IV	4	VIII	8	C	100	MM	2000

Fractions

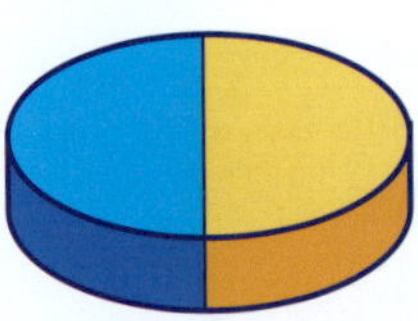

half ½

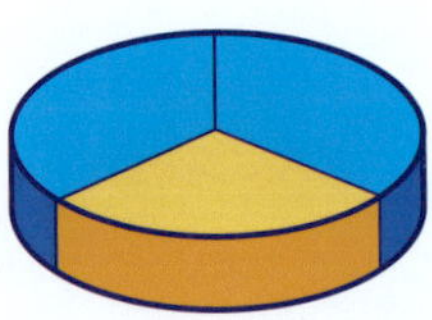

third ⅓

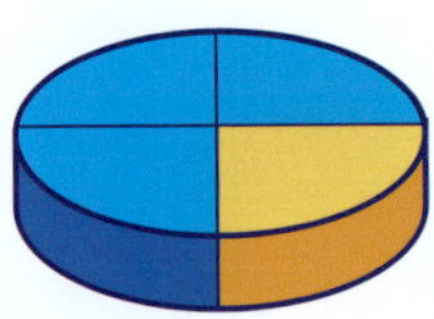

quarter ¼

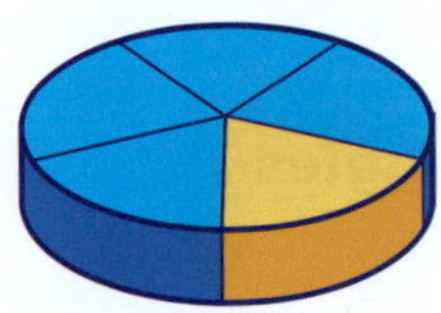

fifth ⅕

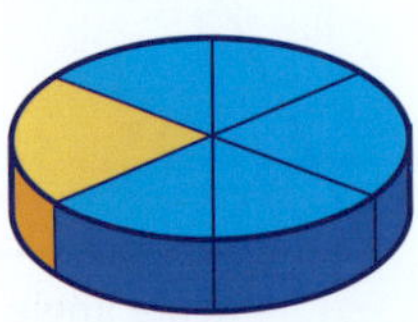

sixth ⅙

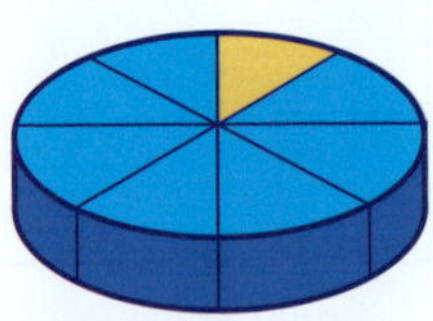

eighth ⅛

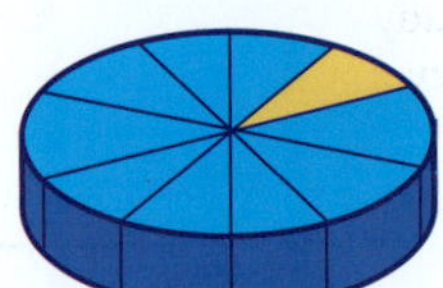

tenth ⅒

Telling the time

a.m.
p.m.
o'clock

half past
quarter past
quarter to

watch
timer
clock

analogue
digital

eleven fifty-five

five to twelve

Measuring time
second
minute
hour
day
week
fortnight
month
year
leap year
decade
century
millennium

Times of day
dawn
sunrise
morning
midday
noon
afternoon
dusk
twilight
sunset
evening
night
midnight

breakfast time
breaktime
playtime
lunchtime
dinnertime
suppertime
bedtime

When/how often?
never
once
twice
rarely
occasionally
from time to time
sometimes
often
soon
frequently
usually
always

Days
Monday
Tuesday
Wednesday
Thursday
Friday
Saturday
Sunday

Months
January
February
March
April
May
June
July
August
September
October
November
December

Seasons
spring
summer
autumn
winter

More time words
yesterday
today
tomorrow

calendar
date
weekend
holiday
birthday
term

Parts of speech

Noun

A **noun** is a person, place, thing, or idea. There are different types of noun.

A noun can be **singular**, which means one ...

book

... or **plural**, which means more than one.

books

Common nouns name people, places, things, or ideas in general. For example, "boy", "dog", "school", "computer", and "happiness" are common nouns.

Proper nouns are the names of particular people, places, or things. They start with a capital letter. For example, "Ben", "France", and "Buckingham Palace" are proper nouns.

Collective nouns

A **collective noun** names a group of things.

a **clutch** of eggs
a **flock** of sheep
a **pack** of wolves
a **litter** of puppies
a **herd** of cows
a **swarm** of bees
a **school** of dolphins

a **shoal** of fish

a **bunch** of grapes

a **pride** of lions

Pronoun

A **pronoun** is used to replace a noun.

I you he, she, it we they	me you him, her, it us them	mine yours his, hers, its ours theirs	myself yourself, yourselves himself, herself, itself ourselves themselves

Personal pronouns are used for a person or thing that has already been named, for example "me", "her", "you", "it". *John jumped for the ball. He caught it!*

Possessive pronouns show that a noun belongs to a person or thing that has already been named, for example, "mine", "theirs", "his", "ours". *That pencil isn't his. It's mine.*

Adjective

An **adjective** describes a noun. For example, "tall", "happy", and "lucky" are all adjectives.

Some adjectives have a **comparative** and a **superlative** form. In most cases, these forms are made by adding **-er** or **-est** to the adjective.

adjective	comparative (more)	superlative (most)
tall	taller	tallest
hot	hotter	hottest
good	better	best
lucky	luckier	luckiest

Verb

A **verb** is an action word. It tells you what people and things do. For example, "sleep", "think", and "play" are all verbs.

Verbs have different forms called **tenses**. A tense shows whether you are talking about the past, present, or future.

past	present	future
I played	*I play* *I am playing*	*I will play*

Adverb

An **adverb** tells you more about a verb. For example, "shyly", "brightly", and "happily" are all adverbs. Many adverbs end in the suffix **-ly**.

How did Mary and Brian talk?
They talked loudly.

Other adverbs tell you where, when, or how often something happens.

where: outside, inside, here, there
when: today, soon, immediately
how often: never, frequently, often, always

Prepositions

Prepositions link two nouns or pronouns, to show how they are connected to each other.

- Prepositions may tell you the **place** of something in relation to another thing:

  She found the book ***on*** *the table.*
  We saw the ball ***beneath*** *the bush.*

- Prepositions may indicate **movement**:

  The dog ran ***towards*** *us.*
  They walked ***along*** *the beach.*

- Prepositions may indicate **time**:

  I got to stay up ***until*** *ten o'clock.*
  We went on holiday ***for*** *a week.*

through

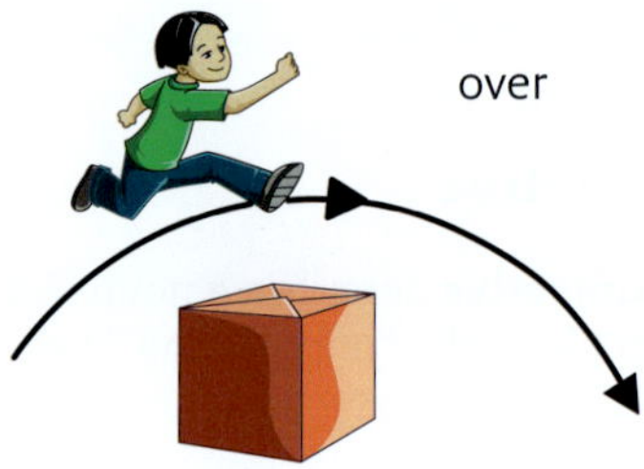

over

down up

about

amid

at

for

against

like

around

off on

beneath

by

from

beyond

behind

beside

Prepositions

inside

across

above below

of

near

towards

to

in

with

upon

till

until

since

under

between

Prefixes

A **prefix** is a group of letters added to the beginning of a word. It changes or adds to the meaning of the word: **tele**scope, **mis**understand, **semi**circle.

Prefix	Meaning	Example
anti-	opposite of, against	anticlockwise
arch-	chief	archbishop
auto-	self	autobiography
co-	together	cooperate
com-	together	compare
contra-	against	contradict
de-	take away	defrost
dis-	opposite of	disappear
em-	in	embark
ex-	former	ex-partner
extra-	more	extraordinary
fore-	before, in front of	forecast
il-, im-, in-, ir-	not	illegal, impossible, inaccurate, irrational
inter-	between	international
micro-	very small	microscope
mid-	middle	midday
mini-	smaller	minibus
mis-	wrong	misspell
mono-	one	monologue
multi-	many	multitude
non-	not	nonfiction
over-	too much	overgrown
poly-	many	polygon
post-	after	post-war
pre-	before	prehistoric
pro-	supporting	pro-European
re-	again	reappear
semi-	half	semicircle
sub-	below	submarine
super-	over, more than	supersonic
tele-	at a distance	telephone
trans-	across	transport
ultra-	beyond	ultraviolet
un-	not	unkind
under-	under, not enough	underestimate

Suffixes

A **suffix** is a letter or group of letters added to the end of a word. It can change the tense of a verb from present to past, as in *talk* to *talked*.

Suffixes can also:

- change nouns into other nouns: child – child**hood**; friend – friend**ship**; art – art**ist**.
- change nouns into verbs: length – length**en**; fright – fright**en**.
- change nouns or verbs into adjectives: drink – drink**able**; use – use**ful**; harm – harm**less**.
- change adjectives into adverbs: slow – slow**ly**; happy – happi**ly**; quick – quick**ly**.
- change verbs or adjectives into nouns: happy – happi**ness**; enjoy – enjoy**ment**; invite – invit**ation**.
- change nouns to be feminine: lion – lion**ess**; prince – princ**ess**.
- change a noun to a diminutive (a word that shows something is small): kitchen – kitchen**ette**; pig – pig**let**.

Suffix	Meaning	Example
-able, -ible, -uble	able to be	enjoyable, edible, soluble
-ant, -ent	a doer	attendant, resident
-dom	condition, rank, territory	freedom, earldom, kingdom
-ee	one who is	employee
-er	a doer	farmer, miner, teacher
-er	more	higher, lower
-ess	used to make the feminine	goddess, princess
-est	most	hardest, lightest
-ful	full of	truthful
-hood	state of	childhood
-ic	belonging to	prehistoric
-ish	like	boyish
-ism	belief	Judaism, Buddhism
-ist	a doer	artist
-itis	inflammation of	appendicitis
-ize, ise	used to make verbs	realize, advertise
-less	free from	thoughtless, smokeless
-let	small	booklet, piglet
-ly	used to make adverbs	hotly, sleepily
-ment	used to make nouns	pavement
-ness	state of being	kindness
-oid	like	cuboid
-ology	study of	biology
-or	a doer	sailor, actor
-ous	used to make adjectives	dangerous
-ship	state of being	friendship
-some	tending to	tiresome
-ty	showing condition	cruelty
-wards	in a direction	southwards

Where words come from

Days of the week

Most of the days of the week were named by the Saxons. The Saxons came from Denmark and Germany to live in Britain over 1500 years ago.

Sunday is named after the **sun**.

Monday is named after the **moon**.

Tuesday is named after **Tiu**, the Saxon god of war and of the sky.

Wednesday is named after **Woden**, leader of the Viking gods.

Thursday is named after **Thor**, the Saxon god of thunder and lightning.

Friday is named after **Frigga**. She was the goddess of marriage, and sat on a throne beside her husband, Woden.

Saturday is named after **Saturn**, the Roman god of farmers and farming.

Months of the year

The months of the year were given their names by the Romans.

January is named after **Janus**, the Roman god of doorways and beginnings.

February is named after **Februa**, a Roman festival when people were purified.

March is named after **Mars**, the Roman god of war.

April's name comes from the Latin word **aperire**, meaning "to open". Spring is when the year "opens".

May is named after **Maia**, a Roman goddess connected with growth.

June is named after the Roman goddess **Juno**, queen of the gods.

July was named after **Julius Caesar**, army general and ruler of Ancient Rome.

August was named after the Roman emperor **Augustus**.

September comes from the Latin word **septem**, meaning "seven". The Roman year used to begin in March, so September was their seventh month.

October comes from the Latin word **octo**, meaning "eight". October was once the eighth month.

November comes from the Latin word **novem**, meaning "nine". November was once the ninth month.

December comes from the Latin word **decem**, meaning "ten". December was once the tenth month.

Words from other languages

Many words we use today come from other languages. Here are some examples.

Latin: adolescent, adverb, benefit, calculate, castle, evaporate, human, industry, literature, manual, observe, square, video.

Greek: acrobat, autograph, colossal, history, hour, ozone, pathetic, telephone.

French: banquet, café, chef, oboe, tapestry, torch, vinegar.

Old English: barn, beetle, bless, cluster, daisy, Easter, ooze, sibling, Thursday, welcome.

Arabic: genie, kebab, sofa, syrup.

Hindi: bungalow, juggernaut, jungle, thug, yoga.

Spanish: alligator, cockroach, crusade, grenade.

Italian: ballet, brave, macaroni, pasta, picturesque, profile, quarantine, spaghetti, squadron, zany.

Here are a few more words from other languages, with an explanation of how they got their names! Look up the words in the dictionary, and then read the explanations below.

appendix
This word comes from the Latin for "the part that hangs". Your appendix hangs at the end of your large intestine. The appendices of this book come at the end.

biscuit
The old French word for twice is *bis*, and the old French for cooked is *cuit*. Put them together and you get biscuit, which meant "cooked twice". Food was cooked like this to make it crisp.

essay
The French word *essayer* means "to try". When someone writes an essay, they are trying to put their ideas down in writing.

hazard
The Arabic word *az-zahr* means "the dice", and the word *hazard* was once used to mean all games played with dice. It came to have a different meaning because games of dice were associated with the dangers of gambling and losing money.

ketchup
Ke-tsiap was a sauce originally invented by the Chinese. It was made of fish and spices. Over time, people added tomatoes and changed the recipe to the sauce that we know today.

Tips for tricky words

Sometimes thinking of a silly phrase or sentence can help you remember how to spell tricky words. Here are some examples:

beautiful
Big elephants are useful.

qu words (q is always followed by u)
The Queen always carries an umbrella.

See how many of these you can remember. Then see if you can think up some of your own!

all right
It's either all right or all wrong.

believe
Believe has a lie in it.

piece
Have a piece of pie.

February
You say "br" in February because it's cold.

receive
R-e-c-e is very easy.

different
One thing differs from another.

hear
You hear with your ear.

separate
Separate has a rat in it.

library
Look into books. Reach and read yours.

friend
I'm seeing my friend on Friday, which comes at the end of the week.

necessary
Necessary has one collar and two socks (one **c** and two **s**'s!).

there
There is a place like here.

weather
We eat in all kinds of weather.

whose
Whose hose is that?

because
Ben eats cake and uses six eggs.

Sound it out!

Another good way to remember the spelling of some words is to sound out their different parts. Try these!

answer
ans-wer

cupboard
cup-board

Wednesday
Wed-nes-day

together
to-get-her

Look, say, cover, write, check!

- **Look** at the word in the dictionary and point to it.
- **Say** the word out loud, and then spell it out.
- **Cover** the word up, remembering what it looks like.
- **Write** the word down on a piece of paper and say it out loud again.
- **Check** your spelling against the dictionary.
- If you got it wrong, cover the page again and **try again!**

Tricky words to learn

The words on this list are tricky, so learn all of them to be a top speller!

address
among
autumn
awful
balloon

beginning
breakfast
build
careful

certain
course
definite
does
everybody
exciting
exercise
guess
interest
necessary
people
really
remember

rhyme
scissors

sentence
straight
through
trouble
until
usually
whole

Punctuation

ABC	A **capital letter** is used at the beginning of a sentence and for proper nouns.	*My brother Jim lives in New Zealand.*
.	You put a **full stop** at the end of a sentence.	*This is a sentence.*
?	You put a **question mark** at the end of a question.	*Can you come to my party?*
,	You use a **comma** to separate parts of a sentence or items on a list.	*She brought sandwiches, crisps, apples, and juice to the picnic.*
!	You use an **exclamation mark** at the end of a sentence to show a strong feeling.	*Wow!*
'	An **apostrophe** is used in contractions and to show belonging.	*I didn't mean to break my brother's toy.*
" " **' '**	**Speech marks** show where speech begins and ends.	*"I like your hair," she said.*
-	You use a **hyphen** to join together words or parts of words.	*I'm left-handed.*
( )	**Brackets** are used to show that something is not part of the main text.	*My cousin (the one from America) is coming to stay.*
—	A **dash** can be used instead of brackets, or to show a change of subject.	*My best friend — besides you — is George.*
:	You can use a **colon** for several things, for example in front of a list.	*You will need the following: strong walking boots, a map, and a compass.*
;	A **semicolon** is used to separate different parts of a sentence or list, or to show a pause.	*The pizza choices are: cheese; onions, peppers, and mushrooms; ham and pineapple; pepperoni; or sausage.*

The Earth and Space

The Solar System

Earth, our planet, is one of eight planets that travel around the Sun. These planets make up the Solar System. The path that a planet follows around the Sun is called its orbit, and the Sun's gravity keeps the planets in their orbits. The planets are all at different distances from the Sun and take different lengths of time to orbit it.

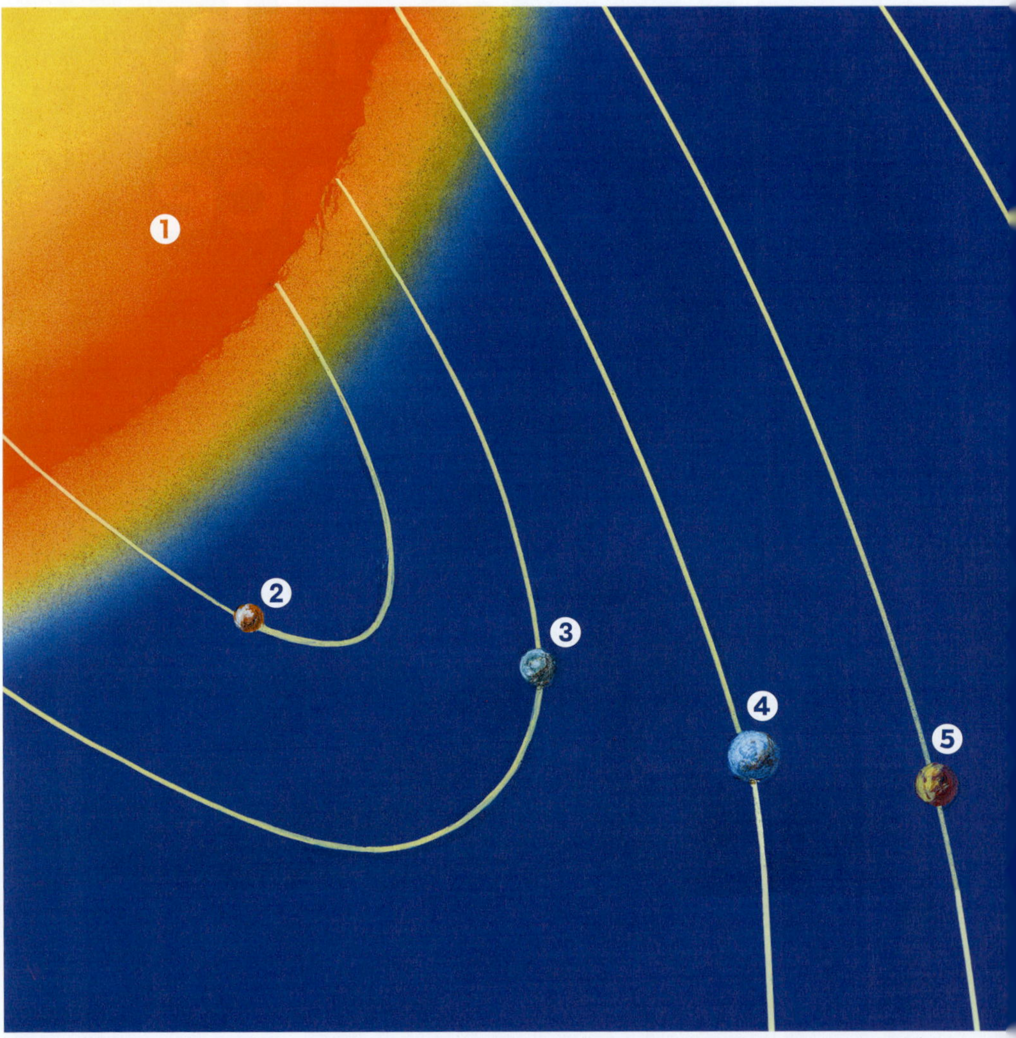

❶ The **Sun** is the fiery centre of our Solar System.

❷ **Mercury** is a small, hot, rocky planet with a very thin atmosphere. It takes 88 days to orbit the Sun.

❸ **Venus** is slightly smaller than the Earth, and is extremely hot and covered in thick clouds of acid. It takes 225 days to orbit the Sun.

❺ **Mars** is a rocky planet, sometimes called the Red Planet because it is covered in iron oxide dust. It takes 687 days to orbit the Sun.

❻ **Jupiter** is the largest of the planets. It is a huge ball of gases that takes 12 years to orbit the Sun.

❼ **Saturn** is an enormous, bright planet surrounded by rings made up of small pieces of ice. It takes nearly 30 years to orbit the Sun.

❽ **Uranus** is huge ball of gas covered in blue-green clouds. It has rings around it that may be made of pieces of ice. It takes 84 years to orbit the Sun.

❾ **Neptune** is a large, bluish ball of gas. It has a ring system, and is orbited by at least thirteen moons. It takes 165 years to orbit the Sun.

❹ **Earth** has breathable air in its atmosphere, temperatures that are not too extreme, and plenty of water, all of which mean that we can live here. It takes just over 365 days (one year) to orbit the Sun.

The Earth

Earth is the only planet in the Universe known to support life! It is a living planet, with plently of water, trees, plants, and breathable air, protected by its atmosphere. It is the third planet from the Sun and is the largest of the four rocky inner planets. Oceans, at least 4 kilometres deep, cover nearly 70 per cent of the Earth's surface. It has one moon, which is the only other place to be visited by people from Earth. It takes the Earth 365 days and 6 hours (one year) to orbit the Sun.

A satellite view of the Earth

A cross-section of the Earth

The Earth was formed around 4600 million years ago. In the beginning it was not solid, but molten. Over time the outside has cooled to form a hard, rock **crust**.

Beneath the crust is another layer of rock called the **mantle**. The mantle is very hot but does not melt completely because of great pressure.

At the centre of the Earth is the **core**. The **outer core** is liquid, but it is thought that the **inner core** is solid.

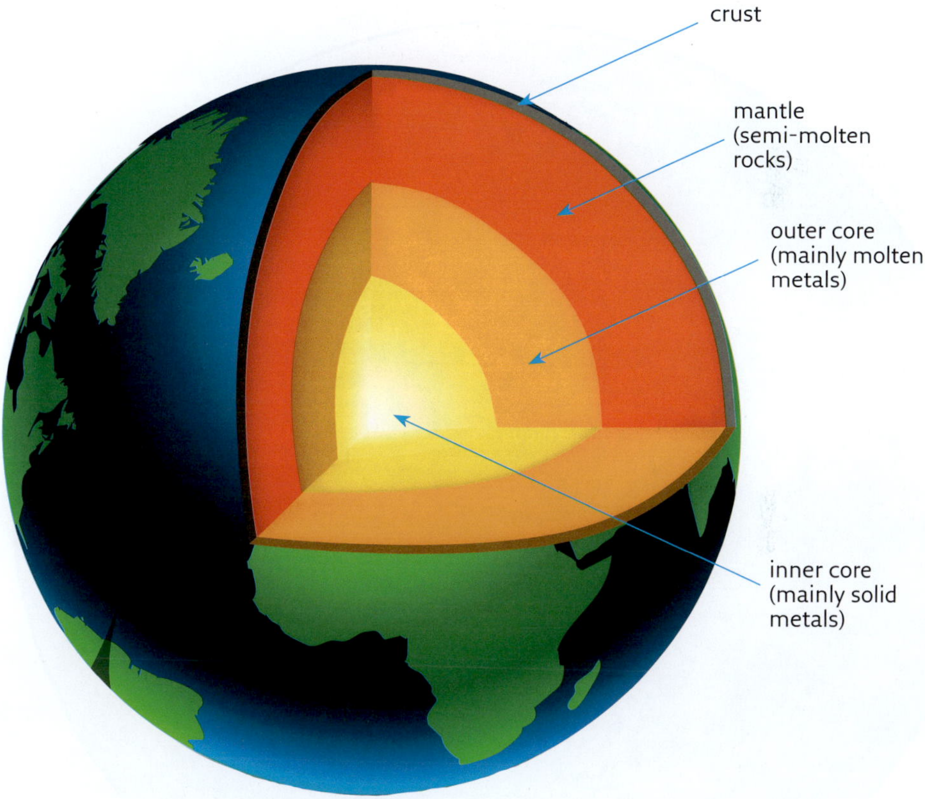

The Moon

The Moon is Earth's only natural satellite. It is the second brightest object in the sky after the Sun and is thought to have formed from the debris when a planet-sized object collided with Earth billions of years ago. It is the only object, other than Earth, that human beings have set foot on. Although the Moon's appearance changes because of its phases, you are only ever able to see one side of it, as it always faces Earth.

There are a lot of dark patches on the Moon, which are flat areas of old lava flows which look like seas. The surface is very mountainous and there are peaks nearly as high as Mount Everest (the highest mountain on Earth). The surface also has a lot of craters, such as Plato, Copernicus, and Tycho.

Phases of the Moon

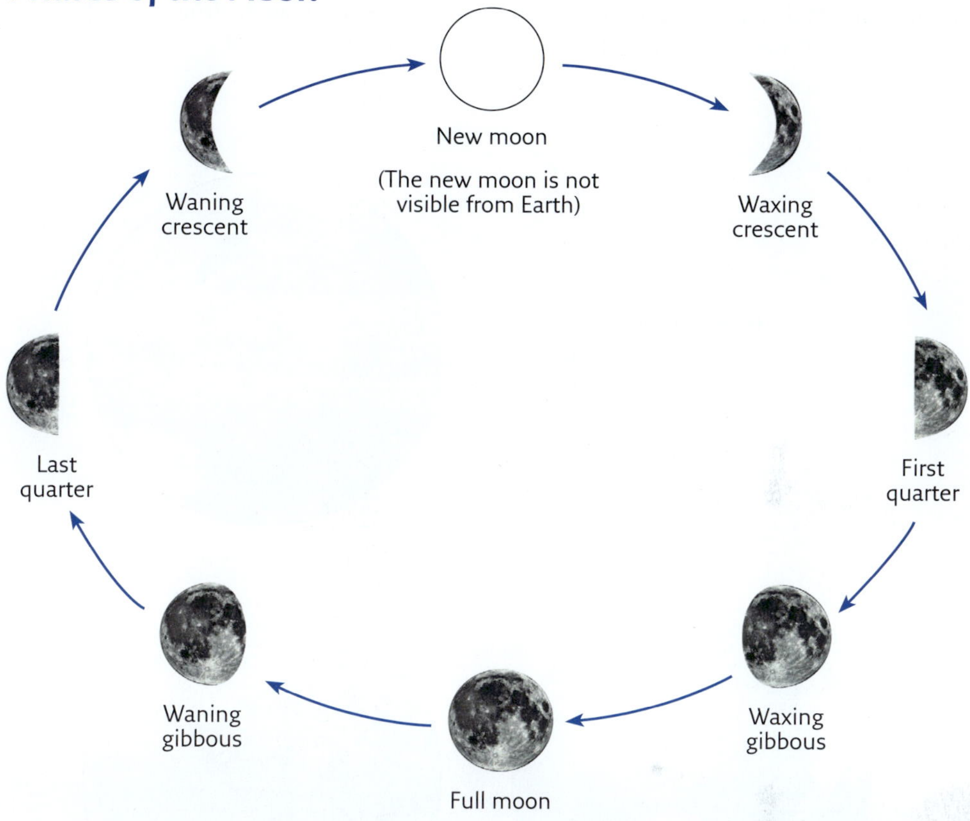

What is an eclipse?

A lunar eclipse occurs when the Earth passes between the Sun and the Moon.

A solar eclipse occurs when the Moon passes between the Sun and the Earth.

Continents

These globes show the seven continents: North America, South America, Antarctica, Europe, Asia, Africa, and Oceania. Globes are the only way to show the true size and shape of the continents. However, flat maps are often more convenient.

North America lies between the Atlantic and Pacific Oceans.

Antarctica encircles the South Pole.

South America stretches south towards the South Pole.

Europe is one of the smallest continents.

Asia is the largest continent.

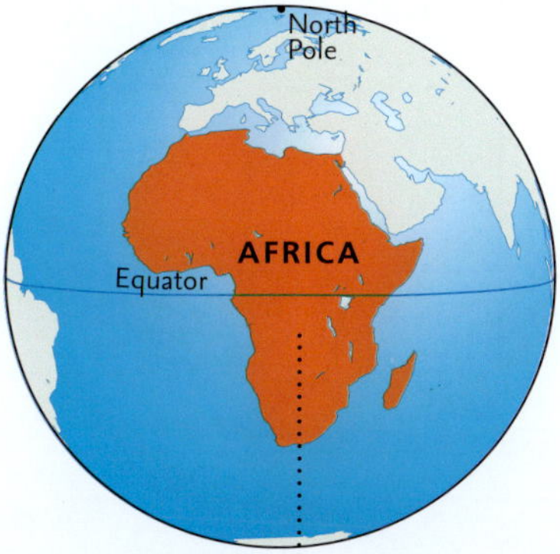

Africa straddles the Equator.

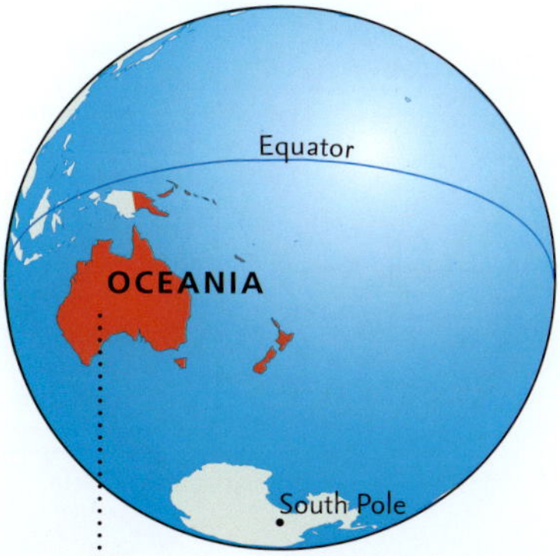

Oceania is made up of Australia, New Zealand, and many small islands.

Mountains, rivers, and oceans

Highest mountains

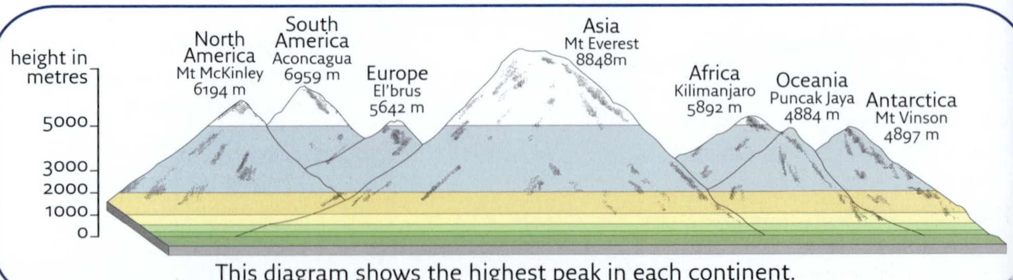

This diagram shows the highest peak in each continent.

Longest rivers

Africa	Nile - 6695 km
S America	Amazon - 6516 km
Asia	Chang Jiang - 6380 km
N America	Mississippi-Missouri - 5969 km
Europe	Volga - 3688 km
Oceania	Murray-Darling - 3672 km

The Nile is the world's longest river. The Amazon is slightly shorter but carries much more water as it flows through the rainforest.

The Earth's surface

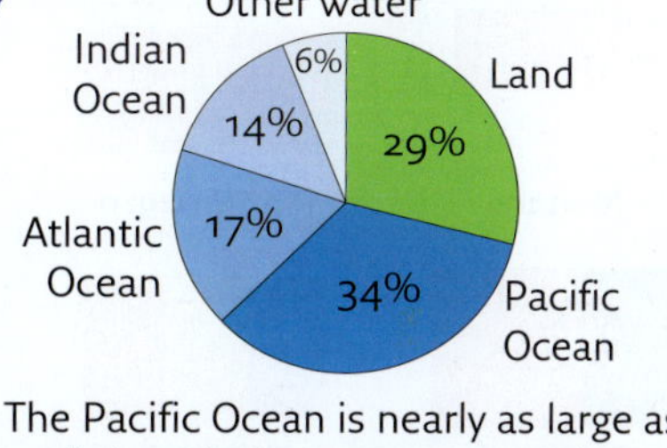

The Pacific Ocean is nearly as large as all the other oceans put together.

Flags of the world

Here is a selection of flags from around the world:

EUROPE

Albania

Andorra

Armenia

Austria

Azerbaijan

Belarus

Belgium

Bosnia and Herzegovina

Bulgaria

Croatia

Cyprus

Czech Republic

Denmark

Estonia

Finland

France

Georgia

Germany

Greece

Hungary

Iceland

Ireland

Italy

Latvia

Liechtenstein

Lithuania

Luxembourg

Macedonia

Malta

Moldova

Monaco

Montenegro

Netherlands

Norway

Poland

Portugal

Romania

Russia

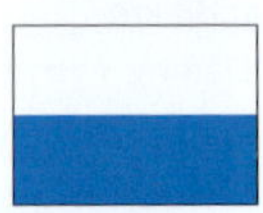
San Marino

Serbia

Slovakia | Slovenia | Spain | Sweden | Switzerland

Ukraine | United Kingdom | Vatican City

AFRICA

Algeria | Angola | Benin | Botswana | Burkina Faso

Burundi | Cameroon | Cape Verde | Central African Rep. | Chad

Comoros | Congo | Congo, Dem. Rep. of | Côte d'Ivoire | Djibouti

Egypt | Equatorial Guinea | Eritrea | Ethiopia | Gabon

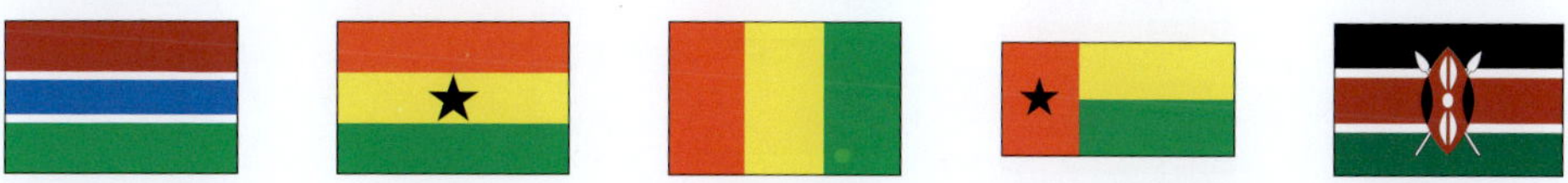

The Gambia | Ghana | Guinea | Guinea-Bissau | Kenya

Lesotho | Liberia | Libya | Madagascar | Malawi

Mali | Mauritania | Mauritius | Morocco | Mozambique

Flags of the world

Namibia

Niger

Nigeria

Rwanda

São Tomé and Príncipe

Senegal

Seychelles

Sierra Leone

Somalia

South Africa

South Sudan

Sudan

Swaziland

Tanzania

Togo

Tunisia

Uganda

Zambia

Zimbabwe

ASIA

Afghanistan

Bahrain

Bangladesh

Bhutan

Brunei

Cambodia

China

East Timor

India

Indonesia

Iran

Iraq

Israel

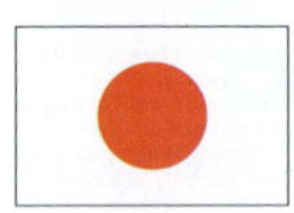
Japan

Jordan

Kazakhstan

Kuwait

Kyrgyzstan

Laos

Lebanon

Malaysia | Maldives | Mongolia | Myanmar | Nepal

North Korea | Oman | Pakistan | Philippines | Qatar

Saudi Arabia | Singapore | South Korea | Sri Lanka | Syria

Taiwan | Tajikistan | Thailand | Turkey | Turkmenistan

United Arab Emirates | Uzbekistan | Vietnam | Yemen

NORTH AMERICA

Antigua and Barbuda | Bahamas | Barbados | Belize | Canada

Costa Rica | Cuba | Dominica | Dominican Republic | El Salvador

Grenada | Guatemala | Haiti | Honduras | Jamaica

Flags of the world

Mexico

Nicaragua

Panama

St Kitts and Nevis

St Lucia

St Vincent and the Grenadines

Trinidad and Tobago

United States of America

SOUTH AMERICA

Argentina

Bolivia

Brazil

Chile

Colombia

Ecuador

Guyana

Paraguay

Peru

Suriname

Uruguay

Venezuela

OCEANIA

Australia

Fiji

Kiribati

Marshall Islands

Micronesia, Fed. States of

Nauru

New Zealand

Palau

Papua New Guinea

Samoa

Solomon Islands

Tonga

Tuvalu

Vanuatu

Picture credits

Photo credits

P8 © clivewa*, P18 © Vitalii Hulai* (newt), P18 © picturepartners* (frog), P20 © Hurst Photo*, P23 © Andreas Zerndl*, P28 © JIANG HONGYAN*, P35 © Dmitry Skutin*, P38 © padu_foto*, P45 © dgcampillo*, P46 © trusjom*, P48 © Lisa S.*, P51 © Oliver Wilde*, P55 © Lightspring*, P57 © Dan Breckwoldt*, P65 © Seregam*, P67 © Pozezan*, P71 © Hurst Photo*, P74 © mama_mia*, P88 © Andaman*, P92 © Drew Rawcliffe*, P95 © Marcos Mesa Sam Wordley*, P100 © SurangaSL*, P106 © Josef Hanus*, P108 © CraigBurrows*, P120 © Venus Angel* (double bass), © vnlit* (dragonfly), P125 © Bas Meelker* (dyke), P126 © Juergen Faelchle*, P130 © Eric Isselee*, P135 © andrea crisante*, P146 © ladyphoto*, P154 © KIM NGUYEN* (both photos), P158 © Sombra*, P161 © Karramba Production*, P163 © Alex Mit*, P167 © Denis Kichatof*, P169 © Blue Marble: Next Generation. NASA's Earth Observatory, P171 © JLR Photography*, P177 © Lebedinski Vladislav*, P190 © Africa Studio*, P193 © Harvepino*, P195 © Denis Burdin*, P205 © Eric Isselee*, P217 © Kbiros*, P218 © takayuki*, P220 © Andy Lidstone*, P221 © howamo*, P226 © Berents*, P241 © Anan Kaewkhammul*, P245 © MAHATHIR MOHD YASIN*, P249 © Mehmet Cetin*, P256 © defpicture*, P259 © Jose Ignacio Soto* (mummy), P265 © Vishnevskiy Vasily*, P270 © Matthias G. Ziegler*, P281 © Nid santana*, P283 © Alexey U*, P300 © de2marco*, P304 © kavram*, P309 © Mmaxer*, P317 © WitR*, P318 © muratart*, P323 © fivespots*, P327 © BlueOrange Studio*, P329 © Pal Teravagimov*, P334 © Dan Schreiber*, P340 © bom*, P346 © puchan*, P353 © Nattika*, P360 © Finomax*, P362 © natrot*, P367 © Sashkin*, P376 © Sirichai Puangsuwan*, P382 © Santi Rodriguez*, P391 © xavier gallego morell*, P393 © Brovkina*, P395 © EpicStockMedia*, P402 © jorisvo*, P408 © Richard Griffin*, P412 © Michiel de Wit*, P416 © Sergey Dzyuba*, P422 © holbox*, P425 © Jaromir Chalabala*, P431 © ChrisVanLennepPhoto*, P435 © Bildagentur Zoonar GmbH*, P440 © InnaFelker*, P441 © Carlos Romero*, P446 © JeniFoto*, P451 © ILYA AKINSHIN*, P459 © funkypoodle* (left), © Pressmaster* (right), P460 © LanKS* (book), © rzstudio* (books), © EM Arts* (grapes), © Rich Carey* (fish), © EastVillage Images* (lions), P467 © Garsya*, P469 © Viet Gallery* (balloons), P474 © NASA, P476 © Lick Observatory, P477 © Lick Observatory (Moon), © Primo_Cigler* (lunar eclipse), © Vladimir Wrangel* (solar eclipse)

Artwork credits

P187 © artform*, P268 © gst*, P398 © velirina*, P475 © Webspark*

Artwork on pages 21, 25, 30, 34, 37, 60, 68, 80, 81, 86, 97, 99, 111, 125, 141, 173, 184, 209, 212, 232, 236, 259 (muscle), 271, 278, 290, 293, 321, 337, 338, 366, 378, 387, 406, 419, 420, 433, 456, and 457 appeared in the first edition of the *Collins Primary Illustrated Dictionary*. The illustrators for the first edition were Tim Archbold, Cy Baker, Simone Boni, Maggie Brand, Tamsin Cook, Joanne Cowne, Luigi Crittone, William Donohoe, Richard Draper, Luigi Gallante, Jeremy Gower, Nick Harris, Christian Hook, Felicity House, Hans Jenssen, Sharon MacCausland, John Mack, Kevin Maddison, Tony Morris, Pat Murray, Chris Orr Associates, Malcolm Porter, Sebastian Quigley, Steve Roberts, Mike Saunders, Peter Scott, Siena Artworks, Hayley Simmons, Gill Thomblin, Phil Weare, Steve Weston, Sarah Wimperis, Ann Winterbotham, and Sue Woollatt.

Artwork on pages 196, 229, 264, 289, and 326 Emily Skinner

Cover artwork and artwork on pages 11, 14, 41, 52, 56, 62, 69, 78, 112, 116, 119, 123, 133, 136, 148, 150, 162, 170, 180, 189, 198, 203, 215, 225, 235, 237, 248, 251, 254, 269, 272, 275, 280, 287, 294, 296, 312, 333, 342, 351, 357, 361, 370, 385, 400, 404, 414, 423, 429, 438, 444, 452, 453, 458, 462, 463, 466, 468, and 469 by Q2A Media Services Private Limited

*from Shutterstock.com

Panto's for Life, not just for Christmas

ANDY FORD

www.andyfordcomedian.com

ISBN: 978-1-7394104-1-4

Andelle books

DEDICATION

I dedicate this book to my beloved Mother Irene Bertha Alice Mogford who passed away in 2023 and my treasured Father in Law Mike whom Michelle and I lost in 2021, both forever in our thoughts.

FORWARD

The Dictionary says....

Forward: in the direction that one is facing or travelling; towards the front.

Forward: onward so as to make progress.

As I look back on my life I choose to remember how I continued to look forward at any given time, whether to plan my next career or life move or to bounce back from challenges and seek to somehow improve my prospects and opportunities in the future. The memories are unavoidably from the past but the motivation was and is undoubtedly.... always to continue my forward trajectory.

Andrew Mogford

CONTENTS

THE WEST COUNTRY COMEDY STAR AND PANTOMIME LEGEND ANDY FORD TELLS THE STORY OF HIS LIFE

ANDREW FORD

tonight Matthew I'm gonna
be Donny Osmond!!

CHAPTER 1

'This blessed plot, this earth, this realm, this Whipton!'

Knee high to a grasshopper

Hello there.... Welcome to the book of my life.... Flipping heck, let me say that again but a little bit slower... Welcome... to... the... Book... of... my... life!! Wow how good does that sound? I have always wanted to do this, if only to see if it all looks more interesting in print! Now, everything you read in this book is written by me, well typed by me, I had to go for the modern technology thing after sadly snapping my last remaining Quill. I have to thank Hayden for helping to get me started by quizzing me about my career, cheers bud I'm grateful as it helped to get the memory juices flowing.

It probably sounds superfluous to say, but I've loved it all, the successes, the challenges, the weird stuff and everything in between. I just like being me the person who is always doing stuff and really doesn't have an off switch. So you are all very welcome to feel sorry for my wonderful Wife Michelle who has to live with this 24/7, what a trouper! I know it all sounds a bit Reggie Perrin (google it, it's a comedy series from the past starring Leonard Rossiter) 'but I didn't get where I am today', without the love of a

lot of special people and you'll probably hear their names a few times throughout this masterpiece. Now here's the problem with me putting all this stuff down for posterity, my mind leaps all over the place and when I talk about one thing, something else tends to jump in and take my train of thought elsewhere, whether it's relevant or not. Dear readers I will do my best to be chronological with all this, but I wouldn't hold your breath if I were you, however, if you're up for a bit of flip-flopping backwards and forwards through the decades then please join me on this epic journey!

I am very proud to say that my career has lasted over 50 years, taken me all around the world and given me the chance to work along side some fantastic World Famous Stars of Stage and Screen particularly in the field of Pantomime, my absolutely favourite genre, of which there is loads more later in this book..... no jumping to that bit yet though, cause if you're gonna read my book you gotta go through it all from the beginning... sorry, but them's the rules. Right, enough waffling boy let's get down to the nitty gritty!

Right then, here we go..... Andrew Ernest Mogford was born in Exeter on the 23rd of February in 1957

to Rene and Ern Mogford. Obviously everything in those days was in Black and White so my naturally colourful personality took a while to break through. Young Andrew lived with his Mum, Dad and sister Sandra in a council flat in Lloyds Crescent in Whipton, Exeter, not very far from the centre of the village where there was an awesome chip shop.

Me and my sister Sandra and I
Can still get into those trousers btw!

The flat must have been too small for the growing Mogford family, so after a while the council moved them into a Terraced council house in Hillyfield Road, literally just around the corner from their flat. That was actually the last move they ever made, and that house became (and to this day still is) the backdrop to all the Mogford's *goings on* over the years, that building has seen everything! After a while in the new home my parents were blessed with another child, Helen was born in February of 1961 in the room next to my bedroom (and I'm not proud of this by the way), but when my Dad woke me up one night to see my new born sister I was slightly less than impressed.

Me and my sisters, I think I'm the one in the middle...
Yep pretty sure!

Nothing to do with Helen, I adore my younger sibling, it's just that I like my kip and being woken up in the middle of the night to be introduced to a screaming baby at close quarters was probably not at the top of my to do list at the age of 4... sorry Helen, love you x.

Well, as far back as I can remember, I've always wanted to perform, 'On that bombshell!' I hear you cry. It probably all started at Whipton Barton Infants where on my first day my mum took me to school and unfortunately it was all predictably dramatic, and one might even say that I was a bit of a diva, I suppose. My mother walked me there on my first day but my little brain didn't realise that after securing my safe arrival she would leave me... I sobbed like a baby apparently, and it must have been so annoying that the teacher made me sit in the corner of the classroom all by myself and drink my milk, outrageous I know but yes Ladies and Gents, that's the first impression I made on everyone. Andrew Mogford is in the room!

I must have recovered from the trauma pretty quickly though because when we kids were playing during the lunch time in our school playground and it started to rain... (Peter Kay's, 'it's spitting', comes

to mind) the dinner ladies would rush us all into the hall and put me on the stage to entertain all the other children. I was four, maybe five, I'm not sure, but the thing is there must have been a reason for them to put me onto that stage. Whether I'd been messing around and making my friends laugh before, I don't know, but somehow I managed to occupy the interest of all my young short attention span contemporaries in the Infant School from the stage. One of the things I used to do was sing a version of Tommy Steele's *Little White Bull* which was really popular at the time, But I've also got this cloudy memory of just running around and stuff to keep them interested; colour and movement you see, what a crowd pleasing format!

So that was my earliest memory of entertaining, but when I moved up to the primary school (which was next door to the infants) I got the chance to join the school choir. There is the possibility that happened because they couldn't shut me up, but to be fair I did sound pretty angelic in those days, and so the natural progression was to be accepted into the local church choir too. Yep I was an official Choirboy!!

I earned money singing at weddings on a Saturday, two and six to be exact twelve and a half pence in new money. As soon as the service was over, I'd run like a crazed marathon runner to St James Park football ground in Exeter (a couple of miles from the church) to watch my beloved Exeter City and not only could I afford to gain entry, but there was also enough money left to buy a Pasty and a Bovril, sweet! Being the Head Choirboy I was often called upon to sing solos at certain weddings, *'Jesus Joy of man's desiring'*, that sort of thing and get extra dosh... come on! So between the infant school and the head choirboy thing I just kept performing.

Me as Head Choirboy with my mates and our Brilliant Vicar Rev. Moellar

Sometimes it was a hastily arranged show with my cousins Steven, Ian and Nicola as well as my sisters after tea on a Sunday night to entertain our parents and aunts and uncles in our front room. On other occasions it was putting on Circuses and other stuff in various neighbour's gardens, including at the back of Kim and Wendy's house which was down the road from us, Their Mum was great for letting all the kids up the street play there, we all loved her. When I put on these dodgy productions my friends were required to purchase a raffle ticket to watch, (yes I was indeed charging people to come and watch me perform from the age of about seven or eight) even then I just knew that this is what I'd be doing for the rest of my life cause it put me in the spotlight and made me happy.

Sandra was the eldest of us siblings and Helen was the baby of our family group. My big sister went into nursing and Helen had various jobs including being a Post Office telephone operator at one point, but neither of them ever had the performing bug. We're all completely different really and that's a good thing, imagine if they were like me seeking attention all the time… the horror!

If I did a show at home, I might try to rope them in to do a bit, and they would join in if pressed but were somewhat reluctant. However I did find a willing participant in the guise of my Cousin Steven.

Here I am with my beautiful Granny Willis, my Sisters and my cousin Steven... In the Days before we were Rock stars!

We were both in the church choir and therefore we loved singing in public, once we even cut a record together in a small recording booth at Butlins in Minehead. How it worked was that you had to put the money in the slot, go inside the booth and when the light came on sing your heads off, we weren't sure when to stop because there wasn't a light for that, so the song just cut off mid sentence. The thing is though, a record popped out at the end of it all and that was mega exciting. I haven't seen or heard

it for many years but there is an ongoing search in my family to find this lost treasure and if it's ever located it will surface on Social Media I can assure you of that!

Steven went down the proper job route, became a detective constable eventually and had a fantastic career in the Force. Long before he became a copper though we used to perform together as a duo and we quite brilliantly named our act.... wait for it, **the Junior Cousins,** I know, where did that come from? We used to enter talent contests in Exeter often winning by singing *California Here I come (*an Al Johnson Song and the one that we did on the record!), *'Oh when the Saints go Marching in'* and stuff like that. At the time we were about nine or ten and I carried on performing forever but Steven as I said was more sensible than me and did the responsible member of society thing by making policing his job for life.

Most of my childhood memories are based on or around entertaining, because it was performing that gave me the most enjoyment and made me feel like I was a someone, a someone who could do things that other people would secretly like to be able to do. It also made me feel quite powerful I suppose.

I was and still am an over sensitive soul, to illustrate how vulnerable I was, once after a church youth group I remember someone being really horrible to me when we were walking home from the club. For some reason he really tore into me saying, *'You're always trying to make people laugh and nobody likes you'*. It really hurt me and to be fair I still don't handle criticism any better now, I keep waiting for that hard skin to develop but it's probably not going to happen at this stage of my life is it? Having said that though, I'm pretty sure that the aforementioned spiteful moment made me want to perform even more, so I suppose I used it for motivation in the end. After I had first cried my eyes out in my bedroom of course.

I was always a bit different to my friends in as much as on a Monday night in Exeter at St George's Hall, there was a disco for teenagers where you went to meet girls and dance and all that malarkey which I secretly wanted to do, especially the meeting girls bit but I was always very shy when I wasn't singing or performing so I never went. I was the odd one out of the friends in our road really as they all used to go there, even Sharon the Girl who lived down the Road and the one that I believed I was in love with from the age of eight or whatever it was, sad eh?

I was mates with the cool kids up our street but was never really one of them, I remember once that Paul (no surnames here) said that I should learn how to snog properly and undo a girl's bra at the same time! What a challenge... he'd arranged for him and one of the girls up our road to show me how it's done and Sharon agreed to have little snog with me to help me out. That was much appreciated and as we were kissing Paul said to me, 'Undo the bra, make your move Andrew'. Flipping eck what a Klutz I was, snog and undo the bra?... The kissing stuff was difficult enough on it's own for this shy boy but dealing with the mechanics of ladies underwear was a step too far. I have never been able to and still can't... multitask!! Rub my tummy and simultaneously pat my head? You're having a laugh!

Picture the scene if you dare, I was groping away like a daddy longlegs looking for a way to get out of a closed window (not convinced that analogy works but you get the idea) and then I happened to glance across at Paul and Susan to see how they were getting on and they were laughing their heads off at me attempting the snogging version of the Krypton Factor! It was all a set up to take the mickey out of me.... but take the positives Andrew you got to snog Sharon for a little while.

I'm not sure to this very day if she was part of the wind up, but even if she was I forgive her. I really did make some great friends growing up in Hillyfield Road... Paul, Tony, Alison, Barry, Sue, Stephen, the other Paul, Clive and his sisters, Bernie, Christine, Kim, Wendy, my sisters Sandra and Helen and of course Sharon, apologies if I forgot any names there. We were Whipton's version of the Bash Street Kids from the Beano, and we used to do everything up that road, all of life was there.... Fetes, Football Tournaments, Circuses, Topsy Turvy days, skipping competitions and on and on infinitum; what a fantastic place and time to grow up in.... Hillyfield Road For Ever!

But dear readers my Monday nights were quite different from all the disco nonsense that everyone else seemed to participate in. My Uncle Edgar (Mum's brother) had given me a banjo as a present (not sure how he got it but let's not go there shall we, he was a bit of a loveable rogue) and although they were struggling financially my parents managed to find the money to pay for Banjo lessons given to me by a guy from our church who played the guitar and quickly taught himself how to play the Banjo so that he could earn the extra dosh teaching me...

Me tearing it up somewhere on the Banjo acquired for me by my Uncle Edgar

So my Monday nights would consist of me and my Dad in my bedroom with him teaching me all the old songs, actually I think he mostly did it for the chance to sing... he really loved his singing did my father! While everyone was going out learning how to socialize meet girls and french kiss, I was learning songs like, There is a tavern in the Town', Rock 'n' Roll eh??

Andy's Animal Idioms

Idiom

Like an Elephant in a fridge

meaning

Someone who just doesn't fit in

CHAPTER 2

'Who seeks and will not take when once 'tis offered. Shall never find it more'

Christmas1969

My dad was a postman and he and all his workmates would only have one delivery on Christmas Eve in the 1960s so after that delivery they would go to a social club in Exeter called Willey's Club (That's the actual name guys, you can't make this stuff up), and there was a postman called Les Chadwick, who played guitar and sang and they'd all love to have a good old sing song with him. I don't know where that's gone nowadays... thank you XBox! Anyway, one of the postman said to my Dad, 'Bring your boy down to join in Ern', and Dad explained that he didn't drive so his mate said, 'I'll go and pick him up'. He drove my father back to our house and I got into the car with my Banjo and we all made our way to the Club. Now bear with here cause this was a long time ago, but mainly all I can remember is being both unbelievably terrified and exceedingly excited at the same time. When I got there I tuned my Banjo up with Les's guitar and he was very encouraging as I could tell he realised how nervous I was, he said, 'Just stay strong, look down at your Banjo and if you don't know the chords, keep playing no one will

know', that was undoubtedly some of the best advice I've ever received in my career... thanks Les you are much missed lovely man.

Well that was my first live performance as a vocal instrumentalist and I even did a couple of songs all by myself. Unbeknownst to me the social secretary of the club we were playing in was watching this singalong and said, 'What are you doing tonight Andrew?' I said, 'Well nothing really', and he asked me if I wanted to do a little show that evening in their club, thank goodness I wasn't planning on washing my hair that night. Well that was my first paid gig, I got £3, yes three of your English pounds dear readers, this was an absolute fortune for a 12 year old in 1969, probably the equivalent fee today would be about £10,000.... btw no calculator was used in this possibly less than accurate calculation.

That night a small time agent was in the club watching me perform and he duly booked me to do some shows in pubs and clubs around Exeter.

Warning, what you are about to read is scandalous!

To be fair he wasn't the most trustworthy of people, he'd normally turn up to the gigs and pay me at the end of the night. For example I used to do a regular spot at a Pub called The Nog Inn which was in Feniton (near Honiton) on a Sunday night, sometimes driven there by my Uncle Les Harris (the husband of my Mum's Sister Auntie Sylv) or by my Uncle Les Mogford my Dad's brother who would take us there in his Hillman Minx. I know that detail is not integral to the story but he asked me to put it in the book, so there it is, how's that Uncle Les you're featured!

The agent used to pay me £2 for the show, but one week he was ill and couldn't come, so at the end of the gig my Dad asked the manager of the pub for my payment and he said, 'Same fee as normal?' Dad said yes please and he duly gave him £5.... how about that, ripping off a 12 year old kid.

But it didn't stop me from doing what I wanted to do and by the way I've been ripped off far worse than that over the years, but you keep going and 54 years later I'm still gigging, take that you scoundrel from my past.

Look at me I'm a professional, paying at venues
So Damp that flowers grew on the stage curtains

Here's who I am and where I came from in a nutshell; my Dad's name is Albert Ernest Mogford, but everyone called him Ernest because his dad was called Albert and by calling him by his second name it stopped any confusion! Clear as mud? So why didn't they just call him Ernest?

My Late Mum's name was Irene Bertha Alice Willis and her Mum was also called Rene... of course she was! I'm not sure why all the other names are in there but it must be to do with grandparents etc.

Gran and Grandad Willis
My Mum's Parents

Now my Dad's parents were Albert and Louisa (nee Adams) Mogford and they lived in Looe Road near St David's Station in Exeter.

My Granny and Grandad Mogford
who lived in Looe Road, Exeter

We would often go round to their house on a Saturday night for family get togethers... it was normally quite busy as my Dad had 3 brothers so when they brought their spouses and children with them (my cousins, Cheryl and Sonia, don't think Selena and Mark were born by then... sorry I'm just thinking out loud) it was pretty full. I was only six when my Grandad died so my memories of him are limited, but the overwhelming feeling was one of love.

My Dad said that his father had quite the temper when he was younger but I never saw that, and my abiding memory is one of sitting on his lap in the corner of their front room on his arm chair whilst he peeled oranges for me and my sisters to eat. That makes me smile even now so I'm happy to go with that.

My Granny Mogford always did a little spread for us to nibble on during the evening and she also loved her singing, so our get togethers would inevitably end up with the record player out and a good old fashioned sing along to Guy Mitchell, Jim Reeves, Connie Francis and other popular Artistes of the time.

My Gran always found a reason to sing including joining a small choir at the old age pensioners club in her twilight years. Boy she was a strong stubborn lady, I wish I could have developed some of her outer shell, that would have been handy as I negotiated my way through this ruthless business we call SHOW!

So the thing is I was always surrounded by singing, therefore it seemed quite natural for me to take my first steps into this business as a vocalist, it was a long time before I became a comedian.

Back to my Dad for a moment, he always wanted to be a performer, so I was more or less living out his ambitions for him. My mother lost her dad when she was 16 and had to become head of the family at that tender age as my beautiful Granny Willis had apparently fallen apart at the loss of her Husband (my Grandad Willis) and being the eldest she just got on with it and took full responsibility for her siblings Edgar, Sylvia and David as well as looking after her Mum... She just did stuff!!

I remember as a very small child that my Mum would have to do two jobs and she'd walk Sandra and me (snug in my Pram) into town from Whipton, which is a suburb of Exeter and my dad who was walking back from finishing his job (either on the scaffoldings or whatever he was doing at the time) would meet us part way and walk us home whilst my mother made her way into the City to do her evening job. The thing is, even with all that toil from my parents, we never had any money. As mentioned earlier Dad didn't drive in those days so we went everywhere on public transport if we could afford to.

I know it's a bit of a cliché but we really did make our own entertainment; My Mum wasn't a brilliant musician or anything but somehow she taught herself how to play the piano.... I know!! Where did that come from? Anyway next to our kitchen there was a little room where we used to keep the coal (our very own coal bunker for our open fire in the front room), but they cleaned the area out and made it like an extra living space and that became our mini music room. So we'd all sit down and Mum would play the piano, yes folks we had an upright piano in the room given to us by a family member or friend, anyway my beloved Mother would bash away at the piano keys probably hitting all the

wrong bass notes, but she could pick out a melody with her right hand and we'd all sing along. Mum was actually quite musical, but didn't have the flare or desire to pursue her natural talent unlike my Dad who would sing at the drop of a hat and always longed to be a performer but seemed (in the end) to be happy enough to leave the stagework to me and bask in the successes of my fledgling career.

I suppose you could say he was part father and part roady, however with him not being able to drive to my local gigs, we reached them via a bus journey starting at the bottom of Hillyfield Road in Whipton. We'd board the double decker together and I'd put my banjo under the stairs while we travelled, I still have that banjo case although to be fair it is falling to pieces. Because I was still quite young, Dad would always accompany me to the venues and I'll never forget that once on Mum and Dad's Wedding anniversary which fell on Boxing Day, he wanted to come to a show at the Devon Yeoman Pub in Beacon Heath in Exeter and that caused a massive argument between them. Mum was understandably quite offended that he would (it seemed to her) rather spend their Anniversary with me at a gig than with her. But he just loved it and couldn't see past going to a gig... not cool Dad, don't think you really thought that one through.

So that was me growing up. Lots of joy in our family, loads of loving care from my wonderful Mum, oodles of enthusiasm from my dad and an unbreakable closeness to my sisters, even though they had no desire to do what I do. My sister Sandra once said to me years later, 'How can you live your life like that? You don't know for definite how much money you're going to earn each year and how do you cope with the uncertainty?' I said that I just can't live any other way. It wasn't a conscious plan, I was born a performer so the decision was made for me long before I appeared here and it's what I'm going to do until I die.

This was our family unit, loving, loyal and tight knit!

Sandra had a great career by the way, she was a State Registered nurse and became a ward sister and all that lot, very successful in her chosen career and bloody good at it, I'm so proud of her. Helen was a few years younger than me and always seemed to be heading for motherhood, she has 4 children and 2 grandchildren as I write this today and is a completely doting and brilliant mother as is Sandra to her 2 children and many grandkids. Sometimes I think that I could have been a better parent myself, however I have two wonderful children and three grandchildren who love me very much so I feel really lucky that my pursuit of a career didn't cause as many problems for them in their life as some might imagine. I suppose it was just *what Dad did* and they got on with it.

Justin, me and Alisha trying to work out how to start this music recording type contraption!

I love my children who along with my grandkids are the apple of my eye. My life would be nothing without them, but they know who I am as well, in fact, my daughter Alisha used to sing and dance in some shows with me, and my Son Justin became a performer too for a while and I used to say to them.... and btw this wouldn't go into the book of good parenting, I used to say, 'Remember kids, we're not normal'. So there you have it.... me in a nutshell!

I properly got into comedy much later on, eventually doing a joke or two in between songs to attempt to pad out my set. However my whole trajectory changed when I met my Wife Michelle.

She just got me and knew who I was in an instant. A few years ago I wrote a play, called Funny Ha Ha about the life of a comedian, there's a line in it (based on true events) where his ex wife says to him, "Why didn't you get a job at the Post Office, a good regular job, we'd be better off now?" and the comedian says "Because I'm a comedian, I was born a comedian, there was nothing injected into me when I first arrived on this planet to make me funny,

I'm just me! You knew who I was when you met me, and that's probably what appealed to you in the first place, so please don't try to change me now. I can't change who I am'.

Andy's Animal Idioms

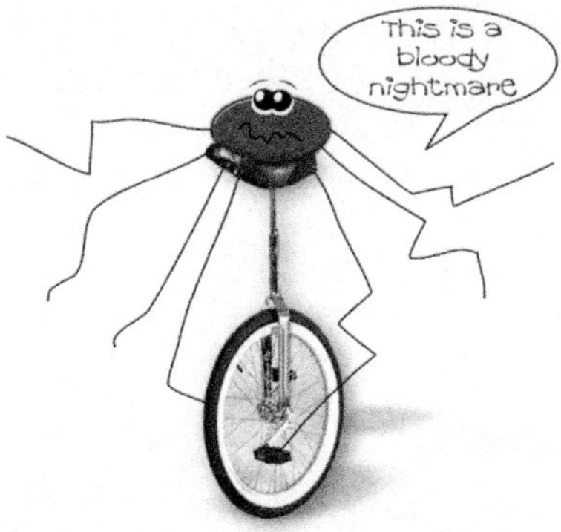

Idiom

Like a Spider on a unicycle

meaning

Someone who overcomplicates things

Craig Revel Horwood

Strictly Come Dancing BBC TV

'After having the honour of working with Andy in Cinderella at the Bristol Hippodrome, Christmas 2022, I can safely say that the rumours are true... Andy Ford, West Country Comic Legend, fab-u-lous comedy writer, generous, professional leading pantomime performer and one of the nicest people you'll ever be fortunate to meet'.

CHAPTER 3

'Love Labours Lost'

Married at a young age

I first got married at 20 years of age to Chris, we'd met at one of my Dance Band gigs and apparently she thought I looked a bit like Donny Osmond or David Cassidy, which to be fair I did a bit in those days and I'd wear a white suit on purpose. I was like the heart throb of the group, because the guys were a lot older than me, I was 16 and they were all mid thirties. I was introduced to her at the dance where we were playing by her step father Wally and her Mum Bet who loved to ballroom dance and often came to our gigs, and within two years (yep that quick) we were married. I don't know why we went down that road quite so quickly as looking back I don't believe I was ready for it all, but there are no regrets here.

Chris delivered our daughter Alisha in November of 1979 when I was 21, she was a breech birth and it was traumatic for both Mother and Daughter, our little girl spent weeks in a special care baby unit where she was wonderfully cared for by the fantastic NHS staff at the Royal Devon and Exeter Hospital. I would talk to my daughter every day

when she was in that incubator and promised her that I would always look after her. Justin was born in 1982 when I was 25 and although not quite as traumatic as Alisha's birth his delivery involved the use of forceps, boy did he let us know that he would have preferred a smoother entry... ear plugs anyone!

My first Wife Chris and I were together for sixteen years. I didn't know how to be a parent, I just winged it really. I was a performer and I sang songs for a living so I used what I was competent at to entertain my kids. My daughter would join in with me and rather than read them stories like a proper Dad would, we would sing songs together and stuff. I don't know what their memories of it are now, but they just grew up living with a performer and got on with it. I think we were a happy family unit at that time, we both loved our kids with a passion and I was happily forging my way in the business whilst being rewarded for it financially, enabling us to buy the house and all that sort of thing. Also I was writing songs and stuff and had a 4 track portable recording studio which I used to create multitrack versions of my compositions. I was always so flipping enthusiastic and I offered to create music for productions at the Bassett's Farm Primary School in Exmouth, the one my kids went to. I did

tracks for Bugsy Malone and my daughter played one of the lead roles namely Blousey Brown, and before you say anything it wasn't nepotism, she was really good! I also did the music for Ulysees the Musical and my son played the title role in that too; again he was just good for the part, you're sounding a bit defensive here Andrew.... for goodness sake people, I put no pressure on the school, but to be fair it does sound a bit dodge doesn't it? It wasn't, they were both just natural performers, I was and still am very proud of their performances in those shows.

Alisha and me about to swim the Channel...

Talking of schools reminds me of my own halcyon days in those educational establishments, (you see how I flip backwards and forwards through time in this book, I did warn you) and although I wasn't a genius in that regard I did alright. I received four GCE O levels, that's back in the days before they put extra letters in there amalgamating the GCE with the CSE creating the GCSE...(Stay with me here... focus) I got a GCE in English Language, Maths, French and Russian.

However when I was at school, all I wanted to do was perform and I got the chance to do just that in different Gilbert and Sullivan productions at Hele's Grammar School in Exeter. Playing either a sailor, a pirate or a Sister, Cousin or Aunt in our versions of HMS pinafore and the Pirates of Penzance, I couldn't get enough, I never managed to secure the lead roles but I didn't mind as long as I got on that stage!

Performance has always been the conveyor belt I've used to lead me through my life, I'd wave and nod at the stuff, either side of it, (you know... real life) but in the end, performing always came first. I think after all these years though, I'm starting to get the life/showbiz balance a little bit better and that's

down to getting older and seeing things from a slightly different angle. My wife Michelle has been the greatest friend I could ever have with the patience of a saint, and her support on and off of the stage has helped me to treasure stuff outside of my all consuming profession.

Me and Michelle Discussing our Council Tax Bill

I adore being a Grandad by the way, and one day hopefully a great grandad and would you believe it, I am now (tangent) also addicted to camping. I know, who would have ever believed that? But I love it! Michelle and I manage a few breaks every year with our two shih tzu doggies Stan and Ollie, they get packed into the car with the camping gear and they flipping love it. Cooking breakfast outside of our tent on the gas griddle in the early mornings is almost like heaven for me now..... again.... I never saw that coming. I camp therefore I am!

Poetry Corner

The Remote Control

You are the desired object,
you're a joy for one to hold,
it's a power thing where you're concerned
I praise you're name manifold

(That means lots, it's nothing to do with
a car exhaust or anything)

A wondrous array of buttons,
encased in voluptuous black,
an infra red thingy at the front
and sod all at the back.

Everybody wants you,
grabbing, shoving, pushing,
but when it all gets far too much,
you hide behind my sofa cushion

CHAPTER 4

'If music be the food of love, then play on'

Playing in Bands

So I'm really happy gigging away at the age of 12 to 14, (here we are back on the Time, Space, Continuum thingy) playing local venues once maybe twice a week. I always had money piled up on my dressing table in my bedroom at home and I was able to impress my mates by treating some of them to a chocolate bar from the school tuck shop at break time courtesey of my burgeoning career. Yep life was good, and then (*hold the phone*) I was asked if I wanted to sing with a local band called the Harry Brown Trio.

Harry was the pianist and his son Cliff (who was a hairdresser in Exeter) played the drums and sang, and somehow it was me they asked to join them, I'm not sure what happened to the other member of the trio, or maybe it was just a duo before I joined. Anyhoo, to me this was like the Big Time, as they did actual summer seasons at Devon's equivalent of Las Vegas… Dawlish Warren! How had they heard of me and what was my appeal from their point of view? Doesn't really matter… it was me they wanted... end of!

Now Harry was in his 60s I believe and his Son Cliff was 40 or so, quite a bizarre age gap with me being added into the mix don't you think? They were probably going for the *'Little Jimmy Osmond'* ambience in the set up of the band. So it happened and I really loved it, as far as I was concerned this was me being a professional entertainer, the stuff of dreams. That first summer season at a holiday camp, I learned so much and just adored all the attention, but more was to come within a year or so.

I think it was my parents who saw the advert in the Express and Echo (Exeter's leading publication) re: a local dance band who were auditioning for a lead singer. The band was 'The Vic Palmer Combo', who were without doubt Devon's premier function band at the time. So my Dad took me on a Sunday Morning trip to a Hall somewhere in the Mount Pleasant area of Exeter not that far from St James' Park where Exeter City play. We walked in and I was quite nervous but when I saw all their equipment spread out and heard the power of their sound, it all just blue me away. Harry Brown and Dawlish Warren felt like another world away compared to the professional feel of Vic's band. I'm sure they didn't expect to see a 16 year old auditioning, but they were very welcoming so I went for it, I sang my socks off and got the job. Again I

was the youngest in the band by far and I loved all the focus on me singing at the front of the stage. However I had no idea what a steep learning curve I was about to face and climb at the hands of these older and wily dance band musicians.

The Vic Palmer Sound, Exeter's Premier Dance band in the 1970s
Also known as the Hair Bear Bunch!

The line up was Vic Palmer on the Hammond organ and synthesiser, Paul Hiley (an Ex Professional Orchestral Percussionist from London) on the drums and Bass player Stuart Boyles an ex rock band bassist who I thought was the coolest dude ever. He was, handsome, moody and the women who came to the shows absolutely loved his bad boy charms. I thought his magnetism was something I wanted to aspire to but I knew I could never pull it off, particularly at such a young age but boy did those years teach me a lot.

On some of our first shows I would be out front singing and suddenly from behind me I'd hear the drummer shout, 'Dance around the stage a bit for God's Sake, you look like a statue Andrew, move your ass to the music!!' What was I gonna do? They were years older than me, so I just did what I was told.... *#besttrainingever.* Boy it was a good band and I loved the regular work which was twice, sometimes three times a week.

So now I really had made it, and the young girls who came to the shows seemed to like me too, particularly when we played local village Hall Hops in the West Country. Of course I was starting to believe my own publicity, I was 17 years old and

girls were coming to see me sing, it was what 7 or 8 year old Andrew could only have ever dreamed of and it was happening now. However there was the odd occasion when I wished that I had perfected the old bra-undoing exercise from my past. Things were going so well but oh fickle fortune, what had you planned next for me? The fall was always gonna happen of course, but it was more literal than you or I could ever have imagined.

So we were playing at a Village Hall in Dulverton near Tiverton I believe, I was wearing blue jeans, a big round collar shirt and a fur coat (it was the seventies) and after setting up our gear on the stage we popped into the local pub for a pre-show drink. It was awesome being the young one, I'd sit in the corner waiting for the guys to bring me a drink from the bar, because at 17 I looked a lot younger than my age and there was no way that I would ever have been served with any alcohol. Anyway when the drinks were finished we left the pub to go back to the venue for the show and as we walked out of the doors there were quite a few girls there who got really excited when they saw me… 'OMG it's Andy!!' they shouted. I duly smiled and waved at them, unfortunately as previously discussed I've never been that good at multi-tasking and with all the waving and smiling going on I forgot to look

down at where I was walking. I missed the curb and fell smack on my face, scraping my knee, ripping my jeans and to my horror the blood just started pouring out. Arrange these words into a well known phrase or saying... *Pride, Fall, the, before....* Congratulations you've got it! I looked up expecting to view their concern for me but the young ladies in question were in absolute hysterics, I've never seen such uncontrollable laughter, (Tena lady could have made a fortune at that instant) and it was all aimed at me! What a life lesson to learn.

Oi Mogford! Who Do you think you are?

The Village Hall hops were one side of the job, but we were also booked for proper functions where we would play up to 3 to 4 hours hours for Ballroom dancing. This is where the Dance Band apprenticeship was so helpful, I was singing everything from Waltzes to Quicksteps to the latest pop songs. It was so good to get that musical training whilst learning how to work a crowd at the same time. Sometimes though the gigs were epic, I can remember doing a few 8pm to 2am dances, but I was just a sponge at the time enjoying and drinking in all the experiences. The journey home after the gigs was also a fantastic memory, we talked about everything in those early hours, Sex, Politics, the Universe (ostensibly why were we here?) and various other topics, but to be fair it was mostly sex. One of my favourite things after a show was to get back to Exeter at about 3am in the morning and gather with other musicians at the late Night Burger Van known as *'Mother's'* at the top of Fore Street where we'd all chat about how our gigs had gone, it was really bonding.

Vic Palmer was the man who gave me my stage name btw, it happened one Sunday night when we were playing at a posh restaurant called the Fisherman's Cot, near Tiverton in Devon.

Vic was about to introduce me on to the stage when he said, 'I don't know what to call you, I can't say please welcome our singer, Andrew Mogford that'll sound crap... hang on I've got it!' Then he said it, ***'Please welcome our vocalist Andrew Ford'.*** So that was it, from that moment in time I was Andrew or Andy Ford, so the ***Mog*** had been decapitated from my surname and it wasn't really as painful as one might imagine. Don't think my Mum and Dad were over impressed though, but hey that's Rock n Roll!

Around this time for some reason I had taken a part time job as an apprentice ladies Hairdresser at the nearby Salon where Mum used to get her hair done. I think it was probably because my mother wanted me to have a proper career as well as me singing in a band, which I don't think she was ever convinced would be a job for life. Anyway I really enjoyed it for a while, cause I adored the ladies and getting to chat and flirt with them when they came in for a shampoo and set was great fun. I also did a weekly day release course at Exeter College (I was the only male in the class... awesome) to learn other hairdressing skills I would need should I continue down this road. It was also around that time in the 1970s when the country was being plunged into darkness regularly and the working week was

reduced cause of strikes and power cuts and all that malarkey. Not one of the happiest times in our nation's history but like everyone else, we muddled our way through it all at the Salon. David was the main hairdresser, it was his own business and one of the other hairstylists working there was called Sally, and I thought she was absolutely gorgeous. I probably enjoyed the job because of getting the chance to spend time near her, but I was also very popular with the older ladies who came in.

Being the apprentice I would be the one who'd wash their hair and I think some of them quite liked being shampooed by a seventeen year old lad. Some of the clients gave me firm instructions as to how they wanted their hair to be washed, one lady in particular used to say, *'Use your nails Andrew I don't mind if you're a bit rough!'* I know!.... if I'm honest she scared me just a little bit. As I say, I was still singing with Vic's band at the time and occasionally after getting back late from a gig I would struggle to stay awake at the salon during the day. On this one occasion I was washing a lady's hair and I dozed off for a second, fell forward slightly and smashed her head on the sink!! OMG, it scared me to death but luckily she was OK about it and no blood was spilt, but it was a lawsuit waiting to happen!

Vic is no longer with us he passed a few years back but without being a part of his Band I don't think that I would still be doing what I do today.

A while after I'd left in the late seventies I found out that Stuart our Bass player had died, not even sure how old he was at the time but it was even worse to discover that apparently he had taken his own life, I couldn't believe it, I'd always held him up in my mind as being a rock star, ladies man and the perfect role model to a young aspiring wannabe musician... in fact everything I wanted to be as a teenager but now he was gone, and in such tragic circumstances. I often think of Stuart today, wondering why it ended the way it did for him... I miss you my friend.

Logical Nursery Rhymes

Humpty Dumpty sat on a wall,
Humpty Dumpty had a great fall
All the Kings horses
and all the Kings men
did absolutely nothing
cause it was only an egg!

CHAPTER 5

'To unpathed waters, undreamed shores'

My own band Choosy

You know me, I have to keep challenging myself, and after having been in Vic's Band for nearly four years it was time to try something new. So I started my own band which I called *'Choosy featuring Andrew Ford'.*

'What sort of name is that?' I hear you say, well now I suppose I'll have to tell you the story of how I came up with the name. Before I share this mind you, I must let you know that it's on condition you don't hold it against me... thank you, I'll continue.... Being a young lad I had read more than one or two cheeky books in my youth let me put it that way, and I'd rather enjoyed reading the really funny but quite rude Confessions of A Window Cleaner (and other professions) series, later to grace the big screen with Robin Askwith always in the lead roles. There was a whole load of them and they made me smile.... Forgive me father, for I have laughed. Anyway this one '*confessions*' book had a scene where a sexy bored housewife was seducing the window cleaner in the kitchen and the line that stayed with me was this... 'We were rolling around

the floor in a sexual frenzy, arms and legs everywhere and at one point my foot kicked out and knocked over the swing bin and the contents spilled out all over the kitchen floor. At one point as the passion intensified I found myself staring at an empty tin of cat food with the words, ***Choosy, a satisfied cat or your money back!!*** written on the label'. Well that made me scream with laughter and so when I had to come up with a name for my Band it was there staring me in the face...lol.

What a talented bunch of musicians with absolutely no Dress sense!

I was more or less doing the same sort of thing with Choosy as when I was in the Dance Band before, but with younger people around me and I was in control of it all. There were a few different line ups over the years, I worked with Richie Burns (a brilliant drummer who is still gigging) and after he left Adrian Waters took up that mantle in my band. My excellent Bass player was Steve Moorman who I now believe runs a tavern somewhere in Greece, he really worked the stage well with me at our shows and for a while we had Arthur Cooke (another special talent) on Lead Guitar, but in the early days it was Neil Govier who went on to become an entertainments agent that helped me out by playing Bass at a few gigs. The band was very successful for a local group of lads and we even spread our wings at one point, travelling to the North East of England to do shows in the Working Men's Clubs in 1980! Impressed? You won't be when you hear how our first gig went.

We left Exeter early in the morning, and I had hired some lights to make our show even more sensational. Well after the epic journey up we were playing the same night in a massive great Club in Gateshead I believe. Greetings with the Social Secretary were exchanged and we set up on stage, ready to give the North East Audiences a show the

likes of which they'd never seen before. Lights... check.... Musical amplification... check..... sound test... check.... Put on my Elvis Costume made for me by my Auntie Sylv... check! The audience came in, the social secretary took to the stage and said, *'Ladies and Gentlemen please welcome all the way from the South West of England, The sensational showband Choosy featuring Andrew Ford!!'* Our drummer Adrian starts playing the tom toms a la Ronnie Tutt at the start of a gig at the MGM Grand Hotel in Las Vegas and I rushed out in my Elvis gear and started singing C.C. Rider when.... Flipping disaster!

The stage went dark and all the sound stopped!! Pitch Black and Silence was our first offering to the good people of the North East, with the exception of our drummer playing on for a while until he realised that it had all come to a grinding halt. Obviously we had to take a break and try to sort it out. So there we were in our stage gear, screw drivers in hand, opening up and checking electricity plugs to see why it all went wrong. We discovered that the lights we'd hired weren't wired tightly and hey presto it all fused... perfect. Probably the first time anyone had witnessed Elvis rewiring a plug on stage! We sorted it eventually, but what an introduction to clubland.

It was on that trip that we played in a venue a couple of miles from where my future wife was living, she would have only been 11 at the time. But I have to say the whole working in the North East Clubs thing really was an eye opener, and during that tour I experienced my first stripper on a Sunday lunchtime, you see it wasn't all doom and gloom.

We had to do two spots in a club in Acklam, Middlesborough and were told that a lady was gonna perform in between. Well perform she certainly did, and very entertaining it was too.... That's all you're getting here! But from the beginning the whole set up was a culture shock for me, seeing all the beers being lined up along the bar, and the staff diligently waiting for the doors to open, anticipating the inevitable influx. Suddenly it happened, right on cue hundreds of blokes entered the club and headed straight for the bar for their Sunday lunchtime drink and stripper fest before returning to their homes for Sunday Lunch.

It was all alien to me, I'd certainly never experienced anything like it in my obviously sheltered life in Whipton. Every day is a school day!

As always I tried to create opportunities for my Band to take off, we did a local ITV talent show called South West Showcase hosted by Police 5's Shaw Taylor and we even entered a Live touring Version of Opportunity Knocks presented in theatres by Hughie Green after they binned his TV show. Hughie liked us and invited me into his dressing room before the show to give me a bit of a pep talk, telling me how good he thought we were and to go out and give the show the big and bright start it needed.

Whilst biding our time backstage before curtain up at the Princess Theatre in Torquay, this happened... I bumped into Freddie Starr a huge Comedy Star in the 1980s who had come in to see Hughie I'm assuming, as it was Opportunity Knocks that gave him his big break. I said, *'Hello Freddie how are you?'*, he said '*Oh I'm OK',* then he punched me in the stomach! Really that's what happened, I don't know if he was on anything or just in a bad mood or didn't like the look of me but it really flipping hurt and to this day I have no idea why he did it. Poor form Mr Starr.

After a fair bit of touring I decided to end the band and concentrate on a solo career. I had little or no

solo work to start with but I did have a typewriter. I wrote what I thought was a fantastic letter selling myself as a self contained Guitar/Vocalist to venues in the South West. I then went to a photocopy shop or possibly the local library to get about 50 of them printed off, and with the help of yellow pages I sought out potential venues in the area that might want to book me. I licked 50 envelopes and 50 stamps and posted the lot in order to get myself some work. Only 2 replied, but one booked me twice a week and the other once a week, so from nothing I was gigging three times a week,

I looked for work and found it... I suppose that has always been my philosophy as it is to this very day.

My fledgling solo career the work cheques were smaller than the ones on my jacket

Andy's
Animal Idioms
Does anyone else hear creaking?
Idiom
Like a Walrus on an ironing board
meaning
Someone who is close to their breaking point

Lesley Joseph

TV Comedy Star, Birds of a Feather

'I am thrilled to see that there is now a biography on the legend that is Andy Ford (Andrew Mogford).... I had the pleasure of working with Andy on a record breaking show a couple of years ago .... He is loved by the audiences and now we can read his journey to success! Bravo!'

CHAPTER 6

'All the World's a stage and all the men and women merely players'

'The Camp entertainer'

I started running holiday camps from about the age of 25, it all came about because I managed to get a gig or two at a holiday camping site in East Devon and the shows went so well that I decided to go in to see the owner and offer him my services to create a full entertainments programme for this holiday camp with myself as the front man. He went for it and we never looked back. I ended up running Ladram Bay in East Devon for 10 years, and eventually Challaborough Bay in South Devon, near Plymouth for 4 years.

I first introduced Ollie the Otter at Ladram Bay, as the camp was near a village called Otterton with the river Otter flowing through it, and me being the genius that I am, I came up with the idea of the holiday camp mascot being an Otter and even created a Kiddies Club that the younger holiday makers could join. We had club badges, a membership card and a Kiddie club chant which was shouted at the start of each Club meeting, 'Squeak, squeak, squeak, hip hip hooray, we are the

Otters of Ladram (Challaborough) Bay!' I wrote loads of songs and stories of Ollie's adventures and I recorded them all onto cassettes, which I sold to the holiday makers as souvenirs of their time there. It was a way of maximizing my income but also I loved creating all the stories and the songs, which I wrote and recorded in lots of different musical styles.

Rocking the holiday camp scene
I had such a good time!!

Apparently the camping and caravan holiday re-bookings went from 20% to 70% after I took over the entertainment, and I also introduced green coats which was based on the Butlins Red Coat model and

made a fortune for the owner, a farmer and haulage business man Mr. Carter.

He was such a lovely old guy, and at one point he actually put money into a record that I made, so it was great working with him and at one point he also offered me the chance to be part of the company hierarchy which I politely declined, but I did feel really appreciated.

As I say I ran the camps for years and years and it rewarded me with family holidays in Florida and a good quality of life. My children Alisha and Justin would occasionally join me on the stage at Ladram

bay during the finals week at the end of each season.

Sell it guys, sell it, they're loving us!!

They were a bit hit with the holiday makers as they sang and strutted their stuff around the stage like young professional entertainers... I guess it's what they had grown up knowing how to do and boy did they do it well!

The two holiday camps I ran were quite different but I loved them both, I suppose you'd say Ladram Bay was more of a holiday maker venue and

Challaborough was more of a weekend break type of place for the good people of Plymouth, but the crowd reaction was just as good at either venue, I was just so lucky to meet so many lovely people who chose to spend their spare time watching me and Ollie entertain.

At the same time as putting all the Ollie the Otter tapes together to sell at the camps, I was writing songs for 'Andy Ford' to perform and record which the holiday makers could purchase if they wanted, and they kindly did. Cause I loved doing the song creation thing I have to say I was quite prolific at it and I managed to coerce a few of my lovely friends in the business to help me. Mike Beckett aka Gribbles played guitar and helped me with chord sequences and stuff cause he was a better musician than me but he was an admirer of how I could write a unique tune and put lyrics together almost immediately. We worked really well as a team and sitting in my ridiculously small studio space creating songs that had never been imagined before really helped me to keep my enthusiasm going. The holiday camp thing was great and lucrative but I really needed the creative bit to run alongside it all.

Paula Kerrison who sang on My Pillow Talk Album
Oh God how 80s were we?

One of the ladies that I booked to play at the camp for me on a Sunday was Paula Kerrison a keyboard player and a great singer to boot.

She was also really keen to help with the recording of my songs, adding lead and backing vocals to the tracks on my ***Pillow Talk*** Album. Also my dear friends Paula Mitchell from the cabaret Duo Cass and Crystal (whose lovely Dad Gordon duplicated the cassettes for me) and Jim Burnett a Bass player from Exeter, helped me to create my ***When I'm in your Arms*** album alongside Gribbles. I recorded all these cassettes and sold them at the camps as well as the Kiddie stuff.

I also had some help on that side of things too, with a professional artist called Mike Punter. He regularly visited the Ladram Bay camp for breaks from his home in Bristol with his Wife Gill and their daughters Amy and Jen; we got chatting one day and from then on he started working on some Ollie illustrations for me and our friendship continues today. So I was very lucky to get the help of some really talented friends which helped to keep me focused on creation, the thing that keeps me alive.

During the mid to late eighties whilst this was all going on I was also getting some work as an extra on television programmes. I'd contacted a casting director in Bristol and he managed to get me a few walk on opportunities. I even appeared on one of

the most famous episodes of *Only Fools and Horses*. It was the show where Del Boy fell through the Bar! Towards the end of the programme Rodney meets Cassandra in a Night Club and they have a romantic dance, well if you look carefully you'll see a young outrageously handsome lad with pushed up jacket sleeves (it was the eighties) dancing with a young lady behind them… that was little ol' me.

Next time you watch that you'll have to do the pause thing! I was also on a few episodes of Casualty, at one point being pushed around A&E in a wheel chair, and in the script I was referred to as 'Man with Leg'.

As mentioned earlier Mr Carter financed my first ever record (if you discount the one in the Booth at Butlins), and Graham Sclater my publisher and I travelled to London to record it with the help of some fantastic session musicians. The A side was called Sitting Pretty and was indeed a pretty generic pop song that I had written many years earlier, and actually recorded a very rough version of once in the Hospital Radio Studios in Exeter with my mate DJ Martin Ball. The B side was a Rock 'n' Roll song called Teenage Love.

Graham entered them both for the Eurovision Song Contest, British Entry that year. The top 8 as chosen by a panel were then performed on TV for the British public to decide which one they wanted. Apparently, although Teenage Love wasn't in the top 8 it was just outside finishing in the top 12. So close eh? Never mind, other stuff to do.

Male model from the 80s come in please you're time is up!

I self financed a second single recording a Reggae version of *Groovy kind of love*, the old Mindbenders hit from the 60's. Not sure how this next bit came about, but a couple of musicians with local records

to their names were given the chance to have them played in front of the Radio One Roadshow crowd on the seafront in Exmouth before the show went live to the nation. My record received the crowd's approval and it was the one chosen to be played live on Radio One, also I was interviewed on stage by ***ooh!*** Gary Davis the DJ.

My publisher told me that EMI loved the song and were going to promote it for me... This was it everyone! This was it! Spoiler alert..... this wasn't it. Andy Ford is the Man who's had more beaks than a Kit Kat lol! (other chocolate biscuits are available).

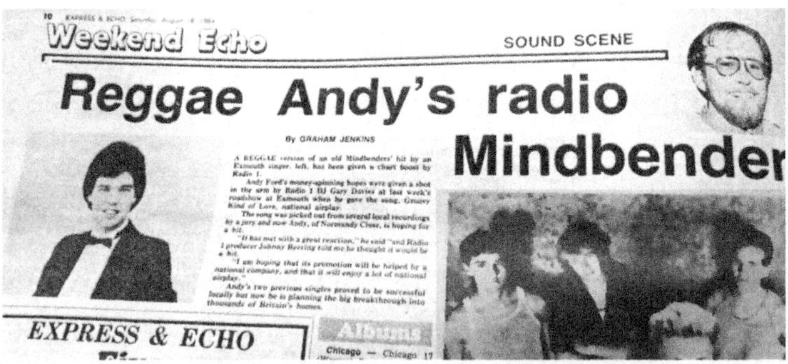
Weekend Echo

SOUND SCENE

Reggae Andy's radio Mindbender

By GRAHAM JENKINS

A REGGAE version of an old Mindbenders' hit by an Exmouth singer, left, has been given a chart boost by Radio 1.

Andy Ford's money-spinning hopes were given a shot in the arm by Radio 1 DJ Gary Davies at last week's roadshow at Exmouth when he gave the song, Groovy Kind of Love, national airplay.

The song was picked out from several local recordings by a jury and now Andy, of Normandy Close, is hoping for a hit.

"It has met with a great reaction," he said "and Radio 1 producer Johnny Beerling told me he thought it would be a hit.

"I am hoping that its promotion will be helped by a national company, and that it will enjoy a lot of national airplay."

Andy's two previous singles proved to be successful locally but now he is planning the big breakthrough into thousands of Britain's homes.

EXPRESS & ECHO

Chicago — Chicago 17

But there's more! In the late 80s I performed on a talent show called The Fame Game hosted by Tim Brooke Taylor. I was placed in the comedians

section hosted by Stan Boardman, where the aim was to get as many laughs as possible and avoid being virtually hooked off the stage by the audience. I had survived one week and was coming back to smash it the next week Ladies and Gentlemen. Unfortunately not seen by TV viewers, the audience in the studio could see the comedians all lined up waiting for their chance, and a couple of places behind me was a lady dressed as a nun. I tell you what, if I was in the crowd I'd have voted the comedians off to make sure that I got to see what this lady could do.

So my bit went ok, but as I suspected the audience were looking to see *The Nun* on stage and before long the rest of us were hooked off and she got her chance. To be fair there's nothing to be that disappointed about as the Nun was in fact Caroline Alhearn getting her first TV exposure. So I suppose you could say that I was with her for the launch of her TV career. What a fantastic and greatly missed talent, Royal Family, The Fast Show, Mrs Merton etc, that Lady was much loved and deservedly so. Yet another comic genius taken far too early. However the Fame Game experience would stand me in good stead for when the Big Big Talent Show came around, about 10 years later.

So back to the holiday camp thing, which was great for a while but the thought of going down that road forever (which I believe Chris was in favour of) just wasn't what I wanted to do, as I was always looking for new challenges and the chance to get my name about. The relationship with Chris wasn't the main problem, it was more that we both held completely different visions for our future and that was the main thing that seemed to cause the divide between us. I'd created the situation with the holiday camps and the money was flowing, but now it was time for the next thing. I've never been one for standing still and patting myself on the back, I just wanted to stretch my horizons you know, let more people see me and become a better comedian as well. It's the same stuff that motivated the little lad from Whipton to perform in people's gardens.

A mortgage and large pension had never been the pot of gold at the end of my rainbow, and if I had stopped where I was then, I would never have been able to fill this book with what followed. I have always been unable to turn off my ambition, but that's a part of what makes me... me I suppose, though I do understand that it can be really frustrating for some.

Unfortunately I have been given the super-power of being able to drive people up the wall from time to time without even trying! My Bad.

CHAPTER 7

'Hear my soul speak of the very instant that I saw you, did my Heart fly at your service'

My Michelle

The great thing about my relationship with Michelle, is that she's never tried to change who I am. She saw me, she recognised who I was immediately and has given me complete unconditional love and support ever since.

I won the lottery when I met this Lady. I'm not saying we live in a Disney type of argument free relationship, I mean who does? Boy does she gives me stick, but it's only because she cares about me. She knows that my first thoughts are always for her happiness and it's the same the other way around. To be fair I must be a pain in the arse to share a home with as comedians can be difficult to live alongside, you're either brilliantly funny or a manic depressive, there's not a lot in between and that's gotta be frustrating for anyone. The reason so many comics die young of heart attacks and stuff is because of the stress of it all. I'm not asking for sympathy though as it's my choice to do what I do; when you're out there making it look easy, it's the biggest buzz in the world, however you are also aware every night before you walk out onto the

stage that this might be the time that nobody likes you and the laughs just don't come, so you're carrying all that self created pressure. When you've been as highly successful as say someone like Tony Hancock with his regular appearances on our Television screens in the 60s and then find yourself becoming completely paranoid that the next series is not going to be as funny, that's how you end up in a hotel room in Australia (Tony Hancock took his own life in 1968). Imagine that, he actually ended up believing at one point that all he needed to do was to drill a hole into his head to let the pressure out, how depressed and paranoic did that unmatched talent become.

But the other side of it is that since I was this little boy that we've just been talking about, I could never do anything else. I'm so grateful that I have someone who sort of steers me away from the stressful side of things. I mean, Shell and I have always said to each other that we would live in a cardboard box together if we had to, and knowing you have that in your life gives you license to try everything, because I know at the end of it all, she's going to love me. Going through the inevitable decline and break up of my first marriage and the forming of our partnership, we experienced lot of pressure from some of my family, but it just made

us stronger. These things are never smooth and mistakes are made on all sides but we knew that we were forever the moment we met.

Here we are in the Wild West, I'm the one shooting the light bulb!

So it was 1991 that we first locked eyes on each other and that was when my life story changed completely, it was like, where the hell have you been? Michelle was stage managing a cabaret group from a drama school in London I believe and they were doing musical shows around the holiday sites in Cornwall, so that's how our paths crossed as we were working in the same venues during that summer season. Her life was putting on shows and my life had always been about putting on shows so it was a great fit. She was originally a theatre designer creating stage sets and stuff and after a while she started designing sets for me too. We just knew that this is the way we should be living our life.

She was twelve years younger than me and still is by the way, but in 1991 I was 34 and wearing a tuxedo suit on stage singing New York, New York at the end of the act wearing a trilby hat, and performing like a stereotypical cabaret act was expected to. One of the first things she said to me was, 'Why don't you dress like a 34 year old instead of a 50 year old? and why did you do those gags?' I said, 'Well, that's what everyone does', she said, 'Do you think they're funny'? I said, 'No, not particularly, some of them are ok I suppose'.

Then this was the big one... 'Why don't you do the stuff that you think is funny and make your career about what you want to do?' It was like, wow, what a chat up line, no one's ever said anything like that to me before. She was right of course!

I had a roadie at the time called Mickey who was great, and I could try material out in the car on the way to gigs with him, he'd shout out subjects to me and I'd have to talk about it and make it funny for 60 secs at a time before he hit me with another subject. Mickey liked the surreal stuff too so I started down that road recreating my comedy persona and material.

It was like a whole new world had just been opened up to me, allowing me to follow in the footsteps of my comedy heroes who had influenced me so much when I was growing up. The material was all so off the wall and I loved performing it.

I once finished a gig by eating a ham sandwich. I said to the audience, 'I've had a great night, thank you for laughing and I'd like finish tonight's show by eating a ham sandwich'. So I took it out of the bag and I ate it on the stage in front of them, the

whole sandwich. I finished it and then I said good night and walked off. Interestingly I found out years later that Danny Kaye did a Royal Variety Show and came out saying, 'Good evening, what a lovely honour to be at the Variety Show, it's all been very busy today what with rehearsals and everything so much so that I was unable to grab any lunch however I did managed to find this backstage, so if you just bear with me'. He then sat on the front of the stage and ate an apple... in the royal variety show! WOW!!! I didn't know he'd done that, but it certainly served as an affirmation for what I was doing now.

I just kept trying new things at this one particular venue where I was booked every Sunday night throughout the Summer season, I always finished the show with some surreal comedy. One week we played the Teddy Bear's Picnic tune over the P.A. system, and I came out with all these cute little toy bears that I'd bought cheaply in a pound shop or something and placed them all around the stage, which quickly became quite full of teddy bears and then the music changed.... the BBC test match music started up and I could hear the whole crowd go, 'NO!!'.

I picked up a cricket bat and my roadie bowled the teddy bears at me, so I hit them all over the venue and when the music finished I just said good night.

But that made me laugh, maybe in the back of my mind I was trying to recreate something like the Monty Python Fish Slapping dance from the early seventies. Anyway the upshot of all that surreal content was that for two years I struggled to get a gig because all the agents said, 'You know, you used to be a good, safe act, we could put you anywhere, we can't put that out'.

However I kept believing and so did Michelle in fact it was she who put together a short video of my slightly surreal comedy style film clips to send to ITV's Big Big Talent Show. I got my spot on the show because of that video and subsequent audition, the main thing they liked was that I was funny but also different, and from there I was asked to appear on the Royal Variety Performance.

Poetry Corner

Do you like cheese?
Do you like cheese?
Do you like cheese?
will you tell me please

Do you like bread?
Do you like bread?
I like bread and I'll eat it
til I'm dead!

Do you like butter?
Do you like butter?
I like butter and it
sets my heart a flutter

Do you Like shrimps?
Do you like shrimps?
even Polar Bears like shrimps
I'm not sure about chimps

Do you like me?
Do you like me?
I'm sorry about my
insecurity

But I like you?
yes I really like you?
and maybe one day we'll be best friends
if you like me too

Do you like Silence.....?

CHAPTER 8

'The best thing you can do when you are hurting is to do something, find a place of new beginnings'

Back to the drawing board

When I first started recreating Andy Ford's comedy in order to get myself to the next stage, I basically took a child's physicality and put it into an adult's body, because we all know that when a child is being petulant, their physical reaction is predictable and acceptable, but the same movements and expressions expressed by an adult look awkward, silly and naturally comedic. So that was my basis really, innocent and infantile comedy delivered with clever punchlines. However I don't think comedians ever grow up completely, because just like a small child, all comics need is to be loved. That's what we want.

A successful comedian once said to me that fundamentally, we walk out onto that stage naked and ask people to love us. All I've got are these jokes and my personality, that's it. Johnny Casson put it this way, 'All I want is a laugh, I'm not asking for a kidney'. It's just our way of saying, 'Do you love me? You do? That's fantastic..... You don't? Well, that has really upset and hurt me, so much so

that I'm not ever going to want to perform again.... at least for 24 hours or so'.

That's who we all are, insecurity personified! We're also a very competitive bunch us comedians, however we love each other too. The camaraderie exists because if you were to strip us bare, you'll see that we all possess the same scars of rejection, but we keep coming back and that's how we improve. As an experienced older comic once said to me, 'You can't be a good comedian, without being a bad one first!' It's a learning process but it never ends.

My aim was to make myself stand out by being different... love me or hate me I needed you to remember me. I have always been a creative and so I started to write comedy that made me laugh, and the surreal stuff usually jumped into my head first.

I suppose it all goes back to me lying in my bed at night listening to my Redifusion radio set all by myself in my room and just laughing. As a young lad radio shows like I'm Sorry I'll read that again, I'm sorry I haven't a clue and (eventually when the BBC got round to replaying their classic shows)...The GOONS (starring Peter Sellars, Spike

Milligan and Harry Secombe) which was my favourite. I think it was their show that opened the door to the surreal side of my brain.

Every Sunday as a family we'd have our Sunday roast, then listen to Two Way Family Favourites on the radio which was a request show on the light programme including messages from family members working in the armed forces overseas. We enjoyed it but my favourite bit was the comedy shows that followed, including the Jimmy Clitheroe Show, Ken Dodd, The Navy Lark, Round the Horne and all those sorts of programmes... I just loved them all. So when the Andy Ford reinvention process got underway it was to those memories I turned to for inspiration, particularly the genius that was Spike Milligan.

I started writing daft poems and logical nursery rhymes which I gradually introduced into my performances. Not only was the material new, but no one else was doing it cause it came out of my head. I have to be honest here and say some stuff was stronger than others and performing it live was the only way to find out what worked.

I have never been scared to try new things and being a creative (luckily for me) there always seems to be more ideas coming my way on my comedic conveyor belt. Whether it is poems, comedy songs, nursery rhymes, impressions, animal idioms,

pantomime sketches or new jokes, the stuff just keeps coming and I am so grateful that it does, but I will never take it for granted. My self penned material and the individual way I choose to deliver it is what makes me.... me, be that for better or worse.

Super, smashing Great

In the build up to the Royal Variety show in 1997 I was booked to appear on an ITV show called Talking Telephone Numbers which was presented by Philip Scholfield and Claudia Winkleman. I'd worked out a routine to last about 5 mins and obviously I was keen to avoid the material that I was gonna use in the upcoming Command Performance. Michelle and I were introduced to Jim Bowen the Bullseye Legend backstage and he was due to film a comedy routine for the show after me, we got chatting and he told me that he had seen my Big Big Talent Show spot and was very generous with his praise.

Anyway my time came to film and after Philip's introduction I ran out and went straight into it. My opening gambit was me shouting to the audience,'*Give me a Y!!'* to which they all

replied... *Y!!!* and I came back with, *'Cause I asked you to',* not the funniest line in the history of comedy but It had the desired impact getting big laughs from the crowd and from there I was all set up to continue with the rest of my material.

However after about a minute the floor manager came onto the set waving his hands saying... *'Stop... Stop... Mic problem'.* Apparently the microphone I was wearing had stopped working, and as the show wasn't going out live the sound guy just replaced my Mic in front of everyone and we set back to Philip's intro and went again. *'Ladies and Gentlemen it's Andy Ford!'*

Same again out I ran and shouted, *'Give me a Y'* which again got a laugh from the audience but not quite as big as the first time as they had already heard it before... anyway I just kept going when... would you believe it? There he was again my very good friend the floor manager with the waving hands.... '*Stop another Mic problem'.* So again I had to reset and could see Jim Bowen go over to my Wife Michelle and put his arms around her saying, '*He'll be ok he's a good Comedian he'll deal with it don't worry'.*

Jim Bowen
what a lovely bloke!

What a gent btw and I know Michelle really appreciated that, however my brain was now ticking over like a flipping train... what am I gonna do, they've heard my opening line twice now, they're not gonna laugh at it again. But somehow I kept focused and made a snap decision in my brain....

Come on Andrew trust yourself! Philip now introduces me for the 3rd time and I take to the stage shouting, *'Give me a Y!!'*, the crowd responds with '*Y*' and I come back with... '*I have no idea!!*' BOOOOM!! It worked so well because the audience had been through the 2 false starts and were sort of

routeing for me at that point, so they were delighted and surprised when I changed it up.

If you watch this clip on my youtube channel you'll just see the 3rd version, but bear in mind when you watch, what had happened before. The comradeship given to me that night by the late great Jim Bowen was so appreciated by this TV novice, what an awesome thing to do sir... bless you Jim x

CHAPTER 9

'Such stuff as dreams are made on'

The Royal Variety Performance

OK so the Royal Variety Show 1997 ... still with me? Good, well it was a quite magnificent evening. My Lady looked a million dollars in her Frank Usher dress and I got the chance to hob nob with some incredible stars like Celine Dione, The Spice Girls, Michael Boulton, the two Ronnies and many more.

Dressed to kill...lol !

Because the Victoria Apollo Theatre didn't have enough room backstage to host everyone on the show we had all been given rooms at a Hotel nearby, so we came out of the stage door and made our way to the hotel to change and stuff. At one point I was walking back to the Hotel at the same time as the Spice Girls, I was just behind them, so that felt fairly bizarre walking amongst all the flashing camera light bulbs. Obviously because it was the Royal Variety show there was security everywhere and you were never far from a guard.

Talking of the Spice Girls, I was in the auditorium waiting for my moment to rehearse when they took to the stage. Whilst they were rehearsing the guy who had designed the stage set was taking pictures of the Ladies on his construction, but no one told the girls who he was and they went (how can I say this without getting into trouble) completely upstage about being photographed as they assumed he was paparazzi. He just happened to be the lovely chap that created the set on which we were all to perform. I'm happy to say the slightly emotional outburst from a couple of the ladies didn't last long and calm was restored, but I'll give you the full story if you ask me at one of my gigs.

The whole Royal Variety thing was surreal from beginning to end with this lad from Exeter being surrounded by so many stars wherever he looked. Joe Pasquale called me over when he saw me and we had a lovely chat, he was very encouraging, telling me that it would be fine and that I was gonna have a great spot. Lovely chap Joe, of whom there is more to come in this book. So I get to do my rehearsal and Comedy Producer Michael Hurl joins me on stage with Nigel Lythgoe who was directing. I run through my stuff and they give me some pointers and advice about the cameras and where to look for certain punchlines etc. Really helpful they were, and Nigel said that even if the crowd weren't fantastic for each gag, I should still keep my focus and that it would look great on the telly.

Shell came back to the Hotel with me before the show started and to be fair she was her usual chilled self, but try as I might it was difficult to stay calm on one of the biggest nights of my life. So the show started and I got the chance to see some of it from the wings while I was waiting to do my spot. At one point I was standing there watching next to Sir Trevor Macdonald. No way! I hear you cry, to which I reply...Yes way! Me and Trev hanging out and waiting to do our thang!

I must have walked 3 miles backstage before my

moment came about and there wasn't that much available space in the wings but I just couldn't stand still. Des O'Connor was hosting and doing all the linky bits between the Stars and he was simply brilliant. So eventually it was my turn to take to the stage, I was one of 4 acts from the Big Big Talent Show on ITV, I think I was second or third on in our bit. Jonathan Ross introduced me and I just went for it, I ran out onto the stage and did my material in front of Her Majesty the Queen and Prince Philip and I loved the experience. Just as I'd been advised the audience took a while to lock in to my style but then they seemed to get it, and that first big laugh.... Wow it was so empowering, and helped me to smash on through the spot, and I was very proud of what I did.

Me giving it stick on
The Royal Variety Show

Michelle didn't really watch me that much from her seat in the auditorium as she was totally fixated on

observing the Queen and Prince's reaction to see if they liked me. Prince Philip's seat was not facing the stage completely as apparently protocol dictates that he can't sit with his back to the Sovereign, so it was angled slightly away from the stage. When I was on Michelle said that he turned his body so that he could watch me properly and laughed away at my antics along with Her Majesty who smiled and appeared to be enjoying it all.

After my moment had passed my mind was still spinning from what had just happened and I made my way from the Theatre to the hotel to change into my tuxedo suit in preparation for the Royal meet and greet after the show. It was really dark outside but I felt safe walking back with all the security detail around. I popped into the lift to go to my room and shared it with Brian Conley who was doing the same thing as me, and I have to say he was very jolly and friendly so another treasured moment from the whole experience. On my return to the Theatre the show was still happening so I went into the pub next door which was taken over for the evening and used as a green room/waiting area.

I met Joe Pasquale in there and he encouraged me to join him, Michael Ball and Jonathan Ross for a drink (complimentary of course). That bit is etched

into my memory as the banter was really hilarious, I fed off of their confidence and knowledge of how the big time goes. As I say, great stuff for me the human sponge to soak up. We had a few drinks, then the word came that the show was over and we were all to gather backstage to meet her Majesty. Suddenly this was all too real, but I never imagined that when this special moment came about, I would get to meet my Queen ever so slightly inebriated! Needless to say I wasn't the only one in that relaxed condition. So we're standing there and I looked down to see her approaching....OMG... here we go!

Me meeting Her Majesty
Wow... It really happened

The flash bombs were going off and I could hear polite laughter emanating from further down the line. I braced myself and then..boom! ... there she was right in front of me holding out her hand to

shake mine. She told me that she thought my show was funny at least that's what I assume she said. I definitely heard the word funny and lost most of the rest of it because of the hubbub around us. But her smile to me was simply glorious and her eyes were shining, in a way that suggested her Majesty was very slightly tipsy... just like me. If she was, who could have blamed her, it was her 50th Wedding Anniversary after all.

What a moment that was, I'd performed for my sovereign and she told me she liked it. You can't ever take that away from me.

After the Show Michelle and I were ferried in a Limo to the Dorchester hotel for the after show Ball. The Ray McVay Orchestra were the function band that night and as we passed through an area just outside the main room, a group of people all bedecked in their poshest frocks and suits gave me a hearty round of applause as I walked pass them and into the VIP bit. They were smiling and shouting well done to me, and that just added to the overall feeling that tonight was the start of something really big for me.

We sat at our table in the ballroom and the Director Nigel Lythgoe came over to me and said that he thought I did a fantastic spot and that I would be delighted when I see it go out on the TV. What a night, everywhere you looked in that ballroom there were big stars and I got the chance to chat with many of them.

My Manager and I had shared the finances to purchase the back page of the showbiz publication *The Stage and Television today*, it costed us £500 each but there was going to be a big picture of me announcing to the world that I was on the Royal Variety Show. We were all set for success and felt ready! So in the days after the show was recorded I made my way to London for rehearsals for my first Theatre Pantomime, Peter Pan. I'll tell you more about that Panto later. Very kindly one of the Cast Carrie Anne who was playing Wendy let me stay at her place in London for the rehearsal period.

Whilst I was there I received a phone call from my Wife Michelle and I instantly knew something was wrong, it sounded like she'd been crying and then she told me that my Manager Brian had rung her to say that because of time restraints and the fact that the Royal Variety Show had overrun, they were

cutting my spot from the final edit. So unfortunately for me my spot wasn't going to go out on the TV, and all I could think was, you're kidding me, how can this be happening?.... This is my dream!!! I wasn't the only one to miss out though as Stephen Mulhearn (Mr Saturday Night on ITV) didn't make the broadcast either, the fact that he and I were sandwiched in between the first and last of the Big Big Talent Show Acts, made it the easiest bit of editing to cut us out.

With Lydia Griffiths from theBig Big Talent Show and our Doggie Eric

Stephen's rise still managed to continue after all this though and Kudos to him! I was completely and utterly devastated but then I thought, hey Andrew you still did it.... you did the Royal Variety Show and you met your Queen.

She loved it, shook your hand and thought you were funny, and it was such an honour to meet and perform for her and will remain in my heart as one of the greatest moments of my career.

That being said, I couldn't speak for what seemed like an eternity and my dear wife was waiting and crying on the other end of the phone. But I also knew that with Michelle's love I could get through anything. I certainly didn't see it coming though, as I'd gone well on the night, and Nigel the Director was waxing lyrical to me at the Dorchester Hotel, I was even featured on the ITV advert for the show for God's sake..... but no, that was it. It was really tough on Michelle to have to make that call, but my manager Brian said that he couldn't handle it and asked my Wife to do the heavy lifting there.

To say I walked around in a trance for a couple of days was an understatement, but thank goodness I had a Panto to rehearse and concentrate on, that really helped me to think about other stuff.

I suppose not making the final cut for the Royal Variety Show was one of the lowest points of my life and it took a while to come back from. I'm not ashamed to say that I did feel down, and one day whilst walking on the beach in Bournemouth I considered just walking into the ocean, to end it all.

Pretty dramatic eh? For God's sake Andrew it's only a telly show, get a grip. Fortunately after a couple weeks of feeling sorry for myself, my endlessly supportive wife Michelle said, 'Right that's long enough are you gonna get over yourself and get on with life or just disappear up your own....', fill in the blank dear readers!! To be fair some people in the business were absolutely cruel and horrible to me about not being on the telly version, you know the *'Kick 'em when they're down'* merchants, but most of that came from jealousy I guess, after all I did the Royal Variety and they didn't.

But there was good news coming in over the Pantomime run as well. Obviously other cast members in the show knew of my Variety woes and were very supportive, and on one occasion someone brought me in a copy of the Sun newspaper with an interview with Bob Monkhouse and at one point when asked about whom he thought might break through and become the next comedy star, he mentioned my name..... yes my name! He had seen me on the Big Big Talent Show and loved my style. How much more of an affirmation do you need Andrew.... that's Bob talking about you for God's Sake. Then a few days later someone else said that Des O'Connor was on Steve Wright in the afternoon

on Radio 2 and he said that he also loved my comedy after working with me on the Royal Variety and that people should expect to see me soon on his show! Time to forget about walking into the ocean I guess.

That all happened during the Panto season but just days after the *not making it on to the broadcast thing,* lots of my fellow comedians were sending me messages of support, there really is a strong comradeship in Comedy as I said. I had many phone calls from Joe Pasquale checking that I was OK, letters from Jimmy Cricket, kind words from so many other comics and that really raised me up again.

In retrospect, obviously I would still have wished for a different outcome as regards the missed TV exposure. But I have to say that I learned so much being around people at the top of their game. The show itself is often described as a graveyard for comedians as the somewhat privileged audience is not particularly primed for stand up and when John Lennon said you can sing along or rattle your jewellery he was spot on. But I observed and took it all in, some of the comedians struggled but what I found fascinating was that their body language

stayed positive even when hardly anyone was laughing. Their experience had taught them to hold a confident pose after a punchline, give it a few beats then continue, which gave room for the TV editors to fill the gap with laughter so that it looked like they were storming it. Sorry if that shatters any illusions but TV is TV!!

Michelle and I were special guests at the late Queen's Platinum Jubilee concert outside of Buckingham Palace in 2022 and were horrified to hear a superstar singing completely out of tune on the show. We were convinced that her career was over so when we got back to our hotel after the concert we watched it back on Youtube and surprise!!! ... the audio of her singing had been simultaneously replaced for TV viewers with a version where she was in perfect pitch and a lot of the camera shots were from a distance so it wasn't easy to tell that the voice didn't sync up with the recording.... The power of telly eh?

Andy's
Animal Idioms
This is quite simply ridiculous!
Idiom
Like a Pig on a surfboard
meaning
Someone who is heading for a fall

Rob Rinder MBE

Judge Rinder TV Star

'Pain produces the most profound comedy.. Andy Ford's life is rich with both. a must read'

CHAPTER 10

'One Man in his time plays many parts'

The Joy of Pantomime

So let's talk about Pantomime the genre that completely changed my career trajectory and my life! Before I had the chance to appear in Panto, I was a big fan. I have a vague memory of me taking my kids to see a production in a village Hall in East Devon in the mid 80s and I remember thinking I would love to do that! It was an Amateur Dramatic Society show, and these wonderful local productions raise funds to get their shows on and rely heavily on people giving up their free time to create something special at Christmas for their community. Power to the *AmDrams* that's what I say, they give people the chance to appear on the stage maybe for the first time, and who knows what they might go on to achieve following that opportunity.

Another much stronger memory is when I took my family to see Aladdin at the Theatre Royal in Plymouth in the 1980s. The big name in the show was Female impersonator Danny La Rue, but it was the comedian Allan Stewart playing Wishy Washy

who stole the show, took the plaudits and won the audience's affections. He did an hilarious skit on Michael Jackson singing a George Formby song, which I thought was brilliant.

He really owned the stage that night, but interestingly many years later when Allan and I were working together on a cruise ship and had become table tennis buddies (there's not a lot to do on a sea day), we would chat about the business and our personal experiences and I told him about the first time I had seen him live in Plymouth.

He told me that Danny La Rue was not overly impressed at how well he was going down in the show. Apparently Danny was overheard on the phone to the producers saying,' Too much Wishy darling!' In other words, he wanted them to restrain Allan a bit, maybe reducing his time on stage or something so that he didn't go so well.... insecure much? I completely believed him when he told me that story as I have encountered that scenario myself on more than one occasion.

I don't know about Allan but when I encounter it, I just want to go bigger and better. That night in

Plymouth fired me up with ambitions of shining like Allan did in Panto, but how could I get into it, I had no idea. After getting together with Michelle I was struggling a bit for work because of my new style and I was looking for more opportunities to express myself and earn money. I remember going to the Whitehall Theatre in London to do an audition for a cruise line, and so true to my belief system I did the spot in my new style and surprisingly (to me) they loved it. There then followed quite a few years performing on Airtours Cruises. The agency that booked me was Openwide International and they were looking for different styles of acts to present to their new clientele on board, just great timing for me I guess.

So for the next few years Michelle and I spent our summers cruising around the Mediterranean Ocean getting the chance to regularly visit some wonderful places, we were having fun and for the most part the shows were going great. However eventually a new cruise director (the equivalent of a holiday camp entertainments manager) came on board and instantly took a dislike to my style and went out of his way to make life difficult for me. The joy of cruising with my girl was tarnished for us and the whole experience was feeling less enjoyable. I tend to thrive on positivity and encouragement, that's

what fires me up, and when that's not there then maybe it's the time to look elsewhere. But as my Wife says, you should look for the best possible outcome in situations, which might not always be exactly what you think it is or should be at any particular time!

I continued getting work where possible and whilst gigging for one particular Agent in the Bristol area, I was offered the chance to do a panto and the hairs on the back of my neck stood up at the prospect. For years I'd been aware that the John Mills agency did a touring pantomime and it was definitely on my *things to achieve* list. However when the offer came it was to take part in an Adult Touring Panto. Now I've always prided myself on trying to keep my act as family orientated as possible, but this opportunity just had to be seized and also as Michelle was booked to be the Stage Manager we were able to keep working together… bonus.

The show was directed and written by ex TV Comedy Star Brian Marshall who had just left one of the top entertainment agencies in London to start up his own Artiste management business representing Performers and TV personalities. The Panto was fairly traditional with dirty jokes and

skits added, but hey it was still panto and it was something that I was desperate to do.

I'd read the script and was offered the chance to put in some of my own gags and to my delight and relief I was asked to perform in my normal way which was great as I certainly didn't want my delivery to change despite the fact that this show was aimed at adults.The show was called, wait for it.... ***Jack and his Beanstalk!!*** All very self explanatory I feel. I have to tell you that I worked with some wonderful people on that show including Adrian Varcoe from Bristol *the sequinned comedian* as he was known, a really fabulous Drag comedy performer.

The Brilliant Adrian Varcoe
Bristol's best!

Michelle and I got very close to Adrian and we'd even stop over at his house occasionally on our Panto tours. He was just so funny, and in his camp acidic way he would say, 'Look I've worked with Bradley Walsh, Brian Conley and Joe Pasquale, would you hurry up and get famous... you're knackering my CV!' I simply adored him and when he was lost to cancer years later, we joined with many famous faces at his funeral service paying respect to a much loved talent and friend.

The female lead on our Panto with an absolutely brilliant and powerful voice was Sarah Devonshire who Michelle and I also became very close with, so much so that she even sang at our Wedding more of which later.

So the gag for this Panto was that the Giant was played by a Dwarf... Kenny Baker no less, the guy who was inside of R2D2 in Star Wars. The late and much missed Kenny was an absolute joy to work with and had been in the business for many years, playing harmonica with the Minitones on lots of variety bills and TV shows. Anyway during the panto Kenny would do a spot of his comedy and harmonica playing, a bit dated for our audiences but well executed by him. So he'd start with a song, then go into some jokes about the war and finish on a harmonica bit. However one night things went how can I put it.... slightly awry. Kenny went on to do his spot which roughly lasted for 8 to 10 minutes during which the rest of the cast would have a break backstage, and certain members of our troupe would take a quick nicotine hit. One of the cigarette smoking members of our cast played the Sado Masochistic character of Miss Whiplash in the Panto (I told you it was an Adult show) and was referred to by the Giant as Whippy. By the way before I forget it, the main joke written to explain

the reason that a Dwarf Actor was playing the Giant went like this....

Female Actor	Who are you?
Kenny	I'm the Giant
Female Actor	Well you don't look like a Giant to me
Kenny	It's my day off!!

Fabulous eh? Anyway back to the incident, witnessed by my wife who watched it all from the wings. Kenny sang his opening number which was *All of me, why not take all of me* (you probably had to be there), played his harmonica and then started shouting for Miss Whiplash to come back on stage, however as explained she had taken her wig off and was sitting with her feet up having a cigarette when Michelle burst into the green room and shouted Miss Whiplash you're needed on stage.

What a sight as she ran from the back of the theatre, skirt pulled up to her knickers adjusting her

Wig and trying to rezip her kinky boots as she hopped and charged towards the stage. When she appeared there next to him Kenny said, 'Where the hell have you been, I've been calling you for ages'. So they got through the rest of that scene and Kenny exited the stage on the same side as Michelle was running the show from. He stood in front of her, looked up and said, 'What happened.... *(moment of realization)...* Oh No, I forgot to do my act!'.... just Precious!!

During this tour we played an adult only weekend at Butlin's in Ayr, on the Scottish West Coast. OH MY ACTUAL GOD!! Yes, true the agent had put our show out as an adult Panto, which would seem to fit into the general feel of the adult weekend scenario, but we were way out of our depth here. We had to follow male and female strippers who were more or less presenting a live sex show, and comedians who would do more than make your Granny blush, she'd have a heart attack. Blue was most definitely the colour and we were like a fish out of water!

By the time we started our show the audience were completely hammered and within a few minutes were baying for Blood, or Sex.... or both. It was one of the most intimidating situations that I had ever faced, so I did my opening bit and got off as soon as I could.

The other comic on our show tried hitting the crowd with heckler stoppers, you know quick one liners to shut them up, but to no avail, in fact it just made them more aggressive. At one point they started rhythmically clapping their hands and singing... 'Get them off, get them off, get them off', and I can assure you dear readers that it was not a request for us to strip but more of an order to get off the stage.

The cast members who were on at this point realised that it was all getting a bit too feisty and therefore it was time to go and headed straight into the wings, but the guys in the Pantomime Cow costume weren't really aware of the animosity and because of the thickness of the costume which impaired their ability to hear properly, they just heard a stifled version of the crowd singing and clapping so assumed that it was all fun audience participation. Our Cow then proceeded to dance enthusiastically on centre stage in the middle of all this mayhem! What a sight, a dancing Cow being pelted by beer glasses and the like, it was Armageddon!

Security were running around like headless chickens and at one point we were locked into our dressing rooms for our own safety. After a while the

situation calmed and we were able to make our escape out of the back door of the complex, with the help of security guards, who broke our stage set down in five minutes and shoved it on to the back of the bus in a heart beat.

Then, to the backdrop of drunken ladies relieving themselves onto the pavement outside the auditorium (what a lovely sight) and some of the gentlemen who were still able to remain vertical, projectile vomiting for Britain, the bus made it's bid for freedom. However Shell and I had been towing her Dad's Caravan with us for this part of the tour to save on accommodation costs and we had to make our way to our car first in order to make our escape. BTW thank you Butlin's at Ayr for that unique experience, what a joy!

Andy's Animal Idioms

Idiom

Like a Bunny wearing a condom

meaning

Something that is not likely to happen

Billy Pearce

Comedy Star and Panto Royalty

'I'm old school and there aren't many comedians who make me belly laugh but the wonderful Andy Ford is one of them. A very funny, lovely, talented man with very funny bones and one of the nicest people in showbiz I've ever met OR and He makes me sick! If it needs to be longer ….'

CHAPTER 11

'The path is smooth that leadeth on to danger'

Is this how it all ends?

So we left the Holiday centre and started on the journey to Michelle's parents home near Teeside. We'd decided it was too long a journey to do all in one go, especially after what we'd just been through, so after a few hours we pulled into a lay by on the side of the road for the night. Not sure if we were in the Scottish Borders or the Lake District but wherever it was we woke up to the most beautiful landscape we'd ever seen, it was stunning and made our hearts sing.

After a bit of breakfast we and our doggie Eric headed off to complete our journey with a couple of rest days looming before the show would be at the City Hall of Varieties in Leeds, a place I was so looking forward to playing as I'd watched many of my heroes play that Theatre on The Good Old Days on telly and the thought of performing on that same stage excited me greatly.

It was a lovely day but the further south we dropped the more windy it became. By the time that we had made it to the A66, I was starting to feel tired so Michelle took over the driving. Eric was sitting on

my lap as I dozed. Michelle had just negotiated a hilly part of the road overtaking a tractor en route and was just coming down the other side when the wind picked up considerably.

We were now on Bowes Moor which I found out afterwards was a notoriously bad area for strong gusts of wind. Our car started picking up speed and the caravan started snaking behind us, I heard Michelle scream as the car veered towards the central barrier. She was taught not to break too severely with the van in tow, but trying to drive out of it wasn't working either. With a loud crash we hit the barrier and suddenly we heard what sounded like an explosion as the caravan ripped itself free from our car and flew through the air towards the field beside us. The momentum of that spun us over and at one point Michelle's head smashed through her driver's side window and actually touched the road underneath us as we were still moving. She told me after that she kept thinking to herself at that moment, 'If I don't close my eyes, I won't die'. Somehow I escaped any serious injury, maybe because I was half asleep and therefore my body wasn't tense. We landed on the side of the road and there was a slightly humorous moment when as the car righted itself, Eric our doggie now freed from my grasp slid first one way along the dashboard top

then back to me.

The silence was so eerie after the crazy sounds we'd just experienced during the crash. It was then that Michelle noticed that the Tractor we had not long passed and a lorry driver had blocked the road behind us when they saw what was happening so that passing traffic wouldn't add to the problem. Someone (I don't know who) called the police and ambulance service and they arrived really quickly I think, time wasn't making much sense at that moment. Michelle's door was jammed as was mine but somehow I was able to open my window and climb out of our squashed vehicle. I'm not exactly sure how but I did manage to get Michelle out as well, she was very shaky and her head was bleeding. Then to my horror I realised that our nearly full Calor Gas Bottle from the Caravan had seemingly flown threw the air and landed upright next to our car... how lucky were we to avoid that missile? A couple of cars had now pulled up in front of us and they were doing their best to help including inviting Shell to sit on their back seat, she was truly grateful but worried that she might get blood onto their upholstery and didn't want her bloody appearance to scare their baby. Strange the concerns that go through your mind in a crisis.

So the Police and Ambulance turn up and the first thing the Officer said to Michelle was, 'Were you in this car?' Shell said that we had been and he said that he couldn't believe we were talking to him and had survived, to be fair the car looked a bit like it had been through a mangle. Shell and I got into the ambulance and the policeman took Eric with him back to the station to look after whilst we were being taken care of at the Darlington Memorial Hospital, ironically the place where my lovely Wife was born. Anyway when we arrived I called Michelle's Mum to let her know what had happened and then we were checked in and triaged, as I say I was incredibly lucky but Shell had the worst of it. She had a cat scan and a few other checks and procedures but they ultimately thought that she would be ok to go home to her Mum's to rest. I can only imagine how her Mother felt driving over to the place where she had given birth to her daughter not knowing if it would be the last time she'd see her.

Mercifully she wasn't as bad as first thought, her head was bleeding quite badly and they had to put a flipping enormous bandage round and round her head, poor girl she looked like she was changing into a mummy fancy dress costume, either that or

impersonating John Cleese on Fawlty Towers doing the sketch about the Germans, and before you say anything my girl was laughing at the vision she encountered in the mirror too. But somehow we'd survived, and we're both convinced that someone or something was watching over us. Michelle's Mum picked us up and the relief and simultaneous concern for her daughter was written large on her face for all to see. What a life changing moment we went through that day, we had both thought that we'd lost the other, but no... we still had lots more to achieve... together.

We've still got lots more to Do!

After all of that I still managed somehow to really enjoy being in that Panto even though I had to swear a couple of times in it which I wasn't happy about, cause it was still Panto and that's what I wanted to do.

During the run I signed to Brian Marshall the director and he represented me for quite a few years after that. From that show I was booked to be the comedian in a touring Country Music show called *Forever in Blue Jeans,* and following that John Mills asked me to do his family touring Panto which I considered to be the Holy Grail at the time and was delighted to perform in them for a couple of years, alongside Michelle who stage managed as always.

Viv Danning played the Baron Hardup/Sultan type roles and always did his own little spot in the shows showcasing his fabulous impressions and musical abilities that he'd been using for many years in the Comedy Showband Omen, and many years later we worked together on a couple of shows about West Country Legend Adge Cutler where Viv's Tuba playing skills were a great asset to our productions. The director of these touring pantos was Ben Murphy another great friend and an outrageous musical comedy performer, Sarah was still the female lead with Adrian as the Dame. The tours were exhausting but fantastic.

One night for example we got to our overnight accomodation, namely a Travelodge at 3am in the

morning and we were up at 5am to get on the road again in order to arrive at a venue in South Wales ready to do a 10.30 am show for school children... oh did I not say that we carried the set and P.A. system into the venues, put up the stage set each day and took it down after the shows ready to stash it in the back of the coach til the next morning? How remiss of me! It was relentless but also fantastic, I learned so much from those touring days and I'm pretty sure that the comedian you see in front of you now in Pantomime is a product honed on the road touring in those productions... that was my apprenticeship! There are some clips from those days on my Youtube channel if you fancy a little look.

CHAPTER 12

'Like as the waves make towards the pebbled shore'

My first Theatre Panto

During those touring days my Manager Brian would bring Panto producers in to see me with the hope that they would want to book me for an actual Theatre Pantomime. Eventually he did the deal with E&B productions run by Pantomime Empresario Paul Elliot and I was booked as Mr Smee to appear at the Bournemouth Pavilion, I think the fact that I was about to appear on the big big talent show on telly helped to sway their decision. I have mentioned the whole Royal Variety debacle that happened whilst I was appearing in this Panto but I've sort of passed over other details of the show experience.

I turned up at rehearsals in London to meet my co-star Ted Rogers from TVs 321 Fame. We instantly hit it off and I was so excited to be working with this comedy legend. However during the rehearsal process the producers noticed that Ted was struggling to remember script and direction and decided to take him off the show. I was devastated as was Ted I'm sure, and to make matters worse the show was booked to do a week's stint at the Bristol

Hippodrome before going on to our full run at the Bournemouth Pavilion. Now there were only 2 days left before we opened in Bristol and the bosses had taken our star off the show... what were we going to do?

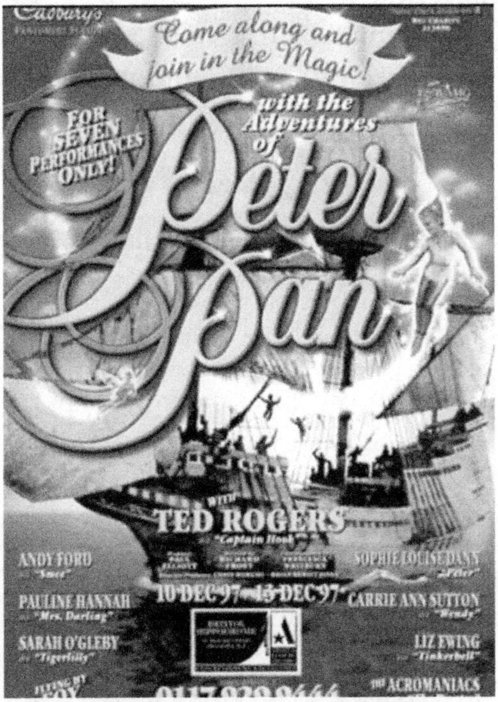

Last minute an *old school* experienced professional Actor called Leon was booked to take Ted's Place, but he had no chance of learning it all in such a short space of time, so for some of the scenes he actually held a script in order to get through them.

The guy was just brilliant, and the whole of the 7 day run at the Hippodrome passed without major incident. This Pantomime appearance was my first at this illustrious theatre and I loved it, who would have ever thought that I'd go on to play there so many times? One day after a performance of the Panto in Bristol Paul Elliot walked into my dressing room with a bottle of Cutty Sark Whisky and thanked me for saving his show! Success tasted lovely that night.

I'm guessing Leon wasn't available for the Bournemouth dates and he was replaced by Sean Canning who played Captain Hook brilliantly, ably assisted on stage by our fabulous Peter Pan who was musical star Sophie Louise Dann. The lovely Carrie Ann Ford played Wendy and it was her apartment that I was staying in when I received the infamous Royal Variety call from my wife, but I have to say that being on stage at Bournemouth for my first Theatre Panto was exhilarating and positive.

The Pantomime was well received and my performance as Smee was taking the plaudits not only from the audiences but the local press as well... I just wanted to do more of these shows.

So after the successful Panto run in Bournemouth which didn't produce very much in the way of earnings, we were really starting to struggle financially. The Royal Variety Show affair and the predicted TV offers that just didn't materialise combined to make me feel like a bit of a failure. Ridiculous really as I'd just smashed my first Theatre Pantomime, but the mind works in funny ways sometimes and at that point all I could see was a half empty glass.

The work dried up again and things got so bad that I actually signed on the dole hoping that we could get help towards the rent for our house in Cropredy Oxfordshire where we were living. This was the first time in my life that I ever asked our government benefits system for help, but things were not looking good work wise for me. What a split screen moment eh? Three months earlier I was standing on a stage performing for the Queen surrounded by global stars and here I was queuing up at an unemployment centre in Banbury asking for financial help! From the sublime to the ridiculous, but I couldn't handle it, I was so embarrassed that I just stopped claiming, we were determined to get through this any way we could. I don't think we ever bought anything to eat that didn't have a Tesco Value label on it, and we also collected kindling and

branches whilst walking our doggie Eric along the canal to burn on our fire in the front room so that we didn't have to use the heating, whatever cutbacks we thought would help... we did them. Throughout it all we stood strong and positive together.

Michelle and I had always said that we would live in a cardboard box if we had to, so one way or another we were gonna get out of this. I kept pushing my manager to find me work all the time this was going on and fortunately he found me some. He managed to secure me a spot for the summer season at the Central Pier in Blackpool on the Frank Carson Show....THANK GOD!!

All the fun of the Pier
With Frank Carson in 1998

So Shell and I sorted out our digs for the run and off we went to Blackpool with our doggie Eric. To this day I'm not conved that Frank Carson's audience was the perfect fit for my humour, but my spots seemed to go well and we had a good time performing and socialising in the Showbiz capital of the North that summer.

We were young
we were foolish
we were soaked
to the skin...Yay
Blackpool

The flying Dutchman bar was the venue that most of Blackpool's performers would go to after their shows and we'd all chat and network together, it

really was quite a community. In a town like that where Entertainment was the number one thing, everyone seemed to know everyone else's business. The word spread that the assistant producer of the Des O'Connor Show was coming up to watch Johnny Casson (a fantastic, experienced, really funny Northern Comedian and lovely chap) perform his act one night at the Viking Show Bar, with a view to booking him for Des's prime time TV show.

As I mentioned Des had said earlier that year on the Steve Wright radio show that he wanted to put me on his telly show, and I kept pressing my manager to sort it with their production team, but to no avail. Brian said he'd been trying but there was nothing positive to report yet. So dear readers it was time for me to step up and go headlong into the fray to make this happen.

Michelle and I went to the Viking bar the night of the assistant producer's visit, and as well as watching Johnny and loving his show, I tracked down Des's representative and started chatting with him at the bar as you do. I told him that I did the Royal Variety with Des and that I believe he wanted me on his show, so he said, send me your Showreel and I'll see what I can do. So now I had a name, an

address and providing I got this to him pronto I should still be in his head. I posted the video the next day!!

At the time Michelle and I were into our positive mantras and we'd been reading the Louise L Hay book, *'You can heal yourself'* (a great read btw), so we were visualising and attempting to stay positive about everything. I was even looking into the front room mirror everyday and telling myself that I could open doors and make things happen because I was a good comedian and deserved to be successful... that sort of thing. Anyway, one day I was talking to my reflection as you do being positive when the phone rang. It was my manager Brian, he said, 'Are you still funny?', and I said,'I'm hilarious!' he said,'Good cause you're on the Des O'Connor show next Wednesday!!'

I'd made it happen!! Again! I told everyone in our cast about my news as well as Joe Pasquale (who was playing at the Grand Theatre) when we met up for a drink and he offered to go through my material with me before I went to London, as he'd done Des's show loads of times and knew how it all worked. We all went to Gigi's Greek Restaurant in Blackpool and after the meal which Joe kindly paid

for, I went through the gags. It was pretty safe material and Joe said, yep mate that should work fine, but there was something in the back of my mind that made me say, 'But this is the stuff I really want to do Joe!' I then proceeded to do my poem Ode to a garlic Crusher to him. He laughed and said, 'You have got to do that Andy, that's you, it's really funny!' That was exactly what I needed and wanted to hear and so it was definitely going into the show!

We had to go down to London for a script read through with the Producer Colin Fay and the Show comedy writer Neil Shand (the guy who had written for everyone, I mean everyone...Cooper, Eric and Ernie, Dawson... everyone), I went through it all including the Garlic Crusher and they liked what I'd written so it was all go for next week's show. I'm not sure whether the producers in Blackpool had given me the night off to record the TV spot or how they sorted it but anyway it was all happening.

Shell and I checked into our hotel near to where the show was to be filmed, made ourselves comfortable and when the time was right we were asked to make our way to ITV's Teddington Lock Studios to record my part on the show. This was happening!

I was sent to make up and whilst I was being beautified in walks flipping Catherine Zeta Jones, I kid you not. She smiled, I smiled, it was a very moving and tender moment but over in a heartbeat.... and strangely neither of us talk about it to this very day, some things are best left unsaid. But we'll always have..... '*the make up room*'.

Whilst waiting to go onto Des's Show I had been strategically positioned behind the Stage set Lift doors through which I would make my entrance. The positive mental attitude thing was still very strong with me at that time and I was meditating, affirming and mantra-ing like nobody's business backstage before Des introduced me, and when I heard him say my name I just ran out and hit that stage like a whirlwind. Mr. O'Connor was the most perfect and engaging host, with the unmatched ability to make the whole chat look natural and spontaneous. There was an autocue on stage behind me for him to read the questions he needed to ask in order to set up my comedy for me. It was all going swimmingly until he started talking about relaxing and asking me if I played Golf. For a mili-second my brain said what the *@$#! is he saying? Then I remembered one of the things that Joe had told me in the restaurant in Blackpool, he said that Des's eyes weren't that great so occasionally he

might ask you the wrong question if he can't see the autocue very well. Thanks Joe, I quickly leaned slightly to one side and took a quick peek at the autocue behind me and saw that the question should have been about TV. I said in reply to him, 'Well to be honest Des I'm not that great at relaxing but I do love to watch TV, and by the way I have to tell you that there has been trouble in Telly Tubbyland'.... then into my gags...phew! If you watch that clip on Youtube you can see the momentary confused look on my face and the subsequent lean to check out the autocue.

Look! I really made Des laugh!

But the thing is that I'd saved it, and then I just kept going on with my material which also included the Garlic Crusher and the audience absolutely loved it. When it went out on the telly the editor actually

changed the running order of my routine slightly and placed that poem at the end of my spot because it had received such a great reaction in the studio, and I was absolutely delighted with that. The whole experience was just fantastic, I had actually just stormed one of the shows that I had so wanted to appear on, and it was Prime Time Telly Ladies and Gentlemen!

Des showing me that ear wax
Is no barrier to success

It led to many more TV appearances with Des who just loved to promote new comedians. BTW the line up for the show I appeared on when it was broadcast was Des O'Connor, Glenda Jackson, Ben Elton, Cliff Richards, Shania Twain and..... Andy

Ford!! BOOM! I was so upset when this star entertainer and chat show Legend passed away… I will forever be grateful for the opportunities and the friendship that you gave me Des...RIP you Star x

Poetry Corner

You, you're my Garlic Crusher
you flavour up my life,
you save me half an hour's chopping
and all the stress and strife.

You, you're my Garlic Crusher,
you aid my butter taste,
I love to squeeze your handles
and watch the Garlic push through your face.

You, your my Garlic Crusher
lying in the drawer
waiting for me to take you out
but I don't mean to the Cinema.

You, you're my Garlic Crusher
you cost me two pounds twenty,
I realise with you around
my life is not so empty.

You, you're my Garlic Crusher.

CHAPTER 13

Our bodies are our gardens to the which our wills are gardeners

Real Life

As well as all the showbizzy stuff happening that summer, real life also knocked on our door. Whilst chatting with my daughter on the phone one night she said that she had discovered a small lump on her neck and a few days later she was told that she had been diagnosed with Thyroid Cancer and was being fast tracked for an operation. She was only about 18 years old, I told her that I was coming down to Devon to be with her and she told me not to travel but to stay where I was. 'You can't do anything Dad stay there and I'll make sure the hospital let's you know how the operation goes'. I felt numb, but of course she was right and we chatted as much as we could in the lead up to the operation.

On the day it happened I was expecting the call to tell me that her surgery had finished and hopefully had been a success. It was all meant to take a few hours but nearly six had passed and I couldn't get any information. Eventually I had to go to work at the Central Pier and whilst I was in my dressing

room waiting for the start of the show, the phone rang. It was the hospital and they said that the procedure had gone on a lot longer than expected but that it was a success and Alisha was in her bed recovering.

I cried, Michelle held me tight and then my intro music started up and I was straight onto the stage! That night went really well strangely enough, with so much on my mind you would have thought that I would be distracted, but when life throws tough moments at me for some reason my performance feels even more focused than usual, it's happened quite a few times now. Weird eh? Maybe it's just my mind and body overcompensating or me immersing myself in my job as a coping mechanism, I'm not really sure.

After a few days we left Blackpool at about 5am one morning and drove to Exeter to see my daughter in the hospital bearing a cassette tape of Blackpool performers including the big stars sending her messages of love and encouragement for her recovery. She didn't know that we were coming and the look on her face when she saw us there will stay with me for the rest of my life. She squealed with delight and the emotion was palpable, unfortunately

we couldn't cuddle her as she had to stay in her sealed room because of the radiation that she was receiving. But we were together and that was all that mattered, we couldn't stay that long as she was quite weak and needed her rest so we were back on the road to Blackpool after an hour or so and just about made it back in time to do the evening show! Alisha has since told me that our visit plus the lovely messages on the tape really helped her to get through it all. My daughter has been through so much in her young life and not all of it is documented here, but she managed to beat the cancer and is now living a healthy life, love you forever darling you make me very proud.

Me and my Strong, Beautiful Daughter Alisha x

My Son Justin has also created a fantastic life for himself after some earlier teenage challenges which I'm proud to say he got himself through. Together with his wonderful Wife Lynn I'm so happy to say that he has gifted us 3 magnificent and adorable grandchildren, whom I love with an absolute passion.

Me and Justin Absolutely Smashing The Father And son Contest x

Things weren't easy for either of my children whilst my marriage split was happening, and for a while I wasn't able to see or visit them because of various

family pressures, but it didn't stop me from trying. Throughout that period I just kept writing letters to my children, telling them how much they were loved and eventually our relationship got a positive reboot when we were able to see each other again (which is what we all needed) and it has never looked back.

Sometimes we Adults don't handle all that emotional mess too well do we? They don't teach you how to deal with all that relationship stuff when you're in school or college do they? You just have to muddle through and do the best you can, but in the end love is always the answer and the way forward.

Me and my lovely lot
How lucky am I?

Meanwhile back at the show business end of this story, the two years of getting hardly any work melted away because I was suddenly doing The Big Big Talent, the Royal Variety and the Des O'Connor Show regularly, performing the material that I wanted to do. It was such an interesting and exciting period in my life, all created by Michelle and me!

CHAPTER 14

'A wise man knows himself to be a fool."

My comedy heroes

As far as my career is concerned the music came first, but I was always in love with comedy. I started doing short comedic bits when I eventually formed my own band, so if one of the musicians on stage broke a string, I'd fill in with a couple of gags then eventually 2 became 4 and so it progressed to the point where I was doing 5 minutes of comedy here and there and just loving the sound of the laughter. To be fair, it was my first wife, Chris who said to me, 'You're organizing all these gigs, fronting them, singing the songs, paying everybody but it's you that people want to see'.

So as mentioned earlier I became a solo artiste with my guitar and drum machine playing pubs and clubs, I started to earn more money and it was during these gigs that I kept introducing more and more humour which made me happy. The comedy that brought me so much joy as a young lad was now becoming an integral part of my act and in a strong way helping to map out my destiny.

Things done well and with a care, exempt themselves from fear'

My **Eric and Ernie** story

My comedy journey really began with watching my heroes Eric and Ernie on the telly and eventually getting to see their live show! I was eleven years old and I went to Hele's Grammar School in Exeter, one day some guys who were involved with a local spastics society (as it was then known) came to the school to ask for volunteers to help collect money from the audiences of the Morecambe and Wise show that was coming to Exeter.

I gratefully received permission from Mum and Dad to take part in the charity collections. The shows took place over two nights and there was a fantastic bill.... Mrs Mills on the piano who was just great and really whipped up the crowd, Ray Allen and Lord Charles the TV Ventriloquist, Norman Vaughan the host of Sunday Night at The London Palladium, Des Lane the Penny Whistle man, and the Johnny Wiltshire Sound who held the whole show together musically. Well the first half was great and during the interval we set to, collecting charitable donations from the audience. Then came the second half.... Eric and Ernie.

I was actually sitting on the steps of the auditorium in between the seats to watch it all... this was obviously well before health and safety had been invented! So it all happened in front of my very eyes, and I was just rolling around the steps of the auditorium in hysterics. It was simply the funniest thing I'd ever seen in my life. I'd loved them on TV, but live, oh God, they were just making stuff up on the spur of the moment. I was watching pure genius and I took it all in.

Then it was time for the Second show on the first night, and I'm watching it thinking Oh, Eric has done that ad lib line again because it had gone so well in the first show. It wasn't until the next night that I realized all the ad lib bits were rehearsed. If you say that to some people, they might be slightly disappointed that it hadn't happened by mistake on the night they were watching and I often get that in panto, you know, when something '*goes wrong*', was that meant to happen? For some reason, if an ad lib is rehearsed, people feel duped. I didn't feel duped, I felt exhilarated and excited by it. They've made it look like there are mistakes in there, but they're not mistakes... no, it was all just set up brilliantly by this wonderful double act who had been honing their comedy for many years. My inner sponge was in overdrive, and I was drinking it all in.

Ernie was the best feed ever, Eric was just the funniest of men and they had a love and trust of each other that I don't think will ever be surpassed.

I watched a comedy masterclass!

That experience completely changed my life, I knew that I wanted to be a comedian right there in that moment. It wouldn't happen for a fair few years, but that was the catalyst for what eventually was to come. After their show they came out front to meet us charity type collecting people, but I was too nervous to go and shake their hand. Can you believe that? My comedy heroes were standing right

in front of me and somehow I couldn't push myself forward to meet them, there's a life lesson right there!

'Better a witty fool than a foolish wit'

Norman Wisdom

Many years later, when I was working with Frank Carson in Blackpool, Norman Wisdom was doing a Saturday Night Lottery TV show with Bradley Walsh at the Grand Theatre, and we went in to see the rehearsals for it. Norman was honing a comedy routine with Bradley in which he was eating an apple, not sure why apples keep coming up in this book but hey it must be a metaphor for something!

The unique and brilliant
Norman Wisdom

So Norman was there on stage, he finishes his rehearsal, and starts walking out. Michelle said, 'Go say hello, don't do what you did with Eric Morecambe, go and speak to him'. I went up to the great man and I said, 'I'm Andy Ford, I'm playing with Frank Carson on the Central Pier'. He said, 'I hear you're doing really well there', and we shook hands... me and Norman Wisdom shook hands!

I'm so grateful that I grew up at a time when I could watch these masters of comedy and then get the chance to meet some of them whilst pursuing my own comedy career years later.

and just like that....

Tommy Cooper came on to my personal radar a few years after Eric and Ernie, but I soon realized what a complete genius he was. I never saw him live or ever met him and those are big regrets for me. Sometimes we don't even realise how affected we have been by someone, for example I do an impression of a man who's never seen a strawberry in his life, and I walk forward, look down on the floor and say, 'What's that?' How Tommy Cooper is that line?? Nothing's new in comedy I suppose, but it's the way you do it... thank you for that Frank Carson!

Tommy Cooper...
The first comedy influencer!

I used to do a gag about a shrimp with a wooden crutch walking around in a circle at a doctors waiting room. It had been to an underwater singles party the night before, I said something like how did you hurt your leg and it's reply was, 'I was chatting up some shellfish but I think I must have pulled a muscle'. I used to do this whole routine with physical comedy thrown in and it was even featured on one of my videos. It wasn't until after I'd written it that I saw it in a joke book and I thought, I'm obviously not the first person to come up with creating that one, but it doesn't matter because it was formed in my own brain so I'm doing it! The

genius that was Tommy Cooper inspired many more comedians than just me, his character based comedy was just simply the best and in my humble opinion will never be surpassed.

I used to be worried to death about doing other people's gags, but now I realize that I could do a joke that other comedians have done for years, and it would feel completely different because no one else would perform it in the way that I do. As I get older I'm not so concerned about that anymore, funny is funny and as long as my creative process is still involved I'll perform it.

Bob Monkhouse once said to Cornish Comedy Legend Jethro, 'That joke you did on Des O'Connor about Red Adair the other night, everyone knows that gag, but you did a line in there that was the funnier than the gag'. It was about Red Adair the famous oil spillage fire fighter, and someone had called him about extinguishing an oil fire, and Red says, 'Well I can't come now, I'm papering the landing!!' Nothing to do with the gag, everything to do with who Jethro was, and that was what made it funny.

So now I know who Andy Ford is. I know how to do stuff that makes me laugh, and I'm playing to a fan base of people that want me to do it. That's fantastic... I can stand on the stage and say, 'I'm going to do a roly poly for you Ladies and Gentleman', then fail to execute it properly and say, 'Oh, I didn't quite make it did I?' My audiences laugh at the physical humour and love the fact that I didn't do the roly poly, how ridiculous is that?.. I think that everyone should have a good dose of Silly everyday!

'Conversation should be pleasant without scurrility, witty without affectation'

Time well spent with **Jethro**

I was lucky enough to work many times with Jethro who now is sadly no longer with us, and once again as I've mentioned before, we comedians have this kindred spirit thing where we can sit down and talk about what it is we do for hours on end. Some nights after a show at Jethro's club we would sit there, just him and me talking about why certain words or numbers were funny. I know it sounds a bit like we were contemplating our own navels but we really find this stuff interesting. Armed only with a bottle of scotch and our love of comedy we would while away two to three hours getting deep and

meaningful but most of the time cracking each other up! He once said to me that although we haven't got any diplomas or anything like that to hang on the wall, we had learned enough during our careers to know how to survive, and that's a big deal. RIP Funny Man x

Jethro and I just chatted and I loved it!

Logical Nursery Rhymes

Jack and Jill
went up the hill
to fetch a pail of water

Jack fell down
and broke his crown
and Jill got arrested
for pushing!

Steve McFadden

TV Star Phil Mitchell Eastenders

'I was introduced to Andy by Barbara Windsor after his show in Bristol and having seen his work and then working alongside him, he really is the nicest man in show business and very funny and talented to boot'.

CHAPTER 15

'The evil that men do lives after them'

I cannot forgive!

I have agonised for quite some time about whether to put this into my book, it was a difficult decision but in the end I chose to tell you about this moment in my life because I refuse to consider myself a victim. I am a survivor and I came through this, carrying on with my life to do all the stuff you've been reading about here. I struggled to find where to put this painful memory in, but now seems as good a point as any other so let's do this Andrew.

Now this happened when I was a young lad in the local church choir, I got on well with everyone there and loved rehearsals every week as we used to play football in the church grounds beforehand. Of course we always got into trouble for that, but I loved the singing side of things too. Our Vicar was the Reverend Moellar, one of the loveliest people I ever met, in fact at Christmas when we used to go Carol singing around local hospitals and care homes we would always sing Good King Wencleslas together, him taking the role of the King and me doing the page bits. I also loved playing table tennis with him regularly at our Church Youth Club on a Wednesday. The fact that he trusted me to do a

good job when singing solos at weddings etc. meant a lot to me. The only time I'd ever seen him sad was when his Wife passed away and we sang at her funeral, this giant of a father figure and our trusted Vicar was suddenly a broken man in front of my eyes, I think it was the first time I'd ever witnessed grief up close and it had a massive impact on me.

Our Choirmaster was Percy Thorne and he was such a good bloke you know? Dedicated to playing every week at all the services and taking the choir rehearsals too. With him and the Vicar supporting me the church became a wonderfully safe environment for me where I could express myself. He sadly passed away during a church service one Sunday, I believe he choked, I'm just grateful that I wasn't there on that occasion, I don't think that I could have handled witnessing his demise cause he meant the world to me and he was such a mentor. His son was proud to take over the organ playing and choir duties after the loss of his father.

But everything changed for me when I was sexually assaulted one day by an adult male chorister. For obvious reasons no names will be used in this, but he was a regular member of our choir and seemed to be there for a long time, every one of us lads

knew him as a friendly chap who would always have a laugh with us. He seemed to hone in on me more than the others and I had guessed that it was just because he liked me. I was only about 8 or so and had no idea that I was actually being groomed, he also befriended my parents when he saw them on a Sunday and like all of us they thought he was a nice chap.

One day he said he was leaving our choir because he was to become a choirmaster/ church organist in another parish a long way away. He asked my parents if it was OK for me to join him for a short trip to Somerset one day as he was going to look at a church organ that his new employers were hoping to buy.

He was our friend for God's sake, they weren't gonna say no and of course I was enthusiastic for the adventure, especially as my Dad didn't drive so it wasn't very often that I got to travel in a car. We set off and chatted I guess, looked around this church organ factory for a while then made our way back. I really can't remember where it was, but he pulled over in some country lane or wherever and all I can remember is that this man started stroking my head and eventually placed his hand inside my

trousers. I was 8 years old and completely petrified, he said something along the lines of... *'what's this then?'* and I was so terrified that all I can remember saying was, *'I don't know'*. Whether I have blanked any more of this event from my mind I'm not sure, but I believe that he stopped fairly soon after that and took me home. I never told my parents a thing about it, whether that was because I felt ashamed and blamed myself or whether I was aware that if I told them my Dad would kill him and go to prison I'm not sure... but in my young head it just felt right to say nothing. I'm not sure if I ever saw him again, I think he left quite soon after that... but I'll never forget what he did to me and I'll never forget his name. I still find it difficult to forgive him as the hurt and inner turmoil continued for many years.

My biggest regret from the whole sordid incident is the overwhelming guilt that I now feel for the boys I'll never know whose lives I could have changed and protected if I had reported this monster at the time... I'm so sorry if any of them had to go through the same thing. However I'm proud to say that I've recovered from it all, I didn't become his Victim and I determinedly refused to let it affect the rest of my life. No little man, your evil has never stopped me from living the life I want, you didn't win!

CHAPTER 16

'If this be magic, let it be an art lawful as eating'

The Wizard of Oz

Next up on my Panto journey was The Wizard of Oz at the Hexagon Theatre in Reading. This really felt like a step up for me. Dorothy was played by Michaela Strachan from TVs the Hit Man and Her and now much loved by the nation for the Spring Watch shows on the BBC, and the Tin Man was played by ex Crossroads Actor Tony Adams, both lovely people and a joy to work with. I was booked to play the Scarecrow and Michelle was also hired to be our assistant stage manager on the show.

On the first day of rehearsals we turned up with our little Shih tzu dog Eric to meet our fellow cast members and director. Michaela immediately took a shine to Eric and it wasn't long before she was rolling around the rehearsal floor playing with him. Tony Adams was there with his lovely dog Ryan, a slightly beefy looking Jack Russell and we were told that Ryan had been booked to play Dorothy's dog Toto in the Panto. Michaela however wanted our dog Eric to be Toto.

We explained that he wasn't a trained acting type dog but just our domestic pet, however she was adamant that she wanted Eric. So after discussions with the producers our dog was booked as Toto. This worried Shell and I slightly as we couldn't guarantee that he'd behave on stage. We needn't have worried though, he was fantastic and even seemed to learn his entrances. If he was in the wings and his entrance music started playing, he'd stand up in preparation of his big moment. We were so proud of him, every night right at the beginning of the show Michaela would run onto the stage with Eric, then hold him in her arms whilst she sang *Somewhere over the rainbow.* It was so sweet as Eric really loved Michaela and most nights he would stare at her as she sang… magical. However on one of our three show days that changed dramatically.

I remember it was show number three and we were all a bit tired including our Dog Eric. Sometimes on a three show day as a performer, when you get to that final performance, you're never too sure whether you've already done a certain line or whether that was in the show before... honestly your mind can go to mush. I think Eric had a bit of a sleep between shows and Michaela seemed to be aware that he was as tired as the rest of us.

Shell recalls that Michaela was in the wings with Eric before her first entrance and was playing with him, trying to get him perky and interested in doing the show, but he wasn't showing that much willing. When the music played our Dorothy tried to run onto the stage as normal with Eric following behind her, but for this show he seemed to have downed tools and refused to trot or even walk. He was more or less dragged onto the stage and that was just the start of it.

She held him in her arms to sing Somewhere over the rainbow and the full theatre could hear Eric growling (picked up on her head mic) as he wasn't that impressed at doing another show. Unfortunately that wasn't the only incident in the performance!

At the end of the Wizard of Oz story there is that famous bit where Dorothy says goodbye to the Lion, Tin Man and Scarecrow, then clicks her heels together to go back to Kansas. Never work with children or animals is the famous acting expression, exhibited in all it's glory on this particular night. Michaela was talking to the other characters with Toto (our Eric) by her side, I think the tiredness must have overwhelmed our little doggie as he rolled over onto his side with exhaustion and just lay there prostrate on the stage. That got a good laugh from the audience, but the best was yet to come.

Standing there with my fellow actors, Tony as the Tin Man, Simon the Cowardly Lion and the wonderful Sarah Jane Buckley who played the good witch Glynda (now a lovely friend) we were all horrified to see Eric start to lick his doggie bits on stage in front of everyone!

I have to tell you, utter mayhem ensued, the audience were screaming with laughter and the professional actors on stage just couldn't get their lines out as they tried to stifle their hysteria, the whole place descended into complete uproar! Thank you Eric.

Poetry Corner

I have a potted plant on a tray,
I water it most every single day,
I water in the morning,
at lunch and dinner too
Oh no, It's floated away!

CHAPTER 17

'For those who love, time is eternal'

Our Quirky Wedding

Michelle and I were married on the 7th November 1999, soul mates tying the knot.

Our Wedding was completely camp and over the top and took place at the Stephen Joseph Theatre in the round in Scarborough. The perfect setting to declare our love to the world. We'd actually been together for 8 years before we got married which gave us plenty of time to plan and boy did it all pay off. Michelle designed the whole thing, it was an underwater theme as her star sign is Cancer and mine is Pisces. She dressed the stage with a sand effect painted cloth and papier mache brightly coloured fish which she made herself and in fact once when I had returned home from a cruise, I walked into our front garden to be greeted by all these painted fish drying on the lawn... Surreal. She also made a massive Anchor out of cardboard and papier mache which looked superb and after chatting with the technical guys at the theatre they managed to put a water lighting effect on it all from above, it just looked fantastic.

My Girl building the stage set for her own wedding ceremony... as you Do!

Michelle's bridesmaid Jane Losing The plot During the wedding preparation

I did a background music track for when people were entering the auditorium, I combined *Handle's Water Music* with dolphin sound effects... perfect. Michelle had wrapped up sweets... black jacks, fruit salads, flying saucers etc. in newspaper cones to give to our guests as they made their way into the theatre auditorium after leaving a video message for us on a strategically placed camera, they also received some bubbles to blow over us at the end of the service instead of confetti... good idea eh? The whole thing smacked of the *'Hey let's put on a show'* attitude, which is exactly who we are. Alan Ayckbourn the world famous playwright and producer is the boss of this theatre and he was quite enthusiastic for us to be married there, I think he found the whole *dressing a stage set for a wedding* thing fascinating and amusing at the same time. He sent us a lovely card and wished us all the best when we went into his office to meet him the day before the wedding.

My family had come up from Devon for the service and this was a big deal for me as relationships had been strained for a while after the end of my first marriage, so the whole experience of having my family there to witness my declaration of love for this wonderful lady on our Wedding Day was cathartic for me.

Our little niece Lilly was dressed as a mermaid and Michelle had also made her own wedding dress. Is there nothing this woman can't do? During the service there was a song by our long time friend Sarah Devonshire and she was joined by my daughter Alisha harmonising. This was the first time she'd sung since the cancer operation and there wasn't a dry eye in the place.

My son Justin was my best man and Michelle's sister Rachelle and best friend Jane were the bridesmaids alongside my Alisha. I even painted a dolphin on a room divider which we placed in the foyer, I was very proud of that.

Michelle's mum along with with her flower arranging friends created the most wonderful scene in the theatre foyer, and I have to say that many people did so much to make our day extremely special and we were so grateful. The underwater theme continued all through the service including

us signing the marriage certificate to the sound of *Under the Sea* from the Little Mermaid Disney film. When the signing was completed the music changed to *I've got you (I feel good)* by James Brown and we literally danced our way off the stage... being filmed as we did so by local BBC TV and ITV Camera crews!

The party that followed was awesome and as a lot of our guests were entertainers, many of them got up to sing and entertain everyone, the whole thing was magical. Pardon the pun but we really pushed the boat out that day... the happiest day of my life.

'I would not wish any companion in the world but you'

Our Honeymoon

It had been our dream for quite a while to spend our honeymoon in Cancun, Mexico and Michelle in particular wanted to swim with the dolphins so we were determined to make this come true. At the time we couldn't afford to pay for it all in one go but whenever we had monies coming in we would pop into the travel agents in Banbury and pay some towards our holiday. It was our first time in the Caribbean together and we had booked an Adult

Only, All Inclusive hotel for our honeymoon adventure. We were determine to have a lovely time and although we had limited spending funds, there was enough for the things that we wanted to do. Our home at the time was in Winderton near Shipston on Stour in Oxfordshire just outside of Banbury, and we lived in a little cottage style bungalow.

When we were ready to make our way up North for the Wedding we had to transport all the props that Michelle had made so we hired a van. It was expensive but needs must and we knew that we would get our £400 deposit back after returning the vehicle and that would made up a great chunk of our honeymoon spending funds.

The journey up to Michelle's parents home in North Yorkshire was plain sailing… until we turned off of the North York Moors to travel the last 2 miles to their house where we would be staying until the Wedding. Within 300 yards of driving down that lane...Bang! An Owl flew into our windscreen and a massive crack appeared on it. First thoughts were one of concern for the unfortunate bird obviously but that quickly changed with the realization that we had just lost our deposit, ergo our spending

money had been instantly slashed in half. But there was nothing we could do about it so, onwards and upwards.

A few days after the wedding we flew to Cancun and were transported to our Hotel. It looked fantastic, the staff there were so friendly and this was our first contact with the lovely Mexican people who we would grow to love even more. The thing about this all inclusive resort was that we seemed to be the only people who ventured outside of the complex. As my Wife says, 'What's the point in going to another country if you don't have a look around, try the local delicacies and see the sights'. We booked a trip to Chichen Itza, (the Mayan Pyramids and surrounding ancient city ruins) and whilst there took in all the culture and heritage on offer, not only on our Honeymoon but on many subsequent visits.

One really romantic memory was our Lobster Dinner sunset cruise on the Nichupte Lagoon in a replica Galleon. Lovely food and drink under the Stars, sharing the experience with my new Wife, what more do you need Andrew? It was heaven and we were experiencing it together.

Sunset cruise on the lagoon in Cancun...
No life jackets so we held on for dear life!

Yep the lack of funds reduced some of the activities we could do but we still managed the Dolphin Swim experience that Michelle was so looking forward to. I was a bit apprehensive as I don't swim a well as Shell but with our life jackets on I felt more confident and it was fab.

In fact a few years later when we returned again to Cancun we booked in a for a ***trainer for a day*** experience where we learned more about dolphins and had extra time with them. There were meant to be about 6 or 8 of us on the experience that day but for some reason the others didn't show and we had

the Dolphins all to ourselves. Michelle was in her element swimming in with a mother and baby dolphin and then we got the chance to swim with the big Daddy *Itza*.

The trainers said that we could go in without life jackets if we wanted, so (stupidly from my point of view) we did. At one point when we were swimming with this magnificent animal the trainer sought to show us how dolphins would react around an injured dolphin or human if a shark was in the vicinity.

They swim around in a circle at great speed so that the shark doesn't get the chance to attack. Well obviously there were no sharks, but swim around us at speed he certainly did. Shell loved it but with all the waves caused by the speed of Itza's swimming I was struggling to stay on the surface and was thrashing around like a four year old on their first swimming lesson, to the delight and hysteria of the trainer and my Wife…. It's ok folks I'm only drowning… hilarious isn't it? Their laughter increased even more at one point when unbeknownst to me a flipping great turtle was swimming up behind me and heading right between my legs!! Yes very droll!

One of our lovely places in the world

We completely fell in love with the area and the Mexican people on that visit and on one of our subsequent hotel stays we secured a return flight for a week later than planned and booked ourselves into a Hotel in the Down Town area of Cancun to extend our holiday and live amongst the local people. That was it for us, we loved it so much that on future visits we found our own private accommodation and just booked flights with the travel company. Our Mexican experience went up and up from that point…. more to follow later in the book. So basically our honeymoon was wonderful,

we made the money stretch and we'd found our own Paradise, thank you Universe.

CHAPTER 18

'The Play's the thing'

The Buttons debut

The pantomimes kept coming in, and the next year I was at the Lyceum Theatre in Sheffield and this was my first show since tying the knot with my Michelle. I worked alongside Sarah Jane Buckley again, she played the Fairy Godmother in Cinderella. Our Prince charming was Jansen Spencer from Neighbours, a lovely guy, quite nervous about doing his first panto but a confident young man to share the stage with.

Also on the show was Andrew Ryan who played one of the Ugly sisters and years later he was to become my director for the Pantomime Snow White at the Bristol Hippodrome in 2022, what a nice chap. You see, you never know when your paths are likely to cross again in the future.... I love this business.

Sarah and I shared our accommodation in Sheffield, we had one double room and one single so we had to keep changing rooms when our partners visited us. However Ladies and Gentleman I must tell you that I was a tad nervous on this production possibly because it was my first Pantomime in the North of England. I was always confident of my own abilities but I started to worry about how my West Country accent would work in this region of the country, but what is it they say? People are people and funny is funny! I had a flipping ball that year in Sheffield and even rode the tram!

In 2000 Michelle was now working a fair bit for Theatre Clwyd in North Wales as Stage Manager on many in-house shows and tours, so when I wasn't busy working myself I would tag along and that's how I got the chance to meet lots of talented Actors including Eric Potts, more of him later. I suppose it was during some of those chats that I started to

realise how much Actors admired the skill sets of the stand up comedian, I found this fascinating and at the same time somewhat encouraging as I had always for some reason felt like we in our game were the poor relations to the legit Acting fraternity.

In 2000 Michelle and I worked in different parts of the country.

I went to Croydon where I performed in the first of 3 pantos at the Peggy Ashcroft Theatre alongside Chris Jarvis from Children's TV and Kate Ritchie who played Sally on *Home and Away* the Australian Soap and Michelle was in North Wales.

What a lovely lady Kate was by the way, we spent loads of time together and really bonded having great fun on what I believe was her first panto. That was also my first time playing alongside Bryan Burden who played the Dame. I learned so much working with this experienced panto performer and over the years Michelle and I became firm friends with him and his lovely Wife Andi. We were to play together several times and I treasure every show performing alongside him. It was my first time breaking up my gags so that they still worked when being presented by two people, Bryan taught me how to do that and it really was a great help going forward.

Here's an example of how to adapt a joke so that two people can perform it. I'd normally deliver this gag like this... I took my dog to the vet for a check up and he said, 'I've got to put him down', so I said, 'why?' and he said, 'because my arms are aching!'

Here's the rewrite

Muddles	I took our doggie Billy to the vets today mum
Dame	Oh yes, he was due for a check up wasn't he? What did the vet say?
Muddles	said he had to put him down
Dame	but why Son?
Muddles	cause his arms were aching!
Dame	Oh stop messing around Muddles, we've got work to do here....

Sounds quite straight forward to do but it completely changes the feeling that the comic is just there to do gags and also develops the relationship

between our characters on stage, making it seamless as we carried on with the rest of the script. Bryan taught me how to make my comedy relate to the storyline, something I'd never really thought about before. Maybe that sounds all obvious and not particularly important but in the world of Panto that give and take is what makes it all work.

Getting some invaluable panto tuition
From Bryan Burden

When I first came up with the idea of doing my Pop Idols panto routine, it was him I spoke to about it and he said, instead of singing the punchlines why don't you mime and dance to the original recordings. That was a fantastic suggestion and the way it has stayed ever since. I have used that

routine in many pantos next to some massive stars and it always works, so thanks Bryan for tweaking the routine for me... you are a gent.

Poetry Corner

Fridge Magnet

I'm a Fridge Magnet kinda guy,
I just buy 'em
and stick 'em on my fridge

CHAPTER 19

'An honest tale speeds best being plainly told'

Stories to break the ice at parties!

No. 1

Many years back, in fact not long after Michelle and I got together, we combined to place an ad in the Stage and Television Today newspaper. I announced in it that I needed to be famous, asking if anyone out there was able to help me. Michelle designed that advert for me and yes I suppose it was a bit of a bizarre thing to do, but as I've mentioned a few times already you gotta try these things. I wasn't convinced that we'd get any feedback, but you never know, and to my delight I received a phone call from a journalist who wrote silly stories for newspapers and magazines and thought that my enthusiasm and boldness would be a good fit for some of his less than copper bottomed stories.

He'd been writing for many years about the seedier side of life on publications like the News of the world and other tabloids. It was a fairly sinister, covert world that he was part of and to be honest I think that he was done with skulking around, secretly recording people and writing stories around

personal tragedies and affairs etc. occasionally putting his own safety at risk. So he had decided to jump ships over to the lighter side of journalism and make up some silly little stories to make people smile, which the newspapers and coffee table magazines gobbled up.

He wrote so many scenarios for me to present and it was all good clean fun. There was the story about me being addicted to Brussel Sprouts, which gave me a couple of TV appearances, another about playing my ukelele to a couple of drivers who were stuck in a traffic jam to calm down their burgeoning road rage. Crazy eh? but I managed to get lots of media opportunities on the back of these tall tales. He knew that whatever he could come up with, I'd be able to sell it.

The most successful of all these was a story about my snoring at night seemingly being able to help our houseplants grow quicker than normal!! Ridiculous I know, but I did loads of telly and radio interviews on the back of it, including being featured all morning long on ITV's Good Morning Britain (or whatever it was called at the time) in an enormous green house where I was being featured intermittently throughout the show with their on the

scene reporter measuring the size of the foliage to see how much it had grown during their broadcast! Another off shoot (excuse the pun) of this story was when a journalist from the Sun turned up and took some pictures of Michelle and myself lying in bed with me holding a plant and pretending to snore, and that Ladies and Gentlemen was printed on page 3 of the Sun. Michelle told some of her mates that she was now an official page three girl...lol.

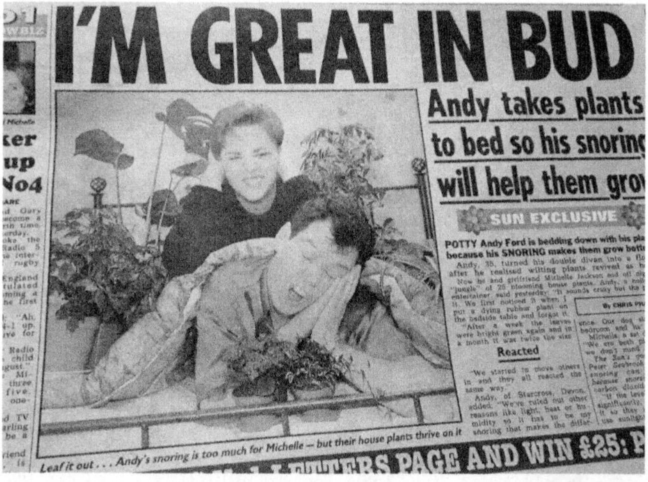

I'M GREAT IN BUD

Andy takes plants to bed so his snoring will help them grow

SUN EXCLUSIVE

POTTY Andy Ford is bedding down with his plants because his SNORING makes them grow better.

Andy, 35, turned his double divan into a ... after he realised wilting plants revived as he ...

Now he and girlfriend Michelle Jackson ... "jungle" of 25 blooming house plants. Andy, ... entertainer, said yesterday: "It sounds crazy but ... it. We first noticed it when I put a dying rubber plant on the bedside table and forgot it.

"After a week the leaves were bright green again and in a month it was twice the size.

Reacted

"We started to move others in and they all reacted the same way."

Andy, of Starcross, Devon, added: "We've ruled out other reasons like light, heat or humidity so it has to be my snoring that makes the difference.

By CHRIS ...

Leaf it out . . . Andy's snoring is too much for Michelle – but their house plants thrive on it

One of the stories was written around the idea of me being on tour away from my wife and because I was missing her so much I had made a cardboard cut out of her to take around the country to stop me

from pining. Silly yes, but loads of interest from the press and by the way I wouldn't have a clue where to start with the making of a cardboard cut out of my wife, so Michelle did it for me. You see, teamwork!

Eventually we will get to the ice breaking moment here.... A few months on from this story doing the rounds, I was booked to appear on ITV's Today with Des and Mel show again. I always looked for a big impact on my entrance and as I still had the cardboard cut out....

I decided to walk on to the ITV set carrying this prop and then delivering some comedy material written around it, culminating in a poem about my cardboard cut out Wife which went...

I have a cardboard cut out Mrs Ford,

I take her with me even when abroad,

and though you'll think this line's intentional,

just because she's two dimensional,

from time to time she looks a little bored!

She's my flat mate, she's my bestest fold up friend,

you should try it Des, maybe we'd start a trend,

cause when your true loves far way, and you're lonely day by day,

here's a new one that can drive you round the bend!

It went down well in the studio and at the end of my spot I left the stage area with my cardboard wife tucked under my arm, which made it slightly difficult to open the green room door at the back of the studio space. However as I approached it, the door seemed to open automatically and I slowly and awkwardly made my way into the room, as I entered this voice said,*' Well done Andy that was brilliant, really funny'.* I looked up to see that it was in fact ROD STEWART who was also on the show that day.... and that dear readers is a story I've used a few times to break the ice at parties and it's all true!

No. 2

Here's another special moment from my life that I love to share.... one night I was doing a solo gig at the County Hotel in Taunton, Somerset and during the interval I was chatting away with some of the audience. A lady came up to me to say how much she enjoyed my performances and that she had often gone to Ladram bay to watch me sing and was a fan of my voice. She then told me that she used to be a professional singer years before on the Billy Cotton Band Show on Television.

At this point my heart was in my mouth because as a young lad I loved that show and watched it every

week. There was a female vocalist in Billy's band called Kathy Kay and I just adored her, in fact whenever she came on the screen I would kiss the TV set. I asked her what her stage name was and when she said Kathy Kay my face must just have beamed.... *'But I really love you'* , I said and She said that she loved me too. *'Can I have your autograph please?'* I asked and she said, *'Only if I can have yours too!'* So that's what we did, right there and then, she signed for me and I signed for her, a completely surreal moment but oh how I wish we could have done selfies in those days! Dear Kathy Kay you made my life in a heartbeat, just goes to show you never know who's out there watching when you do your stuff.

No. 3

I was once the recipient of some fabulous advice from a showbiz legend one afternoon in the grounds of the Royal Devon and Exeter hospital. Well that sounds dodgy for a start doesn't it? But it was a charity day or something and I was booked to perform some songs during the afternoon. Not wishing to miss a chance of self promotion, I had some photo business cards with me for people to take if they wanted to book me in the future. Apparently one of these cards had made it's way to the tent where TV Star Larry Grayson was signing

copies of his new book. I was introduced to him and he complimented me on my performance and my photo card, then he imparted some of the best advice I've ever been given. He said that I shouldn't audition for opportunities but rather invite people that could help advance my career to one of my shows. It's very subtle but the difference is really big, if they see you working then you're already successful and that's more appealing than asking for a break via an audition. That was very astute, and I'm grateful he passed that on to me, and btw I thought that Larry in his heyday was one of the funniest men I'd ever seen and here he was helping me… just brilliant.

No. 4

Whilst working at Theatre Clwyd my Wife Michelle worked as Stage Manager to the brilliant Playwright, Director and Producer Ed Thomas. Whilst one of his plays was performing in Cardiff I tagged along with Michelle to watch the Production and enjoy the after show party at the Director's house. It was great being surrounded by Actors and I always enjoyed the banter, as I say the respect from them towards my profession was always fascinating to me. Whilst having a drink in the kitchen I got chatting away to this lovely chap. He asked me my name and what I did and he seemed

genuinely interested in comedy so we had a great conversation. During the discourse I asked him his name and, he said he was called Rhys and that he was an actor. The penny then dropped as I'd heard someone at the venue mention there was a rumour that this Actor was at the performance in Cardiff. The guy chatting away to me was none other than Rhys Ifans, he of Notting Hill fame and a million other films and TV shows. Upon realising who I was talking to I decided to not flag up the fact that I was aware of his celebrity, cause he seemed to be happy thinking that I had no idea who he was and that would have been a very different experience for him. We really had a good old friendly chin wag and strangely after a while I almost convinced myself that I wasn't aware of his fame and our interesting chat continued for quite a while… just two bloke drinking and chatting!!

No. 5

Whilst I was working for Jim Davidson's Pantomime company in Croydon and after rehearsals one day, me and some fellow cast members were transported to Jim's house near Dorking to record some background vocals and stuff for the show. He had a fair size recording studio in the grounds of his house which I'm pretty sure was once owned by Oliver Reed the Film Actor.

It was very opulent. The recordings went great and afterwards we were shown to Jim's inside pool where we all gathered to have a few drinks before going back to our digs. I have to say that he was a good host, but at one point whilst we were all sitting around chatting he looked at me and said, 'Oi Comic, have you sorted your opening for the Panto yet?' Suddenly everyone's looking at me, Jim, his mates, studio technicians and all of our cast... So I say, 'Yep all ready!' Then he says, 'OK do it!'

Well that took me back a bit, but I believed in my material and myself so I stood up next to his pool and started doing my routine. I was getting good laughs from everyone and so I kept going with it until he says..., 'Alright that's enough, you can sit down now'. I have since learned that Jim likes to test people and see how they react in different circumstances, well react is what I did, and a few years later I was chatting with some of his Production people who were there at the time and was told that I got quite a few brownie points that night for facing up! Is that ice I can hear breaking?

Logical Nursery Rhymes

Two little dicky birds
sitting on the wall,
one named Peter,
one named Paul

Fly away Peter,
Fly away Paul,
Oh no we can't we're fingers!

CHAPTER 20

'I shall no more to sea, to sea'

The Cruising Quandry

My Career on cruise ships wasn't the most rewarding or inspiring time of my life, I have to tell you that I've walked off stage to the sound of my own footsteps occasionally, I don't know a comedian that hasn't, but that doesn't make you a failure, it's sort of comedy's way of helping you to fine tune either your act or to find a different audience demographic to perform in front of. When I used to do all these cruise ships the usually elderly audiences knew that there was a comedian on that night but had no idea on the style that they were about to watch as the comedian wasn't '*Famous*'.

It was pot luck as to whether they would like his or her show, and whether it fitted in with their own personal sense of humour. If it worked well for me on stage the people would be queuing out the doors ready for my second show, but if it didn't I would be ignored around the ship. The contrast couldn't have been any more extreme.

The only way around these opposing scenarios seemed to be to conform and do generic comedy material as performed by a great percentage of cruise ship comedians, (which was never an option for me) or stop putting myself through this by not taking any more cruise ship bookings. But throughout all the ups and downs of my Cruise Ship experience the one thing I can never regret is the wonderful array of beautiful people (some now friends for life) that I met on the ocean. Being stuck on a big floating metal box for days on end during an Atlantic crossing for example gives you the time to bond and create long lasting relationships with other artistically minded folk. Michelle and I treasure the memories of our cruises to the Amazon River in Brazil where she actually hugged a sloth in the Jungle, I kid you not.

Meeting the locals in the Amazon Rain Forest

Most people don't even get the chance to visit the Amazon Rain Forest once in their life, well we did it twice and they paid us for the privilege, how great is that? It was a pleasure to work alongside the brilliant and multi talented Richard Sykes on those trips as well as some other beautiful friends. On another cruise Shell joined me for a visit to Iceland and we even danced on the deck in the sunshine at two in the morning, what an experience that was. The cruise ship thing was probably a better fit for some of my contemporaries rather than it was for me, but at times it was fantastic and Michelle and I have some wonderful friends and fabulous memories from those cruising days.

Chatting up the Mermaid in Copenhagen!

However whenever I was at sea my mind was often thinking about the upcoming Panto for that year, the bit that I was really looking forward to. I feel

blessed to have done so many of them playing next to some of my TV idols who then ended up being my friends, how lucky am I?

It was also around this time that I was chosen to play Patrick the Baker alongside the fantastically gorgeous and talented Naomi Wilkinson in Channel 5's award winning children's TV programme Havakazoo and I loved it. It was fairly full on though, we filmed in Bristol at the studios near Arnos Vale and we recorded 64 episodes in 4 weeks.

Havakazoo!

It was a year or so since I'd done Des's prime time show and ITV had taken it off air so I was looking to get some more TV exposure somehow and this opportunity arose, I went to the audition and I'm delighted to say that they gave me the job. The show was set in a fictional Flour Mill and Patrick and his sister Patricia ran Pat-a-Cake Bakeries, assisted by a weird looking robot called Messy. There were also puppet characters like Watchdog, Plum and a couple of fleas that lived on Watchdog called Tik and Tok, all brilliantly executed by Puppeteers Marcus Clarke and his wife Helena Smee. We became a family very quickly and shared a fantastic rapport on and off camera. Our director was the lovely John Rowe who adored his comedy and was really happy for me to try out different things on the show.

It was such a funny show and to be given license to play with your comedy on TV was a real gift and I'm eternally grateful to him for that. In every episode Naomi (Patricia) would sing a song about something or other and I would comically act it out using whatever props were provided. It doesn't get any simpler than that and producing laughs purely through body language (as the audience were obviously too young for gags) was a challenge gratefully accepted. Although I didn't completely

base my Character on one of my childhood heroes namely Mr Pastry who was a firm children's TV favourite in the 1960s, (real name Richard Hearn) his silliness was always in the back of my mind as I filmed it all. The show was repeated many times, in fact it was on air for over 4 years, which was great for me as I could use it on the posters for my Pantomimes and it helped with my billing.

When the series ended I pushed for another show idea that I had called Mo and Joe's magic Theatre. The scenario was that Mo and Joe were two mannequins in a fancy dress shop and at night when the shop was closed they'd come to life and sing nursery rhymes with their puppet friends with the music for the rhymes being arranged in various styles, big band swing to reggae to Rock n Roll for example and all performed inside a magical toy theatre designed and created by my wife Michelle. Pretty simple idea with potential so we were grateful that Channel 5 let us do a pilot show on the cheap to see if we could make the series happen.

Marcus and Helena were part of it too, creating brand new puppet characters for the show which was directed by John Rowe again.

I was Joe and TV presenter Anna Williamson played Mo. I thought that we'd done a good job although unfortunately it didn't get commissioned, but hey you can't win if you don't buy a ticket! Give it a go that's my motto!

Logical Nursery Rhymes

Goosey Goosey Gander
where shall I wander?
upstairs, downstairs
in my Lady's chamber.

There I saw an old man
who wouldn't say his prayers
so I took him by the left leg
and threw him down the stairs
Committing murder!!

CHAPTER 21

'Frame your mind to mirth and merriment'

The Eastenders sidekick?

In 2001 I was paired with an Eastenders Legend in the shape of Letitia Dean (Sharon) at the Orchard Theatre in Dartford. Michelle was also booked for panto that year but not with me, instead she was working with Director Jim Davidson at the Theatre in Croydon with Stephen Mulhearn, Darren Day and Mr Blobby... what a line up! They were doing Jim's family panto Cinderella, he wasn't appearing in it but he put the whole thing on through his theatre production company which also produced our Pantomime in Dartford. This Snow White panto gave me the chance to work with Bryan Burden again so every day was a school day and we had the best time, Letitia herself was such a ball of fun and we bonded on and off the stage to make for a fantastically successful run, I really enjoyed my time in Kent.

The next year in 2002 I was booked to appear at Northampton's Derngate Theatre as Smee alongside Eastenders bad boy Nasty Nick Cotton playing the Captain and the fabulous Kirsten O'Brien who played Peter Pan. This year Michelle

and I got the chance to work together again and that was really lovely, and because Northampton wasn't far from where we were currently living we would drive home after each show and sleep in our own bed which is a very rare thing when you're doing Pantomime.

On one night we had an incident in our show when Kirsten fell off of the Big Rock on the stage set and damaged her arm, people were running around everywhere back stage wondering what was gonna happen. Yes she was in a lot of pain but somehow Kirsten managed to get herself through the rest of the Panto before going to hospital... we knew how bad it was but she never let the audience know....what a pro.

It was also on that Pantomime that I first did my Pop idols routine with our Captain Hook, Mr. Altman and the audience fell about as he delivered the punchline which was an hilarious impression of Kylie Minogue. John and I are still in contact to this day and I'm proud to call him a friend. Panto really is the gift that keeps giving and it was also on that show that I had the first chance to try out my comedy pirate line up sword routine which I've used many times in various shows ever since. I love

writing these routines and mostly the producers of the pantos have been happy to use my input, I've gotta tell you when you see an audience react positively to a routine that you have put together from scratch, it's a great feeling.

'Lord luv a Duck!'
3 Eastenders co stars in a row!

In 2003 I was performing yet again back at the Peggy Ashcroft Theatre in Croydon as Wishy Washy in Aladdin and this time Michelle was working on the show with me again.

To say this year was full of incident is an understatement, I have so many stories that I'd need another book to cover it all! To be fair most of the

situations to which I refer were humorous, but may not have seemed so at the time. The Aladdin to my Wishy Washy was Dean Gaffney from Eastenders and 'I'm a Celebrity', a guy that I got on with really well, we certainly had fun together on that show.

He had loads of celebrity friends and it was quite interesting to meet lots of them when they came in to watch our show. One day I'm standing there chatting to Katie Price aka Jordan who came to the theatre to watch with her then young son Harvey, all a bit surreal, then I hear this voice behind me say, *'Good God you're funny mate',* and I turn around to see Richard Blackwood standing in front of me being nothing but complimentary... that was sort of how that run went really.

I'd written a couple of comedy routines for Dean and myself which we delivered together and at the end of one of them we would skip off stage a la Eric and Ernie, alas on this particular day I hadn't physically warmed up properly beforehand. So the routine ended and we turned with hands raised to mimic the Morecambe and Wise stage exit when I felt a twinge on my first skip and pulled my right calf muscle.

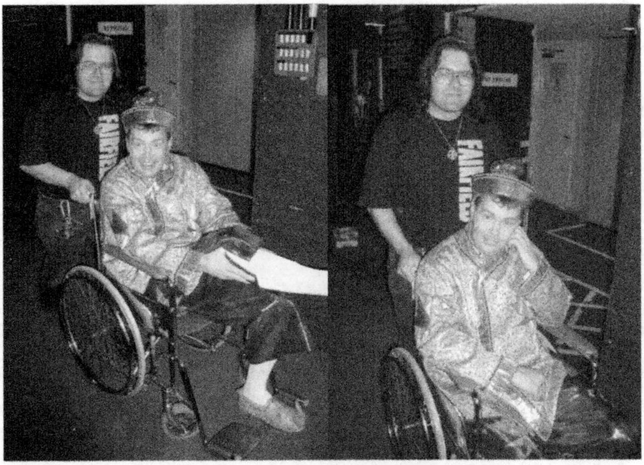

I was on a roll (literally)
In this version of Aladdin!

Flipping eck it hurt and I really struggled to walk but the worst thing was that in this production for some reason my entrances seemed to change from one side of the stage to the other and most of them were very close together.... Nightmare! I was finding it difficult to make it to the opposite side of the stage in time for my entrances, so our quick thinking Stage manager Jim Patterson grabbed a wheelchair from somewhere and started wheeling me behind the scenes from side to side so that I made it on cue. The funniest thing to me however was when we got to the required spot to make my entrance he'd simply tip the wheelchair forward and literally pour me onto the stage, it must have looked

ridiculous in the wings, but I never missed an entrance or a show.... thanks Jim for being on the ball.

Once again my Wife Michelle worked with me on this show, she sort of lived on the stage left wing running it from there as our DSM (Deputy Stage Manager). Towards the end of the interval on one of our matinees, Michelle had been given clearance from the front of house manager, which tells her that the interval is over and the audience were ready for the start of the second half of the Panto.

So we took our positions on stage ready to perform our opening song of Act two, which was a rewriting of the Friends TV show theme tune. As I recall most of the main characters in our pantomime were part of the opening of the second half, so the music started, the curtain went up and we all started singing, but to everyone else's horror and my amusement, the lights in the auditorium were up full. I could see an usher right in front of me selling ice cream from the front of the stage and loads of people coming back from the toilets and other places to retake their seats.

It was mayhem, and my first thoughts as a comedian was to jump off the stage and guide people back to their seats for comic effect, so that's just what I did, you know...seize the moment and all that. It worked great and caused much hilarity out front as everyone was aware that the second half shouldn't really have started yet. My natural instinct was to make the situation funny and entertaining, but after the Panto ended I was told by the Company Manager that the senior Actress in the cast was very angry with me and I was told to go and apologise to her for my conduct. Obviously I felt vindicated in doing what I did because of the situation and thinking on my feet is what comics have to do in a circumstance like that.

Anyway for cast harmony (much as I didn't see any need to apologise for being a comedian) I went into her room where she tore me off a strip! She said that I had embarrassed her by jumping off the stage and would I be doing that on every show from now on. I said that I probably wouldn't as I didn't see that situation ever happening again. In the end I didn't apologise to her for what I did, but I did apologise if it made her feel unhappy. Anyway we didn't actually kiss and make up but we're still friends and found a way through it all.

Andy's Animal Idioms

Idiom

Like a Hedgehog in ballet shoes

meaning

Someone trying to be something they are not

CHAPTER 22

'With mirth and laughter let old wrinkles come'

Today with Des and Mel

As mentioned Des O'Connor's evening show had ended its run on ITV which was disappointing for me because I had started to become a regular guest on his show. But suddenly up he pops on daytime Television in 2003 accompanied by the lovely Melanie Sykes with a show called *Today with Des and Mel.*

The format was tweaked a bit from Des's evening show but he was still having comedians on the set, so of course as soon as I saw the show on my telly I was all over it. I contacted the production company and Des agreed to have me on and in fact I became a regular on their show. You see... you never know when things are gonna come around again, you just have to be ready and go for it!

During one of the occasions that I was at the studio to do the show, Des invited me into his dressing room and we sat there just the two of us chatting away. How lucky was I to have a supporter like him on my side, and on one occasion he actually said to

me, 'Welcome back to the studios Andy, good grief you're on this show more than I am!' He also signed his Autobiography for me during our chat and it meant the world, these are the moments that no one else sees, but I hold them in my heart.

Looks like I tickled Melanie Sykes

TV shows and starring Pantomime roles meant that I was living the dream. It was all plain sailing from here without the slightest possibility of encountering a spanner strategically placed in the works... mmm... I don't think so. What has experience taught you Andrew?

Now I'm a bit hazy about the timing of this next bit, but if I remember correctly the Jim Davidson Pantomime company that I was working for had closed down for some reason after the 2003 season, so I was forced to look for a different Panto Producer to work with for the next year. Whilst chatting with some other companies re: Panto 2004, I was told by one producer that they were keen to book me but that they wanted me to perform as a Dame.

Now I greatly appreciate the skill sets needed to do this role, but at the age of 45 I really wasn't interested in doing that, mainly because I loved the lead comic gig and felt that I was still doing it well; afterwards I learned that there was a real problem finding people to play Pantomime Dames so that was why it was asked of me. When I was told that they couldn't offer me anything else I was gutted and thought that my panto career could be over there and then.

I contacted a producer friend that I'd met during my touring days and although he didn't have the budget that I was used to, he really wanted me to do his show in 2004 in Doncaster. He was also happy to employ Michelle alongside me as the Deputy Stage Manager so, by pooling our resources we were just

able to make it viable for us. The production of Cinderella was staged at the Civic Theatre in Doncaster and I was cast as Buttons alongside one of my late teenage crushes Maureen Nolan of Nolan Sisters fame.

I was stupidly excited to work with Maureen and when we met up for rehearsals, the first thing I said to her was...I love you! She laughed and so did my Wife thank God! Maureen was great in the role of

Fairy Godmother and we even got the chance to do a duet on stage together.... Note to a younger me... 'You see what can happen when you believe...., one day you'll be singing on stage with Maureen Nolan for godnesss sake', it really was a dream come true.

Anyway calm down Andrew... now Sue Douglas the brilliantly funny actress and former wife of comedy legend and Carry On star Jack Douglas was also on the show playing The wicked step mum and every day was a pleasure as I learned new comedy skills next to this fantastic performer who had only the year before been working as a foil to one of my Comedy heroes Billy Pearce. There was lot of friendship going around amongst the cast of this show, we even had an *Arrow words* club backstage. For the uninitiated Arrow words is a form of crossword puzzle and myself, Sue Douglas and Maureen formed a little team, so that when one or more of us were on stage the ones left in the dressing rooms would keep the Arrow Word going.

It was all progressing well until one show when Maureen got so into the puzzle that she missed her entrance. I was out front at the back of the auditorium ready to make my first appearance as Buttons, Sue as the Wicked Step Mother had just put Cinderella into a trance like state where she had

to stand motionless as the drummer did sound effects on the cymbals to symbolize the trance and this was the point where the Fairy God Mother was meant to come onto the stage and unfreeze our heroine with her wand. But as I say Maureen was oblivious this day and Michelle kept putting out calls over the backstage tannoy, '*Miss Nolan this is your call to the stage..... Miss Nolan please come to the stage your cue is coming up.....Miss Nolan to the stage immediately as you've missed your entrance*!!'

I couldn't do any thing about it as I was out front waiting for my cue, and the cymbal sound effects seemed to be going on forever. Eventually Maureen heard the call and ran to the wings Michelle recalled, but just as she was about to go on she realised that she'd left her wand in the dressing room so ran all the way back to get it!! Just brilliant, it was undoubtedly the longest stage freeze in the history of Panto poor Shari (Cinderella) stuck there unable to do anything to get out of it.

But I have to tell you Maureen Nolan was just the most fun and professional lady to work with, however if I may, I have one more story about this Nolan Sister to share with you all... now a lot of the songs in the pantomime were written by the

producer to help him avoid paying PRS Copyright charges to the theatre, and as such we were not all that confident in singing them.

Anyway at the end of Act One, Cinderella is in the coach with real ponies btw and I was standing on the back as the Coachman, artificial snow was falling and there were children on stage pretending to ice skate making a really pretty picture. Throughout this beautiful scene Maureen the fairy Godmother was singing one of these specially written songs for the Panto, when her mind hit a brick wall regarding the lyrics. The tune was there but the words were gone, but being the trouper she is she just kept going. Roy Walker's *'Say what you see'* from Catchphrase comes to mind, so Maureen just kept singing about what was in front of her.

It was just fabulous, the audience were treated to classic lines like.... *'the lovely Cinderella is sitting in her coach, and oh the snow is falling with the children all around, look there's Buttons standing on the back'* ... and on and on it really was delicious, I could hardly breathe with laughing so much but Ladies and Gentlemen she got through it and the audience never knew, what a pro... and btw I still love her!

The thing that all these experiences were affirming to me was that wherever I was doing Pantomime around the country, the response was always the same and this West Country Comedian could ply his trade anywhere!

In fact I filmed my Live and Lovely DVD at that theatre in Doncaster after the Panto had finished and the audience were just great!

Poetry Corner

Oh Vacuum cleaner,
you mean the world to me,
you're standing there so upright
with your attachments, more than three

I've seen you in a tight corner
and the back seat of my car,
and if I had a long extension lead
I'd take you to the beach

Oh vacuum cleaner
cleaning up the world,
ridding us of dog hairs
and human ones straight and curled

You waltzed across my carpet
you crashed into my life
and now I feel so close to you
will you be my wife?

Oh Vacuum cleaner
some people think I'm sad
to fall in love with a cleansing implement,
don't tell my mum or the milkman

For they don't understand me,
don't think they'll ever know
the power of your suction
unless they possess a similar model.

CHAPTER 23

'This above all; to thine own self be true'

I've just gotta do stuff!

I can't keep still for long and I'm easily bored so over the next few years in between Pantomimes and other shows I just kept creating stuff that might open up an opportunity to break through that TV barrier.

Because my poems on Des's shows had always gone down well, I decided to write more and with a bit of help from my mate Jim Birmingham (Comedian Arnold Gutbucket) and Aiden Bell, I filmed some of them to create a sort of TV programme called *Peddling Poetry.* What a blast, we were filming my own TV series and we could do whatever we wanted, awesome.

We got permission from the local B&Q to film a video for my poem *The Kitchen sink* at about 6am in the morning, before the store opened for the day, and we filmed in loads of other weird places too, from car parks to country lanes as we created comedy videos for the other poems. We were making stuff up as we went along really but we did

have a blast filming this wacky content, it was like we were school kids again messing around.

I loved filming my poetry shows!

Years before all this though, I'd created a character called Malcolm Localperson who was quite a simple soul but very loveable and originally my poems were written for him. However gradually the surreal side of Malcolm was integrated into Andy Ford's persona and I took over the bulk of the poetic performing. If you look on my Youtube channel you can still find some videos of Malcolm.

Malcolm Localperson

Yes the poetry stuff was all really silly but the thing was there seemed to be no one else out there doing that and so I pitched it to Channel 4. Ok I didn't get a bite at that time, but hey it's still on my Channel and as Shell says you just put it out there and see what comes back, you never know it might be just what someone is looking for one day. Aren't I the eternal optimist? Enthusiasm is my middle name after all.... It's not though is it? It's Ernest!

I was on a roll now and couldn't stop writing, during breaks and sea days on the ships I would compose comedy radio scripts about my newly created daft West Country Detective called Inspector Biggins. It was my throw back and tribute to the Round the Horne radio programme I suppose, in particular the funny plays that they'd perform with Kenneth Williams and others at the end of their shows.

I was loving creating these stories and even got the chance to record one of them with my very good friend from Cinderella in Doncaster Sue Douglas, she is a brilliant vocal actress and she played all the female roles on the radio play, her husband David Kellar voiced various other characters and I was the Inspector. Once again I edited it all myself and it took me over 100 hours, but I did it. I still think that Inspector Biggins might take off one day, but of course I do... that's just me. You gotta be in it to win it!

Also one time when we were in Mexico on holiday I wrote a play about the Life of a comedian, an idea that had been flying around in my head for quite a while. I called it Funny Ha Ha, basically it was about me and included nods to the Royal Variety

disappointment and earlier marriage woes, but all done using artistic license so that no one would be upset. I so enjoyed writing it and once I had started typing I couldn't stop, the Play just poured out of me it was wonderful therapy. I think it's really funny, hang on Andrew.... I know it's really funny! (that's better) but with some tragedy thrown in there for good measure.

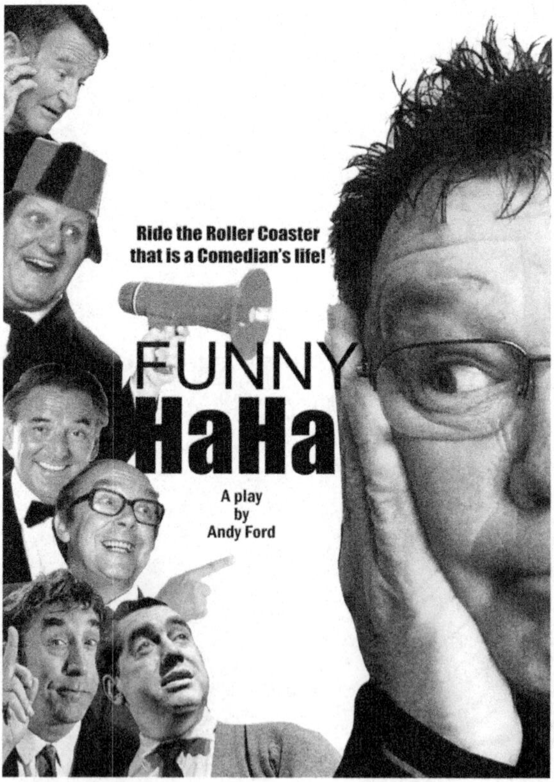

In 2009 I even got the chance to perform it Live at the Market Theatre in Hitchin with Jonathan Ross's lovely Mum Martha recording the voice of the comedian's ex Wife, her husband Tony playing the comic's agent on the phone and it was he who also directed the whole thing for me. I'm proud of that play and was happy to bring it to the stage. We filmed it in the theatre with a live audience and my mate Les Dennis watched it a little while ago on my Youtube channel. He said he loved it, that it summed up the life of a comedian really well and was really complimentary about my writing too. Cheers Les.

Why do I do it all?

Well I have to keep trying these things now while I'm alive. What's it they say? 'You're a long time Dead'.

Poetry Corner

You're a long way from miserable
with a Grapefruit in your hand,
very pink or yellowy,
Floridian or Outspan.

Fleshy fruit for everyone,
tingling on your tongue,
perfect for your breakfast
or later as a starter

You're more than Citrus segments,
you're pleasing to the eye,
maybe that's why people like you
unless you have a really good publicist

CHAPTER 24

'If you tickle us, do we not laugh?'

The Magnificent Ken Dodd

Another special moment for me was when I was doing Pantomime at the Theatre Royal in Nottingham, once again performing alongside Bryan Burden as the Dame. His dad was Albert Burden, a very successful variety act from the past, and it was he that had actually given Ken Dodd his first paid gig on one of his shows. So whilst we were there on our panto run, the aforementioned Ken was performing for one night only in the concert hall next door.

Bryan said, 'Let's go and meet him'. So we went backstage and I was introduced to him, really... one of my all time comedy icons in the flesh for goodness sake! He was so lovely and friendly, and he said to me, 'Haven't we met before? Yes I'm sure we have, it was in police line up wasn't it?' I thought that was brilliant and if I close my eyes I can live it over and over again, that memory will never fade.

I thoroughly enjoyed his live show which I think he kept down to just the three hours that night! What a

man! A true comedy legend with a superb comic brain and delivery... there will never be another like Ken.... it's impossible.

Meeting Ken was an absolute honour!

I was delighted to be playing alongside Claire Sweeney, John McCardle and the lovely Keavey Lynch from the 90s pop group Bewitched (who have recently had a relaunch) at the Theatre Royal in Nottingham in 2005. The show was Snow White and I was booked as Muddles working as I say, alongside Bryan Burden again and I'm delighted that our comedy was well received by the audience and the press alike.

This was the run where the Panto Production Company that I was going to eventually work with for 10 years first saw me live. The producer came into my dressing room after the show to say that they were a new company but were gonna be putting on some big shows and were very interested in working with me. It didn't happen for a couple of years but Nottingham was the place where the plans were hatched.

The following year I was asked to reprise the Muddles role again but this time back in Croydon where the Wicked Step Mother was to be played by the late and much loved Berni Nolan. I was so looking forward to working with this lady that I could have burst, and it became everything that I could have ever wanted it to be.

We performed some comedy sketches together and it was such a joy, not only was she a fabulous singer but she really did have wicked sense of humour, one night catching me out. At the end of the sketch where she had to be horrible to me she unexpectedly planted a smacker of a kiss on my lips during our last show, I panicked for a milli-second wondering what was afoot, and Shell thought it was hilarious. Berni was such a lovely friend as was her husband Steve and precious daughter Erin.

I know people can wax lyrical about their memories of working with someone who is no longer with us but being able to share the stage with such awesome talent as Berni and of course Barbara Windsor will forever be considered by me as my most fulfilling accomplishments.

Berni was just fantastic with a wicked twinkle in her eye!

Andy's Animal Idioms

Idiom

He's got a Lobster in his pocket

meaning

Someone who is tight with money

. CHAPTER 25

'A man may fish with the worm that hath eat of a king, and eat of the fish that hath fed of that worm'

All at Sea on my Birthday

After the Croydon Panto with Berni was over we headed off to our beloved Cancun in the February of 2007 for a good rest, and this time it was also to celebrate my 50th Birthday. When we arrived there, and after getting through customs which always took for flipping ever *#nightmare*, we jumped in a cab and made our way to Mayu Arana's apartment at Quintas del Mar, where we'd stayed on many occasions. It was at the opposite end of Cancun far away from the commercialised Hotel Strip and that's why we loved it so. We just preferred mixing with the locals rather than the Tourists and we certainly got better bang for our buck in that part of Mexico's Caribbean coast.

To illustrate this point, on one night we went into a local bar and restaurant which was situated in the Down Town area of the City and was only ever frequented by locals. We entered, sat down and ordered our food and drinks. As it was unusual for any non-locals to eat there, we received quite a few stares of incredulity from the other diners but in a

nice way and eventually we were all laughing and smiling together. A smile is most definitely the best currency you can ever take with you when you're abroad.

That night we must have spent about 3 hours or more at the venue, we ate until we could eat no more, similarly with the alcohol consumption and we were serenaded a couple of times by local musicians whom we always tipped. The whole experience was just brilliant and only cost us about £15, so when we had family and friends staying with us in Cancun on the occasion that we actually spent 6 weeks on holiday there, we revisited that locals restaurant and gave everybody a night to remember at El Crucero.

Our apartment was right on the sea front and next to a little beach called Playa del Ninos which is spanish for Beach of the Children. It was very much a locals beach and we had fun observing all the comings and goings on that seafront, for example every Sunday morning we would witness families arriving there, quite often on the back of a truck with the kids on the floor and granny sitting on a plastic chair which was not secured to anything by the way, in fact we've even seen whole families

arrive on one motor cycle... unbelievable. Health and safety in Mexico? I don't think so!

Then at one point this guy would walk into the sea and start Baptizing people in the Caribbean Ocean, what a sight with everyone watching from the shore and then surrounding them with love and hugs after the ceremony. Boy oh boy did our balcony enable us to spend lots of time people watching, wow, all of life is there.

The day before my 50th Shell left the apartment and said that she was going out to sort my birthday surprise. I suppose I was a bit worried because we weren't in a tourist area per se, but she didn't go far as it happened and the area around our apartment felt safe.

Whilst walking on our nearby beach Michelle saw a sign advertising fishing trips and she knew that I was desperate to go Deep Sea fishing in the Caribbean, so she went in and in her best pigeon spanish asked if she could book a trip for my birthday. Somehow she says that with neither of them completely understanding each other they seemed to get the gist of their agreement. Michelle

paid the $100 and then she left the restaurant with only a piece of paper with a handwritten receipt and gracias at the bottom trusting that it would all work out OK.

My Birthday morning was fantastic, as it always was with a wonderful breakfast in the apartment after which Shell said that the day might be a bit of a disaster as she'd booked something but wasn't convinced it was all gonna happen.

When the time came we turned up at the place where she had booked our trip and to our delight and relief they were waiting for us. We followed two Mexican guys down to what seemed to be a rowing boat with a small outboard engine resting on the shoreline, following their hand gestured instructions we proceeded to get into the boat and put on our life jackets.. mexican sizes mind you, so we had to be squeezed into them... I ended up looking like the Michelin Man and Shell had her Bust tightly and safely ensconced under her chin... it was all very snug. I'm just trying to paint a picture here folks! So off we set, Mr and Mrs Tightfit on a motorised rowing boat, but now this deep sea fishing adventure was really happening.

We'd seen fishing trips advertised around cancun on the bigger fishing boats and the costs were outrageous (probably aimed at the American tourist market) but we were getting the low budget version and it was raw and exciting. We headed off at a good lick hitting the waves hard as we went and the adrenalin was flowing. Then after about 20 mins or so we stopped, I don't know how far out we were but the Cancun Hotel strip was just a blur on the horizon.

I was given a rod and encouraged to start fishing, one of the guys was fishing too, I wasn't really sure what to expect but when he got a bite and started playing with the line like proper fishermen do, I was beside myself with excitement, what had he got?..... Flipping eck it was a Barracuda, I'm not even joking and my first thought was where the hell are they gonna put that? On the deck in front of us was the answer. Well you've never seen two British people move so fast, at lightening speed we made our way to the back of the boat and the only sound that could be heard besides the thrashing about of the Barracuda was the laughter of two Mexicans!

After our first catch the guys opened a couple of small beers for us to celebrate which we thought was great fun, anyway the Barracuda kept being caught, one even by me I think you'll find, Michelle too had success getting a couple of fish and of course the beers kept flowing. At one point I must have hooked a monster cause it took my line and rod too and the fishermen laughed and gestured that it was enormous. Even without my rod they put together a makeshift version of fishing gear wrapping the line around what looked like the inside of a small tyre to me. Because our mindset was that we were going fishing not sunbathing we didn't cover ourselves in sun cream and in the

middle of the ocean on a small boat without a canopy we had no real protection against the searing heat but hey there were always the beers!

When the fishing was all done the guys started the journey back at break neck speed, hitting every wave again but unfortunately by now Michelle and I were the not so proud owners of unbelievably full bladders which combined with the lack of onboard toilet facilities made for a traumatic return to the shore. We were desperate for the loo and every time the wave crash happened we'd look at each other not knowing whether to laugh or cry.... We both saw the comedy in the situation, but the hilarity didn't make it any less painful.

Upon our arrival we both ran towards the restaurant like Usain Bolt and the relief was palpable. We then went back to the boat and had a photo with the guys holding up the barracuda we'd all caught. They asked us how many we wanted and we said one, I mean what were we gonna do with 5 barracuda in our apartment. So we assume the others went into the restaurant to be part of that night's menu.

What a flipping experience, well done Shell, it was exciting, scary, great fun and boy should we have realised what was to come after drinking all those beers. The most brilliant birthday ever! That night the fun continued with Shell cooking the Barracuda in garlic on our cooker in the apartment, and that added to the birthday feast that she prepared for my special day. We had the music playing and danced in the moonlight on our balcony looking over the Caribbean Ocean.... just perfect.

VIVA MEXICO!!

Logical Nursery Rhymes

Mary had a little lamb
it's fleece was white as snow,
and everywhere that Mary went
the lamb was sure to go

It followed her to school one day
this was against the rules,
it used a GPS tracking system
this lamb was
no one's fool

So now she'd never be alone
the lamb would track her down,
and running out of options
Mary headed out of town

The Lamb was here, the lamb was there
it wouldn't let her be,
so Mary did what she had to do
and ate it for her tea

CHAPTER 26

'To be or not to be: that is the question'

Starsky and the Fonz!

Things changed for me the next year as I had left my then manager and started to work for new producers. The first show I did for them was in Bromley, and was Peter Pan, I played Mr Smee next to a Hollywood legend! I kid you not, Paul Michael Glaser the original Starsky from the US 70s TV series was Captain Hook. I have to admit I was quite nervous about working with him, but I need not have worried, we just hit it off and I have to say he played the comedy bits with me with such fun and respect.

Starsky and Putz!

Excuse me Captain but you look
A little bit like that flipping Starsky!

Michelle and I stayed in Croydon for this panto season with our lovely friend and Military Musical Director Adrian Beckett. During the run I spent loads of time off stage with Paul and of course that all helped to keep the on stage feeling great.

Iconic moment alert!! On one afternoon show Paul's friend David Soul who played Hutch in the classic TV show came in to watch our Panto and afterwards he came backstage for a chat. So picture this, little old me perched between two Hollywood Icons who were showering me with praise..... wake up Andrew, wake up you must be dreaming! But I

wasn't, the only frustrating thing was that I forgot to get a picture of us all together.

Then on another performance Barbara Windsor came in to watch the show with her husband Scott who worked for the production company and was the guy that signed me up to do the shows. It was the first time that I had actually met her, but that night after the show she reaffirmed to me that although we were both disappointed that our planned Panto in Nottingham didn't happen (more info to follow later) because of a sudden illness, she was determined that when she eventually did Pantomime again it would be with me and of course she was completely true to her word. She also loved

the show with Paul and me btw, and I love that picture of us all together at the after show party.

Heyyy!! It's me and the fonz!

Henry Winkler is a Gent, a Genius and all round Good Guy! There I've said it, how on earth could I have ever imagined as a spotty teenager that one day I would be the Fonz's sidekick.

As a young lad I was obsessed with watching Happy Days every Saturday with The Fonz, Richie and the rest of the Cunninghams. TV shows didn't get any bigger than this one and the Fonz was the character that people around the world took to their heart.

The producer of Peter Pan in Bromley had said to me that he was considering teaming me up with Henry in Milton Keynes as I'd done so well in Bromley and he took me to see Bradley Walsh performing in Aladdin after our run had finished to check out the Theatre where I was likely to be for the next year. I was taken into Brad's dressing room before the show and he was not only friendly but also complimentary, he told me that he'd heard that I'd stormed it in Bromley and he believed that I was on an upward trajectory in our business.

Just stop there for a moment everyone..... do you realize how important that was for me to hear, and it just made me feel so special. He didn't have to say all that but he did because he meant it and he knew that I would really appreciate it coming from him. He was giving back there, just such a lovely thing to do to a fellow performer.

So in 2008 it happened, I turned up to meet Henry on the first day of rehearsals. The fact that I was even able to talk to him filled me with pride. Then I had a moment.... Pull yourself together Andrew you've got a job to do. I'd written a fair bit of the comedy for the show but Henry wasn't over sure whether he wanted to do it all as I believe he'd had

one or two *moments* next to a comedian in a previous production and was slightly wary.

However we marched on with rehearsals and Henry and I started to get a good rapport going and I really turned into a sponge again watching every thing he did and learning from him, even the way he handled stage direction and press interviews etc.

He was so professional and friendly but never ever backed himself into a corner where he agreed to do something that wasn't right for him, but it was all done with a friendly air and full of love. I've never met anyone else quite like him. Everyone that's worked with me knows that I keep coming up with ideas in rehearsal for the comedy bits of the show.... It can probably get annoying for fellow artistes sometimes but when the muse is on the ideas keep coming. If on one of these sporadic new idea moments I would suggest something to Henry he'd either say, yes let's try it or I like the concept but just look at it again maybe and let's see what we all think then. In other words, no... it needs working on., but he always kept you onside. I'm telling you the man is a genius.

Anyway as our show (which also featured the fabulous Louisa Lytton as Peter Pan) started to take shape I said to the director that I really thought the pop idols thing would work better if I did it with Henry and not one of the other pirates. He agreed and said, 'Why don't you suggest it to him'. Well one day when it was just Henry, me and the director going through our stuff in the rehearsal room, I actually said out loud that I think he should do this routine with me as I believed we could make it fantastic together. Bold eh? Henry said,' well then let's try it and see how we get on'.

That was music to my ears, and so we started running the routine together and of course I listened to all his suggestions and he to mine and

between us we created a routine that was lauded by the press as one of the highlights of the show. Thanks Henry, this sponge loved working next to you.

As mentioned the press loved our Panto and I was happy to read all their nice reviews until I got to one from The Leighton Buzzard Gazette. Anyway everything had been positive until this piece, I mean this critic really hated me and slagged me off remorselessly. She just kept writing how bad she thought I was, and although it was the only bad review for me, it was the one I kept thinking about.

I couldn't sleep, my confidence took such a knock, eventually I went into Henry's dressing room and told him about what I was going through and he gave me the best advice that I've ever been given in my life, in fact right up there with Larry Grayson's words from years before. I told him how awful this woman had been to me, and I asked him how he dealt with bad reviews and without a second's hesitation he said, 'I don't read them'..... Boom!! How perfect was that?

He wondered why I was reliant on a journalistic opinion of my performance when I knew how well I was doing, as I could hear it in the audience response every night. He said that theirs is the only review that mattered. What a pro and a good friend to me during our time together in Milton Keynes, a memory I will always treasure.

Me, Louisa and Henry having fun in Milton Keynes

CHAPTER 27

'I like this place'

The Bristol Hippodrome

In 2009 I was asked by the panto producers if I wanted to go to the Bristol Hippodrome to play Muddles in Snow White and it ended up being the first of 7 consecutive appearances in Pantomime at that fantastic Frank Matcham Theatre.

I was told that I would have a fair bit of input to the script for the show and that excited me. Of course I wanted to put my Pop Idols routine in and it ended up being one of the best ever versions of it. I was honoured to perform the sketch alongside West End Star Liz Robertson (It's on my Youtube channel if you fancy a look) who absolutely threw herself into it, she really was a delicious Wicked Queen but oh so willing to send herself up for comedy, an absolute gift for any comedian to work with.

Also on the show was the beautiful Kara Tointon who played Snow White, we bonded immediately in rehearsals as she was so happy to be there doing Panto for the first time I believe. I was struck by what a lovely voice she had but strangely she wasn't convinced about how good she was. For a TV Star from Eastenders to be not over confident was a surprise to me,

I kept telling her how good she was and that eventually she would go on to do musicals in the West End and stuff. She laughed at me but I just had a feeling, and many years later whilst I was watching TV in my dressing room at the Hippodrome, a new version of the Sound of Music was airing with Kara in the lead role of Maria....

Singing like an Angel. I cannot tell you how proud of her I felt and sent her a text to say how wonderful it was to see and hear my Snow White becoming a massive musical star in front of my eyes! You see... I do know what I'm talking about sometimes.

Working with Kara, what a talent!

The prince in our production was Joe Swash who wasn't there for the whole rehearsal process as he was doing ITV2's I'm a celebrity after the main show thingy... you know what I mean. Anyway when he eventually was able to join us we had to really concentrate the rehearsal around adding Joe to our show.

He picked it up really quickly and was happy to do some comedy routines with me, he used his naughty school boy type of personality to the ultimate in our sketches and was always slightly unpredictable and cheeky on stage.

EVENING POST 9

STEALING THE SHOW

Unsung hero Andy is the real king of city's great pantomime

REVIEW

Crowning Andy as king

Liz Webster

I love coming to work in the morning and the great thing here is that I can connect with the audience even more – they get the jokes about Chipping Sodbury

Andy Ford

The Pantomime was really well received and in fact the local Bristol Evening Post wrote a fabulous review calling me *The King of Panto*.... I have to tell you that made me proud and happy.

A career changing event happened during that Panto in 2009 at the Bristol Hippodrome. The manager of the theatre came into my dressing room and asked me if I would do a stand up comedy show there as the crowds seemed to love my performance in the Panto. That really was an affirming moment as when I walked out onto the stage to do my show, the audience went crazy before I even said anything! I cannot put into words how that made me feel.

So that's when the penny dropped and after comedy stints in pantomime venues around the country I made sure to book myself back into the theatres for a night of stand up. That's a long winded way of saying I'm happy with who I am, who I play to and with the choices and decisions I've made, it was a financial gamble to pull out of the cruise ship work but although it was scary for a while, in the long run it was the right thing to do for my heart, career and well being.

Logical Nursery Rhymes

Incey Wincey Spider
climbing up the spout,
down came the rain
and washed the spider out

Out came the sunshine
and dried up all the rain
but Incey Wincey Spider
had unfortunately
already drowned

CHAPTER 28

'Women will love her that she is a woman more worth than any man; men, that she is the rarest of all women'

Dame Barbara Windsor

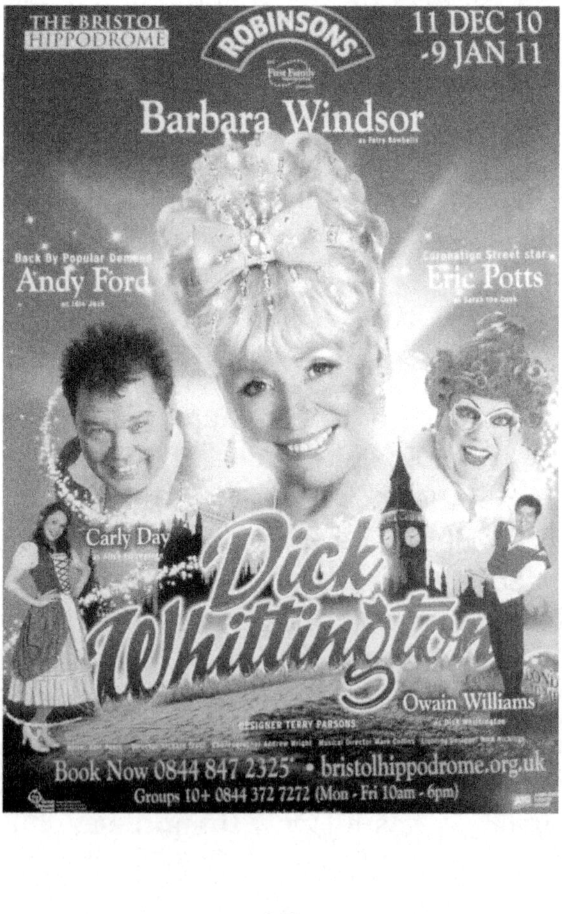

Now I really must give you the set up to my Barbara Windsor Pantomime experience. Around 2003/4 I was a regular guest on ITV's Today with Des and Mel Show and at that time I was doing Pantos for Jim Davidson's Family Pantomime company. One day Jim rang me and asked if I wanted to work the next year at the Theatre Royal in Nottingham with Barbara Windsor in Cinderella. Well that blew me away and he went on to explain that she had been watching me on Des's show and said to her husband Scott, *'That's my Buttons!'* I said that I would love to, it's a no brainer as she was one of my heroes, in fact I remember queuing up to watch her in the Carry On films at the Cinema in Exeter when I was a lad.

It certainly was a *pinch me* moment and Jim set the wheels in motion for it all to happen. Unfortunately Barbara was taken quite ill during that year and had to pull out of the show. My first thought was one of concern for Barbara and hoping she'd recover, but also tinged with a bit of disappointment that my childhood hero wouldn't be on the stage with me in Panto. Her husband Scott said to me when we next met up that Barbara was also really upset that we couldn't do the show together, and he told me that she promised to make it happen if she ever did Panto again. It was a lovely thing to say, but to be

honest at that point I wasn't sure if it would ever happen.

After the rip roaring success of Snow White in 2009 at the Bristol Hippodrome, I received a phone call from the producers to tell me that they would like me to perform there again for the following season. He teased me by saying that this would be a very special production but he couldn't tell me who it might be with at that stage. It was all very mysterious, but in my heart I kept thinking.... could it happen? I'd heard a rumour that Barbara was about to leave Eastenders so to be honest part of me was putting 2 and 2 together and getting 8 million!!

Then I got the call... it was going to take place, and Barbara had insisted that I should be with her. Apparently 2 of the main clauses on her contract were... the production had to be with a new stage set and that Andy Ford was the lead comic. Yes folks I was on Barbara Windsor's flipping contract. I was literally dancing with delight around the house at the wonderful news. I was going to be on a Panto poster next to my boyhood idol and ladies and gentlemen... it don't never not get any better than that!

We turned up in London to start our rehearsals and it was then that the reality hit me, this was happening. Barbara and I just teamed up immediately and it felt like I was working with my best mate. Also on the show as the Dame was a very good friend of Michelle and me, Mr Eric Potts. Shell had worked with him on projects for Theatre Cymru and I had joined them all on various tours to keep my wife company. Eric and I hit it off by talking about comedy and in fact he even came to our wedding. So to be working with him and Barbara made me feel that all my Christmases had come at once.

Strangely when we started a read through of the script on the first day of rehearsals the enormity of it all seemed to hit me and I really struggled to get my lines out properly. To me it just didn't sound funny and for a moment the confidence just drained out of me... completely weird. But as the Director started to rehearse us for different scenes the belief came back and it felt good again.

Looking back I'm convinced that my mind shut down a bit because it all meant so much to me and I was putting ridiculous amounts of pressure on myself to be the finished item straight away. If I'm honest with myself, I think I was so desperate to impress Barbara that I froze and the stupid thing was that I'd got the gig because she wanted to work with me. Oh my word Mogford sometimes you are so complicated....as my wife would say, *'Just go with the flow Andrew'*.

So it was happening and we moved to Bristol to put together the finishing touches to our show before the opening night. Well I am delighted to say that the audiences and press loved us and the reviews were incredible, this just kept getting better and better. But away from the stage the real action was taking place in the Artistes dressing rooms, for I

was getting the chance to spend quality time with Barbara and that was the real reward. Being *'Old Pros'* Barbara and I would always get to the theatre at least 2 hours before curtain up so that we wouldn't feel rushed and could do all our pre show preparations at a leisurely pace. This also gave us loads of time to chat and bond, which was the best bit. Although Barbara was the star she didn't choose dressing room number one she picked number two which was right opposite mine so that basically our doors opened up to each other. Many happy hours ensued with us drinking cups of tea and chatting on my sofa, her life story was a masterclass in how to fight against the odds to succeed and I was getting all of that info one to one. If you haven't yet seen the TV play about Barbara's life then please seek it out and watch, boy was she a fighter.

Like many of you reading this, our first views of Barbara would have been in the Carry On films where she went on to become a massive star, but interestingly she earned very little from those movies. She told me that she had never owned her own house until she did Eastenders, I know, unbelievable eh? The Carry Ons were produced on a very limited budget but sold world wide, although apparently not that much of the monies accrued found it's way to the Artistes. The publicity and profile that the performers received from these films however enabled them to take on other more lucrative opportunities.

My lovely friend Scott Mitchell, Barbara's husband has written a brilliant book about his life with her and it's so worth a read. She talked with me at length about those Carry On experiences, from her first meeting on set with Kenneth Williams through to Sid James's relentless pursuit of her affections.

The Kenny thing was brilliant, apparently he could be a bit diva-ish on set and was well known for his occasionally acidic tongue so when Barbara was first introduced to him he was more than slightly rude to her. Without hesitation she came back with a retort that I couldn't possibly tell you in this book,

but it's effect was to make Kenneth Williams roar with laughter. Immediately he knew that Barbara could certainly handle herself and it was her self confidence that endeared her to him, so from that moment on they were besties.

She once said to me, '*Who else in the Carry Ons would you like to know about Andy?*' I said, 'What was Frankie Howerd like', and without even a moments thinking time she looked at me and said, '*Miserable Bastard!*'

The more we chatted the more I was in awe of her, yet conversely the more comfortable I felt myself becoming in her company. On one notable occasion as we were sitting there the Deputy Stage manager announced over the tannoy in my room that it was the *half hour call*, which meant that it was time to call a brief stop to our chat and to get ready for the show. As she got up to go into her room she said, 'You like Kenny don't you Andy?' I said that I loved him and she said, 'Alright darling', and went out the door. I closed and locked it behind her as I was about to take a quick shower. After showering and putting on some underwear I unlocked the door in case wardrobe or someone needed to get in, when I opened the door a book fell into my room.

It was called Born Brilliant the authorised biography of Kenneth Williams. I quickly opened it to discover a message written by Barbara to me, it went..

Dear Andy, it's been so wonderful working with you, you are simply the best. I hope you continue to rise and rise in our profession, and become the star you so rightly deserve to be, lots of love Barbara Windsor X 2010.

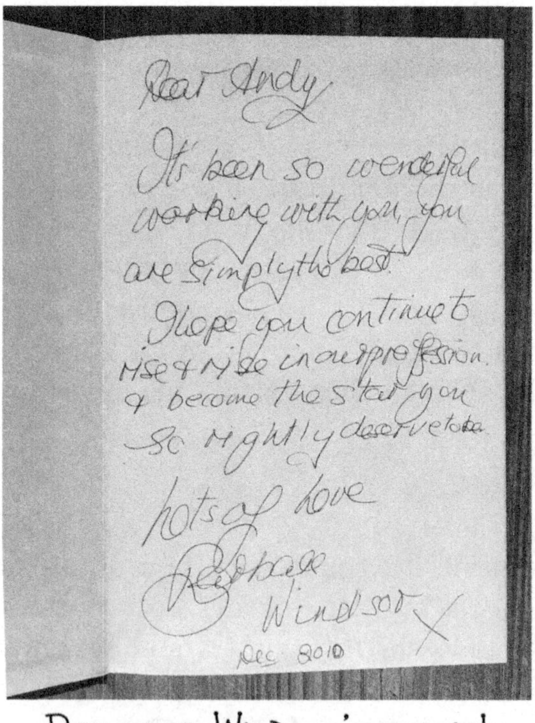

Barbara Windsor's special Message to me

WOW!! Right? Without wishing to offend anyone this was my equivalent of Moses getting the ten Commandments from God. What else could I do but burst into her room to thank her, discovering our Fairy Bowbells standing there in her Bra and Knickers being fitted with a mic by our soundman. Completely oblivious to the situation I said *'Barbara thank you so much, this is so lovely'*, and back came her reply, *'That's alright darling!'* Then Scott says, (looking at us both in our underwear) *'Well this has to be the oddest conversation I've ever witnessed!'*

Of course Barbara is one of the most iconic and popular entertainers in the history of our business, and because of this she was continually getting famous visitors to her dressing room before and after the shows. She was good friends with Matt Lucas and David Walliams from Little Britain, BGT and Bake Off etc. and on one matinee Matt came back to see her.

She asked me if I could bring him up on stage for the songsheet bit that I always do towards the end of the Panto as she thought it would be funny. I said of course, and we arranged for the ushers to bring up 4 children as usual plus Matt. It turned out to be a hoot as Matt is just such a naturally funny man,

and he did all his...*Yeah but no but..* comedy stuff from the telly and I interviewed him as if he were a child.... Brilliant. Well after the show Matt came into my dressing room and said that he had just sat for 2 hours in a theatre learning about comedy by watching me! I kid you not dear listeners and on the following Monday he went on to BBC 1's One Show to say that I was just about the funniest man alive. How lovely was that? We're still in contact through our mutual friend Rob Rinder and I hope to spent more time in his company at some point, a real gentleman.

This guy is lovely!

The other side of all this loveliness of course was that I was getting to watch Barbara the consummate

professional work at really close quarters. She was in her seventies at the time but her energy levels never fell, such a great performer. At one point in the piece I would do a solo comedy spot in the Panto and if I turned my head to the right I could see Barbara there in the wings watching me every show. After my spot one day she said, *'You changed a word today darling didn't ya?'* and I said *'Yeah I did, I just thought I'd try it'*, and she said *'Do you think it was funnier?'* and I said *'Yes I think it was ok'* and she came back...*'OK darling'*, in other words if it ain't broke don't fix it. She even did me the honour of performing the punchline to my Pop Idols routine with her never to be forgotten impression of Lady Gaga. A boy can't ask for any more than that....

Barbara ws always so lovely to my family, here she is with my inlaws!

When they did a whole feature in the Daily Mail about Barbara, they printed her top 12 photos from her life and career. There was a picture with the Queen and with her Dad and Scott of course but one of them with was me….. really! That makes me feel so special. During one of our backstage discussions I discovered that we both started our careers on the same day, it was on Christmas Eve in 1950 that Barbara did her first Pantomime in a theatre as a juvenile and on the same date but in 1969 I was booked to do my first professional gig.

So secretly I arranged with our fantastic Panto Dame Eric Potts and other cast members to do a presentation to her on Stage after the evening show on Christmas Eve as it was her 60th Anniversary in the business. She was very moved when at the end of my normal curtain call speech (which we always split between us) I announced to the audience that we were celebrating a special moment in the career of our national treasure Barbara Windsor…. I'll never forget that night, it was one of those '*I was there'* moments and the audience went absolutely crazy.

During that wonderful production of Dick Whittington in Bristol there was talk of the show going on to Wimbledon the next year with me and Barbara again. When our run ended Michelle and I went off to Mexico for a holiday, we absolutely love it there and we once again rented our apartment right on the seafront where we would drink our morning coffee with the Caribbean Ocean in all its glory right in front of us... perfect eh?

Whilst there we got a phone call from Scott to say that Barbara wouldn't be doing Panto again next season as this year's production was a bit too much for her. I can't be sure of course but in hindsight

Barbara's reduced work load from that point on suggests that the illness that eventually took her from us was sadly starting to have an effect on her well being.

RIP you complete Legend, the world is a sadder place without you Barbara. Xx

A man with unique funny bones!

by **Scott Mitchell**

Actor, Agent, Producer

'When my late wife Dame Barbara Windsor decided to do her last professional pantomime in 2010/11, there was only one man she asked for to be in her cast! That man was Andy Ford and he completed Barbara's dream of one last perfect Panto!!! Thanks Andy!! For your talent and friendship.'

CHAPTER 29

'Give every man thy ear'

David Hasselhoff and me

So no repeat of the dream team for 2011, instead the producers wanted me to stay in Bristol which I was honoured and more than happy to do, cause I'd completely fallen in love with the venue and it's fabulous audiences. The thing was though, I had no idea who I would be working with on the show. When the announcement was made you had to pick me up off of the floor.... Only David *flipping* Hasslehoff!

Yes dear readers he of Baywatch and Knight Rider fame. I was gonna share the stage with one of the most famous people on the planet... again! The stars just kept coming and I was loving every moment.

Michelle will tell you that when I know what the subject matter of the next panto is going to be, and who I'll be working with, the writing muse just starts for me. Doesn't matter if the show is 9 or 10 months away, I keep thinking about it and try to come up with something fresh to do in front of our audiences. I remember this next moment so clearly, I was in an airport somewhere in Scandinavia having a coffee, when this idea came into my head.

Now I knew that David wasn't necessarily a comedy performer, but he was (and of course still is) a larger than life character with a big booming voice and a presence and confidence the likes of which I've never witnessed before or since. So how could I make this work together on stage? For some reason the song *The wind beneath my wings* kept going around my head and I could visualise David as Hook singing it to Mr Smee as a thank you for his loyalty.

The Hoff experiencing that annoying voice in his ear!

I'd already being toying with the idea of Smee acting like a therapist to Hook, probing his thoughts about the crocodile eating his hand etc. I think the reason that it formed in my head was because I remembered the famous video of David uploaded by his daughter that went viral around the world with him on the floor asking for a hamburger or something. It wasn't particularly flattering for him at the time but he'd obviously bounced back from it all and never seemed to take himself completely seriously. So the idea of the song came from the psychoanalyst idea I guess.

The comedy wrote itself really once I'd set up the scenario in my head, basically David would sing the song in his inimitable way with me as Smee interjecting all the way through with comedy quips.... This sort of thing...

Hook sings... *It must have been cold there in my shadow*

Smee replies *Yep it was flipping freezing...*

Hook again... *to never have sunlight on your face....*

Smee.... *That's alright I saved a fortune in Nivea....*

and on and on, as I say the comedy just jumped out at me. I remember going to a production meeting in London to present my script ideas to the producers and they were happy to go with it.

The next thing I had to do of course was to make it work with our Star. Imagine little ol' me meeting the HOFF for the first time in rehearsals. I shook his

hand and looked up at him, he seemed about 6 foot 12… in fact the only other person that I've worked with that was as tall as David was Craig Revel Horwood. So we get to the Wing beneath my wings scene and I'm really nervous.

Obviously David had seen the script and didn't seem to be anti any of it so that was good. The psychiatrist bit went well in rehearsal and then we moved on to the song. It seemed to be going swimmingly, I remember thinking, *'Flipping 'eck Andrew, you're getting away with this'.* Then after one run through of the musical piece he says to me, *'What's a Budgie?'* So dear reader just to clarify, the lyrics went

HOOK…. *I could fly higher than an eagle*

SMEE….. *or possibly a budgie!*

I explained that a budgie was short for budgerigar, the pet bird people would keep in a cage in their houses and the fact that it was so small it would work comically next to his line about flying higher than an eagle. I suppose because David had never heard of a budgie he wasn't convinced that it would

work. He said to me, *'A Budgie? Is that funny?'* I tried to convince him that it would get the desired reaction, and luckily for me later that day our juvenile ensemble came in to watch some of the rehearsals and when we got to the budgie bit they all laughed their heads off. David turned to me and winked, that was it, I knew he trusted me then!

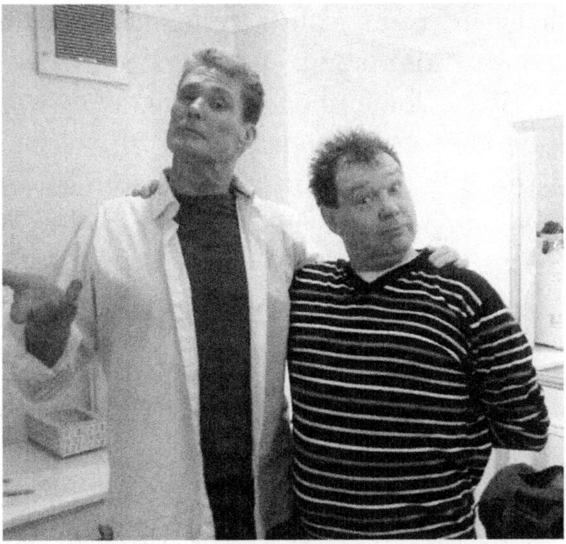

Two Blokes Relaxing in their Dressing Room!

What a joy he was to work with and he has such a lovely caring side that most people probably aren't aware of. For example, I was really struggling with my voice during the run and he went out and

bought some fresh ginger for me to cut up and put in my hot lemon and honey drink to help me. How lovely was that? So back to the Wings sketch... I am delighted to inform you that I believe the routine was a triumph and he just threw himself into it... Thanks David that will always remain as one of my favourite ever moments in Panto (again you can watch it on my Youtube channel).

Also I'd just like to add here that David, Lesley Joseph, Rob, Barbara Windsor, Henry Winkler and many more stars that I have worked with have always appreciated and had time for the audience. After the shows they would come to the stage door and chat, sign autographs and do the selfie thing until everyone had got what they wanted no matter how long it took, it's what I do as well and my mantra has always been, *No audience No Career!*

Without you guys we'd have no one to play to, so there would be no point, I firmly believe that we are here to entertain but that appreciation is a two way street. On the rare occasion that I work with someone who isn't keen to put themselves out to meet the public it really upsets me.

One year I worked in Panto with someone who seemed to be only there for the glory and the cheque which didn't sit comfortably with me. This person even wore some of their ordinary clothes under their walk down costume at the end of the show so that when the curtain came down they could get out of the theatre in a couple of minutes and not have to face the public afterwards at the stage door! Obviously no names to be mentioned here, but if you don't care about the people who come to watch why should they care about you.... Rant now over, thank you for your attention!

Logical Nursery Rhymes

Mary Mary quite contrary
how does your garden grow?

With silver bells
and cockle shells
but nothing in the way
of vegetation

Chapter 30

'The more I give to thee, The more I have, for both are infinite'

The Centenary and beyond

I was about to take part in my 4th consecutive Panto at the Glorious Bristol Hippodrome and the love from the audiences felt really warm and got stronger each year, this was of course always reciprocated by me. Who ever could have imagined that I'd be involved in a mutual appreciation society but I was very grateful and completely loved it.

Our Pantomime season in 2012/13 was quite different, for a start it was my first experience of having a character in the panto being played by two people. How was this going to work? Getting the rapport with a fellow performer takes time in rehearsal but after 2 weeks of the panto I'll have to reset and try to get that feeling of teamwork again without the time to set it properly.

The Slave of the ring was to be performed by Loose Women's Carol McGiffin for the first two weeks and then it would be ITV This Morning presenter and Big Brother winner Josie Gibson from Bristol for the second two weeks. Also on the bill were Britain's Got Talent Dance Troupe Flawless, who were great fun and fabulous to watch. Carol and Josie had never done panto before as far as I'm aware and they were both very nervous about doing the show.

As Carol was performing the role first it was she that joined our pre-show rehearsals in Bristol, I wasn't sure what to expect as I knew that she was quite the hard hitting journalist with the odd opinion or two. But I needn't have worried she was just a joy and we had some lovely chats during our time together.

Carol was quite self deprecating about her performance in Panto and suggested to me on many occasions that maybe this would be her first and last Pantomime performance as she felt outside of her comfort zone.

I hope her performing insecurities didn't stop her from enjoying the experience with me on stage, there were lots of laughs between us out there and I thought that she was a lovely lady.

Carol was flipping lovely!

Being a Bristol girl as I mentioned, Josie had been a visitor to our pantos at the Hippodrome over the years so she was very aware of my work and very complimentary to me. We have remained in touch ever since and I couldn't be happier for her TV successes now working on ITV, a charming natural lady who grasped the nettle and delivered in her first Panto that year, plus being a couple of West Country Bumpkins on that show together, how could we not have fun?....we did!

Having a Gurt Lush time with Josie Gibson!

My one regret from that Pantomime was not getting to do a comedy dance routine with Flawless. There wasn't anything like that written into the script for us to perform together so that was a shame from my perspective and during our chats in the run, the lads from Flawless said to me that they would liked to have put something together for us to perform. Never say never though, who knows what's to come in the years ahead.

Also on the show was an Actor who I had grown up watching in the sitcom *'Cuckoos Nest'* that was really popular in the 1970s. David Roper was his name and we bonded instantly, I loved hearing all his showbiz stories and he was a big fan of comedians, and loved working with me on comedic script ideas which as I say is something that I've witnessed from many a legit Actor. They love what we do, it's humbling but something that I've experienced many times, it's probably because we do it on the hoof so to speak. Yes we have a script to work from, but we also have license to play a bit and we're able to use our stand up experiences to help us when things go wrong or out of kilter on the show.

Another great memory from that year was standing on the stage and telling people on a certain performance that they were there on the day that the Bristol Hippodrome was celebrating 100 years since it's opening! I got the chance to lead the crowd in a rousing chorus of Happy Birthday for the Theatre… fantastic!

The following year I had the chance to reprise my favourite role of Buttons in Cinderella again in Bristol. I've always adored the challenge of this character, yes he's the comedic friend of the audience and in love with Cinderella but there's

always my favourite scene in the piece which happens just after Cinders is forced to rip up her ticket to the Ball and it's Buttons job to comfort and look after her. It's so rewarding for a comedian to do a scene where he or she has to straddle comedy and tragedy, especially when the main Character is badly treated in the play. I just love developing a rapport with my Cinderella and on this occasion it was so lovely to play that scene with Suzanne Shaw who you might remember from the Pop Group Hearsay in the 1990s. We both threw ourselves into the storyline and the kitchen scene was always the one that gave me the most pleasure, it was heartfelt and real from both of our perspectives and a memory I will treasure always.

On this show I won my first Panto award for the UK's best entrance in a pantomime!

'I'd rather have a fool to make me merry'

LIVE to the Nation in 2014, followed by the Merseyside experience

Never work with Children or Animals they say... well this year I was going to do both, not only in front of our wonderful Bristol Audience but the whole nation...LIVE! There had been mutterings about doing a Live Broadcast of our Panto the year before, but it didn't come to anything.

Anyway this year it was gonna happen. Our show at the Hippo was Dick Whittington, the Show that I had done only 4 years before with Barbara Windsor, but our line up was completely different.

For a start we had a very famous dog and Movie Star on the Show called Pudsey, you might remember him from Britain's Got Talent along with his handler and all round lovely girl Ashleigh Buttler. Cbeebies star Ben Faulks aka Mr Bloom was Dick and Eric Potts directed and played the Dame.

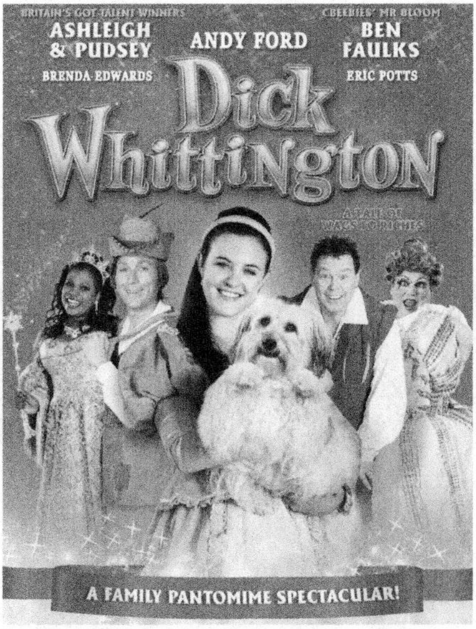

This panto was also fairly controversial in as much as it had a 3D cartoon Scene in the show (I can hear the Panto traditionalists now in uproar), during which the audience were encouraged to don their 3D specs to appreciate it all. Of course Panto keeps changing throughout the years, there are even murmurs that in Victorian times performers and audiences alike were maligning the way Pantomime had changed. But as far as I'm concerned Panto has to stay relevant and modern and embrace the new technologies available in order for this treasured genre to survive. Speaking of technology, the plan was for our show was to be streamed Live via satellite to Cinemas all around the Kingdom and even to parts of Europe.

Great Dame Eric Potts and me smashing it!

My wife and her friends went into a Cinema in Teeside to watch it. Yes there were pressures because we'd only performed this show twice on the first day and now we would be playing to potentially millions around the country... first thoughts were, don't forget any of the script Andrew! Between us the cast all decided to treat the occasion like any other gig with the odd nod to people watching from afar.

Luckily for us, the audience that day were as fantastic as always and Michelle told me that the atmosphere from the Theatre had come across well in the Cinema. People were joining in with the Panto back and forth and reacting as if they were in our Theatre. I think once again the experience of performing live on the Des and Mel show on ITV on quite a few occasions had stood me in good stead for this moment and I really embraced it. Since then the video of the show has been viewed on Amazon Prime Video by many more millions all around the world.... Makes me feel quite proud.

Following that unique Panto moment, I next had the pleasure of working on a cruise ship with Liverpudlian Comedy Legend Pauline Daniels. She was booked to present her magnificent version of

Willey Russell's Shirley Valentine on board and I was there to do a couple of cabaret spots. We immediately hit it off (that comedy camaraderie thing again) and I managed to talk the Cruise Director into letting us do a show together one night. It was on this trip that Pauline invited me to play the male character in a comedy play that she was producing and directing later that year (2015) at the Brian Epstein Theatre in Liverpool. The production was called Waiting for Gateaux, by Ed Waugh and Trevor Wood from the North East of England. It was brilliantly funny and well written but embedded in the hilarious script was the chance for me to act in some of the more serious and emotional scenes too, and that excited me.

So I made my way to Liverpool to meet up with all the ladies on the show to start our rehearsal process, oh did I not say, I was the only bloke on it… fantastic! It was a show about a weight watchers club of sorts and gave me the opportunity to be self deprecating, which is really appealing for a comic. Mind you with famous professional actresses like Lynn Francis and Suzanne Collins from Brookside as well as the young and talented Emma Lisi and Pauline herself, I needed to up my acting game.

I loved it… some of the acting disciplines were alien to me but I was keen to learn, the girls certainly helped me and the whole experience was just fabulous, the press loved us too it was a real success! Pauline was my love interest in the piece which was a new experience for me, I thoroughly enjoyed that and she also let me play with the physical comedy too, at one point Pauline and I were performing a really funny musical workout to the strains of Push it by Salt and Peppa which brought the house down.

Looking back on my life I'm so glad that I get to try all these things, new experiences equals growth... thanks ladies a pleasure to work with you all.

Working alongside These fantastic Women was just brilliant!

Pauline Daniels

Comedy Star, Actress and Liverpudlian Legend

'Andy is a unique funny man who I have the utmost respect for, he worked for me in a great play called Waiting For Gateaux a few years ago, his first venture as an actor and he smashed it, he's boss in every way!

We met on a cruise a few years ago and I was privileged during Covid to be one of his lock down guests on his online Variety Show.

He works hard and it shows, a real trooper and I love him

CHAPTER 31

'I bear a charmed life'

Me and Warwick Davis

I had briefly met Warwick in 2009 when I appeared in Snow White at the Bristol Hippodrome, he was advisor to the 7 Dwarves on our show. So I was excited to be joining up with him again but this time on the stage.

The first week of rehearsals took place without Warwick and the other Dwarves, it was all rather odd and without going into detail, it wasn't the happiest of ships to be sailing on. I'd bonded with the fabulous Andy Day (he of Andy's Dinosaur adventures on CBBC), we really enjoyed each other's company and were happy working together, but I wasn't as comfortable as usual. However that all changed when Warwick turned up. The show seemed to flow a lot better with his presence there and he made me feel really supported. We moved into our dressing rooms and very quickly became the odd couple, chatting about comedy at the drop of a hat, speaking of which I was wearing a pork pie type of hat at the time and I bought one each for Warwick and Andy which made them laugh.

The Management!

Another undoubted highlight on the show as well was our fabulous Wicked Queen Kim Ismay, a quite sensational actor and a comedian's joy to work alongside... what a treasure!

Also on the show was Aardman's Shaun the Sheep, who couldn't speak so we had to find stuff for him to do that didn't involve any sound. I came up with the idea of Shaun being a great impressionist so he just stood there and did his brilliant impression of a cloud with legs etc.... Oh how the crowd laughed...lol.

This show really was a great success and during the run Warwick and I talked about writing a panto together.

Near the end of the run the Producers came in and thanked me for my performance and asked if I would come back to the Hippodrome for Aladdin, but this time they wanted me to play Widow Twankey. Not again, (I thought to myself) I'd been through this before, and I really didn't want to frock up for Panto plus I felt that other actors would do it better than me. So although the reaction was great for our show I was a little down when asked to do the dame thing again.

After it had all finished I kept talking with Warwick about writing our Pantomime. He had been booked to appear in Woking the next year and wanted me to be on the show. The producers seemed happy with this and although it was a big wrench for me after 7 consecutive years at the Bristol Hippodrome I was going to Woking with Warwick as his co-writer and Assistant Director. In the end the Producers changed their minds about presenting Aladdin in Bristol and put on Cinderella instead starring Torville and Dean, which I heard was brilliant!

I loved my new roles in the show and I found it great to suddenly be asked by Warwick on stage during rehearsals..., *'This prose is not long enough to cover the transition Andy can you write me another verse please?'* Yep I'm on it I thought, and within a couple of minutes I'd filled the gap with extra script. Those challenges really excited me and overall I found the entire experience exhilarating. Warwick's Daughter Annabelle and his Son Harrison played 2 of the Dwarves in the piece and it was great spending time with them too. Shout out to Warwick's fantastic Wife Sammy who was always there when I needed to chat and struck up a great friendship with my Wife Michelle.

Great fun with Warwick and Annabelle!

The production company that we were working for were finishing at the end of this season (I'd found out on the grapevine), and so I was thinking that I needed to sort something out for the next Panto season as Warwick had also told me that his TV commitments were increasing and that he wouldn't be able to fit Panto in next year.

The word went around that another couple of producers from a rival production team were coming in to see the show on one of the matinees. The actress in our show who told me about it also said afterwards that they had really enjoyed my performance. So that was it, after the Panto I wrote to them direct, thanked them for coming to see our show in Woking and asked if they thought that they

could use me in any of their shows for the next season. Like I say you've just gotta do these thing, and the reply came back, 'Yes Andy we'd love to work with you and we'll be in contact soon!' Boom!

Andy's Animal Idioms

Idiom

Like a Pelican fishing in the bath

meaning

Something that is not likely to achieve a lot

CHAPTER 32

'his ceremonies laid by, in his nakedness'

Barely a lonely walk!

Dear friends and readers of a nervous disposition, I have to tell you of a momentous night that occurred betwixt the pantomimes of 2016 and 2017.

Are you sitting comfortably? Then I'll begin...

It happened in Scarborough in North Yorkshire and the tickets for this life changing event were purchased for me by my beautiful wife as a birthday present. So two of the greatest events of my life took place in this popular Yorkshire seaside town, first of course my wedding to Michelle in 1999 and then..... wait for it.... my first Status Quo concert 17 years later.

Don't you dare skip this bit!

I have long been a Quo fan and the thought of seeing them live had excited me greatly for many years. I was so beside myself with anticipation that my toilet visits increased exponentially the closer we got to showtime. For this special evening we were joined at the gig by Michelle's Uncle George and his lovely Wife Jenny. George is a year older than me so we grew up listening to and loving the same sort of music. To be fair we were like

schoolboys in the build up to that show. News had just recently broken that the Guitarist and one of the founding members of Quo Rick Parfitt had been taken ill so wouldn't be performing that night, obviously that was chastening news, but as they say...The Show must go on, and go on it most certainly did with a vengeance.

What a party
Me and the Quo!

As this was my first experience of a Quo gig I wasn't fully prepared for the start… it was Epic! The build up track started, it was orchestral and really loud with small snippits of their hits integrated into

the arrangement, the tension was building…. then suddenly they just walked out, I could hardly breathe. Francis Rossi turned his back on the crowd in preparation and the guy who was taking Rick's place adopted the stance, legs open with guitar at the ready.

I wasn't prepared for what this was about to do to me... The rhythm guitar riff for their opening song *Caroline* started, Francis turned around and began the icon lead guitar licks and it all took off right in front of my eyes. I CRIED LIKE A BABY! I had found my bliss in that moment…. You can call it sad if you want, but when something reaches you, What you gonna do? I was in Rock n Roll heaven, George and I were 16 again and no one can ever take that moment away from me.

If only that were the solitary mega moment of the night, but sadly and humiliatingly it's not. We made our way back to the bed and breakfast accommodation via a local pub where we finished the evening in style. Then we all retired for the night agreeing on a time for us to meet up at breakfast the following morning. Our room was fairly snug let's put it that way, with a really small toilet behind a sliding concertina type door.

As I am now a member of the older male fraternity, I often visit our toilet facilities a few times every night. The loo was on my side of the bed and in the early hours I got up to do what I had to do, obviously very sleepy after expending so much energy at the gig, I opened the door and stepped through, closing it behind me so as not to disturb Michelle. Then it hit me! I was in the hallway outside of our room and in case I'd forgotten to mention it, I sleep naked occasionally and this was one of those times. I had no key to let myself back in, so what's a boy to do in this predicament?

There were doors to other bedrooms all around me and shouting to Michelle might have wakened other guests. It was the nightmare scenario that I'd dreamt of many times. So this sad little naked man began to tippy tap on the door praying that Michelle would hear but that no one else would. Thank God she did, but when the door was opened and she saw me there as nature intended my loyal life companion just burst into maniacal laughter. Thanks my darling!

I shuffled past her guffawing and got back into the room. Oh the relief to be inside. Now if any of you know my Wife, you'll be aware that the first thing

she did at breakfast was to recall the previous night's events in great detail, of course she did. Michelle even shared my embarrassment with the landlady, and it was she who told me something that chilled me to the bone.

The B&B had security cameras inside and outside of the building. I couldn't move with fear, imagining that the world and his wife might eventually see my naked night time excursion. But she was teasing me as the cameras in question were installed one floor below us, however this didn't stop George renaming me... ***The naked Rambler***, thanks mate!

Andy's Animal Idioms
No Pingu no Cry!!
Idiom
Like a Penguin in Jamaica
meaning
Someone who looks out of place

CHAPTER 33

'O Hero, what a Hero hadst thou been'

Playing Adge Cutler

2017 turned out to be a great year for me affirmation wise, in as much as I won the Lost Review Best Live Comedy Show UK award that year and I was also inducted into the Panto Archive Hall of Fame. So that was nice! Also I played West Country Legend Adge Cutler in a musical play about this life.

I had been approached by a guy from Bristol called Neil Maggs a few years previously who had a long held dream of producing a show about Adge, and after seeing me perform in Panto at the Bristol Hippodrome he had decided that it was me he wanted me to play the role of Adge. I had been a fan of the Wurzels for years and always had a soft spot for Adge when I was younger, in fact I used to sing many of his songs in my gigs around the Exeter Pubs and clubs.

I went through the script he'd sent me and I thought it was a good basis for a potential Stage show, but needed a bit of resetting and rewriting to make it work, plus I wanted to add more comedy to it. However it was only on reading the story of Adge's success and untimely demise that I realised that there was a real connection between myself and this legendary entertainer. I discovered that Adge had passed away in a car accident in the early hours of May 5th 1974 after a show at the Crystal Room in Hereford the night before.

Whilst going through the story I found out that the support act to Adge and the Wurzels on that last show was Aiden J Harvey. On the night that Adge passed away, the same performer did a cabaret spot

in Exeter at the Clifton Hill Labour Club and the resident band was the Vic Palmer sound with me as the lead singer.

After all these years I suddenly remembered that when Aiden turned up for a sound check at the venue in Exeter, he told us what had happened to Adge Cutler. We were devastated and I know that we played a few of his songs that night as a tribute. The thing is I didn't think any more of it until I read Neil's script and realised that the last person to play alongside Adge worked with me on his very next show....

At that moment I felt a close connection and that motivated me to play the part even more. The show entitled *Drink Up Thy Cider* went out for the first time in 2017 at the Redgrave Theatre in Bristol and after a bit of tweaking and rewriting it was well received.

During our rehearsal period a chap walked into the hall in Bristol that we'd hired and said that he was looking for Adge Cutler. I was taken aback until he introduced himself as John Miles the man who managed Adge and help to create the Wurzel

phenomenon. He'd come in to see how it was all progressing, what a surprise that was for me and the cast.

He was very encouraging, a true gent, and eventually he went on to become my manger too, in fact we sealed the deal with a handshake in exactly the same way that he did with Adge back in the 1960s.

The show was a success and a couple of years later I resurrected the role again but this time in my self penned production, *Don't tell I tell 'ee* where I played Adge performing in a concert setting with his band as he had done throughout his career. I

included some story telling of Adge's life and it was a show that I really enjoyed. My mate from the early panto days Viv Danning joined me on the show playing the Tuba, and Harry Haden-Brown was our keyboard/accordion player and musical director.

Great fun working with my mate Viv again!

In 2021 after the lockdown Neil and I decided to resurrect the Musical Drink up thy Cider and this time I wrote some new songs for it to make it more of a complete musical.

Me and the cast of Drink Up Thy Cider 2021

I wrote incidental songs about how he named the band, how his accident had happened and others things around his story. Julian Charles played John Miles and Diane Jacobson was Adge's Wife Yvonne. The show also featured Andy Coogan as Acker Bilk and Tommy Banner from the Wurzels, Viv Danning my mate as John Macey, Jake Palmer as Pete Budd, plus fantastic cameo performances from Emma Bunce, Michaela Sidney, Francesca Carly and the much missed Bristolian Comic Stoney Garnett as George Rollings he of *Drink Up Thy Cider George* fame. We had a fabulous Live Band too lead by Felix Surbe and a terrific group of dancers.

Once again the shows went down great with the West Country audiences every night as we smacked them right between the eyes with no holds barred Wurzel classics. The shows were a riot and a great way of showing love for our West Country heritage, I was pleased with doing my bit to keep Adge's name and Legacy alive. My wife Michelle helped me to direct the show and also ran the whole shooting match from the sound booth as the Deputy Stage Manager.

CHAPTER 34

'But here's the joy my friend and I are one'

Smee and Steve McFadden

In 2017 I was booked for the first time by the Qdos Pantomime company to appear at the wonderful Theatre Royal in Plymouth as Smee alongside Steve McFadden who plays Phil Mitchell in Eastenders. So for me this was another new beginning and I was delighted to be embracing this opportunity in my home county of Devon. Steve and I had met briefly a couple of times before, once literally a fleeting glance when he came in to visit Kara Tointon and Joe Swash backstage during Snow White in Bristol in 2009 and a bit more of a chat in Barbara's dressing room in 2010.

You never knew who you were gonna see in Barbara's room, one day I went in and heard the dulcet tones of Dot Cotton saying, *' 'Oh 'ello Andy!'* June Brown was hilarious and a great joy to be around. The day that she came in she was accompanied by her TV son John Altman AKA Nasty Nick Cotton, my Panto buddy from Northampton. Isn't my life great?!!

Anyway Peter Pan in Plymouth that's what we were talking about here, and as mentioned earlier in this book I'd always wanted to play at the Theatre Royal ever since seeing Allan Stewart with Danny La Rue there, and now I was booked to do it. Not only that, I was second on the Bill and the only two faces featured on the poster were Steve's and mine. That's a big deal in our world and for this company to have that faith in me on my first show for them, made me feel very special.

We went to Plymouth to do the launch and Steve was as friendly as I remembered, and when I asked him if he was ok doing a couple of my self penned sketches if the producers saw fit to include them into the script he said, 'Whatever you want me to do mate, I'll do it because I trust you!' That meant the world to me and we went on to have a fantastic

season in Plymouth together, enjoying each other's company, going out to some fabulous restaurants and all that bonding stuff… just fabulous. Steve is a true gent and a good friend!

The other great thing about being at that theatre was the fact that I could meet up again with loads of my Plymothian friends who used to come to see me when I was running nearby Challaborough Bay all those years ago. As I say Steve and I remain good buddies to this day and we performed together again on another panto run a couple years later in Dartford where we reprised our roles in Peter Pan.

Panto BUDDies!

Now what's that famous expression? Write about what you know! Well a few years ago as my body started to develop more aches and pains and as I could feel myself falling behind with the latest technologies and trends, I did what any self respecting ageing comedian would do.... I wrote about it.

Whilst chatting with lovely Steve McFadden one day in my dressing room in Plymouth I just had a vision of older blokes trying to look cool on the dance floor to impress the young ladies. Steve's immediate reaction was to laugh and I thought there's something here that I could make work.

Another thought was to get some famous middle aged men to perform it with me and release it as a prostate cancer charity record. You see how my brain works, all that came from the one idea and I hadn't even written the song yet. The idea kept niggling away at me and one day I went into my studio and out came the song... *Dad Dancing*!

Dad Dancing!

I was really pleased with it and it made me want to film the video to help promote it. My original idea was to have a load of older blokes doing this dance but that would take a whole lot of arranging and studio time costs a fortune, so as usual I did it in my own way. With a green screen erected in our front room I started filming the various bits for the video,

playing 3 different middle aged men. The final edit took me forever to do, but I wasn't paying for any of it, it was just me doing stuff in my studio, as usual I was the writer, performer, director, editor, musician and songwriter. I love losing myself in these projects and when I see the final edit, it just makes me feel great (most times) and fires me up to do more.

I sent the video to my Manager John Miles and he absolutely loved it and so once again I bounced off that positive reaction to create even more. The next self penned mid life crisis song was written followed by four others. Six Mid life crisis comedy songs that came from an idea and chat with a mate in my dressing room. I just have to keep creating, it's what keeps me going! I suppose I carry on doing all this stuff because you never know what might come of it. I remember sitting in the green room at Thames TV Studios in Teddington Lock in 1998 just before an appearance on *Des O'Connor Tonight* chatting to a very successful entertainment agent. He said that he believed I had a good chance of making it because I was different. I said to him that maybe the missing piece for me was a big time agent, and he said something that I'll never forget.

His view was, yes of course Agents and managers are important but no one will ever sell you as well as you sell yourself. That struck me because of course no one else could possibly know what I can do as much as me, and no one can care as much about it as I do either. That's why I continually try new stuff I suppose, more reasons if you will to publicise and promote myself. Some stuff is obviously more successful than others but you can't win the lottery if you don't by a ticket. Plus and I really can't stress this enough.... I love doing it all, I just adore being me... full on, slightly annoying at times some might say but always doing things in good faith, keeping myself busy and trying to entertain.

There's not really an off button with me... hang on, yes there is, it's called sleep. When we go to bed at night Michelle always reads to try to come down from whatever she's been doing that day. For me it's completely different, as soon as my head hits the pillow I'm gone. When I'm on, I'm on and I like creating stuff and filling my days with various projects until I sleep.

The other day someone said to me that they'd spent hours watching videos on my YouTube channel, so I

actually logged on and took a look at it all...OMG it goes on forever. There's so much stuff on there, some of it's advertising upcoming shows etc, but the majority of it is performing and creating, like the mid life crisis songs and the FacebookLive shows. When I think of it, all those shows that I did online like the variety show and the happy chats and all that, they've happened within the last couple of years. Some people don't do all that in their lifetime! Keep going Boy!

I'll never retire! Some people say you can't live to work, you go to work to live. But they're equal for me because if you took my work away, my wife would divorce me. I think that if I couldn't do what I do, I'd implode, I can't ever imagine sitting in an office.

. CHAPTER 35

'Words are easy, like the wind, faithful friends are hard to find'

Dick Whittington in Devon

Hey Plymouth I'm back!!

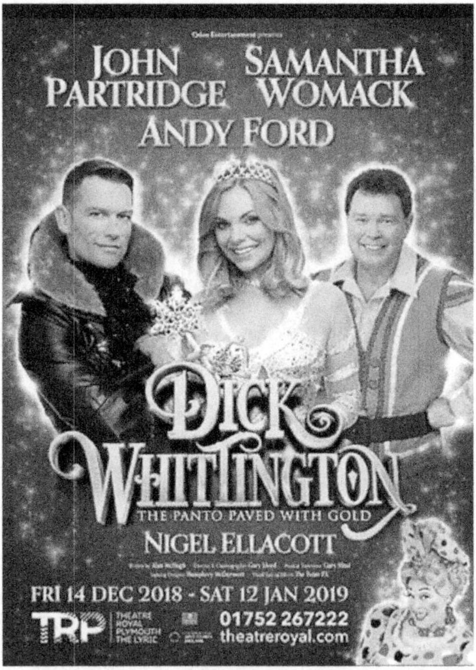

The Panto company wanted me to go back to Devon the next year and I was absolutely delighted to do it. I played Idle Jack in Dick Whittington, alongside Sam Womack, John Partridge and Legendary Panto Dame Nigel Ellacott. I believe that Nigel and I had

crossed paths many years earlier but this was my first chance to share the stage with him. He has well been established as one of the Country's top Panto Dames and it was great to experience that up close and personal. With Nigel's excellent comedy timing and great on stage generosity we revelled in each others company up there on that stage.

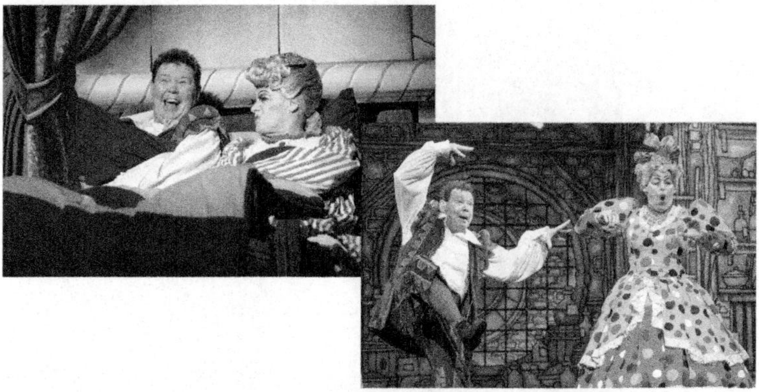

Most of the comedy scenes in this show were just me and the Dame, which meant that we were carrying nearly all the humour on our shoulders..... hang on a minute Andrew, rewind.... let's say that again....most of the comedy scenes in this show featured Nigel and I... and we flipping loved it! There that's better. This was also the year that I won my second Great British Pantomime award for the best song sheet in the country. It was called the

Jolly Janner and I wrote it especially for the good folk of Plymouth and boy did they sing their heads off when i performed it there.

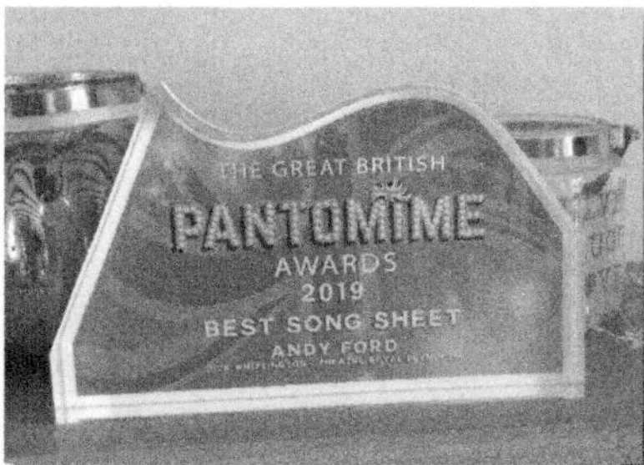

My second Great British Pantomime award!

I'm not sure if many other Panto comics write their own song sheets, but I've done it for years now and there is nothing better than watching the audience sing along in traditional style at the end of a Pantomime, especially when it's to my song. Sadly since Covid the chance to interview children on stage during the song sheet hasn't been possible, but hopefully that'll return soon as you can get some fantastically funny output from the younger audience members if you ask the right questions!

I've loved creating all these song sheets over the years....

I'm in love with my Babber 2010 Bristol

The Pasty Song (Yo ho ho, yum yum yum) 2011 Bristol/ 2017 Plymouth

Chop Suey 2012 Bristol

The Jolly Janner 2018 Plymouth

Pirates on the Ocean 2019 Dartford

Proper Gurt Lush 2021 Bristol

The West Country Song 2022 Bristol

Following that 2018 Panto appearance in Plymouth I was booked back at the Theatre Royal to perform my Stand Up Comedy Show and it was not only a great night but also a sell out! It's really lovely to be in demand in the South West but meanwhile on my Social media platforms there was a whole debate going on about whether I should be in Plymouth or Bristol. Fortunately I don't make that decision, but I can tell you it's great when people from Bristol come down to see me in Plymouth and similarly when the good folk of Plymouth travel to Bristol to watch me in Panto. It's quite overwhelming. You're a lucky boy Andrew.

From Plymouth to Dartford then! As mentioned Steve McFadden and I resurrected our roles of Hook and Smee in Kent in 2019. This year it was a bit closer to home for our Captain Hook compared with Devon and therefore we didn't get so much free time together as Steve was returning to his home in London after the shows each night.

However it was another joyful season working with my very good friend. I was staying with my family in Dartford for the run, and after it was done Michelle and I packed our bags for a well deserved break in glorious Mexico, but there were murmurings of a global virus starting to take hold.

Like most of the country we weren't sure how seriously to take it all and just carried on with our

post Pantomime holiday plans. The growing crisis did seem a long way away when we were lying on sunbeds on our favourite beach... Playa Tortugas in our beloved Cancun, but the world had changed a fair bit on our return.

Poetry Corner

Place mats annoy me,
I'm sorry but they do,
lying there on my nice table cloth,
they think they're so special.

Place mats annoy me,
I'm sorry but they do
and I think it's great
to slam down a plate,
that brings them down a peg or two

CHAPTER 36

'In these times, you stand on distance'

2020 Lockdown

So we sort of knew Lockdown was coming and all of us needed to find a way to get through it, cause everything changed on the decision to virtually shut down our country. I had booked in a Spring comedy tour for 2020 and tickets had already been sold so I was feeling bad for the people that were gonna be disappointed, me included, as I just love going out there and performing. That was the big thing for me, I wasn't able to do what I do and as all comedians know you have to keep working and honing your comedy in front of a live audience to bed in new material and keep it all flowing and fresh. So what to do?

I'm just one of those people who needs to do stuff, to be fair I'm a bit of a nightmare on holiday. If Michelle is lying on the beach reading a book I'm probably walking up and down the beach trying out material in my head, so the thought of doing nothing was scary! Then I thought, I have a fantastic following on my Facebook social media platform and I've often gone Live to everyone with career updates and chat, why don't I use that

situation to actually perform a Live Show of comedy. The technology was in place and I was chomping at the bit to perform so why not? Sounds straight forward doesn't it? A no brainer! Well I quickly realised that it was gonna take over my whole life. But to be fair there wasn't a lot else for me to do, so I say again, why not?

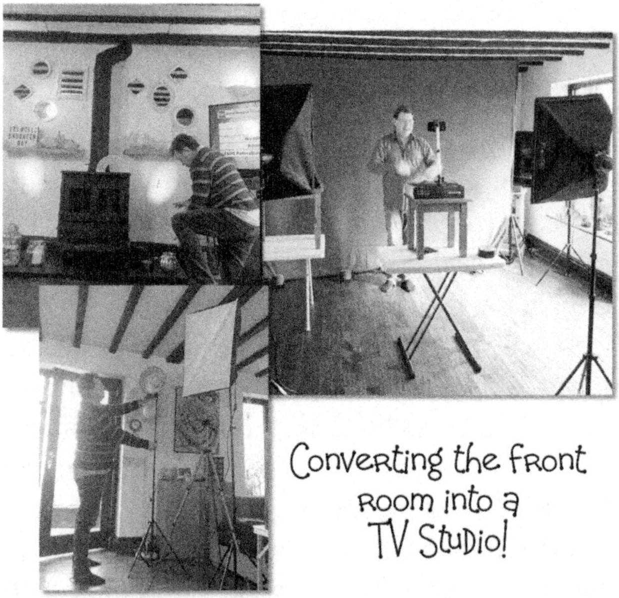

Converting the front room into a TV Studio!

The original plan was to do one live show on a Sunday night from our front room and see how it went, but when I saw the viewing figures for it I had

to pick myself up off the floor! ITV had kindly invited me onto their newscast to talk about what I was about to do because at that time I think I was probably one of the first comedians to actually do a live comedy show on the internet during the Lockdown, and the publicity was a great help in bringing in viewers for the show which went out on Mother's day in March of that year.

Well over ten thousand people tuned in to watch me live on Facebook! I could never have imagined that was about to happen when I was setting everything up for the broadcast in the afternoon. Luckily my Wife is used to my crazy hair brained schemes and helped me to create this event. I wanted it to look a bit Tellyish so I put up a blue backdrop in front of the fireplace and used some coloured uplighters to make it look as good as I could get it. My phone was placed in a stand which was on top of a couple of tables, I had to push the sofa back to give myself enough room to perform, the dogs must have wondered what the hell was going on. I set up my ipad just out of shot on my right hand side so that I could tap it to play music when required. I'd thought of everything except... what it was actually gonna feel like when I went live! It suddenly hit me, you're not gonna hear any laughter, how are you gonna time the next gag? How long is too long? Will

anyone actually be watching? Oh yes and why did I ever think this was a good idea? Michelle stayed in her studio upstairs and was the point of contact with my audience. Replying to their comments and occasionally coming down into the front room to give me some birthday requests to read out, so it looked like a one man show but I couldn't have made it happen without Michelle.

I know that I was a pain in the arse in the build up to the show on the day and as usual we discussed it as a mature married couple does... fill in the blanks! I somehow have the ability to drive my Wife up the wall whilst making her proud at the same time.

I have to say the reaction on Social media to the first live show was fantastic and very humbling, and that's what made me want to keep going with it. The thing that I didn't really take into consideration was the unquestionable camaraderie that these Sunday Night shenanigans helped to develop. I read the messages and I saw the photos that people had sent in every week to know that they felt part of something bigger outside of their own situation. The whole Sunday night live thing took on a life of it's own, with many messages coming in from people living alone and they told me that the shows made

them feel part of a community. Who could have guessed it would have that effect? I listened to what everyone was saying, for example they weren't over impressed with the blue backdrop but wanted to actually see our front room, so for better or worse that's what I did. I also had a little message board which I put behind me during the shows thanking the NHS workers for all they were doing during the lockdown.

I was live to the World every Sunday!

To shake it up a bit I started to introduce different themes to the shows, originally as an idea to stimulate the comedy input.... eg 'NHS theme', I might talk about my visits to the doctors with various medical gags put in there. One week I did a

fancy dress theme and I was flabbergasted by all the costume photos that my audiences sent to me. There were groups of people setting up zoom calls to watch the show together and react like an audience in a theatre laughing together. People can be very creative when they have a reason to be, necessity is the mother of invention and all that.

To my great surprise and delight I started getting messages from Facebook viewers who were watching me live all around the world, apparently I was on at lunchtime in the USA, Canada and Mexico and breakfast time in Australia. It does rather blow my mind to think that someone was sitting in their kitchen in Sydney wearing their PJ's, eating cornflakes and watching me standing in my front room doing a comedy show.

Of course there was no financial reward involved, the performances were given for free, but the thing is that by making myself do this every week it really helped to keep me alive as a comedian. As the weeks passed by I spent the majority of my time collating new material and rehearsing for each Live Sunday Night Extravaganza. My aim was to not repeat a gag and I think that I just about got away with that for the full run.

Eventually Shell said, this will be the 10th week, you need to give yourself a little bit of a break, and I thought, Yeah, I do, actually, because it was rewarding but exhausting. The added incentive was that I could have my Wife's world famous Sunday Roasts again!! We normally eat around 7pm on a Sunday Night but that was impossible when I was doing the *Lives* because the front room was in uproar and my brain was racing with what was about to happen, so not the best way to enjoy a classic Sunday Roast Dinner.

So I took a week off but then I started planning what I could do next.... on that bombshell eh? Within a few weeks I was posting a brand new online variety show edited with videos from my showbiz friends who were also stuck at home and frustrated that they couldn't perform, so they kindly donated their talents for me to include on the broadcasts. I hosted the programmes as well, it seemed to be logically the next thing to do after the success of the live comedy shows.

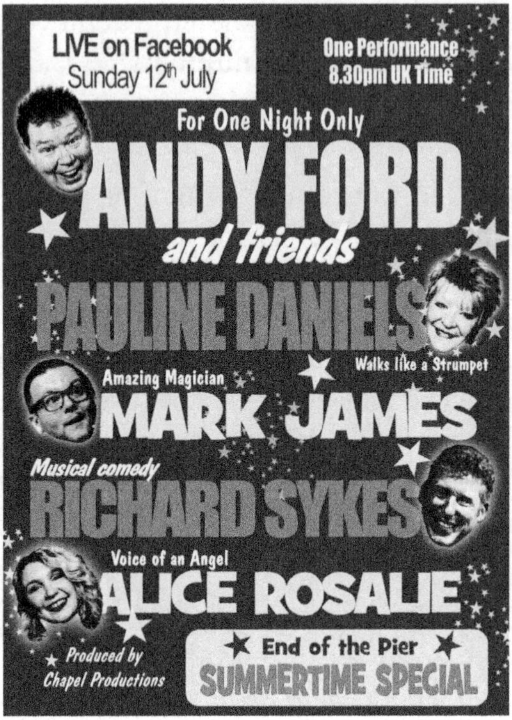

I've just gotta do stuff, I might have said that before by the way!! By spending the week editing the show and pre scheduling it to go out on a Sunday, I could not only sit back and watch it live with my Facebook followers and friends, but I could also comment along with them at the same time as eating my Sunday Roast… Winner winner Chicken *(or occasionally Roast Pork)* Dinner!

'A victory is twice itself when the achiever brings home full numbers'

Our Pandemic VE Day Celebrations

Ironically 2020 turned out to be one of the busiest years of my life. Do you remember the VE celebrations that year? At the time we were living in a charming little Village in County Durham called Middlestone, and as a community there was a will to celebrate the end of the second world war on the 75th anniversary. Lockdown restrictions had been slightly lifted but people could only meet up outside and at a distance.

So Michelle and I set to in putting on a *'bit of a do'*, for our little village. The local village pub was gonna bring drinks out to the gathered masses and everyone had to stay social distanced with their family groups on the village green. Some of the villagers decked their houses in the union flag and sat in their gardens to enjoy the festivities. There was something quintessentially British about the whole, 'We're gonna do this whatever the circumstances' routine. The stiff upper lip and all that, very Churchillian.

VE Day eh!
Let's put on
a show!

So I downloaded lots of wartime music as well as Rule Britannia, Land of hope and Glory and all that sort of thing. I set up my PA system outside of our flag bedecked front door and I hosted the whole event with quizzes and stuff, then at 3pm I patched in BBC radio who were playing Churchill's famous end of war speech and I went straight into Rule Britannia after he said, 'God save the King'. It was a spine tingling moment if I say so myself and to see all our fellow villagers waving their flags and singing was something I will always remember.

Distance seems to be bad for some but not for me'

Socially distanced Panto 2020 in Plymouth

Following my panto in Dartford I was asked to go back to the Bristol Hippodrome after 4 years away for the next year's show but Covid messed that up completely and so I'd given up on doing Panto in 2020, but to my surprise I received an offer later in the year to be part of a socially distanced Pantomime Production at the Theatre Royal in Plymouth. I had no idea how it was all gonna work, or whether anyone would come to watch it, but as things had been completely wiped out earlier in the year, the thought of getting the chance to do panto was very exciting.

The show was Robinson Crusoe and the cast included the brilliant Les Dennis as the Dame, Coronation Street's Connor McIntyre as the Captain and Dame's love interest, Simon Webb from the 90's pop group Blue as Robinson and me as his silly brother Billy. It was a very small cast for obvious reasons, our fantastic female performers were Jenny Dale from CBBC as the baddie with Charlotte Haynes as the leading Lady and Robinson's girlfriend plus the wonderful Emily Harrington as the Fairy. We had 3 dancers, a troupe of acrobats and that was it. We never met the tumblers until the dress rehearsal and even when we did it was always at a distance of at least 2 metres.

On the first day of rehearsals we all turned up to be immediately tested for Covid 19. Although we'd all been on Zoom calls to discuss how the process was going to play out it was still a bit of a shock to the system when it all started happening. So the first time I met Les, I had to wave at him from a short distance and my first thought was how the hell are we gonna make his funny performing in different post codes on the stage! Les was a joy to be around and a fountain of comedy knowledge which I was happy to dive into.

When you're doing a production like this, (I'm guessing it was the first of it's kind) you sort of have to trust the process and your fellow performers.

My routine became digs, taxi, rehearsal at the theatre and back to my digs. That was it, obviously we couldn't socialize and even had to keep our distance from each other whilst in the wings waiting for our cue. Our seats were all 2 metres apart and we sat there in the dark wearing a mask waiting for our cue to go on, at which point we'd remove the mask and make our way onto the stage. The entrances were staggered as much as possible by our director Jonathan Kiley who did a great job in turning a good script into a really funny show to watch particularly in these unique circumstances.

Waiting for our Cue backstage 2 metres apart!

The bizarre continued when we got out there as we looked out on an audience who were all masked, spread out into family groups or as they were then called, bubbles. It was very weird but still fantastic to hear that first muffled audience laugh, something that I'd missed so much that year. Plymouth wasn't the only place that a socially distanced Panto was booked for, but as the spread of the virus increased in speed as well as voracity we ended up being the last Panto standing in Britain until we had to close 3 days before we were meant to... so all in all we did really well and I was so grateful to have that one off experience, making some fabulous new friends in a unique setting.

Plymouth Panto favourite Andy Ford takes on the role of Billy Crusoe, Robinson's not so bright brother, and even in this strange and challenging year, he is able to delight the audience with every appearance on stage. His normal cheer of hello boys and girls may be gone to prevent too much shouting, but everyone was more than willing to join in with 'friendly little wave'. He had the audience in stitches in his scenes alongside Dennis and McIntyre with hilarious tongue twister and lip sync scenes. They may have to send apart from each other, but they are still able to make the audience laugh

Great review for our Socially Distanced Panto!

CHAPTER 37

'Full of joy and mirth.... Joy, gentle friends!'

Lesley, Rob and Craig

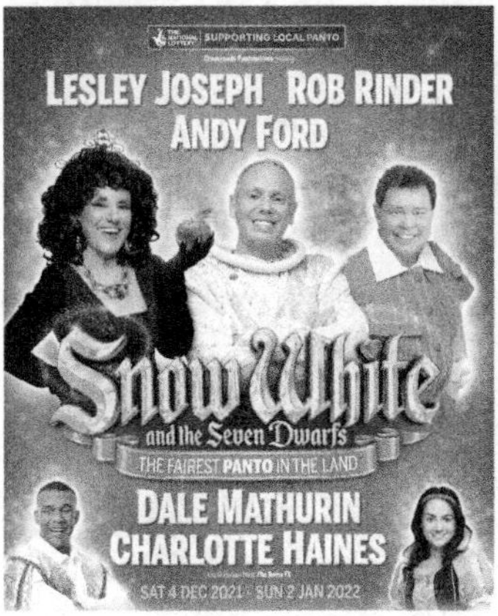

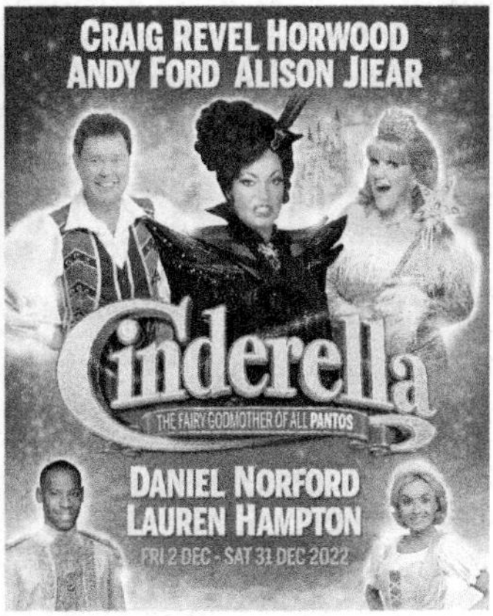

I have to say the excitement that was building up all around the land at the thought of our wonderful British tradition of Pantomime being able to return to the stage in all it's glory was tangible. As I say, I was one of the lucky ones who didn't miss out on Panto in 2020, but with Lockdown restrictions being lifted in 2021 it felt like it was gonna happen big time this year! I was booked to return to the magnificent Bristol Hippodrome for my 9th Panto and it had been 5 years since I tread the boards

there as the Pantomime Comic, so I was already beside myself with anticipation. Then I heard that British Comedy Legend Lesley Joseph from Birds of a Feather was playing the Wicked Queen and I was fit to burst. Not another comedy hero to work alongside Andrew? Fabulous!

Also booked for this production was Rob Rinder (he of Judge Rinder fame) in his first ever Panto, and Charlotte Haines as Snow White whom I worked with on our socially distanced Panto in Plymouth the year before, the difference this time was that we got the chance to hug (we'd kept 6 foot apart for 6 weeks on that show). So the launch date was set and we all turned up for the photo shoot and press call in Bristol. As usual I was nervous about meeting the star names, keen as always to set up a rapport with them.

I was directed into a room to change into my costume for the shoot and there was Rob Rinder sharing the room with me. I said hi, and he just threw his arms around me, told me that he was a big Andy Ford fan and was so excited at learning the ropes of Panto from me!! Well (as a friend of mine used to say without realising that she always got this expression wrong) You could have knocked

me down with a sledge hammer! (The original expression was you could have knocked me down with a feather btw).

When stars Become friends!

Rob was a delight and I just loved being in his company from the get go, what a flipping joy he is to be around. So that went well and then to my delight Lesley was just as welcoming and I immediately thought that this season was gonna be brilliant… spoiler alert, it was! I had comedy Dance routines with Rob (who had just recently stormed Strictly Come Dancing), an adapted Abbot and Costello sketch originally entitled ***Who's on first***

base to perform with Lesley Joseph, and a *Twelve days of Christmas* song with them and Dale Mathurin who played the Prince. There was a lot to learn but I couldn't wait to get started. So we met up again a couple of months later to rehearse in London, I was booked into my hotel but Rob insisted that I stay with him at his place, so I did and was made to feel very welcome. I know it sounds luvvie like to say that we all got on and it was fabulous etc.... but it's true and that is so important when you're putting on an epic like Snow White and the Seven Dwarves in just 2 Weeks, the cast getting on well comes across to the audience and they are happier and enjoy the whole experience more if they can see that we're just having a ball together performing for them.

Right then, the Abbot and Costello thing.. Lesley and I were both nervous about doing it as it was so intricate and difficult to learn and execute.

Here's a little bit of it…

Wicked Queen	Now Muddles I want you to deliver these invitations to the ball to 3 of my toy boys, Mr Who, Mr What, and Mr. I don't know. Mr Who lives in the 1st house, Mr What lives in the 2nd house, and Mr I don't know lives in the 3rd house
Muddles	Who lives in the first house?
Wicked Queen	Yes
Muddles	What?

Wicked Queen	No he lives in the 2nd house
Muddles	Who lives in the 2nd house?
Wicked Queen	No, Who lives in the 1st house, What lives in the 2nd House
Muddles	I don't know
Wicked Queen	No he lives in the third house
Muddles	Who lives in the 3rd house….. etc…..and on and on.

But learn it and execute we did, and I really loved it every time it came around in the show, but we both felt nervous for each performance as we never wanted to get it wrong. I don't know if I've said this before, but trusting your comedy partner is a really

special thing and the more confident we became with the routine the more we enjoyed it.

Iconic moment alert!!

One day during the interval and after a particularly good Abbot and Costello routine, Lesley walked into my room and said, '*Andy Ford, I really love working with you!*' Boom! Another gem for the memory box, thanks Lesley I really loved working with you too.

Now performing comedy routines with Rob was hilarious, as I just made him laugh and watching him crumble next to me in hysterics every night was one of the most pure and joyful things I've ever experienced. It wasn't all plain sailing that year though, Covid was still lingering and we were

testing twice everyday and doing our best to not gather in public houses or restaurants etc. because of the possibility of getting the virus and not being able to perform. Word had got around the industry that some shows were closing because of another Covid flare up and we in the cast would wear our masks into the stage wings only to remove them just before going on.

We were being very good however we did lose a few dancers and crew to the virus during the season, although we were all proud that we kept the show going for the entirety of its run. Like I did the year

before in Plymouth, I kept myself away from people in tight spaces and returned to my digs by myself each night after the shows finished. Oh it really was a great year of Panto and very much a feeling that things were starting to return to normal.

'For here, I hope, begins our lasting joy'

Working with Strictly's Craig Revel Horwood in Bristol 2022

OK, now this really was a special occasion for me, not only was I returning to the Hippodrome again, but it was to be my 10th Pantomime performance on that stage! Plus as mentioned, the part of Buttons is a treasured role for me, Comedy, Tragedy and empathy all in one show... it's by far my favourite Panto character.

When I was at this theatre the year before in Snow White, I noticed a poster advertising the following year's Panto with a picture of Craig Revel Horwood on it and I was hoping that I might be involved as he has been on my wish list of people to work with for many years. Michelle and I have a very good friend called Denny and she is a brilliant theatre wardrobe mistress who also made a brief appearance with me once on stage in Doncaster and was featured on my

Live and Lovely DVD. Anyway, she is a great laugh and we often swap stories regarding the lighter side of our profession. She was Craig's dresser on many occasions and had told us that he was great fun and a joy to work with, so I was hoping that one day our onstage partnership would come to pass.

The producers offered me the chance to team up with Mr Revel Horwood in Bristol and I was delighted. Once again the old press call and publicity launch took place well before rehearsals, and it was the chance to meet up with my fellow cast members and get to know them a bit. Not only was it the first chance to meet Craig which was a pleasure and a joy, but I also met the powerful, outrageous and darn right sensational Alison Jiear who was to play our Fairy Godmother. She and Craig had worked together many times I believe, not only in the UK but in Australia where they both come from.

Me and the tallest Dame in history!

Another dynamic in the show for me was getting the opportunity to see what a positive effect the genre of Panto can have on someone's life and career. Bristol born Lauren Hampton was for many years in the juvenile ensemble at the hippodrome and would dance away behind us lead characters whilst learning all about stage presence and delivery etc. In fact on one of my Panto Diaries (A vlog of happenings behind the scenes during panto rehearsals) filmed about 14 years previously, I

interviewed two of our young dancers about how they were enjoying the process of putting on a pantomime, plus their ambitions for the future.

The girls were Georgia Pegg and Lauren Hampton who I'm pleased to say continue to have fantastic careers in this business of ours with Lauren even going on to star in Mama Mia in the West End. I could never have imagined then that the young girl I was interviewing would be sharing the stage with me as my Cinderella, nor the fact that it was happening in the City of her birth. What a fabulous story!

So back to our show which turned out to be everything I could have wished for. Without naming everybody who appeared on this show, I just need to say that the whole cast was bursting with talent and for the first time ever in my career I got the chance of playing opposite two fabulous actresses as the Step Sisters. It took me by surprise a bit when I saw their names on the script as I'd only ever worked with men in drag in that role. But Catherine and Leanne smashed it and we even got the opportunity to do my famous Pop idols routine together which was a real hoot.

With Leanne, Catherine, Alison and Lauren!

Working alongside an old pro like Craig was great and it was interesting to see how the audience reacted when they discovered that not only could he dance but was also the owner of one of the most powerful voices you'll ever hear. That's the thing with being famous for one thing I suppose, people were so used to seeing him being tough on contestants on Strictly Come Dancing that they were unaware of what a long and successful career he'd had in the business before getting the Strictly gig.

The show went really well and the restrictions of the last two years seemed to be melting away, however that didn't stop me from having a drama of

my own. In 2021 I had pulled a couple of leg muscles on the run and was determined not to do that again, yeah right… this is me and somehow I have been blessed with the ability to do the wrong thing time and time again. As I say I was definitely gonna be learning from past mistakes and that's why I joined in with the physical warm up on stage every day to make sure my leg muscles were stretched and warm before the curtain up. However right at the beginning of one physical warm up session, because I had requested a song for us all to loosen up to, namely Mike Oldfield's *Indulce jubilo* which is a bright, fun old folk song with a festive feel, I started messing around with one of our dancers and got a bit carried away kicking my legs like a flipping lunatic…. Ping! There it was... I'd pulled a muscle during physical warm up which I was only doing to prevent me from pulling a muscle! You can't make this stuff up, what a div Andrew.

I went into Craig's dressing room to share my stupid muscle pull news and his reaction was priceless, he said, *'You're not going off are you?'* and I said that I'd never missed a panto performance in my career and wasn't gonna start now. To which he replied, *'That's good cause you're going on even if I have to push you on in a wheelchair!'* I laughed and told him about how that had actually happened once many years back in Croydon.

During this season, to commemorate my tenth show in the Theatre Pantos my Star was put up in the Bristol Hippodome's Foyer and I was presented with a replica to keep from Ben Phillips the manager. What an honour, thanks everyone.

What a magical Pantomime it was and to cap it all, Lauren and I would soar over the heads of the audience in a magical coach with flying horses on the way to the ball at the end of the first half of our show every night. You see, right there is why Pantomime is so important, it lifts your spirits in a way that no other genre can, not only for children but for all the generations that come to see it.... Long live Panto!

Andy's Animal Idioms

Idiom
Like a Chameleon in a paint factory
meaning
Someone who has too many choices

Chapter 38

'...and all my mother came into mine eyes and gave me up to tears'

A Mother's Love

As I write this today, it's not that long since the passing of my lovely Mum. She had been ill for quite a while with this bloody awful dementia thing. To watch her deteriorate in front of our eyes was horrendous, but as a family you somehow have to deal with it. Of course it was terrible for my Dad, as

they had been together since they were 19 years old and were both in their 90's when Mum passed. I am sure you'll all agree that a Mother's love is so important and she was not only adored me, my sisters, my Dad, all the grand children and great grandchildren but she was also our protector.

I remember once as a young lad at our local primary school, I was roped into a scheme to nick some apple wine from the staff room. You'll obviously be aware if you know me at all that it's not an idea that I'd come up with, I was afraid of my own shadow at that age. But two of my mates were a bit more daring than me, and they had decided to do it after school one day.

So ladies and Gentlemen, little ol' me Andrew Ernest Mogford, was the designated lookout on this quest...OMG. When it began, my mates (I've kept their surnames a secret in case anyone from Scotland Yard is reading this) Christopher and Graham made their way into the staff room and I was standing just outside looking for anyone that may be coming so that I could warn them, (this might read better if you start humming the mission impossible theme about now). They entered and I waited, suddenly I could hear shouting, it was an

adults voice, we'd been rumbled! Bravely I ran away like Forrest Gump on speed, you couldn't see me for dust! I ran straight home and went to my room, hoping no questions would be asked about my frenetic arrival and the copious amount of sweat I was emitting. I seemed to get away with it and the next morning I got myself ready for school, as it happened it was also the day that I went to my cub/scout meeting so I wore my cub uniform to school.

On arrival I was ushered to the headmaster's office because my mates had obviously dobbed me in, they had told the headmaster that I was part of it, how could they? Our punishment that day was to walk into every class in the school and tell the teachers and our fellow pupils, what we had done and how bad we were for doing it. I know, horrendous eh? I was about 8 or 9 and I knew that this was gonna be tough and might brand me for life, but because I was a bit of a performer and used to entertain my friends in the playground, Christopher and Graham told me that I had to do the talking. They were both a lot bigger and tougher than me so I wasn't gonna argue with them. We made our way into the classrooms and I talked through it all every time in every room. It wasn't nice but I seemed to be handling it OK, that was

until we went into Harry Nutting's Class!! This most flamboyant of teachers decided that we should be humiliated for our crimes and encouraged the children in his class to ridicule us. It was horrible, and because I was in my cub uniform he really laid into me and I started crying. Now I know that if you do wrong there should be repercussions, but come on I was only 8 or so and I can still remember the humiliation as if it happened yesterday.

When I got home I told my Mum what had happened, and I was not aware of what happened next until I was an adult. My mother went straight to the school and demanded to see the head teacher. *'How dare you do that to my Andrew, he's a good boy, maybe he got in with the wrong crowd but abject humiliation in front of everyone it's not right!'* I believe he apologised to my mum and there didn't seem to be any further punishment for me. But looking back on it all now, I feel so much love and respect for what she did for her son. I wasn't the brightest spark but I wasn't a bad lad and she would never let me get treated in that way, now that's what you call a protector.

I'm sure you guys have some dodgy memories of school too but on one occasion on a parents night,

you know the sort of thing, your Mum and Dad turn up to speak to your teacher and he or she let's them know how you're doing, well on this one occasion I was close enough to hear what my teacher Mrs Bentley was saying to my Parents. Imagine hearing this… *'I'm sorry Mrs Mogford, Andrew is fairly enthusiastic but I don't really think he's going to make anything of his life*'. My mother was horrified, she didn't cause a scene but she got out of there fairly sharpish. I mean, come on there was no need for that, and in fact I did struggle for a while, particularly as in the next school year I went into Harry Nutting's class!

Yep it was all downhill until the following year when I was put into Mr's Hands Class, she had the reputation of being fierce and none of the pupils seemed to like her. However this lady changed my life, yes she was strict but encouraging when you tried hard. For the first time ever I started getting A's in my report cards and as it was my last year at the primary school with the help of her tuition I passed my eleven plus exam. Thank you Mrs Hands, you'll never know what you did for me but I will always be grateful. My parents burst with pride when they knew I'd made it to Grammar school, not bad for a lad that was going to make nothing of his Life eh?!

It's sometimes not until someone is gone that you realise what a really great friend they were, and my Mum was my best friend throughout my youth, she gave me fantastic counsel on whatever I was worried about, she was always there to talk things through. My dear Mother was always my biggest supporter, but her continual worry that I might not succeed at some point was never that far away in her mind. In short she was a worrier, not sure why or where that came from but it was just part of her make up.

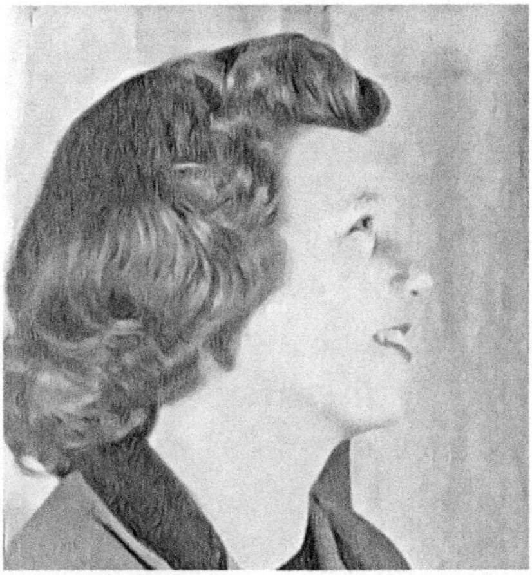

I know this sounds slightly strange but on a Thursday night (I think it was) at about 9.30pm my Mother and I would sit down to watch Monty

Python's Flying Circus every week. Don't think it was to her comedy taste or anything but she knew how much I loved it, so while my sisters were upstairs getting ready for School on a Friday, and Dad was maybe in bed early to get up at silly o'clock for work the next morning or having a swift half with his mates, we'd be sitting there together on the settee. It was always so special to be in her serene company and I treasured every one on one moment with her, but she was also a pretty ruthless table tennis player, good grief Andrew that's a tangent! I know, but when I was thinking about the front room just then, I suddenly pictured my Mum and I playing table tennis on our dining table with the two extended flaps at the end, so let's talk about it. We'd flip them up, lock them in place and attach the net so that we could hold the Mogford table tennis tournaments, all five of us would take part but Mum normally won as she had such an awesome serve.

Throughout my life she was so proud of my achievements and cared about me so much. We were regular church goers in our family and Mum was quite religious, we actually were confirmed together in our Church in Lloyd's Crescent by the Bishop of Crediton, yep me and Mum kneeling there together.

Me, Mum and Justin having fun on his wedding Day!

My sisters who live in Exeter, did most of the looking after Mum as the dementia kicked in and I am so grateful to them for their love and support of our parents. I live in the North of England now which makes sense for us because we are closer to Michelle's Mum for whenever she needs us, which has become even more important since the sad passing of my beloved Father in Law Mike in 2021, therefore I didn't get as much time with Mum during the latter stages of her illness as I would have liked, thank goodness for video calling!

On one occasion I came down to visit my mother in a Nursing home in Exeter and the staff kindly made us comfortable in a room just off the main building so that we could have a private conversation together and some tea and cake. I quickly realised how much she had deteriorated and the slightest thing would start her crying. I wasn't expecting this but the most unexpected swapping of roles happened that day. Mum had turned into the child and I was the caring parent. If she cried I'd say that we weren't gonna do tears today as this is a special time with us being together and she'd nod and stop crying just like I would do when I was young and she'd give me the same instruction.

That was probably one of the hardest things to see, this wonderful Lady in front of me reduced to child like reactions. However the visit was truly wonderful and happy and we just loved each other's company as we've always done despite this cruel situation. When it was time for me to leave I'll never forget her looking at me and saying, 'On your way home Andrew can you drop me off in town?' Wow, that hit me hard as we'd just spent a lot of the time reminiscing and at certain moments during our conversation, things seemed quite like they'd always been… but that statement from her smacked me right in between the eyes. She could hardly walk

but her mind refused to accept it, and wanted her to carry on with life like she used to. When I got to the car I cried at the realization that she was really going.

I never made it to her bedside before she passed although I tried so hard. Sandra rang me in the morning and it was obvious that Mum wasn't long for this world, so within an hour I was up, dressed and ready to leave. Michelle did me a quick breakfast and I hit the road from North Yorkshire to the South West. Dad wasn't at the nursing home

that morning but was keen to be with mum so he'd got himself dressed and was waiting for me to pick him up when I got to Exeter. Sadly Mum went downhill quickly at the end and I was just outside of Taunton when Helen rang me to say that it was over.

I know we were prepared for it but when you actually hear the words it's real. I rang Shell immediately and her concern was for me driving with that news in my head, she said there's no point in rushing just be safe. So I rang my children to tell them about their Gran and carried on with my journey to Exeter.

When I arrived at Hillyfield Road and walked into the front room Dad stood up ready to go to see Mum and I had to tell him the news. Well I've never heard my Father scream like that before, he howled and pounded his head against my chest sobbing his heart out. All I could do was hug him and to be honest it was the longest we had ever held each other in our lives, my Dad needed to cry at the loss of his dear Wife and I was there for him. I was scared as to how I was going to deal with it beforehand, but it all happened naturally and we were just there for each other.

That Lady meant the world to me and my life was better for all the lovely memories. The other day I was listening to the Mike and the Mechanics song, The Living Years, which is about telling people what they mean to you and sorting out your differences while you're still alive to do it. It made me realise how happy I was that the relatively short period of time that there was any distance between my parents and me had ended when they came to our Wedding in Scarborough in 1999.

The breakdown of my first marriage was unfortunately a bit acrimonious and there was a period of painful estrangement from my Mum and Dad and other members of my family. I know it hurt them as much as it hurt me and when the barriers were breached and we could resume our relationships it meant the world to all of us. I kept thinking when I was listening to that song, imagine if we didn't sort it out and she had passed with us not talking. That thought horrifies me and sorting our differences out was one of the best things that I have ever done in my life, no situation is ever perfect but your parents are your parents forever.

Another thing that I am so proud of is setting up my Ipad one day and interviewing my parents, I think it was in 2015. They chatted away about their Lives to me, how they met, the war years, struggling financially but always doing what was needed to make our upbringing so wonderful. That is there now for all future generations of our family.... so go on, when you get chance to chat to your parents about their life.... film it. You'll have that forever and it'll be a lovely source of comfort when they're no longer around. I asked my Sisters if they were OK with me doing the Eulogy at Mum's service and they were happy for me to do it. When I sat down to compose the speech I wasn't sure where to start, but to be honest when I got going on it the words just

flowed and the love I have for that lady made telling people what she meant to us all, one of the easiest thing I've ever had to write.

Sleep well dear Mum you are missed but loved forever.

CHAPTER 39

'It is a wise father that knows his own child'

Me and Dad the Dream Team

Being the only two males in our family group my Dad and I were unsurprisingly close. I know I talked about him earlier in this epic publication but there is more I need to say about my lovely Father. He was my vocal coach, football coach and my number one cheer leader. All the songs he taught me from his youth stood me in good stead for the band work I would eventually take on.

There weren't that many teenagers in the early seventies that could reel off Guy Mitchell and Connie Francis songs, but when they were required in my dance band career I had them all well rehearsed thanks to my Dad.

As regards the football coach thing, well we would play football any time, any where. As well as his regrets for not living the entertainer's life that I have been lucky enough to enjoy, Dad was also a frustrated footballer and a bloody good one by the way. When he was in the army he played for his battalion team and he was the only amateur player in the side, the others were all professional including many from Division One the equivalent of the premier league nowadays.

I know that one of his team mates was John Bond the ex Norwich player for example, and Dad told me that when the team sheet was put up in Barracks before any game the players names were followed by their professional team. The list included names like West Ham Utd, Stoke City etc... for my Dad it said Ern Mogford Exeter YMCA, but he was proud of that and I believe he was a quick and tricky inside right who kept his place in the side on merit. Michelle and I took Dad back to

his old barracks when we were living nearby in Oxfordshire and it was a fantastic trip down memory lane for him and gave Mum the chance to see where Dad was based, I am so glad that we could do that for him.

My two Dads, one as a young recruit and one back at base as an older man!

He told me that when he was a teenager he had a trial for Exeter City, but he had a paper round to do beforehand and for some reason the papers were delayed that day and by the time he'd finished, cycled home, got changed into his football kit and rode to St James Park, the other lads who were there for a trial were already on the pitch training with the Exeter City staff and he felt too embarrassed to let them know he was there because of his late arrival. It does break my heart rather when I hear that story.

We loved our football me and my Dad and I'll never forget sharing that Day in 1966 with him, my Mum and Sisters when our England won the World Cup. I was only nine at the time and when Haller scored that first goal for West Germany I was so upset and traumatised that I went and hid myself behind the settee and wouldn't come out until we equalized. You see I never failed to see the drama in a moment... 'I thought it was all over'.... to quote someone, 'But it turned out nice again', to quote someone else...lol.

Now Exeter City has always been a big part of my life and in the early nineties I wrote a song for the team that is still played after the games in the

stadium. My son Justin sang on it too and one night when we were at the game at St James' Park as City got promoted, we ran onto the pitch at the final whistle with all the other fans and danced around as they played our song over the tannoy, now that was brilliant! Only recently when I updated the song, my Grandson Dylan joined me and his Dad on the recording (I'm also pleased to say that Dylan is up the Park for most home games now, so the Mogford Exeter City supporting legacy continues) and my Father loves that.

4 Generations of Mogford Boys!

So like I say we loved our football did me and my Dad and sometimes took the chance to play even when maybe it wasn't appropriate. Like when Mum was at work and the girls were in their rooms upstairs Dad and I would turn the oblong shaped fire guard in the front room around and use it as goal posts, with my Dad smashing the ball at me from 2 yards away and me in the goal punching the ball clear. I can't remember how many vases and trinkets we smashed but it was a fair few! Outrageous really but boy did we have fun, but as Dad got older and was less able to run around the fields with me like he used to, we still got our football fix.

My Dad's brother Les was also a good player and on a Sunday morning Dad and I would go to the JLC Fields in Exeter and watch him play for local team Windsor United. I loved going and before the games would start as part of his warm up routine my Uncle Les would kick the ball around with me, and it made me feel special.

As mentioned before, my Dad was my Roadie in the early days and travelled to all the gigs with me. He loved it of course but I could still embarrass him occasionally by taking out my trusty kitchen knife

during the show to tighten up the tuning pegs on my banjo that would occasionally work themselves loose. I didn't care... if the Banjo needed tuning it needed tuning and I can still see him covering his face with embarrassment as I did it during a show. Hopefully I've become a bit more professional since then, but of course I would invite him up on stage with me from time to time to sing, usually to *Won't you come home Bill Bailey* which is his favourite song in the whole wide world. I loved to do that for Dad cause I knew what it meant to him.

Take it away Dad......

Being Exeter lads we of course love Exeter City Football club and he used to take me to matches as indeed I did with my son when he was old enough. In April of 1964 Exeter secured promotion by drawing 0-0 away to Workington and we City Fans all waited for them to return to our fair City… wait for it… on the train. I suppose the M5 wasn't around then and a trip to Cumbria must have felt like travelling to the other side of the world. Anyway we all gathered there, the local press took pictures and I have one with me on my Dad's shoulders right behind my Exeter football hero Alan Banks… I will treasure that pic forever.

Growing up with an enthusiastic, music loving, pub singing Dad obviously shaped the direction of my Life and I know that without him I probably wouldn't have lived the Life I have and this book might have been considerably smaller. My perfectly imperfect but fantastic Father is my hero!

CHAPTER 40

'Pray, do not mock me: I am a very foolish fond old man '

In conclusion...

I've been on this planet for a fair while now, and it's still brilliant, I mean really brilliant. Every day when I wake up I think... 'I'm a comedian, how fabulous is that?' Yeah I know the old adage that you can't please all of the people all of the time, but for most of my life the people have pleased me. So in summing up where I am in my life.... I'm right here typing away and planning the sequel to this book! Who know's what tomorrow brings?..... be honest you sang that then didn't you? But to live a full and happy life you gotta laugh haven't you? As I said to myself whilst naked in front of the mirror this morning. But seriously folks (hughie Green jumped into my head then for some reason, that's a reference that no one under 50 is gonna get) you have to get out there and do stuff if you can.

I am so grateful that you are all a part of my life, from the people who tuned in to watch me every week during the lockdown to the people who buy tickets to see me on stage. Whether it's in Panto or on my stand up comedy tours, you're always truly

appreciated, it's lovely to see you at the gigs and to occasionally work with some of my best mates like Paul Burling and Steve Hewlett as well as many others.

Performing makes me happy and now it gives me the opportunity to shine a light on some emerging talents and of course encourage them, like the brilliant female vocalist Francesca Carly who supports me on the road as well as our fabulous Sorella Dancers.

Francesca Carly and me having fun on tour!

We are all the result of our life decisions and looking back I wouldn't change anything, to quote Sir Elton, *'I'm still standing, better than I ever did, looking like a true survivor feeling like a little kid'.*

Anyway.... Moving on, there's still lots to do... some of it on stage as a comedian, a writer and some of it just being a loving Husband to Michelle, a devoted Dad to Alisha and Justin and a fun Grandad to Dylan, Sophie and Evie Rene....I love it all, thanks for reading... see you soon,

I'm off camping!

yours sincerely,

Andrew Ernest Mogford

AKA Andy Ford xx

'O Excellent! I love long life better than figs'

Artwork © Michelle Jackson-Mogford

Acknowledgements

A big shout out to everyone who has been part of my journey, it has been impossible to name everyone in this book, but I want you all to know how glad I am that you have been part of my life tapestry. Thank you to Hayden for interviewing me at the start of this process, also my grateful thanks to William Shakespeare for the Chapter Quotes… cheers Bill.

ABOUT THE AUTHOR

Andy Ford is a professional Comedian and comedy writer whose career has so far spanned 54 years. He is married to Michelle and is Father to Alisha and Justin and Grandfather to Dylan, Sophie and Evie Rene. He hails from Devon and spends his life creating.... and he just loves doing that!!

www.andyfordcomedian.com

Andelle books

Printed in Great Britain
by Amazon

25426286R00225